Praise from the Expe[rts]

"While numerous texts address using SAS and other statistical packages for biostatistical analysis, there has been no text addressing how to use SAS Enterprise Guide for this purpose. Jim's book is thus a uniquely valuable resource for the many biostatistics faculty members, including myself, who seek to provide students with hands-on experience with a statistical package that is both user-friendly and powerful."

Albert G. Crawford, Ph.D., MBA, MSIS
Assistant Professor, Department of Health Policy
Thomas Jefferson University

"*Statistics Using SAS® Enterprise Guide®* offers multiple opportunities. It is most suitable for a beginner wishing to learn both SAS Enterprise Guide and statistics. Alternatively, for someone with knowledge of SAS Enterprise Guide or statistics, it will offer a chance to become proficient in both."

Karol Katz, M.S.
Programmer Analyst
Yale University School of Medicine

"I recommend this book as the main book for a basic, non-technical course in statistics and as a supplement for a technical course. In either case, it provides the foundation for using SAS Enterprise Guide as the tool for doing statistics. It is important to introduce future users of statistics to their future interface to SAS, the premier software package in statistics."

John C. Hennessey, Ph.D.
Mathematical Statistician
Social Security Administration

Statistics Using SAS® Enterprise Guide®

James B. Davis

The correct bibliographic citation for this manual is as follows: Davis, James B., 2007. *Statistics Using SAS® Enterprise Guide®*. Cary, NC: SAS Institute Inc.

Statistics Using SAS® Enterprise Guide®

Copyright © 2007, SAS Institute Inc., Cary, NC, USA

ISBN 978-1-59047-566-9

All rights reserved. Produced in the United States of America.

SAS Institute Inc., SAS Campus Drive, Cary, North Carolina 27513.

1st printing, April 2007

SAS® Publishing provides a complete selection of books and electronic products to help customers use SAS software to its fullest potential. For more information about our e-books, e-learning products, CDs, and hard-copy books, visit the SAS Publishing Web site at **support.sas.com/pubs** or call 1-800-727-3228.

SAS® and all other SAS Institute Inc. product or service names are registered trademarks or trademarks of SAS Institute Inc. in the USA and other countries. ® indicates USA registration.

Other brand and product names are registered trademarks or trademarks of their respective companies.

Contents

Acknowledgments

I thank SAS Press for supporting this project. I am especially grateful to Donna Sawyer Faircloth for her excellent work, untiring efforts, and positive attitude. I am also especially grateful to Julie Platt for her continued support.

I thank SAS for its support. I always received the latest software. I received multiple beta copies of SAS Enterprise Guide. I am grateful to all those who answered my questions and offered advice. I appreciate the time they gave, the high quality of their work, and their friendly attitude. Additional thanks go to Kathy Underwood, Technical Editor; Monica McClain, Technical Publishing Specialist; Mary Beth Steinbach, SAS Press Managing Editor; Patrice Cherry, Designer; and Jennifer Dilley, Technical Publishing Specialist.

I thank all those who have reviewed this book. I appreciate the time they gave, the high quality of their work, and their professional attitude. I have been able to incorporate many of their suggestions. I have tried to meet the expected standard of quality implicit in all comments.

I thank all the students who, over the years, did their assignments with Base SAS software, SAS/ASSIST software, the Analyst Application, and SAS Enterprise Guide software. They inspired me to write this book. I always had them in mind as I worked.

Introduction to SAS Enterprise Guide

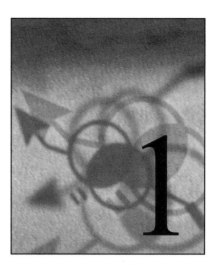

1.1   First Look at SAS Enterprise Guide

1.1.1   Projects

Our work in SAS Enterprise Guide focuses on data sets, tasks, and output files.

* Data sets are files that contain the measurements, counts, and categorizations collected from individuals and objects. Data sets are discussed in Chapter 2, "Working with Data."

* Tasks are interfaces for underlying SAS software. All the data management and the statistical analysis discussed in this book are supported by tasks.

* When a task produces output, it produces the output in a file.

o The file may be some form of text file, such as an HTML file or a Microsoft Word file. The file may be a SAS data set.

o Options related to these files are generally under a Results heading.

Activity in SAS Enterprise Guide is organized into *projects*. A project is a record of the data sets that have been opened, the tasks that have been run, the results that have been produced, and the relationships between these objects. One project at a time is opened in SAS Enterprise Guide.

A project is represented graphically as a project tree in the Project Explorer and as a process flow diagram in the Project Designer. See Figure 1.2 and Figure 1.3.

The information about the project is in a *project file*. A project file can be saved and copied. It can contain many types of items. In particular, a project file can contain:

- Shortcuts to the data sets that have been opened.

- Details about the tasks that have been run.

- Output files that are not data sets.

- Shortcuts to output data sets.

1.1.2 New Project

SAS Enterprise Guide opens with the window in Figure 1.1. An existing project can be opened or a new project can be created.

Figure 1.1 Welcome Window

For the current discussion, select **New Project** (🦌). SAS Enterprise Guide opens with a new project. See Figure 1.2.

Selecting **New SAS Program** (📄) creates a new project and opens a window for writing code.

Selecting **New Data** (📄) creates a new project and opens a window for creating a new SAS data set.

Figure 1.2 SAS Enterprise Guide Window Opening with a New Project

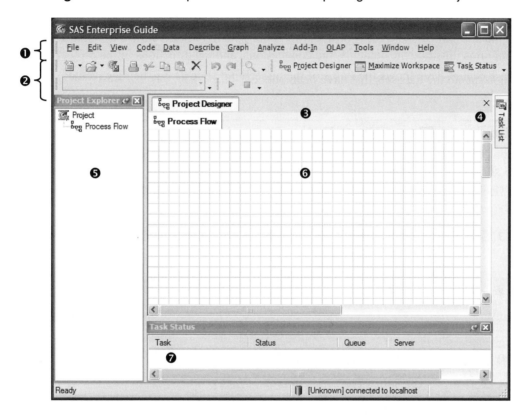

The numbers in Figure 1.2 identify the main areas of the SAS Enterprise Guide window.

❶ Menu bar. Everything can start from here. The menu bar is referenced throughout the book.

❷ Toolbars. See the "Toolbars" section.

❸ Workspace. This contains the Project Designer and any opened files. The Project Designer contains one or more process flow diagrams. See ❻.

❹ Task List. This lists all the tasks both by category and by name.

❺ Project Explorer. The name of the project is at the top. The elements of the project are listed below in project tree form. The default name of a new project is Project. This is changed to the name of the project file when the project is saved. The new project shown in Figure 1.2 contains an empty process flow diagram named Process Flow. See ❻.

> By default the Task List window is unpinned (⊣ or ⊠). The window opens when the cursor is above its tab. It stays open as long as the cursor is over the window.
>
> By default the Project Explorer window is pinned (⊣ or ⊙). The window opens with the SAS Enterprise Guide window and stays open.
>
> Clicking an unpinned icon changes the window to pinned. Clicking a pinned icon changes the window to unpinned.

   ➏   A process flow diagram in the Project Designer. The name Process Flow is a default name and can be changed. A project can contain many process flow diagrams. These diagrams illustrate the contents, the connections, and the directions in the project.

   ➐   Task Status. This shows the status of the underlying code as it is being executed.

1.1.3 Common Elements of Projects

This section uses Example 3.9 in Section 3.6 to present elements that are common in projects. Figure 1.3 shows the SAS Enterprise Guide window after completion of both examples in Section 3.5. The process flow diagram Example 3.9 is seen in the Project Designer.

Figure 1.3 SAS Enterprise Guide Window Applied to the Examples in Section 3.5

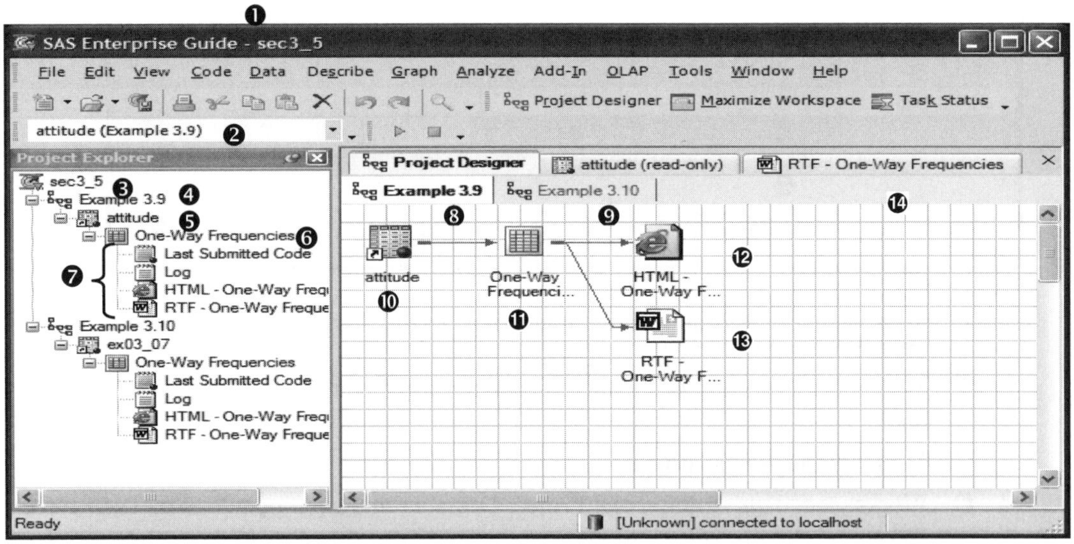

The numbers in Figure 1.3 identify elements of the current project.

   ➊   The project name sec3_5 in the title bar. The project file is sec3_5.egp.

   ➋   The active data set is Attitude on the Example 3.9 process flow diagram.

   ➌   The project name sec3_5 at ▓ in the Project Explorer.

   ➍   The icon ᵇₑₒ indicates a process flow diagram. This section of Project Explorer is associated with the process flow diagram Example 3.9.

❺ The icon ▦ indicates a shortcut for a SAS data set. This shortcut is for the Attitude data set. The shortcut is also in the Example 3.9 process flow diagram.

❻ The One-Way Frequencies task has been applied to the Attitude data set.

❼ Files associated with running the One-Way Frequencies task:

Last Submitted Code is the underlying SAS code.

Log has the details associated with the task's execution.

HTML - One-Way Frequencies is the task output in HTML format.

RTF - One-Way Frequencies is the task output in rich text format.

❽ ⬚⬚ Example 3.9 is the tab of the process flow diagram showing in the Project Designer.

❾ ⬚⬚ Example 3.10 is the tab of a hidden process flow diagram in the Project Designer.

❿ Attitude is the data source for the One-Way Frequencies task in the Example 3.9 process flow diagram.

⓫ The One-Way Frequencies task has been applied to the Attitude data set. The same output is in two files.

⓬ HTML - One-Way Frequencies is the task output in HTML format.

⓭ RTF - One-Way Frequencies is the task output in rich text format.

⓮ RTF - One-Way Frequencies tab in the workspace.

1.1.3.1 Opening a Data Set

Example 3.9 begins with opening the SAS data file Attitude on the local computer. A more general discussion is in Section 2.2.6, "Opening an Existing SAS Data File."

1. From the Standard toolbar, the Open icon (📂) is selected.

2. Then **Data** is selected from the drop-down menu.

3. **Local Computer** is selected on the Open Data From window. See Figure 1.4.

Figure 1.4 Open Data from Window

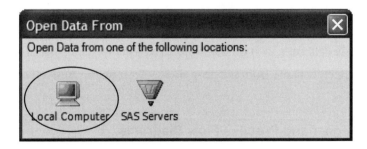

4. The Open From My Computer window opens. In Figure 1.5, the author has navigated to the Data Appendix folder in his computer. The SAS data file Attitude is opened.

5. Labels and shortcuts for the SAS data file Attitude appear in the Project Explorer and Project Designer. See ❺ and ❿ in Figure 1.3.

Figure 1.5 Open from My Computer Window

1.1.3.2   Active Data

When a task opens, it uses the data set that is currently designated as the *active data set*. The name of the active data set is shown in the Active Data toolbar.

- See ❷ in Figure 1.3 and ❹ in Figure 1.12.
- The toolbar shows Attitude (Example 3.9). The active data set is Attitude in the Example 3.9 process flow diagram.

To select a data set to be active:
- Click the example data set's icon on the Project Explorer or the Project Designer.
- Alternatively, select its name from the drop-down menu on the Active Data toolbar.

1.1.3.3   Project Designer and Process Flow Diagrams

The Project Designer contains the project's *process flow diagrams*. A process flow diagram (PFD) graphically represents:

- data sets, tasks, and results associated with the project
- relationships between these objects

A new project opens with one PFD named Process Flow. A PFD name can be changed. A project can have multiple process flow diagrams.

To change a PFD name:
From the Project Designer:

1. Right-click the name on the PFD tab identified by the PFD icon (⬚⬚⬚).
2. Select **Rename** from the pop-up menu. The Rename window opens.
3. Enter the new name in the entry box. Click **OK**.

From the Project Explorer:

1. Right-click the name by the PFD icon (⬚⬚⬚).
2. Select **Rename** from the pop-up menu. The name is in a box for editing.
3. Change the name. Press **Enter** on the keyboard or click a region on the screen outside the editing box.

To add a new PFD:
From the menu bar, select **File ▶ New ▶ Process Flow**.

From the Standard toolbar, select **Create New Item In Project ▶ Process Flow**.

From the Project toolbar, select **New Process Flow**.

Figure 1.3 has two process flow diagrams. See ❽ and ❾. They are named Example 3.9 and Example 3.10. The former is seen in the workspace.

- The Attitude data set (❿) is the data source for the One-Way Frequencies task (⓫).
- The output of the task is in an HTML file (⓬) and a Microsoft Word RTF file (⓭). See Output 1.1 in the "Output" section.

1.1.3.4   Formats for Results

Results can be in five formats. See Figure 1.6. HTML, PDF, and RTF formats can be sent to external viewers. See Figure 1.7.

- HTML: This is the default format. HTML is the basic Web browser format. See the icon at ⓬ in Figure 1.3. See Output 1.1 in the "Output" section.
- PDF: Portable document format opens with Adobe Acrobat Reader.
- RTF: Rich text format opens with Microsoft Word. See the icon at ⓭ in Figure 1.3. The RTF output is in Output 3.7 in Section 3.6.2, "Task Output and Interpretation for Example 3.9."
- SAS Report: A SAS format.
- Text output: Plain text format.

To select result formats and viewers:

From the menu bar:

1. Select **Tools ▶ Options**.
2. The Options window opens. Select **Results General** on the left. The Results General options are shown in Figure 1.6.
3. Check the desired formats.
4. HTML, PDF, and RTF can be viewed within SAS Enterprise Guide or in an external viewer. See the viewer options in Figure 1.7. The default is Enterprise Guide.
5. When finished, click **OK**.

Figure 1.6 Results General Options with HTML and RTF Selected

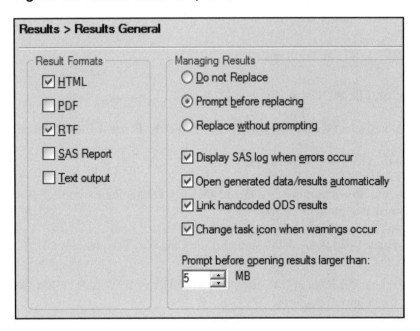

Figure 1.7 Viewer Options

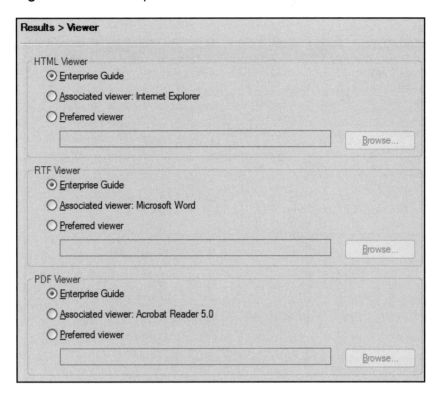

1.1.3.5 Tasks

Almost all tasks have the same format as the One-Way Frequencies task shown in Figure 1.8.

- There is a selection pane on the left that lists groups of options. See ❷.
- Once selected, the group of options appears in the task window under the group title. See ❸.
- Help messages for items in the task window are shown beneath the options area. See ❺. This is discussed in the "SAS Enterprise Guide Help" section.

The Titles group of options is common to most tasks and is discussed in general in Section 1.2. It controls the titles and the footnotes in the task output.

The One-Way Frequencies task is discussed in Section 3.6.2, "Instructions for Creating Frequency Distributions with the One-Way Frequencies Task."

Figure 1.8 One-Way Frequencies Task with Task Roles Showing

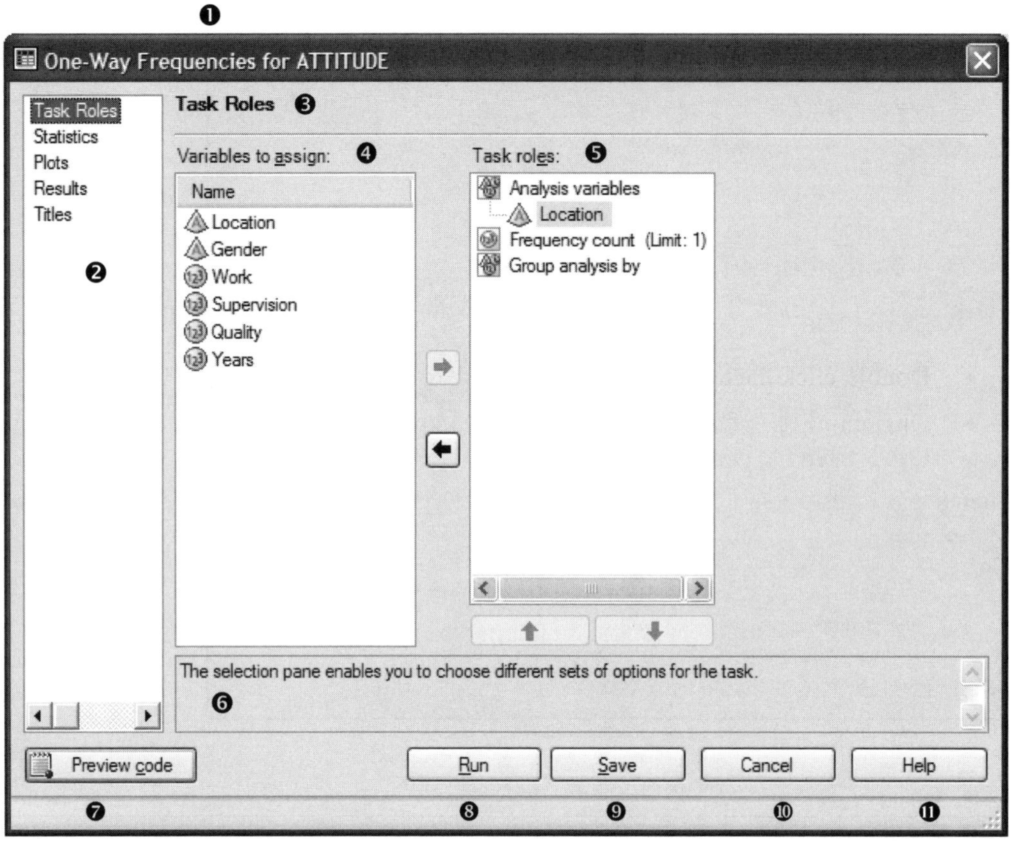

The numbers in Figure 1.8 identify elements of the One-Way Frequencies window that is showing the Task Roles options.

❶ Task name and data source in the title bar: One-Way Frequencies is being applied to the Attitude data set.

❷ Selection pane: **Task Roles** is selected.

❸ Title of options group: **Task Roles**.

❹ **Variables to assign** lists the variables in the data source. The red bell (⚠) indicates character data. The blue ball (⑫) indicates numeric data.

❺ **Task roles** lists roles appropriate for the task. A variable is assigned to a role by dragging it from **Variables to assign** to the role. A variable can be removed from a role by dragging back to the **Variables to assign** box. The arrows can also be used to assign and remove variables.

> The roles Group analysis by, Frequency count, and Relative weight are common to many tasks. These are discussed in general in Section 1.2.2, "Common Task Roles."

❻ Help for items in the task window. Message in Figure 1.8 is for the selection pane.

❼ **Preview Code** shows the underlying SAS code. New code can be inserted.

❽ **Run** executes the task.

❾ **Save** closes the task window and keeps changes. The task is not executed.

❿ **Cancel** closes the task window without saving changes.

⓫ **Help** opens SAS Enterprise Guide Help for the current task options.

1.1.3.6 Repeating a Task

A task can be reopened, the options changed, and the task repeated. To reopen a task:

- Double-click the task icon in the Project Explorer or in the Project Designer.

- Or right-click the task icon in the Project Explorer or in the Project Designer. Select **Open** from the pop-up menu.

When a task is run or saved again, the window in Figure 1.9 asks how the results are to be handled.

Figure 1.9 Choices for the Results of a Repeated Task

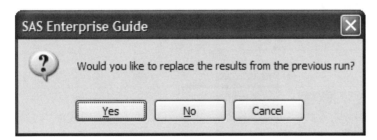

The question is "Would you like to replace the results from the previous run?"

- **Yes** replaces the old output with the new output.

- **No** adds a new section in the Project Explorer and a new branch in the Project Designer for the repeated task and the associated files.

- **Cancel** returns to the task window.

1.1.3.7 Output

The output for Example 3.9 is in Output 1.1. It is in HTML format, which is the default format for results. The output in RTF format is in Output 3.7 in Section 3.6.3, "Task Output and Interpretation for Example 3.9." Virtually all output in this book is in RTF format. When that is the case, titles are not repeated and the footnotes are dropped.

Output 1.1 Output for Example 3.9 in HTML Format

One-Way Frequencies
Results

The FREQ Procedure

Location of Office				
Location	Frequency	Percent	Cumulative Frequency	Cumulative Percent
Central	7	29.17	7	29.17
North	8	33.33	15	62.50
South	9	37.50	24	100.00

Generated by the SAS System (Local, XP_HOME) on 19NOV2005 at 10:22 AM

One-Way Frequencies
Plots

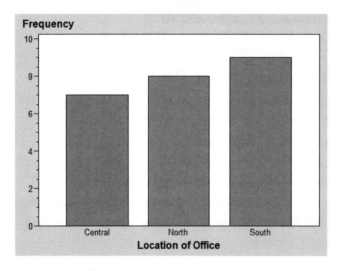

Generated by the SAS System (Local, XP_HOME) on 19NOV2005 at 10:22 AM

1.1.3.8 Simple Color Changes with Interactive Graphs

The background color and the color scheme of all the interactive graphs have been changed in this text. The ActiveX control and Java applet output formats are interactive.

The background color of the graph in Output 1.1 has been changed to white. The color scheme has been changed from custom to grayscale. The result is Output 1.2.

Output 1.2 Example 3.9 Graph with Grayscale Color Scheme and White Background

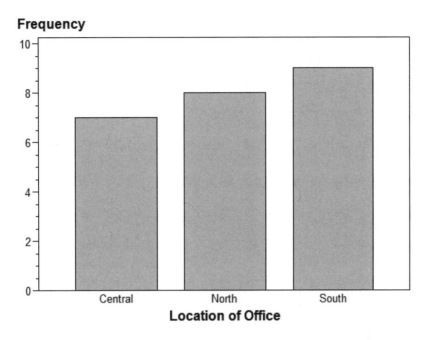

To change the color scheme and the background color:

1. Right-click the graph and select **Graph Properties** from the pop-up menu.
2. The Properties window appears.
3. The **Graph** tab is shown in Figure 1.10.
   a. At **Scheme**, select the desired color scheme from the drop-down menu. **Grayscale** is selected in Output 1.2. See Figure 1.10.
   b. At **Background**, click [...] to open the Background color palette. Select the desired color. White is selected in Output 1.2. Click **OK** to return to the Properties window. The selected color is shown in the box to the right of **Background**.
4. Click **OK** when finished.

Figure 1.10 Properties Window for Interactive Graphs

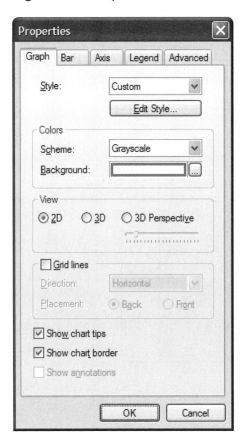

1.1.4 Working with Project Files

Projects can be opened, closed, and saved on the **File** menu. Items ❶ through ❹ in Figure 1.11 are for projects. Item ❺ is not for projects. It is included here to help avoid confusion.

Figure 1.11 Project Items and Save Text Items on File Menu

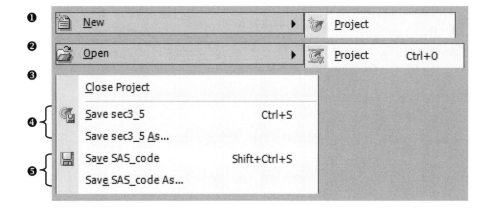

The circled numbers in Figure 1.11 refer to the following:

    ❶ **New ▶ Project** creates a new project. See Figure 1.2.

❷ **Open ▶ Project** opens an existing project. See the "Opening a Project" section below. Recent projects are listed near the bottom on the **File** menu.

❸ **Close Project** clears the Project Explorer and the Project Designer. Opened files are closed.

> If there are unsaved changes when any of the previous three items are selected, a window will appear asking whether changes are to be saved.

❹ **Save** *current-project-name* saves the current project to the same file and location. **Save** *current-project-name* **As** is used to save the current project to a different file or location. See the "Saving a New Project or Saving a Project As" and "Saving the Current Project" sections below.

❺ **Save** *file-name* and **Save** *file-name* **As** save SAS code files and other text files. The two items are inactive until such a file is selected.

A project takes on the name of its project file.

- In Figure 1.3 in the "Common Elements of Projects" section, the project name is sec3_5. See ❶ in the title bar and ❸ at top in the Project Explorer.
- The project file is sec3_5.egp.

Project files can be opened from and saved to a Windows folder or a SAS Enterprise Guide binder.

- SAS Enterprise Guide is a Microsoft Windows client application. A project file is opened and saved in the standard manner.
- A SAS Enterprise Guide binder is a virtual folder corresponding to a folder on the computer or a server. For information about adding binders, refer to *SAS Enterprise Guide Explorer: User's Guide*.

1.1.4.1   Opening a Project

Windows folder
1. From the menu bar, select **File ▶ Open ▶ Project**.
2. The Open Project window opens. Select **Local Computer**.
3. The Open From My Computer window opens.
4. **Files of type** is set to Enterprise Guide Project Files (*.egp).
5. Navigate to and open the desired file.

SAS Enterprise Guide Binder
1. From the menu bar, select **File ▶ Open ▶ Project**.
2. The Open Project window opens. Select **SAS Servers/Folders**.
3. The Open From SAS Servers/Folders window opens.
4. Select **Binders** on the left-hand side.

5. **Files of type** is set to Enterprise Guide Project Files (*.egp).

6. Navigate to and open the desired file.

1.1.4.2 Saving a New Project or Saving a Project As

Windows Folder

1. If saving a new project, select **File ▶ Save Project** from the menu bar or select the **Save Project** icon on the standard toolbar.

2. If saving as, select **File ▶ Save** *current-project-name* **As** from the menu bar.

3. The Save *current-project-name* To window opens. Select **Local Computer**.

4. The Save As window opens.

5. **Save as type** should be Enterprise Guide Project Files (*.egp).

6. Navigate to the desired folder and save the file.

Enterprise Guide Binder

1. From the menu bar:

    a. If saving a new project, select **File ▶ Save Project**.

    b. If saving as, select File ▶ **Save** *current-project-name* **As**.

2. The Save *current-project-name* To window opens. Select **SAS Servers/Folders**.

3. The Save To SAS Servers/Folders window opens.

4. Select **Binders** on the left-hand side.

5. **Files of type** is Enterprise Guide Project Files (*.egp).

6. Navigate to the desired binder and save the file.

1.1.4.3 Saving the Current Project

To save the current project to the same location:

1. From the menu bar, select **File ▶ Save** *current-project-name*.

2. On the standard toolbar, select **Save** *current-project-name*.

1.1.5 Toolbars

The four of the five toolbars shown in Figure 1.12 are alternatives to the menu bar. The exception is ❹, the Active Data toolbar.

Figure 1.12 Available Toolbars

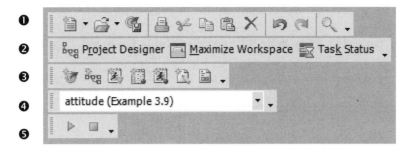

❶ Standard toolbar has icons that are also seen in the **File** and **Edit** menus.

    o First group:

        ▪ **Create New Item In Project** and **Open** add objects to the project.

        ▪ **Save** *current-project-name*

    o Second group: **Print**, **Cut**, **Copy**, **Paste**, **Delete**

    o Third group: **Undo**, **Redo**

    o Fourth group: **Find** (to search for text in data files and code files that are opened in the workspace)

❷ View toolbar has icons that are also seen in the **View** menu.

    o **Project Designer** opens process flow diagrams in the work space. See Project Designer and Process Flow Diagrams in Section 1.1.3, "Common Elements of Projects."

    o **Maximize Workspace** unpins and closes other windows.

    o **Task Status** opens the Task Status window.

❸ Project toolbar has icons that are also seen by selecting **File ▶ New: New Project**, **New Process Flow**, **New Stored Process**, **New Data**, **New Code**, **New Note**, or **New Report**.
This toolbar is not automatically shown. To show this toolbar, select on the menu bar: **View ▶ Toolbars ▶ Project**.

❹ Active Data toolbar names the active data set. The active data set can be selected from the drop-down menu on the toolbar.

Figure 1.3 shows Attitude (Example 3.9). The active data set is Attitude on the Example 3.9 process flow diagram. See Active Data Set in Section 1.1.3, "Common Elements of Projects."

❺ Control toolbar ❺ has icons that are also seen in the **Code** menu. These are used when executing SAS code. The icons are Run and Stop.

1.1.6 SAS Enterprise Guide Help

SAS Enterprise Guide has a thorough Help capability.

- From the menu bar, select **Help ▶SAS Enterprise Guide Help**. See Figure 1.13.

Figure 1.13 SAS Enterprise Guide Help

- o The online SAS Enterprise Guide manual is available on the **Contents** tab.
- o The Index, Search, and Favorites capabilities are available. Index and Search are based on a wide range of SAS manuals.
- **F1** on the keyboard provides context-sensitive help.
  - o For example, the window in Figure 1.14 appears after you click on a process flow diagram and press **F1**.
  - o SAS Enterprise Guide Help displays the appropriate page from the online manual. The page is highlighted on the **Contents** tab. In Figure 1.14, the page **About process flows** is discussed in the "Working with Process Flows" section of the **Contents** tab.
- **Help** provides help for the current task options. See ❶ in Figure 1.8 in the Tasks section. Clicking **Help** opens SAS Enterprise Guide Help to the appropriate page in the online manual. The page is also highlighted on the **Contents** tab.
- Help is shown in the task windows for specific options. See ❻ in Figure 1.8 in the Tasks section. Also see Figure 1.15 below. In Figure 1.15, the cursor is hovering over **Frequencies and percentages with cumulatives**.
- The What is …? window describes selected options. In Figure 1.16, the cursor is hovering over **Maximize Workspace** in the View toolbar. To open this window, select **View ▶ What is**.
- The tutorial "Getting Started with SAS Enterprise Guide" is an excellent way to become familiar with SAS Enterprise Guide. It works through examples using data that is comes with the software. To start the tutorial, select **Help ▶Getting Started Tutorial**.

Figure 1.14. About the Process Flow Window in SAS Enterprise Guide Help

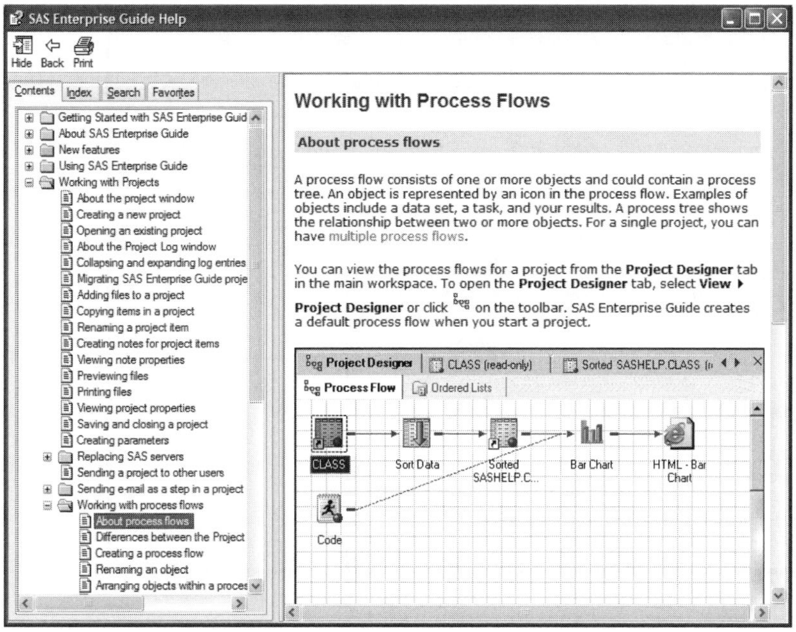

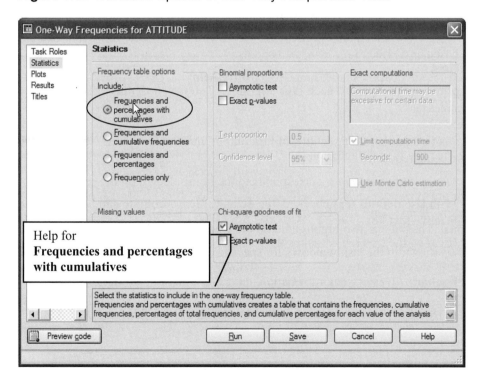

Figure 1.15 Statistics Options in One-Way Frequencies Task

Figure 1.16 What is ... ? Describes Maximize Workspace on View Toolbar.

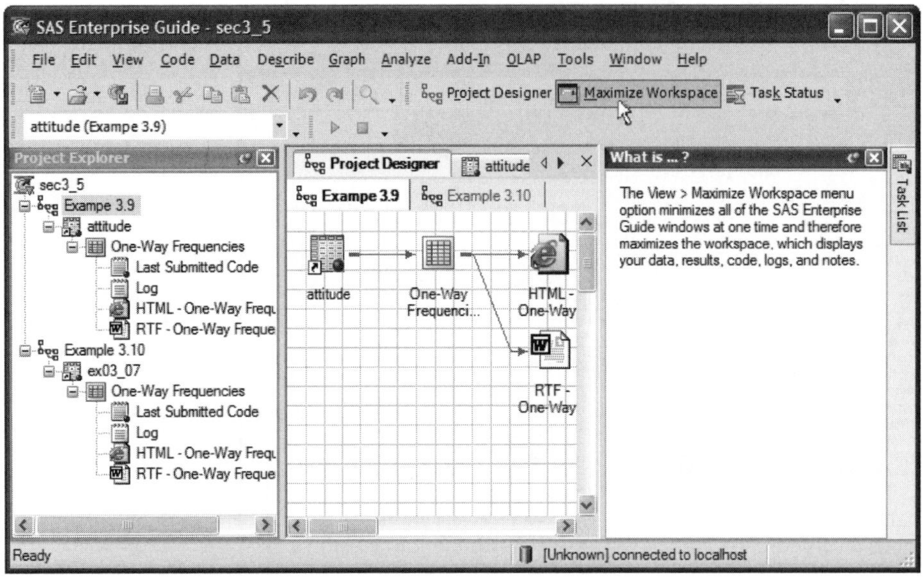

1.2   Titles and Common Task Roles

Instructions for most tasks refer back to this section. The Titles group of options is common and is discussed here. Three task roles that occur often are also discussed here.

1.2.1   Titles

The Titles options are the same in each task. Figure 1.17 shows the Titles options for the One-Way Frequencies task.

- Section lists the possible sections of task output plus the footnotes. Checked sections are those being requested.

- Text for section: *item-name* corresponds to the item selected on the section list.
  - o With **Use default text** checked, the default title or footnote can be seen in the inactive text box.
  - o Clearing the check box makes the text box active. The title or footnote can be edited.

The default **Footnote** gives system information, date, and time. For example:

Generated by the SAS System (Local, XP_HOME) on 19NOV2005 at 10:22 AM

Figure 1.17 Titles Options in the One-Way Frequencies Task

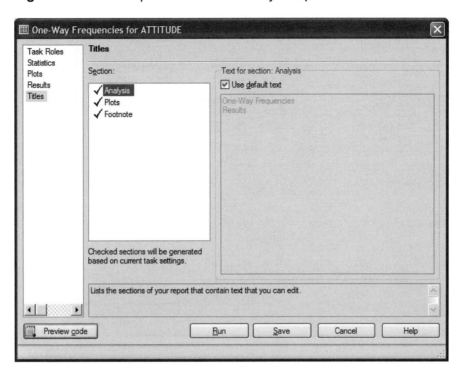

1.2.2 Common Task Roles

Group analysis by, Frequency count, and Relative weight task roles are fairly common and are discussed here.

- Group analysis by: Variables assigned to this role create groups of observations. All observations having identical rows in these variables form a group. The task is applied separately to each group. The task output is in a single file but there are separate results for each group.

  In Figure 1.18, Gender is assigned to the Group analysis by role. The Gender values F and M create two groups in the analysis variable Location. The One-Way Frequencies task is applied separately to each group.

  When a variable is assigned to this role, the variable's **sort order** drop-down menu appears. See Gender sort order on the right in Figure 1.18.

  o The unformatted values may be sorted in ascending (the default) and descending order, if **Sort by variables** is selected.

  o If **Sort by variables** is not selected, the groups are listed in the order that the values occur in the data.

Figure 1.18 Task Roles Options in One-Way Frequencies Task

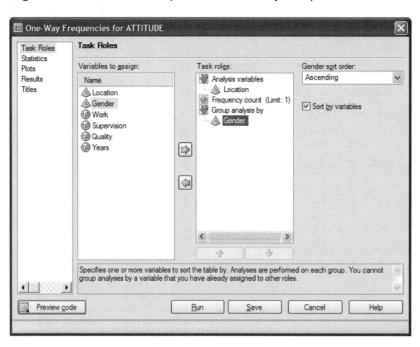

- Frequency count: The rows of this variable list the frequencies that the respective observations occur in the sample. If no variable is assigned to the Frequency count role, all the frequencies are assumed to be 1.

- Relative weight: The rows of this variable list weights that the respective observations are given. If no variable is assigned to the Relative weight role, all weights are 1.

Working with Data

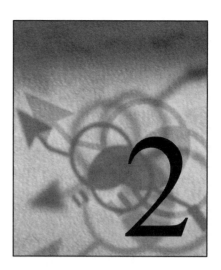

2.1 Introduction

This chapter presents topics necessary for working with data. These topics include SAS data sets, data sets in Excel and other formats, and the Query Builder.

The different file types are covered in Section 2.2 and Section 2.3. See Figure 2.1.

Figure 2.1 Data Can Be Read from Different File Types

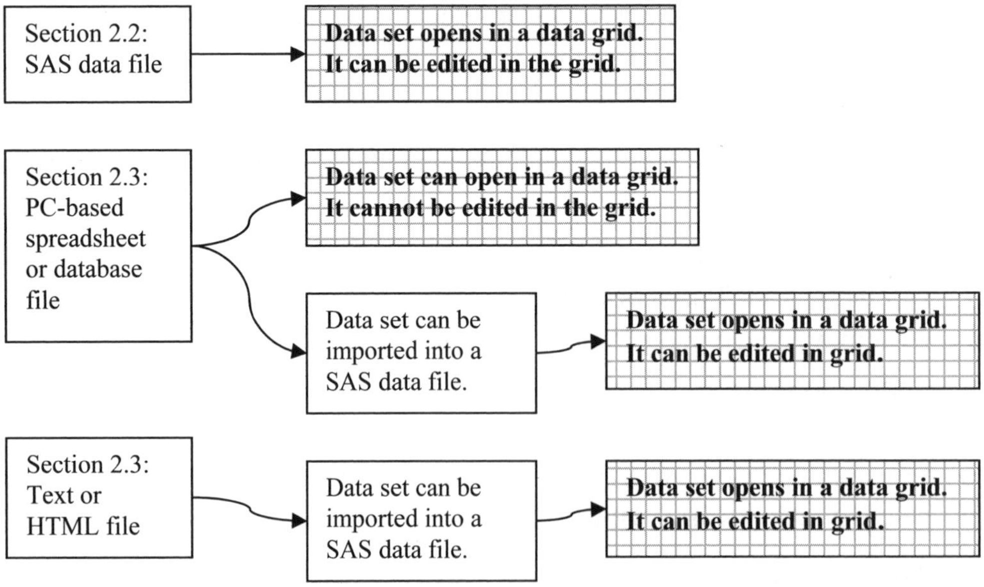

The Query Builder is a versatile data management tool. Among its capabilities are:

- filtering data
- selecting and changing the properties of output data

- sorting data
- replacing data
- creating new data
- grouping and summarizing data

2.2 SAS Data Sets

Data are the measurements, counts, and categorizations obtained from individuals or objects. A single measurement, count, or categorization is a *data value* or, simply, a *value*. Data are stored in *data sets*.

A data set is a table with columns corresponding to *variables* and rows corresponding to *observations*:

- A variable is a collection of values associated with a specific measurement or characterization.
- An observation is a collection of values associated with a single individual or object.

Figure 2.2 shows data set Ex02_01 in a SAS Enterprise Guide data grid. The data are from a class of 10 students. There are seven variables (Name, FI, MI, Test1, Test2, Test3, and Status) and 10 observations.

- The red bell (⚠) indicates character data. Name, FI, MI, and Status are character variables.
- The blue ball (🔵) indicates numeric data. Test1, Test2, and Test3 are numeric variables.

Some data are *missing*. One student does not have a middle initial (MI). Some test scores are absent. Only one student has a nonblank status value.

- A missing character value is represented by a blank.
- A missing numeric value is represented by a dot.

The icon (📇) to the left of the data set name in Figure 2.2 indicates that this is a SAS data set. In addition to the data values and variable names, a SAS data set contains information regarding the properties of the variables. See Section 2.2.1, "Variable Properties."

Figure 2.2 Data from a Class of Ten Students

	Name	FI	MI	Test1	Test2	Test3	Status
1	Alexander	W	J	95	76	80	
2	Chen	Z		84	96	87	
3	Davidson	A	K	100	88	100	
4	Davis	M	T	68	68	75	
5	Jackson	K	B	92	92	92	
6	Jones	G	H	.	75	68	
7	MacDonal	M	B	56	32	.	
8	Matthews	G	A	.	.	.	W
9	Robertson	A	T	95	80	84	
10	Rosen	J	S	95	92	100	

2.2.1 Variable Properties

Variable properties control how a variable is identified (name and label), whether it contains character or numeric data (type), its read-in form (informat), its display form (format), and the number of bytes used to store each value (length).

2.2.1.1 Name

- Variable names can be up to 32 characters in length.

- Names can start with any character. Names can include blanks.

- Letters in a variable name may be lowercase (cat), uppercase (CAT), or a mixture of both (Cat). Letter cases are for presentation only. For example, cat, CAT, and Cat would refer to the same variable.

There are some reserved names such as _N_ and _ERROR_. To avoid using a reserved name, it is good idea not to use names that begin with underscores.

2.2.1.2 Label

A variable label may have up to 256 characters. In some output, variable labels can replace variable names. In other output, variable labels are printed next to variable names.

Variable labels can be displayed instead of variable names in the data grid. See Figure 2.3.

To display variable labels instead of variable names in the data grid:
1. On the menu bar, select **Tools** and then **Options**.
2. When the Options window opens, select **Data General** from the selection pane on the left.
3. Check **Use labels for column names**.
4. Click **OK**.

To turn off the option, repeat the steps but clear the check box at **Use labels for column names**.

Figure 2.3 Data Labels Are Displayed for Data Set Ex02_01

	Last Name	First Initial	Middle Initial	Test 1 score	Test 2 score	Test 3 score	Enrollment Status
1	Alexander	W	J	95	76	80	
2	Chen	Z		84	96	87	
3	Davidson	A	K	100	88	100	
4	Davis	M	T	68	68	75	
5	Jackson	K	B	92	92	92	
6	Jones	G	H	.	75	68	
7	MacDonald	M	B	56	32	.	
8	Matthews	G	A	.	.	.	W
9	Robertson	A	T	95	80	84	
10	Rosen	J	S	95	92	100	

2.2.1.3 Type

A column is either character or numeric. In the variable heading, a red bell (⚠) indicates character data and a blue ball (◉) indicates numeric data. See Figure 2.2 and Figure 2.3. There can be special types of numeric data: dates (▦), time (🕐), and currency (💲).

2.2.1.4 Length

Length is the number of bytes used to store the variable's values. The default length for a numeric variable is 8. The default length for a character variable is 12.

The length of a numeric variable can be between 3 and 8. With a length of 8, the largest possible exact integer is 9,007,199,254,740,992, and numbers with decimals are accurate to 15 digits. With a length of 3, the largest possible exact integer is 8,192, and numbers with decimals are accurate to 3 digits. Numeric variables of less than 8 bytes are never necessary in this text.

The length of a character variable can be between 1 and 32767. Character values are stored one character per byte. The length of a variable is the maximum number of characters that can be stored per data value.

The format width and informat width of a character variable should correspond to its length. If the length is 25, the format should be $25. and the informat should be $25., for example. Formats and informats are discussed next.

2.2.1.5 Formats (Display Formats)

A *format* determines the column width and how the values are displayed. Formats are also called *display formats*.

For example, the F12.2 numeric format permits at most 12 characters, which can be digits, - prefix, decimal point, and E exponent notation. All numbers are displayed with 2 decimal places. The stored values are not affected by the format.

The F12.2 format is a specific case of the F$w.d$ (or $w.d$) numeric format, where values have at most w characters and are displayed with d decimal places. However, this is not the default numeric format.

Default Numeric Format

BEST12.0 is the default numeric format:

- Values are displayed with at most 12 characters, which can be digits, - prefix, decimal point, and E exponent notation.

- The zero in Best12.0 is ignored.

- Numeric values are aligned on the right side of the column.

- BEST12.0 does not display commas, dollar signs, and date notation.

- With BEST12.0 format:

    o Integers are written without decimal points. One sees 10 instead of 10.00.

    o Unnecessary decimals are not added to a number. One sees 10.01 instead of 10.0100.

    o Otherwise, the number of decimal places is whatever fits within 12 characters. One would see 10.123456789 and 100.12345678.

- In general, this is the BEST$w.d$ format, where values have at most w characters and d is ignored.

Default Character Format

Character format names begin with dollar signs. For a character variable, $12. is the default format. Values are displayed with at most 12 characters. Character values are aligned on the left side of the column. In general, this is the $$w.$ format, where values can have at most w characters.

2.2.1.6   Informats (Read-in Formats)

An *informat* determines how a value is entered. Informats are also called *read-in formats*.

Default Numeric Informat

F12.0 is the default numeric informat. The F12.0 informat is also written as the 12.0 informat.

- Values can have at most 12 characters, which can be digits, - prefix, decimal points, and E exponent notation.

- The zero in F12.0 is ignored. The number of decimal places in an entered value overrides the zero in F12.0.

- Commas, dollar signs, and date notation cannot be entered with F12.0 informat.

- In general, this is the F$w.d$ informat, where values can have at most w characters and d is ignored.

Default Character Informat

Character informat names begin with dollar signs. For a character column, $12. is the default informat. Values can have at most 12 characters. In general, this is the $$w.$ informat, where values can have at most w characters.

2.2.2 Data Set Locations: Folders, Binders, and Libraries

SAS Enterprise Guide opens SAS data files from Windows folders, SAS Enterprise Guide binders, and SAS data libraries.

- SAS Enterprise Guide is a Microsoft Windows client application. Data files are opened from Windows folders in the standard manner.

- SAS Enterprise Guide binders are virtual folders corresponding to folders on the computer or a server. Binders are created by the SAS Enterprise Guide Administrator software.

- SAS data libraries are locations defined with the SAS software. These are discussed here.

2.2.2.1 SAS Data Libraries

A SAS library is a collection of SAS files that is identified by a *libref*, a shortcut name. Since SAS Enterprise Guide operates in the Windows environment, folders are generally used instead of libraries. However, Work, EC, and Sasuser libraries are used. All are automatically created by SAS Enterprise Guide.

Work Library

The Work library is a temporary folder that contains files needed for a SAS Enterprise Guide session. When one exits SAS Enterprise Guide, the folder is deleted.

When a new SAS data set is created, it opens by default in the Work library. The data set is deleted at the end of the SAS Enterprise Guide session. To save the new data, you must export the contents of the data set to a file in a permanent folder. See "Creating a New SAS Data Set."

EC Libraries

An EC library is a temporary library created by SAS Enterprise Guide. The name of this library includes the EC prefix. This library is reserved for software use only.

Sasuser Library

The Sasuser library is a permanent folder that contains files needed by SAS Enterprise Guide. The actual folder depends on which version of Windows is being used:

- For Windows NT, Sasuser refers to C:\WINNT\Profiles\user-id\Personal\My SAS Files\9.1.

- For Windows 2000, Windows XP, and Windows Server 2003, Sasuser refers to C:\Documents and Settings\user-id\My Documents\My SAS Files\9.1.

Many SAS Enterprise Guide tasks can produce results in SAS data sets. By default, these data sets are stored in the Sasuser library. They are permanent in the sense that they are not automatically deleted by SAS software.

2.2.3 Rules for SAS Data Set Names

- A SAS data set name can be up to 32 characters in length.

- A SAS data set name must start with a letter or underscore. The remaining characters must be letters, numbers, or underscores.

- A SAS data set name cannot contain blanks.

- Letters may be lowercase, uppercase, or a mixture of both. Data set names are processed by SAS in uppercase regardless.

2.2.4 Opening a New SAS Data Set

One of the items on the Welcome to SAS Enterprise Guide window is **New Data** (⊞).

1. There are a number of ways to open a new data grid:

   - From the menu bar, select **File ▶ New ▶ Data**.

   - From the Standard toolbar, select **Create New Item In Project ▶ Data**.

   - From the Project toolbar, select the New Data icon (⊞).

   - Right-click on a Process Flow window and select **New ▶ Data**.

   Each of the above actions opens page 1 of 2 of the New Data window: **Specify name and location**. See the top window in Figure 2.4.

   - Name: The default data set names are Data, Data1, Data2, …. Names must follow certain rules. See Section 2.2.3, "Rules for SAS Data Set Names." The data set name is changed to Sections in Figure 2.4.

   - Location: A new SAS data set opens in the Work library. The Work library is a temporary folder that is deleted when SAS Enterprise Guide closes. To save a data set that is in the Work library, you must export it to a file in a permanent folder. See Section 2.2.8, "Exporting a Data Set."

2. Click **Finish** to open a new data grid with 6-character columns, A through F, and 12 empty rows.

> In a newly created data set, the variable type changes from character to numeric if a number is the first data value entered.
>
> To change this behavior, select **Tools** on the menu bar and then **Options** on the drop-down menu. At **Data General**, clear the check box at **Use cell value to determine column type**. This needs to be done before opening **New Data**.

3. Click **Next** to open page 2 of 2 of the New Data window: **Create columns and specify their properties**. See the bottom window in Figure 2.4.

   - Columns: Initially, 6 character columns, A through F, are listed. New columns can be added to the list. Listed columns can be duplicated, moved, and deleted.

   - Column Properties: The column names, labels, date types, and other properties can be changed.

4. Click **Finish** to open a new data grid with the specified columns and 12 empty rows. See Figure 2.6. Data values can be entered and edited. See Section 2.2.7, "Working in a Data Set."

2.2.5 Example 2.1: Creating a New Data Set

A new data set is created in this example. The data set has 2 numeric variables and 2 character variables. The length, the display format, and the read-in format are changed for one of the variables.

Example 2.1

1. Open page 1 of 2 of the New Data window by using one of the means presented at the beginning of Section 2.2.4, "Opening a New Data Set." See the top window in Figure 2.4.

2. Enter **Sections** at **Name**.

   At **Location**, the default—the Work library—is not changed.

3. Click **Next** to open page 2 of 2 of the New Data window. See the bottom window in Figure 2.4. Properties for 4 columns are entered.

   a. 1st column: Name is **Section**. **Label** is **Course section**. Change **Type** to **Numeric**. **Group** stays **Numeric**. **Length** stays 8. The default numeric **Display format** (BEST12.0) and the default numeric **Read-in format** (F12.0) are not changed. See Figure 2.5a.

   b. 2nd column: **Name** is **Time**. Label is **Class time and day**. **Type** stays **Character**. **Group** stays **Character**. **Length** stays 12. The default character **Display format** ($12.) and the default character **Read-in format** ($12.) are not changed.

   c. 3rd column: **Name** is **Location**. **Label** is **Classroom location**. **Type** stays **Character**. **Group** stays **Character**.

      i. **Length** is changed to **25**. See Figure 2.5b.

      ii. Click the Display format row, and the Display format selector icon (⊞) appears. A Format window opens with **Character** selected in **Categories** and **$w.** selected in **Formats**. (Display formats are also simply called formats.) **Overall width** is changed to **25**. See Figure 2.5c. Click **OK** to return to the New Data window.

      iii. Click the read-in format row. The Display format selector icon (⊞) appears. A Format window opens with **Character** selected in **Categories**, and **$w.** selected in **Informats**. (Read-in Formats are also called informats.) **Overall width** is changed to **25**. See Figure 2.5d. Click **OK** to return to the New Data window.

   d. 4th column: **Name** is **Enrollment**. **Label** is **Class enrollment**. **Type** is changed to **Numeric**. **Group** stays **Numeric**. **Length** stays **8**. The default numeric **Display format** (BEST12.0) and the default numeric Read-in format (F12.0) are not changed. See Figure 2.5e.

4. Columns E and F are deleted. Click **Finish**. The new Sections data set is opened with 12 empty rows. See Figure 2.6. Data values are entered in 2 rows. The remaining rows are deleted. See Figure 2.7.

5. The Sections data set is put in read-only mode: Click **Data** on the menu bar and then **Read-only**. In Figure 2.7, **(read-only)** appears next to the data set name.

At this point, the Sections data set is still in the temporary Work library. To make it permanent, you must copy it to another folder. See Section 2.2.8, "Exporting a Data Set."

Figure 2.4 New Data Window Pages 1 (Top) and 2 (Bottom)

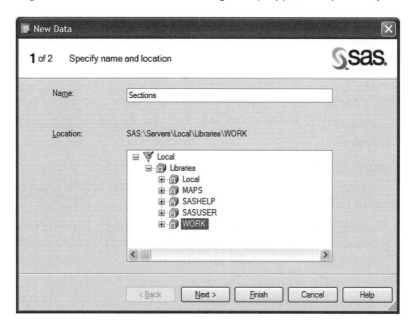

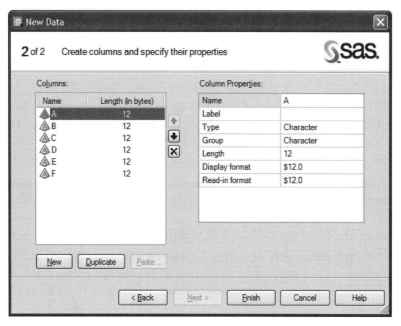

Figure 2.5 (a) Section Properties; (b) Location Properties; (c) Display Format Window for Location; (d) Read-in Format Window for Location; and (e) Enrollment Properties

(a)

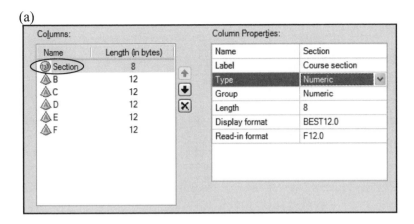

(b)

(c)

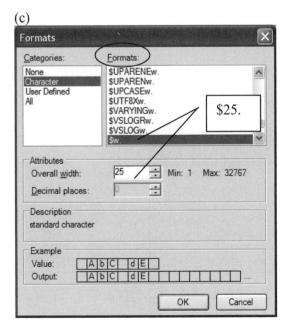

(d)

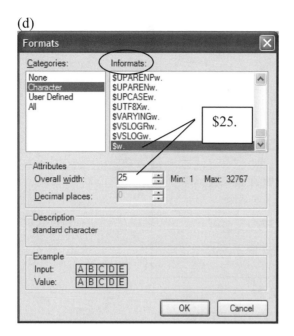

(e)

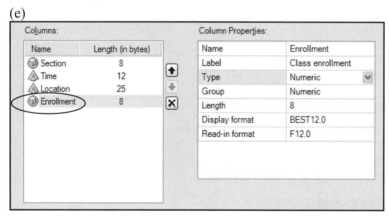

Figure 2.6 New Sections Data Set

Figure 2.7 Sections Data Set with Values and in Read-only Mode

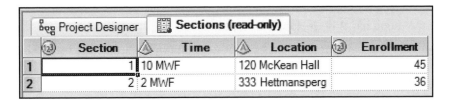

2.2.6 Opening an Existing SAS Data File

A *data file* is a file containing a data set. A SAS data file is a SAS system file with the extension
*.sas7bdat, *.sd7, or *.sd2. The data set in a SAS data file opens by default in a data grid.

Figure 2.8 SAS Data Files Open by Default in a Data Grid

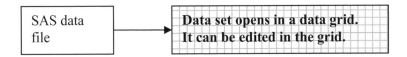

SAS Enterprise Guide opens SAS data files from the following locations: a Windows folder, a
SAS library, or a SAS Enterprise Guide binder.

2.2.6.1 Windows Folder

SAS Enterprise Guide is a Microsoft Windows client application. A data file is opened in the
standard manner.

To open a data file in one of the computer's folders:

1. Select one of the following:

   - From the menu bar, select **File ▶ Open ▶ Data**.

   - Or from the Standard toolbar, click the **Open** icon (📂). Then select **Data** from the
     drop-down menu.

   - Or right-click a Process Flow window and select **Open ▶ Data**.

2. Select **Local Computer** in the Open Data From window.

3. From the Open From My Computer window, navigate to and open the desired file.

2.2.6.2 SAS Libraries

When a SAS data set is from a SAS library, it is given a name that combines the library name and
the data set name Library_name.data_set_name.

As examples, Work.data1 is the data set Data1 from the Work library, and
SASUSER.QURY4357 is the QURY4357 data set from the Sasuser library. Upper- and
lowercase in data set names do not matter.

To open a data file from a SAS library:

1. Select one of the following:

    *   From the menu bar, **File ▶ Open ▶ Data**.

    *   Or from the Standard toolbar, click the Open icon (📂). Then select **Data** from the drop-down menu.

    *   Or right-click on a Process Flow window and select **Open ▶ Data**.

2. Select **SAS Servers** in the Open Data From window.

3. On the Open From SAS Servers window, select servers in the selection pane on the left.

4. The result is the list of available servers. Navigate to and open the desired file.

2.2.6.3   SAS Enterprise Guide Binder

A binder is a virtual folder corresponding to a folder on the computer or a server. Binders are created by the SAS Enterprise Guide Administrator software.

To open a data file from a SAS Enterprise Guide binder:

1. Select one of the following:

    *   From the menu bar, select **File ▶ Open ▶ Data**.

    *   Or from the Standard toolbar, click the Open icon (📂). Then select **Data** from the drop-down menu.

    *   Or right-click on a Process Flow window and select **Open ▶ Data**.

2. Select **SAS Servers** in the Open Data From window.

3. On the Open From SAS Servers window, select **Binders** in the selection pane on the left.

4. The result is the list of available binders. Navigate to and open the desired file.

2.2.7 Working in a Data Grid

SAS data sets can be edited in the data grids. Observations and variables can be added and deleted. Data values can be entered and edited. Variable properties can be changed.

> **Changes are made directly to the data set.** You will not be asked whether any changes are to be saved. Any changes are immediately saved.

Manipulating data is best done with queries. See Section 2.4, "Query Builder."

A data grid must be in *update mode* in order to make changes. A newly created SAS data set opens in update mode. An existing data set does not. See Section 2.2.7.1, "Read-only and Update Modes."

New data is entered by:

*   typing data into the cells of the data grid

*   copying and pasting from another source

*   dragging and dropping from another source

To edit a data value:

1. Move the cursor cell to the value.

2. Enter the new value.

3. To insert or delete characters, click the cell. A blinking vertical cursor line appears.

The arrow keys are used to navigate around the grid. The **Enter** key moves the cursor cell to the beginning of the next row.

2.2.7.1   Read-only and Update Modes

An opened data set is in one of two modes:

*   *read-only* mode:
    o   The data is protected and no changes can be made.
    o   **(read-only)** is displayed in the data set's Workspace tab.
    o   An existing SAS data set opens in read-only mode. See Figure 2.2.
*   *update* mode:
    o   The data can be edited and the variable properties can be changed.
    o   **read-only** is absent in the data set's Workspace tab.
    o   A newly created SAS data set opens in update mode. See Figure 2.6.

To switch from read-only mode to update mode:

1. Click **Data** on the menu bar then click **Read-only** to deselect the check mark (✔).

2. Click **Yes** when prompted. See Figure 2.9. The **(read-only)** notation disappears from the title bar of the data set window.

Figure 2.9 Prompt When Switching to Update Mode

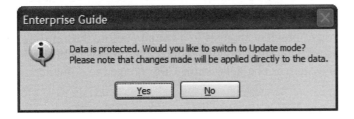

To switch from update mode to read-only mode:

1. Click **Data** on the menu bar.

2. Click **Read-only**. **Read-only** is checked (✔) in the **Data** menu, and **(read-only)** appears next to the data set name.

2.2.7.2   Changing Properties in an Existing Variable

To open a variable's Properties window:

1. The data must be in update mode in order to make changes to variable properties.

2. Right-click the variable name in the data grid.

3. Select **Properties** from the drop-down menu.

Properties Window

Figures 2.10 and 2.11 show the Properties option groups. The data is in update mode. Figure 2.10 shows the properties of the character variable Name. Figure 2.11 shows the properties of the numeric variable Test1. Both variables are from data set Ex02_01 in Figure 2.2.

- general options:
  - name and Label entry boxes
  - type and Group drop-down lists and the Group icon
    - Character variables show a red bell (⚠). Character variables are not subdivided into groups. The only Group for character variables is Character.
    - General numeric variables show a blue ball (123). Special types of numeric data are date (▦), time (🕐), and currency ($¥). Group for a numeric variable may be Numeric, Data, Time, or Currency.
  - length (in bytes) entry box.
- Formats options are a list of formats and entry boxes in the Attributes region. See "Formats (Display Formats)" in Section 2.2.1, "Variable Properties."
  - In Figure 2.10, the selection is the $12. character format. At most 12 characters are displayed. Character values are aligned on the left.
  - In Figure 2.11, the selection is the BEST12. numeric format. Values are displayed with at most 12 characters, which can be digits, - prefix, decimal point, and E exponent notation. Numeric values are aligned on the right. The software selects the best way to display the data.
- Informats options are a list of informats and entry boxes in the Attributes region. See "Informats (Read-in Formats)" in Section 2.2.1, "Variable Properties."
  - In Figure 2.10, the selection is the $12. character informat. At most 12 characters can be entered.
  - In Figure 2.11, the selection is the 12. numeric informat. At most 12 characters (digits, - prefix, decimal point, and E exponent notation) can be entered.
- Confirm options enables you to preview changes to a column before they are applied to the data grid. Previewing is particularly useful when the type of the variable is changed. This occurs when numbers written as character values are changed to numeric values.

Click **OK** when finished.

Figure 2.10 General Formats, Informats, and Confirm Options for the Character Variable Name

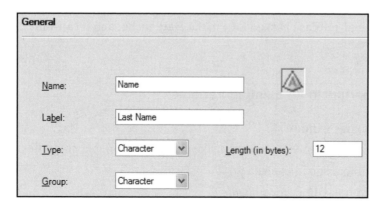

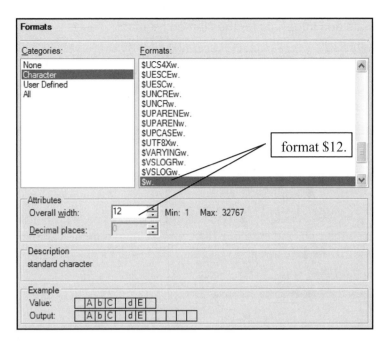

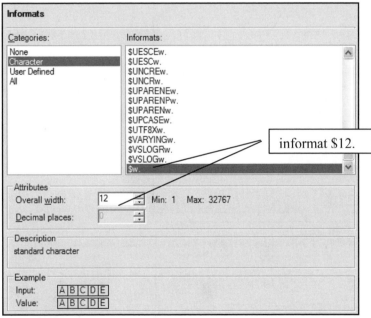

Figure 2.11 General Formats and Informats for the Numeric Variable Test1

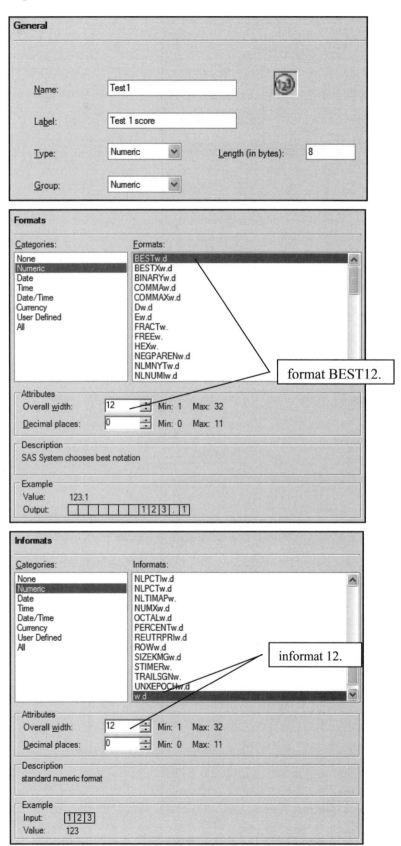

2.2.7.3 Inserting Columns

To insert a new blank column:

1. The data grid must be in update mode.

2. Click the header of the column that will be next to—before or after—the new column.

3. From the menu bar, select **Data ▶ Columns ▶ Insert**. Or, right-click the highlighted column and select **Insert Column**.

   The Insert window opens.

4. In the Insert the new column box, select whether the new column is to be to the left or to the right of the selected column.

Insert Window

The Insert window is similar to the Properties window discussed in Section 2.2.7.2, "Changing Properties in an Existing Variable." Figure 2.12 shows the general options of the Insert window.

Values can be computed from a wide variety of expressions. An expression can be entered at **Expression**. The Advanced Expression Editor is opened by clicking ⬚. See Section 2.4.9, "Computed Columns: Building Expressions."

Click **OK** when finished.

Figure 2.12 shows the general options for inserting the location character variable.

Figure 2.12 General Options on the Insert Window

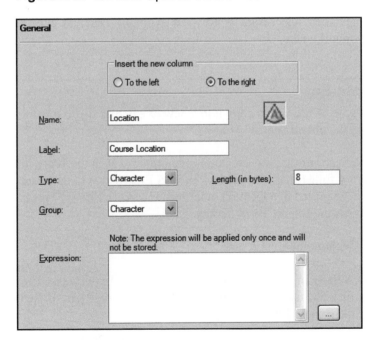

2.2.7.4 Deleting Rows and Columns

With the data grid in update mode, select a row or a column by clicking its header. Multiple rows or columns can be selected by clicking a row or a column header, holding down the **Shift** key, and using the arrows on the keyboard.

Any one of the following will delete selected rows or columns:

- From the menu bar, select **Edit** and then select **Delete**.
- From the Standard toolbar, select **Delete**.
- Right-click a highlighted row or column. Then select **Delete rows** or **Delete**.
- Pressing the **Delete** key.

2.2.7.5   Inserting and Appending Rows

The data grid must be in update mode.

Pressing the **Enter** key with the cursor on the last row adds new rows to the end of the data set.

Up to 999 rows at a time can be inserted anywhere.

To insert a row:
1. Click the row header where one or more rows are to be inserted.
2. From the menu bar, select **Data**, then **Rows**, and then **Insert**. Or, right-click the highlighted row and select **Insert rows**.
3. The Insert Rows window opens. Select whether the new rows are to be inserted above or below. Type in or select the number of rows to insert. Click **OK**.

Appending a row opens a blank row at the top of the data set. New values can be entered. The row is then added to the end of the data set when the **Enter** key is pressed.

To append a row: From the menu bar, select **Data ▶ Rows ▶ Append**. Or, right-click the highlighted row and select **Append a row**.

2.2.8 Exporting a Data Set

To *export* a data set—or any type of file—is to copy it to a new or existing file, but without replacing it in the project with the output file.

For example, the new data set Sections that was created in Example 2.1 is in the Work library. The Work library is a temporary folder that is deleted when SAS Enterprise Guide closes. To save the data set, it needs to be exported to a location other than the Work library. This is explained in the "Instructions for the Export Task" section.

Files can be exported with or without the Export task.

- Selecting **Export As A Step In Project** from a menu opens the Export task. The result of the task is the output file. The task icon and data set shortcut become part of the project. See "Instructions for the Export Task."
- Selecting **Export** from a menu enables navigation to a folder for the output file. No change is made to the project. See "Exporting without the Task."

2.2.8.1 Instructions for the Export Task

Open the Export task in one of the following ways:

- From the menu bar, select **File ▶ Export ▶ Export As A Step In Project**.
- Right-click the Project Explorer or Project Designer icon of the file to be exported. Select **Export _____ As A Step In Project** from the pop-up menu. The blanks would be the file name.

Listed below are the pages of the Export task. The third in the list—Modify additional options for the output file—does not appear for some output files, including the SAS data file.

- Select the file to export.

  The first page lists the project files that can be exported. Select the file to be exported from the list. In Figure 2.13, the Sections data set is selected on page 1.

- Select a file type for the output file.

  The second page lists the possible file types. SAS Data File (*.sas7bdat) is the selection on page 2 in Figure 2.13.

- Modify additional options for the output file.

  This page is available for some types of output files where column labels can be used for column names. To apply this option, check **Use labels for column names**. This is not an option for SAS data files, which have both column names and column labels.

- Specify the location and name for the output file.

  The file is exported to the local computer or a SAS server. Click **Edit** to navigate to the desired location for the output file and to name the file. On page 3 in Figure 2.13, the path for the output file is C:\Documents and Settings\Owner\My Documents\My SAS Files\Sections.sas7bdat.

- Confirm the selections you have made.

  Page 4 in Figure 2.13 confirms that the Sections data set will be exported as a SAS data file to a permanent folder.

  When you are ready to export the file, click **Finish**. The task adds an Export File icon and an output data set icon to the Project Explorer and to the Project Designer. See Figure 2.14 for the Project Designer icons.

Figure 2.13 Pages 1 of 4 through 4 of 4 of the Export Task

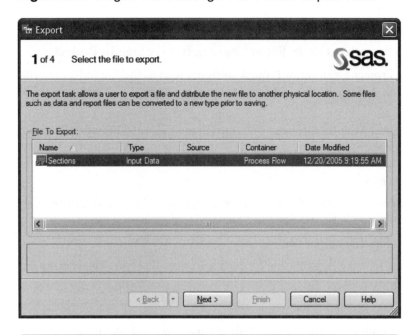

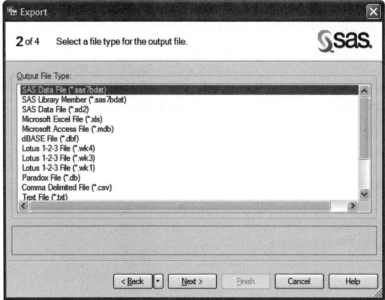

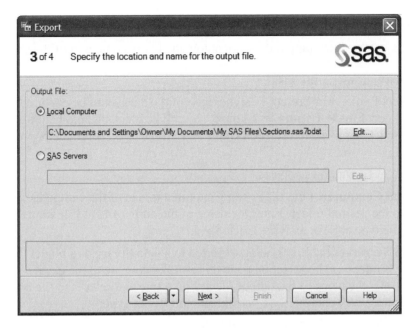

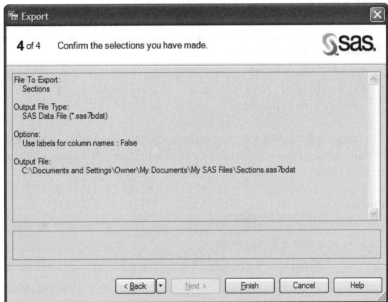

Figure 2.14 Export File Icon and Sections Output Data Set Icon

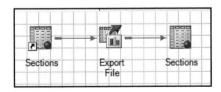

2.2.8.2   Exporting without the Task

When the Export task is not used, the output does not automatically become part of the project.

To export a data set without using the task:

1. Select the Project Explorer or Project Designer icon of the data set to be exported. From the menu bar, select **File ▶ Export ▶ Export _____**. The blanks would be the data set's name. Or right-click the icon, and select **Export ▶ Export _____** from the pop-up menu.

2. The Export _____ To windows appears.

    a. Select **Local Computer** if the file is being exported to one of the computer's folders. Navigate to the desired folder. Enter the name of the output file at **File name** and select the file type at **Save as type**. Click **Save**.

    b. Select **SAS Servers** if the file is being exported to a data library or a binder. Select **Servers** or **Binders** on the selection pane on the left. Navigate to the desired library or binder. Enter the name of the output file at **File name** and select the file type— when other than SAS data files are permitted—at **Files of type**.

    c. Click **Save**.

2.2.9   Changing Data Set Shortcuts

When a project file and associated data sets are copied to another computer, it is very possible that data set shortcuts need to be changed. Also, changing a data set shortcut is a way to replace a temporary data set in a project with an exported permanent version.

Figure 2.15 shows the file names before and after the temporary data file Data1 is replaced by a permanent file. The complete name of the temporary file is Work.Data1. It means that the data file Data1 is in the Work data library.

To change a data set shortcut:

1. Select the shortcut icon of the data set ▦. From the menu bar, select **File ▶ Properties**. Or right-click the icon and select **Properties**.

2. The Properties for _____ window appears. The blanks would be the data set name.

3. At the General options, **File Name** shows the SAS library name or Windows path of the current data set.

4. Click the **Change** icon. See Figure 2.15.

5. The Open data window appears.

    a. Select **Local Computer** if the new file is in one of the computer's folders. Navigate to the folder and select the desired file. Click **Open**.

    b. Select **SAS Servers** if the new file is in a data library or a binder. Select **Servers** or **Binders** on the selection pane on the left. Navigate to the library or binder and select the desired file. Click **Open**.

6. Click **OK** on the Properties for _____ window.

Figure 2.15 File Names Before (Top) and After (Bottom) the Temporary File Data1 Is
Replaced by a Permanent File

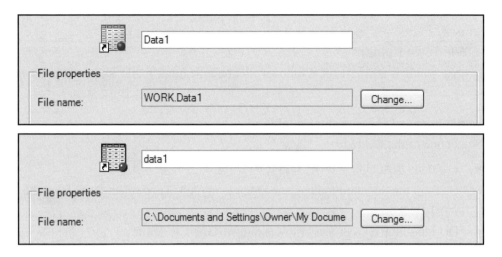

2.3 Data Sets in Other Types of Files

A data set in a PC-based spreadsheet or database file can be opened directly into a data grid or it
can first be imported into a SAS data file. A data set in a text or HTML file must first be imported
into a SAS data file. See Figure 2.16.

Figure 2.16 Data Sets Can Be Read from Different File Types

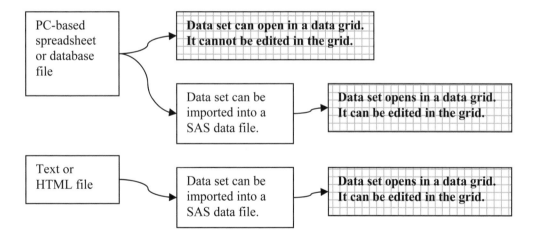

If a data set in a PC-based spreadsheet or database file is to be opened directly into a data grid,
the sequence is to first open the file and then select "as is" when prompted by the Open Data
window. See Section 2.31, "Opening Other Types of Files" and Example 2.2.

Importing a data set from a file that is not a SAS file into a SAS data file is done with the Import
Data task. See Sections 2.3.3 through 2.3.6.

2.3.1 Opening Other Types of Files

A file that is not a SAS file can be opened from anywhere except from SAS data libraries.

2.3.1.1 Windows Folder

SAS Enterprise Guide is a Microsoft Windows client application. A file is opened in the standard manner.

To open a file in one of the computer's folders:

1. Select one of the following:

    - From the menu bar, **File ▶ Open ▶ Data**.

    - Or from the Standard toolbar, the Open icon (📂). Then select **Data** from the drop-down menu.

    - Or right-click on a Process Flow window: **Open ▶ Data**.

2. The Open Data From window opens. Select **Local Computer**.

    The Open From My Computer window opens with **Files of type** set to **All Known Data Files**. These file types are listed below:

    - SAS data files (*sas7bdat, *.sd2)
    - Microsoft Excel files (*.xls)
    - Microsoft Access files (*mdb)
    - dBase files (*.dbf)

    - Lotus 1-2-3 files (*.wk?)
    - Paradox files (*.db)
    - Text files (*.txt, *.csv, *.asc, *.tab)
    - HTML files (*.htm, *html)

3. Navigate to and open the desired file.

2.3.1.2 SAS Enterprise Guide Binder

A binder is a virtual folder corresponding to a folder on the computer or a server. Binders are created by the Enterprise Guide Administrator software.

To open a data file from a SAS Enterprise Guide binder:

1. If the binder list is not showing, select **View ▶ Binder List**.

2. The result is the list of available binders. Navigate to the desire binder. Double click the desired file or drag the desired file onto the process flow diagram.

2.3.2 Example 2.2: Opening Directly from an Excel File

The data set in Figure 2.17 is opened directly into a data grid. The steps outline the process.

The data set is in worksheet Ex02_01 of the Excel file Ex02_01.xls, which, in this example, is in one of the computer's folders.

Example 2.2

1. From the menu bar, select **File ▶ Open ▶ Data**.

2. The Open Data From window opens. **Local Computer** is selected.

3. In the Open From My Computer window, the appropriate folder is opened and **ex02_01** is selected. Click **Open**.

4. The Open Tables window appears with the list of the Excel file spreadsheets and named regions. See Figure 2.18.

   - A name that includes $ refers to an entire spreadsheet. In Figure 2.18, Ex02_01$, Sheet2$, and Sheet3$ refer to the spreadsheets in Ex02_01.xls.

   - A name that does not include $ refers to a named region. In Figure 2.18, the name Ex02_01 refers to the rectangular region from A1 to G11 in the Ex02_01 spreadsheet. There is nothing else in the spreadsheet.

   In this case, Ex02_01$ is selected. Then **Open** is clicked.

5. The Open Data window appears with the two choices for opening the spreadsheet. See Figure 2.19.

   a. **as is** (▤). The data set is opened directly into a data grid.

   b. **as a SAS data set** (▦). The Import Data task opens.

   Select **as is**. The result is in Figure 2.20. The name of the new data set in Enterprise Guide is Ex02_01(ex02_01$). The icon 🐝 indicates that this is associated with an Excel file.

Figure 2.17 Spreadsheet Ex02_01 of Excel File ex1_02.xls

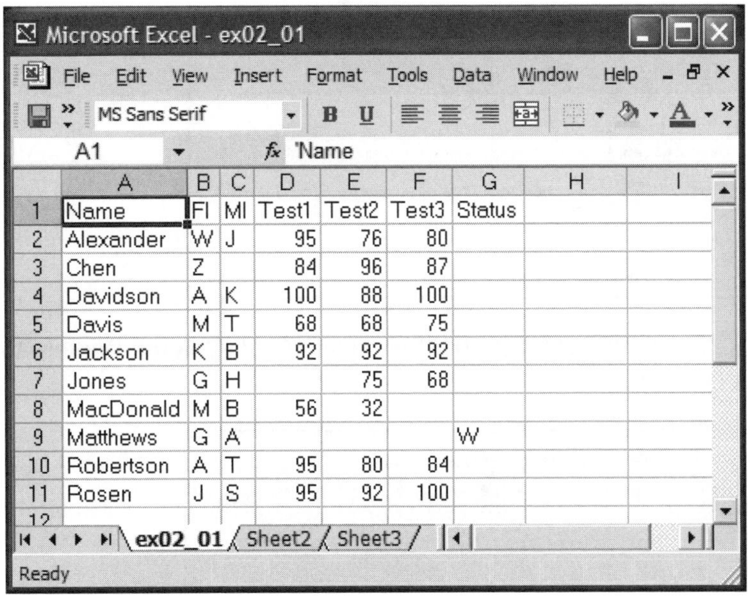

Figure 2.18 Spreadsheet Ex02_01 Is Checked

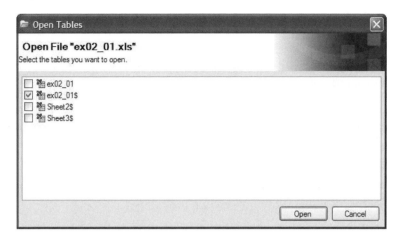

Figure 2.19 The Top Icon Opens the Spreadsheet As Is. The Bottom Icon Opens the Import Data Task.

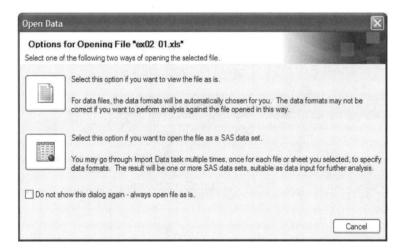

Figure 2.20 Data Set Ex02_01(ex02_01$) in a Data Grid (Column Widths Are Resized from the Default)

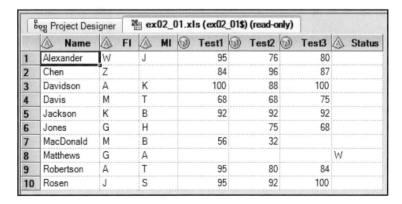

	Name	FI	MI	Test1	Test2	Test3	Status
1	Alexander	W	J	95	76	80	
2	Chen	Z		84	96	87	
3	Davidson	A	K	100	88	100	
4	Davis	M	T	68	68	75	
5	Jackson	K	B	92	92	92	
6	Jones	G	H		75	68	
7	MacDonald	M	B	56	32		
8	Matthews	G	A				W
9	Robertson	A	T	95	80	84	
10	Rosen	J	S	95	92	100	

2.3.3 Importing Data

To *import* a data set is to copy it from a file other than a SAS file into a SAS data file. This is done with the Import Data task.

Example 2.3 illustrates importing a data set from an Excel file. Example 2.4 and Example 2.5 illustrate importing data sets from text files.

The Import Data task is opened by either selecting the file first or by selecting Import Data first.

To select the file first:

1. To open a file that is not a SAS file, select **as is** or **as a SAS data set** in the Open Data window. The file is added to the project in its original format, and the Import Data window opens. See the "Region to Import" section below.

2. In the case of a text file that has previously been added "as is" to the project, right-click the file icon and select **Import Data**. The Import Data window appears. See the "Region to Import" section below.

To select import data first:

1. From the menu bar, select **File ▶ Import Data**.

2. The Open Data window appears.

   - If the file is in one of the computer's folders, select **Local Computer**. Navigate to the folder and select the desired file. Click **Open**. If the file is a PC-based spreadsheet or database file, select the spreadsheet or table to be imported. See Figure 2.18 in Example 2.2.

   - If the file is in a binder, select **SAS Servers**. Then select **Binders** on the selection pane on the left of the Open window. Navigate to the binder and select the desired file. Click **Open**. If the file is a PC-based spreadsheet or database file, select the spreadsheet or table to be imported.

3. The file is added to the project in its original format and the Import Data window opens. See the "Region to Import" section below.

2.3.3.1 Region to Import

The Import Data window opens with the **Region to Import**. See Figure 2.21 in Example 2.3 and Figure 2.30 in Example 2.5. The rows to be read are selected here.

1. Check **Specify line to use as column heading** if columns headings are present. Then select the appropriate row number on the right.

2. **Import entire file** is checked by default. Other options are available to read specific rows.

2.3.3.2 Text Format

The Text Format options are available when importing from a text file. See Figure 2.27 in Example 2.4 and Figure 2.31 in Example 2.5.

1. In the **Format** box, indicate how the data is structured:

   - **Delimited**: Values are separated in the rows by a comma, tab, or other character.

   - **Fixed Width**: Values are aligned in columns.

2. If **Delimited** is selected, identify the character in the **Delimiter** box. See Figure 2.27 in Example 2.4.

3. If **Fixed Width** is selected, then the field break window opens. See Figure 2.31 in Example 2.5. Lines identify the columns. An arrow identifies the location of a column's first character. Click to insert a line. Double-click to delete a line. Drag a line to move it.

2.3.3.3 Column Options

Column Options show the column properties of the imported data set. See Figure 2.22 in Example 2.3 and Figure 2.32 in Example 2.5. These properties are the same as in Section 2.2.1, "Variable Properties." Display format and read-in format are format and informat, respectively, in the same section.

2.3.3.4 Results

The Results options set the name and location of the new SAS data set. See Figure 2.23 in Example 2.3. The default names are IMPW, IMPW_0000, IMPW_0001, IMPW_0002 …. The default location is the Sasuser library. The data set name and the SAS library can be changed by clicking **Browse**.

To save the data set to a Windows folder or a SAS Enterprise Guide binder, export the data set after the task is complete.

When you are finished selecting options, click **Run**. The task adds an Import Data icon and an icon for the new SAS data set. See Figures 2.24, 2.28, and 2.33.

2.3.4 Example 2.3: Excel File

The data set in Figure 2.17 in Example 2.2 is imported into a SAS data set. The steps outline the process. The first five steps are the same as in Example 2.2. The data set is in worksheet Ex02_01 of the Excel file Ex02_01.xls, which, in this example, is in one of the computer's folders.

Example 2.3
1. From the menu bar, select **File ▶ Open ▶ Data**.
2. The Open Data From window opens. **Local Computer** is selected.
3. In the Open From My Computer window, the appropriate folder is opened and Ex02_01 is selected. Click **Open**.
4. The Open Tables window appears with the list of the Excel file's spreadsheets and named regions. See Figure 2.18 in Example 2.2.
    a. A name that includes $ refers to an entire spreadsheet. In Figure 2.18, Ex02_01$, Sheet2$ and Sheet3$ refer to the spreadsheets in Ex02_01.xls.
    b. A name that does not include $ refers to a named region. In Figure 2.18, the name Ex02_01 refers to the rectangular region from A1 to G11 in the Ex02_01 spreadsheet. There is nothing else in the spreadsheet.
    c. In this case, Ex02_01$ is selected. Then click **Open**.

5. The Open Data window appears with the two choices for opening the spreadsheet. See Figure 2.19 in Example 2.1.

   a. **as is** (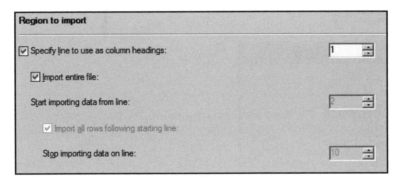). The data set is opened directly into a data grid.

   b. **as a SAS data set** ( ). The Import Data task opens.

6. Here, **as a SAS data set** is selected.

7. The Import Data window opens with the Region to Import options. See Figure 2.21. Here, the column heading will be read from row 1, and the entire data set will be read.

8. The Column options window identifies the column names and properties. See Figure 2.22. No changes have been made here. Empty columns can be added and removed with the Add and Remove icons.

9. The Results options set the name and the location of the new SAS data set. See Figure 2.23. Here, the new data set is SASUSER.IMPW_000B. The new data set is named IMPW_000B and it is saved in the Sasuser library. No changes have been made here.

10. Clicking **Run** on the Import Data window executes the task. An Import Data icon and an icon for the new data set are added to the process flow diagram and the project tree. See Figure 2.24. The new data set opens in the workspace. Except for the name, the data set is the same as in Figure 2.2.

Figure 2.21 Region to Import Options

Figure 2.22 Column Options

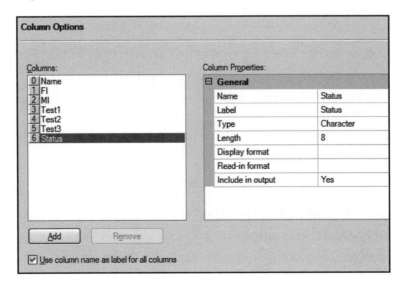

Figure 2.23 Results Options

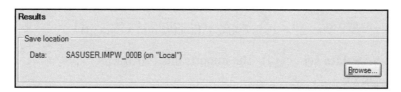

Figure 2.24 Shortcut for Excel Worksheet, Import Data Icon, and Output SAS Data
Set Icon

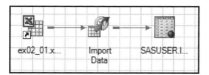

2.3.5 Example 2.4: Delimited Text File with Column Headers

The data set in Figure 2.25 is imported into a SAS data set. The steps outline the process.

Column headers and the data values are separated by commas. The data set is in text file
Ex02_01.txt, which in this example is in one of the computer's folders.

Figure 2.25 Ex2_01.txt

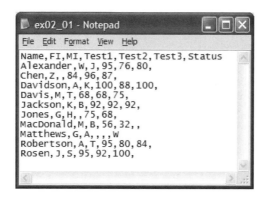

Example 2.4

1. From the menu bar, the following sequence of items is selected: **File ▶ Open ▶ Data**.

2. The Open Data From window opens. Local Computer is selected.

3. In the Open From My Computer window, the appropriate folder is opened and Ex02_01
   is selected. **Open** is clicked.

4. The Open Data window appears with the two choices for opening the text file. See Figure
   2.26.

   a. **as is** (📄). The data set is opened directly into a data grid.

   b. **as a SAS data set** (📄). The Import Data task opens.

5. Here, **as a SAS data set** is selected.

6. The Import Data window opens with the Region to Import. See Figure 2.21 in Example
   2.3. Here, the column headings will be read from row 1 and the entire data set will be
   read.

7. The Text Format window has the options for how data values are to be read. See Figure 2.27. Here, the data is delimited, and the delimiter is a Comma.

8. The Column options window identifies the column names and properties. See Figure 2.22 in Example 2.3. No changes have been made here.

9. The Results options set the name and the location of the new SAS data set. See Figure 2.23 in Example 2.3. Here, the new data set name would be similar to SASUSER.IMPW_000B. By default, it is saved in the Sasuser library.

10. Clicking **Run** on the Import Data window executes the task. An Import Data icon and an icon for the new data set are added to the process flow diagram and the project tree. See Figure 2.28. The new data set opens in the workspace. Except for the name, the data set is the same as in Figure 2.2.

Figure 2.26 The Top Button Opens the Text File As Is; the Bottom Button Opens the Import Data Task

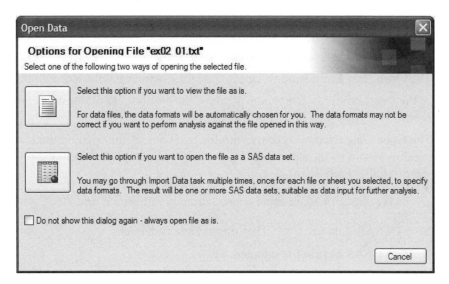

Figure 2.27 Text Format Options

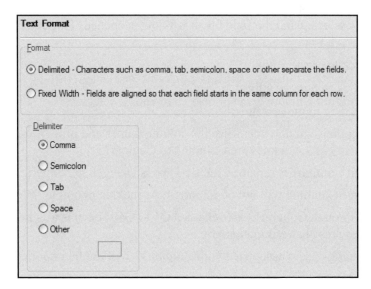

Figure 2.28 Shortcut for Ex02_01.txt, Import Data Icon, and Output SAS Data Set Icon

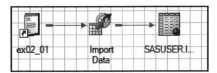

2.3.6 Example 2.5: Fixed-Width Text File without Column Headers

The data set in Figure 2.29 is imported into a SAS data set. The steps outline the process.

The data values are in fixed-width format. Column headers are not present. The data set is in text file Ex02_04.txt, which in this example is in one of the computer's folders.

Example 2.5

1. From the menu bar, select **File ▶ Open ▶ Data**.

2. The Open Data From window opens. Local Computer is selected.

3. In the Open From My Computer window, the appropriate folder is opened and Ex02_05 is selected. The **Open** button is clicked.

4. The Open Data window appears with the two choices for opening the text file. The window would be the same as in Figure 2.26 in Example 2.4 except the window would refer to Ex02_05.txt.

   a. **as is** (🗎). The data set is opened directly into a data grid.

   b. **as a SAS data set** 🗎 . The Import Data task opens.

5. Here, **as a SAS data set** is selected.

6. The Import Data window opens with the Region to Import. See Figure 2.30. Here, there is no line for column headings to specify. The entire data set will be read.

7. Text Format has the options for how data values are to be read. See Figure 2.31. Here, Fixed Width is selected and the field break window is opened. Thirteen columns are identified.

   • Single-click to create a line.

   • Double-click to remove a line.

   • Select and drag to move a line.

8. The Column options window identifies the column names and properties. See Figure 2.32. The default column names are Column1 to Column13.

   a. The 3-digit Column1 is renamed ID. Its Type is changed to Numeric.

   b. The 9-space Column2 will not be imported. At Include in output, No is selected.

   c. Column3 through Column12 are renamed Q1 to Q10. Each is a 1-digit column. The Type for each is changed to Numeric.

   d. The remaining spaces associated with Column13 will not be imported. At Include in output, No is selected.

9. The Results options set the name and the location of the new SAS data set. The window would be the same as in Figure 2.23 in Example 2.3 except for the digits in the name. No changes are made here.

10. Clicking **Run** on the Import Data window executes the task. An Import Data icon and an icon for the new data set are added to the process flow diagram and the project tree. See Figure 2.33. The new data set opens in the workspace. See Figure 2.34.

Figure 2.29 Ex02_05.txt in Microsoft Notepad

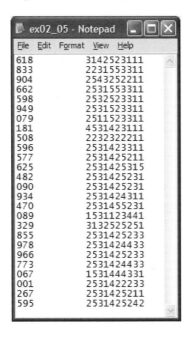

Figure 2.30 Region to Import Options

Figure 2.31 Text Format Options

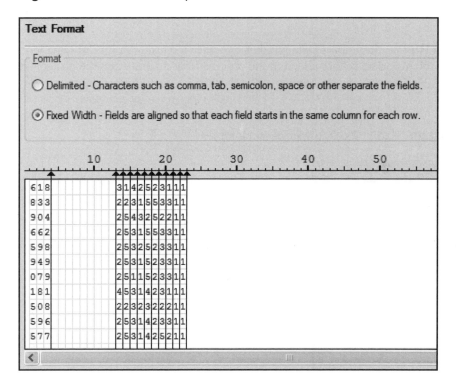

Figure 2.32 Column Options

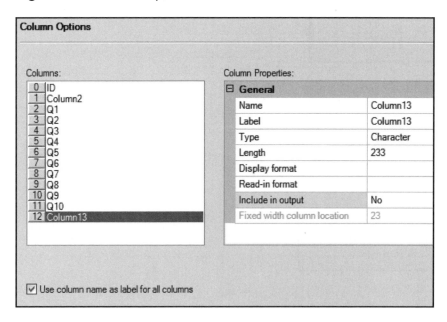

Figure 2.33 Shortcut for Ex02_05.txt, Import Data Icon,
and Output SAS Data Set Icon

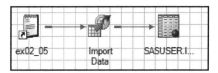

Figure 2.34 Data Set SASUSER.IMP_000C in a Data Grid (Column Widths Are Resized from the Default)

	ID	Q1	Q2	Q3	Q4	Q5	Q6	Q7	Q8	Q9	Q10
1	618	3	1	4	2	5	2	3	1	1	1
2	833	2	2	3	1	5	5	3	3	1	1
3	904	2	5	4	3	2	5	2	2	1	1
4	662	2	5	3	1	5	5	3	3	1	1
5	598	2	5	3	2	5	2	3	3	1	1
6	949	2	5	3	1	5	2	3	3	1	1
7	079	2	5	1	1	5	2	3	3	1	1
8	181	4	5	3	1	4	2	3	1	1	1
9	508	2	2	3	2	3	2	2	2	1	1
10	596	2	5	3	1	4	2	3	3	1	1
11	577	2	5	3	1	4	2	5	2	1	1
12	625	2	5	3	1	4	2	5	3	1	5
13	482	2	5	3	1	4	2	5	2	3	1
14	090	2	5	3	1	4	2	5	2	3	1
15	934	2	5	3	1	4	2	4	3	1	1
16	470	2	5	3	1	4	5	5	2	3	1
17	089	1	5	3	1	1	2	3	4	4	1
18	329	3	1	3	2	5	2	5	2	5	1
19	855	2	5	3	1	4	2	5	2	3	3
20	978	2	5	3	1	4	2	4	4	3	3
21	966	2	5	3	1	4	2	5	2	3	3
22	773	2	5	3	1	4	2	4	4	3	3
23	067	1	5	3	1	4	4	4	3	3	1
24	001	2	5	3	1	4	2	2	2	3	3
25	267	2	5	3	1	4	2	5	2	1	1
26	595	2	5	3	1	4	2	5	2	4	2

(Project Designer / SASUSER.IMPW_000C (read-only))

2.4 Query Builder

The Query Builder is a powerful data management tool. Each application of the Query Builder manages data through a *query*, which is a set of instructions requesting actions with one or more data sources.

When discussing queries, it is standard practice to use the words *table*, *column*, and *row* instead of data set, variable, and observation. See Table 2.1. Table is the general classification. A data set is a type of table.

Table 2.1 Query Terms Used instead of Statistical Terms

Statistical Terms	Query Terms
data set	table
variable	column
observation	row

This section covers the following Query Builder capabilities:

- Select and change the properties of the columns to be included in the results.
- Filter rows of data.
- Sort the rows according to the values in one or more columns.
- Replace data values.

- Create new data values with the Advanced Expression Editor.
- Group and summarize the data.
- Combine multiple tables.

2.4.1 Opening the Query Builder

The Query Builder can be opened in either of the following ways:

- Select **Data ▶ Filter and Query**.
  - o The Query Builder opens with the table named in the Active Data toolbar.
  - o If the project does not contain a data set, an Open Data window appears. Navigate to and open the table to be queried. The Query Builder opens with the selected table.
- In the Project Explorer or the Project Designer, right-click the icon of a table to be queried. Select **Filter and Query** from the pop-up menu. The Query Builder opens with the selected table. See Figure 2.35.

The Query Builder opens with the table and its variables listed in the left-hand pane. In Figure 2.35, the Query Builder is opened with the baseline table.

- The name of the query is at **Query name**. The query name appears in the Project Explorer and the Project Designer. In Figure 2.35, the name is **Query for baseline**. This can be changed.
- The name of the output table is at **Output name**.
  - o In Figure 2.35, the output table is SASUSER.QUERY_FOR_BASELINE_0012. That is, the results will be in table QUERY_FOR_BASELINE_0012 located in the SASUSER library.
  - o Click **Change** to change the name or library. To save the output table in a Windows folder, it is easiest to export it after it is produced by the query. See Section 2.2.8, "Exporting a Data Set."

Figure 2.35 Baseline Table in the Query Builder. Variables Names (and Labels) Listed in Left-hand Pane

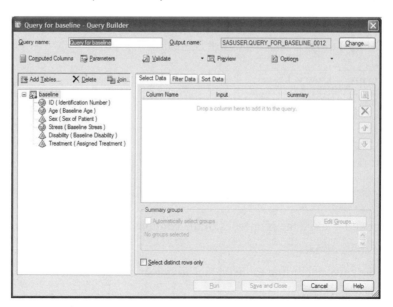

2.4.2 Selecting Data

The **Select Data** tab lists the output columns.

- To add all columns in a table to the query, drag the table name from the left-hand pane to the box on the **Select Data** tab. Alternately, right-click the table name on the left-hand pane and select **Add All Columns to Selection** on the pop-up menu.

- To add a single column to the query, drag the column name from the left-hand pane to the box on the **Select Data** tab. Alternately, double-click the column name. Also right-click the column name and select **Add to Selection** on the pop-up menu.

- To add multiple columns to the query, hold down **Ctrl** on the keyboard and select the column names on the left-hand pane. Drag the selected column names to the box on the **Select Data** tab, or right-click among the selected column names and select **Add to Selection** on the pop-up menu. In Figure 2.36, variables Age, Sex, Stress, and Disability have been added to the query.

Figure 2.36 Variables Added to Select Data Tab

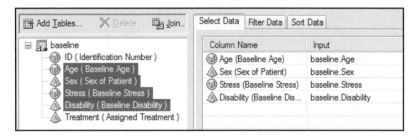

2.4.2.1 Column Properties

The names and labels (in parentheses) of the output columns are listed under Column Name. The origin of each column is listed as input_table.input_column under Input. See Figure 2.37.

The name and label of an output column can be changed on the **Select Data** tab. First, select the column's row. Then, single-click the Column Name cell. In Figure 2.37, the second cell is ready for editing.

Figure 2.37 Select Data Tab with Second Column Name Cell Ready for Editing

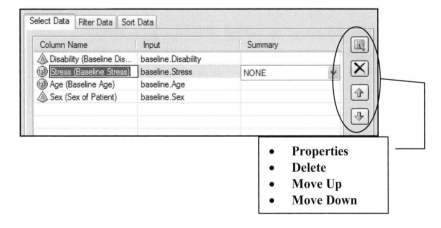

Figure 2.38 shows the Properties for the Stress (Baseline Stress) window. The parts of the window are listed below. Alias, Label, and Format can be changed.

Figure 2.38 Properties for Stress (Baseline) Window

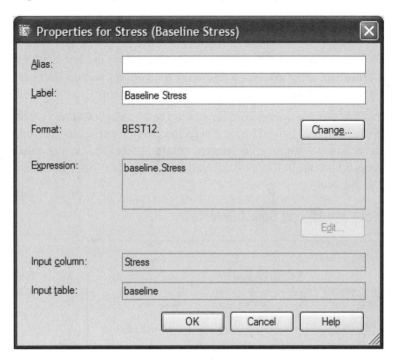

- Alias: The *alias* is the name of the column in the query and in the output. The default alias is the variable name.
- Label: The label for the output column.
- Format: The display format for the output column. See Section 2.2.1.5, "Formats (Display Formats)," and Section 2.2.1.6, "Informats (Read-in Formats)."
- Expression: The column in **input_table.input_column** form or the expression that defines this column. See Section 2.4.7, "Computed Columns: Recode a Column," and Section 2.4.9, "Computed Columns: Building Expressions."
- Input Column: Name of the original column.
- Input Table: Name of the original table.

To change the alias, label, and format of an output column:
1. Select the column's row and click **Properties**. Alternatively, double-click the **Column Name** or **Input** cell.
2. The Properties for _____ window opens.
3. Click **OK** to return to the Query Builder.

2.4.2.2 Deleting Columns

Deleting a column from the Select Data grid means it will not be in the output table. It may still be used for filtering and sorting. Deleting a column from the Select Data grid does not delete it from the input table.

To delete a column from the **Select Data** grid, select its row and click **Delete** on the right. See Figure 2.37.

2.4.2.3 Moving Columns

The order that the columns are listed on the **Select Data** tab is the order that they are listed in the output table. To move a column up or down in order, select its row and click **Move Up** and **Move Down** on the right. The order of the columns in Figure 2.37 is changed from Figure 2.36.

2.4.3 Filtering Rows: The WHERE Filter

There are two types of filters: the WHERE filter and the HAVING filter. This section considers the WHERE filter. Both filters are created on the **Filter Data** tab of the Query Builder.

- A *WHERE filter* instructs a query to include only the *rows* where a specified condition is met. WHERE filters are applied at the beginning of the execution of a query. In particular, WHERE filters are applied before the creation of any summary functions or summary groups.

- A *HAVING filter* is applied after the creation of any summary functions or summary groups. HAVING filters instruct a query to include only the *summary groups* having a specified condition. See Section 2.4.11, "Creating a Table of Means, Sums, and Other Statistics."

The following WHERE filter is applied in Figure 2.39. It instructs the query to include the rows of the columns listed on the **Select Data** tab that correspond to the rows of the Stress column in the baseline table that have values greater than 60.

baseline.Stress > 60

- Column names are qualified by their table names. The column **Stress** in the table baseline becomes baseline.Stress.

- In Figure 2.39, baseline.Stress is listed on the **Select Data** tab. This is not required. Filters can be created with any of the columns in the left-hand pane.

- The comparison rule ">" is an *operator*. See Table 2.2. The column name and the comparison value, baseline.Stress and 60, are the *left operand* and the *right operand*.

- The filter definition is added to a query in Figure 2.39. It will filter the "raw data," as opposed to filtering the results of summary functions.

Figure 2.39 Filter the Raw Data — WHERE Filter — Area on the Filter Data Tab

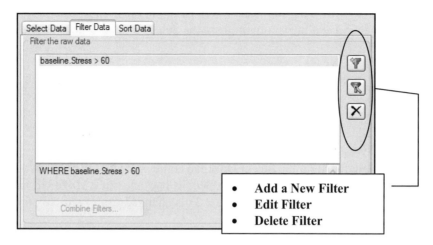

2.4.3.1 Operators

The operators in Table 2.2 are used to create filter definitions. The operators are discussed after the table.

Table 2.2 Filter Operators

Operators	Notation	Examples
Equal to	=	= 50, = 'Female'
Not Equal to	<>	<> 50, <> 'Female'
In a list of values	IN(value, value, …)	IN(2,3,4), IN('VA','NC','DC')
Not in a list of values	NOT IN(value, value, …)	NOT IN(2,3,4), NOT IN('VA','NC','DC')
Greater than	>	> 50
Greater than or equal to	>=	>= 50
Less than	<	< 50
Less than or equal to	<=	<= 50
Between	BETWEEN *a* AND *b*	BETWEEN 50 AND 60
Not between	NOT BETWEEN *a* AND *b*	NOT BETWEEN 50 AND 60
Is missing	IS MISSING	
Is not missing	NOT IS MISSING	
Is null	IS NULL	
Is not null	NOT IS NULL	
Contains	CONTAINS	CONTAINS 'stat'
Does not contain	NOT CONTAINS	NOT CONTAINS 'stat'
Matches pattern	LIKE	LIKE 'D%'
Does not match pattern	NOT LIKE	NOT LIKE 'D%'
Sounds like	=*	=* 'carry'
Does not sounds like	NOT =*	NOT =* 'carry'

Equality and Inequality Operators (=, <>, <, <=, >, >=)

These operators can be applied to both numerical and character data.

- Numbers: Standard order is used with missing values (denoted by periods) that are less than any number.

- Character values:

  o Character values are compared character by character and left to right.

  o When two values have different lengths, comparison is made as if blanks are added to the smaller value.

  o Blanks are less than all other characters. Digits are less than all letters. Uppercase letters are less than lowercase letters. See Table 2.3. As examples, 'top' = 'top', ' top' < 'top', and 'Top' < 'top'.

Table 2.3 English-Language ASCII Sequence

blank!"#$%&'()*+,- ./0123456789:;<=>?@
ABCDEFGHIJKLMNOPQRSTUVWXYZ [\ ] ^_
abcdefghijklmnopqrstuvwxyz{}~

IN Operator

The IN operator would include all values that equal any one of those in the parentheses. As examples, IN(2, 3, 4) would include all values equal to 2, 3, or 4; IN('VA', 'NC','DC') would include all values equal to VA, NC, or DC. Spaces outside paired quotation marks are ignored and can be added for clarity.

BETWEEN-AND Operator

For example, BETWEEN 50 AND 60 would include all values greater than or equal to 50 and less than or equal to 60. It is equivalent to the algebraic expression $50 \leq x \leq 60$.

IS NULL and IS MISSING Operators

IS NULL and IS MISSING can be used with both character and numerical data. They would include all missing values: the blank for character data and the period for numerical data. When NOT is applied, the result is all nonmissing values.

CONTAINS Operator

The CONTAINS operator would include all values containing a specific set of characters. The comparison is case-sensitive. For example, CONTAINS 'stat' would include state, Biostatistics, and thermostat, but not Statistics.

LIKE Operator

The LIKE operator would include all values containing a specific pattern of characters. The comparison is case-sensitive. There are two special characters used with the LIKE operator: the percent sign (%) and the underscore (_).

- Percent sign (%): A percent sign can be replaced by any number of characters.

- Underscore (_): An underscore can be replaced by any single character.

LIKE 'D%' would include all values beginning with D, such as Daniels and Donald. LIKE '_I' would include values such as HI and MI.

Sounds-like Operator

The sounds-like operator (=*) would include values with similar spelling. For example, =* 'carry' would include Care, Carey, Carr, and Cary.

2.4.3.2   Creating WHERE Filters

Filters are created on the **Filter Data** tab of the Query Builder. See Figure 2.35.

To create a WHERE filter:

1.   Drag a column to be the left operand from the left-hand pane to the Filter the raw data area. See Figure 2.39 shown earlier.

   The Edit Filter window appears. See Figure 2.40.

   The **Column** field contains the column name qualified by its table name: **table_name .column_name**. See Figure 2.40.

2.   At **Operator**, select the filter operator. In Figure 2.40, **greater than** is selected.

   There are one or more value entry boxes depending on which operator is selected. In Figure 2.40, there is one **Value** entry box where 60 is entered.

   The resulting filter definition, **baseline.Stress > 60**, is shown in the **Filter definition** box.

   Character values need to be in quotation marks. The default is for the **Enclose values in quotes** check box to be clear when the column is numeric and to be checked when the column is character.

3.   Click **OK** to add the filter. See Figure 2.39.

Figure 2.40 Edit Filter Window

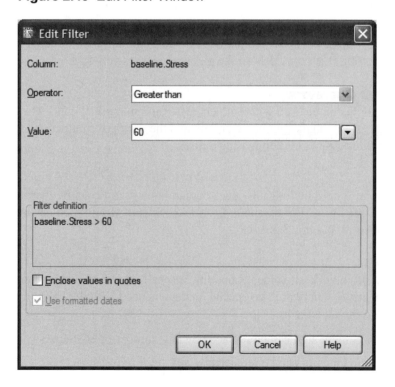

Entering and Selecting Values

Values can be entered or selected.

- Entering values: Numbers can be entered. Character constants must be in quotation marks. Variable names must be in the form of table_name.column_name.

- Selecting values: Click the down arrow (▼) or **Add** for the IN operator at the value entry box. A window opens with the **Values** tab showing. Click **Get Values**. The icon changes to **More Values**. The unique values from the column are listed. Select from the list. In Figure 2.41, **Severe** is selected.

More Complex Filters

More complex filters can be created with the Advanced Expression Editor. See Advanced Expression Editor in Section 2.4.9, "Computed Columns: Building Expressions."

To create a filter with the Advanced Expression Editor, click **Add a New Filter** (see Figure 2.39) and select **New Advanced Filter** from the pop-up menu.

Figure 2.41 Creating Baseline.Disability = Severe by Selecting from Column Values

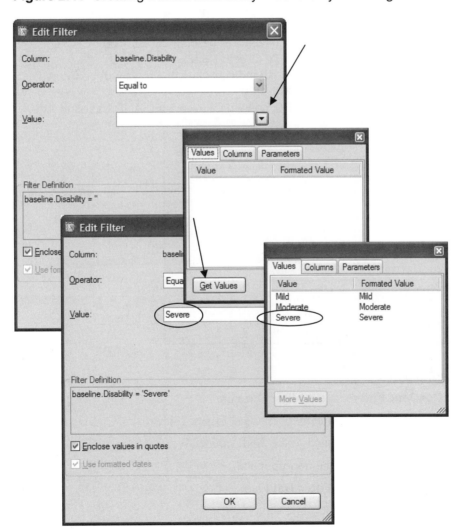

2.4.3.3 Connectives

The filter connectives are AND and OR.

- AND: A row is included if its values agree with both conditions in the combined filters.
  - As an example:

    baseline.Stress > 60 AND baseline.Age > 45

  - Only rows with both baseline.Stress values greater than 60 and baseline.Age values greater than 45 would be included.

- OR: A row is included if its values agree with at least one condition in the combined filters.
  - As an example:

    baseline.Stress > 60 OR baseline.Disability = Severe

  - Only rows with baseline.Stress values greater than 60, baseline.Disability values equal to Severe, or both conditions would be included.

To create additional filters:

When an additional filter is created, the default is to connect it with AND. In Figure 2.42, the filter baseline.Age > 45 is automatically connected to baseline.Stress > 60 by AND.

The WHERE statement on the **Filter Data** tab indicates how the rows will be filtered.

Figure 2.42 Filter Data Tab with WHERE baseline.Stress > 60 AND baseline.Age > 45

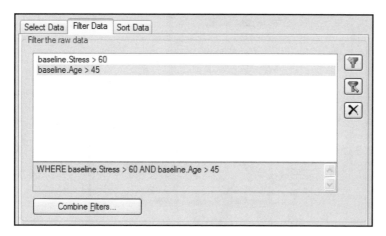

To change AND to OR:
1. Click **Combine Filters** on the **Filter Data** tab.
2. The Filter Combination window opens. See Figure 2.43.
3. Click the down arrow (▼) next to the AND connective.
4. Select **Change to OR** on the pop-up menu.
5. Click **OK** to return to the **Filter Data** tab.

Changing OR to AND is done in the same way.

Figure 2.43 Filter Combination Window with OR Connecting baseline.Stress > 60 and
baseline.Disability = "Severe"

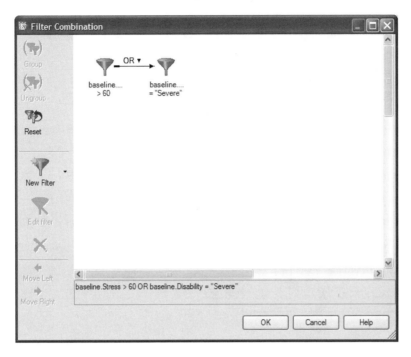

Figure 2.44 Filter Data with WHERE baseline.Stress > 60 OR baseline.Disability = "Severe"

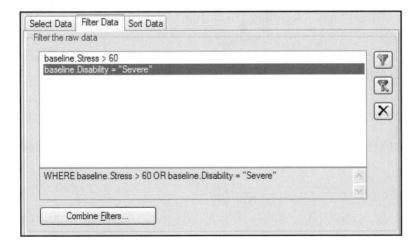

2.4.4 Sorting Rows

The query sorts values in one or more variables, moving the rows accordingly.

In Figure 2.45, variables Disability and Stress are selected for sorting. The Disability values will be sorted first in descending order: Severe, Moderate, and Mild. Then the Stress values will be sorted in descending order within each Disability group.

In Figure 2.36, baseline.Disability and baseline.Stress are listed on the **Select Data** tab. This is not required. Rows can be sorted by any of the columns in the left-hand pane.

Figure 2.45 Sort Data Tab

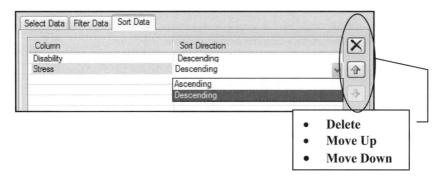

The characters in Table 2.4 are listed in the sorting order used in Windows.

Table 2.4 English-Language ASCII Sequence

blank!"#$%&'()*+,- ./0123456789:;<=>?@
ABCDEFGHIJKLMNOPQRSTUVWXYZ [\ ] ^_
abcdefghijklmnopqrstuvwxyz{}~

To sort the rows:

1. Drag a column to be sorted from the left-hand pane to the box in the **Sort Data** tab. See Figure 2.45.

2. The default **Sort Direction** is **Ascending**. To change to **Descending**, select a column's Sort Direction cell and select **Descending** from the drop-down menu.

3. The order that variables are listed is the order that they will be sorted. Use **Move Up** and **Move Down** to change the order.

2.4.5 Output

Query output can be in the three types of tables: data table, data view, and report. The default is data table.

- A data table is a SAS data file. See Figure 2.46.

- A data view is a virtual data table. Its values are updated each time the query opens in the Query Builder.

- A report is a table in one of the following formats: HTML, PDF, RTF, SAS report, or text. See Figure 2.47, Output 2.1, and Figure 2.48.

To change the default query output:

1. On the menu bar, select **Tools ▶ Options**.

2. The Options window opens. Select **Query** on the selection pane.

3. At the Query options, select **Data table**, **Date view**, or **HTML** from the **Save query result as** drop-down menu.

4. If **HTML** is selected, other formats can be selected from the Results General options on the Options window.

5. Click **OK** when finished.

To override the default:

1. On the Query Builder window, click **Options**.

2. Select **Option for This Query** on the pop-up menu.

   The Results Options window opens.

3. In the **Result format** box, check **Override preferences set in Tools ▶ Options**. Select **Data table**, **Date view**, or **Report**.

4. Click **OK** when finished.

Figure 2.46 Query Output as Data Table

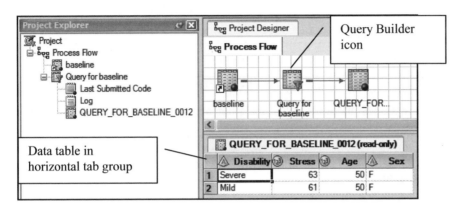

Figure 2.47 Query Output in Reports

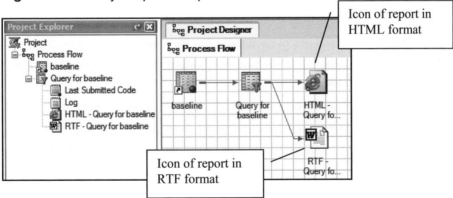

Output 2.1 Report in RTF Format

Baseline Disability	Baseline Stress	Baseline Age	Sex of Patient
Severe	63	50	F
Mild	61	50	F

Figure 2.48 Report in HTML Format

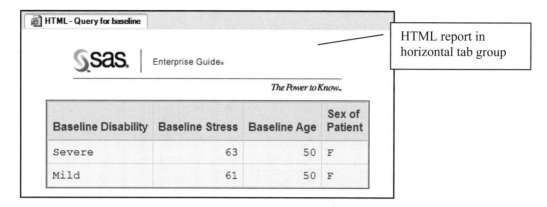

2.4.6 Examples 2.6 to 2.8: Selecting, Filtering, and Sorting

These examples show the results of the selecting, filtering, and sorting requested in Figure 2.35 to Figure 2.45.

2.4.6.1 Baseline Data

The baseline table in Appendix 1 represents information from 52 patients at the beginning of a clinical trial of a drug for headaches. The table contains the following columns:

- ID: Each patient is assigned an identification number.

- Age and Sex: The age and sex of each patient is recorded.

- Stress: Intensity of emotional stress is measured with 50 being average. Higher scores indicate greater intensity.

- Disability: Baseline disability is classified as mild, moderate, or severe.

- Treatment: Each patient is randomly assigned to a treatment: the new drug at a 5-milligram dosage (N05), the new drug at a 10-milligram dosage (N10), a standard drug (ST), or a placebo (PL).

Example 2.6

Create a query for the following information:

1. Select the columns Disability, Stress, Age, and Sex. The columns should be in the preceding order in the output.

2. Include only the rows with Stress values greater than 60.

3. The rows should be sorted first in the descending order of the Disability values and then in the descending order of the Stress values.

Example 2.7

Create a query for the same information as in Example 2.6.1, but include only the rows with Stress values greater than 60 and Age values greater than 45.

Example 2.8

Create a query for the same information as in Example 2.6.1, but include only the rows with Stress values greater than 60 or the Disability value Severe.

2.4.6.2 Solutions and Output

Example 2.6

The baseline table in Appendix 1 is opened in the project. See Figure 2.35.

1. Drag **Age**, **Sex**, **Stress**, and **Disability** from the left-hand pane onto the **Select Data** tab. See Figure 2.36. **Disability** is moved to the top of the list. **Stress** is moved to the row below it.

2. Open the **Filter Data** tab.

   a. Drag **Stress** from the left-hand pane. The Edit Filter window opens. See Figure 2.40. Column is baseline.Stress.

   b. At **Operator**, select **greater than** from the drop-down list.

   c. At **Value**, enter 60 in the entry box.

   d. Click **OK** to close the Edit Filter window.

3. The **Sort Data** tab is opened.

   a. Drag **Disability** from the left-hand pane. The **Sort Direction** is changed to **Descending**.

   b. Drag **Stress** from the left-hand pane. The **Sort Direction** is changed to **Descending**. See Figure 2.45.

4. Click **Run** on the Query Builder window.

Figure 2.49 Output for Example. 2.6 as a Data Set

	Disability	Stress	Age	Sex
	QUERY_FOR_BASELINE_0012 (read-only)			
1	Severe	71	45	F
2	Severe	63	41	M
3	Severe	63	50	F
4	Severe	61	38	F
5	Mild	61	50	F

Example 2.7

This exercise is done with the previous query in the project. Double-click the Query Builder icon for Example 2.6.

1. With the **Filter Data** tab open, drag **Age** from the left-hand pane. The Edit Filter window opens. Column is baseline.Age.

   a. Select **Operator**, **greater than** from the drop-down list.

   b. At **Value**, enter 45 in the entry box.

   c. Click **OK** to close the Edit Filter window.

   d. The **Filter Data** tab opens with WHERE baseline.Stress > 60 AND baseline.Age > 45. See Figure 2.42.

   There are no other changes from Example 2.6.

2. Click **Run** on the Query Builder window.

3. Click **Yes** when a window opens asking, "Would you like to replace the results from the previous run?" The output is shown in Figure 2.47, Output 2.1, and Figure 2.48.

Example 2.8

This exercise is done with the query for Example 2.7 in the project. Double-click the Query Builder icon for Example 2.7.

1. To delete the second filter from the query: On the **Filter Data** tab, select **baseline.Age >** **45** and click the **Delete** button.

2. Drag **Disability** from the left-hand pane. The Edit Filter window opens. Column is baseline.Disability.

   The default **Operator** is **equals**. That is not changed.

   a. Click the down arrow (▼) at **Value**. A window opens with the **Values** tab showing.

   b. Click **Get Values** and select **Severe** from the list. See Figure 2.41.

   c. Click **OK** to close the Edit Filter window.
      The **Filter Data** tab opens with WHERE baseline.Stress > 60 AND baseline.Disability = "Severe".

3. To change AND to OR, click **Combine Filters**.

   The Filter Combination window opens.

   a. Click the down arrow (▼) next to the **AND** connective.

   b. Select **Change to OR** on the pop-up menu.

   c. Click **OK** to return to the **Filter Data** tab.
      The **Filter Data** tab opens with WHERE baseline.Stress > 60 OR baseline.Disability = "Severe". See Figure 2.44.

   There are no other changes from Example 2.7.

4. Click **Run** on the Query Builder window.

5. Click **Yes** when a window opens asking, "Would you like to replace the results from the previous run?" The output is below.

Figure 2.50 Output for Example 2.8 as a Data Set

	Disability	Stress	Age	Sex
1	Severe	71	45	F
2	Severe	63	50	F
3	Severe	63	41	M
4	Severe	61	38	F
5	Severe	60	54	M
6	Severe	60	40	F
7	Severe	59	34	F
8	Severe	59	44	F
9	Severe	58	33	F
10	Severe	57	33	M
11	Severe	53	38	F
12	Severe	53	46	M
13	Severe	52	40	M
14	Severe	47	33	M
15	Mild	61	50	F

QUERY_FOR_BASELINE_0012 (read-only)

2.4.7 Computed Columns: Recoding a Column

Recoding a column replaces specific values or ranges of values with new values. The replacement values become a new column. In Example 2.9, Female and Male replace F and M. Also, Mild, Moderate, and Severe replace numerical values based on three ranges.

Computed columns are managed with the Computed Columns window in the Query Builder. New columns can be added. Existing columns can be edited, deleted, and renamed.

2.4.7.1 Computed Columns Window

Click **Computed Columns** on the Query Builder. This opens the Computed Columns window.

1. If creating a new column, select **New**. Then select **Recode a Column** from the pop-up menu.
   a. Select the column to be recoded from the Select Item window. Then click **Continue**. The Recode Column window opens.
   b. At **New column name**, change the default name, if desired.
2. If editing an existing recoded column, select the column from the list and click **Edit**. The column's Recode Column window opens.

The Recode Column window is shown in Figure 2.53.

2.4.7.2 Replacement Rules

The rules defining how the values in the column are to be recoded are listed in the **Replacements** box. New replacement rules can be added. Current rules can be removed.

Clicking **Add** opens the Specify a Replacement window:

1. Specific values are recoded on the **Replace Values** tab. See Figure 2.52.
   - A value to be replaced can be entered. Click a row on the **Replace Values** tab to open an entry box.
   - A value can be selected. Click **Get Values**. The unique values from the column are listed. Select from the list. To select multiple values, hold down the **Ctrl** key while selecting. Click **OK** to return to the Specify a Replacement window.
   - Enter the replacement value in the **With this value** box.
   - To delete a value, click its row and press **Delete**. To change a value, click its row and click again to open the entry box. Values in the **With this value** box can be edited.

   Click **OK** to return to the Recode Column window.
2. Ranges of values are recoded on the **Replace a Range** tab.
   a. Three types of ranges are possible.
      - For the range from a to b (all values x where $a \leq x \leq b$), both **Set a lower limit** and **Set an upper limit** should be checked.
      - For the range b or lower (all values x where $x \leq b$), only **Set an upper limit** should be checked.
      - For the range a or higher (all values x where $x \geq a$), only **Set a lower limit** should be checked

   b. Enter the desired range limits in the entry boxes. If a limit is a column value, it can be selected. Click the down arrow (▼). The unique values from the column are listed. Select from the list.

   c. Enter the replacement value in the **With this value** box.

   d. Values in the entry boxes can be edited.

   e. Click **OK** to return to the Recode Column window.

2.4.7.3 Finishing Up

1. Assign a default replacement value at **Replace all other values with**. See Figure 2.53. There are three choices:

    • **The current value**: This is the default selection. No replacement is made. This selection is not available when numeric values are replaced with character values and character values are replaced with numeric values.

    • **A missing value**: Values are replaced with a period if the replacement values are numeric and with a blank if the replacement values are character.

    • **This value**: If this is selected, the entry box on the right becomes active. Enter the replacement value there.

2. Determine the **New column type**: **Character** or **Numeric**.

3. When finished, click **OK** on the Recode Column window to return to the Computed Columns window. Click **Close** to return to the Query Builder window.

2.4.8 Example 2.9: Recoding Values and Ranges

This example shows the results of recoding values and ranges of values. It continues using the baseline data table used in Example 2.6.

Example 2.9

Use the following tables to recode the Sex and Stress columns. Name the new columns Sex and Stress Category. Create an output table that also includes the columns Age and Treatment. Include only rows where Treatment is N05.

Sex values	Replacement values
F	Female
M	Male

Ranges of Stress values	Replacement values
0 to 40	Mild
41 to 60	Moderate
61 and higher	Severe

2.4.8.1   Solutions and Output

The baseline table in Appendix A is opened in the project. Right-click the icon and select **Filter and Query** from the pop-up menu.

To begin and to recode sex:

1. **Age** and **Treatment** are dragged from the left-hand pane to the **Select Data** tab.

2. Click **Computed Columns** to open the Computed Columns window.

3. Click **New** and then select **Recode a Column** from the pop-up menu.

4. Select **Sex** on the Select Item window and click **Continue**. The Recode Column window opens. The **New column name** is changed to **Sex**.

5. Click **Add**. The Specify a Replacement window opens.

   a. Click **Get Values**. The unique values in **Sex** are listed. See Figure 2.51. **F** is selected. Click **OK**.

   b. Returning to the Specify a Replacement window, enter **Female** at **With this value**. See Figure 2.52.

   c. Click **OK** to return to the Recode Column window.

Figure 2.51 List of Unique Values in Sex

Figure 2.52 Female to Replace F in Specify a Replacement Window

Figure 2.53 New Sex Column Defined in Recode Column

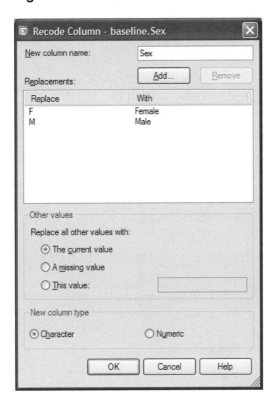

6. Click **Add** again. The Specify a Replacement window opens.

   a. Click **Get Values**. The unique values in **Sex** are listed. **M** is selected. Click **OK**.

   b. In the Specify a Replacement window, enter **Male** at **With this value**.

   c. Click **OK** to return to the Recode Column window. See Figure 2.53.
      The default selection for **Replace all other values with** remains as the current value.
      The **New column type** remains as **Character**.

7. Click **OK** on **Recode Column** to return to the Computed Columns window.

To recode stress:

1. Click **New** and then select **Recode a Column** from the pop-up menu.

2. Select **Stress** on the Select Item window and then click **Continue**. The Recode Column window opens.

3. Change the **New column name** to Stress Category.

4. Click **Add**. The Specify a Replacement window opens. Open the **Replace a Range** tab.

   a. **Set a lower limit** is checked and 0 is typed in the entry box.

   b. **Set an upper limit** is checked and 40 is typed in the entry box.

   c. **Mild** is entered at **With this value**. See Figure 2.54.

5. Click **OK** to return to the Recode Column window.

Figure 2.54 Mild to Replace Stress Values 0 to 40 in Specify a Replacement
Window

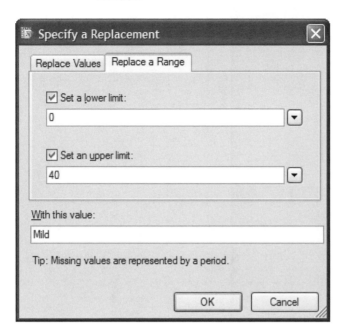

6. Click **Add**. The Specify a Replacement window opens. Open the **Replace a Range** tab.

   a. **Set a lower limit** is checked and 41 is typed in the entry box.

   b. **Set an upper limit** is checked and 60 is typed in the entry box.

   c. **Moderate** is entered at **With this value**.

   d. Click **OK** to return to the Recode Column window.

7. Click **Add**. The Specify a Replacement window opens. The **Replace a Range** tab is opened.

   a. **Set a lower limit** is checked and 61 is entered in the entry box.

   b. **Severe** is entered at **With this value**.

   c. Click **OK** to return to the Recode Column window. See Figure 2.55.

8. The **New column type** is changed to **Character**.

9. The default selection for **Replace all other values with** becomes **A missing value**.

10. Click **OK** to return to the Computed Columns window. See Figure 2.56.

11. Click **Close** to return to the Query Builder window. See Figure 2.57.

Figure 2.55 Stress Category Column Defined in Recode Column

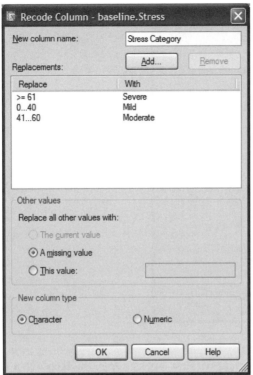

Figure 2.56 Computed Columns with Sex and Stress Category

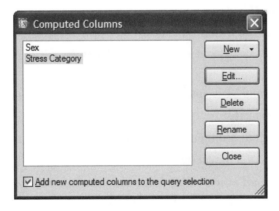

Figure 2.57 Select Data Tab for Example 2.9

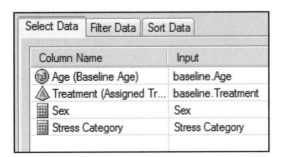

To finish up:

1. Create the filter on the Filter Data tab: **WHERE baseline.Treatment = "N05"**.
2. Click **Run** on the Query Builder window. Output 2.2 shows the output table as a report in RTF format.

Output 2.2 Output for Example 2.9 as a Report in RTF Format

Baseline Age	Assigned Treatment	Sex	Stress Category
33	N05	Female	Moderate
65	N05	Male	Moderate
40	N05	Female	Moderate
46	N05	Male	Moderate
58	N05	Male	Mild
49	N05	Male	Mild
50	N05	Female	Severe
40	N05	Male	Moderate
47	N05	Female	Moderate
53	N05	Female	Moderate
65	N05	Female	Moderate
43	N05	Female	Moderate
42	N05	Male	Moderate
44	N05	Female	Moderate
55	N05	Male	Moderate
58	N05	Male	Moderate

2.4.9 Computed Columns: Building Expressions

Data values can be created from a wide variety of expressions. The expressions are created in the Advanced Expression Editor. See Figure 2.58. The statistical functions and the conditional expressions available in the Advanced Expression Editor are discussed in this section.

Figure 2.58 Advanced Expression Builder with Data Tab and with Functions Tab

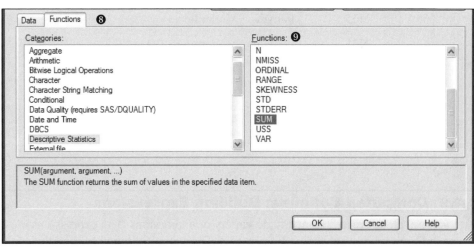

2.4.9.1 Advanced Expression Editor

The Advanced Expression Editor (see Figure 2.58) consists of the following:

- **Expression Text** box (at ❶): The expression is entered here with or without the assistance of the operator buttons, **Data** tab, and **Functions** tab. Copying, cutting, and pasting are done with **Ctrl+C**, **Ctrl+X**, and **Ctrl+V** on the keyboard.

- Operator buttons

  ❷ add, subtract, multiply, divide, or raise to power.

❸ AND and OR are useful in conditional expressions. NOT is used to negate operators. See Table 2.2.

❹ Comparison operators are equal, not equal, less than, less than or equal to, greater than, greater than or equal to, and sounds like.

❺ Grouping symbols are parentheses, quotation marks, left bracket, right bracket, left brace, right brace, and comma.

- **Data** tab with the **Available variables** list on the left (at ❻) and the **Variable values** list on the right (at ❼).
  - ○ **Available variables** lists the tables and variables that are listed on the **Select Data** tab.
    - ▪ If a table is selected, its columns are listed in the **Variable values** box.
    - ▪ If a column set is selected, its unique values are listed in the **Variable values** box.
  - ○ To insert a column or value into the **Expression Text** box:
    - ▪ Select it in the **Variable values** list and click **Add to Expression**.
    - ▪ Or double-click it in the **Variable values** list.
  - ○ At the top in Figure 2.58, the Ex02_01 table is selected and its columns are listed.
- **Functions** tab with the **Categories** list on the left (at ❽) and the **Functions** list on the right (at ❾).
  - ○ To insert a function into the **Expression Text** box:
    - ▪ Select it in the **Functions** list and click **Add to Expression.**
    - ▪ Or double-click it in the **Functions** list.
  - ○ At the bottom in Figure 2.58, **Descriptive Statistics** and the **SUM** function are selected. Help for **SUM** is at the bottom at ❿.

To open the Advanced Expression Editor:

1. Click **Computed Columns** on the Query Builder. This opens the Computed Columns window. Computed columns are managed in this window. New columns can be added. Existing columns can be edited, deleted, and renamed.

2. If creating a new column, select **New**. Then select **Build Expression** from the pop-up menu.

3. If applying the Advanced Expression Editor to an existing column, select the column from the list and click **Edit**.

   The Advanced Expression Editor window opens.

To finish:

1. Click **OK** to close the Advanced Expression Editor and return to the Computed Columns window.

   The window lists a default name for a new column, such as **Calculation1**.

2. To change a name, select it and click **Rename**. The name can then be edited.

3. Click **Close** to return to the Query Builder window.

2.4.9.2 Statistical Functions

Statistical functions are available in the Aggregate and the Descriptive Statistics categories. Both categories contain many of the same functions. However, aggregate functions are applied column-wise and descriptive statistics are applied row-wise.

Aggregate Functions

An aggregate function has a single argument. As examples:

- AVG(baseline.Age) produces the average of all values in the Age column of the baseline table.
- AVG(math_predict.SATMath + math_predict.SATVerbal) produces the average of all the sums of the SATMath and SATVerbal values of the math_predict table.

The result is a column with all rows containing the same value, unless the column is *grouped*. See Section 2.4.11, "Creating a Table of Means, Sums, or other Statistics." In that case, groups of rows contain the same value.

Most functions are qualified by {**All**} or {**Distinct**}.

- {**All**} indicates that the function is applied to all values.
- {**Distinct**} indicates that the function is applied to the set of distinct values.

Exceptions are:

- **COUNT {*}** is the number of missing and nonmissing values.
- **FREQ** (frequency) is the same as **N{All}**, the number of nonmissing values.

Also, in the table, **AVG** (average) is the same as **MEAN**. The aggregate functions are listed in Table 2.5.

Descriptive Statistics

A descriptive statistic function has multiple arguments. The function is applied to all the values in each of the rows.

For example, **SUM(math_predict.SATMath, math_predict.SATVerbal)** produces a sum for each pair of **SATMath** and **SATVerbal** values of the **math_predict** table. The result is a column with potentially many values.

Table 2.5 Statistical Functions in the Aggregate and the Descriptive Statistics Categories

Aggregate Functions	Descriptive Statistics	Name	Formula/Symbol
✓		AVG (average, same as the mean)	$\overline{x} = \dfrac{\displaystyle\sum_{i=1}^{n} x_i}{n}$
✓		COUNT (number of nonmissing values)	
✓		COUNT {*} (total number of missing and nonmissing values)	
✓	✓	CSS (corrected sum of squares)	$\displaystyle\sum_{i=1}^{n}\left(x_i - \overline{x}\right)^2$

Aggregate Functions	Descriptive Statistics	Name	Formula/Symbol
✓	✓	CV (coefficient of variation)	$\dfrac{s}{\overline{x}} 100\%$
✓		FREQ (frequency, number of nonmissing values)	
	✓	KURTOSIS (positive if tails heavier than normal probability distribution, negative if lighter, 0 if same)	$\left(\dfrac{n(n+1)}{(n-1)(n-2)(n-3)} \dfrac{\sum\limits_{i=1}^{n}(x_i - \overline{x})^4}{s^4} \right)$ $- \dfrac{3(n-1)^2}{(n-2)(n-3)}$
✓	✓	MAX (maximum value)	
✓	✓	MEAN	$\overline{x} = \dfrac{\sum\limits_{i=1}^{n} x_i}{n}$
✓	✓	MIN (minimum value)	
✓	✓	N (number of non-missing values)	n
✓	✓	NMISS (number of missing values)	
	✓	ORDINAL (the kth smallest of the missing and nonmissing values)	
✓		PRT (*p*-value for Student's *t* test on the hypotheses $H_0 : \mu = 0$ versus $H_1 : \mu \neq 0$)	$2P(t > \lvert \text{t Value} \rvert)$
✓	✓	RANGE	$\text{Max} - \text{Min}$
	✓	SKEWNESS (positive if distribution is right-skewed, negative if left-skewed, 0 if symmetric)	$\dfrac{n}{(n-1)(n-2)} \dfrac{\sum\limits_{i=1}^{n}(x_i - \overline{x})^3}{s^3}$
✓	✓	STD (standard deviation)	$s = \sqrt{\dfrac{\sum\limits_{i=1}^{n}(x_i - \overline{x})^2}{n-1}}$
✓	✓	STDERR (standard error)	$\dfrac{s}{\sqrt{n}}$

Aggregate Functions	Descriptive Statistics	Name	Formula/Symbol
✓	✓	SUM	$\displaystyle\sum_{i=1}^{n} x_i$
✓		SUMWGT (sum of weights)	$\displaystyle\sum_{i=1}^{n} w_i$
✓		T (test statistic for Student's t test on the hypotheses $H_0 : \mu = 0$ versus $H_1 : \mu \neq 0$)	$\dfrac{\overline{x}}{\left(\dfrac{s}{\sqrt{n}}\right)}$
✓	✓	USS (uncorrected sum of squares)	$\displaystyle\sum_{i=1}^{n} x_i^2$
✓	✓	VAR (variance)	$s^2 = \dfrac{\displaystyle\sum_{i=1}^{n}\left(x_i - \overline{x}\right)^2}{n-1}$

2.4.9.3   Conditional Expressions

A *conditional expression* assigns values depending on which condition in a list of conditions is true. Conditional expressions are automatically created by SAS Enterprise Guide when recoding a column. More general expressions are possible using the Advanced Expression Editor.

Table 2.6 shows the "short" and "else" form of the conditional expression. They are identified as **CASE{short}** and **CASE{else}** in the Functions list.

Values are assigned to a new column as the values in each row of the table made by the columns in the **Select and Sort** tab are evaluated.

- Each row is evaluated by every *when condition* in the order that the when conditions are listed.

- If a when condition is true, its *result expression* is applied to the corresponding row in the new column. A result expression can be a constant (for example, 2 or F) or it can be an expression.

- If none of the when conditions is true and there is an *else* statement, the else statement's result expression is applied. Otherwise, a missing value is assigned.

Table 2.6 Short Conditional Expression, and Else Conditional Expression

```
CASE
WHEN <whenCondition> THEN <resultExpression>
WHEN <whenCondition> THEN <resultExpression>
END
```

```
CASE
WHEN <whenCondition> THEN <resultExpression>
WHEN <whenCondition> THEN <resultExpression>
ELSE <resultExpression>
END
```

2.4.10 Examples 2.10 to 2.14: Computing Values

2.4.10.1 Student Grades

The data set Ex02_01 in Figure 2.59 has information from 10 students.

- **Name**, **FI**, and **MI** contain the last names, first initials, and middle initials of the student.

- **Test1**, **Test2**, and **Test3** are test scores.

- **Status** is the enrollment status, with W indicating a student who has withdrawn from the class.

Figure 2.59 Data from a Class of 10 Students. Column Widths Are Resized from the Default.

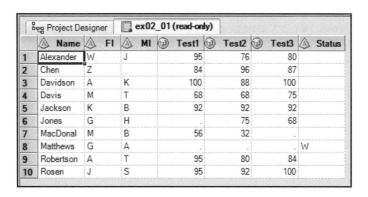

	Name	FI	MI	Test1	Test2	Test3	Status
1	Alexander	W	J	95	76	80	
2	Chen	Z		84	96	87	
3	Davidson	A	K	100	88	100	
4	Davis	M	T	68	68	75	
5	Jackson	K	B	92	92	92	
6	Jones	G	H	.	75	68	
7	MacDonal	M	B	56	32	.	
8	Matthews	G	A	.	.	.	W
9	Robertson	A	T	95	80	84	
10	Rosen	J	S	95	92	100	

Example 2.10
Create a query so that only the rows with Status values not equal to W are included. Do not include the Status column in the output.

Example 2.11
Continue Example 2.10. Compute Score1: the mean test score as the sum of the three tests divided by 3. Give 0 points to missing tests.

Example 2.12
Continue Example 2.11. Compute Score2: the mean test score as the mean of the nonmissing tests.

Example 2.13
Continue Example 2.12. Compute Score3: the mean of the best two tests.

Example 2.14
Determine the Grade for each student based on Score3. Use the following ranges.

Score3 ranges	Grade
$0 \leq \text{Score3} < 60$	F
$60 \leq \text{Score3} < 70$	D
$70 \leq \text{Score3} < 80$	C
$80 \leq \text{Score3} < 90$	B
$90 \leq \text{Score3} \leq 100$	A

2.4.10.2 Solutions and Output

Example 2.10
Open the Ex02_01 table in the project. Right-click the icon and select **Filter and Query** from the pop-up menu.

1. Drag all the columns but **Status** from the left-hand pane to the **Select Data** tab.

2. On the **Filter Data** tab, drag **Status** to the **Filter the raw data** box.

   a. The Edit Filter window opens with Column being Ex02_01.Status and **Enclose values in quotes** being checked.

   b. Operator is set to **Not equal to**.

   c. The down arrow (▼) at **Value** is clicked. **Get Values** is clicked from the **Values** tab on the opened window. **W** is selected from the list.

   d. **W** appears in the **Value** entry box. The **Filter Definition** is Ex02_01.Status ◇ 'W'.

   e. **OK** closes the **Edit Filter** window.

   f. The **Filter Data** tab has the statement WHERE Ex02_01.Status ◇ "W".

Example 2.11
1. Click **Computed Columns** on the Query Builder. This opens the Computed Columns window.

2. **New** is selected. From the pop-up menu, **Build Expression** is selected.

3. The **Advanced Expression Editor** window opens.

   a. The sum of the three tests is:

   SUM(ex02_01.Test1, ex02_01.Test2, ex02_01.Test3)

   The **SUM** function adds the nonmissing values in the respective rows. If there is at least one nonmissing value, this essentially gives 0 points to missing values in a sum. If all the values are missing, the result is a missing value.

   The **SUM** function is used instead of plus signs, as in Ex02_01.Test1 + Ex02_01.Test2 + Ex02_01.Test3. With the $+, -, *, /, **$ operators, the result is a missing value if any operand is a missing value.

For example, SUM(., 100) is 100, while ". + 100" is a missing value (.).

The sum divided by 3 is:

SUM(ex02_01.Test1, ex02_01.Test2, ex02_01.Test3)/3

Spaces can be removed. Spaces and new lines can be added except within a keyword (in capital letters) or a column name.

   i. On the Functions tab, select **Descriptive Statistics** in the Categories list. SUM is double-clicked in the Functions list.
SUM(<numValue>,<numValue>) appears in the **Expression Text** box.

   ii. The **<numValue>** placeholders are replaced with column names: On the **Data** tab, Ex02_01 is selected by default in the **Available variables** box. Double-clicking **Test1** in the **Variable values** box produces Ex02_01.Test1 in the **Expression Text** box. Commas are required between column names. The list of column names must be enclosed in parentheses.

   iii. Divided by 3 — /3 — is added.

   iv. The result is shown in Figure 2.60.

b. Click **OK** on the Advanced Expression Editor window to return to Computed Columns. The window lists a default name for the new column, such as **Calculation1**.

c. Select the default name and click **Rename**. In Figure 2.61, the default name is replaced by **Score1**.

Figure 2.60 Expression for Example 2.11 Is Entered

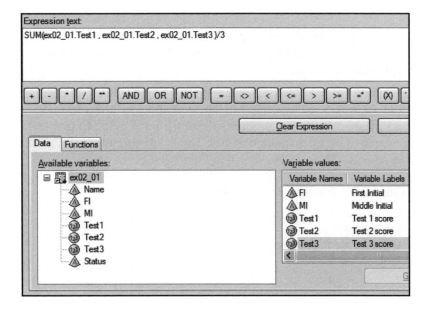

Figure 2.61 Default Name Replaced by Score1

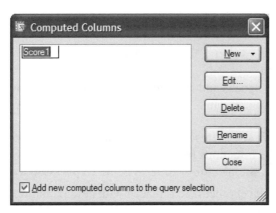

Example 2.12

1. **New** on **Computed Columns** is selected. From the pop-up menu, **Build Expression** is selected.

2. The Advanced Expression Editor window opens.

   The mean of the nonmissing tests is:

   MEAN(ex02_01.Test1, ex02_01.Test2, ex02_01.Test3)

   The MEAN function computes the mean of the nonmissing values in the respective rows. For example, MEAN(80, 90, 100) is 90 and MEAN(80, 90, .) is 85. If all the values are missing, the result is a missing value.

   Spaces can be removed. Spaces and new lines can be added except within a keyword (in capital letters) or a column name.

3. On the **Functions** tab, **Descriptive Statistics** is selected in the **Categories** list. **MEAN** is double-clicked in the **Functions** list. MEAN(<numValue>,<numValue>) appears in the **Expression Text** box.

4. The **<numValue>** placeholders are replaced with column names: On the **Data** tab, Ex02_01 is selected by default in the **Available variables** box. Double-clicking **Test1** in the **Variable values** box produces Ex02_01.Test1 in the **Expression Text** box. Commas are required between column names. The list of column names must be enclosed in parentheses. The result is shown in Figure 2.62.

Figure 2.62 Expression for Example 2.12

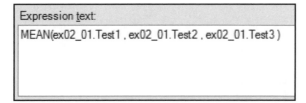

5. Click **OK** on the Advanced Expression Editor window to return to Computed Columns. The window lists a default name for the new column, such as **Calculation1**.

6. The default name is selected and **Rename** is clicked. The default name is replaced with **Score2**.

Example 2.13

1. **New** on Computed Columns is selected. From the pop-up menu, **Build Expression** is selected.

2. The Advanced Expression Editor window opens.

   The mean of the best two tests is:

   SUM(

   ORDINAL(2, ex02_01.Test1, ex02_01.Test2, ex02_01.Test3),

   ORDINAL(3, ex02_01.Test1, ex02_01.Test2, ex02_01.Test3))

   /2

   Spaces can be removed. The functions do not have to be on separate lines. Spaces and new lines can be added except within a keyword (in capital letters) or a column name.

   The Ordinal function is in Descriptive Statistics.

   - ORDINAL(2, ex02_01.Test1, ex02_01.Test2, ex02_01.Test3) produces the second smallest value among the three values, whether missing or nonmissing. Missing values are treated as less than any number.

   - ORDINAL(3, ex02_01.Test1, ex02_01.Test2, ex02_01.Test3) produces the third smallest value among the three values. In effect, it produces the largest value of the three.

   - The SUM function adds nonmissing values. The result is shown in Figure 2.63.

   Figure 2.63 Expression for Example 2.13

   ```
   Expression text:
   SUM(
   ORDINAL(2, ex02_01.Test1 , ex02_01.Test2 , ex02_01.Test3 ),
   ORDINAL(3, ex02_01.Test1 , ex02_01.Test2 , ex02_01.Test3 ))
   /2
   ```

3. Clicking **OK** on the Advanced Expression Editor window returns to Computed Columns. The window lists a default name for the new column, such as **Calculation1**.

4. The default name is selected and **Rename** is clicked. The default name is replaced with **Score3**.

5. **Close** is selected and the three new computed columns are added to the query. At this point, **Score3** needs to be added to the query so that it can be used in creating the **Grade** computed function next.

Example 2.14

1. **Computed Columns** is clicked on the Query Builder. This opens the Computed Columns window.

2. **New** is selected. From the pop-up menu, **Build Expression** is selected.

3. **Yes** is selected to retrieve values for the computed columns. See Figure 2.64. **No** would be appropriate if the new column did not involve any computed columns.

Figure 2.64 Do You Want to Get Retrieve Values for the Computed Columns?

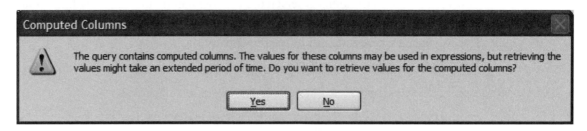

4. The Advanced Expression Editor window opens.

The Grade column is created with the following conditional expression:

CASE

WHEN 0 <= CALCULATED Score3 < 60 THEN 'F'

WHEN 60 <= CALCULATED Score3 < 70 THEN 'D'

WHEN 70 <= CALCULATED Score3 < 80 THEN 'C'

WHEN 80 <= CALCULATED Score3 < 90 THEN 'B'

WHEN 90 <= CALCULATED Score3 <= 100 THEN 'A'

END

Spaces can be removed. The statements do not have to be on separate lines. Spaces and new lines can be added except within a keyword (in capital letters) or a column name.

5. On the **Functions** tab, **Conditional** is selected in the **Categories** list. **CASE {short}** is double-clicked in the **Functions** list. The result is:

CASE WHEN <whenCondition> THEN <resultExpression> WHEN <whenCondition> THEN <resultExpression> END

6. The first **<whenCondition>** placeholder is replaced with an inequality:

a. On the **Data** tab, **Current Query** is selected in the Available variables box. Double-clicking **Score3** in the **Variable values** box inserts **CALCULATED Score3** into the expression box.

b. Numbers and symbols are added to produce 0<= CALCULATED Score3 < 60.

7. The first **<resultExpression>** placeholder is replaced with **'F'**.

8. The remaining WHEN statements are added in a similar way.

- WHEN{simple} in the Conditional functions creates WHEN <whenCondition> THEN <resultExpression>.

- Copying, cutting, and pasting can be done with **Ctrl+C**, **Ctrl+X**, and **Ctrl+V** on the keyboard.
  The result is shown in Figure 2.65. The conditional expression is put on 5 lines so it could be fully shown.

Figure 2.65 Expression for Example 2.14

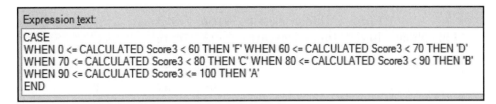

Expression text:

```
CASE
WHEN 0 <= CALCULATED Score3 < 60 THEN 'F' WHEN 60 <= CALCULATED Score3 < 70 THEN 'D'
WHEN 70 <= CALCULATED Score3 < 80 THEN 'C' WHEN 80 <= CALCULATED Score3 < 90 THEN 'B'
WHEN 90 <= CALCULATED Score3 <= 100 THEN 'A'
END
```

9. Clicking **OK** on the Advanced Expression Editor window returns to Computed Columns. The window lists a default name for the new column, such as **Calculation1**.

10. The default name is selected and **Rename** is clicked. The default name is replaced with **Grade**.

11. When finished, select **Close**.
     Score1, **Score2**, **Score3**, and **Grade** are added to the left-hand pane and to the **Select Data** tab. See Figure 2.66.

12. Click the **Run** button on the Query Builder window. Output 2.3 shows the output table as a report in RTF format.

Figure 2.66 Select Data Tab for Examples 2.10 through 2.14

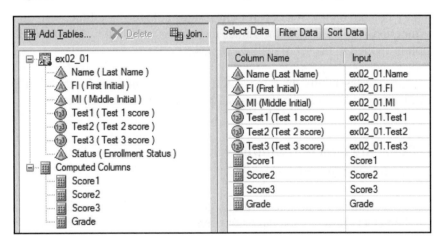

Output 2.3 Output for Examples 2.10 through 2.14 as a Report in RTF Format

Last Name	First Initial	Middle Initial	Test 1 score	Test 2 score	Test 3 score	Score1	Score2	Score3
Alexander	W	J	95	76	80	83.66667	83.66667	87.5
Chen	Z		84	96	87	89	89	91.5
Davidson	A	K	100	88	100	96	96	100
Davis	M	T	68	68	75	70.33333	70.33333	71.5
Jackson	K	B	92	92	92	92	92	92
Jones	G	H	.	75	68	47.66667	71.5	71.5
MacDonald	M	B	56	32	.	29.33333	44	44
Robertson	A	T	95	80	84	86.33333	86.33333	89.5
Rosen	J	S	95	92	100	95.66667	95.66667	97.5

2.4.11 Creating a Table of Means, Sums, and Other Statistics

The Summary column on the **Select Data** tab assigns column-wise functions. See Figure 2.67. A summary function is applied to all the values unless it is qualified by **DISTINCT**. In that case, the function is applied to the set of distinct values.

These functions are essentially the same as the aggregate functions described in Section 2.4.9, "Computed Columns: Building Expressions." See Table 2.5.

2.4.11.1 Summary Function Output

If **Automatically select groups** is checked:

- Summary values are produced for the groups defined by the unique rows of the columns on the **Select Data** tab that have not been assigned summary functions.
- When all the columns on the **Select Data** tab are assigned summary functions, the output is a single row of summarized values.

If **Automatically select groups** is unchecked, groups can be defined on the Edit Groups window.

If the **Select Data** tab contains a column that is not being summarized and is not a group-by column, the output contains all rows of the column. A summarized column would contain the same value for all the rows, unless there are group-by columns. In which case, a summarized column would have the same value for all the rows in each group.

To create a table of means, sums, and other summary statistics:

1. Drag the columns to be included in the output table to the **Select Data** tab.
2. For a column to be summarized:
   a. Click its cell in the **Summary** column to open the drop-down list and select the desired summary function. See Figure 2.67.
   b. A default name appears in the **Column Name**. A new column with the default name appears on the left-hand pane.

3. To change the name or add a label, open the properties window for the column: Select the row and click the **Properties** icon. Or double-click the column's **Column Name** or **Input**.

4. If **Automatically select groups** is checked, groups are created by the unique rows of the columns that have not been assigned summary functions.

5. To create groups using columns that are not on the **Select Data** tab, clear the check at **Automatically select groups**. Click **Edit Groups** and use the Edit Groups window.

2.4.11.2 Filtering Groups: The HAVING Filter

A *HAVING filter* determines which groups are included in the output. It is applied after any row filters —WHERE filters — are applied and after the creation of summary functions and summary groups.

A HAVING filter is created on the **Filter Data** tab using the list box, filter, the summarized data. The procedure is the same as creating a WHERE filter. See Section 2.4.3, "Filtering Rows: The WHERE Filter."

2.4.12 Example 2.15: Summary Table

Example 2.15 creates a summary table. It uses the **baseline** data table described in Example 2.6 through 2.8.

Example 2.15

Create a table with the average ages and the average stress scores for the patients in the treatment groups.

2.4.12.1 Solutions and Output

The baseline table in Appendix 1 is opened in the project. Right-click its icon and select **Filter and Query** from the pop-up menu.

Example 2.15

1. **Treatment**, **Age** and **Stress** are dragged from the left-hand pane to the **Select Data** tab. See Figure 2.67.

2. The average values for **Age** and **Stress** are selected.

   In the **Summary** column of each, **AVG** is selected from the drop-down list.

   The default names of the two new columns are **AVG_OF_Age** and **AVG_OF_Stress**.

   Automatically select groups is checked, by default. Beneath the check, **baseline.Treatment** is listed as the group-by column.

3. Click **Run** on the Query Builder window. Output 2.4 shows the output in RTF format.

Figure 2.67 Left-hand Pane and Select Data Tab for Example 2.15

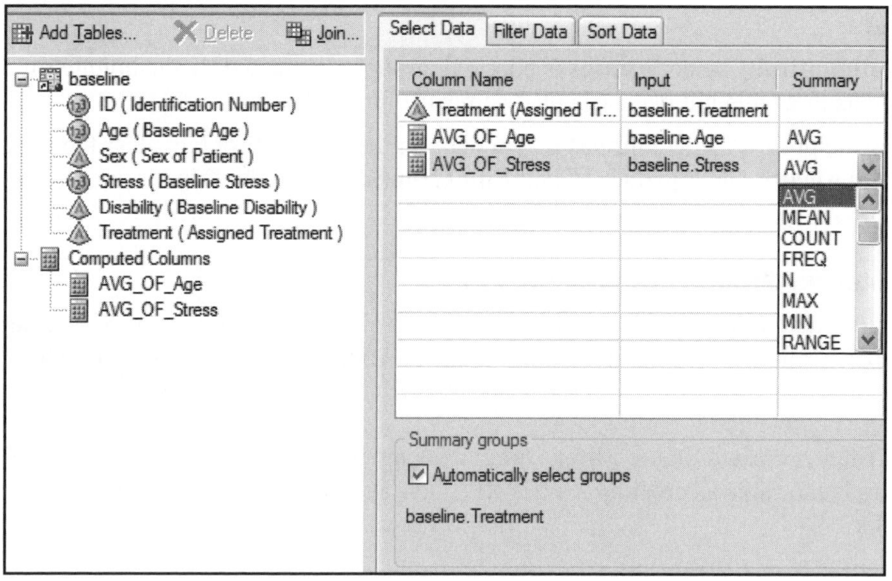

Output 2.4 Output for Example 2.15 as a Report in RTF Format

Assigned Treatment	AVG_OF_Age	AVG_OF_Stress
N05	49.25	47.9375
N10	47.6875	52.1875
PL	40.625	48.375
ST	43	49.33333

2.4.13 Multiple Tables in Queries

When the Query Builder contains multiple tables, the tables are combined with *joins* to create a single, larger table. A join connects the rows of one table with the rows of another table. Four types of joins are discussed here.

When a table is added, it joins with another table in the Query Builder.

- In Example 2.16 and Example 2.17, a table of experiment results is joined with a table of baseline data through columns of patient identification numbers in the two tables.

- In Example 2.18, a table of student data is joined with a table of course section data through columns of course section numbers in the two tables.

2.4.13.1 Joins

Cartesian Product

The basic join is the *Cartesian product* of the two tables. Each row of the first table is connected to every row of a second table. Below, **table_a** joins with **table_b** by means of a Cartesian product. The resulting table is on the left, **cartesian_product_ab**. The **x** column in **table_b** becomes **x1** when it is included in the **Select Data** tab.

table_a	
x	**w**
1	11
2	12
3	13
4	14

table_b	
x	**y**
2	21
3	22
4	23
5	24

cartesian_product_ab			
x	**w**	**x1**	**y**
1	11	2	21
1	11	3	22
1	11	4	23
1	11	5	24
2	12	2	21
2	12	3	22
2	12	4	23
2	12	5	24
3	13	2	21
3	13	3	22
3	13	4	23
3	13	5	24
4	14	2	21
4	14	3	22
4	14	4	23
4	14	5	24

Inner Join

The default is the *inner join*. It includes those rows from the Cartesian product that have matching values in a pair of assigned columns, one column from each table.

The inner join of **table_a** and **table_b** is below **inner_join_ab**. The assigned columns are the **x** columns in the tables. The inner join connects the rows of **table_a** and **table_b** that have the same **x** value.

Also below is **table_c**. Its **x** column has repeated values. The inner join of **table_a** and **table_c** is **inner_join_ac**. The assigned columns are the **x** columns in the tables. The inner join connects each row in the first table with every row in the second table that has a matching value.

inner_join_ab			
x	**w**	**x1**	**y**
2	12	2	21
3	13	3	22
4	14	4	23

table_c	
x	**z**
1	31
2	32
2	33
3	34
3	35
3	36

inner_join_ac			
x	**w**	**x1**	**z**
1	11	1	31
2	12	2	32
2	12	2	33
3	13	3	34
3	13	3	35
3	13	3	36

Left Outer Join

A *left outer join* contains the inner join rows plus the rows from the first table that have no matching values in the pair of assigned columns. The left outer join of **table_a** and **table_b** and the left outer join of **table_a** and **table_c** are below.

left_join_ab			
x	w	x1	y
1	11	.	.
2	12	2	21
3	13	3	22
4	14	4	23

left_join_ac			
x	w	x1	z
1	11	1	31
2	12	2	32
2	12	2	33
3	13	3	34
3	13	3	35
3	13	3	36
4	14	.	.

Right Outer Join

A *right outer join* contains the inner join rows plus the rows from the second table that have no matching values in the pair of assigned columns. The right outer join of **table_a** and **table_b** and the right outer join of **table_a** and **table_c** are below.

right_join_ab			
x	w	x1	y
2	12	2	21
3	13	3	22
4	14	4	23
.	.	5	24

right_join_ac			
x	w	x1	z
1	11	1	31
2	12	2	32
2	12	2	33
3	13	3	34
3	13	3	35
3	13	3	36

Full Outer Join

A *full outer join* contains the inner join rows plus the rows from the two tables that have no matching values in the pair of assigned columns. The full outer join of **table_a** and **table_b** and the full outer join of **table_a** and **table_c** are below.

full_join_ab			
x	w	x1	y
1	11	.	.
2	12	2	21
3	13	3	22
4	14	4	23
.	.	5	24

full_join_ac			
x	w	x1	z
1	11	1	31
2	12	2	32
2	12	2	33
3	13	3	34
3	13	3	35
3	13	3	36
4	14	.	.

2.4.13.2 Adding a Table to the Query

1. It is recommended that tables be added from the **Tables and Joins** window: Click **Join** above the left-hand pane. The window opens with tables and joins that currently exist in the query. See Figure 2.71.

2. Select **Add Tables**.

3. The Open Data window opens with a list of locations that include the local computer, SAS servers (and binders), and the current project. Navigate to and open the desired file.

4. The Query Builder attempts to create a join between the new table and a table already in the Query Builder. It searches for a pair of columns with the same name and type (numeric or character).

5. If a link is found, the list of columns in the new table appears in **Tables and Joins** with a *join line* connecting it to an existing table. See Figure 2.72.

   a. There is a *join indicator* on the connecting line. The filled area in the join indicator identifies the type of join. See Table 2.7. An arrow on the join line points to the second table in the join.

   Table 2.7 Join Types

   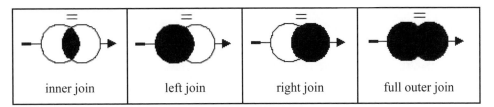

inner join	left join	right join	full outer join

   b. The equal signs in Table 2.7 indicate that rows in the existing table and the new table are connected when they have equal values in the assigned columns. Other comparisons can be selected.

   c. A label appears that identifies the join when the cursor is over the join indicator. See Figure 2.72.

   d. The type of join and comparison can be changed by double-clicking the join indicator or right-clicking the join indicator and selecting Modify Join from the pop-up menu. The Modify Join window opens. See Figure 2.68.

   Figure 2.68 Modify Join Window with the Join from Example 2.16

   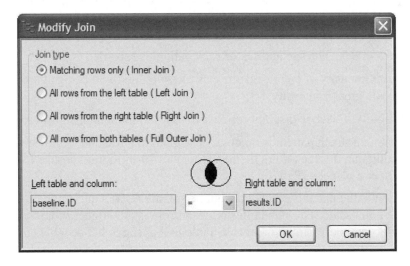

6. To replace a join:

   a. Delete the current join by right-clicking the join indicator and selecting **Delete Join** from pop-up menu.

   b. Create the desired join by:

      • Dragging the column in the first list onto the column in the second list.

      • Or right-clicking the column in the first list. Select **Join ____ with**, the second table, and the column in the second table from the pop-up menus. See Figure 2.75.

7. If no columns with the same name and type are found, the message in Figure 2.69 appears. Click **OK** and the list of columns in the new table appears. Apply step 6b above to create a join manually.

Figure 2.69 Message Indicating No Automatic Join

8. When finished, click **Close** to return to the Query Builder window.

2.4.14 Example 2.16: Automatic Join

Example 2.16 combines two tables that are linked by columns that uniquely identify each row in both tables.

2.4.14.1 Example 2.16: Baseline Data and Clinical Trial Results

The baseline table in Appendix 1 represents information from 52 patients at the beginning of a clinical trial of a drug for headaches. The table contains the following variables:

- ID: Each patient is assigned an identification number.

- Age and Sex: The age and sex of each patient is recorded.

- Stress: Intensity of emotional stress is measured with 50 being average. Higher scores indicate greater intensity.

- Disability: Baseline disability is classified mild, moderate, and severe.

- Treatment: Each patient is randomly assigned to a treatment: the new drug at a 5-milligram dosage (N05), the new drug at a 10-milligram dosage (N10), a standard drug (ST), or a placebo (PL).

After one month, the patients complete a quality-of-life (QOL) questionnaire. The QOL scores are on a 100-point scale. The standardized mean score is 50. Higher scores indicate a better quality of life. The scores are in the results table in Appendix 1. The table contains the following variables:

- ID: These correspond to the ID values in baseline.

- QOL: These are the patient QOL scores.

The tables are partially shown in Figure 2.70.

Example 2.16

Combine the baseline and results tables with an inner join. Use the ID columns to join the tables.

Figure 2.70 Baseline and Results

	ID		Age		Sex		Stress		Disability		Treatment
1	228		38	F			53		Severe		N10
2	282		33	F			58		Severe		N05
3	333		35	F			43		Moderate		ST
4	341		54	M			60		Severe		N10

results (read-only)

	ID		QOL
1	228		59
2	282		42
3	333		36
4	341		52

2.4.14.2 Solutions and Output

The baseline table is opened in the project. Its icon is right-clicked and **Filter and Query** is selected from the pop-up menu.

1. **Join** is clicked to open the Tables and Joins window. The window opens with a list of the columns in baseline. See Figure 2.71.

2. **Add Tables** is selected. The results data set is located and opened.

3. The Query Builder automatically finds a numeric column named ID in baseline and results. The list with the results columns opens with the desired join. See Figure 2.72.

Figure 2.71 Tables and Joins Window Containing Baseline

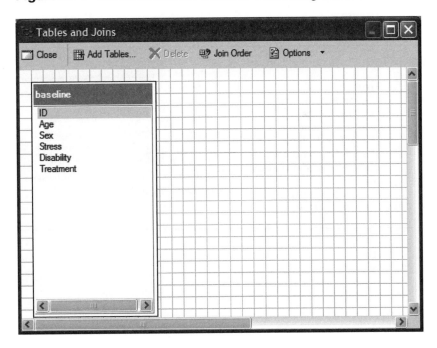

Figure 2.72 Tables and Joins Window with Baseline and Results Being Joined

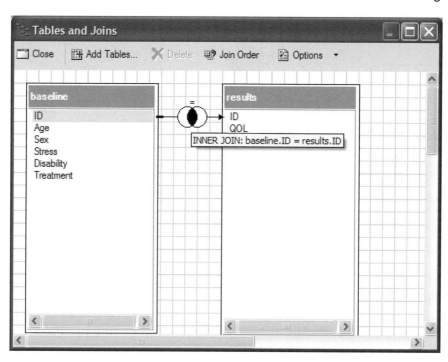

4. **Close** is clicked to return to the Query Builder window. The columns of both baseline and results are listed in the left-hand pane. See Figure 2.73.

5. All columns but ID in results are added to the **Select Data** tab. If the column were added, it would be given the name **ID1**.

6. **Run Query** is clicked. Output 2.5 shows the first 10 rows of the output table as a report in RTF format.

Figure 2.73 Left-hand Pane and Select Data Tab after Results Are Added

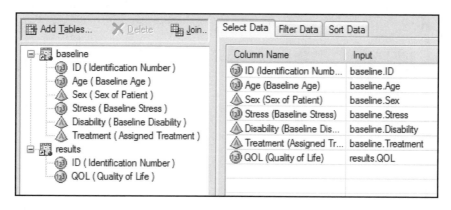

Output 2.5 First 10 Rows for Example 2.16

Identification Number	Baseline Age	Sex of Patient	Baseline Stress	Baseline Disability	Assigned Treatment	Quality of Life
228	38	F	53	Severe	N10	59
282	33	F	58	Severe	N05	42
333	35	F	43	Moderate	ST	36
341	54	M	60	Severe	N10	52
344	45	F	71	Severe	N10	59
345	52	M	41	Mild	ST	65
374	42	M	48	Moderate	N10	55
379	42	M	46	Mild	PL	37
405	48	F	54	Mild	N10	73
435	38	F	53	Moderate	PL	28

2.4.15 Example 2.17: Manual Join

This example shows how a manual join would be necessary in Example 2.16. Here, the column of identification numbers in the second table has the name Number and not ID. The second table is now named results2. See Figure 2.74.

Figure 2.74 Baseline and Results2

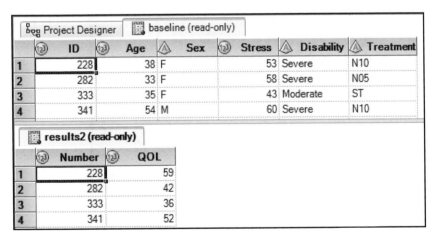

Because baseline and results2 do not have columns with the same name, a join will not be automatically found. The error message in Figure 2.69 would appear. It is necessary to manually join the tables with ID in baseline and Number in results2. See Figure 2.75.

Example 2.17

1. **ID** is right-clicked in the **baseline** list.

2. **Join ID with**, the table **results2**, and the column **Number** are selected from pop-up menus.

Figure 2.75 Manual Join with ID in Baseline and Number in results2t

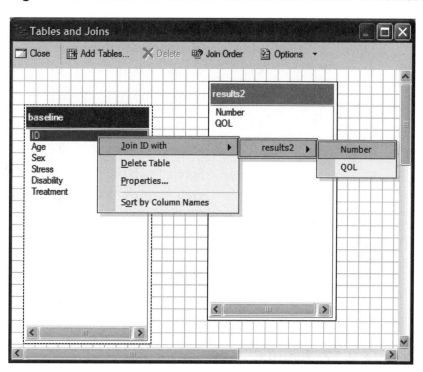

Figure 2.76 Tables and Joins Window with Baseline and results2 Being Joined

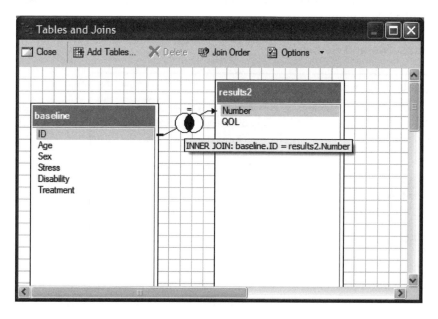

2.4.16 Example 2.18: Repeated Linking Values

This example combines two tables that are joined by columns that do not both have unique values. The process of joining these tables is the same as in Example 2.16.

2.4.16.1 Course Section Data and Student Data

The Ex02_12_sections table at the top in Figure 2.77 contains meeting times and locations for two sections of a university course. The Ex02_12_students table at the bottom in Figure 2.77 contains names of the students assigned to the two sections.

The Ex02_12_sections table contains the following variables:

- Section: the course section number
- Time: the time and days that the section meets
- Location: the classroom where the section meets

The Ex02_12_students table contains the following variables:

- Name, FI, and MI: the last name, first initial, and middle initial of each student.
- Section: the assigned course section

Figure 2.77 Ex02_12_sections (Top), Ex02_12_students (Bottom)

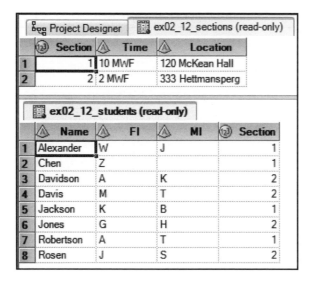

The tables Ex02_12_sections and Ex02_12_students are combined with the two Section columns joining the tables. Each row in Ex02_12_sections combines with every row in Ex02_12_students that has the same Section number.

Example 2.18

Combine the Ex02_12_sections and Ex02_12_students tables with an inner join. Use the **Section** columns to link the tables.

2.4.16.2 Solution

Output 2.6 Results for Example 2.18

Course Section Number	Course Time	Course Location	Last Name	First Initial	Middle Initial
1	10 MWF	120 McKean Hall	Alexander	W	J
1	10 MWF	120 McKean Hall	Chen	Z	
2	2 MWF	333 Hettmansperger Hall	Davidson	A	K
2	2 MWF	333 Hettmansperger Hall	Davis	M	T
1	10 MWF	120 McKean Hall	Jackson	K	B
2	2 MWF	333 Hettmansperger Hall	Jones	G	H
1	10 MWF	120 McKean Hall	Robertson	A	T
2	2 MWF	333 Hettmansperger Hall	Rosen	J	S

Descriptive Statistics

3.1   Introduction to Statistics

3.1.1 Statistical Inference

The science of statistics is principally the science of *statistical inference*. Measurements and characterizations of individuals or objects are analyzed with the goal of making conclusions about quantities and qualities that describe the complete group from which the individuals or objects are drawn.

Data are collected within a *population* and analyzed collectively as a *sample*. In Figure 3.1, the dots represent data. *Inferences* are made about the population based on the analysis of the sample.

- *Data* are the measurements, counts, and categorizations obtained from individuals or objects. A single measurement, count, or categorization is a *data value* or, simply, a *value*. Data are stored in *data sets*. See Chapter 2, "Working with Data."

- Depending on the context, an *observation* can be a single value, some of the values, or all of the values obtained from an individual or object. In statistical theory, a sample is a collection of observations. Samples are the focus in this chapter.

- In statistical theory, a population is the collection of potential observations from all persons or objects of interest. Probability is used to describe populations. See Chapter 4, "Inferences from One Sample."

- Statistical inference is descriptive statistics analyzed in the context of the laws of probability. Statistical inference begins in Chapter 4, "Inferences from One Sample," and continues with each following chapter.

Figure 3.1 Process of Statistical Inference

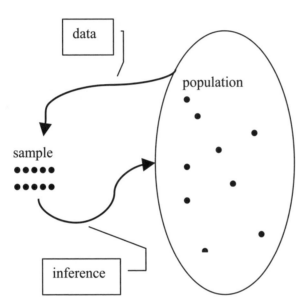

3.1.2 A Statistic

A *statistic* describes a feature of one or more variables. All the statistics defined in this chapter are one-variable statistics. An example of a one-variable statistic is n, the number of nonmissing values in a given variable.

In order to define statistics, mathematical notation is necessary. As in algebra, the symbol for a variable is a lowercase letter: $x, y, z \ldots$.

Data values associated with a variable are written with subscripts. All n data values associated with the variable x are written as $x_1, x_2, \ldots, x_n$, or equivalently as x_i, $i = 1, \ldots, n$.

Descriptive statistics include both statistics and graphs to describe samples. Taken together, statistics and graphs turn raw data into usable information.

3.1.3 Example 3.1: Basic Ideas

3.1.3.1 Employee Data

In order to monitor attitudes, 24 employees are randomly selected and asked to complete a psychological questionnaire. Evaluation of the questionnaire results in three scores measuring different attitudes. The scores and other information are shown in the Attitude data set in Figure 3.2.

Figure 3.2 A Sample of Employees, a Data Set, and a Sample of Data Values

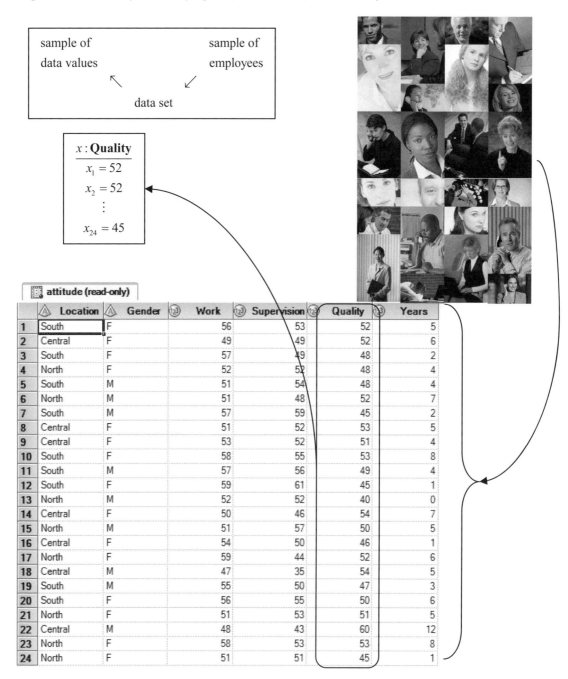

	Location	Gender	Work	Supervision	Quality	Years
1	South	F	56	53	52	5
2	Central	F	49	49	52	6
3	South	F	57	49	48	2
4	North	F	52	52	48	4
5	South	M	51	54	48	4
6	North	M	51	48	52	7
7	South	M	57	59	45	2
8	Central	F	51	52	53	5
9	Central	F	53	52	51	4
10	South	F	58	55	53	8
11	South	M	57	56	49	4
12	South	F	59	61	45	1
13	North	M	52	52	40	0
14	Central	F	50	46	54	7
15	North	M	51	57	50	5
16	Central	F	54	50	46	1
17	North	F	59	44	52	6
18	Central	M	47	35	54	5
19	South	M	55	50	47	3
20	South	F	56	55	50	6
21	North	F	51	53	51	5
22	Central	M	48	43	60	12
23	North	F	58	53	53	8
24	North	F	51	51	45	1

The figure also shows:

sample of data values ← data set → sample of employees

$$x : \text{Quality}$$

$$x_1 = 52$$

$$x_2 = 52$$

$$\vdots$$

$$x_{24} = 45$$

attitude (read-only)

The Attitude data set contains six values for each of the 24 employees. There are six variables. The first two are character and the last four are numeric.

- **Location** identifies the employee's branch office.
- **Gender** identifies the employee as female or male.
- **Work** measures an employee's attitude toward their tasks and responsibilities.
- **Supervision** measures an employee's attitude toward their supervisors.
- **Quality** measures an employee's attitude toward the company's quality program.
- **Years** is the number of years an employee has been with the company.

Consider the sample of Quality scores.

- $n = 24$
- In terms of the variable x, the sample $x_1, x_2, \ldots, x_{24}$ is:

$$x_1 = 52 \quad x_2 = 52 \quad x_3 = 48 \quad x_4 = 48 \quad x_5 = 48 \quad x_6 = 52 \quad x_7 = 45 \quad x_8 = 53 \quad x_9 = 51 \quad x_{10} = 53$$
$$x_{11} = 49 \quad x_{12} = 45 \quad x_{13} = 40 \quad x_{14} = 54 \quad x_{15} = 50 \quad x_{16} = 46 \quad x_{17} = 52 \quad x_{18} = 54 \quad x_{19} = 47 \quad x_{20} = 50$$
$$x_{21} = 51 \quad x_{22} = 60 \quad x_{23} = 53 \quad x_{24} = 45$$

3.2 Listing Data

The List Data task does just that: it lists the data.

- The order of the variables in the output is arranged in the task.
- Column headings can be either the variable labels (the default option) or the variable names.
- Row numbers can be included (the default option) or not. Row numbers can be replaced by the values in one or more identifying columns. These columns might be names or identification numbers, for example.
- Rows can be listed in groups. These groups are called *by groups*.
- The number of rows can be included in the output.
- The sum of data values can be included in the output.

3.2.1 Example 3.2: Listing Data

Basic applications of the List Data task are illustrated here.

- Applying the task is discussed in Section 3.2.2, "Instructions for the List Data Task."
- The results are in Task Output for Example 3.2.

This example uses the Attitude data set shown in Figure 3.2 in Example 3.1. See "Attitude" in Appendix 1.

Example 3.2.1

List the data in the Attitude data set.

Example 3.2.2

List the **Work**, **Supervision**, and **Quality** Attitude scores by **Location**. Do not include row numbers but do print the number of rows.

3.2.2 Instructions for the List Data Task

Open the List Data task in one of the following ways:

- From the menu bar, select **Describe ▶ List Data**.

- On the **Task by Category** tab of the **Task List**, go to the **Describe** section and click **List Data**.

- On the **Task by Name** tab of the **Task List**, double-click **List Data**.

The List Data task has three groups of options: Task Roles, Options, and Titles. The Titles group of options is discussed in Chapter 1, "Introduction to SAS Enterprise Guide." The Titles options control the titles and the footnotes in the task output.

3.2.2.1 Task Roles

Click **Task Roles** on the selection pane to open this group of options. A variable is assigned to a role by dragging its name from **Variables to assign** to a role in **Task Roles**. See Figure 3.3. A variable can be removed from a role by dragging it back to **Variables to assign**. The right and left arrows and the resulting pop-up menus can also be used. To select more than one variable at a time, press **Ctrl** on the keyboard while selecting.

- **List variables**: These are the variables to be listed. The order that the variables are listed below **List variables** is the order that they are listed from left to right in the output.

- **Group analysis by:**
  o If a single variable is assigned to the Group analysis by role, the rows are grouped by its unique values. These are *by-group values*. The default is to list the groups in the ascending order of the by-group values. Descending order can be selected. See discussion in Section 1.2.2, "Common Task Roles." If **Sort by variables** is not selected, the groups are listed in the order that the by-group values occur in the data.

  o If multiple variables are assigned to the Group analysis by role, the rows are grouped by the unique rows of these variables. If **Sort by variables** is selected, the by-group values are sorted in the order that the variables are listed below Group analysis by.

- **Page by**: The variable in the Page by role must also be assigned to the Group analysis by role. A new page begins for each by-group value.

- **Total of**: Sums of the values in these numeric variables are included at the bottom of the output.

- **Subtotal of**: The variable in the Subtotal of role must also be assigned to the Group analysis by role. Subtotals of the variables in the Total of role are included for each by-group value in the variable in the Subtotal of role.

- **Identifying label**: The values in these variables replace the row numbers in the output. If the formatted values are different from the stored values, the formatted values are used.

Figure 3.3 shows the Task Roles window for Example 3.2.1. All the variables are assigned to List variables.

Figure 3.4 shows the Task Roles window for Example 3.2.2. Work, Supervision, and Quality are assigned to List variables. Location is assigned the Group analysis by role. This causes the Location sort order menu and Sort by variables selection box to appear. In the resulting Output 3.1, the by groups are sorted in the ascending order of the unique Location values.

Figure 3.3 Task Roles in the List Data Task for Example 3.2.1

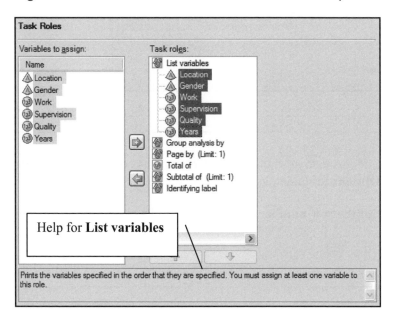

Figure 3.4 Task Roles in the List Data Task for Example 3.2.2

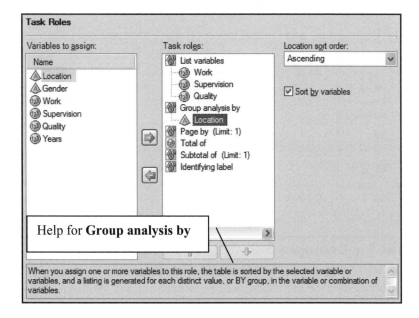

Figure 3.5 Options in the List Data Task for Example 3.2.1

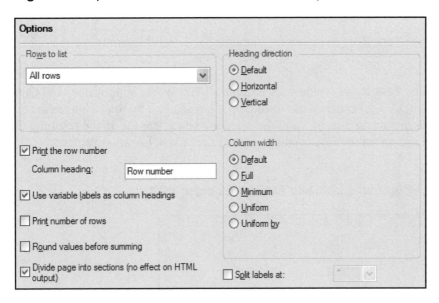

3.2.2.2 Options

Click **Options** on the selection pane to open this group. These items control the appearance of the output. Figure 3.5 shows **Options** for Example 3.2.1. These are the default selections.

For Example 3.2.2, the **Print the row number** check box would be cleared and **Print number of rows** would be checked.

3.2.2.3 When Finished

When you are finished assigning variables to roles and selecting options, click **Run**. The task adds a List Data icon and one or more output icons to the process flow diagram. See Figure 3.6. The results for Example 3.2 are in Output 3.1 and Output 3.2.

Figure 3.6 Example 3.2 Data, Task, and Output Icons on the Process Flow Diagram

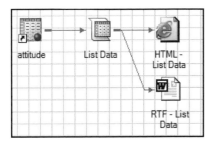

3.2.3 Task Output for Example 3.2

Output 3.1 has the results for Example 3.2.1, and Output 3.2 has the results for Example 3.2.2. In both cases, the column headings are the variable labels. In Output 3.2, the by groups are identified by the Location variable label and the unique Location values.

Output 3.1 Report Listing: Results for Example 3.2.1

Row number	Location of Branch Office	Gender	Work	Supervision	Quality	Years with company
1	South	F	56	53	52	5
2	Central	F	49	49	52	6
3	South	F	57	49	48	2
4	North	F	52	52	48	4
5	South	M	51	54	48	4
6	North	M	51	48	52	7
7	South	M	57	59	45	2
8	Central	F	51	52	53	5
9	Central	F	53	52	51	4
10	South	F	58	55	53	8
11	South	M	57	56	49	4
12	South	F	59	61	45	1
13	North	M	52	52	40	0
14	Central	F	50	46	54	7
15	North	M	51	57	50	5
16	Central	F	54	50	46	1
17	North	F	59	44	52	6
18	Central	M	47	35	54	5
19	South	M	55	50	47	3
20	South	F	56	55	50	6
21	North	F	51	53	51	5
22	Central	M	48	43	60	12
23	North	F	58	53	53	8
24	North	F	51	51	45	1

Output 3.2 Report Listing: Results for Example 3.2.2

Location of Branch Office=Central

Work	Supervision	Quality
49	49	52
51	52	53
53	52	51
50	46	54
54	50	46
47	35	54
48	43	60
N = 7		

Location of Branch Office=North

Work	Supervision	Quality
52	52	48
51	48	52
52	52	40
51	57	50
59	44	52
51	53	51
58	53	53
51	51	45
N = 8		

Location of Branch Office=South

Work	Supervision	Quality
56	53	52
57	49	48
51	54	48
57	59	45
58	55	53
57	56	49
59	61	45
55	50	47
56	55	50
N = 9		

3.3 Histograms

Histograms are used with continuous data and discrete data with a large number of distinct values. A histogram presents a sample as a virtual pile of numbers.

- A *frequency histogram* consists of rectangular bars with the base of each bar representing an interval of numbers and the height of each bar representing the number of values in the interval at the base. A histogram interval is called a *class*.

- A *percentage histogram* is essentially the same as a frequency histogram but with the height of each bar representing the percentage of the sample of values in the class at the base.

Both types of histograms produce the same shape for a given sample but have different axes for bar heights. Figure 3.7 shows frequency and percentage histograms with depth, giving them a three-dimensional appearance. Both histograms indicate that the sample has a relatively large number of values near 50 and relatively few values near either 40 or 60.

Figure 3.7 Frequency and Percentage Histograms

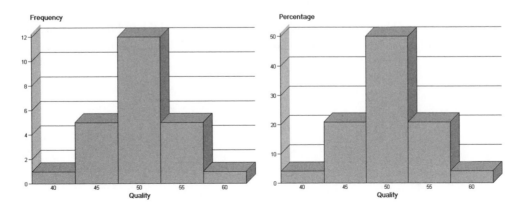

Each class has the form $[a,b)$, which means all the numbers x such that $a \le x < b$. If a value is greater than or equal to the left class boundary a and less than the right class boundary b, it is counted as being in the class $[a,b)$.

- The *class width* is the distance between the left and right boundaries: $b - a$.
- All classes should have the same width.
- Taken together, the classes have no gaps and should cover all the values in the sample.
- The *class midpoint* is the number midway between the class boundaries. The midpoint of $[a,b)$ is $(a+b)/2$. Classes in SAS Enterprise Guide are represented by their midpoints.
- Since the class widths are the same, midpoints are equally spaced and the common width is equal to the common distance between adjacent midpoints.

The midpoints in Figure 3.7 are 40, 45, 50, 55, and 60. The class width is 5.

It is generally not necessary to compute the class boundaries from midpoints, but it can be done easily.

- The left-hand boundary is equal to the midpoint minus half the class width. The left-hand boundary of the class with midpoint 40 is 37.5.
- The right-hand boundary is equal to the midpoint plus half the class width. The right-hand boundary of the class with midpoint 40 is 42.5.

The classes in Figure 3.7 are $[37.5, 42.5)$, $[42.5, 47.5)$, $[47.5, 52.5)$, $[52.5, 57.5)$, and $[57.5, 62.5)$.

Classes can be automatically determined by the SAS software or they can be determined by the person analyzing the data. See Section 3.3.2.3, "Appearance."

Recognizable shapes suggest that the data result from a stable and predictable process. The following are often seen in data:

- A *bell-shaped* histogram is approximately symmetric with most of the values in the center and fewer values distributed nearly equally in both the left and right tails. See Figure 3.7 and Figure 3.8 (a).
- A *uniform* histogram is approximately symmetric with roughly the same number of values in each class. See Figure 3.8 (b).
- A *right-skewed* histogram has most of the values on the left and the rest distributed in a longer tail on the right or positive side. See Figure 3.8 (c).
- A *left-skewed* histogram has most of the values on the right and the rest distributed in a longer tail on the left or negative side. See Figure 3.8 (d) and Figure 3.17.

Figure 3.8 Histograms That Are Approximately (a) Bell-shaped and (b) Uniform Histograms That Are (c) Right-Skewed and (d) Left-Skewed.

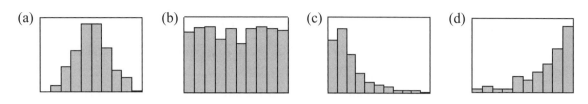

3.3.1 Example 3.3: Creating a Histogram

This example illustrates basic applications of the Bar Chart task.

- The Bar Chart task is discussed in "Instructions for Creating a Histogram with the Bar Chart Task."

- The results are in "Task Output, Interpretation, and Analysis for Example 3.3."

3.3.1.1 Scores Measuring Attitude toward Supervision

In order to monitor employee attitudes, 24 randomly selected employees are asked to complete a standardized psychological questionnaire. Evaluation of the questionnaire results in a number of scores measuring different attitudes. One of these scores measures the employee's attitude toward his or her supervisors. Scores above 50 indicate a positive attitude; scores below 50 indicate a negative attitude. The 24 scores are below. The data is also in the Supervision column of the Attitude data set in Appendix 1.

| 53 | 49 | 49 | 52 | 54 | 48 | 59 | 52 | 52 | 55 | 56 | 61 |
| 52 | 46 | 57 | 50 | 44 | 35 | 50 | 55 | 53 | 43 | 53 | 51 |

Example 3.3.1

Create a frequency histogram of the scores. Allow the SAS software to determine the classes.

1. Determine the midpoint of the class with the smallest frequency.
2. Determine the midpoint of the modal class, the class with the greatest frequency.

Example 3.3.2

Create a percentage histogram of the scores. Use midpoints 35, 40, 45, 50, 55, and 60. Label the bars with the percentage values.

1. Determine the midpoint of the class with the smallest percentage.
2. Determine the midpoint of the modal class, the class with the greatest percentage.

3.3.2 Instructions for Creating a Histogram with the Bar Chart Task

Open the Bar Chart task in one of the following ways:

- From the menu bar, select **Graph ▶ Bar Chart**.

- On the **Task by Category** tab of the **Task List**, go to the **Graph** section and click **Bar Chart**.

- On the **Task by Name** tab of the **Task List**, double-click **Bar Chart**.

The Bar Chart task has four major groups of options: Bar Chart, Task Roles, Appearance, and Titles. The Titles group of options is discussed in Chapter 1, "Introduction to SAS Enterprise Guide." The Titles options control the titles and the footnotes in the task output.

3.3.2.1   Bar Chart

A histogram is a special type of a simple vertical bar chart. **Simple Vertical Bar** is the default selection for the Bar Chart options. See Figure 3.9.

Figure 3.9 Bar Chart Options in the Bar Chart Task for Example 3.3

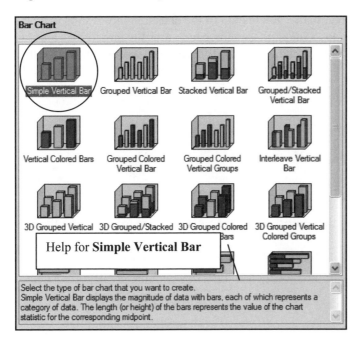

3.3.2.2   Task Roles

Click **Task Roles** on the selection pane to open this group of options. A variable is assigned to a role by dragging its name from **Columns to assign** to a role in **Task roles**. See Figure 3.10. A variable can be removed from a role by dragging it back to **Columns to assign**. The right and left arrows and the resulting pop-up menus can also be used.

- **Column to chart**: A chart is created based on the values in this variable.
- **Sum of**: Bar charts can be created where heights of the bars are sums or means of a second variable.
- Group charts by:
  - o If a single variable is assigned to the Group charts by role, a chart is created for each group identified by its unique values. These are by-group values. By default, the groups are listed in the ascending order of the by-group values. Descending order can be selected. See Section 1.3.
  - o If multiple variables are assigned to the Group charts by role, the charts are grouped by the unique rows of these variables.

In Figure 3.10, Supervision is assigned to the Column to chart role.

Figure 3.10 Task Roles in the Bar Chart Task for Example 3.3

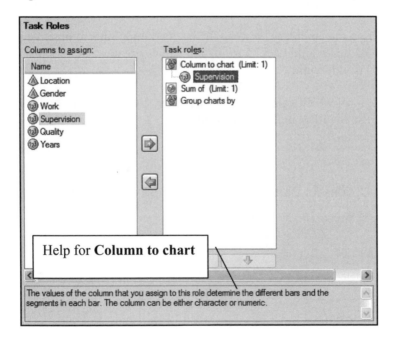

3.3.2.3   Appearance

Click **Appearance** on the selection pane to open this group of options. Bar, Options, Chart Area, and Advanced are presented here.

- Bar options:
  - o For Example 3.3.1, no action is required here. However, bar colors are changed to gray for the benefit of this black-and-white text. This is done with the color pallet in the **Bar appearance** box. See Figure 3.11.

    o   Example 3.3.2 asks that midpoints be entered. See Figure 3.12.

        ·   Check **Specify number of bars** and select **Specify the bar values**.

        ·   Midpoints are entered using the following description:

$$m_1 \text{ to } m_L \text{ by } w \quad \text{where} \begin{cases} m_1 \text{ is the first midpoint.} \\ m_L \text{ is the last midpoint.} \\ w \text{ is interval width.} \end{cases}$$

        ·   For Example 3.3.2, the midpoints "35, 40, 45, 50, 55, 60" are entered as 35 to 60 by 5.

        ·   Then **Add** is clicked.

Important: When specifying midpoints one needs to be sure that the classes contain all the data. Otherwise misleading results are possible.

The Bar Chart task constructs a simple bar chart so that the first interval goes from negative infinity to the boundary between the first and second midpoints. In terms of Example 3.3.2 that would be $-\infty$ to 37.5. All values below 37.5 are associated with the first midpoint.

The last interval goes from the boundary between the last two midpoints to positive infinity. In terms of Example 3.3.2 that would be 57.5 to ∞. All values greater than or equal to 57.5 are associated with the last midpoint.

The midpoints do not control which values are represented by the histogram. To restrict the values being analyzed, use the filter in the Query Builder.

Figure 3.11 Appearance Options for Bars in the Bar Chart Task for Example 3.3.1

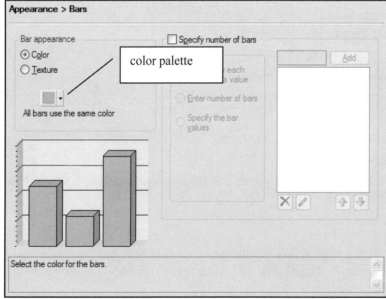

Figure 3.12 Specifying Midpoints for Example 3.3.2

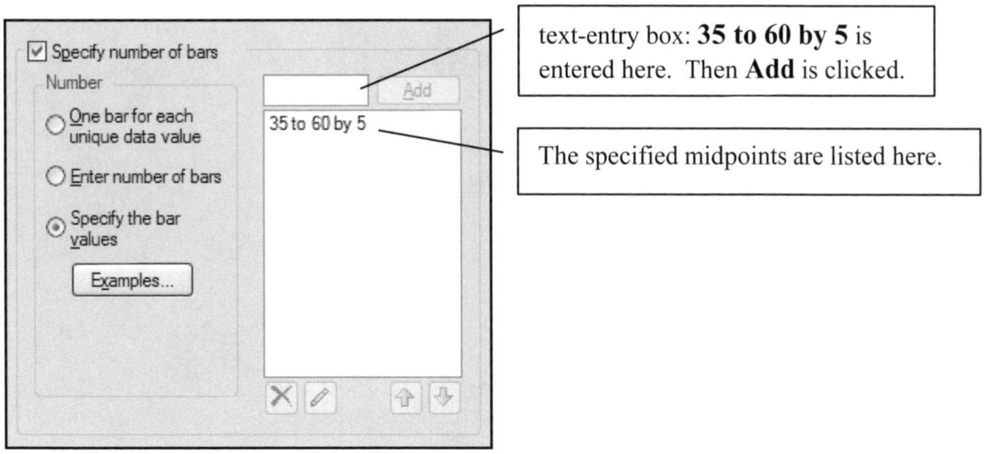

- Options: Histogram classes have no gaps. This is represented by no space between the bars. This is the selection for both Example 3.3.1 and Example 3.3.2. See Figure 3.13.
  - At the drop-down menu at **Bar Size**, select **Set spacing**.
  - An entry box appears. Change the default value to 0. The sample bars show the spacing when the window is reset. To reset, click another option group on the selection pane and then return.
- Chart Area options: This is the selection for both Example 3.3.1 and Example 3.3.2. See Figure 3.14.
  - **Chart background color**: This controls the color around the histogram. White is selected on the color palette.
  - **Draw frame around plot area**: The plot area is the region defined by the axes. The frame is controlled only for two-dimensional graphs. The frame adds top and right-hand lines to complete a rectangle with the horizontal and vertical axes. Controlling the planes created with a three-dimensional line requires code.
  - **Plot area background color**: This controls the color in the plot area. **Draw frame around plot area** must be checked for this color palette to be active.
- Advanced options:
  - For Example 3.3.1, no action is required here. A frequency histogram is requested and, by default, the **Statistic used to calculate bar** is **Frequency**.
  - For Example 3.3.2:
    - A percentage histogram is requested. The **Statistic used to calculate bar** is changed to **Percentage**. See Figure 3.15.
    - Also, percentage-value labels are requested for the bars. Check **Additional statistical value to show next to bar**. Select **Percentage** from the drop-down menu.

Figure 3.13 Appearance Options for Layout in the Bar Chart Task for Example 3.3

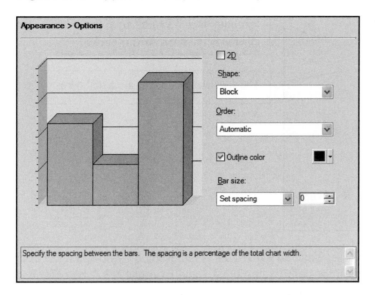

Figure 3.14 Appearance Options for Chart Area in the Bar Chart Task for Example 3.3

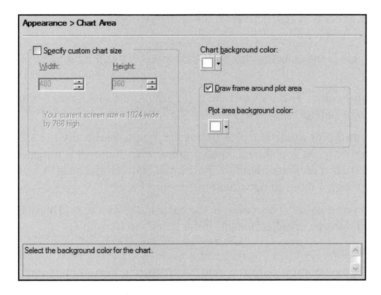

Figure 3.15 Advanced Appearance Options in the Bar Chart task for Example 3.3.2

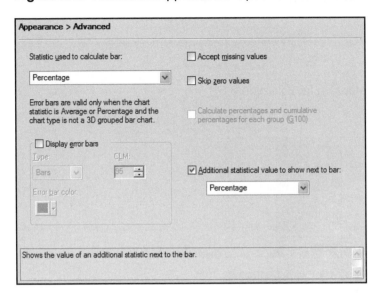

3.3.2.4   When Finished

When finished assigning variables to roles and selecting options, click **Run**. The task adds a Bar Chart icon and one or more output icons to the process flow diagram. See Figure 3.16. The results for Example 3.3 are in the "Task Output, Interpretation, and Analysis for Example 3.3" section.

Figure 3.16 Example 3.3 Data, Task, and Output Icons on the Process Flow Diagram

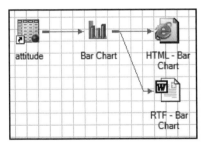

3.3.3 Task Output, Interpretation, and Analysis for Example 3.3

3.3.3.1 Task Output

Figure 3.17 Frequency Histogram for Example 3.3.1

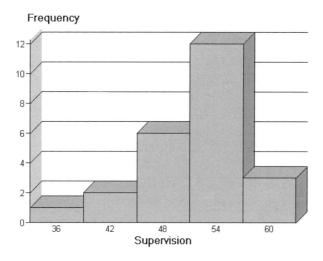

Figure 3.18 Percentage Histogram for Example 3.3.2

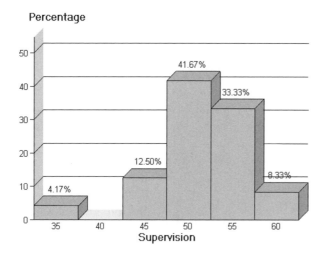

3.3.3.2 Interpretation

The histogram in Figure 3.17 is left skewed. The bulk of the observations are on the right with fewer and fewer observations tailing off to the left. The histogram in Figure 3.18 shows that the left tail might be the result of an *outlier*, a statistically unusual observation, with the remaining observations being roughly bell-shaped. Outliers are discussed in Section 3.5, "Measures of Position."

3.3.3.3 Analysis

Example 3.3.1
- 36 is the midpoint of the class with the smallest frequency.
- 54 is the midpoint of the modal class.

Example 3.3.2
- 40 is the midpoint of the class with the smallest percentage.
- 50 is the midpoint of the modal class.

3.3.4 Example 3.4: Grouped and Stacked Histograms

A grouped histogram presents multiple histograms in a single graph. A stacked histogram is a single histogram with the bars partitioned to display group frequencies or percentages.

Example 3.4 has the scores from Example 3.3 in groups. Grouped histograms and a stacked histogram are requested.

3.3.4.1 Scores Grouped by Location

Psychological tests are given to 24 randomly selected employees. Scores measuring employee attitude towards supervision are analyzed. New to this example is the fact that the employees come from three different offices. The offices are identified by their location: Central, North, and South. The data is below.

Central				North				South			
49	52	52	46	52	48	52	57	53	49	54	59
50	35	43		44	53	53	51	55	56	61	50
								55			

Example 3.8.1
Construct grouped frequency histograms of the scores at the three offices. Allow the SAS software to determine the classes.

Example 3.8.2
Construct a stacked frequency histogram of the scores at the three offices. Allow the SAS software to determine the classes.

The scores and locations are shown in the data grid below. Note that the table of data becomes two columns. The scores are in the Supervision column and the classification values are in the Location column.

The Attitude data set is in the data grid. All variables except Location and Supervision are hidden.

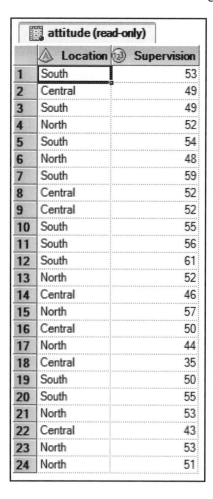

	Location	Supervision
1	South	53
2	Central	49
3	South	49
4	North	52
5	South	54
6	North	48
7	South	59
8	Central	52
9	Central	52
10	South	55
11	South	56
12	South	61
13	North	52
14	Central	46
15	North	57
16	Central	50
17	North	44
18	Central	35
19	South	50
20	South	55
21	North	53
22	Central	43
23	North	53
24	North	51

3.3.5 Instructions for Creating Grouped and Stacked Histograms with the Bar Chart Task

The only changes from the "Instructions for Creating a Histogram with the Bar Chart Task" are at the Bar Chart and Task Roles options.

3.3.5.1 Bar Chart

The **Bar Chart** options are shown in Figure 3.9.

- To create a grouped histogram, select **Grouped Vertical Bar**. This is the selection for Example 3.4.1.

- To create a stacked histogram, select **Stacked Vertical Bar**. This is the selection for Example 3.4.2.

3.3.5.2 Task Roles

Each to the two options listed above adds a role to the Bar Chart task roles.

- The Group bars by role is added when **Grouped Vertical Bar** is selected. The result is a single graph with histograms created for the groups identified by this variable. This is the selection for Example 3.4.1 with Location assigned to the Group bars by role.

- The Stack role is added when **Stacked Vertical Bar** is selected. The result is a single histogram with the bars partitioned to display the frequencies or the percentages associated with the groups identified by this variable. This is the selection for Example 3.4.2 with Location assigned to the Stack role.

3.3.6 Output and Interpretation for Example 3.4

3.3.6.1 Output

Figure 3.19 Grouped Histogram for Example 3.4.1

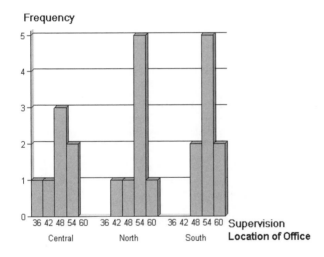

Figure 3.20 Stacked Histogram for Example 3.4.2

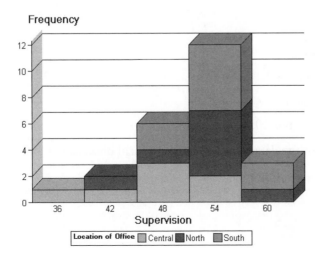

Comment
"Location of Office" is the label of the Location variable.

3.3.6.2   Interpretation

The supervision scores at the South and North offices are generally higher than at the Central office. In Figure 3.19, the midpoints of the three modal classes, going from left to right, are 48, 54, and 54. In Figure 3.20, only two scores from the Central office are in the two bars representing the two highest classes.

3.4 Basic Statistics

A *statistic* is a number that describes a characteristic of a sample, a sample being a collection of observations. Table 3.1 is a sample consisting of the number of emails received by a person on 5 mornings.

Table 3.1 E-mail Data

| 2 | 4 | 1 | 5 | 10 |

Let the variable be x: the number of e-mails received. In terms of the variable x, the sample is:

$$x_1 = 2 \quad x_2 = 4 \quad x_3 = 1 \quad x_4 = 5 \quad x_5 = 10$$

An index variable is used to make the notation manageable. Here, the index variable is i.

- x_i, where $i = 1,\ldots,5$, means x_1, x_2, x_3, x_4, x_5.

- $\sum_{i=1}^{5} x_i$ means the sum (Σ) of the values x_1 through x_5: $\sum_{i=1}^{5} x_i = x_1 + x_2 + x_3 + x_4 + x_5 = 2 + 4 + 1 + 5 + 10 = 22$

It is not too much of an exaggeration to say that the following statistics are the best known, most used, and most important.

- *Number of observations* in a sample, denoted by n in the text and N in the output
    For Table 3.1, $n = 5$.

- *Minimum*: the smallest observation
    For Table 3.1, the minimum is 1.

- *Maximum*: the largest observation
    For Table 3.1, the maximum is 10.

- *Mean*: a value at the center of the data representing the typical observation

The formula is $\bar{x} = \dfrac{\sum\limits_{i=1}^{n} x_i}{n}$. That is, the sample mean ("x-bar") is equal to the sum of the observations x_1 through x_n divided by n. For Table 3.1,

$$\bar{x} = \frac{2+4+1+5+10}{5} = \frac{22}{5} = 4.4\,.$$

- *Standard deviation*: a measure of how far the observations are spread out or dispersed from the center

The formula is $s = \sqrt{\dfrac{\sum\limits_{i=1}^{n}\left(x_i - \bar{x}\right)^2}{n-1}}$. The important thing to notice about the standard deviation formula is that it is based on the *deviations* $x_i - \bar{x}$, the differences between the observations and the sample mean. The resulting statistic measures how far the observations are spread out from the mean.

For Table 3.1, $s = \sqrt{\dfrac{\left(2-4.4\right)^2 + \left(4-4.4\right)^2 + \left(1-4.4\right)^2 + \left(5-4.4\right)^2 + \left(10-4.4\right)^2}{5-1}}$

$$s = \sqrt{\frac{\left(-2.4\right)^2 + \left(-0.4\right)^2 + \left(-3.4\right)^2 + \left(0.6\right)^2 + \left(5.6\right)^2}{5-1}}$$

$$s = \sqrt{\frac{5.76 + 0.16 + 11.56 + 0.36 + 31.36}{4}}$$

$$s = \sqrt{12.3}$$

$$s = 3.5 \ \left(\text{Rounded to the same number of decimal places as } \bar{x}\right)$$

One would think that the best measure of the dispersion of the data would be the *average deviation*, $\sum\limits_{i=1}^{n}\left(x_i - \bar{x}\right)\big/n$. But deviations always sum to 0. Therefore, the average deviation is always 0. For Table 3.1, $\sum\limits_{i=1}^{5}\left(x_i - \bar{x}\right)\big/5 = \left(-2.4 - 0.4 - 3.4 + 0.6 + 5.6\right)/5 = 0/5 = 0$.

- The deviations are squared to create positive numbers: $\sum\limits_{i=1}^{n}\left(x_i - \bar{x}\right)^2$

- What one gets is almost the mean of the squared deviations. This is the *sample variance*: $s^2 = \sum\limits_{i=1}^{n}\left(x_i - \bar{x}\right)^2 \big/ \left(n-1\right)$. It is not a true mean because of the division by $n-1$ instead of n. (This is done for estimation purposes. Division by $n-1$ results in a better estimate of the population variance σ^2 than division by n.)

- The problem with the sample variance is that it is measured in square units. Examples are $\left(\text{miles}\right)^2$, $\left(\text{voters}\right)^2$, and $\left(\text{points}\right)^2$. For Table 3.1, $s^2 = 12.3 \ \left(\text{e-mails}\right)^2$. A measure in original units is required.

- The square root of the variance is a measure in the original units. The result is the *standard* deviation. For Table 3.1, $s = 3.5$ emails.

Figure 3.21 Sample from Table 3.1 on the Number Line with Deviations and Statistics

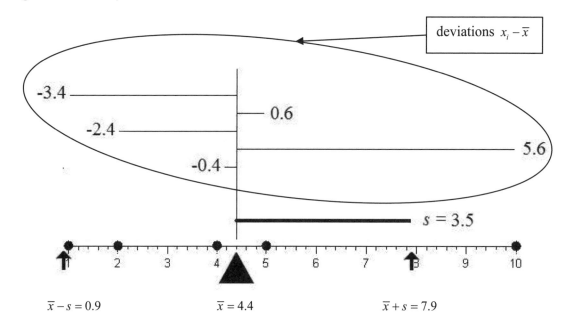

$$\bar{x} - s = 0.9 \qquad \bar{x} = 4.4 \qquad \bar{x} + s = 7.9$$

Figure 3.21 shows the mean (▲) as the balance point of the sample from Table 3.1. As is generally the case, most of the sample is between the values determined by $\bar{x} - s$ and $\bar{x} + s$. The sample deviations are shown above the number line. The sample standard deviation s takes on the role of the average deviation.

3.4.1 Information Provided by the Mean and the Standard Deviation Together

The Empirical Rule and Chebyshev's Theorem describe how the mean and standard deviation work together. Chebyshev's Theorem is true for all data sets. Empirical Rule, also called the 68-95-99.7 Rule, is most accurate when describing data having bell-shaped histograms.

3.4.1.1 Chebyshev's Theorem

At least $\left(1 - 1/k^2\right)100\%$ of the observations are between $\bar{x} - ks$ and $\bar{x} + ks$, for $k > 1$. In particular, the theorem states the following:

- At least 75% of the observations are between $\bar{x} - 2s$ and $\bar{x} + 2s$.
- At least 89% of the observations are between $\bar{x} - 3s$ and $\bar{x} + 3s$.

3.4.1.2 The Empirical Rule (or the 68-95-99.7 Rule)

- Approximately 68% of the observations are between $\overline{x} - s$ and $\overline{x} + s$. That is, it is generally the case that *most* observations are within one standard deviation of the mean.

- Approximately 95% of the observations are between $\overline{x} - 2s$ and $\overline{x} + 2s$. That is, it is generally the case that *almost all* observations are within two standard deviations of the mean. Observations more than two standard deviations from the mean are considered unusual.

- Approximately 99.7% of the observations are between $\overline{x} - 3s$ and $\overline{x} + 3s$. That is, it is generally the case that *all* observations are within three standard deviations of the mean. Observations more than three standard deviations from the mean are considered very unusual.

Figure 3.22 illustrates the Empirical Rule. The sample observations are points on the number line, and the histogram represents their distribution. The inner circle has a center at $\overline{x}$ on the number line and a radius s. Most of the observations fall within the inner circle. The outer circle has the same center but has a radius of $2s$. All or almost all of the observations fall within the outer circle.

Figure 3.22 Illustration of the Empirical Rule

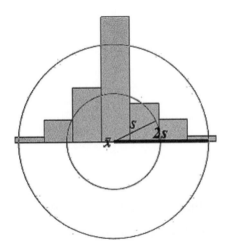

3.4.2 Example 3.5: Computing Basic Statistics

This example illustrates computing basic statistics with the Summary Statistics task.

- The Summary Statistics task is discussed in Section 3.4.3, "Instructions for Computing Statistics with the Summary Statistics Task."

- The results are in the Section 3.4.4, "Task Output, Interpretation, and Analysis for Example 3.5."

3.4.2.1 Scores Measuring Different Attitudes

In order to monitor employee attitudes, 24 randomly selected employees are asked to complete a standardized psychological questionnaire. Evaluation of the questionnaire results in the following scores.

Work	Supervision	Quality
56	53	52
49	49	52
57	49	48
52	52	48
51	54	48
51	48	52
57	59	45
51	52	53
53	52	51
58	55	53
57	56	49
59	61	45
52	52	40
50	46	54
51	57	50
54	50	46
59	44	52
47	35	54
55	50	47
56	55	50
51	53	51
48	43	60
58	53	53
51	51	45

- **Work** measures an employee's attitude toward their tasks and responsibilities.
- **Supervision** measures an employee's attitude toward their supervisors.
- **Quality** measures an employee's attitude toward the company's quality program.

Scores above 50 indicate a positive attitude; scores below 50 indicate a negative attitude.

The data is in the Attitude data set in Appendix 1.

Example 3.5.1

Determine the number of observations, the mean, the standard deviation, the minimum, and the maximum for each variable.

Example 3.5.2

For **Supervision**:

1. Create a histogram using the Bar Chart task.
2. Compute $\bar{x} - s$ and $\bar{x} + s$. What percent of observations are between these values?
3. Compute $\bar{x} - 2s$ and $\bar{x} + 2s$. What percent of observations are between these values?

3.4.3 Instructions for Computing Statistics with the Summary Statistics Task

Open the Summary Statistics task in one of the following ways:

- From the menu bar, select **Describe ▶ Summary Statistics**.
- On the **Task by Category** tab of the **Task List**, go to the **Describe** section and click **Summary Statistics**.
- On the **Task by Name** tab of the **Task List**, double-click **Summary Statistics**.

The Summary Statistics task has five major groups of options: Task Roles, Statistics, Plots, Results, and Titles. The Titles group of options is discussed in Chapter 1, "Introduction to SAS Enterprise Guide." The Titles options control the titles and the footnotes in the task output.

3.4.3.1 Task Roles

Click **Task Roles** on the selection pane to open this group of options. A variable is assigned to a role by dragging its name from **Variables to assign** to a role in **Task roles**. See Figure 3.23. A variable can be removed from a role by dragging it back to **Variables to assign**. The right and left arrows and the resulting pop-up menus can also be used.

- **Analysis variables**: Statistics are computed for each variable in this role. The order that the variables are listed here is the order that they are listed in the output. See Figure 3.23.
- **Classification variables**: Statistics are computed for each group created by the variables in this role. All the statistics for these groups are in a single table. See Example 3.6 and Section 3.4.6, "Instructions for Computing Basic Statistics for Groups."
- **Copy variables**: These are identification variables. The maximum or minimum value of an identification variable assigned to this role is included in the output. The choice between maximum and minimum is one of the Results options.
- **Group analysis by**: Statistics are computed for each group created by the variables in this role. The statistics for each group are in a separate table. See Example 3.6 and Section 3.4.6, "Instructions for Computing Basic Statistics for Groups."

Frequency count and Relative weight task roles are discussed in Section 1.2.

In Figure 3.23, the data is in the Attitude data set. Work, Supervision, and Quality are assigned to the Analysis variables role.

Figure 3.23 Task Roles in the Summary Statistics Task for Example 3.5

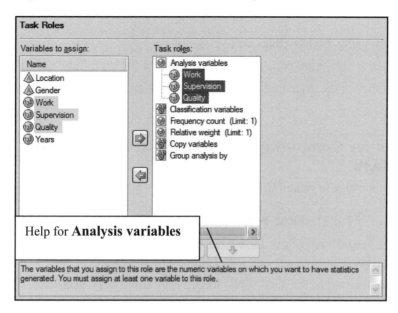

3.4.3.2 Statistics

The Statistics group of options includes Basic, Percentiles, and Additional options. The Basic options are shown in Table 3.2. The Percentiles are presented in Section 3.5.

Mean, **Standard deviation**, **Minimum**, **Maximum**, and **Number of observations** are the default selections. The number of decimal places for the statistics can be set with the **Maximum decimal places** drop-down menu. The default setting is **Best fit**, which generally results in 7 decimal places. See Figure 3.24.

Table 3.2 Basic Statistics

Mean	$\overline{x} = \sum\limits_{i=1}^{n} x_i \Big/ n$
Standard deviation	$s = \sqrt{\sum\limits_{i=1}^{n} \left(x_i - \overline{x}\right)^2 \Big/ (n-1)}$
Standard error	$s/\sqrt{n}$ (Estimates the standard deviation of the sample mean $\sigma/\sqrt{n}$)
Variance	$s^2 = \left(s\right)^2$
Minimum	smallest value
Maximum	largest value
Range	**Maximum−Minimum**
Sum	$\sum\limits_{i=1}^{n} x_i$
Sum of weights	$\sum\limits_{i=1}^{n} w_i$ (When there is a variable in the **Relative weight** role)
Number of observations	number of nonmissing values
Number of missing values	number of missing values

Figure 3.24 Basic Options for Statistics in the Summary Statistics Task for Example 3.5

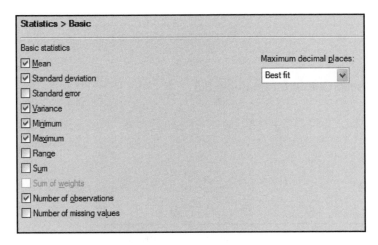

3.4.3.3 Plots

The Plots options include the Histogram and the Box and whisker plots. This text uses the Bar Chart task to compute histograms. The box-and-whisker plot is discussed in Section 3.5.2.

3.4.3.4 When Finished

When finished assigning variables to roles and selecting options, click **Run**. The task adds a Summary Statistics icon and one or more output icons to the process flow diagram. See Figure 3.25. The results for Example 3.5 are in Output 3.3.

Figure 3.25 Example 3.5 Data, Task, and Output Icons on the Process Flow Diagram

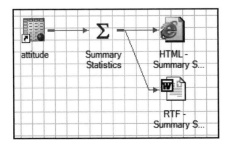

3.4.4 Task Output, Interpretation, and Analysis for Example 3.5

3.4.4.1 Output

Output 3.3 Summary Statistics Output for Example 3.5

Summary Statistics
Results

The MEANS Procedure ❶

❷ Variable	❸ Label	❹ Mean	❺ Std Dev	❻ Minimum	❼ Maximum	❽ N
Work	Work	53.4583333	3.6113248	47.0000000	59.0000000	24
Supervision	Supervision	51.2083333	5.4929137	35.0000000	61.0000000	24
Quality	Quality	49.9166667	4.1169498	40.0000000	60.0000000	24

3.4.4.2 Interpretation

❶ The underlying SAS procedure is the MEANS procedure.

❷ Variable name

❸ Variable label

❹ $\bar{x}$

❺ s, the standard deviation

❻ minimum value

❼ maximum value

❽ number of nonmissing values

3.4.4.3 Analysis

Example 3.5.1
The statistics are shown in Output 3.3.

Example 3.5.2
The following histogram of the Supervision values is created in Example 3.3.

Figure 3.26 Histogram of Supervision Scores

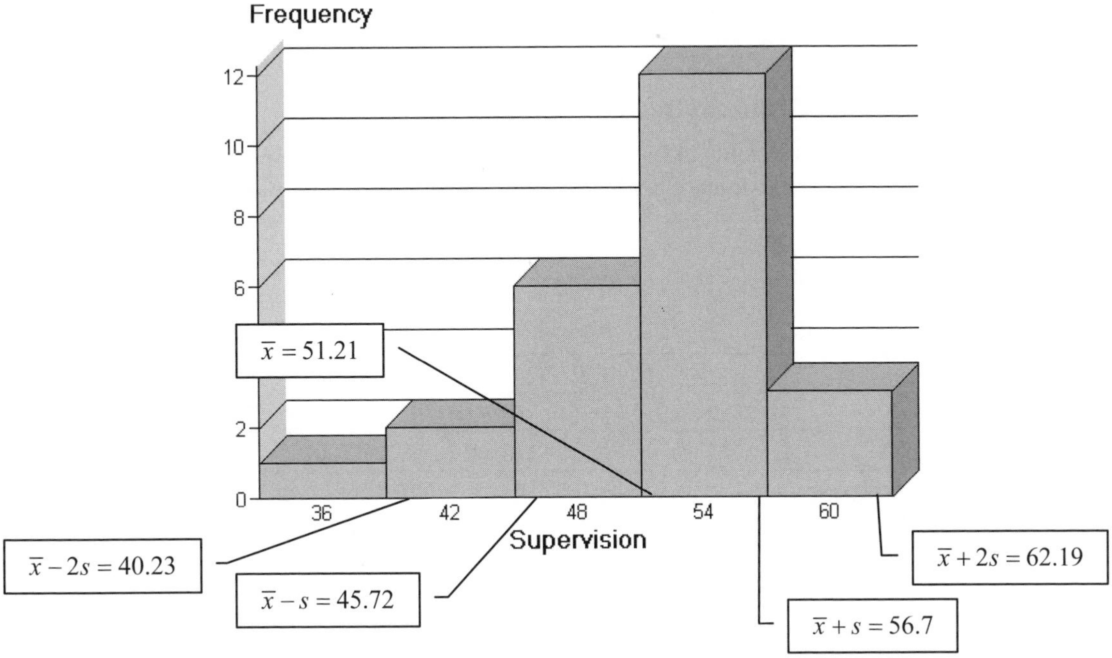

Frequency

$\bar{x} = 51.21$

$\bar{x} - 2s = 40.23$

$\bar{x} - s = 45.72$

$\bar{x} + s = 56.7$

$\bar{x} + 2s = 62.19$

Supervision

For convenience, $\bar{x}$ and s are rounded to 2 decimal places.

$$\bar{x} - s = 51.21 - 5.49 = 45.72 \text{ and } \bar{x} + s = 51.21 + 5.49 = 56.70$$

There are 18 of 24 or 75% within one standard deviation of the mean. See Figure 3.27.

$$\bar{x} - 2s = 51.21 - 2(5.49) = 40.23 \text{ and } \bar{x} + 2s = 51.21 + 2(5.49) = 62.19$$

There are 23 of 24 or 96% within two standard deviations of the mean. See Figure 3.27.

The results are consistent with what is predicted by the Empirical Rule. Most of the values are within one standard deviation of the mean. Almost all the values are within two standard deviations of the mean.

Figure 3.27 Supervision Values in Ascending Order

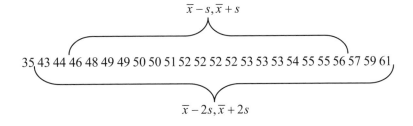

$\bar{x} - s, \bar{x} + s$

35 43 44 46 48 49 49 50 50 51 52 52 52 52 53 53 53 54 55 55 56 57 59 61

$\bar{x} - 2s, \bar{x} + 2s$

3.4.5 Example 3.6: Basic Statistics for Groups

Variables in both the Classification variables and the Group analysis by roles separate the data into groups. Statistics for all groups defined by the first role are in a single table. Statistics for the groups defined by the second role are in separate tables. Both roles can be applied at the same time.

3.4.5.1   Scores Grouped by Location and Gender

Psychological tests are given to 24 randomly selected employees. Scores measuring employee attitude towards supervision are analyzed. In this example, the employees are grouped by gender (F, M) and office location (Central, North, South). The data is below.

		Location															
		Central					North					South					
Gender	F	49	52	52	46	50	52	44	53	53	51	53	49	55	61	55
	M	35	43				48	52	57			54	59	56	50		

Determine the number of observations, the mean, the standard deviation, the minimum, and the maximum for each of the six groups in the data. Assign Location to the Classification variables role and Gender to the Group analysis by role.

The data is shown in the data grid below. Note that the table of data becomes three columns.

The Attitude data set is in the data grid. All variables except Location, Gender, and Supervision are hidden.

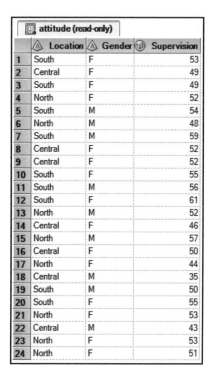

3.4.6 Instructions for Computing Basic Statistics for Groups

These instructions extend the Task Roles options in "Instructions for Computing Statistics with the Summary Statistics Task."

3.4.6.1 Task Roles

The Classification variables and the Group analysis by roles for the Summary Statistics task are presented here.

- **Classification variables**: Statistics are computed for each group created by the variables in this role. All the statistics for these groups are in a single table. When a variable is assigned to this role, the **Class level** box appears. See Figure 3.28.
  - o The **Sort by** drop-down menu lists four sorting criteria.
    - **Data set order**: The order of the Location values in the Attitude data set is South, Central, and North.
    - **Formatted values**: The Create Format task can provide alternate presentation values for data values.
    - **Descending frequencies**: The descending-frequency order of the Location values in the Attitude data set is South, North, and Central with 9, 8, and 7 values, respectively.
    - **Unformatted values**: This is the default selection. It is the sorting order of the values as they exist in the data set. The sorting order of the Location values in the Attitude data set is Central, North, and South.
  - o The **Sort order** drop-down menu lists **Ascending** (the default) and **Descending**.
    - With respect to **Data set order**, **Descending** reverses that order.
    - With respect to **Descending frequencies**, **Ascending** results in ascending frequency order.
  - o The **Missing values** drop-down menu lists **Exclude** (the default) and **Include**. Missing values can identify a group for analysis (**Include**) or can identify values to be excluded from the analysis (**Exclude**).
  - o **Allow multi-level formats**: Allows overlapping format labels if such a format has been created.
- **Group analysis by**: Statistics are computed for each group created by the variables in this role. The statistics for each group are in a separate table. When a variable is assigned to this role, the variable's **sort order** drop-down menu appears.
  - o The unformatted values can be sorted in **Ascending** (the default) and **Descending** order, if **Sort by variables** is selected.
  - o If **Sort by variables** is not selected, the groups are listed in the order that the by-group values occur in the data.

Figure 3.28 Task Roles Options Showing Class-Level Location Box for Example 3.6

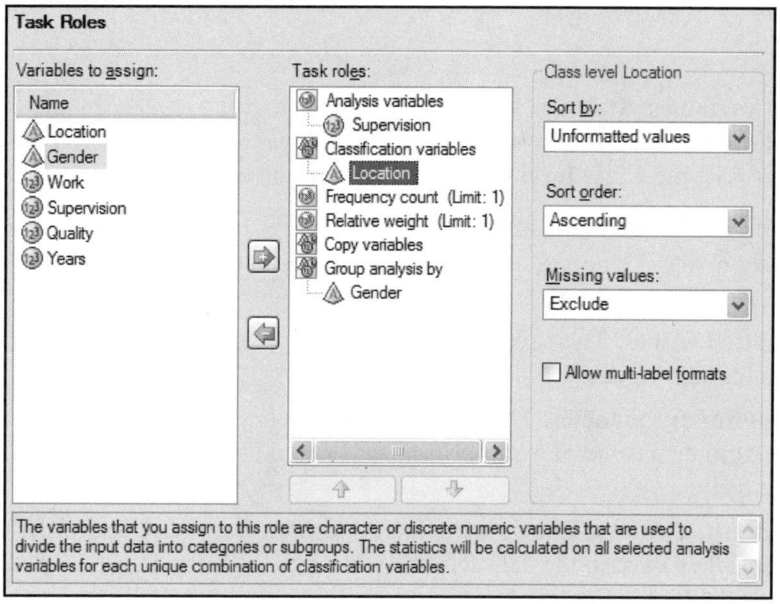

3.4.7 Task Output and Interpretation for Example 3.6

3.4.7.1 Task Output

Output 3.4 Summary Statistics Output for Example 3.6

Summary Statistics
Results

The MEANS Procedure
Gender=F ❶

		Analysis Variable : Supervision Supervision ❷				
❸	❹					❺
Location of Office	N Obs	Mean	Std Dev	Minimum	Maximum	N
Central	5	49.8000000	2.4899799	46.0000000	52.0000000	5
North	5	50.6000000	3.7815341	44.0000000	53.0000000	5
South	5	54.6000000	4.3358967	49.0000000	61.0000000	5

Gender=M ❶

Analysis Variable : Supervision Supervision						
Location of Office	N Obs	Mean	Std Dev	Minimum	Maximum	N
Central	2	39.0000000	5.6568542	35.0000000	43.0000000	2
North	3	52.3333333	4.5092498	48.0000000	57.0000000	3
South	4	54.7500000	3.7749172	50.0000000	59.0000000	4

3.4.7.2   Interpretation

❶ The gender values are, in ascending order, F and M.

❷ Name of the analysis variable is Supervision. Its label is also Supervision.

❸ Location of Office is the label of the classification variable Location.

❹ The number of classification values.

❺ The number of nonmissing analysis values.

3.4.8 Basic Statistics from Frequency Distributions

Data can be presented in terms of a *frequency distribution*. This essentially consists of two variables: one variable contains the distinct data values and the other contains the frequencies that the values occur in the sample.

Table 3.3 is a frequency distribution of grades and a frequency distribution of grade points for a college class. The grade point distribution is represented by a bar char in Figure 3.29. Bar charts for discrete data and frequency distributions for character values are discussed in Section 3.5.

Table 3.3 Frequency Distribution of Grades and Grade Points

Grade	GradePoint	Frequency
A	4	3
B	3	6
C	2	8
D	1	1
F	0	2

Figure 3.29 Bar Chart of Frequency Distribution

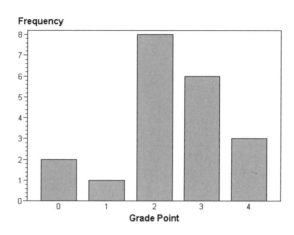

The following is the same data in "raw" form, but in descending order:

4   4   4   3   3   3   3   3   3   2   2   2   2   2   2   2   2   2   1   0   0

- Let the variable x represent the GradePoint values.
- Let the variable f represent the Frequency values.

In terms of the variables x and f, the sample is:

$$x_1 = 4 \quad f_1 = 3$$
$$x_2 = 3 \quad f_2 = 6$$
$$x_3 = 2 \quad f_3 = 8$$
$$x_4 = 1 \quad f_4 = 1$$
$$x_5 = 0 \quad f_5 = 2$$

Expressions for the number of observations, the mean, the variance, and the standard deviation for a frequency distribution of numeric values are below. The computed values for Table 3.3 are to the right. Let k be the number of distinct x values. For Table 3.3, $k = 5$.

- $$n = \sum_{i=1}^{k} f_i \qquad\qquad n = 3 + 6 + 8 + 1 + 2 = 20$$

- $$\bar{x} = \frac{\sum_{i=1}^{k} x_i f_i}{n} \qquad\qquad \bar{x} = \frac{4 \cdot 3 + 3 \cdot 6 + 2 \cdot 8 + 1 \cdot 1 + 0 \cdot 2}{20} = \frac{47}{20} = 2.35$$

- $$s^2 = \frac{\sum_{i=1}^{k}\left(x_i - \overline{x}\right)^2 f_i}{n-1}$$

$$s^2 = \frac{(4-2.35)^2 \cdot 3 + (3-2.35)^2 \cdot 6 + (2-2.35)^2 \cdot 8 + (1-2.35)^2 \cdot 1 + (0-2.35)^2 \cdot 2}{20-1}$$

$$= \frac{24.55}{19} = 1.2921$$

- $s = \sqrt{s^2}$ $\qquad\qquad$ $s = 1.14$ (Rounded to the same number of decimal places as $\overline{x}$)

3.4.9 Example 3.7: Basic Statistics for Frequency Distributions

The Summary Statistics task is applied to the grade point frequency distribution in Table 3.3. The table is data set Ex03_07 below.

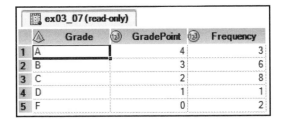

- GradePoint is assigned to the **Analysis variables** role.
- **Frequency** is assigned to the **Frequency count** role.

3.4.10 Task Output for Example 3.7

Output 3.5 Summary Statistics Output for Example 3.7

Summary Statistics
Results

The MEANS Procedure

Analysis Variable : GradePoint Grade Point				
Mean	Std Dev	Minimum	Maximum	N
2.3500000	1.1367081	0	4.0000000	20

3.5 Measures of Position

The sample mean, variance, and standard deviation are based on sums of values, where the order of the values does not matter. *Quantile* statistics, on the other hand, are based on sorted data.

The most important quantiles are the *median* and the *quartiles*.

- The median is the middle value among the sorted data. The median is often represented by $\tilde{x}$ — "x-tilde".

- The first, second, and third quartiles divide the sample into four equal or nearly equal groups. The three quartiles are denoted as Q_1, Q_2, and Q_3, respectively.

Percentiles are quantiles expressed in terms of percentages. For example, the 90th percentile is a value above approximately 90% of the observations and below approximately 10%. The 90th percentile is denoted by P_{90}.

The median and the quartiles are also percentiles.

- $Q_1 = P_{25}$
- median $= \tilde{x} = Q_2 = P_{50}$
- $Q_3 = P_{75}$

Some quantile statistics are shown against sorted data in Figure 3.30. The values are from the dt_min variable in the Defect_study data set in the Appendix. They are the total minutes of downtime per day observed in a study of the production of automobile parts.

Figure 3.30 Sorted dt_min Values

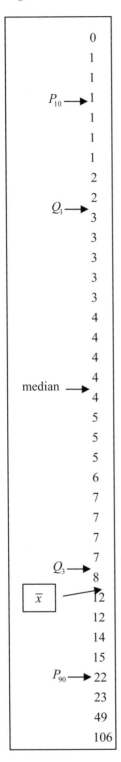

The median, like the mean $\overline{x}$, is a measure of the center of the data. It represents the typical value. When the data has a skewed distribution, the median is generally a more typical value than the mean. When the data has a symmetric distribution, the median and the mean are generally both typical values.

- The left-hand histogram in Figure 3.31 is skewed right. It is based on the dt_min values in Figure 3.30. The median is 4. The mean is 9.86, which is shown in Figure 3.30 to be greater than Q_3. That is, $\bar{x}$ is not typical here since it is larger than 75% of the values.

- The right-hand histogram in Figure 3.31 is symmetric. It is based on the Quality values in the Attitude data set in the appendix. The median is 50.5 and the mean is 49.92. Both values are in the middle of the data and are typical values.

Figure 3.31 Skewed and Symmetric Histograms

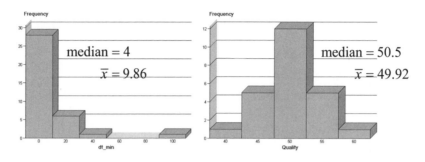

3.5.1 Computing Percentiles

There are a number of ways to compute sample percentiles. Five definitions are listed in SAS Enterprise Guide Help.

To see the percentile definitions:
1. Go to SAS Enterprise Guide Help: **Help ▶ SAS Enterprise Guide Help**.
2. Type **calculating percentiles** with the quotes in the **Search** entry box. Click **List Topics**.
3. Double-click **Calculating Percentiles** in the **Select Topic** list.

Definition 5, Empirical distribution function with averaging, is presented here.

The kth percentile ($0 < k < 100$) is represented by P_k. It is a value above approximately k% of the observations and below approximately $(100 - k)$%.

The n observations are sorted in ascending order. Ordered observations are represented using parentheses in the subscripts: $x_{(1)} \le x_{(2)} \le \ldots \le x_{(n)}$. The first in order and smallest is $x_{(1)}$, the second smallest is $x_{(2)}$, and so forth.

1. The number $\left(\dfrac{k}{100}\right) n$ is calculated. It is equal to $m + d$ where m is the integer part and d is the fractional part.

2. If $d = 0$, then $P_k = \dfrac{\left(x_{(m)} + x_{(m+1)}\right)}{2}$.

3. If $d > 0$, then $P_k = x_{(m+1)}$.

Some percentiles are computed below.

Table 3.4 Percentile Calculations Applied to the dt_min Values in Figure 3.30

Quantile	Percentile	$\left(\dfrac{k}{100}\right)n$	Result
median	P_{50}	$.50(36) = 18$	$\dfrac{x_{(18)} + x_{(19)}}{2} = \dfrac{4+4}{2} = 4$
Q_1	P_{25}	$.25(36) = 9$	$\dfrac{x_{(9)} + x_{(10)}}{2} = \dfrac{2+3}{2} = 2.5$
Q_3	P_{75}	$.75(36) = 27$	$\dfrac{x_{(27)} + x_{(28)}}{2} = \dfrac{7+8}{2} = 7.5$
	P_{10}	$.10(36) = 3.6$	$x_{(4)} = 1$
	P_{90}	$.90(36) = 32.4$	$x_{(33)} = 22$

3.5.2 Box-and-Whisker Plots

A box-and-whisker plot represents the middle 50% of the data with a rectangular box and identifies the median with a line through the box. Lines, or whiskers, are extended from the box to the largest and smallest values that are not statistically unusual. These lines represent the top and bottom 25% of the data. Statistically unusual observations are called *outliers* and are individually identified. See Figures 3.32 and 3.33.

3.5.2.1 Components of a Box-and-Whisker Plot

A box-and-whisker plot applies four statistics:

- Q_1, median, Q_3
- *interquartile range*: $IQR = Q_3 - Q_1$

In SAS Enterprise Guide, box-and-whisker plots are drawn against a vertical scale. See Figure 3.32. The components are:

- A rectangle from Q_1 to Q_3.
- A horizontal line through the rectangle at the median.
- A vertical line from the bottom of the rectangle to the smallest observation at or above the *lower fence* at $LF = Q_1 - 1.5(IQR)$.
- A vertical line from the top of the rectangle to the largest observation at or below the *upper fence* at $UF = Q_3 + 1.5(IQR)$.
- Observations beyond the two fences are considered outliers and are individually identified.

Figure 3.32 Components of a Box-and-Whisker Plot

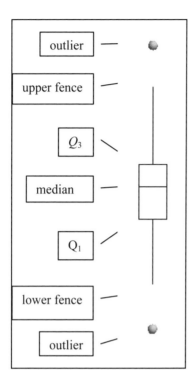

The box-and-whisker plot in Figure 3.33 is based on the dt_min values in Figure 3.30. Its components are computed below. The statistics Q_1, the median, and Q_3, are from Table 3.4.

$$Q_1 = 2.5$$

$$\text{median} = 4$$

$$Q_3 = 7.5$$

$$IQR = 7.5 - 2.5 = 5$$

$$LF = Q_1 - 1.5(IQR) = 2.5 - 1.5(5) = -5$$

$$UF = Q_3 + 1.5(IQR) = 7.5 + 1.5(5) = 15$$

The box-and-whisker plot in Figure 3.33 has:

- a rectangle from 2.5 to 7.5, representing the middle 50% of the data
- a horizontal line through the rectangle at 4, the median.
- a vertical line from the bottom of the rectangle at 2.5 to 0, the smallest observation that is not statistically unusual
- a vertical line from the top of the rectangle at 7.5 to 15, the largest observation that is not statistically unusual
- outliers: 22, 23, 46, 106

Figure 3.33 Box-and-Whisker Plot of dt_min Values

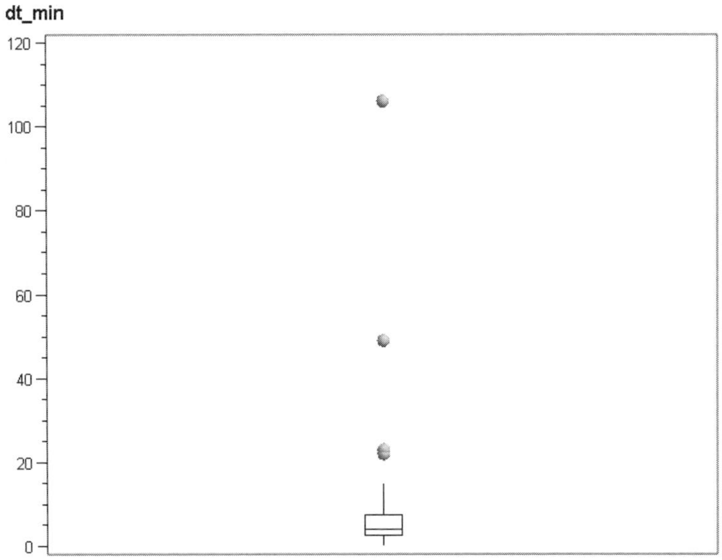

3.5.3 Example 3.8: Percentiles and Box-and-Whisker Plots

This example produces percentiles and box-and-whisker plots with the Summary Statistics task.

- The Summary Statistics task is discussed in the "Instructions for Producing Percentiles and Box-and-Whisker Plots with the Summary Statistics Task" section.

- The results are in the "Task Output and Interpretation for Example 3.8" section.

Statistics for all the groups defined by the variables in the Classification variables role are in a single table. Box-and-whisker plots for these groups are in a single graph and are plotted against the same scale.

Statistics for the groups defined by the variables in the Group analysis by role are in separate tables. Box-and-whisker plots for these groups are in separate graphs and are plotted against different scales.

3.5.3.1 Scores Grouped by Location

Psychological tests are given to 24 randomly selected employees. Scores measuring employee attitude towards supervision are analyzed. The employees come from three different offices: Central, North, and South. The data is below.

Central				North				South			
49	52	52	46	52	48	52	57	53	49	54	59
50	35	43		44	53	53	51	55	56	61	50
								55			

Example 3.8.1
Compute the follow statistics for the scores at the three offices:
P_{10}, Q_1, median, Q_3, P_{90}.

Example 3.8.2
Create box-and-whisker plots for the scores at the three offices. Compare the box-and-whisker plots by creating them in a single graph. That is, the Location variable should be assigned to the Classification variables role.

The scores and locations are shown in the data grid below. Note that the table of data becomes two columns. The scores are in the Supervision column and the classification values are in the Location column.

The Attitude data set is in the data grid. All variables except Location and Supervision are hidden.

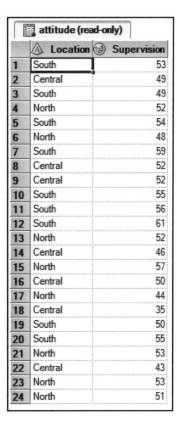

	Location	Supervision
1	South	53
2	Central	49
3	South	49
4	North	52
5	South	54
6	North	48
7	South	59
8	Central	52
9	Central	52
10	South	55
11	South	56
12	South	61
13	North	52
14	Central	46
15	North	57
16	Central	50
17	North	44
18	Central	35
19	South	50
20	South	55
21	North	53
22	Central	43
23	North	53
24	North	51

3.5.4 Instructions for Producing Percentiles and Box-and-Whisker Plots with the Summary Statistics Task

These instructions add the Percentiles and the Plots options to the instructions found in "Instructions for Computing Statistics with the Summary Statistics Task."

For Example 3.8, Supervision is assigned to the Analysis variables task role and Location is assigned to the Classification variables task role. All selections are cleared in the Basic Statistics options.

3.5.4.1 Percentiles

A number of percentiles are available. The Quantile method should be Order statistics. At the left in Figure 3.34, P_{10}, Q_1, median, Q_3, and P_{90} are selected. The number of decimal places is set with the Basic options. The default setting is **Best fit**, which generally results in 7 decimal places.

3.5.4.2 Plots

At the right in Figure 3.34, **Box and whisker** is selected.

Figure 3.34 Options for Percentiles (Left), Options for Plots (Right)

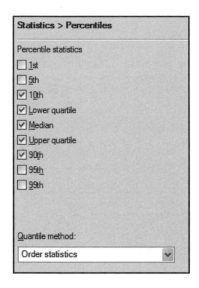
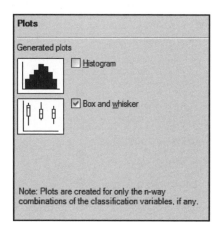

3.5.5 Task Output and Interpretation for Example 3.8

3.5.5.1 Task Output

Output 3.6 Summary Statistics Output for Example 3.8

Summary Statistics
Results
The MEANS Procedure

Analysis Variable : Supervision Supervision					
❶	❷	❸		❹	❺
Location of Office	10th Pctl	Lower Quartile	Median	Upper Quartile	90th Pctl
Central	35.0000000	43.0000000	49.0000000	52.0000000	52.0000000
North	44.0000000	49.5000000	52.0000000	53.0000000	57.0000000
South	49.0000000	53.0000000	55.0000000	56.0000000	61.0000000

Summary Statistics
Box and Whisker Plots

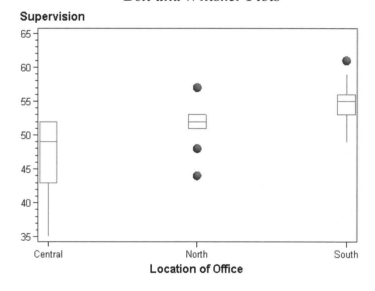

3.5.5.2 Interpretation

❶ Location of Office is the label of the classification variable Location.

❷ P_{10}

❸ Q_1

❹ Q_3

❺ P_{90}

3.6 Frequency Distributions for Discrete Data

Discrete values are viewed as separate and not part of a continuous scale. Character values are always discrete. Counts and numeric classifications are discrete. Both the Grade and GradePoint variables in Table 3.5 contain discrete data. The data represent grades and grade points for a college class.

Table 3.5 Grades and Grade Points

Grade	D	B	A	C	A	B	C	F	A	C	B	C	C	C	C	B	F	B	B	C
GradePoint	1	3	4	2	4	3	2	0	4	2	3	2	2	2	2	3	0	3	3	2

Discrete data are summarized with the following distributions:

- The *frequency distribution* lists the number of occurrences of each distinct value in the sample.
- The *percent distribution* lists the percentage of occurrences of each distinct value in the sample.
- The *cumulative frequency distribution* lists a running total of the frequencies.
- The *cumulative percent distribution* lists a running total of the percentages.

Table 3.6 presents the four distributions for the character variable Grade in a single table. Table 3.3 in Section 3.3 presents the frequency distribution for the numeric variable GradePoint.

Table 3.6 Distributions for the Grade Variable

Grade	Frequency	Percent	Cumulative Frequency	Cumulative Percent
A	3	15	3	15
B	6	30	9	45
C	8	40	17	85
D	1	5	18	90
F	2	10	20	100

The distributions are often represented by bar charts and pie charts. Figure 3.35 shows the vertical frequency bar chart of the data in Table 3.6. Figure 3.36 shows a frequency pie chart and a three-dimensional percentage bar chart of the same data.

Figure 3.35 Frequency Bar Charts for the Grade Values

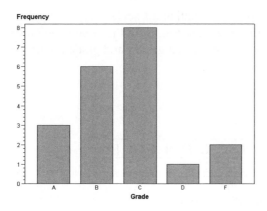

Figure 3.36 Pie Chart and Three-Dimensional Percentage Bar Chart of the Grade Values

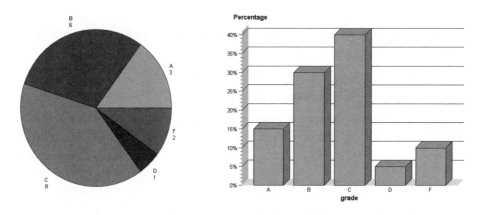

3.6.1 Example 3.9: Working with Character Data

This example produces distributions and charts with the One-Way Frequencies task.

- The One-Way Frequencies task is discussed in the instructions for "Creating Frequency Distributions with the One-Way Frequencies Task."

- The results are in "Task Output and Interpretation for Example 3.9."

3.6.1.1 Office Locations

In order to monitor employee attitudes, 24 randomly selected employees complete a standardized psychological questionnaire. Evaluation of the questionnaire results in a number of scores measuring different attitudes. In addition to the scores, the location of each employee's office is recorded. The employees come from three offices: Central, North, and South.

The results are in the Location column of the Attitude set in Appendix 1. Attitude is in a data grid with all columns but Location hidden.

attitude (read-only)	
⚠ **Location**	
1	South
2	Central
3	South
4	North
5	South
6	North
7	South
8	Central
9	Central
10	South
11	South
12	South
13	North
14	Central
15	North
16	Central
17	North
18	Central
19	South
20	South
21	North
22	Central
23	North
24	North

Example 3.9.1

Create the frequency distribution, percentage distribution, cumulative frequency distribution, and cumulative percentage distribution for Location.

Example 3.9.2

Create the following charts:

- two-dimensional frequency vertical bar chart

- two-dimensional frequency pie chart

- three-dimensional percentage bar chart

3.6.2 Instructions for Creating Frequency Distributions with the One-Way Frequencies Task

Open the One-Way Frequencies task in one of the following ways:

- From the menu bar, select **Describe ▶ One-Way Frequencies**.

- On the **Task by Category** tab of the **Task List**, go to the **Describe** section and click **One-Way Frequencies**.

- On the **Task by Name** tab of the **Task List**, double-click **One-Way Frequencies**.

The One-Way Frequencies task has five groups of options: Task Roles, Statistics, Plots, Results, and Titles. The Titles group of options is discussed in Chapter 1, "Introduction to SAS Enterprise Guide." The Titles options control the titles and the footnotes in the task output.

3.6.2.1   Task Roles

Click **Task Roles** on the selection pane to open this group of options. A variable is assigned to a role by dragging its name from **Variables** to **Roles**. See Figure 3.37. A variable can be removed from a role by dragging it back to **Variables**. The right and left arrows and the resulting pop-up menus can also be used.

- **Analysis variables**: Distributions are created for each variable in this role. Location is assigned to this role in Figure 3.37.

Frequency count and Group analysis by are discussed in Section 1.2.

Figure 3.37 Task Roles in the One-Way Frequencies Task for Example 3.9

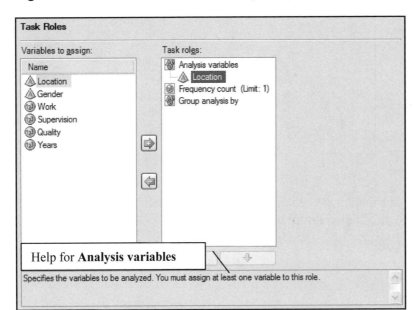

3.6.2.2   Statistics

Four tables are available in the **Frequency table options** box:

- All four distributions: **Frequencies and percentages with cumulatives**. This is the default.

- Both frequency distributions: **Frequencies and cumulative frequencies**

- Both noncumulative distributions: **Frequencies and percentages**.

- Only frequency distribution: **Frequencies only**.

Missing values can be included as an analysis value. In the **Missing values** box:

- Selecting **Show frequencies** results in the number of missing values being included in the frequency column in the output.

- Selecting **Include in calculations** results in the number of missing values being included when all frequencies, percentages, and cumulative totals are calculated.

Figure 3.38 Statistics Options in the One-Way Frequencies Task for Example 3.9

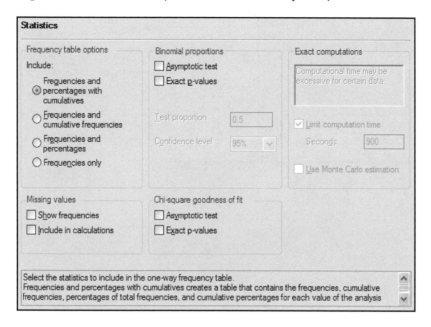

3.6.2.3 Plots

Two-dimensional horizontal and vertical frequency bar charts can be selected here. A vertical frequency bar chart is selected at the top in Figure 3.39. To create a pie chart and a three-dimensional percentage bar chart, see the comments after Figure 3.41 in Section 3.6.3, "Task Output and Interpretation for Example 3.9."

3.6.2.4 Results

The Results options include how the values in the Analysis variables are sorted in the output. The **Order output data by** drop-down menu lists four sorting criteria:

- **Data set order**: The order of the Location values in the Attitude data set is South, Central, and North.

- **Formatted values**: The Create Format task can provide alternate presentation values for data values.

- **Descending frequencies**: The descending-frequency order of the Location values in the Attitude data set is South, North, and Central with 9, 8, and 7 values, respectively.

- **Unformatted values**: This is in ascending order of the values as they exist in the data set. The sorting order of the Location values in the Attitude data set is Central, North, and South. Unformatted values is the default selection and the selection at the bottom in Figure 3.39.

Figure 3.39 Plots Options (Top), Results Options (Bottom)

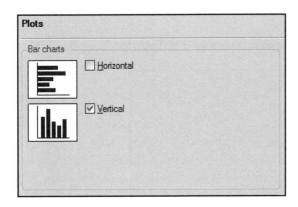

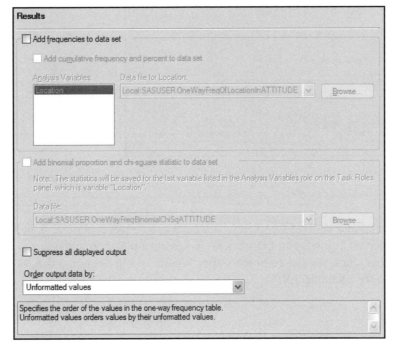

3.6.2.5 When Finished

When finished assigning variables to roles and selecting options, click **Run**. The task adds a One-Way Frequencies icon and one or more output icons to the process flow diagram. See Figure 3.40. The results for Example 3.9 are in Output 3.7.

Figure 3.40 Example 3.9 Data, Task, and Output Icons on the Process Flow Diagram

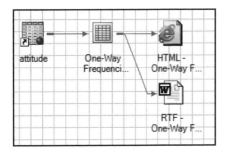

3.6.3 Task Output and Interpretation for Example 3.9

3.6.3.1 Task Output

Output 3.7 One-Way Frequencies Output for Example 3.9

One-Way Frequencies
Results

The FREQ Procedure ❶

Location of Office ❷				
❸ Location	Frequency	Percent	Cumulative Frequency	Cumulative Percent
Central	7	29.17	7	29.17
North	8	33.33	15	62.50
South	9	37.50	24	100.00

One-Way Frequencies
Plots

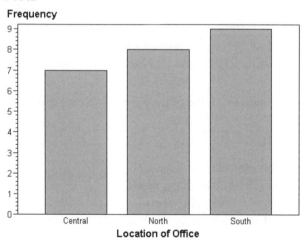

3.6.3.2 Interpretation

❶ The underlying SAS procedure is the FREQ procedure.

❷ Location of Office is the label of the classification variable Location.

❸ Location values

Figure 3.41 Pie Chart and Three-Dimensional Percentage Bar Chart of the Location Values

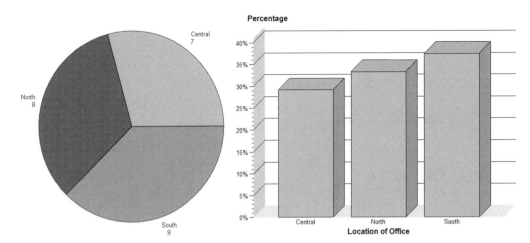

Comment

1. To change from the frequency bar chart in Output 3.7 to the pie chart in Figure 3.41, move the cursor inside the graph and right-click. From the pop-up menu, select **Chart Type**. Then select **Pie**.

2. To change from the pie chart in Figure 3.41 to the three-dimensional percentage bar chart in Figure 3.41:

   a. Move the cursor inside the graph and right-click. From the pop-up menu, select **Chart Type**. Then select **Vertical Bar**.

   b. Again, right-click within the graph. From the pop-up menu, select **Data Options**. With the **Statistic** drop-down menu in the Data Options window, select **Percentage**. Click **OK**.

   c. Again, right-click within the graph. From the pop-up menu, select **Graph Properties**.

      i. On the **Graph** tab, select **3D**.

      ii. On the **Axis** tab:

         1. Select **Vertical** with the **Axis** drop-down menu.
         2. **Label** should be checked. Click **Label Options**. In the Label Options window, **Custom label** should be selected. Write **Percentage** in the entry box. Click **OK**.

      iii. Click **OK**.

3.6.4 Example 3.10: Starting with a Frequency Distribution

The frequency distribution of the GradePoint values in Table 3.3 is below. The GradePoint and Frequency variables are in data set Ex03_07 shown following.

GradePoint	Frequency
4	3
3	6
2	8
1	1
0	2

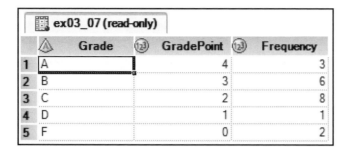

The One-Way Frequencies task is applied to the frequency distribution. A vertical frequency bar chart of the distribution is in Figure 3.29 in Section 3.3.

- GradePoint is assigned to the Analysis variables role.

- Frequency is assigned to the Frequency count role.

3.6.5 Task Output for Example 3.10

Output 3.8 Output for Example 3.10

One-Way Frequencies
Results

The FREQ Procedure

Grade Point				
GradePoint	Frequency	Percent	Cumulative Frequency	Cumulative Percent
0	2	10.00	2	10.00
1	1	5.00	3	15.00
2	8	40.00	11	55.00
3	6	30.00	17	85.00
4	3	15.00	20	100.00

3.7 Summary Tables Task

There might be times when the Summary Tables task is preferred over the Summary Statistics and One-Way Frequencies tasks. Summary Tables needs to be set up, and it does not produce graphs. But it has some important capabilities that the other two tasks do not have. With the Summary Tables task:

- The user designs the output table. The table in Output 3.9 is designed in Section 3.7.5, "Example 3.12: Analysis and Classification Variables."

- BEST*w.d* format is available. The format drops unnecessary zero decimals. In Output 3.9, values such as 51.25, 44, and 37.5 are written without trailing zeros. See the "BEST*w.d*" section.

- Statistics for groups and for the entire sample can be put in the same table. In Output 3.9, there are statistics for each of the three Location of Office groups (Central, North, South) and for the entire sample (All).

- Percentage statistics can be put in the same table as basic and percentile statistics. In Output 3.9, the column ColPctN shows the sample percentages. They are the percentages, down a column, that the classification values occur with respect to the sample size *n*.

Output 3.9 Summary Table for Example 3.12

Summary Tables

Example 3.12	Supervision					
	Mean	**Min**	**Max**	**N**	**ColPctN**	**Median**
Location of Office						
Central	46.714285714	35	52	7	29.166666667	49
North	51.25	44	57	8	33.333333333	52
South	54.666666667	49	61	9	37.5	55
All	51.208333333	35	61	24	100	52

3.7.1 List of Summary Table Statistics

The statistics available with the Summary Tables are in Table 3.7. All statistics available with the Summary Statistics task are listed. The frequency and percentage statistics available in One-Way Frequencies are listed.

Table 3.7 Statistics in the Summary Tables Task

Name	Statistic
ColPctN	percentage of values attributed to a column classification value
ColPctSum	percentage of sum attributed to a column classification value
CSS	corrected sum of squares , $\sum_{i=1}^{n}(x_i - \bar{x})^2$
CV	coefficient of variation, $\dfrac{s}{\bar{x}}100\%$
Max	maximum value
Mean	$\bar{x}$
Median	median
Min	minimum value
N	number of nonmissing values
NMiss	number of missing values
P1, P5, P10, P90, P95, P99	percentiles: $P_1, P_5, P_{10}, P_{90}, P_{95}, P_{99}$
PctN	percentage of values attributed to a classification value
PctSum	percentage of sum attributed to a classification value
Probt	p-value for Student's t test and the hypotheses $H_0 : \mu = 0$ versus $H_1 : \mu \neq 0$, $2P(t > \lvert t \text{ Value}\rvert)$
Q1, Q3	quartiles: Q_1, Q_3
QRange	interquartile range (IQR)
Range	Max − Min
RepPctN	report percentage of values attributed to a classification value
RepPctSum	report percentage of sum attributed to a classification value
StdDev	standard deviation, s
StdErr	standard error of the mean, $s/\sqrt{n}$
Sum	$\sum_{i=1}^{n} x_i$
SumWght	sum of weights, $\sum_{i=1}^{n} w_i$
t	t Value $= \bar{x} \Big/ \left(\dfrac{s}{\sqrt{n}}\right)$, test statistic for Student's t test and the hypotheses $H_0 : \mu = 0$ versus $H_1 : \mu \neq 0$

Name	Statistic
USS	uncorrected sum of squares, $\displaystyle\sum_{i=1}^{n} x_i^2$
Var	variance, s^2

3.7.2 BEST*w.d* Format

BEST format allows the SAS System to select the best notation. For instance, unnecessary zeros are not added to decimals, and integers are written without decimal points. One would see 3.5 instead of 3.50 and 10 instead of 10.00.

In general, this is called the BEST*w.d* format.

- *w* stands for width. Values are displayed with at most *w* characters: digits, - prefix, and decimal point.

- *d* stands for the number of decimal places. However, with BEST format, *d* is ignored.

The maximum number of decimal places is the width that remains following a possible - prefix, an integer part, and a decimal point. With BEST12.0, one would see 10.123456789 and 1000.1234567. The $d = 0$ is ignored. BEST12.0 and BEST12.9 produce the same results.

The default format is 12.2. There can be at most 12 characters and each value has 2 decimal places. See "Summary Tables" in Section 3.7.3, "Instructions for the Summary Tables Task."

3.7.3 Instructions for the Summary Tables Task

Open the Summary Statistics task in one of the following ways:

- From the menu bar, select **Describe ▶ Summary Tables**.

- On the **Task by Category** tab of the **Task List**, go to **Describe** and click **Summary Tables**.

- On the **Task by Name** tab of the **Task List**, double-click **Summary Tables**.

The Summary Tables task has four major groups of options: Task Roles, Summary Tables, Results, and Titles. The Titles group of options is discussed in Chapter 1, "Introduction to SAS Enterprise Guide." Titles options control the output titles and the footnotes.

3.7.3.1 Task Roles

Click **Task Roles** on the selection pane to open this group of options. A variable is assigned to a role by dragging its name from **Variables to assign** to a role in **Task roles**. See Figure 3.42. A variable can be removed from a role by dragging it back to **Variables to assign**. The right and left arrows and the resulting pop-up menus can also be used.

- **Analysis variables**: Variables in this role are made available when constructing the summary table. Statistics can be computed for the variables in this role. See Figure 3.42.

Figure 3.42 Task Roles in the Summary Tables Task for Example 3.11

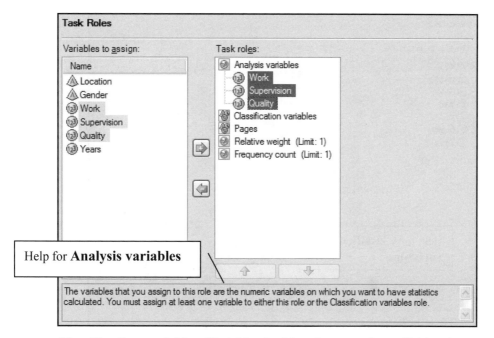

- **Classification variables**: Variables in this role are made available when constructing the summary table. Statistics can be computed for the groups created by the variables in this role. When a variable is assigned to this role, the **Class level** box appears. See Figure 3.43.
  - The **Sort by** drop-down menu lists four sorting criteria:
    - **Data set order**: The order of the Location values in the Attitude data set is South, Central, and North.
    - **Formatted values**: The Create Format task can provide alternate presentation values for data values.
    - **Descending frequencies**: The descending-frequency order of the Location values in the Attitude data set is South, North, and Central with 9, 8, and 7 values, respectively.
    - **Unformatted values**: This is the default selection. It is the sorting order of the values as they exist in the data set. The sorting order of the Location values in the Attitude data set is Central, North, and South.
  - The **Order** drop-down menu lists **Ascending** (the default) and **Descending**.
    - With respect to **Data set order**, **Descending** reverses that order.
    - With respect to **Descending frequencies**, **Ascending** results in ascending frequency order.
  - The **Missing values** drop-down menu lists **Include** (the default) and **Exclude**. Missing values can identify a group for analysis (**Include**) or can identify values to be excluded the analysis (**Exclude**).
  - **Restrict levels to format values**, **Multilevel formats**, and **Heading format** involve working with user-defined formats. That area is not covered in this text.

Figure 3.43 Task Roles in the Summary Tables Task for Example 3.12

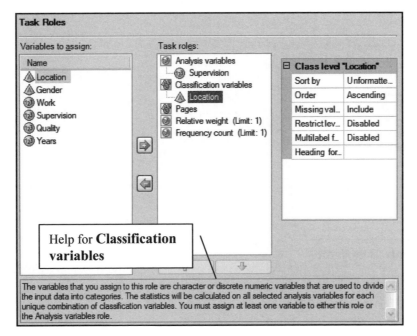

- **Pages**: A separate summary table is created for each group defined by the variables in this role.

Frequency count and Relative weight task roles are discussed in Section 1.3.

In Figures 3.42 and 3.43, the data is in the Attitude data set.

- In Figure 3.42, Work, Supervision, and Quality are assigned to the Analysis variables role. See "Example 3.11: Applying the Summary Tables Task to Example 3.5."

- In Figure 3.43, Supervision is assigned to the Analysis variables role and Location is assigned to the Classification variables role. See "Example 3.12: Analysis and Classification Variables."

3.7.3.2   Summary Tables

A summary table is constructed with the variables and the statistics listed in the following boxes.

- Available variables
  - These are the analysis and the classification variables selected in Task Roles.
  - The All variable is always listed. The All variable is a classification variable with one group: the entire sample.
- Available statistics lists the statistics in Table 3.7

In Figure 3.44, All, Quality, Supervision, and Work are listed in the Available variables box.

Figure 3.44 Summary Tables Options for Example 3.11

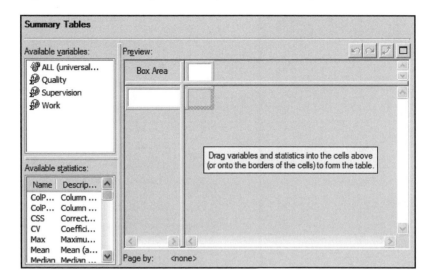

A summary table is constructed by dragging variables and statistics from the boxes to the left and top portions of the Preview table. See Figure 3.44.

Example 3.11 and Example 3.12 show the construction of summary tables.

Depending on the circumstances, the following buttons are active at the upper-right corner of the Preview table:

To apply BEST format to all numerical values in the table:
1. Right-click on the Preview table. Select **Table Properties** from the pop-up menu.
2. Click the **Format** tab. See Figure 3.45. Select **Numeric** from the **Categories** box. Select **BESTw.d** from the **Formats** box.
3. The **Attributes** box becomes active with the default values: **Overall width** is **12** and **Decimal places** is **0**. See Figure 3.45. These values can be changed.
4. Click **OK** when finished.

Figure 3.45 Table Properties Window with Format BEST12.0 Selected

To apply a format to an individual variable's statistics, right-click the variable name in the Preview table and select **Data Value Properties** from the pop-up menu. Continue from the second step above.

To apply a format to a specific statistic, right-click the statistic name in the Preview table and select **Data Value Properties** from the pop-up menu. Continue from the second step above.

To add text to the table's box area:

The box area is the space in the upper-left corner of the table. See Box Area in Figure 3.44.

1. Right-click on the Preview table. Select **Box Area Properties** from the pop-up menu.
2. Select the **General** tab and then **Use the following text**, if necessary. See Figure 3.46. Write the text in the entry box.
3. Click **OK** when finished.

Figure 3.46 Box Area Properties Window for Example 3.11

3.7.4 Example 3.11: Applying the Summary Tables Task to Example 3.5

This example produces the statistics requested in Example 3.5 with the **Summary Tables** task. The results are in Output 3.10.

1. The Summary Tables task is opened. At **Task Roles**, the variables Work, Supervision, and Quality are assigned to the Analysis variables role. See Figure 3.42.

2. At **Summary Tables**:

   a. **Work** is dragged from **Available variables** to the empty row cell in the Preview table. The **Sum** statistic, the default statistic for an analysis variable, appears in the column cell. The variable could have gone to the empty column cell with the statistic appearing in the row cell.

   b. **Supervision** is dragged to the lower border of the Work cell in the Preview table. The border turns blue when the cursor is in the correct position. An arrow points to where the new item will be placed. See below.

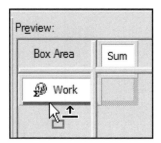

   c. **Quality** is dragged to the lower border of the **Supervision** cell. The **Mean** statistic is dragged onto **Sum**, replacing it. See below.

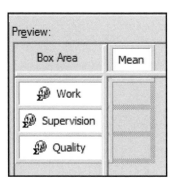

d. The **StdDev** statistic is dragged to the right border of the **Mean** cell in the Preview table. See below.

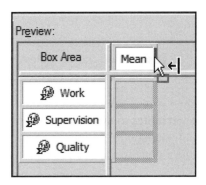

e. One by one, the **Min**, **Max**, and **N** statistics are dragged to the right border of the last cell in the upper portion of the Preview table. See below.

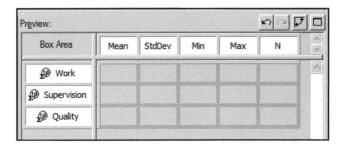

f. The BEST12.0 format is selected for the table. See Figure 3.45.

g. **Example 3.11** is entered for the box area. See Figure 3.46.

3. At **Titles**, the footnote is cleared.

4. Click **Run**.

Output 3.10 Summary Tables Output for Example 3.11

Summary Tables

Example 3.11	Mean	StdDev	Min	Max	N
Quality	49.916666667	4.1169497644	40	60	24
Supervision	51.208333333	5.4929137486	35	61	24
Work	53.458333333	3.61132478	47	59	24

3.7.5 Example 3.12: Analysis and Classification Variables

This example produces the summary table shown in Output 3.9 at the beginning of this section. The Attitude data set is used.

1. The Summary Tables task is opened. At Task Roles, Supervision is assigned to the Analysis variables role and Location is assigned to the Classification variables role. See Figure 3.43.

2. At Summary Tables:

   a. **Location** is dragged from **Available variables** to the empty row cell in the Preview table. The N statistic—the default statistic for a classification variable—appears in the column cell. A variable assigned to the Classification variables role is identified by the two empty sections in its cell. The All variable is dragged to the lower border of the Location cell. See below.

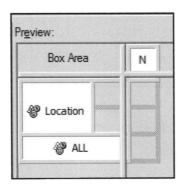

   b. **Supervision** is dragged to the upper border of the N statistic. The **Mean** statistic is dragged onto N, replacing it. See below.

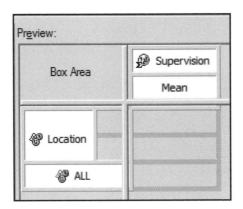

   c. The **Min** statistic is dragged to the right border of the **Mean** cell but below the **Supervision** cell. See below.

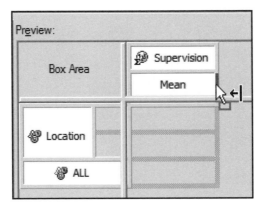

    d.   One by one, the **Max**, **N**, **ColPctN**, and **Median** statistics are dragged to the right border of the last statistic cell. See below.

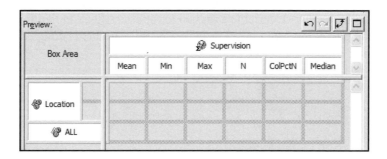

    e.   The BEST12.0 format is selected for the table.

    f.   **Example 3.12** is entered for the box area.

3.   At **Titles**, the footnote is cleared.

4.   Click **Run**.

Inferences from One Sample

4.1   Populations

In statistical theory, a *population* is the collection of potential observations from all persons or objects of interest. All observations discussed in this chapter are values from a single measurement or characterization.

A *parameter* is a number that describes a feature of a population. Greek letters often represent parameters. As an example, the mean of a population of numeric values is denoted by μ (lowercase *mu*). Statistics estimate parameters: $\bar{x}$ estimates μ.

Table 4.1 Parameters Discussed in Chapter 4

Parameter	Parameter Notation	Feature of Population Described by Parameter
mean	μ (lowercase Greek mu)	center of values
standard deviation	σ (lowercase Greek sigma)	spread of values
proportion	p (lowercase Roman p)	proportion having a given characteristic
median	θ (lowercase Greek theta)	center of values

4.1.1 Populations Defined by Categories

Populations can be partitioned so that each value falls into exactly one category. If the categories represent something that is increasing or decreasing, they are described as *ordinal*. Otherwise, the categories are described as *nominal*.

A population of categorical values is described by the proportions or percentages of the population associated with the categories. Table 4.2 shows the racial categories that make up the U.S. population. The data is from the U.S. Census Bureau web site (www.census.gov). The categories are nominal.

Table 4.2 Racial Categories of the U.S. Population

Race	Percentage
White	75.1%
Black or African American	12.3%
Asian	3.6%
American Indian and Alaska Native	0.9%
Native Hawaiian and Other Pacific Islander	0.1%
Other	5.6%
Two or more	2.4%

Table 4.3 represents how parents of school-age children in a particular community rate the quality of the local public schools. The categories are ordinal. These categories become ranks in the Probability Distributions section.

Table 4.3 Quality Ratings of Local Schools by Parents

Quality Rating	Percentage
Bad	20%
Poor	20%
Fair	20%
Good	20%
Excellent	20%

4.1.2 Populations Defined by Random Variables

Populations of numerical values fall under the theory of *random variables*. A random variable is a function—a theoretically applied measurement or characterization—that assigns a number to each person or object of interest. The variable is "random" because its observed value is determined by random selection.

A random variable is either *discrete* or *continuous*.

- A discrete random variable assigns integer values or other isolated points on the number line. Counts and ranks are the assignments of a discrete random variable.

- A continuous random variable assigns real numbers from an interval on the number line. Because each real number has an infinite number of decimals, these values only exist in theory. Rounding always occurs in practice.

4.1.3 Populations and Probability

A probability measurement is a number between 0 and 1 expressing the likelihood that an event occurs in the future. In everyday terms, it is usually a percentage, between 0% and 100%.

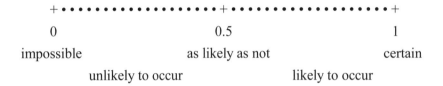

Population proportions can be interpreted as probabilities.

- In terms of categories, the probability that a randomly selected person or object is from a particular category is equal to the proportion of that category in the population. Applying Table 4.2, the probability that a person randomly selected from the U.S. population will be Asian is 3.6% or 0.036.

- In terms of random variables, the probability that the number associated with a randomly selected person or object satisfies some condition is equal to the proportion of values in the population that satisfy the condition.

  - A *probability distribution* describes a population determined by a discrete random variable.

  - A *probability density function* describes a population determined by a continuous random variable.

4.1.3.1   Probability Distributions

A probability distribution assigns a probability to each possible outcome of a discrete random variable. As an example, consider the ordinal categories in Table 4.3.

- In Table 4.4 (a), the random variable X assigns the ranks 1, 2, 3, 4, 5 to the categories bad, poor, fair, good, and excellent, respectively.

- Table 4.4 (b) lists the probability distribution with numerical values x and probabilities $p(x)$. The probability distribution is represented by the bar chart in Figure 4.8.

Capital letters are used to represent random variables and lower case letters are used to represent numbers (as in algebra).

Table 4.4 (a) Random Variable *X*, (b) Probability Distribution of the Random Variable *X*

(a)

	X
Bad	→ 1
Poor	→ 2
Fair	→ 3
Good	→ 4
Excellent	→ 5

(b)

x	$p(x)$
1	0.2
2	0.2
3	0.2
4	0.2
5	0.2

Figure 4.1 Bar Chart of Probability Distribution in Table 4.4 (b)

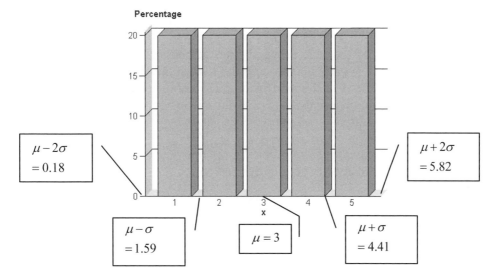

The mean, variance, and standard deviation of the probability distribution become the mean, variance, and standard deviation of the population of numerical values.

- The *mean* μ is the balance point of the distribution. See Figure 4.1. For a probability distribution, $\mu = \sum x \cdot p(x)$, where the sum Σ is computed with all possible values of the random variable. For Table 4.4 (b):

$$\mu = 1 \cdot 0.2 + 2 \cdot 0.2 + 3 \cdot 0.2 + 4 \cdot 0.2 + 5 \cdot 0.2 + 6 \cdot 0.2$$
$$= 0.2 + 0.4 + 0.6 + 0.8 + 1.0$$
$$= 3$$

- The spread of the outcomes from the center is measured by the *variance* σ^2 and the *standard deviation* $\sigma = \sqrt{\sigma^2}$. The variance is measured in squared units and the standard deviation is measured in the original unit. For a probability distribution, $\sigma^2 = \sum (x - \mu)^2 p(x)$, where the sum Σ is computed with all possible values of the random variable. For Table 4.4 (b):

$$\sigma^2 = (1-3)^2 \, 0.2 + (2-3)^2 \, 0.2 + (3-3)^2 \, 0.2 + (4-3)^2 \, 0.2 + (5-3)^2 \, 0.2$$
$$= 0.8 + 0.2 + 0 + 0.2 + 0.8$$
$$= 2$$

For Table 4.4 (b), $\sigma = \sqrt{2} = 1.41$, rounded to 2 decimal places.

It is generally the case that *most* of the population values are between $\mu - \sigma$ and $\mu + \sigma$. In the example, 60% are between $\mu - \sigma = 3 - 1.41 = 1.59$ and $\mu + \sigma = 3 + 1.41 = 4.41$. See Figure 4.1.

Also, it is generally the case that *all or almost all* of the population values are between $\mu - 2\sigma$ and $\mu + 2\sigma$. In the example, 100% are between $\mu - 2\sigma = 3 - 2(1.41) = 0.18$ and $\mu + 2\sigma = 3 + 2(1.41) = 5.82$. See Figure 4.1.

4.1.3.2   Probability Density Functions

A probability density function assigns a probability to each possible interval in the range of a continuous random variable. As an example, consider a situation where it takes a train 5 minutes to pass a railroad crossing. Let X be the time the train has been passing the crossing when a car randomly arrives. The car might arrive at any time during the 5 minutes. All intervals of equal width have the same probability of containing the arrival time.

This is an example of a *uniform probability density function*. See Figure 4.2. The black line represents the probability density function for this example:

$$f(x) = \begin{cases} 0.2, \text{ for } 0 < x < 5 \\ 0, \text{ otherwise} \end{cases}$$

The gray area in Figure 4.2 between the interval (a,b) and $f(x)$ is equal to $P(a < X < b)$: the probability that X is greater than a and less than b.

In terms of the example, $P(a < X < b)$ is:

- the probability that a car randomly arrives when the train has been passing the crossing for between a and b minutes

- the proportion of all cars that arrive at the crossing when the train has been passing for between a and b minutes

Formally, $P(a < X < b)$ is computed using integration:

$$P(a < X < b) = \int_a^b f(x) \, dx$$

But since it is a rectangle, the area can be computed as length times width: $0.2(b - a)$. All intervals with width $b - a$ have the same probability in this example.

Figure 4.2 An Example of a Uniform Probability Density Function

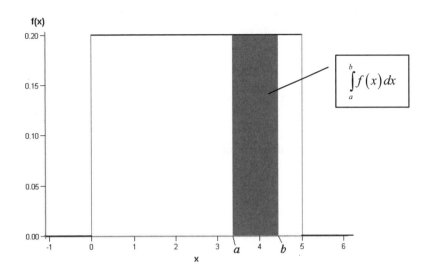

The mean, variance, and standard deviation of the probability distribution become the mean, variance, and standard deviation of the population of numerical values.

- The *mean* μ is the balance point of the distribution. See Figure 4.3. For a probability density function, $\mu = \int x\, f(x)\, dx$, which is integrated over all x where $f(x) > 0$. For Figure 4.3:

$$\mu = \int_0^5 x(0.2)\, dx = 0.1x^2 \Big]_0^5 = 0.1(5)^2 = 2.5$$

- The spread of the outcomes from the center is measured by the *variance* σ^2 and the *standard deviation* $\sigma = \sqrt{\sigma^2}$. The variance is measured in squared units, and the standard deviation is measured in the original unit. For a probability density function, $\sigma^2 = \int (x - \mu)^2 f(x)\, dx$, which is integrated over all x where $f(x) > 0$. For Figure 4.3:

$$\sigma^2 = \int_0^5 (x - 2.5)^2 (0.2)\, dx = \int_0^5 0.2x^2 - x + 1.25\, dx = \frac{1}{15}x^3 - \frac{1}{2}x^2 + 1.25x \Big]_0^5$$

$$= \frac{1}{15}(5)^3 - \frac{1}{2}(5)^2 + \frac{5}{4}(5) = \frac{25}{3} - \frac{25}{2} + \frac{25}{4} = \frac{25}{12}$$

For Table 4.3, $\sigma = \sqrt{25/12} = 1.44$, rounded to 2 decimal places.

It is generally the case that *most* of the population values are between $\mu - \sigma$ and $\mu + \sigma$. In the example, 57.6% are between $\mu - \sigma = 2.5 - 1.44 = 1.06$ and $\mu + \sigma = 2.5 + 1.44 = 3.94$:

$$P(1.06 < X < 3.94) = \int_{1.06}^{3.94} 0.2\, dx = 0.2x \Big]_{1.06}^{3.94} = 0.2(3.94) - 0.2(1.06) = 0.2(3.94 - 1.06) = 0.576$$

See Figure 4.3.

Also, it is generally the case that *all or almost all* of the population values are between $\mu - 2\sigma$ and $\mu + 2\sigma$. In the example, 100% are between $\mu - 2\sigma = 2.5 - 2(1.44) = -0.38$ and $\mu + 2\sigma = 2.5 + 2(1.44) = 5.38$. The total area under a probability density function always equals 1.

$$P(0 < X < 5) = \int_0^5 0.2dx = 0.2x \Big]_0^5 = 0.2(5) = 1$$

Figure 4.3 Roles of μ and σ with the Uniform Probability Density Function

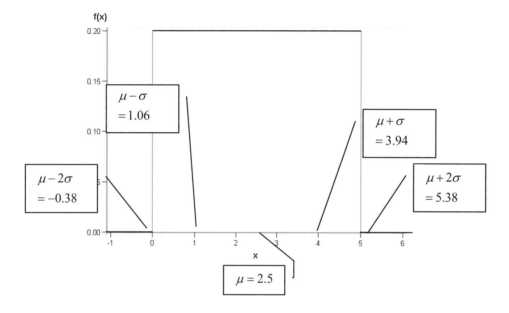

4.1.3.3 Normal Random Variable

The most important random variable in statistics is the *normal random variable*. A population of normally distributed values follows the famous "bell curve." See Figure 4.4. The normal probability density function for a given mean μ and standard deviation σ is:

$$f(x) = \frac{1}{\sigma\sqrt{2}} e^{-0.5(x-\mu)^2/\sigma^2}, \text{ for } -\infty < x < \infty$$

Figure 4.4 Normal Distribution

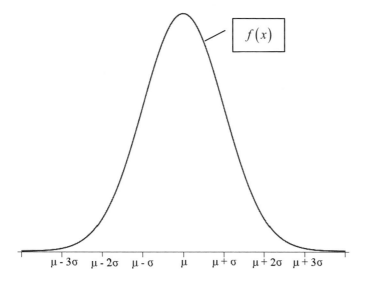

As an example, consider IQ scores. IQ stands for intelligence quotient:

$$IQ = \frac{\text{mental age}}{\text{chronological age}} \times 100$$

IQ scores are normally distributed. See Figure 4.5. The quotient can be any positive value, although IQ scores are generally given as integers.

Let X be the IQ of a randomly selected person. Assume that the $\mu = 100$ (mental age = chronological age) and $\sigma = 16$. The black line represents the probability density function for this example:

$$f(x) = \frac{1}{16\sqrt{2}} e^{-0.5(x-100)^2/(16)^2}, \text{ for } -\infty < x < \infty$$

The gray area in Figure 4.5 between the interval (a,b) and $f(x)$ is equal to $P(a < X < b)$. In this example, $P(a < X < b)$ is:

- The probability that a randomly selected person has an IQ between a and b
- The proportion of all persons having an IQ between a and b

The normal model allows negative values. Here, $P(X < 0) = 0.0000000002$. That probability is interpreted to mean impossible in practice.

Formally, $P(a < X < b)$ is computed using integration:

$$P(a < X < b) = \int_a^b f(x)\,dx$$

However, it is generally determined without integration using textbook tables, calculators, and computers. An interval with width $b - a$ has greatest probability when it is centered at μ. Intervals of the same width have lower probabilities the farther they are from μ.

Figure 4.5 Distribution of IQ Scores with Scores between *a* and *b* Shaded

In a normally distributed population:

- 68% of the values are between $\mu - \sigma$ and $\mu + \sigma$.

- 95% of the values are between $\mu - 2\sigma$ and $\mu + 2\sigma$.

- 99.7% of the values are between $\mu - 3\sigma$ and $\mu + 3\sigma$.

For IQ scores with $\mu = 100$ and $\sigma = 16$, the 68-95-99.7 intervals are (84, 116), (68, 132), and (52, 148). See Figure 4.6.

These same percentages are applied to samples in the Empirical Rule presented in Section 3.3. There, μ is replaced by $\bar{x}$ and σ is replaced by s.

Figure 4.6 Normal Distribution

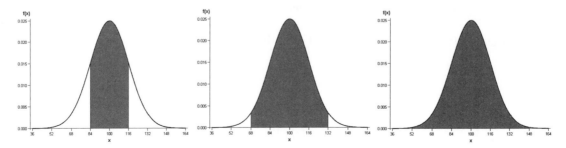

4.2 Sampling Distributions of the Mean

The most impressive thing about statistics is that it can exist as a science. After looking at samples of data, it's difficult to believe that order can be made of randomness. But actually order comes quite quickly. Consider the sample mean $\bar{x}$. It is, for almost all practical purposes, a normal random variable.

The population from which samples are drawn is called the *original population*. A population of sample means is called a *sampling distribution of the mean*.

- **Normal Distribution Theory:** If the original population follows a normal distribution with mean μ and standard deviation σ, then, for a sample size n, the sampling distribution of the mean follows the normal distribution with mean μ and standard deviation $\sigma/\sqrt{n}$.

- **Central Limit Theorem:** If the original population follows any non-normal distribution with mean μ and standard deviation σ, then, for a sufficiently large sample size n, the sampling distribution of the mean approximates the normal distribution with mean μ and standard deviation $\sigma/\sqrt{n}$. Larger sample sizes result in better approximations.

4.2.1 Example 4.1: Sampling Distribution of the Mean

In this example, simulations illustrate the Normal Distribution Theory and the Central Limit Theorem. The code for the simulations is in "SAS Code for Example 4.1 and Example 7.5" in the appendix.

4.2.1.1 Samples from a Normally Distributed Population

Consider a situation where bags of rice are being filled. Assume the weights of rice in the bags are normally distributed with $\mu = 50$ pounds and $\sigma = 0.5$ pounds.

- The normally distributed population of weights is illustrated in Figure 4.7, where the weight values are denoted by x.

- The weights of 1000 bags are simulated and represented by the left histogram in Figure 4.8. In the figure, the weight values are denoted by x.

- One thousand sample means are simulated and represented by the right histogram in Figure 4.8. Each sample has 30 weights. In the figure, the sample means are denoted by xbar.

Figure 4.7 Normal Distribution with $\mu = 50$ Pounds and $\sigma = 0.5$ Pounds

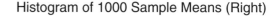

Figure 4.8 Histogram of 1000 Weights (Left)   Histogram of 1000 Sample Means (Right)

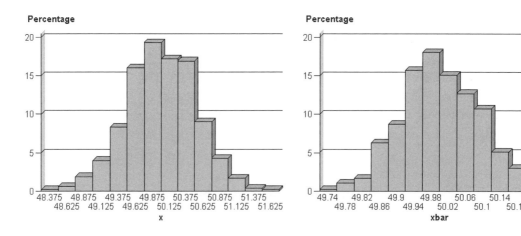

Note the following:

- The histogram of 1000 sample means (the histogram of xbar values on the right in Figure 4.8) approximates a normal distribution.

- Also, the histogram of sample means has midpoints from 49.74 to 50.26. All of the sample means $\bar{x}$ fall close to the population mean $\mu = 50$.

4.2.1.2   Samples from a 5-Outcome Population

A newspaper conducts an opinion poll that asks parents of school-age children to rate the quality of the local public schools. Parents are asked to choose one of five responses: bad, poor, fair, good, and excellent. Assume for the sake of illustration that, if asked, 20% of parents would say bad; 20%, poor; 20%, fair; 20%, good; and 20%, excellent. The responses are assigned numerical values: 1, 2, 3, 4, and 5, respectively.

This example is discussed in Section 4.1. See Table 4.3, Table 4.4, and Figure 4.1. The mean, variance, and standard deviation of the population of numerical values are $\mu = 3$, $\sigma^2 = 2$, and $\sigma = \sqrt{2}$.

Consider a sample of 2 responses. All possible 2-response samples are listed on the left in Table 4.5. Assume the number of parents with school-age children is large enough that the sampling can be considered independent. Then the probability of seeing any particular sample is 1/25 or 0.04. The corresponding sample means and sampling distribution is on the right in Table 4.5. The sampling distribution is represented by the bar chart in Figure 4.9.

Table 4.5 Samples and Sampling Distribution from Probability Distribution in Table 4.3

samples	$\bar{x}$	probability
(1,1)	1	0.04
(2,1) (1,2)	1.5	0.08
(3,1) (2,2) (1,3)	2	0.12
(4,1) (3,2) (2,3) (1,4)	2.5	0.16
(5,1) (4,2) (3,3) (2,4) (1,5)	3	0.20
(5,2) (4,3) (3,4) (2,5)	3.5	0.16
(5,3) (4,4) (3,5)	4	0.12
(5,4) (4,5)	4.5	0.08
(5,5)	5	0.04

Figure 4.9 Bar Chart of Sampling Distribution in Table 4.5

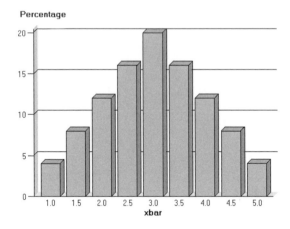

- The mean of the sampling distribution in Table 4.5 is:

$$\mu_{\bar{x}} = 1\cdot0.04+1.5\cdot0.08+2\cdot0.12+2.5\cdot0.16+3\cdot0.20+3.5\cdot0.16+4\cdot0.12+4.5\cdot0.08+5\cdot0.04$$
$$= 0.04+0.12+0.24+0.40+0.60+0.56+0.48+0.36+0.20$$
$$= 3$$

- The variance of the sampling distribution in Table 4.5 is:

$$\sigma_{\bar{x}}^2 = \left(1-3\right)^2 0.04+\left(1.5-3\right)^2 0.08+\left(2-3\right)^2 0.12+\left(2.5-3\right)^2 0.16+\left(3-3\right)^2 0.20+\left(3.5-3\right)^2 0.16$$
$$+\left(4-3\right)^2 0.12+\left(4.5-3\right)^2 0.08+\left(5-3\right)^2 0.04$$
$$= 0.16+0.18+0.12+0.04+0+0.04+0.12+0.18+0.16$$
$$= 1$$

Important Generalizations

- $\mu_{\bar{X}} = \mu$

  The mean of the sampling distribution and the mean of the original distribution are the same. In the computations above: $\mu_{\bar{X}} = \mu = 3$.

- $\sigma_{\bar{X}}^2 = \dfrac{\sigma^2}{n}$ and $\sigma_{\bar{X}} = \dfrac{\sigma}{\sqrt{n}}$

  The variance of the sampling distribution is equal to the variance of the original

  distribution divided by the sample size. Consequently, $\sigma_{\bar{X}} = \sqrt{\sigma_{\bar{X}}^2} = \sqrt{\dfrac{\sigma^2}{n}} = \dfrac{\sigma}{\sqrt{n}}$. This is the

  standard error of the mean or *standard error*, if the context is clear. In Table 4.5, $n = 2$.

  In the computations above: $\sigma_{\bar{X}}^2 = 1$ and $\dfrac{\sigma^2}{n} = \dfrac{2}{2} = 1$.

- Tendency toward a bell-shaped sampling distribution

Figure 4.10 shows 1000 sample means. Each sample has 30 responses, and each response comes from the population described in Table 4.5. Note that the distribution of the 1000 sample means in Figure 4.10 approximates a normal distribution.

Figure 4.10 Histogram of 1000 Sample Means Where the Samples
Are from the Population Represented in Table 4.5

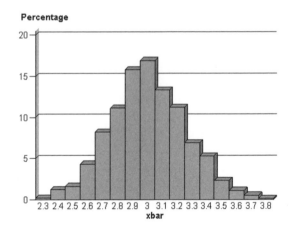

4.2.1.3   Samples from a 2-Outcome Population

A political candidate conducts a poll of 150 voters in which each voter is asked whether they support the candidate. The proportion of voters in the sample that say "yes" estimates the proportion of all voters that support the candidate. Assume that the candidate has support of 60% of all voters.

This example examines the distribution of the sample proportion, which is denoted by $\hat{p}$. Here, the formula for the sample proportion is:

$$\hat{p} = \frac{\text{number in sample that say 'yes'}}{150}$$

The sample proportion $\hat{p}$ is the same as the sample mean $\overline{x}$ when responses are assigned $x = 0$ for "no" and $x = 1$ for "yes." The sum of the x values, $\sum_{i=1}^{n} x_i$, is equal to the number in the sample that say "yes".

$$\hat{p} = \frac{\text{number in sample that say 'yes'}}{150} = \sum_{i=1}^{n} x_i \bigg/ n = \overline{x}$$

The population of numerical responses is modeled by the probability distribution in Table 4.6. The probability distribution is represented by the bar chart in Figure 4.11.

Table 4.6 Probability Distribution for Responses

x	$p(x)$
0	0.4
1	0.6

Figure 4.11 Bar Chart of Table 4.6

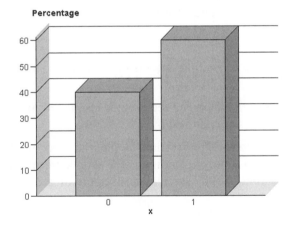

Figure 4.12 shows 1000 sample proportions. Each sample has 150 responses, and each response comes from the population described in Table 4.6. Note that the histogram approximates a normal distribution.

Figure 4.12 Histogram of 1000 Sample Proportions

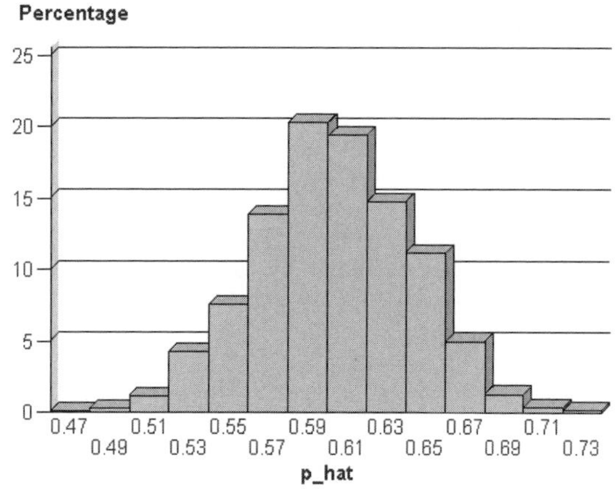

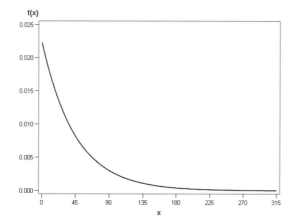

4.2.1.4   Samples from an Exponentially Distributed Population

Consider the time an emergency room patient waits to see a physician. Assume that the mean waiting time is 45 minutes. This situation can be modeled by the exponential distribution with $\lambda = 1/45$. With the exponential distribution, $\mu = 1/\lambda$ and $\sigma = 1/\lambda$. In this example, n $\mu = 45$ and $\sigma = 45$.

- The exponentially distributed population of waiting times is illustrated in Figure 4.13, where the time values are denoted by x.

- The waiting times of 1000 patients are simulated and represented by the left histogram in Figure 4.14. In the figure, the time values are denoted by x.

- One thousand sample means are simulated and represented by the right histogram in Figure 4.14. Each sample has 30 waiting times. In the figure, the sample means are denoted by xbar. Note that the histogram of 1000 sample means approximates a normal distribution.

Figure 4.13 Exponential Distribution with $\lambda = 1/45$

Figure 4.14 Histogram of 1000 Simulated Waiting Times (Left),
Histogram of 1000 Simulated Sample Means (Right)

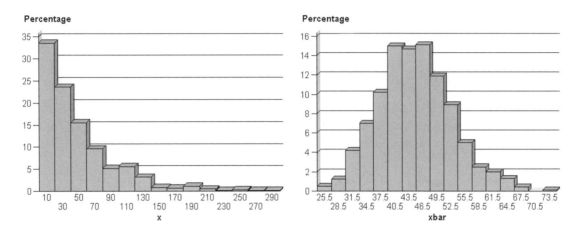

4.2.2 Development of Inferential Statistics

The Central Limit Theorem says that in a sampling distribution of the mean:

- Approximately 68% of the $\bar{x}$ values are between $\mu - \dfrac{\sigma}{\sqrt{n}}$ and $\mu + \dfrac{\sigma}{\sqrt{n}}$.

- Approximately 95% of the $\bar{x}$ values are between $\mu - 2\dfrac{\sigma}{\sqrt{n}}$ and $\mu + 2\dfrac{\sigma}{\sqrt{n}}$.

- Approximately 99.7% of the $\bar{x}$ values are between $\mu - 3\dfrac{\sigma}{\sqrt{n}}$ and $\mu + 3\dfrac{\sigma}{\sqrt{n}}$.

Therefore, approximately 95% of the time, a randomly selected sample mean $\bar{x}$ is within two standard errors $\sigma/\sqrt{n}$ of the true population mean μ :

$$\mu - 2\frac{\sigma}{\sqrt{n}} < \bar{x} < \mu + 2\frac{\sigma}{\sqrt{n}}$$

This is also expressed in the following important form:

$$-2 < \frac{\bar{x} - \mu}{\left(\dfrac{\sigma}{\sqrt{n}}\right)} < 2$$

4.2.2.1   Inference When the Population Standard Deviation Is Known

A *hypothesis test on the population mean* tests the assumption that the mean is equal to a given number, which is denoted by μ_0. If it is *not true* that

$$-2 < \frac{\bar{x} - \mu_0}{\left(\dfrac{\sigma}{\sqrt{n}}\right)} < 2 \ ,$$

then the sample mean $\bar{x}$ is said to be *significantly different* from μ_0. This significant difference is due to one of two things:

- A common event has occurred.
  - The sample mean $\bar{x}$ is actually within two standard errors of the population mean μ.
  - It is not within two standard errors of μ_0 because μ_0 is not equal to and not close to μ.
- A rare event has occurred.
  - The sample mean $\bar{x}$ is not within two standard errors of the population mean μ.
  - It is not within two standard errors of μ_0 because μ_0 is equal to or close to μ.

In a hypothesis test, the first statement is supported because it is more likely to be true.

Estimation of the population mean involves a point estimate and an interval estimate. A point estimate of μ is $\bar{x}$. An interval estimate of μ is the numbers between $\bar{x} - 2\dfrac{\sigma}{\sqrt{n}}$ and $\bar{x} + 2\dfrac{\sigma}{\sqrt{n}}$. The first line below is what one expects to see approximately 95% of the time: a sample mean $\bar{x}$ within two standard errors $\sigma/\sqrt{n}$ of the population mean μ.

$$\mu - 2\frac{\sigma}{\sqrt{n}} < \bar{x} < \mu + 2\frac{\sigma}{\sqrt{n}}$$

$$-\bar{x} - 2\frac{\sigma}{\sqrt{n}} < -\mu < -\bar{x} + 2\frac{\sigma}{\sqrt{n}}$$

$$\bar{x} + 2\frac{\sigma}{\sqrt{n}} > \mu > \bar{x} - 2\frac{\sigma}{\sqrt{n}}$$

$$\bar{x} - 2\frac{\sigma}{\sqrt{n}} < \mu < \bar{x} + 2\frac{\sigma}{\sqrt{n}}$$

After some algebra, the interval estimate is produced in the last line. Approximately 95% of the time, one can expect the interval $\left(\bar{x} - 2\dfrac{\sigma}{\sqrt{n}}, \bar{x} + 2\dfrac{\sigma}{\sqrt{n}} \right)$ to contain the population mean μ.

4.2.2.2   Inference When the Population Standard Deviation Is Not Known

Most often, the population standard deviation σ is not known. In that case, it is estimated by the sample standard deviation s. Then the expressions $\left(\bar{x} - \mu_0\right)/\left(s/\sqrt{n}\right)$, $\bar{x} - 2s/\sqrt{n}$, and $\bar{x} + 2s/\sqrt{n}$ involve two randomly determined values: $\bar{x}$ and s. The *t distribution* is applied here.

A *t* distribution is bell-shaped but slightly shorter and more spread out than the normal distribution. In Figure 4.15, the dotted and dashed curves are *t* distributions. The solid curve is the standard normal distribution: normal distribution with $\mu = 0$ and $\sigma = 1$.

The specific form of the *t* distribution depends on a number called the *degrees of freedom*. For the expressions involving $\bar{x}$ and s, the degrees of freedom are equal to $n-1$. A larger degrees-of-freedom value means a *t* distribution that is closer to the normal distribution. In Figure 4.15, the dotted curve (t10) is the *t* distribution with 10 degrees of freedom. The dashed curve (t29) is the *t* distribution with 29 degrees of freedom.

Figure 4.15 *t* Distributions and Normal Distribution

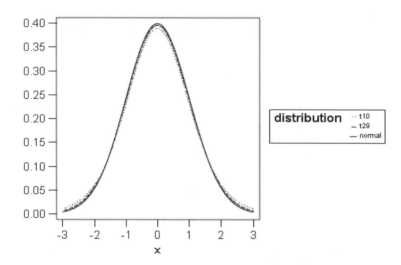

For samples with 30 or more values from a normally distributed population, the foundational sentence changes little: Approximately 95% of the time, a randomly selected sample mean $\bar{x}$ is within twice the *estimate* of the standard error $s/\sqrt{n}$ of the true population mean μ :

$$\mu - 2\frac{s}{\sqrt{n}} < \bar{x} < \mu + 2\frac{s}{\sqrt{n}}$$

or

$$-2 < \frac{\bar{x} - \mu}{\left(\dfrac{s}{\sqrt{n}}\right)} < 2$$

The statistic for the hypothesis test becomes $\dfrac{\overline{x} - \mu_0}{\left(\dfrac{s}{\sqrt{n}}\right)}$ and an interval estimate is

$$\left(\overline{x} - 2\frac{s}{\sqrt{n}}, \overline{x} + 2\frac{s}{\sqrt{n}}\right).$$

In practice, the above statistic and interval estimate can be applied to a sample from any population as long as the population has a mean μ and standard deviation σ. In practice, this means a sample without large outliers. When the sample contains large outliers, nonparametric statistics should be used.

Hypothesis testing and interval estimation are discussed in Section 4.3. The *p*-value is introduced for hypothesis testing. Use of the *p*-value is a more refined way of doing a hypothesis test than comparing a result to −2 and 2. Similarly for interval estimation, more precise critical values replace −2 and 2.

4.3 Inference on the Population Mean and Standard Deviation

This section considers the following areas of statistical inference:

- Hypothesis test on the mean: a determination of whether a numerical statement about a population mean is consistent with the data

- Confidence interval on the mean: a range of numbers where the population mean is believed to be

- Confidence interval on the standard deviation: a range of numbers where the population standard deviation is believed to be

4.3.1 Hypothesis Test on the Mean

In Example 4.2 in this section, food science researchers believe that french fries cooked in a new type of oil have fewer calories than french fries cooked in the oil used by a particular fast food chain. By checking the fast food chain's Web site, it is found that, on average, there are 475 calories in a large serving. The researchers wish to test the claim that, on average, a large serving of fries cooked in the new oil has less than 475 calories.

Here, the symbol μ represents the mean number of calories in all possible large servings cooked in the new oil. Two logically complementary hypotheses are tested:

$H_0 : \mu \geq 475$

$H_1 : \mu < 475$

- H_0 is the *null hypothesis*. Its numerical comparison contains equality.

- H_1 is the *alternative hypothesis*. Its numerical comparison is a strict inequality.

For testing purposes, H_0 is assumed to be true. In Example 4.2, the test assumption is that, on average, a large serving of fries cooked in the new oil has at least 475 calories.

If the sample mean $\bar{x}$ is inconsistent with the null hypothesis by a significant amount—less than 475 by a significant amount—the formal decision is to "Reject H_0." Otherwise, the formal decision is "Do not reject H_0."

In terms of Example 4.2, rejecting H_0 would confirm the researchers' belief that their french fries have fewer calories than the fast food chain's.

The following discussion examines the components of a hypothesis test.

4.3.1.1 Null and Alternative Hypotheses

The process begins with a claim. A claim regarding a population mean is always equivalent to one of six numerical comparisons. See the left column in Table 4.7. However, there are many ways to express these comparisons in words. The middle column in Table 4.7 is not an exhaustive list.

Table 4.7 Numerical Comparisons Involving the Population Mean

Comparison with Symbols	Comparison with Words	Hypothesis
$\mu = number$	the mean $\begin{Bmatrix} \text{is} \\ \text{is equal to} \end{Bmatrix}$ *number*	H_0
$\mu \neq number$	the mean $\begin{Bmatrix} \text{is not} \\ \text{is not equal to} \\ \text{is different from} \end{Bmatrix}$ *number*	H_1
$\mu \leq number$	the mean $\begin{Bmatrix} \text{is less than or equal to} \\ \text{is at most} \end{Bmatrix}$ *number* the mean is *number* or less	H_0
$\mu > number$	the mean $\begin{Bmatrix} \text{is greater than} \\ \text{is bigger than} \end{Bmatrix}$ *number*	H_1
$\mu \geq number$	the mean $\begin{Bmatrix} \text{is greater than or equal to} \\ \text{is at least} \end{Bmatrix}$ *number* the mean is *number* or more	H_0
$\mu < number$	the mean $\begin{Bmatrix} \text{is less than} \\ \text{is smaller than} \end{Bmatrix}$ *number*	H_1

The claim and the negation of the claim, written symbolically, become two logically complementary hypotheses. These are the null hypothesis and the alternative hypothesis.

- The *null hypothesis* is denoted by H_0. H_0 always includes equality ($=, \leq, \geq$).

- The *alternative hypothesis* is denoted by H_1. H_1 is always a strict inequality ($\neq, >, <$).

In Table 4.6, the number that the mean μ is being compared to is denoted by μ_0. It is sometimes called the hypothesized mean. Below are the three possible pairs of null and alternative hypotheses involving the population mean:

$H_0 : \mu = \mu_0$	$H_0 : \mu \leq \mu_0$	$H_0 : \mu \geq \mu_0$
$H_1 : \mu \neq \mu_0$	$H_1 : \mu > \mu_0$	$H_1 : \mu < \mu_0$

A claim may be equivalent to either the null or the alternative hypothesis.

- For the purposes of testing, one assumes that the null hypothesis H_0 is true. The number μ_0 is used for the population mean in computations.

- The hypothesis test concludes with either the decision to reject H_0 or to not reject H_0.

4.3.1.2 Significance Level

H_0 is rejected when the data agrees with H_1. However, it is possible for the data to agree with H_1 and for H_0 to be true. Rejecting H_0 when H_0 is true is called a Type I error. See Table 4.7. Such errors do occur and they are undetectable. The goal is to make them rare.

Going into a hypothesis test, one determines an acceptable Type I error rate. This is called the *significance level*. In more formal terms, the significance level is the probability of making a Type I error.

- It is denoted by α (lowercase Greek alpha). A small α is desirable, such as 0.01, 0.025, 0.05, or 0.10. It is often the case that $\alpha = 0.05$. A significance level α is usually given for textbook problems.

- Decreasing the significance level comes at the expense of increasing the probability of making a Type II error: not rejecting H_0 when H_0 is false. See Table 4.8.

Table 4.8 Type I and Type II Errors

		True State of Nature:	
		H_0 is true.	H_0 is false.
Decision:	Reject H_0.	Type I Error	Correct decision
	Do not reject H_0.	Correct decision	Type II Error

4.3.1.3 Test Statistic

The test statistic for the one-sample *t* test is:

$$t \text{ value} = \frac{\bar{x} - \mu_0}{\left(\dfrac{s}{\sqrt{n}}\right)}$$

The *t* value measures the distance between the sample mean $\bar{x}$ and the hypothesized mean μ_0 in $s/\sqrt{n}$ units. With a fixed sample size *n*, there is a *t* value for every possible sample that can be taken from the original population.

If the original population is normally distributed, the *t* values follow a *t* distribution. The specific *t* distribution depends on a number called the *degrees of freedom*. For the one-sample *t* test, the degrees of freedom are equal to $n-1$.

If the original population is not normally distributed but has a mean μ and a standard deviation σ, the population of *t* values approximates a *t* distribution. Larger sample sizes provide better approximations. In practice, the one-sample *t* test gives reliable results as long as the sample does not contain large outliers.

4.3.1.4 *p*-Value

The *p-value* is a measure of the likelihood that the sample comes from a population where H_0 is true. Smaller values indicate less likelihood. That is, the more the data agrees with H_1, the smaller the *p*-value. In terms of the hypotheses of the one-sample *t* test:

- $H_0 : \mu = \mu_0$ versus $H_1 : \mu \neq \mu_0$: The greater the difference between $\bar{x}$ and μ_0—or equivalently, the greater the difference between the *t* value and 0—the smaller the *p*-value.

- $H_0 : \mu \leq \mu_0$ versus $H_1 : \mu > \mu_0$: The more $\bar{x}$ is greater than μ_0—or equivalently, the more the *t* value is greater than 0—the smaller the *p*-value.

- $H_0 : \mu \geq \mu_0$ versus $H_1 : \mu < \mu_0$: The more $\bar{x}$ is less than μ_0—or equivalently, the more the *t* value is less than 0—the smaller the *p*-value.

In terms of the one-sample *t* test, the *p*-value is formally defined to be the probability that a random sample from a population with mean μ_0 would produce a *t* value at or beyond the current sample value.

If the p-value is small, the event—a random sample from a population with mean μ_0 producing a t value at or beyond to the current sample value—is unlikely to be repeated. If the event is unlikely to be repeated, the event is unlikely to have occurred in the first place. That is, it is unlikely that the current sample has been randomly selected from a population with mean μ_0 and has produced the current t value. The only thing that can be false in that statement is the initial assumption of the hypothesis test: the population has mean μ_0. Therefore, if the p-value is small, it is unlikely that the current sample comes from a population with mean μ_0.

The technical definitions of the p-value are given in Table 4.9. There, the random variable T represents a future value of the test statistic and follows the t distribution with $n-1$ degrees of freedom.

$\Pr > |t|$ identifies the p-value in the one-sample t test task output.

- The test of the hypotheses $H_0 : \mu = \mu_0$ versus $H_1 : \mu \neq \mu_0$ is called a *two-sided test*. See the first graph in Table 4.9. *$\Pr > |t|$ is the p-value for a two-sided test.*

- The tests of $H_0 : \mu \leq \mu_0$ versus $H_1 : \mu > \mu_0$ and $H_0 : \mu \geq \mu_0$ versus $H_1 : \mu < \mu_0$ are called *one-sided tests*. See the second and third graphs in Table 4.9. *The p-values for one-sided tests are computed from the $\Pr > |t|$ value.* See Table 4.9.

SAS code expressions are included in Table 4.9 to aid in the discussion. The p-value is computed using an expression in "Detailed Solutions" in "Example 4.2: Hypothesis Test and Confidence Intervals." In the expressions, t value and $n-1$ represent numbers. A new column can be created with a SAS code expression using the Advanced Expression Builder. See Section 2.4.

Table 4.9 *p*-values for One-Sample *t* Test

Hypotheses	Gray areas correspond to probability statements and are examples.	

$H_0 : \mu = \mu_0$
$H_1 : \mu \neq \mu_0$

$p\text{-value} = 2P\left(T \geq |t\ \text{Value}|\right)$

Task output:
Pr > |t|

SAS code expression:
2*(1-probt(abs(*t* Value),*n* − 1))

$H_0 : \mu \leq \mu_0$
$H_1 : \mu > \mu_0$

$p\text{-value} = P\left(T \geq t\ \text{Value}\right)$

Computed from task output:
   0.5(Pr > |t|), if *t* Value > 0
   1 − 0.5(Pr > |t|), if *t* Value ≤ 0

SAS code expression:
1-probt(*t* Value,*n* − 1)

$H_0 : \mu \geq \mu_0$
$H_1 : \mu < \mu_0$

$p\text{-value} = P\left(T \leq t\ \text{Value}\right)$

Computed from task output:
   1 − 0.5(Pr > |t|), if *t* Value ≥ 0
   0.5(Pr > |t|), if *t* Value < 0

SAS code expression:
probt(*t* Value,*n* − 1)

4.3.1.5 Formal Decision

If the *p*-value is small, the data agrees with H_1. If the *p*-value is less than the significance level, the risk of making a Type I error is acceptable. Therefore, the *p*-value decision rule is the following:

If the p-value < α, reject H_0. Otherwise, do not reject H_0.

Since a hypothesis test begins with the assumption that H_0 is true, concluding a hypothesis test requires one of the following formal statements:

- Reject H_0.
- Do not reject H_0.

The *p*-value is part of the output for all hypothesis tests. It is identified in the output by Prob or Pr as part of an inequality involving a letter representing the test statistic. In the one-sample *t* test, the *p*-value is identified by $\text{Pr} > |t|$.

4.3.1.6   Stating the Decision in Terms of the Problem

"Reject H_0" and "Do not reject H_0" are necessary because they communicate an unambiguous decision. But a hypothesis test should be interpreted beyond these formal statements. Please consider the concluding sentence and concluding observation.

Concluding Sentence

The form of the concluding sentence depends on two independent facts: whether H_0 is rejected and whether the claim is equivalent to the null or the alternative hypothesis. There are four forms of the concluding sentence. See Table 4.10.

When the claim is equivalent to the null hypothesis, the concluding sentence uses the word *reject*. The concluding sentence becomes an expanded version of the formal decision.

When the claim is equivalent to the alternative hypothesis, the concluding sentence uses the word *support*. If the data supports the rejection of H_0, the data supports H_1. If the data does not support rejection of H_0, the data cannot support H_1.

Table 4.10 Concluding Sentences

Formal Statistical Decision	Claim stated as H_0	Claim stated as H_1
Reject H_0.	There is sufficient evidence to reject the claim that ... (claim in words).	There is sufficient evidence to support the claim that ... (claim in words).
Do not reject H_0.	There is not sufficient evidence to reject the claim that ... (claim in words).	There is not sufficient evidence to support the claim that ... (claim in words).

Concluding Observation

"Significantly different" is a phrase that is commonly used in reporting the results of a hypothesis test. It is equivalent to saying that H_0 has been rejected. With regard to the one-sample *t* test, it always refers to the sample mean $\bar{x}$ and the μ_0 value. The phrase may use the word *different*, *greater*, or *less* depending on the H_1 inequality. See Table 4.11.

Table 4.11 Observations: Inequality Equivalent to H_1

Reject H_0.	The sample mean is significantly different/greater/less than μ_0.
Do not reject H_0.	The sample mean is not significantly different/greater/less than μ_0.

4.3.2 Estimation of the Mean

In Example 4.2, food science researchers test the claim that, on average, a large serving of fries cooked in a new type of oil has less than 475 calories. If that claim is supported by the data, the researchers will want to know what the average is when using the new oil. More formally, the researchers want to estimate the mean of the population of calorie values that are associated with all large servings that will be cooked in the new oil.

- The *point estimate* of the population mean, denoted by $\hat{\mu}$, is the sample mean $\overline{x}$. This is the best estimate. The point estimate should be close to μ, but it is unlikely that it will hit the mark exactly.

- An *interval estimate* of the population mean is an interval (a,b)—all the numbers greater than a and less than b—that is likely to contain μ.

- A *confidence interval* is an interval estimate where the likelihood is given an exact value.

- The given likelihood value is called the *confidence level*, which is usually 90%, 95%, or 99%.

4.3.2.1 *t* Distribution Critical Values

In Section 4.3, a rough interval estimate is constructed:

$$\left(\overline{x} - 2\frac{s}{\sqrt{n}}, \overline{x} + 2\frac{s}{\sqrt{n}} \right)$$

For samples with 30 or more values from a normally distributed population, the interval should contain the population mean μ approximately 95% of the time. To set an exact confidence level for any sample size, 2 becomes a variable called a *critical value*.

A critical value for a t distribution is denoted by t_q, where q is between 0 and 1. The critical value t_q is a value on the number line that marks the right q proportion of the distribution. For a fixed q, there is a different t_q value for each degrees-of-freedom value. The degrees of freedom for the confidence interval on the mean is $n - 1$. See Table 4.12.

In Figure 4.16, the proportion of the distribution to the right of $t_{0.025}$ is 0.025. The proportion of the distribution to the right of $-t_{0.025}$ is 0.975. Because of symmetry, $-t_{0.025} = t_{0.975}$. Ninety-five percent of the distribution is between $-t_{0.025}$ and $t_{0.025}$.

Figure 4.16 *t* Distribution with Critical Values

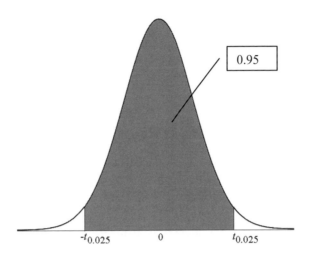

The SAS code expression for t_q is tinv($1-q$,df), where $1-q$ and df represent numbers. The degrees of freedom, df, for the confidence interval on the mean is $n-1$. Table 4.12 contains the code expression and the $t_{0.025}$ critical value for selected degrees of freedom.

Table 4.12 SAS Code and *t* Critical Value for Selected Degrees of Freedom

degrees of freedom	SAS code expression	$t_{0.025}$
10	tinv(0.975, 10)	2.2281
20	tinv(0.975, 20)	2.0860
29	tinv(0.975, 29)	2.0452
39	tinv(0.975, 30)	2.0227
49	tinv(0.975, 49)	2.0096

The One-Sample *t* Test task computes confidence intervals without the user having to supply the critical values. The SAS code expression is included here to aid in the discussion. A confidence interval is computed using the expression in "Detailed Solutions" in "Example 4.2: Hypothesis Test and Confidence Intervals."

Confidence levels are generally equal to 90%, 95%, and 99%. As a group, confidence levels are represented by the notation $(1-\alpha)100\%$. Here, α would be equal to 0.10, 0.05 and 0.01. A $(1-\alpha)100\%$ confidence interval on the mean has critical values $-t_{\alpha/2}$ and $t_{\alpha/2}$.

- For a 90% confidence interval ($\alpha = 0.10$), the critical values are $-t_{0.05}$ and $t_{0.05}$.

- For a 95% confidence interval ($\alpha = 0.05$), the critical values are $-t_{0.025}$ and $t_{0.025}$.
- For a 99% confidence interval ($\alpha = 0.01$), the critical values are $-t_{0.005}$ and $t_{0.005}$.

4.3.2.2 Confidence Interval on the Mean

For a sample from a normally distributed population, a $(1-\alpha)100\%$ confidence interval on the mean μ is:

$$\left(\overline{x} - t_{\alpha/2}\frac{s}{\sqrt{n}}, \overline{x} + t_{\alpha/2}\frac{s}{\sqrt{n}} \right)$$

Consider all possible samples of a fixed size that can be randomly selected from a normally distributed population. There is a 95% confidence interval associated with each sample. Ninety-five percent of the confidence intervals contain the population mean μ, and 5% do not. Suppose a researcher collects a sample and computes a 95% confidence interval. The researcher cannot know whether the interval contains μ. But if the sample was randomly selected, there is a 95% chance that it does.

Figure 4.17 represents 40 95% confidence intervals as vertical lines. The small horizontal mark on each line is the sample mean. The population mean in this simulation is 450. Note that two confidence intervals fail to contain $\mu = 450$. Not every set of 95% confidence intervals has exactly 5% that do not contain the population mean. But on the whole, this is what is occurring.

Figure 4.17 Simulated Confidence Intervals with Two Failing to Contain the Population Mean

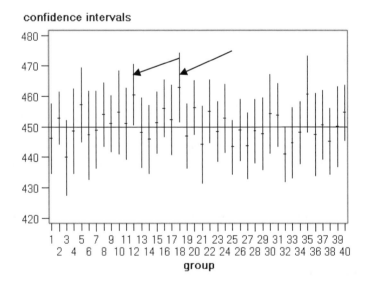

4.3.3 Estimation of the Standard Deviation

The point estimate of the population standard deviation, denoted by $\hat{\sigma}$, is the sample standard deviation s.

The point estimate of the population variance, denoted by $\hat{\sigma}^2$, is the sample variance s^2.

The confidence intervals for the standard deviation and variance are based on the chi-squared (χ^2) distribution.

4.3.3.1 Chi-Squared Distribution Critical Values

A critical value for a chi-squared distribution is denoted by c_q, where q is between 0 and 1. The critical value c_q is a value on the number line that marks the right q proportion of the distribution. For a fixed q, there is a different c_q value for each degrees-of-freedom value. The degrees of freedom for the confidence interval on the standard deviation is $n - 1$. See Table 4.13.

In Figure 4.18, the proportion of the distribution to the right of $c_{0.025}$ is 0.025. The proportion of the distribution to the right of $c_{0.975}$ is 0.975. Ninety-five percent of the distribution is between $c_{0.975}$ and $c_{0.025}$.

Figure 4.18 Chi-Squared Distribution with Critical Values

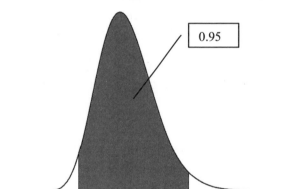

The SAS code expression for c_q is cinv($1-q$,df), where $1-q$ and df represent numbers. The degrees of freedom, df, for the confidence interval on the standard deviation is $n - 1$. Table 4.13 contains code expressions and the $c_{0.975}$ and $c_{0.025}$ critical values for selected degrees of freedom.

Table 4.13 SAS Code and t Critical Value for Selected Degrees of Freedom

degrees of freedom	SAS code expression	$c_{0.975}$	SAS code expression	$c_{0.025}$
10	cinv(0.025, 10)	3.2470	cinv(0.975, 10)	20.4832
20	cinv(0.025, 20)	9.5908	cinv(0.975, 20)	34.1696
29	cinv(0.025, 29)	16.0471	cinv(0.975, 29)	45.7223
39	cinv(0.025, 30)	23.6543	cinv(0.975, 30)	58.1201
49	cinv(0.025, 49)	31.5549	cinv(0.975, 49)	70.2224

The one-sample *t* test task computes confidence intervals without the user having to supply the critical values. The SAS code expression is included here to aid in the discussion. A confidence interval is computed using the expression in the "Detailed Solutions" section in Section 4.3.6, "Example 4.2: Hypothesis Test and Confidence Intervals."

4.3.3.2 Confidence Intervals on the Standard Deviation

For a sample from a normally distributed population, a $(1-\alpha)100\%$ confidence interval on the variance σ^2 is:

$$\left(\frac{(n-1)s^2}{c_{\alpha/2}}, \frac{(n-1)s^2}{c_{1-\alpha/2}} \right)$$

For a sample from a normally distributed population, a $(1-\alpha)100\%$ confidence interval on the standard deviation σ is:

$$\left(s\sqrt{\frac{(n-1)}{c_{\alpha/2}}}, s\sqrt{\frac{(n-1)}{c_{1-\alpha/2}}} \right)$$

The confidence interval above is referred to as *equal tailed* because the area in either distribution tail is $\alpha/2$. The critical values $c_{1-\alpha/2}$ and $c_{\alpha/2}$ may not result in the shortest—most precise—confidence interval. A task option uses critical values that produce the shortest confidence interval. This is a *uniformly most powerful unbiased (UMPU)* confidence interval.

For a sample from a normally distributed population, a $(1-\alpha)100\%$ UMPU confidence interval on the standard deviation σ is:

$$\left(s\sqrt{\frac{(n-1)}{c_{\text{upper}}}}, s\sqrt{\frac{(n-1)}{c_{\text{lower}}}} \right)$$

The critical values c_{lower} and c_{upper} are the closest critical values that have $(1-\alpha)100\%$ of the distribution between them.

Confidence intervals on the standard deviation are more sensitive to the distribution of the original population than confidence intervals on the mean. For samples not from a normally distributed population, the confidence level may not reflect the actual likelihood that the interval contains σ.

4.3.4 Summary of the Hypothesis Test and Confidence Intervals

4.3.4.1 Hypothesis Test

Plan the experiment.

$$H_0 : \mu = \mu_0 \qquad H_0 : \mu \leq \mu_0 \qquad H_0 : \mu \geq \mu_0 \left.\begin{matrix} \\ \\ \end{matrix}\right\} \text{Task requires } \mu_0.$$
$$H_1 : \mu \neq \mu_0 \qquad H_1 : \mu > \mu_0 \qquad H_1 : \mu < \mu_0$$

The significance level is α.

Task computes the statistics.

t Tests			
Variable	**DF**	**t Value**	**Pr > |t|**
analysis variable	degrees of freedom $= n-1$	$t \text{ Value} = \dfrac{\overline{x} - \mu_0}{\left(\dfrac{s}{\sqrt{n}}\right)}$	p-value for $H_0 : \mu = \mu_0$ $H_1 : \mu \neq \mu_0$

Determining the p-value:

Hypotheses	
$H_0 : \mu = \mu_0$ $H_1 : \mu \neq \mu_0$	$p\text{-value} = \left(\mathbf{Pr} > \|\mathbf{t}\|\right)$
$H_0 : \mu \leq \mu_0$ $H_1 : \mu > \mu_0$	$p\text{-value} = \begin{cases} 0.5\left(\mathbf{Pr} > \|\mathbf{t}\|\right), & \text{if } t \text{ Value} > 0 \\ 1 - 0.5\left(\mathbf{Pr} > \|\mathbf{t}\|\right), & \text{if } t \text{ Value} \leq 0 \end{cases}$
$H_0 : \mu \geq \mu_0$ $H_1 : \mu < \mu_0$	$p\text{-value} = \begin{cases} 1 - 0.5\left(\mathbf{Pr} > \|\mathbf{t}\|\right), & \text{if } t \text{ Value} \geq 0 \\ 0.5\left(\mathbf{Pr} > \|\mathbf{t}\|\right), & \text{if } t \text{ Value} < 0 \end{cases}$

Apply the results.

If the p-*value* < α, reject H_0. Otherwise, do not reject H_0.

- Reject H_0. There is sufficient evidence to reject/support the claim that ... (claim in words). The sample mean is significantly different/greater/less than μ_0.

- Do not reject H_0. There is not sufficient evidence to reject/support the claim that ...(claim in words). The sample mean is not significantly different/greater/less than μ_0.

4.3.4.2 Confidence Interval on the Mean

CL stands for *confidence limit* in the task output:

Lower CL Mean	Mean	Upper CL Mean
$\bar{x} - t_{\alpha/2}\dfrac{s}{\sqrt{n}}$	$\bar{x}$	$\bar{x} + t_{\alpha/2}\dfrac{s}{\sqrt{n}}$

4.3.4.3 Confidence Intervals on the Standard Deviation

CL stands for *confidence limit* in the task output:

Lower CL Std Dev	UMPU Lower CL Std Dev	Std Dev	UMPU Upper CL Std Dev	Upper CL Std Dev
$s\sqrt{\dfrac{(n-1)}{c_{\alpha/2}}}$	$s\sqrt{\dfrac{(n-1)}{c_{\text{upper}}}}$	s	$s\sqrt{\dfrac{(n-1)}{c_{\text{lower}}}}$	$s\sqrt{\dfrac{(n-1)}{c_{1-\alpha/2}}}$

4.3.5 Returning to Normal Theory and Central Limit Theorem

Simulations test how well theory works in practice.

- Simulations of inference based on normal distribution theory do well.

- Simulations of inference based on the Central Limit Theorem give mixed results. The Central Limit Theorem depends on the phrase "for a sufficiently large sample size *n*." Some situations need larger samples than others.

- Simulations of inference not based on normal distribution theory or Central Limit Theorem give poor results.

4.3.5.1 Normal Distribution Theory

A simulation generates 10,000 30-value samples from the normally distributed population in Example 4.1. In that population, $\mu = 50$ and $\sigma = 0.5$.

Hypothesis Test

Each sample tests the hypotheses $H_0 : \mu = 50$ and $H_1 : \mu \neq 50$ with the significance level $\alpha = 0.05$. The proportion of rejections is recorded. Since the significance level is the probability of rejecting H_0 when H_0 is true and since H_0 is true here, one expects that proportion to be 0.05.

The proportion of rejections is 0.0496. This is essentially what is expected.

Confidence Intervals

Each sample produced a 95% confidence interval on μ and a 95% confidence interval on σ. The results are as expected.

- 95.04% of the intervals contained $\mu = 50$.

- 94.04% of the intervals contained $\sigma = 0.5$.

4.3.5.2   Central Limit Theorem

Simulations generate 10,000 30-value samples from the 5-outcome population and the exponentially distributed population in Example 4.1.

Hypothesis Test

- The 5-outcome population has $\mu = 3$. Each sample tests the hypotheses $H_0 : \mu = 3$ and $H_1 : \mu \neq 3$ with the significance level $\alpha = 0.05$. The proportion of rejections is 0.0561. This is essentially what is expected.

- The exponentially distributed population has $\mu = 45$. Each sample tests the hypotheses $H_0 : \mu = 45$ and $H_1 : \mu \neq 45$ with the significance level $\alpha = 0.05$. The proportion of rejections is 0.0734. This is somewhat higher than expected. Working with exponentially distributed data may require larger samples.

Confidence Intervals on μ

Each sample produced a 95% confidence interval on μ.

- 5-outcome population: 94.39% of the intervals contained $\mu = 3$. A sample size of 30 does well for the 5-outcome population.

- Exponentially distributed population: 92.66% of the intervals contained $\mu = 45$. This is somewhat smaller than expected. Sample sizes greater than 30 would produce better results.

4.3.5.3   Inference Not Based on Normal Distribution Theory or the Central Limit Theorem

Inference on the standard deviation σ for non-normal populations is not covered by normal distribution theory or the Central Limit Theorem.

Simulations generate 10,000 30-value samples from the 5-outcome population and the exponentially distributed population in Example 4.1. Each sample produces a 95% confidence interval on σ. The results are poor.

- 5-outcome population: 99.84% of the intervals contained $\sigma = \sqrt{2}$. This is much higher than the nominal 95%.

- Exponentially distributed population: 71.56% of the intervals contained $\sigma = 45$. This is much lower than the nominal 95%.

4.3.6 Example 4.2: Hypothesis Test and Confidence Intervals

The hypothesis test and estimation procedures discussed earlier are worked out in detail for Example 4.2. The analysis results can be compared to the one-sample *t* test output in Output 4.2.

4.3.6.1 French Fries

A large serving of french fries at a certain fast food restaurant has an average of 475 calories. The restaurant is experimenting with a new type of oil for cooking french fries. It is claimed that the servings of fries cooked in the new oil have less than 475 calories, on average. The following are the calorie measurements from a sample of servings cooked in the new oil:

465	459	425	433	466	437	532	411	454	470
436	479	484	496	419	472	512	459	470	399
445	418	379	427	477	423	500	430	457	468

The data is saved as Ex04_02. The data column is named calories.

Example 4.2.1

Test the claim that the mean number of calories for all large servings to be cooked in the new oil is less than 475. Let $\alpha = 0.05$.

1. Determine H_0 and H_1.
2. Determine the *p*-value.
3. State the formal decision, the concluding sentence, and the concluding observation.

Example 4.2.2

Estimate the mean number of calories for all large servings to be cooked in the new oil. Construct a 95% confidence interval for this mean.

Example 4.2.3

Estimate the standard deviation of the calorie values for all large servings to be cooked in the new oil. Construct a 95% equal-tailed confidence interval for this standard deviation.

Example 4.2.4

Construct a box-and-whisker plot.

4.3.6.2 Detailed Solutions

To begin the analysis, the Summary Tables task is used to compute the sample size, mean, and standard deviation. See Output 4.1.

Output 4.1 Summary Tables Output for Example 4.2

Summary Tables

	N	Mean	StdDev
calories	30	453.4	34.235089883

Example 4.2.1

The claim is that "the mean number of calories for all large servings to be cooked in the new oil is less than 475."

- The numerical comparison is "the mean ... for all ... is less than 475".
- Symbolically, this is "$\mu < 475$".

Plan the task.

$H_0 : \mu \geq 475$

$H_1 : \mu < 475$

$\alpha = 0.05$

Compute the statistics.

$$t \text{ Value} = \frac{\overline{x} - \mu_0}{\left(\dfrac{s}{\sqrt{n}}\right)} = \frac{453.4 - 475}{\left(\dfrac{34.235089883}{\sqrt{30}}\right)} = -3.45575$$

The degrees of freedom for the one-sample t test is $n - 1$. For Example 4.2, degrees of freedom = 29. Referring to Table 4.9:

p-value $= P(T < -3.45575) = \text{probt}(-3.45575,29) = 0.0008560519$

Apply the results.

Since p-value < 0.05, reject H_0. There is sufficient evidence to support the claim that the mean number of calories for all large servings to be cooked in the new oil is less than 475. The sample mean, $\overline{x} = 453.4$ calories, is significantly less than 475 calories.

Example 4.2.2

The estimate of the population mean is $\overline{x} = 453.4$.

The degrees of freedom for the confidence interval on the mean is $n - 1$. For Example 4.2, degrees of freedom = 29. Referring to Table 4.12:

$t_{0.025} = \text{tinv}(.975,29) = 2.0452$

A 95% confidence interval on the population mean:

$$\left(\bar{x} - t_{.025} \frac{s}{\sqrt{n}}, \ \bar{x} + t_{.025} \frac{s}{\sqrt{n}} \right)$$

$$\left(453.4 - 2.0452 \frac{34.235089883}{\sqrt{30}}, 453.4 + 2.0452 \frac{34.235089883}{\sqrt{30}} \right)$$

$$\left(440.617, 466.183 \right)$$

Example 4.2.3

The estimate of the population standard deviation is $s = 34.235089883$. The degrees of freedom for the confidence interval on the standard deviation is $n - 1$. For Example 4.2, degrees of freedom = 29. Referring to Table 4.13:

$$c_{0.975} = \text{cinv}(.025, 29) = 16.0471$$

$$c_{0.025} = \text{cinv}(.975, 29) = 45.7223$$

A 95% confidence interval on the population standard deviation:

$$\left(s\sqrt{\frac{(n-1)}{c_{.025}}}, s\sqrt{\frac{(n-1)}{c_{.975}}} \right)$$

$$\left(34.235089883\sqrt{\frac{(30-1)}{45.7223}}, 34.235089883\sqrt{\frac{(30-1)}{16.0471}} \right)$$

$$\left(27.2651, 46.0227 \right)$$

4.3.7 Instruction for the One-Sample *t* Test

Open the *t* test task in one of the following ways:

- From the menu bar, select **Analyze ▶ ANOVA ▶ t Test**.
- On the **Task by Category** tab of the **Task List**, go to the **ANOVA** section and click **t Test**.
- On the **Task by Name** tab of the **Task List**, double-click **t Test**.

The *t* test task has five of major groups of options: *t* Test Type, Task Roles, Analysis, Plots, and Titles. The Titles group of options is discussed in Chapter 1, "Introduction to SAS Enterprise Guide." The Titles options control the titles and the footnotes in the task output.

4.3.7.1 *t* Test Type

Select **One sample** for the one-sample *t* test. See Figure 4.19. The two-sample *t* test and the paired *t* test are discussed in Chapter 5, "Inferences from Two Samples."

Figure 4.19 *t* Test Type in the *t* Test Task for Example 4.2

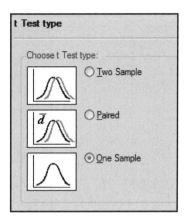

4.3.7.2 Task Roles

Click **Task Roles** on the selection pane to open this group of options. A variable is assigned to a role by dragging its name from **Variables to assign** to a role in **Task roles**. See Figure 4.20. A variable may be removed from a role by dragging it back to **Variables to assign**. The right and left arrows and the resulting pop-up menus can also be used.

Analysis variables: Requested statistics and plots are computed for each variable in this role. The order that the variables are listed here is the order that they are listed in the output. See Figure 4.20.

Group analysis by, Frequency count and Relative weight roles are discussed in Section 1.3.

In Figure 4.20, the data is in the Ex04_02 data set. The variable calories is assigned to the Analysis variables role.

Figure 4.20 Task Roles in the *t* Test Task for Example 4.2

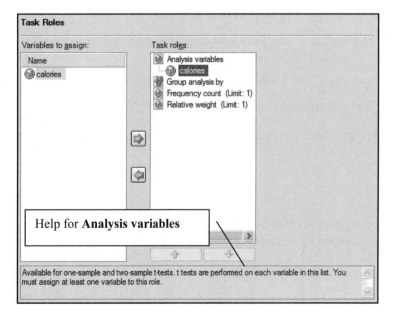

4.3.7.3 Analysis

- The hypothesis test comparison number μ_0 is entered here at Ho =. See Figure 4.21.

- The task reports the *p*-value for the two-sided test $H_0 : \mu = \mu_0$ versus $H_1 : \mu \neq \mu_0$ at Pr > |t|. The *p*-values for one-sided tests ($H_0 : \mu \leq \mu_0$ versus $H_1 : \mu > \mu_0$, $H_0 : \mu \geq \mu_0$ versus $H_1 : \mu < \mu_0$) are computed from the Pr > |t| Value. See Table 4.8.

- A confidence interval on the mean μ is automatically part of the output. Its Confidence level is determined here.

- Equal-tailed and UMPU confidence intervals on the standard deviation σ are requested here. Their confidence levels are the same as for the confidence interval on the mean. At least one confidence interval on the standard deviation σ is always part of the output.

In Figure 4.21, a test of $H_0 : \mu = 475$ versus $H_1 : \mu \neq 475$, a 95% confidence interval on the mean μ , and a 95% equal-tailed confidence interval on the standard deviation σ are requested.

Since Example 4.2 tests $H_0 : \mu \geq 475$ versus $H_1 : \mu < 475$, the correct *p*-value is computed from the Pr > |t| Value in the "Analysis" section of "Task Output, Interpretation, and Analysis for Example 4.2."

Figure 4.21 Analysis Options in the *t* Test Task for Example 4.2

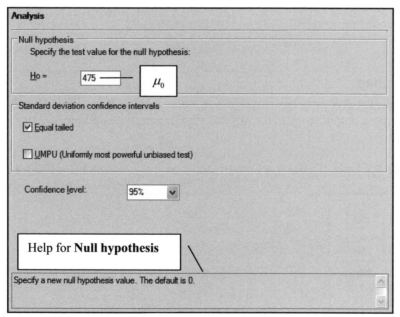

4.3.7.4   Plots

The **Box and whisker** plot is selected in Figure 4.22. Box-and-whisker plots are discussed in Section 3.4.

The one-sample *t* test assumes that the data comes from a normally distributed population. Ideally, the data is not skewed and has no outliers. An *outlier* is an unusually large or small value relative to the rest of the sample. Outliers are individually identified in the box-and-whisker plot.

The task is most reliable when the data comes from a normally distributed population. Nevertheless, it does a good job as long as there are no severe outliers. Severe outliers can cause incorrect results, especially Type II Errors. A Type II Error occurs when the null hypothesis is not rejected when it is false. If the data contains severe outliers, a nonparametric test should be considered.

Figure 4.22 Box and Whisker Selected in Plots Options

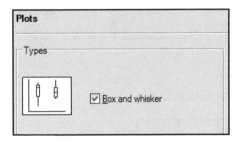

4.3.7.5   When Finished

When finished assigning variables to roles and selecting options, click **Run**. The task adds a *t* Test icon and one or more output icons to the process flow diagram. See Figure 4.23.

Figure 4.23 Example 4.2 Data, Task, and Output Icons on the Process Flow Diagram

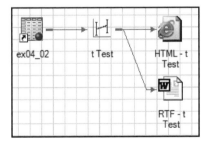

4.3.8 Task Output, Interpretation, and Analysis for Example 4.2

4.3.8.1 Task Output

Output 4.2 One-Sample *t* Test Output for Example 4.2

t Test

The TTEST Procedure

				Statistics			
Variable	**N**	**Lower CL Mean**	**Mean**	**Upper CL Mean**	**Lower CL Std Dev**	**Std Dev**	**Upper CL Std Dev**
calories	30	440.62	453.4	466.18	27.265	34.235	46.023
		❶	❷	❸	❹	❺	❻

Std Err	**Minimum**	**Maximum**
6.2504	379	532

❼

T-Tests			
Variable	**DF**	**t Value**	**Pr > |t|**
calories	29	-3.46	0.0017
	❽	❾	❿

Box Plot

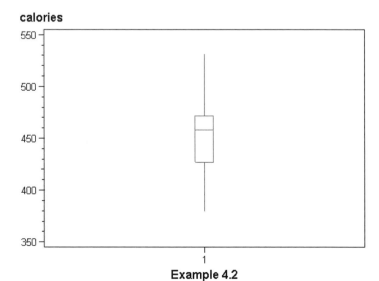

Example 4.2

Comment

The statistics table in Output 4.2 has been edited so that it fits within the margins.

For the box-and-whisker plot, the background is changed to white and the horizontal axis label has been changed from _const to Example 4.2. The dummy classification variable _const is created when there is one sample. To make these changes, move the cursor inside the graph and right-click. From the pop-up menu, select **Graph Properties**.

4. On the **Graph** tab, go to **Background** and select white on the color palette. Click **OK**.

5. On the **Axis** tab:

    a. **Horizontal** is the default selection on the **Axis** drop-down menu.

    b. **Label** should be checked. Click **Label Options**. In the Label Options window, select **Custom label**. Type Example 4.2 in the entry box. Click **OK** to return to the Properties window.

6. Click **OK**.

4.3.8.2 Interpretation

❶ Lower 95% confidence limit for the population mean: $\bar{x} - t_{0.025} \dfrac{s}{\sqrt{n}}$

❷ Sample mean $\bar{x}$

❸ Upper 95% confidence limit for the population mean: $\bar{x} + t_{0.025} \dfrac{s}{\sqrt{n}}$

❹ Lower 95% confidence limit for the population standard deviation: $s\sqrt{\dfrac{(n-1)}{c_{0.025}}}$

❺ Sample standard deviation s

❻ Upper 95% confidence limit for the population standard deviation: $s\sqrt{\dfrac{(n-1)}{c_{0.975}}}$

❼ Estimate of the standard error of the mean: $s/\sqrt{n}$

❽ degrees of freedom: $n - 1$

❾ $t \text{ Value} = \dfrac{\bar{x} - \mu_0}{\left(\dfrac{s}{\sqrt{n}}\right)}$

❿ p-value for test of the hypotheses $H_0 : \mu = 475$ versus $H_1 : \mu \neq 475$. Since t value < 0, the p-value for the test of the hypotheses $H_0 : \mu \geq 475$ versus $H_1 : \mu < 475$ is $0.5(0.0017) = 0.00085$.

4.3.8.3 Analysis

Example 4.2.1

$H_0 : \mu \geq 475$

$H_1 : \mu < 475$

p-value = 0.5(0.0017) = 0.00085. See ❿ in Output 4.2.

Since the p-value < 0.05, reject H_0. There is sufficient evidence to support the claim that the mean number of calories for all large servings to be cooked in the new oil is less than 475. The sample mean is significantly less than 475 calories.

Example 4.2.2

See ❶, ❷, and ❸ in Output 4.2. An estimate of the mean number of calories for all large servings to be cooked in the new oil is 453.4. A 95% confidence interval on the mean number of calories for all large servings to be cooked in the new oil is (440.62, 466.18). In other words, the restaurant is 95% confident that large servings cooked in the new oil have, on average, between 440.62 and 466.18 calories.

Problem 3

See ❹, ❺, and ❻ in Output 4.2. An estimate of the standard deviation of the calorie values for all large servings to be cooked in the new oil is 34.235 calories. A 95% equal-tailed confidence interval for the standard deviation of the calorie values for all large servings to be cooked in the new oil is (27.265, 46.023).

Problem 4

See Output 4.2. There are no outliers.

4.3.9 Example 4.3: Hypothesis Test and Confidence Interval

4.3.9.1 Fitness in Children

Medical researchers examine the fitness of healthy sixth-grade boys (based on "One-Mile Run Performance and Cardiovascular Fitness in Children," by Rowland et al., *Archives of Pediatrics & Adolescent Medicine*, Vol. 153, pp. 845-849). One measure of fitness is the time it takes to complete a one-mile run. The data, in minutes, is below. It is also in the time column of the Boys_fitness data set in Appendix 1.

8.52	12.25	7.15	11.05	10.62	10.25	7.79	10.17	10.26	10.77
12.36	11.02	10.88	12.72	12.37	13.69	9.34	6.04	11.29	11.61
9.72	9.21	7.8	12.66	8.82	7.56	11.87	10.62	9.96	8.02

Example 4.3.1

Test the claim that the mean time required by all healthy sixth-grade boys to run one mile is 11 minutes. Let $\alpha = 0.10$.

1. Determine H_0 and H_1.
2. Determine the *p*-value.
3. State the formal decision, the concluding sentence, and the concluding observation.

Example 4.3.2

Estimate the mean time required by all healthy sixth-grade boys to run one mile. Construct a 90% confidence interval on this mean.

Example 4.3.3

Estimate the standard deviation of one-mile times associated with all healthy sixth-grade boys. Construct a 90% UMPU confidence interval for this standard deviation.

Example 4.3.4

Construct a box-and-whisker plot of the data. Are there any outliers?

4.3.9.2   Output, Comments, and Analysis

Output

Output 4.3 One-Sample *t* Test for Example 4.3

t Test

The TTEST Procedure

Statistics							
Variable	N	Lower CL Mean	Mean	Upper CL Mean	UMPU Lower CL Std Dev	Std Dev	UMPU Upper CL Std Dev
Time	30	9.6275	10.213	10.798	1.5412	1.8873	2.3852

❶ ❷

Std Err	Minimum	Maximum
0.3446	6.04	13.69

T-Tests			
Variable	DF	t Value	Pr > |t|
Time	29	-2.28	0.0299

❸

Box Plot

Time

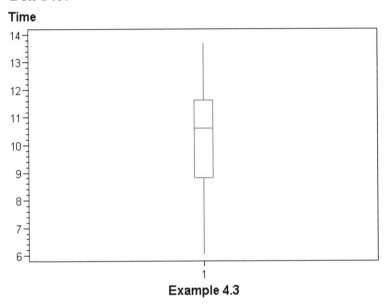

Example 4.3

Comments

The statistics table in Output 4.3 has been edited so that it fits within the margins.

For the box-and-whisker plot, the background is changed to white and the horizontal axis label has been changed from _const to Example 4.3. See the comments after Output 4.2 in "Task Output, Interpretation, and Analysis for Example 4.2."

Analysis

Example 4.3.1

$H_0 : \mu = 11$

$H_1 : \mu \neq 11$

p-value = 0.0299. See ❸ in Output 4.3.

Since the *p*-value < 0.10, reject H_0. There is sufficient evidence to reject the claim that the mean time required by all healthy sixth-grade boys to run one mile is 11 minutes. The sample mean is significantly different from 11 minutes.

Example 4.3.2

See ❶ in Output 4.3. An estimate of the mean time required by all healthy sixth-grade boys to run one mile is 10.213 minutes. A 90% confidence interval on the mean time required by all healthy sixth-grade boys to run one mile is (9.6275, 10.798). In other words, the medical researchers are 90% confident that it takes healthy sixth-grade boys, on average, between 9.6275 and 10.798 minutes to run one mile.

Example 4.3.3

See ❷ in Output 4.3. An estimate of the standard deviation of one-mile times associated with all healthy sixth-grade boys is 1.8873 minutes. A 90% UMPU confidence interval for the standard deviation of one-mile times associated with all healthy sixth-grade boys is (1.5412, 2.3852).

Example 4.3.4

See Output 4.3. There are no outliers.

4.3.10 Example 4.4: Hypothesis Test and Confidence Interval

4.3.10.1 Academic Achievement

A state high school cheerleading association (SHSCA) believes that, on average, its members are better prepared for college than high school students in general. To confirm this, the SHSCA uses the scores from a nationwide academic achievement test. It is known that the mean score is 1000 for all students who take the test. The SHSCA claims that the mean score of its members is greater than 1000. The scores for twenty randomly selected SHSCA members are below.

1280	1020	972	949	1248	1110	1001	971
1156	988	919	826	1096	951	930	1190
1077	702	1018	985				

The data is saved as Ex04_04. The data column is named score.

Example 4.4.1

Test the claim that the mean score of SHSCA members is greater than 1000. Let $\alpha = 0.05$.

1. Determine H_0 and H_1.
2. Determine the p-value.
3. State the formal decision, the concluding sentence, and the concluding observation.

Example 4.4.2

Estimate the mean score of SHSCA members. Construct a 95% confidence interval for this mean.

Example 4.4.3

Estimate the standard deviation of all SHSCA member scores. Construct a 95% UMPU confidence interval for this standard deviation.

Example 4.4.4

Construct a box-and-whisker plot of the data. Are there any outliers?

4.3.10.2 Output, Comment, and Analysis

Output

Output 4.4 One-Sample *t* Test for Example 4.4

t Test

The TTEST Procedure

Statistics							
Variable	N	Lower CL Mean	Mean	Upper CL Mean	UMPU Lower CL Std Dev	Std Dev	UMPU Upper CL Std Dev
score	20	955.18	1019.5	1083.7	104.43	137.32	200.57

❶   ❷

Std Err	Minimum	Maximum
30.706	702	1280

T-Tests			
Variable	DF	t Value	Pr > |t|
score	19	0.63	0.5340

❸

Box Plot

score

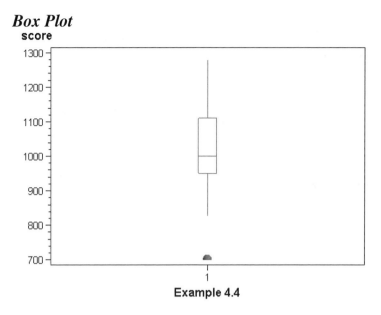

Example 4.4

Comments

The Statistics table in Output 4.4 has been edited so that it fits within the margins.

For the box-and-whisker plot, the background is changed to white and the horizontal axis label has been changed from _const to Example 4.4. See the comments after Output 4.4 in "Task Output, Interpretation, and Analysis for Example 4.2."

4.3.10.3 Analysis

Example 4.4.1

$H_0 : \mu \leq 1000$

$H_1 : \mu > 1000$

p-value $= 0.5(0.5340) = 0.2670$. See ❸ in Output 4.4.

Since p-value ≥ 0.05, do not reject H_0. There is not sufficient evidence to support the claim that the mean score of SHSCA members is greater than 1000. The sample mean is not significantly greater than 1000.

Example 4.4.2

See ❶ in Output 4.4. An estimate of the mean score of SHSCA members is 1019.5. A 95% confidence interval on the mean score of SHSCA members is (955.18, 1083.7). In other words, the association is 95% confident that the mean score is between 955.18 and 1083.7.

Example 4.4.3

See ❷ in Output 4.4. An estimate of the standard deviation of all SHSCA member scores is 137.32. A 95% UMPU confidence interval for the standard deviation of all SHSCA member scores is (104.43, 200.57).

Example 4.4.4

See Output 4.4. There is an outlier. (This example would be a candidate for the sign test and the signed rank test discussed in Section 4.5. However, the outlier is not severe. Neither the sign test nor the signed rank test supports the claim.)

4.4 Inference on a Population Proportion

A proportion is the relative size of the part of a population or a sample of people or objects that has a given characteristic.

- A population proportion is denoted by p, where p is a number between 0 and 1.
  - o It is often referred to as a *binomial* proportion.
  - o A binomial proportion is one of a pair of proportions, p and $1 - p$, that corresponds respectively to the part that has and the part that does not have a given characteristic.
- A sample proportion is $\hat{p} = x/n$, where x is the number in a sample of size n with a given characteristic. The sample proportion $\hat{p}$ estimates the population proportion p.

Tests and confidence intervals on a population proportion are part of the One-Way Frequencies task.

4.4.1 Hypothesis Test on the Proportion

A hypothesis test on a proportion is very similar to a hypothesis test on a mean. Both tests compare a parameter to a number. There is a significance level and a p-value. The formal decision and conclusions are the same. The differences are in the parameter—p replaces μ—and the test statistic. The test statistic is based on the sample proportion $\hat{p}$ and not the sample mean $\bar{x}$.

4.4.1.1 Null and Alternative Hypotheses

In Example 4.5, a study investigates the rate of dental caries (cavities) among school children in a community. The study hopes to show that more than 90% of all the children have no dental caries. The parameter of interest here is a population proportion: the proportion of all the children in the community with dental caries.

The word *proportion* does not appear in the first two sentences of the last paragraph. Rate, risk, and percentage are often used for proportion.

The one-sample test on a proportion begins with a claim about a population proportion. The claim is often expressed in terms of the percentage $100p\%$. In a statistical hypothesis test, the claim must be equivalent to a numerical comparison. Below are the six possible numerical comparisons involving a population proportion:

$p = number$	$p \le number$	$p \ge number$
$p \ne number$	$p > number$	$p < number$

The proportion comparison number in the hypotheses is denoted by p_0. Below are the three possible pairs of null and alternative hypotheses involving a population proportion p:

| $H_0 : p = p_0$ | $H_0 : p \leq p_0$ | $H_0 : p \geq p_0$ |
| $H_1 : p \neq p_0$ | $H_1 : p > p_0$ | $H_1 : p < p_0$ |

A hypothesis test assumes that the null hypothesis H_0 is true. In the one-sample test on a proportion, the number p_0 is used for the population proportion in computations. The data determines whether the assumption should be rejected or not.

The claim in Example 4.5 is that "more than 90% of all the children have no dental caries." The corresponding hypotheses are:

$$H_0 : p \leq 0.90$$
$$H_1 : p > 0.90$$

4.4.1.2   Test Statistics

There are two test statistics associated with the one-sample test on a proportion. The asymptotic test is computationally quick, but it produces approximate p-values. The exact test produces exact p-values, but it may require excessive computing time.

- If $np_0(1 - p_0) \geq 5$, use the *asymptotic test*.

- The condition is true when p_0 is close to 0.5 and the sample size is moderate or larger, or when p_0 is not close to 0.5 but the sample size is large.

- In either case, the sample size is "sufficiently large" enough for the Central Limit Theorem to hold. The distribution of the sample proportion $\hat{p}$ approximates a normal distribution, with larger sample sizes resulting in better approximations. See Example 4.1 in Section 4.2. More formally, the sampling distribution of the proportion is asymptotically normal distribution.

- If $np_0(1 - p_0) < 5$, use the *exact test*. The sample size is not large enough for the Central Limit Theorem to hold.

Example 4.5 tests the claim that more than 90% of the community children have no dental caries. The sample size is $n = 100$. Here, $np_0(1 - p_0) = 100 \cdot 0.9 \cdot 0.1 = 9$. The asymptotic test can be used. Figure 4.24 shows 1000 simulated sample proportions where $H_0 : p = 0.9$ is the case and $n = 100$. The results approximate a normal distribution.

Example 4.6 tests the claim that less than 90% of patients who take a new drug show symptoms after one week. The sample size is $n = 16$. Here, $np_0(1 - p_0) = 16 \cdot 0.9 \cdot 0.1 = 1.44$. The exact test should be used. Figure 4.25 shows 1000 simulated sample proportions where $H_0 : p = 0.9$ is the case and $n = 16$. The results are too skewed to approximate a normal distribution.

Figure 4.24 Simulation of 1000 Sample Proportions Where $H_0 : p = 0.9$ and $n = 100$

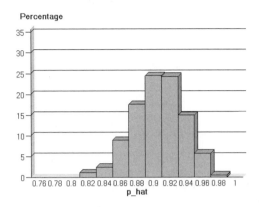

Figure 4.25 Simulation of 1000 Sample Proportions Where $H_0 : p = 0.9$ and $n = 16$

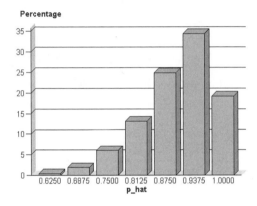

For both tests, the original population of values consists of 1s and 0s. There is a 1 for every person or object described by the given characteristic and a 0 for all other persons or objects. The proportion of 1s in the population is p and proportion of 0s is $1 - p$.

In general, the probability distribution is:

x	$p(x)$
1	p
0	$1 - p$

Asymptotic Test

- The population mean is $\mu = \sum x\, p(x) = 1 \cdot p + 0 \cdot (1-p) = p$.

- The population variance is $\mu = \sum (x - \mu)^2\, p(x) = (1-p)^2 p + (0-p)^2(1-p) = (1-p)^2 p + p^2(1-p) = p(1-p)[(1-p) + p] = p(1-p)$.

Applying the Central Limit Theorem in Section 4.3, the sampling distribution of the proportion approximates the normal distribution with mean p and standard deviation $\sqrt{\dfrac{p(1-p)}{n}}$.

The test statistic is based on the *standardized* sample proportion $\hat{p}$. A statistic is standardized when it is subtracted by its mean and the difference is divided by the standard deviation of the statistic. The standardized sample proportion is denoted by z.

$$z = \frac{\hat{p} - p}{\sqrt{\dfrac{p(1-p)}{n}}}$$

The population of z values approximates the normal distribution with $\mu = 0$ and $\sigma = 1$. This distribution is called the standard normal distribution.

A hypothesis test assumes that the null hypothesis H_0 is true. In the one-sample test on a proportion, the number p_0 is used for the population proportion in the test statistic:

$$z = \frac{\hat{p} - p_0}{\sqrt{\dfrac{p_0(1-p_0)}{n}}}$$

This measures the distance between the sample proportion $\hat{p}$ and the hypothesized proportion p_0 in $\sqrt{p_0(1-p_0)/n}$ units. The denominator $\sqrt{p_0(1-p_0)/n}$ is the *asymptotic standard error under H_0*.

Exact Test

The test statistic for the exact test is x: the number of 1s in the sample taken from the original population.

There is an x value for each sample of size n that can be randomly selected from the original population. The population of x values follows the binomial distribution where the probability of success is p and the number of trials is n.

The test statistic is also x: the number of persons or objects in the sample with the given characteristic. In Example 4.5, x is the number of children in the sample with dental caries (cavities).

4.4.1.3   *p*-Value

The *p-value* is a measure of the likelihood that the sample comes from a population where H_0 is true. Smaller values indicate less likelihood. That is, the more the data agrees with H_1—the more $\hat{p}$ is different than, greater than, or less than p_0—the smaller the *p*-value.

In terms of the one-sample test on a proportion, the *p*-value is the probability that a random sample from a population with proportion p_0 would produce a test statistic at or beyond the current sample value. If the *p*-value is small, it is unlikely that the current sample comes from a population with proportion p_0.

The technical definition of the *p*-value depends on the test and the alternative hypothesis H_1.

- Table 4.14 has the definitions for the asymptotic test. The random variable Z represents a future value of the test statistic and follows the standard normal distribution. In the expressions, z represents a number.

- Table 4.15 has the definitions for the exact test. The random variable X represents a future value of the test statistic and follows the binomial distribution where the probability of success is p_0 and the number of trials is n. In the expressions, p_0, n, and x represent numbers.

SAS code expressions are included in both tables to aid in the discussion. The *p*-values are computed using expressions in Section 4.4.4.2, "Detailed Solutions."

Table 4.14 *p*-Values for Asymptotic One-Sample Test on a Proportion

Hypotheses	**Gray areas correspond to probability statements and are examples.**	
$H_0 : p = p_0$ $H_1 : p \neq p_0$	 $p\text{-value} = 2P\left(Z \geq |z|\right)$	Task output: Two-sided $\Pr > |Z|$ SAS code expression: 2*(1-probnorm(abs(z))
$H_0 : p \leq p_0$ $H_1 : p > p_0$	 $p\text{-value} = P\left(Z \geq z\right)$	Computed from task output: • One-sided $\Pr > Z$, if $z > 0$ • $1 - $ (One-sided $\Pr < Z$), if $z \leq 0$ SAS code expression: 1-probnorm(z)
$H_0 : p \geq p_0$ $H_1 : p < p_0$	 $p\text{-value} = P\left(Z \leq z\right)$	Computed from task output: • $1 - $ (One-sided $\Pr > Z$), if $z \geq 0$ • One-sided $\Pr < Z$, if $z < 0$ SAS code expression: probnorm(z)

Table 4.15 *p*-Values for Exact One-Sample Test on a Proportion

Hypotheses	Graphs represent example distributions. Gray areas correspond to probability statements and represent example values.
$H_0 : p = p_0$ $H_1 : p \neq p_0$	 $p\text{-value} = 2 \cdot \min \left\{ P\left(X \leq x\right), P\left(X \geq x\right) \right\}$ Task output: p-value = (Two-sided = 2*One-sided) SAS code expression: 2*min(1-probbnml(p_0,n,$x-1$),probbnml(p_0,n,x))
$H_0 : p \leq p_0$ $H_1 : p > p_0$	 $p\text{-value} = P\left(X \geq x\right)$ Computed from task output: • p-value = (One-sided Pr >= P), if $\hat{p} > p_0$ • p-value > $1 -$ (One-sided Pr <= P), if $\hat{p} \leq p_0$ SAS code expression: 1-probbnml(p_0,n,$x-1$)
$H_0 : p \geq p_0$ $H_1 : p < p_0$	 $p\text{-value} = P\left(X \leq x\right)$ Computed from task output: • p-value > $1 -$ (One-sided Pr >= P), if $\hat{p} \geq p_0$ • p-value = (One-sided Pr <= P), if $\hat{p} < p_0$ SAS code expression: probbnml(p_0,n,x)

4.4.1.4 Formal Decision

If the p-value is small, the data agrees with H_1. If the p-value is less than the significance level, the risk of making a Type I error is acceptable. Therefore, the p-value decision rule is the following:

If the p-value $< \alpha$, reject H_0. Otherwise, do not reject H_0.

Since a hypothesis test begins with the assumption that H_0 is true, concluding a hypothesis test requires one of the following formal statements:

- Reject H_0.
- Do not reject H_0.

4.4.1.5 Stating the Decision in Terms of the Problem

Concluding Sentence

When the claim is equivalent to the null hypothesis, the concluding sentence uses the word *reject*. The concluding sentence becomes an expanded version of the formal decision.

When the claim is equivalent to the alternative hypothesis, the concluding sentence uses the word *support*. If the data supports the rejection of H_0, the data supports H_1. If the data does not support rejection of H_0, the data cannot support H_1.

Table 4.16 Concluding Sentences

Formal Statistical Decision	Claim stated as H_0	Claim stated as H_1
Reject H_0.	There is sufficient evidence to reject the claim that ... (claim in words).	There is sufficient evidence to support the claim that ... (claim in words).
Do not reject H_0.	There is not sufficient evidence to reject the claim that ... (claim in words).	There is not sufficient evidence to support the claim that ... (claim in words).

Concluding Observation

"Significantly different" is a phrase that is commonly used in reporting the results of a hypothesis test. It is equivalent to saying that H_0 has been rejected. With regard to the one-sample test on a proportion, "significantly different" always refers to the sample proportion $\hat{p}$ and the p_0 value.

The phrase may use the word *different*, *greater*, or *less* depending on the H_1 inequality. See Table 4.17.

Table 4.17 Concluding Observations: Inequality Equivalent to H_1

Reject H_0.	The sample proportion is significantly different/greater/less than p_0.
Do not reject H_0.	The sample proportion is not significantly different/greater/less than p_0.

4.4.2 Estimation of the Proportion

A point estimate of the population proportion p is the sample proportion $\hat{p} = x/n$, where x is the number of observations in the sample with the given characteristic.

As with hypothesis tests, there are two confidence intervals associated with the proportion. The choice between the two depends on whether the sample proportion $\hat{p}$ does a good job of approximating the normal distribution.

- If $n\hat{p}(1-\hat{p}) \geq 5$, use the *asymptotic confidence interval.*

    o The condition is true when $\hat{p}$ is close to 0.5 and the sample size is moderate or larger, or when $\hat{p}$ is not close to 0.5 but the sample size is large.

    o In either case, the sample size is "sufficiently large" for the Central Limit Theorem to hold. The distribution of the sample proportion $\hat{p}$ approximates a normal distribution, with larger sample sizes resulting in better approximations. See Example 4.1 in Section 4.2. More formally, the sampling distribution of the proportion $\hat{p}$ is asymptotically normal distribution.

- If $n\hat{p}(1-\hat{p}) < 5$, use the *exact confidence interval.* The sample size is not large enough for the Central Limit Theorem to hold.

4.4.2.1 Asymptotic Confidence Interval

The asymptotic confidence interval on a proportion is based on the same z value as the asymptotic test:

$$z = \frac{\hat{p} - p}{\sqrt{\dfrac{p(1-p)}{n}}}$$

In the discussion of the asymptotic test in "Hypothesis Test on the Proportion," it is shown that the population of z values approximates the standard normal distribution (the normal distribution with $\mu = 0$ and $\sigma = 1$). The asymptotic confidence interval uses critical values from the standard normal distribution.

Standard Normal Distribution Critical Values

A critical value for the standard normal distribution is denoted by z_q, where q is between 0 and 1. The critical value z_q is a value on the number line that marks the right q proportion of the distribution.

In Figure 4.26, the proportion of the distribution to the right of $z_{0.025}$ is 0.025. The proportion of the distribution to the right of $-z_{0.025}$ is 0.975. Because of symmetry, $-z_{0.025} = z_{0.975}$. Ninety-five percent of the distribution is between $-z_{0.025}$ and $z_{0.025}$.

Figure 4.26 Standard Normal Distribution with Critical Values

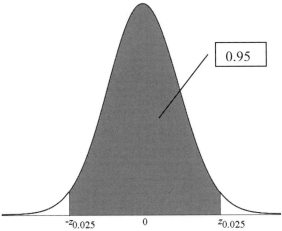

The SAS code expression for z_q is probit($1-q$), where $1-q$ represents a number. Table 4.18 contains the code expression for selected critical values.

Table 4.18 SAS Code and Selected z Critical Values

z_q	SAS code expression	critical value
$z_{0.05}$	probit(0.95)	1.6449
$z_{0.025}$	probit(0.975)	1.9600
$z_{0.005}$	probit(0.995)	2.5758

Confidence intervals are computed without the user having to supply the critical values. The SAS code expression is included here to aid in the discussion. A confidence interval is computed using the expression in Section 4.4.4.2, "Detailed Solution."

Confidence levels are generally equal to 90%, 95%, and 99%. As a group, confidence levels are represented by the notation $(1 - \alpha)100\%$. Here, α would be equal to 0.10, 0.05, and 0.01. A $(1 - \alpha)100\%$ confidence interval on the proportion has critical values $-z_{\alpha/2}$ and $z_{\alpha/2}$.

- For a 90% confidence interval ($\alpha = 0.10$), the critical values are $-z_{0.05}$ and $z_{0.05}$.
- For a 95% confidence interval ($\alpha = 0.05$), the critical values are $-z_{0.025}$ and $z_{0.025}$.
- For a 99% confidence interval ($\alpha = 0.01$), the critical values are $-z_{0.005}$ and $z_{0.005}$.

Confidence Interval on the Proportion

If 95% of the z values are between $-z_{0.025}$ and $z_{0.025}$, the interval

$$\left(\hat{p} - z_{0.025}\sqrt{\frac{p(1-p)}{n}}, \hat{p} + z_{0.025}\sqrt{\frac{p(1-p)}{n}} \right)$$

contains the population proportion p 95% of the time:

$$-z_{0.025} < z < z_{0.025}$$

$$-z_{0.025} < \frac{\hat{p} - p}{\sqrt{\dfrac{p(1-p)}{n}}} < z_{0.025}$$

$$-z_{0.025}\sqrt{\frac{p(1-p)}{n}} < \hat{p} - p < z_{0.025}\sqrt{\frac{p(1-p)}{n}}$$

$$-\hat{p} - z_{0.025}\sqrt{\frac{p(1-p)}{n}} < -p < -\hat{p} + z_{0.025}\sqrt{\frac{p(1-p)}{n}}$$

$$\hat{p} + z_{0.025}\sqrt{\frac{p(1-p)}{n}} > p > \hat{p} - z_{0.025}\sqrt{\frac{p(1-p)}{n}}$$

$$\hat{p} - z_{0.025}\sqrt{\frac{p(1-p)}{n}} < p < \hat{p} + z_{0.025}\sqrt{\frac{p(1-p)}{n}}$$

The confidence interval is created by replacing the asymptotic standard error of the proportion $\sqrt{p(1-p)/n}$ with its estimate $\sqrt{\hat{p}(1-\hat{p})/n}$.

Below is the formula for a $100(1-\alpha)\%$ asymptotic confidence interval on a population proportion p.

$$\left(\hat{p} - z_{\alpha/2}\sqrt{\frac{\hat{p}(1-\hat{p})}{n}}, \hat{p} + z_{\alpha/2}\sqrt{\frac{\hat{p}(1-\hat{p})}{n}} \right)$$

4.4.2.2   Exact Confidence Interval

The exact confidence interval on a proportion consists of all hypothesized values p_0 that would not be rejected by the exact test. A $100(1-\alpha)\%$ confidence interval is all the values between p_{lower} and p_{upper}:

- p_{lower} is the smallest value where the exact test would not reject $H_0 : p = p_{\text{lower}}$, given the significance level α.

- p_{upper} is the largest value where the exact test would not reject $H_0 : p = p_{\text{upper}}$, given the significance level α.

The upper and lower confidence limits (p_{lower} and p_{upper}) depend on critical values from the F distribution. A critical value for the F distribution is denoted by f_q, where q is between 0 and 1. The critical value f_q is a value on the number line that marks the right q proportion of the distribution. The F distribution depends on two degrees-of-freedom values: the numerator degrees of freedom (*ndf*) and the denominator degrees of freedom (*ddf*). In terms of SAS code, f_q is finv($1-q$, *ndf*, *ddf*).

With n being the sample size and x being the number in the sample with the given characteristic, the confidence limits are:

- $p_{\text{lower}} = \dfrac{1}{1 + \left(\dfrac{n - x + 1}{x f_{1 - \alpha/2}} \right)}$, where the numerator degrees-of-freedom value is $2x$ and the

  denominator degrees-of-freedom value is $2(n - x + 1)$

- $p_{\text{upper}} = \dfrac{1}{1 + \left(\dfrac{n - x}{(x + 1) f_{\alpha/2}} \right)}$, where the numerator degrees-of-freedom value is $2(x + 1)$ and

  the denominator degrees-of-freedom value is $2(n - x)$

The formulas are from Leemis and Trivedi (1996).

4.4.3 Summary of the Hypothesis Tests and Confidence Intervals

4.4.3.1 Hypothesis Test

Plan the experiment.

$$H_0 : p = p_0 \qquad H_0 : p \le p_0 \qquad H_0 : p \ge p_0 \left. \vphantom{\begin{array}{c} a \\ b \end{array}} \right\} \text{Task requires } p_0.$$
$$H_1 : p \ne p_0 \qquad H_1 : p > p_0 \qquad H_1 : p < p_0$$

The significance level is α.

Task computes the statistics.

Test of H0: Proportion = p_0	
ASE under H0	asymptotic standard error under H_0: $\sqrt{\dfrac{p_0(1-p_0)}{n}}$
Z	$z = \dfrac{\hat{p} - p_0}{\sqrt{\dfrac{p_0(1-p_0)}{n}}}$
One-sided Pr > Z	p-value for $\begin{cases} H_0 : p \le p_0 \text{ versus } H_1 : p > p_0 \text{ if } z > 0 \\ H_0 : p \ge p_0 \text{ versus } H_1 : p < p_0 \text{ if } z \le 0 \end{cases}$
Two-sided Pr > |Z|	p-value for $H_0 : p = p_0$ versus $H_1 : p \ne p_0$
Exact Test	
One-sided Pr >= P or **One-sided Pr <= P**	p-value for $H_0 : p \le p_0$ versus $H_1 : p > p_0$ if $\hat{p} > p_0$ p-value for $H_0 : p \ge p_0$ versus $H_1 : p < p_0$ if $\hat{p} \le p_0$
Two-sided = 2 * One-sided	p-value for $H_0 : p = p_0$ versus $H_1 : p \ne p_0$

Asymptotic Test (brace grouping the first four rows)

Exact Test (brace grouping the last three rows)

Apply the results.

If the p-value $< \alpha$, reject H_0. Otherwise, do not reject H_0.

Reject H_0. There is sufficient evidence to reject/support the claim that ... (claim in words). The sample proportion is significantly different/greater/less than p_0.

Do not reject H_0. There is not sufficient evidence to reject/support the claim that ... (claim in words). The sample proportion is not significantly different/greater/less than p_0.

4.4.3.2 Confidence Intervals on the Proportion

Binomial Proportion for *analysis variable* = given characteristic		
Proportion (P)	$\hat{p}$	
ASE	estimate of the asymptotic standard error: $\sqrt{\dfrac{\hat{p}(1-\hat{p})}{n}}$	
100(1• α)% Lower Conf Limit	$\hat{p} - z_{\alpha/2}\sqrt{\dfrac{\hat{p}(1-\hat{p})}{n}}$	Asymptotic Confidence Interval
100(1• α)% Upper Conf Limit	$\hat{p} + z_{\alpha/2}\sqrt{\dfrac{\hat{p}(1-\hat{p})}{n}}$	
Exact Conf Limits		
100(1• α)% Lower Conf Limit	Smallest value that would not be rejected by a two-sided exact test with significance level α.	Exact Confidence Interval
100(1• α)% Upper Conf Limit	Largest value that would not be rejected by a two-sided exact test with significance level α.	

4.4.4 Example 4.5: Asymptotic Hypothesis Test and Confidence Interval

The asymptotic hypothesis test and estimation procedures are worked out in detail for Example 4.5.

4.4.4.1 Dental Survey

A study is performed to investigate the rate of dental caries (cavities) among school children in a community. One hundred children are randomly selected and given clinical examinations.

The results are in the CommOne column of the Dental_survey data set in the Appendix. Below, Dental_survey is in a data grid.

	dental_survey (read-only)	
	⚠ **CommOne**	⚠ **CommTwo**
1	N	N
2	N	N
3	N	N
4	N	N
5	N	N
6	N	N
7	C	N
8	N	C
9	N	C
10	N	N

The CommOne column contains the two distinct values: C and N.

The letter C indicates a child with dental caries; the letter N indicates a child with no dental caries.

The value N represents the characteristic of interest, "no dental caries."

The statistics for this example are based on $\hat{p} = x/n$, where x is the number of N's in the sample.

The One-Way Frequencies task selects the first value in "order" for analysis. Order is defined in a number of ways. Here, N is selected for analysis because the order is Data set order. See Figure 4.29.

Example 4.5.1
Test the claim that more than 90% of the children in the community have no dental caries. Let α = 0.05. (Since $np_0(1 - p_0) = 100 \cdot 0.9 \cdot 0.1 = 9$, the asymptotic test is used.)

Example 4.5.2
Estimate the percentage of children in the community that have no dental caries. Construct a 95% confidence interval on that percentage.

4.4.4.2   Detailed Solutions
To begin the analysis, the Summary Tables task is used to compute the frequencies of the values in CommOne. See Output 4.5.

Output 4.5 Summary Tables Output for Example 4.5

Summary Tables

CommOne	
C	**N**
N 7	93

Example 4.5.1

The claim is that "more than 90% of the children in the community have no dental caries."

- The claim in terms of a proportion is: The proportion of children in the community with no dental caries is more than 0.90.
- Symbolically, this is " $p > 0.90$ ".

Plan the task.

$H_0 : p \leq 0.90$

$H_1 : p > 0.90$

$\alpha = 0.05$

Compute the statistics.

$$\hat{p} = \frac{93}{100} = 0.93$$

$$z = \frac{\hat{p} - p_0}{\sqrt{\frac{p_0(1 - p_0)}{n}}} = \frac{0.93 - 0.90}{\sqrt{\frac{(0.90)(0.10)}{100}}} = 1$$

Referring to Table 4.14:

p-value $= P(Z > 1) = 1 - \text{probnorm}(1) = 0.1587$

Apply the results.

Since p-value ≥ 0.05, do not reject H_0. There is not sufficient evidence to support the claim that more than 90% of the children in the community have no dental caries. The sample percentage, 93%, is not significantly greater than 90%.

Example 4.5.2

The estimate of the population proportion is $\hat{p} = \frac{93}{100} = 0.93$.

Since $n\hat{p}(1 - \hat{p}) = 100 \cdot 0.93 \cdot 0.07 = 6.51$, the asymptotic confidence interval is used.

Referring to Table 4.18:

$$z_{0.025} = \text{probit}(.975) = 1.9600$$

A 95% confidence interval on the population proportion:

$$\left(\hat{p} - z_{.025} \sqrt{\frac{\hat{p}(1-\hat{p})}{n}}, \hat{p} + z_{.025} \sqrt{\frac{\hat{p}(1-\hat{p})}{n}} \right)$$

$$\left(0.93 - 1.9600\sqrt{\frac{(0.93)(0.07)}{100}}, 0.93 + 1.9600\sqrt{\frac{(0.93)(0.07)}{100}} \right)$$

$$(0.8800, 0.9800)$$

4.4.5 Instructions for Inference on a Proportion with the One-Way Frequencies Task

Open the One-Way Frequencies task in one of the following ways:

- From the menu bar, select **Describe ▶ One-Way Frequencies**.
- On the **Task by Category** tab of the **Task List**, go to the **Describe** section and click **One-Way Frequencies**.
- On the **Task by Name** tab of the **Task List**, double-click **One-Way Frequencies**.

The One-Way Frequencies task has five groups of options: Task Roles, Statistics, Plots, Results, and Titles. The Titles group of options is discussed in Chapter 1, "Introduction to SAS Enterprise Guide." The Titles options control the titles and the footnotes in the task output.

4.4.5.1 Task Roles

Click **Task Roles** on the selection pane to open this group of options. A variable is assigned to a role by dragging its name from **Variables to assign** to **Task roles**. See Figure 4.27. A variable may be removed from a role by dragging it back to **Variables to assign**. The right and left arrows and the resulting pop-up menus can also be used.

- **Analysis variables**: Statistics are created for each variable in this role. CommOne is assigned to this role in Figure 4.27.
- **Frequency count**: The rows of this variable list the frequencies with which the respective rows of the Analysis variables occur in the sample. If no variable is assigned to the Frequency count role, all the frequencies are assumed to be 1.

The Group analysis by role is discussed in Section 1.2.

4.4.5.2 Statistics

The options for inference on p are in the **Binomial Proportions** box. See Figure 4.28.

- Check **Asymptotic test** for that test.
- Check **Exact p-values** for both the exact test and Asymptotic test.

The hypothesis test comparison number p_0 is entered in the **Test proportion** field.

If at least one test is checked, both the asymptotic and exact confidence intervals on p are part of the output. The common Confidence level is determined here.

In Figure 4.28, an asymptotic test with $p_0 = 0.9$ and 95% confidence intervals is requested.

Frequency table options are discussed in "Instructions for Creating Frequency Distributions with the One-Way Frequencies Task" in Chapter 3, "Descriptive Statistics."

Figure 4.27 Task Roles in the One-Way Frequencies Task for Example 4.5

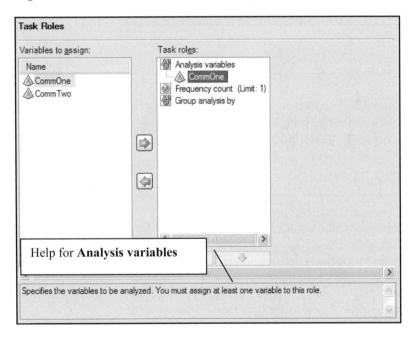

Figure 4.28 Statistics in the One-Way Frequencies Task for Example 4.5

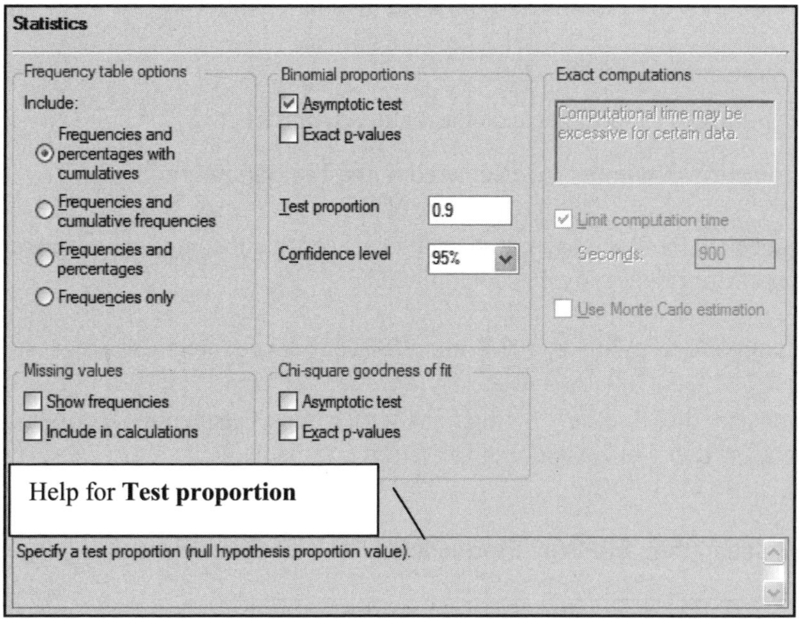

4.4.5.3   Plots

Two-dimensional horizontal and vertical frequency bar charts may be selected here. There is more on plots in "Instructions for Creating Frequency Distributions with the One-Way Frequencies Task" in Chapter 3, "Descriptive Statistics."

4.4.5.4   Results

The Results options include how the values in the Analysis variables are sorted in the output.

The One-Way Frequencies task selects the first value in "order" for a Binomial proportions analysis requested with the Statistics options.

The **Order output data by** drop-down menu lists four sorting criteria:

- **Data set order**: The order of the CommOne values in the Dental_survey data set is N and C. This is the selection in Figure 4.29.

- **Formatted values**: The Create Format task can provide alternate presentation values for data values.

- **Descending frequencies**: According to Output 4.5, the order would be N and C.

- **Unformatted values**: This is the ascending order of the values as they exist in the data set.

Figure 4.29 Results Options in the One-Way Frequencies Task for Example 4.5

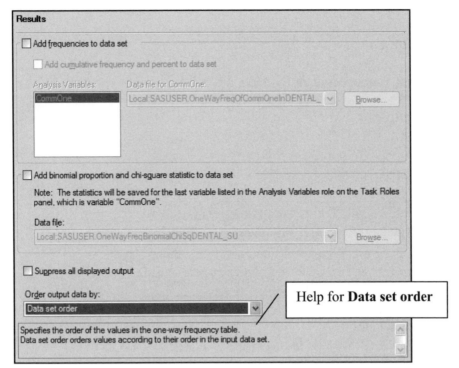

4.4.5.5   When Finished

When finished assigning variables to roles and selecting options, click **Run**. The task adds a One-Way Frequencies icon and one or more output icons to the process flow diagram. See Figure 4.30.

Figure 4.30 Example 4.5 Data, Task, and Output Icons on the Process Flow Diagram

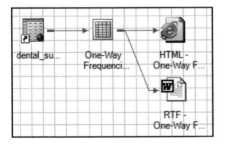

4.4.6 Task Output, Interpretation, and Analysis for Example 4.5

4.4.6.1   Task Output

Output 4.6 One-Way Frequencies for Example 4.5

One-Way Frequencies
Results

The FREQ Procedure

CommOne	Frequency	Percent	Cumulative Frequency	Cumulative Percent	
N	93	93.00	93	93.00	❶
C	7	7.00	100	100.00	

Binomial Proportion for CommOne = N		
		❷
Proportion	0.9300	❸
ASE	0.0255	❹
95% Lower Conf Limit	0.8800	❺
95% Upper Conf Limit	0.9800	❻
Exact Conf Limits		
95% Lower Conf Limit	0.8611	
95% Upper Conf Limit	0.9714	

Test of H0: Proportion = 0.9		❼
ASE under H0	0.0300	❽
Z	1.0000	❾
One-sided Pr > Z	0.1587	❿
Two-sided Pr > |Z|	0.3173	

Sample Size = 100

4.4.6.2 Interpretation

❶ CommOne values in data set order

❷ The analysis is based on the CommOne value N.

❸ Sample proportion $\hat{p}$

❹ Estimate of the asymptotic standard error: $\sqrt{\dfrac{\hat{p}(1-\hat{p})}{n}}$

❺ Lower 95% confidence limit for the population proportion: $\hat{p} - z_{\alpha/2}\sqrt{\dfrac{\hat{p}(1-\hat{p})}{n}}$

❻ Upper 95% confidence limit for the population proportion: $\hat{p} + z_{\alpha/2}\sqrt{\dfrac{\hat{p}(1-\hat{p})}{n}}$

❼ p_0

❽ Asymptotic standard error under H_0: $\sqrt{\dfrac{p_0(1-p_0)}{n}}$

❾ $z = \dfrac{\hat{p} - p_0}{\sqrt{\dfrac{p_0(1-p_0)}{n}}}$

❿ p-value for test of the hypotheses $H_0 : p \le 0.90$ versus $H_1 : p > 0.90$ since $z > 0$

4.4.6.3 Analysis

Example 4.5.1

$H_0 : p \le 0.9$

$H_1 : p > 0.9$

p-value = 0.1587. See ❿ in Output 4.6.

Since p-value ≥ 0.05, do not reject H_0. There is not sufficient evidence to support the claim that more than 90% of the children in the community have no dental caries. The sample percentage, 93%, is not significantly greater than 90%.

Example 4.5.2

See ❸, ❺, and ❻ in Output 4.6. An estimate of the proportion of children in the community with no dental caries is 0.93. A 95% confidence interval on the proportion of children in the community with no dental caries is (0.8800, 0.9800). In other words, the study shows, with 95% confidence, that between 88% and 98% of the children in the community have no dental caries.

4.4.7 Example 4.6: Exact Inference Based on Summarized Data

4.4.7.1   Rare Disease

A drug is developed for a relatively rare disease that has a mortality rate of 90%. The drug is tested on 16 patients. After one week on the new drug, 10 patients continue to show symptoms of the disease.

The raw data is not given in this example. The responses are summarized in the table below and the data grid following. The data set is Ex04_06.

symptoms	frequency
yes	10
no	6

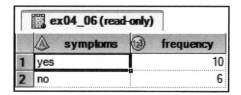

The analysis variable is symptom and the frequency variable is frequency.

The symptoms value "yes" represents the characteristic of interest, "symptoms after one week," The statistics for this example are based on *x*: the frequency of "yes" values.

The One-Way Frequencies task selects the first value in "order" for analysis. **Data set order** is selected with the Results options so that "yes" is selected for analysis.

Example 4.6.1
Test the claim that less than 90% of patients who take a new drug show symptoms after one week. Let $\alpha = 0.05$. (Since $np_0(1-p_0) = 16 \cdot 0.9 \cdot 0.1 = 1.44$, the exact test is used.)

Example 4.6.2
Estimate the percentage of patients with the disease that would show symptoms after one week on the new drug. Construct a 90% confidence interval on that percentage.

4.4.7.2   Detailed Solutions

Example 4.6.1
The claim is "less than 90% of patients who take a new drug show symptoms after one week."

The claim in terms of a proportion: Among the patients who take the new drug, the proportion with symptoms after one week is less than 0.90.

Symbolically, this is $p < 0.90$.

Plan the task.

$H_0 : p \geq 0.90$

$H_1 : p < 0.90$

$\alpha = 0.05$

Compute the statistics.

$\hat{p} = \dfrac{10}{16} = 0.625$

Referring to Table 4.14:

p-value $= P(X \leq 10) = \text{probbnml}(0.90,16,10) = 0.0033$

Apply the results.

Since p-value < 0.05, reject H_0. There is sufficient evidence to support the claim that less than 90% of patients who take a new drug show symptoms after one week. The sample percentage, 62.5%, is significantly less than 90%.

Example 4.6.2

The estimate of the population proportion is $\hat{p} = \dfrac{10}{16} = 0.625$.

Since $n\hat{p}(1-\hat{p}) = 16 \cdot 0.625 \cdot 0.375 = 3.75$, the exact confidence interval is used.

Referring to the Exact Confidence Interval section:

$$p_{\text{lower}} = \dfrac{1}{1 + \left(\dfrac{n-x+1}{x f_{1-\alpha/2}} \right)} = 1/(1+(7/(10*\text{finv}(.05,20,14)))) = 0.3910$$

$$p_{\text{upper}} = \dfrac{1}{1 + \left(\dfrac{n-x}{(x+1) f_{\alpha/2}} \right)} = 1/(1+(6/(11*\text{finv}(.95,22,12)))) = 0.8222$$

4.4.7.3　One-Way Frequencies Task

- **Task Roles**:
  - symptoms is assigned to the Analysis variables role
  - frequency is assigned to the Frequency count role
- **Statistics**:
  - **Exact p-values** is checked
  - **0.9** is entered at **Test proportion**.
  - **90%** is selected at **Confidence Level**.
- **Results**: **Data set order** is selected. The first value in analysis variable symptoms (yes) is used to compute the sample proportion and the exact statistics.

4.4.7.4　Task Output, Interpretation, and Analysis

Task Output

Output 4.7 One-Way Frequencies Output for Example 4.6

One-Way Frequencies
Results

The FREQ Procedure

symptoms	Frequency	Percent	Cumulative Frequency	Cumulative Percent	
yes	10	62.50	10	62.50	❶
no	6	37.50	16	100.00	

Binomial Proportion for symptoms = yes		
		❷
Proportion	0.6250	❸
ASE	0.1210	
90% Lower Conf Limit	0.4259	
90% Upper Conf Limit	0.8241	
Exact Conf Limits		
90% Lower Conf Limit	0.3910	❹
90% Upper Conf Limit	0.8222	❺

Test of H0: Proportion = 0.9		❻
ASE under H0	0.0750	
Z	-3.6667	
One-sided Pr < Z	0.0001	
Two-sided Pr > |Z|	0.0002	
Exact Test		
One-sided Pr <= P	0.0033	❼
Two-sided = 2 * One-sided	0.0066	

Sample Size = 16

Interpretation

❶ symptoms values in data set order

❷ The analysis is based on the symptoms value "yes."

❸ Sample proportion $\hat{p}$

❹ Lower 90% confidence limit for the population proportion

❺ Upper 90% confidence limit for the population proportion

❻ p_0

❼ p-value for test of the hypotheses $H_0 : p \geq 0.90$ versus $H_1 : p < 0.90$ since $\hat{p} < p_0$

Analysis

Example 4.6.1

$H_0 : p \geq 0.9$

$H_1 : p < 0.9$

p-value = 0.0033. See • in Output 4.7.

Since p-value < 0.05, reject H_0. There is sufficient evidence to support the claim that less than 90% of patients who take a new drug show symptoms after one week. The sample percentage, 62.5%, is significantly less than 90%.

Example 4.5.2

See ❸, ❹, and ❺ in Output 4.7. An estimate of the percentage of patients with the disease that would show symptoms after one week on the new drug is 62.5%. A 90% confidence interval on the percentage of patients with the disease that would show symptoms after one week on the new drug is (39.10%, 82.22%). In other words, the study shows, with 90% confidence, that between 39.10% and 82.22% of patients with the disease would show symptoms after one week.

4.4.8 Example 4.7: Data with More Than Two Values

4.4.8.1 Voter Poll

A poll of 423 likely voters examines candidate support a week before an election. There are three candidates in the election: Dodd, Lee, and Smith. Poll participants mark one of the three candidates or undecided. The responses are summarized in the table below and the data grid following. The data set is Ex04_07.

Candidate	Support
Dodd	58
Lee	121
Smith	227
Undecided	17

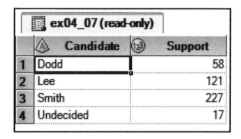

Example 4.7.1

Test the claim that Smith has support among a majority of all likely voters. Let $\alpha = 0.05$.

    a.   Determine H_0 and H_1.

    b.   Determine the p-value.

    c.   State the formal decision, the concluding sentence, and the concluding observation.

Example 4.7.2

Estimate the percentage of likely voters that support Smith. Construct a 95% confidence interval on that percentage.

4.4.8.2 One-Way Frequencies Task

- **Task Roles**:
  - Candidate is assigned to the Analysis variables role
  - Support is assigned to the Frequency count role
- **Statistics**:
  - **Asymptotic test** is checked
  - **0.5** is entered at **Test proportion**.
  - 95% is selected at **Confidence Level**.
- **Results**: **Descending frequencies** is selected so that the Candidate value Smith is first in order.

4.4.8.3 Task Output, Interpretation, and Analysis

Task Output

Output 4.8 One-Way Frequencies Output for Example 4.6

One-Way Frequencies
Results
The FREQ Procedure

❶
Candidate	Frequency	Percent	Cumulative Frequency	Cumulative Percent
Smith	227	53.66	227	53.66
Lee	121	28.61	348	82.27
Dodd	58	13.71	406	95.98
Undecided	17	4.02	423	100.00

Binomial Proportion for Candidate = Smith ❷	
Proportion	0.5366 ❸
ASE	0.0242
95% Lower Conf Limit	0.4891
95% Upper Conf Limit	0.5842
Exact Conf Limits	
95% Lower Conf Limit	0.4878
95% Upper Conf Limit	0.5849

❹

Test of H0: Proportion = 0.5 ❺	
ASE under H0	0.0243
Z	1.5073
One-sided Pr > Z	0.0659 ❻
Two-sided Pr > |Z|	0.1317

Sample Size = 423

4.4.8.4   Interpretation

❶ Candidate values in descending order of frequencies

❷ The analysis is based on the Candidate value Smith.

4.4.8.5   Analysis

Example 4.7.1

$H_0 : p \leq 0.5$

$H_1 : p > 0.5$

See ❺ in Output 4.8.

p-value = 0.0659. See ❻ in Output 4.8.

Since the p-value ≥ 0.05, do not reject H_0. There is not sufficient evidence to support the claim that Smith has a majority of support among all likely voters. The sample proportion is not significantly greater than 0.5.

Example 4.7.2

See ❸ and ❹ in Output 4.8. An estimate of the percentage of likely voters that support Smith is 53.66%. A 95% confidence interval on the percentage of likely voters that support Smith is (48.91%, 58.42%). In other words, the poll shows with 95% confidence that between 48.91% and 58.42% of likely voters support Smith.

4.5   Inference on a Population Median

This section considers inference on a *median* of a population of continuous numerical values. A population median θ (lowercase Greek *theta*) is the 50th percentile in a population of numerical values: 50% of the values are less than the median and 50% are greater.

For a symmetric distribution, the median is at the point of symmetry. If the population mean exists—sometimes it does not, at least in theory—then $\mu = \theta$. See the left distribution in Figure 4.31.

For a skewed distribution, the mean μ is shifted away from the median θ in the direction of the tail. See the right distribution in Figure 4.31.

Figure 4.31 Symmetric and Skewed Probability Distributions

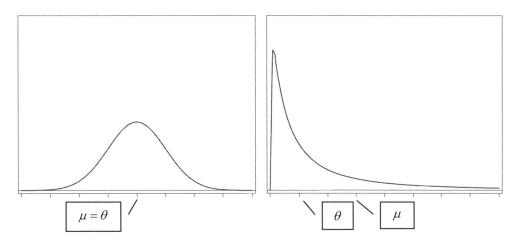

This section presents the Sign Test and the Wilcoxon Signed Rank Test. These tests are *nonparametric* or *distribution-free* alternatives to the one-sample *t* test on a mean.

The one-sample *t* test on a mean is a parametric test. It is based on the parameters of a specific probability distribution. The one-sample *t* test on a mean is based on the unknown parameters μ and σ from a normally distributed population. The test statistic, *t* value $= \left(\bar{x} - \mu_0\right)\big/\left(s/\sqrt{n}\right)$, involves estimates of these parameters. For sufficiently large sample sizes, the assumption of a normal distribution is relaxed. But the reliance on the parameters μ and σ continues.

The Sign Test and the Wilcoxon Signed Rank Test are not based on parameters of a specific probability distribution. Both tests do use the fact that a population median θ—a parameter— exists. But the median always exists. This is not a special assumption.

The Wilcoxon Signed Rank Test and the Sign Test are often considered when the combination of an insufficiently large sample size and a lack of normality in the data—generally outliers and skewness—cause the *t* test to be ineffective.

4.5.1 Hypothesis Test on the Median

4.5.1.1 Null and Alternative Hypotheses

The Sign Test and the Wilcoxon Signed Rank Test are tests on a population median θ. Both tests are analogous to the one-sample *t* test for the population mean μ. The following are the three possible pairs of null and alternative hypotheses, with θ_0 being the given comparison number:

$H_0 : \theta = \theta_0$	$H_0 : \theta \le \theta_0$	$H_0 : \theta \ge \theta_0$
$H_1 : \theta \ne \theta_0$	$H_1 : \theta > \theta_0$	$H_1 : \theta < \theta_0$

4.5.1.2 Sign Test

The Sign Test is based on the number of observations above θ_0, which is the population median under the assumption that H_0 is true. The test eliminates the effect of outliers. The Sign Test only requires that the data be continuous.

The Sign Test is an application of the binomial experiment.

- The number of repetitions is n_t: the number of observations not equal to θ_0. Observations equal to θ_0 are not included in the Sign Test calculations.

- The observations are assumed to be randomly selected.

- The event of interest, called a *success* in the binomial experiment, is an observation being above θ_0.

- Under H_0, the probability of an observation being above θ_0 is 0.5.

- n^+ is the number of observations above θ_0.

Under H_0, n^+ follows a binomial probability distribution with n_t trails and probability of success 0.5. The expected value for n^+ is $n_t(0.5) = n_t/2$. The Distributions task reports the statistic $M = n^+ - \dfrac{n_t}{2}$. In the Sign Test, n^+ is the test statistic and determines the *p*-value.

p-Value

The technical definition of the *p*-value depends on the alternative hypothesis H_1. See Table 4.19. The random variable Y represents a future value of the test statistic and follows the binomial distribution where the probability of success is 0.5 and the number of trials is n_t.

Table 4.19 *p*-Values for the Sign Test

Hypotheses	*p* - value =	Compute Dialog Expression
$H_0 : \theta = \theta_0$		
$H_1 : \theta \neq \theta_0$	$2P(Y \geq n^+)$, if $n^+ - \dfrac{n_t}{2} \geq 0$	$2*(1 - \text{probbnml}(0.5, n_t, n^+))$
	$2P(Y \leq n^+)$, if $n^+ - \dfrac{n_t}{2} < 0$	$2*\text{probbnml}(0.5, n_t, n^+)$
$H_0 : \theta \leq \theta_0$		
$H_1 : \theta > \theta_0$	$P(Y \geq n^+)$	$1 - \text{probbnml}(0.5, n_t, n^+)$
$H_0 : \theta \geq \theta_0$		
$H_1 : \theta < \theta_0$	$P(Y \leq n^+)$	$\text{probbnml}(0.5, n_t, n^+)$

4.5.1.3 Wilcoxon Signed Rank Test

The Wilcoxon Signed Rank Test is based on the ranked differences between the observations and θ_0, the population median under H_0. Positive differences are given positive ranks and negative differences are given negative ranks. Zero differences are ignored. The use of signed ranks instead of the actual values greatly reduces the effect of outliers.

The Wilcoxon Signed Rank Test requires that the observations follow a symmetric and continuous distribution.

As an example, signed ranks are assigned in Table 4.20. Let the x values be data and let $\theta_0 = 10$.

- Signed ranks are based on the absolute value of the differences: $|x - \theta_0| = 9, 5, 2, (0$ differences are ignored), 5, 6, 490. Average ranks are used in the case of ties.
  - The smallest absolute value is 2 and is ranked 1.
  - The second and third smallest absolute values are both 5. Because of the tie, both values are given the average rank of $(2+3)/2 = 2.5$.
  - The next absolute values in order are 6, 9, and 490. They are given ranks 4, 5, and 6, respectively. Note that the rank of the largest absolute value would be 6 regardless of how large it is.
- The r values are the *signed* ranks. Positive differences $x - \theta_0$ are given positive ranks and negative differences $x - \theta_0$ are given negative ranks.

The number of nonzero differences is represented by n_t. In Table 4.20, $n_t = 6$.

Table 4.20 Signed Ranks of Nonzero Differences

x	$x - \theta_0$	r
1	−9	−5
5	−5	−2.5
8	−2	−1
10	0	.
15	5	2.5
16	6	4
500	490	6

Under H_0, θ_0 is the population median. One would then expect the ranks to be evenly distributed between the positive and negative differences $x - \theta_0$. Therefore, under H_0, the mean of the signed ranks is expected to be 0. When $n_t > 20$, the Wilcoxon Signed Rank Test is the one-sample t test applied to the signed ranks. The test statistic is:

$$t \text{ Statistic} = \frac{\bar{r} - 0}{\left(\dfrac{s_r}{\sqrt{n_t}}\right)}, \text{ where } \begin{cases} \bar{r} \text{ is the mean of the signed ranks} \\ s_r \text{ is the standard deviation of the signed ranks} \\ n_t \text{ is number of nonzero differences} \end{cases}$$

When $n_t \leq 20$, the p-value is determined by tables within the SAS program.

The Distribution task reports the statistic $s = \sum r^+ - n_t(n_t + 1)/4$: $\sum r^+$ is the sum of the positive ranks and $n_t(n_t + 1)/4$ is the expected sum of positive ranks under H_0. The relationship between $\overline{r}$ and s is $\overline{r} = 2s/n_t$.

p-Value

The technical definition of the p-value depends on the alternative hypothesis H_1. See Table 4.21. The random variable T represents a future value of the test statistic and follows the t distribution with $n_t - 1$ degrees of freedom.

Table 4.21 p-Values for Wilcoxon Signed Rank Test When $n_t > 20$

Hypotheses	p - value =	Compute Dialog Expression
$H_0 : \theta = \theta_0$ $H_1 : \theta \neq \theta_0$	$2P(T \geq \lvert t \text{ Statistic}\rvert)$	$2*(1 - \text{probt}(\text{abs}(t \text{ Statistic}), n_t - 1))$
$H_0 : \theta \leq \theta_0$ $H_1 : \theta > \theta_0$	$P(T \geq t \text{ Statistic})$	$1 - \text{probt}(t \text{ Statistic}, n_t - 1)$
$H_0 : \theta \geq \theta_0$ $H_1 : \theta < \theta_0$	$P(T \leq t \text{ Statistic})$	$\text{probt}(t \text{ Statistic}, n_t - 1)$

4.5.1.4　Decision and Conclusions

The formal decision and concluding sentence do not change from the one-sample tests discussed in Section 4.3. The concluding observation depends on the particular statistics involved in the test.

If the p-value is small, the data agrees with H_1. If the p-value is less than the significance level, the risk of making a Type I error is acceptable. Therefore, the p-value decision rule is the following:

If the p-value $< \alpha$, reject H_0. Otherwise, do not reject H_0.

Since a hypothesis test begins with the assumption that H_0 is true, concluding a hypothesis test requires one of the following formal statements:

- Reject H_0.
- Do not reject H_0.

When the claim is equivalent to the null hypothesis, the concluding sentence uses the word *reject*. The concluding sentence becomes an expanded version of the formal decision.

When the claim is equivalent to the alternative hypothesis, the concluding sentence uses the word *support*. If the data supports the rejection of H_0, the data supports H_1. If the data does not support rejection of H_0, the data cannot support H_1.

Table 4.22 Concluding Sentences

Formal Statistical Decision	Claim stated as H_0	Claim stated as H_1
Reject H_0.	There is sufficient evidence to reject the claim that ... (claim in words).	There is sufficient evidence to support the claim that ... (claim in words).
Do not reject H_0.	There is not sufficient evidence to reject the claim that ... (claim in words).	There is not sufficient evidence to support the claim that ... (claim in words).

"Significantly different" is a phrase that is commonly used in reporting the results of a hypothesis test. It is equivalent to saying that H_0 has been rejected. With regard to the one-sample test on a median, it always refers to the sample median $\tilde{x}$ and the θ_0 value. The phrase may include the word *different*, *greater*, or *less* depending on the H_1 inequality. See Table 4.23.

Table 4.23 Concluding Observations: Inequality Equivalent to H_1

Reject H_0.	The sample median is significantly different/greater/less than θ_0.
Do not reject H_0.	The sample median is not significantly different/greater/less than θ_0.

4.5.2 Estimation of the Median

The point estimate of the population median θ is the sample median $\tilde{x}$ (x-tilde). Both the point estimate and the confidence interval are based on ordered data. The use of the parentheses in the subscript indicates ordered data:

$$x_{(1)} \leq x_{(2)} \leq \ldots \leq x_{(n)}$$

The smallest value is $x_{(1)}$ and the largest value is $x_{(n)}$.

The sample median is:

- $\tilde{x} = \dfrac{x_{(n/2)} + x_{(n/2+1)}}{2}$ when n is even

- $\tilde{x} = x_{((n+1)/2)}$ when n is odd

The limits for a $(1-\alpha)100\%$ confidence interval on the median θ are applications of the binomial distribution where Y is the number of successes in n_t trials and the probability of success is $p = 0.5$. Let k be the largest integer value for Y such that the cumulative probability is at most $\alpha/2$: $P(Y \le k) \le \alpha/2$.

An approximate $(1-\alpha)100\%$ confidence interval on θ has values greater than or equal to $x_{(k+1)}$ and less than $x_{(n-k)}$. In closed and opened interval notation, that is:

$$\left[x_{(k+1)}, x_{(n-k)} \right)$$

The actual probability associated with the confidence interval is
$$P(k+1 \le Y < n-k) = P(Y \le n-k-1) - P(Y \le k).$$

In theory, this interval consists of all values θ_0 for the hypotheses $H_0: \theta = \theta_0$ and $H_1: \theta \ne \theta_0$ that would not be rejected by the Sign Test. The requirement by the Sign Test that the data be continuous implies in theory that all the sample values are different. Assume that is the case.

- If $x_{(k+1)} \le \theta_0 \le \tilde{x}$, then $n^+ \le n-(k+1)$. If θ_0 equals a sample value, $n_t = n-1$.
  Computing the p-value for the Sign Test:
  $$P(Y \ge n^+ \text{ with the number of trials } n_t = n-1)$$
  $$\ge P(Y \ge n-(k+1) \text{ with the number of trials } n_t = n-1)$$
  $$= P(Y \le k+1 \text{ with the number of trials } n_t = n-1)$$
  $$\ge P(Y \le k+1 \text{ with the number of trials } n_t = n)$$
  $$> \alpha/2$$

  In which case, p-value $> \alpha$. If θ_0 does not equal a sample value and $n_t = n$, the steps are similar and the result is the same.

- If $\tilde{x} < \theta_0 < x_{(n-k)}$, then $n^+ \ge k+1$. If θ_0 equals a sample value, $n_t = n-1$. Computing the p-value:
  $$P(Y \le n^+ \text{ with the number of trials } n_t = n-1)$$
  $$\ge P(Y \le k+1 \text{ with the number of trials } n_t = n-1)$$
  $$\ge P(Y \le k+1 \text{ with the number of trials } n_t = n)$$
  $$> \alpha/2$$

  In which case, p-value $> \alpha$. If θ_0 does not equal a sample value and $n_t = n$, the steps are similar and the result is the same.

4.5.3 Summary of the Hypothesis Tests and Confidence Interval

4.5.3.1 Hypothesis Tests

Plan the experiment.

$$H_0 : \theta = \theta_0 \qquad H_0 : \theta \leq \theta_0 \qquad H_0 : \theta \geq \theta_0$$
$$H_1 : \theta \neq \theta_0 \qquad H_1 : \theta > \theta_0 \qquad H_1 : \theta < \theta_0$$
$$\left. \right\} \text{Task requires } \theta_0.$$

The significance level is α.

Task computes the statistics.

Tests for Location: Mu0=θ_0				
Test		**Statistic**		**p Value**
Student's t	t	$t = (\overline{x} - \theta_0)/(s/\sqrt{n})$	Pr > |t|	*p*-value for $H_0 : \mu = \theta_0$ versus $H_1 : \mu \neq \theta_0$
Sign	M	$M = n^+ - n_t/2$	Pr >= |M|	*p*-value for $H_0 : \theta = \theta_0$ versus $H_1 : \theta \neq \theta_0$
Signed Rank	S	$s = \sum r^+ - n_t(n_t+1)/4$	Pr >= |S|	*p*-value for $H_0 : \theta = \theta_0$ versus $H_1 : \theta \neq \theta_0$

Determining the *p*-value:

Hypotheses	
$H_0 : \mu$ or $\theta = \theta_0$ $H_1 : \mu$ or $\theta \neq \theta_0$	*p*-value = p Value
$H_0 : \mu$ or $\theta \leq \theta_0$ $H_1 : \mu$ or $\theta > \theta_0$	*p*-value = $\begin{cases} 0.5(\text{p Value}), & \text{if Statistic} > 0 \\ 1 - 0.5(\text{p Value}), & \text{if Statistic} \leq 0 \end{cases}$
$H_0 : \mu$ or $\theta \geq \theta_0$ $H_1 : \mu$ or $\theta < \theta_0$	*p*-value = $\begin{cases} 1 - 0.5(\text{p Value}), & \text{if Statistic} \geq 0 \\ 0.5(\text{p Value}), & \text{if Statistic} < 0 \end{cases}$

Apply the results.

If the *p-v*alue $< \alpha$, reject H_0. Otherwise, do not reject H_0.

- Reject H_0. There is sufficient evidence to reject/support the claim that ... (claim in words). The sample mean/median is significantly different/greater/less than θ_0.

- Do not reject H_0. There is not sufficient evidence to reject/support the claim that ... (claim in words). The sample mean/median is not significantly different/greater/less than θ_0.

4.5.3.2 Confidence Interval on the Median

LCL and UCL stand for *lower confidence limit* and *upper confidence limit* in the task output.

		(1-α)100% Confidence Limits Distribution Free		Order Statistics		
Quantile	Estimate			LCL Rank	UCL Rank	Coverage
50% Median	$\tilde{x}$	$x_{(k+1)}$	$x_{(n-k)}$	k	$n-k$	$1-2P(Y \le k)$

4.5.4 Example 4.8: Inference on the Median

4.5.4.1 Net Weight

A company monitors the amount of cereal put into boxes. The target weight is 482 grams. Boxes are randomly selected shortly after being filled. The data below represent the net weight in grams. The values are in the weight column of data set Ex04_08.

224	458	460	465	466	467	467	468	469	470	472	472	472
475	477	479	480	481	482	482	483	484	486	491	496	

Example 4.8.1

Use the Sign Test to test the claim that the median net weight is 480 grams for all boxes filled at the company. Let $\alpha = 0.05$.

Example 4.8.2

Estimate the median net weight for all boxes filled at the company. Construct a 95% confidence interval.

Example 4.8.3

Use the Wilcoxon Signed Rank Test to test the claim that the median net weight is 480 grams for all boxes filled at the company. Let $\alpha = 0.05$.

Example 4.8.4

Construct a histogram and a box-and-whisker plot.

4.5.4.2 Detailed Solutions

Example 4.8.1

Plan the task.

$H_0 : \theta = 480$

$H_1 : \theta \neq 480$

$\alpha = 0.05$

Compute the statistics.

The total number of observations is $n = 25$. Since 1 observation equals 480, $n_t = 24$. The number of observations above 480 is $n^+ = 8$.

$$M = n^+ - \frac{n_t}{2} = 8 - \frac{24}{2} = -4$$

Since $n^+ - \frac{n_t}{2} = 8 - \frac{24}{2} = -4 < 0$, the *p*-value is $2P(Y \leq 8) =$

$2 * \text{probbnml}(0.5, 24, 8) = 2(0.07579) = 0.15158$.

Apply the results.

Since the *p*-value > 0.05, do not reject H_0. There is not sufficient evidence to reject the claim that the median net weight is 480 grams for all boxes filled at the company.

Table 4.24 Ranks and Cumulative Binomial Probabilities for Example 4.8

Weight	y	$P(Y \le y)$
224	1	0.00000077
458	2	0.00000972
460	3	0.00007826
465	4	0.00045526
466	5	0.00203866
467	6	0.00731665
467	7	0.02164263
468	8	0.05387607
469	9	0.11476147
470	10	0.21217811
472	11	0.34501898
472	12	0.50000000
472	13	0.65498102
475	14	0.78782189
477	15	0.88523853
479	16	0.94612393
480	17	0.97835737
481	18	0.99268335
482	19	0.99796134
482	20	0.99954474
483	21	0.99992174
484	22	0.99999028
486	23	0.99999923
491	24	0.99999997
496	25	1.00000000

Example 4.8.2

With a 95% confidence interval, $\alpha/2 = 0.025$. From Table 4.24, $k = 7$ since $P(Y \le 7)$ is the largest probability less than or equal to 0.025.

An approximately 95% confidence interval on θ is:

$$\left[x_{(8)}, x_{(18)} \right) = \left[468, 481 \right)$$

The actual probability associated with the confidence interval is $P(k+1 \le Y < n-k) = 0.97835737 - 0.02164263 = 0.956715$, or 95.6715%.

Table 4.25 Differences and Signed Ranks Example 4.8

weight	diff	signed_rank
224	-256	-24
458	-22	-23
460	-20	-22
465	-15	-20
466	-14	-19
467	-13	-17.5
467	-13	-17.5
468	-12	-16
469	-11	-14.5
470	-10	-13
472	-8	-11
472	-8	-11
472	-8	-11
475	-5	-8
477	-3	-5.5
479	-1	-1.5
480	0	.
481	1	1.5
482	2	3.5
482	2	3.5
483	3	5.5
484	4	7
486	6	9
491	11	14.5
496	16	21

Example 4.8.3

Plan the task.

$H_0 : \theta = 480$

$H_1 : \theta \neq 480$

$\alpha = 0.05$

Compute the statistics.

The data is in the weight column in Table 4.25. The diff column shows the data values minus θ_0: diff = weight − 480.

A signed_rank value is the sign of diff times the average rank of the absolute value of diff. The zero diff value is not ranked.

The number of nonzero differences is $n_t = 24$.

$$s = \sum r^+ - n_t \left(n_t + 1\right)/4 = \left(1.5 + 3.5 + 3.5 + 5.5 + 7 + 9 + 14.5 + 21\right) + \frac{24\left(25\right)}{4} = 65.5 - 150 = -84.5$$

Since $n_t > 20$, the Wilcoxon Signed Rank Test is the one-sample t test for a mean applied to the signed ranks. The results are below:

T-Tests			
Variable	DF	t Value	Pr > |t|
signed_rank	23	-2.72	0.0123

Since the p-value < 0.05, reject H_0. There is sufficient evidence to reject the claim that the median net weight is 480 grams for all boxes filled at the company.

Example 4.8.4
See Output 4.9. The plots are created with the Distributions Analysis task.

4.5.5 Instructions for Applying the Distributions Task for Nonparametric Tests

Open the Distributions task in one of the following ways:

- From the menu bar, select **Describe ▶ Distribution Analysis**.
- On the **Task by Category** tab of the **Task List**, go to the Describe section and click **Distribution Analysis**.
- On the **Task by Name** tab of the **Task List**, double-click **Distribution Analysis**.

Application of Distribution Analysis for nonparametric tests uses the Task Roles, Plots, and Tables option groups. Titles are discussed in general in Chapter 1, "Introduction to SAS Enterprise Guide." The Titles options control the titles and the footnotes in the task output.

Use the selection pane on the left to navigate through assigning data columns to roles and selecting options.

4.5.5.1 Task Roles

Click **Task Roles** on the selection pane to open this group of options. A variable is assigned to a role by dragging its name from **Variables to assign** to a role in **Task Roles**. See Figure 4.32. A variable may be removed from a role by dragging it back to **Variables to assign**. The right and left arrows and the resulting pop-up menus can also be used.

Analysis variables: Requested statistics and plots are computed for each variable in this role. The order that the variables are listed here is the order that they are listed in the output. See Figure 4.32.

Classification variables: Statistics and plots are computed for each group created by the variables in this role. The statistics for each group are on a separate page. Plots for each group are put in single comparative graphs.

The roles Group analysis by, Frequency count, and Relative weight are discussed in Section 1.2.

In Figure 4.32, the data is in the Ex04_08 data set. The variable weight is assigned to the Analysis variables role.

Figure 4.32 Task Roles in the Distribution Analysis Task for Example 4.8

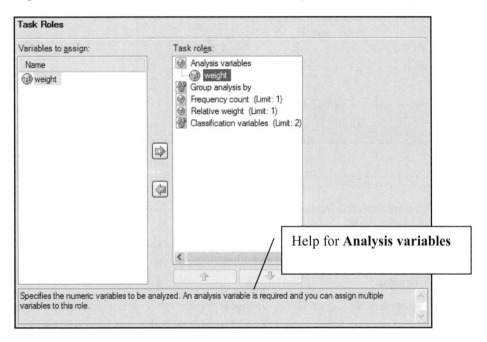

4.5.5.2 Plots > Appearance

The **Histogram Plot** and **Box Plot** are selected in Figure 4.33. The **Background color** is set to white for both plots.

The Distribution Analysis task does not produce interactive graphs.

Figure 4.33 Plots Appearance Options in the Distribution Analysis Task for Example 4.8

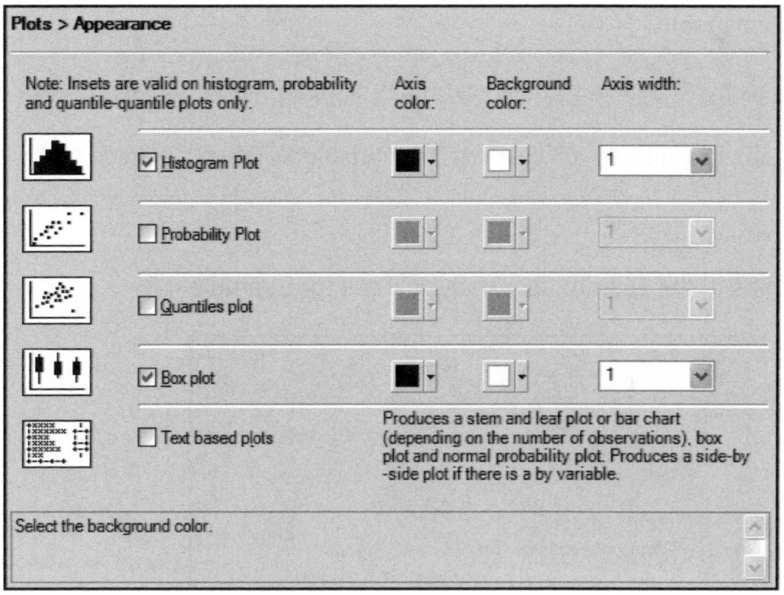

4.5.5.3 Tables

The following tables are selected for nonparametric tests:

- **Basic Measures**: The sample mean, median, mode, standard deviation, variance, range, and interquartile range are shown in this table.

- **Tests of Location**:

  ○ The hypotheses $H_0 : \mu$ or $\theta = \theta_0$ versus $H_1 : \mu$ or $\theta \neq \theta_0$ are tested with one sample t test, Sign Test, and Signed Rank Test. The test statistics and p-values are shown in this table.

  ○ The value θ_0 is entered here. See Figure 4.34 where $\theta_0 = 480$.

- **Quantiles**:

  ○ A list of quantiles, including the sample median $\tilde{x}$, are shown in this table.

  ○ Check **Distribution free** for nonparametric confidence intervals on the population quantiles, including θ. The **Confidence level** is entered here. See Figure 4.34. The default confidence level is 95%.

  ○ **Symmetric** confidence limits is the default and appropriate for the confidence interval on θ. If confidence limits are missing for larger and smaller population quantiles, **Asymmetric** can be selected. In that case, symmetric confidence limits are applied if they exist; asymmetric confidence limits are applied otherwise.

Figure 4.34 Test for Locations (Top) and Quantiles (Bottom) in the Tables Options in the Distribution Analysis Task for Example 4.8

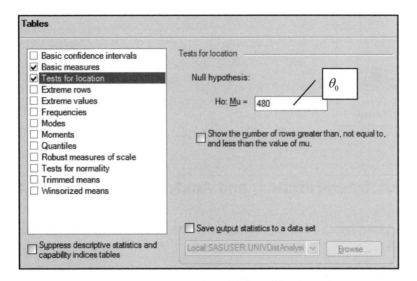

4.5.5.4 When Finished

When finished assigning variables to roles and selecting options, click **Run**. The task adds a Distribution Analysis icon and one or more output icons to the process flow diagram. See Figure 4.35.

Figure 4.35 Example 4.8 Data, Task, and Output Icons on the Process Flow Diagram

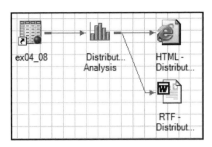

4.5.6 Task Output, Interpretation, and Analysis for Example 4.8

4.5.6.1   Task Output

Output 4.9 Distribution Analysis Output for Example 4.8

Distribution analysis of: weight

The UNIVARIATE Procedure
Variable: weight

Basic Statistical Measures			
Location		**Variability**	
Mean	465.0400	**Std Deviation**	51.08121
Median	472.0000	**Variance**	2609
Mode	472.0000	**Range**	272.00000
		Interquartile Range	15.00000

❶ (marks Median row)

Tests for Location: Mu0=480				
Test		**Statistic**	**p Value**	
Student's t	t	-1.46433	**Pr > |t|**	0.1561
Sign	M	-4	**Pr >= |M|**	0.1516
Signed Rank	S	-84.5	**Pr >= |S|**	0.0123

❷ (Tests for Location header) ❸ (Student's t row) ❹ (Sign row) ❺ (Signed Rank row)

Quantiles (Definition 5)						
		95% Confidence Limits Distribution Free		Order Statistics		
Quantile	**Estimate**			**LCL Rank**	**UCL Rank**	**Coverage**
100% Max	496					
99%	496	.	.	.	.	.
95%	491	486	496	23	25	59.55
90%	486	482	496	20	25	89.48
75% Q3	482	477	491	15	24	96.33
50% Median	472	468	481	8	18	95.67
25% Q1	467	458	472	2	11	96.33
10%	460	224	467	1	6	89.48
5%	458	224	460	1	3	59.55
1%	224	.	.	.	.	.
0% Min	224					

❻ (99%) ❼ (50% Median) ❻ (1%)

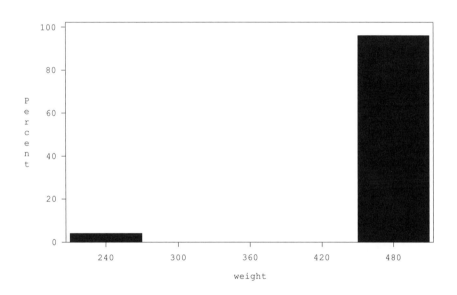

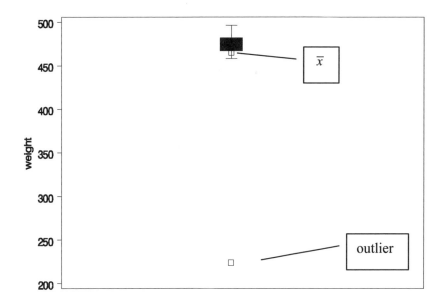

Comment

The box-and-whisker plot produced by the Distribution Analysis task identifies the sample mean $\bar{x}$. In the graph above, $\bar{x}$ is a black box and the outlier is a blue box.

4.5.6.2   Interpretation

❶ Sample median $\tilde{x}$

❷ The hypotheses for Student's one-sample t test are $H_0 : \mu = 480$ versus $H_1 : \mu \neq 480$. The hypotheses for the Sign Test and the Signed Rank Test are $H_0 : \theta = 480$ versus $H_0 : \theta \neq 480$.

❸ Results of the Student's one-sample t test

❹ Results of the Sign Test

❺ Results of the Signed Rank Test

❻ Symmetric confidence limits do not exist in this sample for the 99th and 1st quantile.

❼ Inference on θ: The estimate is $\tilde{x} = 472$. An approximately 95% confidence interval is $[468, 481)$ based on the ranks of the lower and upper confidence limits: $\left[x_{(8)}, x_{(18)} \right)$. The actual probability associated with the confidence interval is 95.67%.

4.5.6.3   Analysis

Example 4.8.1

$H_0 : \theta = 480$

$H_1 : \theta \neq 480$

$\alpha = 0.05$

p-value $= 0.1516$. See ❹ in Output 4.9.

Since the *p*-value > 0.05, do not reject H_0. There is not sufficient evidence to reject the claim that the median net weight is 480 grams for all boxes filled at the company.

Example 4.8.2

An approximately 95% confidence interval is $[468, 481)$. See ❼ in Output 4.9.

Example 4.8.3

$H_0 : \theta = 480$

$H_1 : \theta \neq 480$

$\alpha = 0.05$

p-value = 0.1516. See ❺ in Output 4.49.

Since the *p*-value < 0.05, do not reject H_0. There is sufficient evidence to reject the claim that the median net weight is 480 grams for all boxes filled at the company.

4.5.7 Comparing Student's *t* Test, the Sign Test, and the Signed Rank Test

The Signed Rank Test in the Tests for Location table in Output 4.9 supports rejection of the null hypothesis while Student's one-sample *t* test and the Sign Test do not. If one can assume that the underlying distribution of the population is symmetric and μ exists, then all three tests are on the same parameter. So, does the data support rejection of H_0 or not?

It does. A decision should be based on the Signed Rank Test.

- With the large outlier, the *t* test is not expected to be effective.
- The Signed Rank Test is expected to be effective when the data is at least roughly symmetric and there are few large outliers. This is the case in Example 4.8.
- The Sign Test may not be effective when the Signed Rank Test is. The Sign Test does not take into account the size of the observations. To reject a null hypothesis, the number of values above θ_0 need to be relatively large (if $\theta_0 \leq \tilde{x}$) or small (if $\tilde{x} < \theta_0$).

The tests are compared in four situations below.

4.5.7.1 Data from a Normally Distributed Population

Student's one-sample *t* test is best when the data comes from a normally distributed population. But the Signed Rank Test generally does almost as well. The Sign Test is generally effective only when the number of values above θ_0 is relatively extreme.

The data below is from a normally distributed population with $\mu = \theta = 472$. It is the same data as in Example 4.8 but without the outlier 224. The values are in the weight2 column of data set Ex04_08b.

458	460	465	466	467	467	468	469	470	472	472	472
475	477	479	480	481	482	482	483	484	486	491	496

In the Tests for Location table in Output 4.10, the Student's one-sample *t* test correctly rejects $H_0 : \mu = 480$ and the Signed Rank Test correctly rejects $H_0 : \theta = 480$. The Sign Test can be ignored as being not sensitive enough to identify the difference as significant.

Output 4.10 Distribution Analysis with weight2 Values

Basic Statistical Measures			
Location		**Variability**	
Mean	475.0833	Std Deviation	9.55950
Median	473.5000	Variance	91.38406
Mode	472.0000	Range	38.00000
		Interquartile Range	14.50000

Tests for Location: Mu0=480				
Test		**Statistic**	**p Value**	
Student's t	t	-2.51966	Pr > |t|	0.0191
Sign	M	-3.5	Pr >= |M|	0.2100
Signed Rank	S	-72.5	Pr >= |S|	0.0237

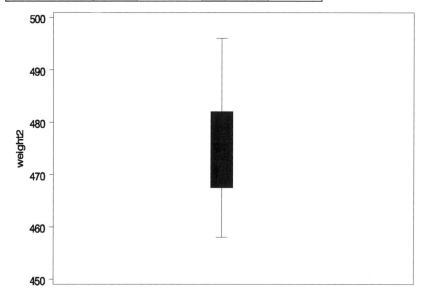

4.5.7.2 Data with Some Large Outliers

The Signed Rank Test often performs better than the Student's one-sample *t* test when deviation from normality is significant but limited. The Sign Test is generally effective only when the number of values above θ_0 is relatively extreme.

The large outlier in Example 4.8 causes the *t* test to be ineffective because of how much it increases the sample standard deviation. The weight data in Example 4.8 is the weight2 data shown earlier with the addition of the outlier 224. Note the changes in the following statistics from the normal weight2 data to the outlier-containing weight data. The statistics for weight2 are in Output 4.10 and the statistics for weight are in Output 4.9.

- $\bar{x} = 475.0833$ for weight2 becomes $\bar{x} = 465.0400$ for weight.
- $s = 9.55950$ for weight2 becomes $s = 51.08121$ for weight.
- $t = -2.51966$ for weight2 becomes $t = -1.46433$ for weight.
- *p*-value $= 0.0191$ for weight2 becomes *p*-value $= 0.1561$ for weight.

The effect of the outlier on the Signed Rank Test is limited to the size of the largest rank. The statistics change little. If anything, they are more significant.

- $S = -72.5$ for weight2 becomes $S = -84.5$ for weight.
- *p*-value $= 0.0237$ for weight2 becomes *p*-value $= 0.0123$ for weight.

The changes in the Sign Test statistics are mostly due to the change in the sample size.

4.5.7.3 Data with Many Large Outliers

Numerous outliers can result in both the Student's one-sample *t* test and the Signed Rank Test being ineffective. The Sign Test is still effective if the number of values above θ_0 is relatively extreme.

The data below is from a population with $\theta = 472$. The values are in the weight3 column of data set Ex04_08b.

```
324   451   452   460   462   465   469   469   470   471   472   472
472   475   475   475   477   479   482   490   509   540   586   766
```

A large number of large outliers are identified in a box-and-whisker plot in Output 4.11. The Sign Test correctly rejects $H_0 : \theta = 480$.

The outliers cause a very large sample standard deviation, which results in a small *t* test. The ranks of the positive differences weight3 $- 480$ are large. This sufficiently balances the more numerous but mostly smaller negative ranks. The result is a small *t* test on the signed ranks.

Output 4.11 Distribution Analysis with Weight3 Values

Basic Statistical Measures			
Location		Variability	
Mean	485.9583	Std Deviation	73.52461
Median	472.0000	Variance	5406
Mode	472.0000	Range	442.00000
		Interquartile Range	13.50000

Tests for Location: Mu0=480				
Test		Statistic	p Value	
Student's t	t	0.397007	Pr > |t|	0.6950
Sign	M	-6	Pr >= |M|	0.0227
Signed Rank	S	-50	Pr >= |S|	0.1570

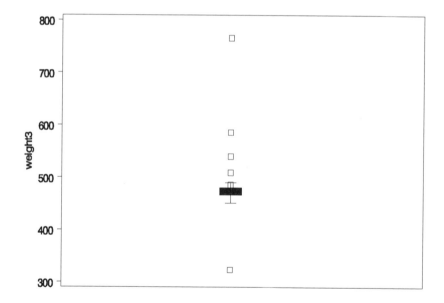

4.5.7.4 Asymmetric Data

Asymmetric data can result in both the Student's one-sample *t* test and the Signed Rank Test being ineffective. Both tests are based on the assumption that the underlying population is symmetric. The Sign Test does not require that assumption.

The data below is from a population with $\theta = 472$. The values are in the weight4 column of data set Ex04_08b.

467	468	468	469	469	470	470	470	470	471	471	472
472	472	473	475	479	479	480	491	492	493	498	501

The box-and-whisker plot in Output 4.12 shows the data to be positively skewed. The Sign Test correctly rejects $H_0 : \theta = 480$.

The large values above $\bar{x}$ cause a large sample standard deviation, which results in a small t test. The ranks of the positive differences weight4 − 480 are large. This sufficiently balances the more numerous but mostly smaller negative ranks. The result is a small t test on the signed ranks.

Output 4.12 Distribution Analysis with weight4 Values

Basic Statistical Measures			
Location		**Variability**	
Mean	476.6667	**Std Deviation**	10.34478
Median	472.0000	**Variance**	107.01449
Mode	470.0000	**Range**	34.00000
		Interquartile Range	9.50000

Tests for Location: Mu0=480				
Test		**Statistic**	**p Value**	
Student's t	t	-1.57857	Pr > |t|	0.1281
Sign	M	-6.5	Pr >= |M|	0.0106
Signed Rank	S	-39.5	Pr >= |S|	0.2370

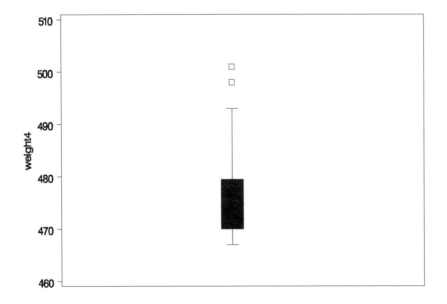

4.6 Reference

Leemis, L.M., and Trivedi, K.S. 1996. "A Comparison of Approximate Interval Estimators for the Bernoulli Parameter." *The American Statistician* 50(1): 63-68.

Inferences from Two Samples

5.1   Connection to Chapter 4

This chapter extends the discussion of inference from one to two samples. In Chapter 4, "Inferences from One Sample," a population mean is tested against a constant using the statistics $\bar{x}$, s and n. See an example below on the left. In this chapter, two population means are compared against one another as seen on the right. The new parameters, sample statistics, and test statistic are reasonably straightforward reapplications of the one-sample concepts.

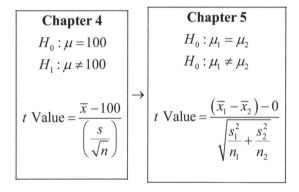

Except for the population proportion, all the parameters discussed in Chapter 4 are covered here in the context of two populations. See Table 5.1. Comparisons of two or more population proportions are covered in Chapter 8, "Table Analysis."

Table 5.1 Parameters Discussed in Chapter 5

Parameter Expressions For Two Populations	Notation
difference of population means	$\mu_1 - \mu_2$
ratio of population variances	$\dfrac{\sigma_1^2}{\sigma_2^2}$
mean difference associated with a population of pairs	μ_d
medians of two populations	θ_1, θ_2
median difference associated with a population of pairs	θ_d

5.2 Inference on the Means and Variances from Two Independent Populations

The two-sample t test is the appropriate test to use when comparing the means and the variances of two independent populations. Two populations are independent when the values in one population are not being paired with the values in the other population. Furthermore, samples are taken from one population without any reference to the other population.

Subscripts are used to identify the two populations and the respective parameters, samples, and statistics. The mean and variance of the first population are μ_1 and σ_1^2. The mean and variance of the second population are μ_2 and σ_2^2. Statistics from the samples taken from the two populations are handled in the same way.

Population	Sample Size	Sample Mean	Sample Standard Deviation	Sample Variance
1	n_1	$\overline{x}_1$	s_1	s_1^2
2	n_2	$\overline{x}_2$	s_2	s_2^2

The input data consists of a column containing the numerical values of two samples and a column of classification values identifying the samples memberships.

The subscripts 1 and 2 are assigned according to the sorting order of the classification values. Sorting is done in numeric and alphabetic order with numbers being first in order, then uppercase letters, then the underscore, and then lowercase letters.

The Two-Sample t Test task produces estimates and confidence intervals on:

- μ_1, μ_2, and $\mu_1 - \mu_2$

- σ_1, σ_2, and the common standard deviation if $\sigma_1 = \sigma_2 = \sigma$

The task output includes three hypothesis tests:

- Folded F test: This tests the equality of the population variances and is generally considered first.

- Pooled *t* test: This tests the hypothesis on the population means if the Folded F test does not reject the assumption of equal variances.

- Satterthwaite *t* test: This test the hypothesis on the population means if the Folded F test does reject the assumption of equal variances.

See the diagram in Figure 5.1.

Figure 5.1 Hypothesis Tests in the Two-Sample *t* Test Task

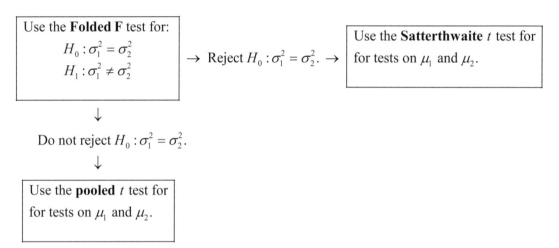

5.2.1 Hypothesis Test on Two Variances

The Folded *F* test assumes that the original populations are normally distributed. When this is not true, the results can be unreliable. See the section on the Folded F Test and Normally Distribution Theory.

5.2.1.1 Null and Alternative Hypotheses

The Folded *F* tests the equality of the two population variances σ_1^2 and σ_2^2. The null and alternative hypotheses are:

$$H_0 : \sigma_1^2 = \sigma_2^2$$
$$H_1 : \sigma_1^2 \neq \sigma_2^2$$

5.2.1.2 Test Statistic

The null hypothesis is equivalent to both of the following:

$$H_0 : \frac{\sigma_1^2}{\sigma_2^2} = 1 \quad \text{and} \quad H_0 : \frac{\sigma_2^2}{\sigma_1^2} = 1$$

A reasonable test statistic would be the ratio of the sample variances s_1^2 and s_2^2. The Folded F test places the larger sample variance on the top and the smaller on the bottom.

$$F \text{ value} = \frac{\max\left\{s_1^2, s_2^2\right\}}{\min\left\{s_1^2, s_2^2\right\}}$$

- This folds a two-tailed test into a right-tailed test.
- If F value $= 9.81$, then the larger population variance is estimated to be 9.81 times the size of the smaller population variance.

5.2.1.3 *p*-Value

The Folded F test assumes that the original populations are normally distributed. In which case, the F values follow an F distribution. See Table 5.2. The specific F distribution depends on two degrees-of-freedom values: the numerator degrees of freedom (ndf) and the denominator degrees of freedom (ddf). For the Folded F test, the numerator degrees-of-freedom value is associated with the sample with the larger variance. The denominator degrees-of-freedom value is associated with the sample with the smaller variance.

- If sample 1 has the larger variance, then ndf $= n_1 - 1$ and ddf $= n_2 - 1$.
- If sample 2 has the larger variance, then ndf $= n_2 - 1$ and ddf $= n_1 - 1$.

The *p-value* is a measure of the likelihood that the samples comes from populations where H_0 is true. Smaller values indicate less likelihood. That is, the more the data agrees with H_1 — the more $\max\left\{s_1^2, s_2^2\right\} / \min\left\{s_1^2, s_2^2\right\}$ is greater than 1 — the smaller the *p*-value.

In terms of the Folded F test, the *p*-value is the probability that random samples from two independent populations with equal variances would produce an F value at or beyond the current value. If the *p*-value is small, it is unlikely that the current samples come from two populations with equal variances.

Table 5.2 has the technical definition of the *p*-value. The random variable F represents a future value of the test statistic and follows an F distribution. In the SAS code expression, F value, ndf, and ddf represent numbers. The SAS code expression is included to aid in the discussion. The *p*-value is computed using the expression in the "Detailed Solutions" section of "Example 5.1: Samples from Populations with Equal Variances."

Table 5.2 *p*-Value for the Folded *F* Test

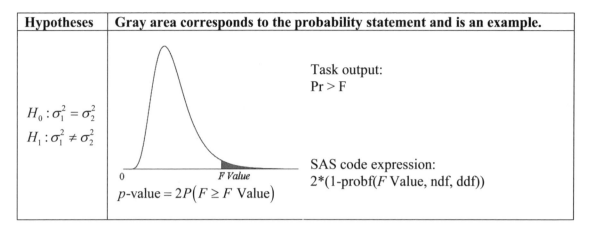

Hypotheses	**Gray area corresponds to the probability statement and is an example.**
$H_0 : \sigma_1^2 = \sigma_2^2$ $H_1 : \sigma_1^2 \neq \sigma_2^2$	Task output: Pr > F SAS code expression: 2*(1-probf(*F* Value, ndf, ddf))

$$p\text{-value} = 2P(F \geq F \text{ Value})$$

5.2.1.4 Decisions and Conclusions

The formal decision and concluding sentence do not change from the one-sample tests discussed in Chapter 4, "Inferences from One Sample." The concluding observation depends on the particular statistics involved in the test.

If the *p*-value is small, the data agrees with H_1. If the *p*-value is less than the significance level, the risk of making a Type I error is acceptable. Therefore, the *p*-value decision rule is the following.

If the *p*-value < α, reject H_0. Otherwise, do not reject H_0.

Since a hypothesis test begins with the assumption that H_0 is true, concluding a hypothesis test requires one of the following formal statements.

- Reject H_0.
- Do not reject H_0.

When the claim is equivalent to the null hypothesis, the concluding sentence uses the word *reject*. The concluding sentence becomes an expanded version of the formal decision.

When the claim is equivalent to the alternative hypothesis, the concluding sentence uses the word *support*. If the data supports the rejection of H_0, the data supports H_1. If the data does not support rejection of H_0, the data cannot support H_1.

Table 5.3 Concluding Sentences

Formal Statistical Decision	Claim stated as H_0	Claim stated as H_1
Reject H_0.	There is sufficient evidence to reject the claim that ... (claim in words).	There is sufficient evidence to support the claim that ... (claim in words).
Do not reject H_0.	There is not sufficient evidence to reject the claim that ... (claim in words).	There is not sufficient evidence to support the claim that ... (claim in words).

Table 5.4 Concluding Observations

Reject H_0.	The sample variances are significantly different.
Do not reject H_0.	The sample variances are not significantly different.

5.2.1.5 Folded *F* Test and Normally Distribution Theory

The Folded F test is not very reliable if the original populations are not normally distributed. In that case, it is recommended that no assumption be made about the equality of the population variances. One would then use the Satterthwaite t test when testing hypotheses on the population means. See the section on "Hypothesis Tests on Two Means."

Simulations have generated 10,000 pairs of independent 30-value samples from populations with equal variances. $H_0 : \sigma_1^2 = \sigma_2^2$ is tested with a $\alpha = 0.05$ significance level. The proportion of rejections is recorded. Since the significance level is the probability of rejecting H_0 when H_0 is true, one expects that proportion to be 0.05.

- Samples are drawn from two independent normally distributed populations where $\sigma_1^2 = \sigma_2^2 = 0.25$. (See Example 4.1 in Section 4.2.) The proportion of rejections is 0.0493. This is essentially what is expected.

- Samples are drawn from two independent exponentially distributed populations where $\sigma_1^2 = \sigma_2^2 = 2025$. (See Example 4.1 in Section 4.2.) The proportion of rejections is 0.2850. This is much higher than expected. Here, the Folded F test rejects too liberally to be reliable.

- Samples are drawn from two independent 5-response populations where $\sigma_1^2 = \sigma_2^2 = 2$. (See Example 4.1 in Section 4.2.) The proportion of rejections is 0.0020. This is much lower than expected. Here, the Folded F test rejects too conservatively to be reliable.

5.2.2 Estimation of the Variances and Standard Deviations

- The point estimates of the population standard deviations σ_1 and σ_2 are the sample standard deviations s_1 and s_2.

- The point estimates of the population variances σ_1^2 and σ_2^2 are the sample variances s_1^2 and s_2^2.

If it can be assumed that the underlying population variances are equal $(\sigma_1^2 = \sigma_2^2 = \sigma^2)$ then the common variance is estimated by the *pooled variance* s_{pooled}^2:

$$s_{pooled}^2 = \frac{(n_1 - 1)s_1^2 + (n_2 - 1)s_2^2}{n_1 + n_2 - 2}$$

The pooled variance is a weighted average of the sample variances. The weights are the degrees of freedom associated with the two samples. The pooled standard deviation is $s_{pooled} = \sqrt{s_{pooled}^2}$.

The confidence intervals for the standard deviations and variances are based on the chi-squared (χ^2) distribution. A critical value for a chi-squared distribution is denoted by c_q, where q is between 0 and 1. The critical value c_q is a value on the number line that marks the right q proportion of the distribution. For a fixed q, there is a different c_q value for each degrees-of-freedom value. Using SAS code, $c_q = \text{cinv}(1-q, \text{df})$. In the expression, $1-q$ and df (the degrees-of-freedom value) represent numbers.

Let i represent the sample number: $i = 1$ or 2. For a sample from a normally distributed population, a $(1 - \alpha)100\%$ confidence interval on the variance σ_i^2 is:

$$\left(\frac{(n_i - 1)s_i^2}{c_{\alpha/2}}, \frac{(n_i - 1)s_i^2}{c_{1-\alpha/2}} \right)$$

The degrees-of-freedom value associated with the critical values is $n_i - 1$. A $(1 - \alpha)100\%$ confidence interval on the standard deviation σ_i is:

$$\left(s_i\sqrt{\frac{n_i - 1}{c_{\alpha/2}}}, s_i\sqrt{\frac{n_i - 1}{c_{1-\alpha/2}}} \right)$$

If it can be assumed that $\sigma_1^2 = \sigma_2^2 = \sigma^2$ and the populations are normally distributed, a $(1 - \alpha)100\%$ confidence interval on the common variance σ^2 is:

$$\left(\frac{(n_1 + n_2 - 2)s_{pooled}^2}{c_{\alpha/2}}, \frac{(n_1 + n_2 - 2)s_{pooled}^2}{c_{1-\alpha/2}} \right)$$

The degrees-of-freedom value associated with the critical values is $n_1 + n_2 - 2$. A $(1 - \alpha)100\%$ confidence interval on the common standard deviation σ is:

$$\left(s_{\text{pooled}} \sqrt{\frac{n_1 + n_2 - 2}{c_{\alpha/2}}}, s_{\text{pooled}} \sqrt{\frac{n_1 + n_2 - 2}{c_{1-\alpha/2}}} \right)$$

The confidence intervals above are referred to as equal tailed because the area in either distribution tail is $\alpha/2$. The critical values $c_{1-\alpha/2}$ and $c_{\alpha/2}$ might not result in the shortest—most precise—confidence interval. A task option produces uniformly most powerful unbiased (UMPU) confidence intervals. The formulas are the same except for the critical value notation. The critical values $c_{1-\alpha/2}$ and $c_{\alpha/2}$ are replaced by c_{lower} and c_{upper}, the closest critical values that have $(1 - \alpha)100\%$ of the distribution between them.

5.2.3 Summary of the Hypothesis Test and Confidence Intervals on Two Variances

5.2.3.1 Folded *F* Test

Plan the experiment.

$H_0 : \sigma_1^2 = \sigma_2^2$
$H_1 : \sigma_1^2 \neq \sigma_2^2$

The significance level is α.

Task computes the statistics.

Equality of Variances					
Variable	**Method**	**Num DF**	**Den DF**	**F Value**	**Pr > F**
analysis variable	**Folded F**	ndf	ddf	$F \text{ Value} = \dfrac{\max\left\{s_1^2, s_2^2\right\}}{\min\left\{s_1^2, s_2^2\right\}}$	*p*-value

- If sample 1 has the larger variance, then $\text{ndf} = n_1 - 1$ and $\text{ddf} = n_2 - 1$.

- If sample 2 has the larger variance, then $\text{ndf} = n_2 - 1$ and $\text{ddf} = n_1 - 1$.

Apply the results.

If the *p*-value $< \alpha$, reject H_0. Otherwise, do not reject H_0.

- Reject H_0. There is sufficient evidence to reject/support the claim that ... (claim in words). The sample variances are significantly different.

- Do not reject H_0. There is not sufficient evidence to reject/support the claim that ...(claim in words). The sample variances are not significantly different.

5.2.3.2   Confidence Intervals on the Standard Deviations

CL stands for *confidence limit* in the task output:

Variable	*group by variable*	N	Lower CL Std Dev	UMPU Lower CL Std Dev	Std Dev	UMPU Upper CL Std Dev	Upper CL Std Dev
analysis variable	*1st group value*	n_1	$s_1\sqrt{\dfrac{n_1-1}{c_{\alpha/2}}}$	$s_1\sqrt{\dfrac{n_1-1}{c_{\text{upper}}}}$	s_1	$s_1\sqrt{\dfrac{n_1-1}{c_{\text{lower}}}}$	$s_1\sqrt{\dfrac{n_1-1}{c_{1-\alpha/2}}}$
analysis variable	*2nd group value*	n_2	$s_2\sqrt{\dfrac{n_2-1}{c_{\alpha/2}}}$	$s_2\sqrt{\dfrac{n_2-1}{c_{\text{upper}}}}$	s_2	$s_2\sqrt{\dfrac{n_2-1}{c_{\text{lower}}}}$	$s_2\sqrt{\dfrac{n_2-1}{c_{1-\alpha/2}}}$
analysis variable	**Diff (1-2)**		$s_{\text{pooled}}\sqrt{\dfrac{n_1+n_2-2}{c_{\alpha/2}}}$	$s_{\text{pooled}}\sqrt{\dfrac{n_1+n_2-2}{c_{\text{upper}}}}$	s_{pooled}	$s_{\text{pooled}}\sqrt{\dfrac{n_1+n_2-\ ?}{c_{\text{lower}}}}$	$s_{\text{pooled}}\sqrt{\dfrac{n_1+n_2-\ ?}{c_{1-\alpha/2}}}$

5.2.4 Hypothesis Test on Two Means

A two-sample *t* test refers to a hypothesis test comparing the means of two independent populations. The task has two such tests: the pooled *t* test and the Satterthwaite *t* test.

Both two-sample *t* tests assume that the original populations are normally distributed. But as with the one-sample *t* test in Chapter 4 ("Inferences from One Sample"), the Central Limit Theorem also applies to the two-sample *t* tests.

5.2.4.1   Null and Alternative Hypotheses

The null and alternative hypotheses in a two-sample *t* test compare the difference of two population means— $\mu_1 - \mu_2$ —to a number, denoted by δ_0.

$H_0 : \mu_1 - \mu_2 = \delta_0$	$H_0 : \mu_1 - \mu_2 \le \delta_0$	$H_0 : \mu_1 - \mu_2 \ge \delta_0$
$H_1 : \mu_1 - \mu_2 \ne \delta_0$	$H_1 : \mu_1 - \mu_2 > \delta_0$	$H_1 : \mu_1 - \mu_2 < \delta_0$

It is often the case that $\delta_0 = 0$:

| $H_0 : \mu_1 - \mu_2 = 0$ | $H_0 : \mu_1 - \mu_2 \leq 0$ | $H_0 : \mu_1 - \mu_2 \geq 0$ |
| $H_1 : \mu_1 - \mu_2 \neq 0$ | $H_1 : \mu_1 - \mu_2 > 0$ | $H_1 : \mu_1 - \mu_2 < 0$ |

In which case, the hypotheses are written in a more convenient form.

| $H_0 : \mu_1 = \mu_2$ | $H_0 : \mu_1 \leq \mu_2$ | $H_0 : \mu_1 \geq \mu_2$ |
| $H_1 : \mu_1 \neq \mu_2$ | $H_1 : \mu_1 > \mu_2$ | $H_1 : \mu_1 < \mu_2$ |

5.2.4.2   Test Statistics

A two-sample *t* test assumes that the original populations are normally distributed. It follows from normal distribution theory that the sampling distributions of the two means are also normally distributed.

- The $\bar{x}_1$ values are normally distributed with mean μ_1, variance $\dfrac{\sigma_1^2}{n_1}$ and standard deviation $\dfrac{\sigma_1}{\sqrt{n_1}}$.

- The $\bar{x}_2$ values are normally distributed with mean μ_2, variance $\dfrac{\sigma_2^2}{n_2}$ and standard deviation $\dfrac{\sigma_2}{\sqrt{n_2}}$.

Theory further says that the $\bar{x}_1 - \bar{x}_2$ values are normally distributed with mean $\mu_1 - \mu_2$, variance $\dfrac{\sigma_1^2}{n_1} + \dfrac{\sigma_2^2}{n_2}$ and standard deviation $\sqrt{\dfrac{\sigma_1^2}{n_1} + \dfrac{\sigma_2^2}{n_2}}$.

When the underlying population variances are known, the test statistic becomes the following. Under H_0, the difference in population means is assumed to be equal to δ_0.

$$z = \frac{(\bar{x}_1 - \bar{x}_2) - \delta_0}{\sqrt{\dfrac{\sigma_1^2}{n_1} + \dfrac{\sigma_2^2}{n_2}}}$$

The population of z values follows the standard normal distribution: the normal distribution with $\mu = 0$ and $\sigma = 1$.

The Central Limit Theorem also applies here: If the two original populations are not normally distributed but have means and standard deviations, the sampling distributions of the preceding statistics ($\bar{x}_1$, $\bar{x}_2$, $\bar{x}_1 - \bar{x}_2$, z) approximately follow the stated normal distributions.

A two-sample *t* test is used when the underlying variances are unknown and must be estimated.

If Variances Are Equal: The Pooled *t* Test

The pooled *t* test is used when the underlying population variances are assumed to be equal. If $\sigma_1^2 = \sigma_2^2 = \sigma^2$, then the common variance is estimated by the pooled variance s_{pooled}^2 below.

$$s_{pooled}^2 = \frac{(n_1 - 1)s_1^2 + (n_2 - 1)s_2^2}{n_1 + n_2 - 2}$$

The pooled variance is a weighted average of the sample variances. The weights are the degrees of freedom associated with the two samples.

The test statistic for the pooled *t* test is:

$$t \text{ Value} = \frac{(\bar{x}_1 - \bar{x}_2) - \delta_0}{\sqrt{\dfrac{s_{pooled}^2}{n_1} + \dfrac{s_{pooled}^2}{n_2}}} = \frac{(\bar{x}_1 - \bar{x}_2) - \delta_0}{s_{pooled}\sqrt{\dfrac{1}{n_1} + \dfrac{1}{n_2}}}$$

When the original populations are normally distributed, the pooled *t* test follows the *t* distribution with $n_1 + n_2 - 2$ degrees of freedom. When the Central Limit Theorem applies, the pooled *t* test approximately follows the *t* distribution.

If Variances Are Not Equal: The Satterthwaite *t* Test

The Satterthwaite *t* test is used when the underlying population variances are not equal, $\sigma_1^2 \neq \sigma_2^2$. Each population variance is estimated by the corresponding sample variance. The test statistic is:

$$t \text{ Value} = \frac{(\bar{x}_1 - \bar{x}_2) - \delta_0}{\sqrt{\dfrac{s_1^2}{n_1} + \dfrac{s_2^2}{n_2}}}$$

The degrees of freedom are given by Satterthwaite's formula below.

Satterthwaite's formula: $\quad v = \dfrac{\left(\dfrac{s_1^2}{n_1} + \dfrac{s_2^2}{n_2}\right)^2}{\dfrac{\left(\dfrac{s_1^2}{n_1}\right)^2}{n_1 - 1} + \dfrac{\left(\dfrac{s_2^2}{n_2}\right)^2}{n_2 - 1}}$

The Satterthwaite t test is an approximate test. When the original populations are normally distributed, the Satterthwaite t test approximately follows the t distribution with v degrees of freedom. When the Central Limit Theorem applies, the Satterthwaite t test approximately follows the same t distribution.

When $n_1 = n_2$ and $s_1^2 = s_2^2$, the Satterthwaite t test and the pooled t test are equal.

5.2.4.3 *p*-Value

The *p-value* is a measure of the likelihood that the samples comes from populations where H_0 is true. Smaller values indicate less likelihood. That is, the more the data agrees with H_1 — the more $\overline{x}_1 - \overline{x}_2$ is different than, greater than, or less than δ_0 — the smaller the *p*-value.

In terms of a two-sample t test, the *p*-value is the probability that random samples from two independent populations with means differing by δ_0 would produce a t value at or beyond the current value. If the *p*-value is small, it is unlikely that the current samples come from two populations with means differing by δ_0.

The technical definition of the *p*-value depends on the alternative hypothesis H_1. See Table 5.5. The random variable T represents a future value of the test statistic and follows the t distribution. The degrees-of-freedom values (df) are:

- df $= n_1 + n_2 - 2$ for the pooled t test

- df $= v$ for the Satterthwaite t test

  Pr > |t| identifies the *p*-values in the Two-Sample t Test task output.

- The test of the hypotheses $H_0 : \mu_1 - \mu_2 = \delta_0$ versus $H_1 : \mu_1 - \mu_2 \neq \delta_0$ is called a *two-sided test*. See the first graph in Table 5.5. *Pr > |t| is the p-value for a two-sided test.*

- The tests of $H_0 : \mu_1 - \mu_2 \leq \delta_0$ versus $H_1 : \mu_1 - \mu_2 > \delta_0$ and
  $H_0 : \mu_1 - \mu_2 \geq \delta_0$ versus $H_1 : \mu_1 - \mu_2 < \delta_0$ are called *one-sided tests*. See the second and third graphs in Table 5.5. *The p-values for one-sided tests are computed from the Pr > |t| value. See Table 5.5.*

SAS code expressions are included in Table 5.5 to aid in the discussion. The *p*-value is computed using an expression in the "Detailed Solutions" section of "Example 5.1: Samples from Populations with Equal Variances." In the expressions, t value and df represent numbers.

Table 5.5 *p*-Values for Two-Sample *t*-Test

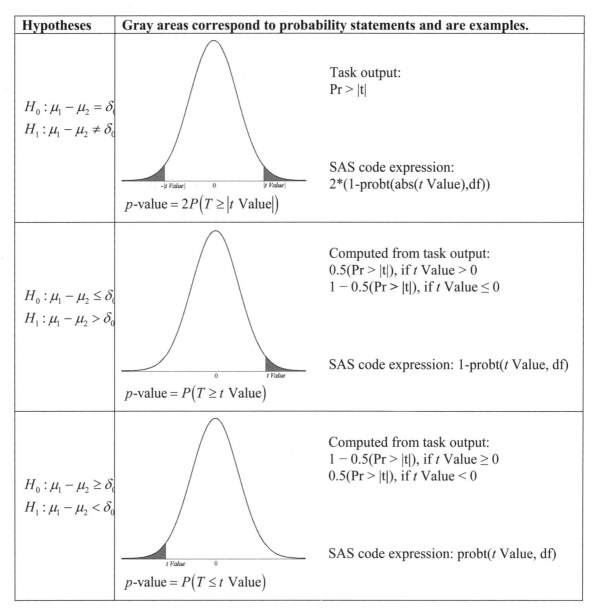

Hypotheses	Gray areas correspond to probability statements and are examples.
$H_0 : \mu_1 - \mu_2 = \delta_0$ $H_1 : \mu_1 - \mu_2 \neq \delta_0$	p-value $= 2P\left(T \geq \left\vert t\ \text{Value} \right\vert\right)$ Task output: $\Pr > \vert t \vert$ SAS code expression: $2*(1-\text{probt}(\text{abs}(t\ \text{Value}),\text{df}))$
$H_0 : \mu_1 - \mu_2 \leq \delta_0$ $H_1 : \mu_1 - \mu_2 > \delta_0$	p-value $= P\left(T \geq t\ \text{Value}\right)$ Computed from task output: $0.5(\Pr > \vert t \vert)$, if t Value > 0 $1 - 0.5(\Pr > \vert t \vert)$, if t Value ≤ 0 SAS code expression: $1-\text{probt}(t\ \text{Value},\ \text{df})$
$H_0 : \mu_1 - \mu_2 \geq \delta_0$ $H_1 : \mu_1 - \mu_2 < \delta_0$	p-value $= P\left(T \leq t\ \text{Value}\right)$ Computed from task output: $1 - 0.5(\Pr > \vert t \vert)$, if t Value ≥ 0 $0.5(\Pr > \vert t \vert)$, if t Value < 0 SAS code expression: $\text{probt}(t\ \text{Value},\ \text{df})$

5.2.4.4   Decision and Conclusions

The formal decision and concluding sentence do not change from the one-sample tests discussed in Chapter 4, "Inferences fromOne Sample." The concluding observation depends on the particular statistics involved in the test.

If the *p*-value is small, the data agrees with H_1. If the *p*-value is less than the significance level, the risk of making a Type I error is acceptable. Therefore, the *p*-value decision rule is the following.

   If the *p*-value $< \alpha$, reject H_0. Otherwise, do not reject H_0.

Since a hypothesis test begins with the assumption that H_0 is true, concluding a hypothesis test requires one of the following formal statements.

- Reject H_0.
- Do not reject H_0.

When the claim is equivalent to the null hypothesis, the concluding sentence uses the word *reject*. The concluding sentence becomes an expanded version of the formal decision.

When the claim is equivalent to the alternative hypothesis, the concluding sentence uses the word *support*. If the data supports the rejection of H_0, the data supports H_1. If the data does not support rejection of H_0, the data cannot support H_1.

Table 5.6 Concluding Sentences

Formal Statistical Decision	Claim stated as H_0	Claim stated as H_1
Reject H_0.	There is sufficient evidence to reject the claim that ... (claim in words).	There is sufficient evidence to support the claim that ... (claim in words).
Do not reject H_0.	There is not sufficient evidence to reject the claim that ... (claim in words).	There is not sufficient evidence to support the claim that ... (claim in words).

Table 5.7 Concluding Observations

Reject H_0.	The difference in sample means is significantly different/greater/less than δ_0. If $\delta_0 = 0$: The sample means are significantly different. Sample mean 1 is significantly greater/less than sample mean 2.
Do not reject H_0.	The difference in sample means is not significantly different/greater/less than δ_0. If $\delta_0 = 0$: The sample means are not significantly different. Sample mean 1 is not significantly greater/less than sample mean 2.

5.2.4.5   *t* Tests, Normal Distribution Theory, and the Central Limit Theorem

Two sets of simulations are considered. In the first set, the population variances are equal and the samples sizes are equal. In the second set, the population variances are not equal and the samples sizes are not equal.

Equal Population Variances and Equal Sample Sizes

Simulations generate 10,000 pairs of independent 30-value samples from populations with equal means and equal variances. $H_0 : \mu_1 = \mu_2$ is tested with a $\alpha = 0.05$ significance level. The proportion of rejections is recorded. Since the significance level is the probability of rejecting H_0 when H_0 is true, one expects that proportion to be 0.05.

- Samples are drawn from two independent normally distributed populations with $\mu_1 = \mu_2 = 50$ and $\sigma_1^2 = \sigma_2^2 = 0.25$. (See Example 4.1 in Section 4.2.) The proportions of rejections are essentially as expected.
  - The proportion of rejections for the pooled t test is 0.0529.
  - The proportion of rejections for the Satterthwaite t test is 0.0529.

- Samples are drawn from two independent exponentially distributed populations with $\mu_1 = \mu_2 = 45$ and $\sigma_1^2 = \sigma_2^2 = 2025$. (See Example 4.1 in Section 4.2.) The proportions of rejections are very close to 0.05.
  - The proportion of rejections for the pooled t test is 0.0499.
  - The proportion of rejections for the Satterthwaite t test is 0.0488.

- Samples are drawn from two independent 5-response populations with $\mu_1 = \mu_2 = 3$ and $\sigma_1^2 = \sigma_2^2 = 2$. (See Example 4.1 in Section 4.2.) The proportions of rejections are very close to 0.05.
  - The proportion of rejections for the pooled t test is 0.0502.
  - The proportion of rejections for the Satterthwaite t test is 0.0502.

Unequal Population Variances and Unequal Sample Sizes

Simulations generate 10,000 pairs of independent samples from populations with equal means and unequal variances. Samples from population 1 have 48 values and samples from population 2 have 12 values. $H_0 : \mu_1 = \mu_2$ is tested with a $\alpha = 0.05$ significance level. The proportion of rejections is recorded. Since the significance level is the probability of rejecting H_0 when H_0 is true, one expects that proportion for the Satterthwaite t test to be 0.05.

- Samples are drawn from two independent normally distributed populations with $\mu_1 = \mu_2 = 50$, $\sigma_1^2 = 0.25$, and $\sigma_2^2 = 1$. (See Example 4.1 in Section 4.2.) The proportions of rejections are high for the pooled t test but essentially as expected for the Satterthwaite t test.
  - The proportion of rejections for the pooled t test is 0.1839.
  - The proportion of rejections for the Satterthwaite t test is 0.0537.

- Samples are drawn from two independent exponentially distributed populations with $\mu_1 = \mu_2 = 45$, $\sigma_1^2 = 2025$, and $\sigma_2^2 = 8100$. (See Example 4.1 in Section 4.2.) The proportions of rejections are high for both the pooled t test and the Satterthwaite t test. Larger sample sizes would produce better results for the Satterthwaite t test.
  - The proportion of rejections for the pooled t test is 0.1887.
  - The proportion of rejections for the Satterthwaite t test is 0.0907.

- Samples are drawn from two independent 5-response populations with $\mu_1 = \mu_2 = 3$, $\sigma_1^2 = 2$, and $\sigma_2^2 = 8$. (See Example 4.1 in Section 4.2.) The proportions of rejections are high for the pooled t test but essentially as expected for the Satterthwaite t test.
  - The proportion of rejections for the pooled t test is 0.1857.
  - The proportion of rejections for the Satterthwaite t test is 0.0563.

5.2.5 Estimation of the Means and the Difference of Means

- The point estimates of the population means μ_1 and μ_2 are the sample means $\overline{x}_1$ and $\overline{x}_2$.

- The point estimate of the difference in the population means $\mu_1 - \mu_2$ is the difference in the sample means $\overline{x}_1 - \overline{x}_2$.

The confidence intervals on the means and the difference of means are based on the t distribution. A critical value for a t distribution is denoted by t_q, where q is between 0 and 1. The critical value t_q is a value on the number line that marks the right q proportion of the distribution. For a fixed q, there is a different t_q value for each degrees-of-freedom value. Using SAS code, $t_q =$ tinv($1-q$,df). In the expression, $1-q$ and df (the degrees-of-freedom value) represent numbers.

- Let i represent the sample number: $i = 1$ or 2. For a sample from a normally distributed population, a $(1 - \alpha)100\%$ confidence interval on the mean μ_i is:

$$\left(\overline{x}_i - t_{\alpha/2} \frac{s_i}{\sqrt{n_i}}, \overline{x}_i + t_{\alpha/2} \frac{s_i}{\sqrt{n_i}} \right)$$

The degrees-of-freedom value associated with the critical value is $n_i - 1$.

- If it can be assumed that the underlying population variances are equal — $\sigma_1^2 = \sigma_2^2 = \sigma^2$ — then the common variance is estimated by the pooled variance s_{pooled}^2 :

$$s_{pooled}^2 = \frac{(n_1 - 1)s_1^2 + (n_2 - 1)s_2^2}{n_1 + n_2 - 2}$$

The pooled standard deviation is $s_{pooled} = \sqrt{s_{pooled}^2}$. A $100(1 - \alpha)\%$ confidence interval on $\mu_1 - \mu_2$ is:

$$\left((\overline{x}_1 - \overline{x}_2) - t_{\alpha/2} s_{pooled} \sqrt{\frac{1}{n_1} + \frac{1}{n_2}}, (\overline{x}_1 - \overline{x}_2) + t_{\alpha/2} s_{pooled} \sqrt{\frac{1}{n_1} + \frac{1}{n_2}} \right)$$

The degrees-of-freedom value associated with the critical value is $n_1 + n_2 - 2$.

- If the underlying population variances are unequal, $\sigma_1^2 \neq \sigma_2^2$, each population variance is estimated by the corresponding sample variance. A $100(1 - \alpha)\%$ confidence interval on $\mu_1 - \mu_2$ is:

$$\left((\bar{x}_1 - \bar{x}_2) - t_{\alpha/2}\sqrt{\frac{s_1^2}{n_1} + \frac{s_2^2}{n_2}}, (\bar{x}_1 - \bar{x}_2) + t_{\alpha/2}\sqrt{\frac{s_1^2}{n_1} + \frac{s_2^2}{n_2}} \right)$$

The degrees-of-freedom value associated with the critical value is Satterthwaite's ν, which is presented with the Satterthwaite t test in the "Hypothesis Test on Two Means" section.

The last confidence interval is not part of the task output, although Satterthwaite's ν is. The lower and upper limits can be computed using SAS code. See Table 5.8.

Table 5.8 SAS Code for Confidence Interval Based on Satterthwaite Degrees of Freedom

Confidence Limits	SAS Code
	• $\bar{x}_1$, $\bar{x}_2$, ν, s_1, n_1, s_2, n_2 represent numbers taken from the Two-Sample t Test task output.
	• .975 results in a 95% confidence interval. .95 would result in a 90% confidence interval and .995 would result in a 99% confidence interval. In general, $1 - \alpha/2$ results in a $100(1 - \alpha)\%$ confidence interval.
$\bar{x}_1 - \bar{x}_2 - t_{\alpha/2}\sqrt{\dfrac{s_1^2}{n_1} + \dfrac{s_2^2}{n_2}}$	$\bar{x}_1$ - $\bar{x}_2$ -tinv(.975, ν)*sqrt((s_1)**2/ n_1 +(s_2)**2/ n_2)
$\bar{x}_1 - \bar{x}_2 + t_{\alpha/2}\sqrt{\dfrac{s_1^2}{n_1} + \dfrac{s_2^2}{n_2}}$	$\bar{x}_1$ - $\bar{x}_2$ +tinv(.975, ν)*sqrt((s_1)**2/ n_1 +(s_2)**2/ n_2)

5.2.6 Summary of Hypothesis Tests and Confidence Intervals on Two Means

5.2.6.1 Hypothesis Tests

Plan the experiment.

$$\left.\begin{array}{lll} H_0: \mu_1 - \mu_2 = \delta_0 & H_0: \mu_1 - \mu_2 \leq \delta_0 & H_0: \mu_1 - \mu_2 \geq \delta_0 \\ H_1: \mu_1 - \mu_2 \neq \delta_0 & H_1: \mu_1 - \mu_2 > \delta_0 & H_1: \mu_1 - \mu_2 < \delta_0 \end{array}\right\} \text{Task window requires } \delta_0$$

The significance level is α.

Task computes the statistics.

T-Tests					
Variable	**Method**	**Variances**	**DF**	**t Value**	**Pr > |t|**
analysis variable	**Pooled**	Equal	$n_1 + n_2 - 1$	$t \text{ Value} = \dfrac{(\bar{x}_1 - \bar{x}_2) - \delta_0}{s_{\text{pooled}}\sqrt{\dfrac{1}{n_1} + \dfrac{1}{n_2}}}$	p-value for $H_0 : \mu_1 - \mu_2 = \delta_0$ $H_1 : \mu_1 - \mu_2 \neq \delta_0$
analysis variable	**Satterthwaite**	Unequal	Satterthwaite's ν	$t \text{ Value} = \dfrac{(\bar{x}_1 - \bar{x}_2) - \delta_0}{\sqrt{\dfrac{s_1^2}{n_1} + \dfrac{s_2^2}{n_2}}}$	p-value for $H_0 : \mu_1 - \mu_2 = \delta_0$ $H_1 : \mu_1 - \mu_2 \neq \delta_0$

Determining the *p*-value:

Hypotheses	
$H_0 : \mu_1 - \mu_2 = \delta_0$ $H_1 : \mu_1 - \mu_2 \neq \delta_0$	$p\text{-value} = (\Pr > \|t\|)$
$H_0 : \mu_1 - \mu_2 \leq \delta_0$ $H_1 : \mu_1 - \mu_2 > \delta_0$	$p\text{-value} = \begin{cases} 0.5(\Pr > \|t\|), & \text{if } t \text{ Value} > 0 \\ 1 - 0.5(\Pr > \|t\|), & \text{if } t \text{ Value} \leq 0 \end{cases}$
$H_0 : \mu_1 - \mu_2 \geq \delta_0$ $H_1 : \mu_1 - \mu_2 < \delta_0$	$p\text{-value} = \begin{cases} 1 - 0.5(\Pr > \|t\|), & \text{if } t \text{ Value} \geq 0 \\ 0.5(\Pr > \|t\|), & \text{if } t \text{ Value} < 0 \end{cases}$

Apply the results.

If the *p*-value $< \alpha$, reject H_0. Otherwise, do not reject H_0.

- Reject H_0. There is sufficient evidence to reject/support the claim that ... (claim in words). The difference in sample means is significantly different/greater/less than δ_0. (If $\delta_0 = 0$: The sample means are significantly different. Sample mean 1 is significantly greater/less than sample mean 2.)

- Do not reject H_0. There is not sufficient evidence to reject/support the claim that ...(claim in words). The difference in sample means is significantly different/greater/less than δ_0. (If $\delta_0 = 0$: The sample means are significantly different. Sample mean 1 is significantly greater/less than sample mean 2.)

5.2.6.2 Confidence Interval on the Means and the Difference on Means

CL stands for *confidence limit* in the task output:

Variable	group-by variable	N	Lower CL Mean	Mean	Upper CL Mean
analysis variable	*1ˢᵗ group value*	n_1	$\bar{x}_1 - t_{\alpha/2}\dfrac{s_1}{\sqrt{n_1}}$	$\bar{x}_1$	$\bar{x}_1 + t_{\alpha/2}\dfrac{s_1}{\sqrt{n_1}}$
analysis variable	*2ⁿᵈ group value*	n_2	$\bar{x}_2 - t_{\alpha/2}\dfrac{s_2}{\sqrt{n_2}}$	$\bar{x}_2$	$\bar{x}_2 + t_{\alpha/2}\dfrac{s_2}{\sqrt{n_2}}$
analysis variable	**Diff (1-2)**		$\left(\bar{x}_1 - \bar{x}_2\right) - t_{\alpha/2}s_{\text{pooled}}\sqrt{\dfrac{1}{n_1}+\dfrac{1}{n_2}}$	$\bar{x}_1 - \bar{x}_2$	$\left(\bar{x}_1 - \bar{x}_2\right) + t_{\alpha/2}s_{\text{pooled}}\sqrt{\dfrac{1}{n_1}+\dfrac{1}{n_2}}$

5.2.7 Example 5.1: Samples from Populations with Equal Variances

This illustrates inference on the means and variances of two populations. The requested analysis includes hypothesis tests, confidence intervals, and a means plot.

- The hypothesis tests and confidence intervals are worked out in the "Detailed Solutions" section below.
- The Two-Sample *t* Test task is discussed in "Instructions for the Two-Sample *t* Test."
- Complete results are in "Task Output, Interpretation, and Analysis" for Example 5.1.

5.2.7.1 Parts Production

The Old River Castings Company makes metal parts for the automobile industry. The company monitors the percentage of metal parts that do not meet quality standards. The parts that do not meet standards become scrap and are reprocessed. The following experiment is designed to answer the question of whether two different products (part #12 and part #237) generate the same percentage of scrap, on average. Because of production requirements, part #12 is produced for 16 days and part #237 is produced for 5 days. The order of production is randomly determined. The percentage of parts that become scrap is computed at the end of each day. The results are below.

Part #12					Part #237				
4	5	4	4	4	20	15	18	16	19
10	6	6	9	9					
7	8	5	7	6					
3									

Estimate the ratio between the larger population variance and the smaller population variance. Test the claim that the variances associated with the two populations of percentage values are equal. Let $\alpha = 0.01$.

Example 5.1.1

If the previous claim is not rejected, estimate the common standard deviation. Construct a 99% equal-tailed confidence interval on the common standard deviation.

Example 5.1.2

Test the claim that the mean percentages of scrap are the same for all #12 parts and all #237 parts. Let $\alpha = 0.01$.

Example 5.1.3

Estimate the difference between the mean percentage of scrap among all #12 parts and the mean percentage of scrap among all #237 parts. Construct a 99% confidence interval on the difference between these population means.

Example 5.1.4

Create a means plot with bars equaling one standard deviation.

Input for the Two-Sample t Test task is a column of numerical data values—the *analysis variable*—and a column of classification values—the *group-by variable*. The analysis variable contains two samples. The sample membership of each value is identified by the corresponding value in the group-by variable.

Inferences are made on the difference of the two population means $\mu_1 - \mu_2$ using the difference of the two population means $\bar{x}_1 - \bar{x}_2$. The subscripts, which indicate the order of subtraction, are assigned according to the sorting order of the classification values. Sorting is done in numeric and alphabetic order with numbers being first in order, then uppercase letters, then the underscore, and then lowercase letters.

The results are in the Ex05_01 data set, shown below.

	PctScrap	PartNo
1	20	237
2	4	12
3	5	12
4	4	12
5	15	237
6	4	12
7	4	12
8	10	12
9	6	12
10	6	12
11	9	12
12	9	12
13	7	12
14	8	12
15	5	12
16	7	12
17	18	237
18	16	237
19	6	12
20	19	237
21	3	12

ex05_01 (read-only)

The analysis variable is PctScrap. The group-by variable is PartNo. The classification values are 12 and 237.

- The subscript 1 is assigned to the classification value that comes first in sorting order. In Example 5.1, subscript 1 refers to part #12.

- The subscript 2 is assigned to the classification value that comes second in sorting order. In Example 5.1, subscript 2 refers to part #237.

5.2.7.2 Detailed Solutions

To begin the analysis, the Summary Statistics task is used to compute some statistics and box-and-whisker plots. See Output 5.1.

The assumption that the samples come from normally distributed populations appears reasonable from the plots: The data are not strongly skewed and there are no outliers.

Output 5.1 Summary Tables Output for Example 5.1

Analysis Variable : PctScrap Percent scrap per day							
Part Number	N Obs	Mean	Std Dev	Variance	Minimum	Maximum	N
12	16	6.0625000	2.1124630	4.4625000	3.0000000	10.0000000	16
237	5	17.6000000	2.0736441	4.3000000	15.0000000	20.0000000	5

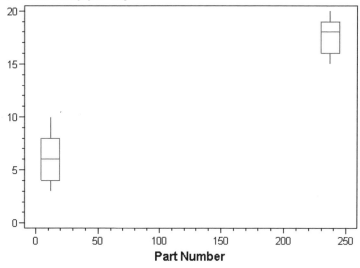

Comment

"Percent scrap per day" is the label of the PctScrap column. "Part Number" is the label of the PctNo column.

Example 5.1.1

The estimate of the ratio between the larger population variance and the smaller population

variance is: $F \text{ Value} = \dfrac{\max\left\{s_1^2, s_2^2\right\}}{\min\left\{s_1^2, s_2^2\right\}} = \dfrac{4.4625}{4.3} = 1.03779$.

To test the claim that the variances associated with the two populations of percentage values are equal:

Plan the task.

$H_0 : \sigma_1^2 = \sigma_2^2$

$H_1 : \sigma_1^2 \neq \sigma_2^2$

$\alpha = 0.05$

Compute the statistics.

$F \text{ Value} = \dfrac{\max\left\{s_1^2, s_2^2\right\}}{\min\left\{s_1^2, s_2^2\right\}} = \dfrac{4.4625}{4.3} = 1.03779$

Since sample 1 (part #12) has the larger variance, the numerator degrees-of-freedom value is ndf $= 16 - 1 = 15$. Since sample 2 (part #237) has the smaller variance, the denominator degrees-of-freedom value is ddf $= 5 - 1 = 4$.

Referring to Table 5.2:

p-value $= 2P\left(F > F \text{ Value}\right) = 2*(1 - \text{probf}(1.03779, 15,4)) = 1.0884109768$, which is interpreted as 1 since probability values are never greater than 1.

Apply the results.

Since p-value ≥ 0.01, do not reject H_0. There is not sufficient evidence to reject the claim that the variances associated with the two populations of percentage values are equal. The sample variances are not significantly different.

Example 5.1.2

The estimate of the common variance and common standard deviation are:

$s_{\text{pooled}}^2 = \dfrac{(n_1 - 1)s_1^2 + (n_2 - 1)s_2^2}{n_1 + n_2 - 2} = \dfrac{(16 - 1)(2.1125)^2 + (5 - 1)(2.0736)^2}{16 + 5 - 2} = 4.42837$

$s_{\text{pooled}} = \sqrt{s_{\text{pooled}}^2} = \sqrt{4.42837} = 2.10437$

The degrees-of-freedom value for the confidence interval on the common standard deviation is $n_1 + n_2 - 2 = 16 + 5 - 2 = 19$.

$$c_{0.995} = \text{cinv}(.005,19) = 6.84397$$

$$c_{0.005} = \text{cinv}(.995,19) = 38.58226$$

A 99% confidence interval on the common standard deviation:

$$\left(s_{pooled}\sqrt{\frac{n_1 + n_2 - 2}{c_{.025}}}, s_{pooled}\sqrt{\frac{n_1 + n_2 - 2}{c_{.975}}} \right)$$

$$\left(2.10437\sqrt{\frac{19}{38.58226}}, 2.10437\sqrt{\frac{19}{6.84397}} \right)$$

$$\left(1.47674, 3.50627 \right)$$

Example 5.1.3

The claim is "the mean percentages of scrap are the same for all #12 parts and #237 parts that are produced."

- Symbolically, this is " $\mu_1 = \mu_2$ " with subscript 1 referring to part #12 and subscript 2 referring to part #237.

- In terms of the difference of means, this is " $\mu_1 - \mu_2 = 0$ ".

For illustration purposes, both the pooled and Satterthwaite *t* tests are computed below. From Example 5.1.1, only the pooled *t* test is needed.

Plan the task.

$$H_0 : \mu_1 - \mu_2 = 0$$
$$H_1 : \mu_1 - \mu_2 \neq 0$$
$$\alpha = 0.01$$

Compute the statistics.

Pooled *t* test:

$$t \text{ Value} = \frac{(\bar{x}_1 - \bar{x}_2) - \delta_0}{s_{pooled}\sqrt{\frac{1}{n_1} + \frac{1}{n_2}}} = \frac{(6.0625 - 17.6) - 0}{\sqrt{4.42837}\sqrt{\frac{1}{16} + \frac{1}{5}}} = -10.701$$

$$\text{degree of freedom} = n_1 + n_2 - 2 = 16 + 5 - 2 = 19$$

$$p\text{-value} = 2P\left(T > \left|-10.701\right|\right) = 2*(1 - \text{probt}(\text{abs}(-10.701),19)) = 0.0000000017 < .0001$$

Satterthwaite t test:

$$t \text{ Value} = \frac{(\bar{x}_1 - \bar{x}_2) - \delta_0}{\sqrt{\dfrac{s_1^2}{n_1} + \dfrac{s_2^2}{n_2}}} = \frac{(6.0625 - 17.6) - 0}{\sqrt{\dfrac{(2.1125)^2}{16} + \dfrac{(2.0736)^2}{5}}} = -10.811$$

Satterthwaite's formula: $\quad \nu = \dfrac{\left(\dfrac{s_1^2}{n_1} + \dfrac{s_2^2}{n_2}\right)^2}{\dfrac{\left(\dfrac{s_1^2}{n_1}\right)^2}{n_1 - 1} + \dfrac{\left(\dfrac{s_2^2}{n_2}\right)^2}{n_2 - 1}} = \dfrac{\left(\dfrac{(2.1125)^2}{16} + \dfrac{(2.0736)^2}{5}\right)^2}{\dfrac{\left(\dfrac{(2.1125)^2}{16}\right)^2}{15} + \dfrac{\left(\dfrac{(2.0736)^2}{5}\right)^2}{4}} = 6.82$

$$p\text{-value} = 2P\left(T > |-10.811|\right) = 2*(1 - \text{probt}(\text{abs}(-10.811), 6.82)) = 0.000015 < .0001$$

Apply the results.

From Example 5.1.1, it is reasonable to assume that the underlying population variances are equal. The pooled t test is used to test the claim in Example 5.1.3.

Since p-value < 0.01, reject H_0. There is sufficient evidence to reject the claim that the mean percentages of scrap are the same for all #12 parts and all #237 parts. The sample means are significantly different.

Example 5.1.4

The estimate of the difference between the population means is
$\bar{x}_1 - \bar{x}_2 = 6.0625 - 17.6 = -11.5375$.

For illustration purposes, both the pooled and Satterthwaite confidence intervals are computed below. From Problem Example 5.1.1, only the pooled confidence interval is needed.

Pooled confidence interval:

- For a 99% confidence interval with $n_1 + n_2 - 2 = 19$ degrees of freedom, the critical value is $t_{.005} = \text{tinv}(.995, 19) = 2.861$.

- A 99% confidence interval on the difference between the mean percentage of scrap among all #12 parts that are produced and the mean percentage of scrap among all #237 parts that are produced:

$$\left((\bar{x}_1 - \bar{x}_2) - t_{.005} s_{\text{pooled}} \sqrt{\frac{1}{n_1} + \frac{1}{n_2}}, (\bar{x}_1 - \bar{x}_2) + t_{.005} s_{\text{pooled}} \sqrt{\frac{1}{n_1} + \frac{1}{n_2}} \right)$$

$$\left((6.0625 - 17.6) - (2.861)\sqrt{4.42837}\sqrt{\frac{1}{16} + \frac{1}{5}}, (6.0625 - 17.6) + (2.861)\sqrt{4.42837}\sqrt{\frac{1}{16} + \frac{1}{5}} \right)$$

$$(-14.62, -8.45)$$

Satterthwaite confidence interval:

- For a 99% confidence interval with 6.82 degrees of freedom, the critical value is $t_{.005} = \text{tinv}(.995, 6.82) = 3.5312$.

- A 99% confidence interval on the difference between the mean percentage of scrap among all #12 parts that are produced and the mean percentage of scrap among all #237 parts that are produced:

$$\left((\bar{x}_1 - \bar{x}_2) - t_{.005}\sqrt{\frac{s_1^2}{n_1} + \frac{s_2^2}{n_2}}, (\bar{x}_1 - \bar{x}_2) + t_{.005}\sqrt{\frac{s_1^2}{n_1} + \frac{s_2^2}{n_2}} \right)$$

$$\left((6.0625 - 17.6) - (3.5312)\sqrt{\frac{4.4625}{16} + \frac{4.3}{5}}, (6.0625 - 17.6) + (3.5312)\sqrt{\frac{4.4625}{16} + \frac{4.3}{5}} \right)$$

$$(-15.306, -7.769)$$

5.2.8 Instructions for the Two-Sample *t* Test

Open the *t* Test task in one of the following ways:

- From the menu bar, select **Analyze ▶ ANOVA ▶ t Test**.
- On the **Task by Category** tab of the **Task List**, go to the **ANOVA** section and click **t Test**.
- On the **Task by Name** tab of the **Task List**, double click **t Test**.

The *t* Test task has five of major groups of options: *t* Test Type, Task Roles, Analysis, Plots, and Titles. Titles are discussed in general in Chapter 1, "Introduction to SAS Enterprise Guide." The Titles options control the titles and the footnotes in the task output.

5.2.8.1 *t* Test Type

Two sample is the default selection. See Figure 5.2 at the top. The one-sample *t* test is discussed in Chapter 4, "Inferences from One Sample," and the paired *t* test is discussed in Section 5.3.

5.2.8.2 Task Roles

Click **Task Roles** on the selection pane to open this group of options. A variable is assigned to a role by dragging its name from **Variables to assign** to a role in **Task Roles**. See Figure 5.2 at the bottom. A variable can be removed from a role by dragging it back to **Variables**. The right and left arrows and the resulting pop-up menus can also be used.

- **Group by**: This variable contains the classification values that identify sample membership. The variable must contain only 2 distinct values.
- **Analysis variables**: Requested statistics and plots are computed for each variable in this role. The order that the variables are listed here is the order that they are listed in the output.

The roles Group analysis by, Frequency count, Relative weight are discussed in general in Chapter 1, "Introduction to SAS Enterprise Guide."

In Figure 5.2, the data is in the Ex05_01 data set. The variable PartNo is assigned to the Group **by** role. The variable PctScrap is assigned to the Analysis variables role.

Figure 5.2 *t* Test Type for Example 5.1 (Top); Task Roles for Example 5.1 (Bottom)

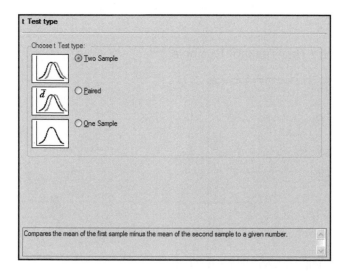

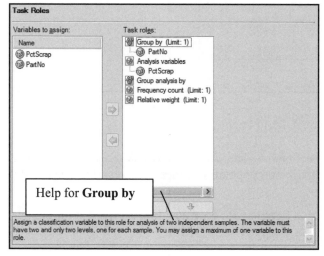

5.2.8.3 Analysis

Figure 5.3 shows the Analysis options.

- The hypothesis test comparison number δ_0 is entered here at Ho =.

- The task reports the *p*-value for the two-sided test $H_0 : \mu_1 - \mu_2 = \delta_0$ versus $H_0 : \mu_1 - \mu_2 \neq \delta_0$ at Pr > |t|. The *p*-values for one-sided tests ($H_0 : \mu_1 - \mu_2 \leq \delta_0$ versus $H_0 : \mu_1 - \mu_2 > \delta_0$, $H_0 : \mu_1 - \mu_2 \geq \delta_0$ versus $H_0 : \mu_1 - \mu_2 < \delta_0$) are computed from the **Pr >** |t| value. See Table 5.5.

- Confidence intervals on the means μ_1 and μ_2 and on the difference of means $\mu_1 - \mu_2$ are automatically part of the output. The common confidence level is determined here.

- Equal-tailed and UMPU confidence intervals on the standard deviations σ_1 and σ_2 and the common standard deviation σ are requested here. Their confidence levels are the same as for the confidence intervals on the means.

In Figure 5.3, a test of $H_0 : \mu_1 - \mu_2 = 0$ versus $H_0 : \mu_1 - \mu_2 \neq 0$ and 99% confidence intervals are requested. Equal-tailed confidence intervals on the standard deviations are also requested.

Figure 5.3 Analysis Options in the *t* Test Task for Example 5.1

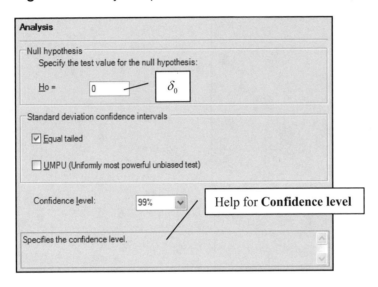

5.2.8.4   Plots

The Plots options are shown in Figure 5.4.

- Box plots are discussed in Section 3.5. The Two-Sample *t* Test task assumes that the data comes from two normally distributed populations. Ideally, each sample is not skewed and has no outliers.

- The means plot represents each sample with a vertical line centered at the sample mean.
  - The sample means are connected.
  - For a basic means plot, the length of the vertical line from its center is one standard deviation. That is, the first vertical line is drawn from $\overline{x}_1 - s_1$ to $\overline{x}_1 + s_1$. The second vertical line is drawn from $\overline{x}_2 - s_2$ to $\overline{x}_2 + s_2$.

A Means plot are selected in Figure 5.4. The length of each vertical line from its center is 1 (1 Unit) Standard deviation.

Figure 5.4 Plots Options in the *t* Test Task for Example 5.1

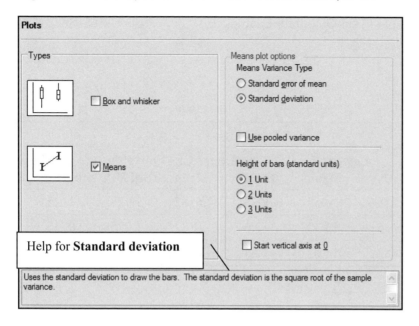

5.2.8.5   When Finished

When finished assigning variables to roles and selecting options, click **Run**. The task adds a *t* test icon and one or more output icons to the process flow diagram. See Figure 5.5.

Figure 5.5 Example 5.1 Data, Task, and Output Icons on the Process Flow Diagram

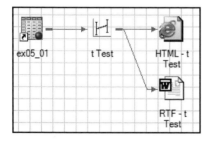

5.2.9 Task Output, Interpretation, and Analysis for Example 5.1

5.2.9.1 Task Output

Output 5.2 Two-Sample *t* Test Output for Example 5.1

t Test

The TTEST Procedure

Statistics								
Variable	**PartNo**	**N**	**Lower CL Mean**	**Mean**	**Upper CL Mean**	**Lower CL Std Dev**	**Std Dev**	**Upper CL Std Dev**
PctScrap	12	16	4.5063	6.0625	7.6187	1.4285	2.1125	3.8143
PctScrap	237	5	13.33	17.6	21.87	1.0758	2.0736	9.1157
PctScrap	Diff (1-2)		-14.62	-11.54	-8.453	1.4767	2.1044	3.5062
			❶	❷	❸	❹	❺	❻

Std Err	**Minimum**	**Maximum**
0.5281	3	10
0.9274	15	20
1.0782		
❼		

T-Tests					
			❽	❾	❿	⓫
Variable	**Method**	**Variances**	**DF**	**t Value**	**Pr > |t|**
PctScrap	Pooled	Equal	19	-10.70	<.0001
PctScrap	Satterthwaite	Unequal	6.82	-10.81	<.0001

Equality of Variances					
Variable	Method	Num DF	Den DF	F Value	Pr > F
PctScrap	Folded F	15	4	1.04	1.0000
		⑫	⑬	⑭	⑮

Means Plot

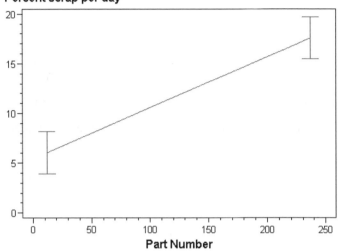

Comment

The **Statistics** table in Output 5.2 has been edited so that it fits within the margins.

5.2.9.2   Interpretation

❶ Lower 99% pooled confidence limit on the difference of population means:

$$\left(\overline{x}_1 - \overline{x}_2\right) - t_{.005} s_{\text{pooled}} \sqrt{\frac{1}{n_1} + \frac{1}{n_2}}$$

❷ Difference of sample means $\overline{x}_1 - \overline{x}_2$

❸ Upper 99% pooled confidence limit on the difference of population means:

$$\left(\overline{x}_1 - \overline{x}_2\right) + t_{.005} s_{\text{pooled}} \sqrt{\frac{1}{n_1} + \frac{1}{n_2}}$$

❹ Lower 99% confidence limit for the common population standard deviation $\sigma_1 = \sigma_2 = \sigma$:

$$s_{\text{pooled}} \sqrt{\frac{(n_1 + n_2 - 1)}{c_{.005}}}$$

❺ Pooled standard deviation s_{pooled}

❻ Upper 99% confidence limit for the common population standard deviation $\sigma_1 = \sigma_2 = \sigma$:

$$s_{\text{pooled}} \sqrt{\frac{(n_1 + n_2 - 1)}{c_{.995}}}$$

❼ Poole estimate of the standard error of the difference of means: $s_{\text{pooled}} \sqrt{\frac{1}{n_1} + \frac{1}{n_2}}$

❽ Satterthwaite allows for unequal variances: $\sigma_1^2 \neq \sigma_2^2$.

❾ Degrees-of-freedom value for the pooled t test is $n_1 + n_2 - 2$. Degrees-of-freedom value for the Satterthwaite t test is ν.

❿ t Value for the pooled t test in Example 5.1 is $t\ \text{value} = \dfrac{(\bar{x}_1 - \bar{x}_2) - 0}{s_{\text{pooled}} \sqrt{\dfrac{1}{n_1} + \dfrac{1}{n_2}}}$. The t value for

the Satterthwaite t test in Example 5.1 is $t\ \text{value} = \dfrac{(\bar{x}_1 - \bar{x}_2) - 0}{\sqrt{\dfrac{s_1^2}{n_1} + \dfrac{s_2^2}{n_2}}}$.

⓫ p-values for the pooled and Satterthwaite t tests of the hypotheses $H_0 : \mu_1 - \mu_2 = 0$ versus $H_1 : \mu_1 - \mu_2 \neq 0$

⓬ Numerator degrees of freedom

⓭ Denominator degrees of freedom

⓮ $F\ \text{Value} = \dfrac{\max\left\{s_1^2, s_2^2\right\}}{\min\left\{s_1^2, s_2^2\right\}}$

⓯ p-value for the hypotheses $H_0 : \sigma_1^2 = \sigma_2^2$ versus $H_0 : \sigma_1^2 \neq \sigma_2^2$

5.2.9.3 Analysis

Example 5.1.1
An estimate the ratio between the larger population variance and the smaller population variance is 1.04. See ⓮ in Output 5.2.

$$H_0 : \sigma_1^2 = \sigma_2^2$$
$$H_1 : \sigma_1^2 \neq \sigma_2^2$$

p-value $= 1.0000$. See ⓯ in Output 5.2.

Since *p-value* ≥ 0.01, do not reject H_0. There is not sufficient evidence to reject the claim that the variances associated with the two populations of percentage values are equal. The sample variances are not significantly different.

Example 5.1.2

See ❹, ❺, and ❻ in Output 5.2. An estimate of the common standard deviation is 2.1044. A 99% confidence interval on the common standard deviation is (1.4767, 3.5062).

Example 5.1.3

$H_0 : \mu_1 - \mu_2 = 0$

$H_1 : \mu_1 - \mu_2 \neq 0$

$\alpha = 0.01$

From Example 5.1.1, one would apply the pooled *t* test here.

p-value < 0.0001. See ⓫ in Output 5.2.

Since *p-value* < 0.01, reject H_0. There is sufficient evidence to reject the claim that the mean percentages of scrap are the same for all #12 parts and #237 parts. The sample means are significantly different.

Example 5.1.4

See ❶, ❷, and ❸ in Output 5.2. An estimate of the difference between the mean percentage of scrap among all #12 parts and the mean percentage of scrap among all #237 parts is −11.54. A 99% confidence interval on the difference between those mean percentages is (−14.62, −8.453). In other words, one can be 99% confident that the mean percentage of scrap among all #12 parts is between 8.435 and 14.62 points less than the mean percentage of scrap among all #237 parts.

Example 5.1.5

See Output 5.2. There are no outliers.

5.2.10 Example 5.2: Samples from Populations with Unequal Variances

5.2.10.1 Treatment for Lead Exposure

Medical researchers investigate a drug for the treatment of children who have been exposed to lead (based on "The Effect Chelation Therapy with Succimer on Neuropsychological Development in Children Exposed to Lead", Rogan et al., *New England Journal of Medicine*, Vol. 344, pp. 1421-1426). One of the effects of exposure is the lowering of IQ. Sixty exposed children take part in the study. Fifty are randomly assigned to receive a placebo and 10 are randomly assigned to receive the drug. After 12 months, the children take IQ tests. The data is on the right.

placebo					drug
68	75	69	61	73	90
66	68	91	71	65	77
63	60	65	62	59	86
76	69	74	72	70	84
62	82	58	55	63	90
66	74	81	80	73	76
77	77	57	70	81	53
81	73	75	78	68	60
66	64	65	74	81	92
59	58	74	56	69	65

Example 5.2.1

Estimate the ratio between the larger population variance and the smaller population variance. Test the claim that the variances associated with the two populations of IQ scores are equal. Let $\alpha = 0.05$.

    1.   Determine H_0 and H_1.

    2.   Determine the *p*-value.

    3.   State the formal decision, the concluding sentence, and the concluding observation.

Example 5.2.2

If the previous claim is not rejected, estimate the common standard deviation. Construct a 95% UMPU confidence interval on the common standard deviation.

Example 5.2.3

Test the claim that the mean IQ of children treated with the new drug is greater than the mean IQ of untreated children. Let $\alpha = 0.05$.

    1.   Determine H_0 and H_1.

    2.   Determine the *p*-value.

    3.   State the formal decision, the concluding sentence, and the concluding observation.

Example 5.2.4

Estimate the difference between the mean IQ of children treated with the new drug and the mean IQ of untreated children. Construct a 95% confidence interval on the difference between these population means.

Example 5.2.5

Construct box-and-whisker plots. Are there any outliers?

Example 5.2.6

Construct a means plot with bars equaling one standard deviation.

The results are in the Ex05_02 data set. The analysis variable is IQ. The group-by variable is treatment. The classification values are placebo and drug.

- The subscript 1 is assigned to the classification value that comes first in sorting order. In Example 5.2, subscript 1 refers to drug.

- The subscript 2 is assigned to the classification value that comes second in sorting order. In Example 5.1, subscript 2 refers to placebo.

The hypotheses being tested are:

$$H_0 : \mu_1 - \mu_2 \leq 0$$
$$H_1 : \mu_1 - \mu_2 > 0$$

5.2.11 Output, Interpretation, and Analysis for Example 5.2

5.2.11.1 Output

Output 5.3 Two-Sample *t* Test for Example 5.2

Test

The TTEST Procedure

Statistics								
Variable	treatment	N	Lower CL Mean	Mean	Upper CL Mean	Lower CL Std Dev	❷ Std Dev	Upper CL Std Dev
IQ	drug	10	67.462	77.3	87.138	9.4592	13.752	25.106
IQ	placebo	50	67.183	69.48	71.777	6.751	8.0818	10.071
IQ	Diff (1-2)		1.4448	7.82	14.195	7.7829	9.1939	11.234

Statistics		
Std Err	Minimum	Maximum
4.3488	53	92
1.1429	55	91
3.1848		

T-Tests					❹
Variable	Method	Variances	DF	t Value	Pr > |t|
IQ	Pooled	Equal	58	2.46	0.0171
IQ	Satterthwaite	Unequal	10.3	1.74	0.1118

❸

Equality of Variances					
Variable	Method	Num DF	Den DF	F Value	Pr > F
IQ	Folded F	9	49	2.90	0.0159

❺　　❻

Box Plot

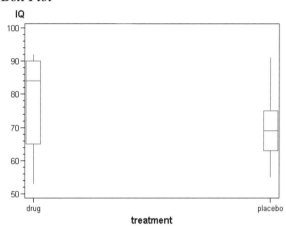

Means Plot

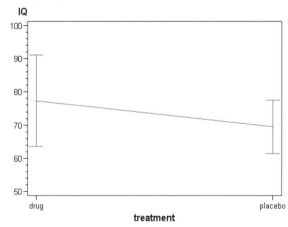

Interpretation

❶ Difference of sample means $\overline{x}_1 - \overline{x}_2$

❷ standard deviations: s_1, s_2, s_{pooled}

❸ Satterthwaite degrees of freedom v

❹ *p*-values for the pooled and Satterthwaite *t* tests of the hypotheses $H_0 : \mu_1 - \mu_2 = 0$ versus $H_1 : \mu_1 - \mu_2 \neq 0$

❺ $F \text{ Value} = \dfrac{\max\left\{s_1^2, s_2^2\right\}}{\min\left\{s_1^2, s_2^2\right\}}$

❻ *p*-value for the hypotheses $H_0 : \sigma_1^2 = \sigma_2^2$ versus $H_0 : \sigma_1^2 \neq \sigma_2^2$

5.2.11.2 Analysis

Example 5.2.1
The estimate of the ratio between the larger population variance and the smaller population variance is: $F \text{ Value} = \dfrac{\max\left\{s_1^2, s_2^2\right\}}{\min\left\{s_1^2, s_2^2\right\}} = 2.90$. See ❸ in Output 5.3.

$$H_0 : \sigma_1^2 = \sigma_2^2$$
$$H_1 : \sigma_1^2 \neq \sigma_2^2$$

p-value = 0.0159. See ❹ in Output 5.3.

Since the *p*-value < 0.05, reject H_0. There is sufficient evidence to reject the claim that the variances associated with the two populations of IQ scores are equal. The sample variances are significantly different.

Example 5.2.2
Since the previous claim is rejected, there is no common standard deviation.

Example 5.2.3
$$H_0 : \mu_1 - \mu_2 \leq 0$$
$$H_1 : \mu_1 - \mu_2 > 0$$

p-value = 0.5(0.1118) = 0.0559. The value 0.1118 at ❷ in Output 5.3 is the *p*-value for $H_0 : \mu_1 - \mu_2 = 0$ versus $H_0 : \mu_1 - \mu_2 \neq 0$. See Table 5.5. The Satterthwaite *t* test is used because of the result of Example 5.2.1.

Since the *p*-value ≥ 0.05, do not reject H_0. There is not sufficient evidence to support the claim that the mean IQ of the children treated with the new drug is greater than the mean IQ of untreated children. The mean IQ of the sample of children treated with the new drug is not significantly greater than the mean IQ of the sample of children taking a placebo.

Example 5.2.4
The estimate of the difference between the mean IQ of children treated with the new drug and the mean IQ of untreated children is 7.82. See ❶ in Output 5.3.

Since the Example 5.2.1 rejected the claim that the underlying variances are equal, the pooled confidence interval in the Output 5.3 is not appropriate. A confidence interval using Satterthwaite degrees of freedom can be computed using SAS code. See Table 5.8. This can be done using the Query Builder.

- For the lower confidence limit:

  expression: 7.82-tinv(.975,10.3)*sqrt((13.752)**2/10+(8.0818)**2/50)

  value: −2.1593

- For the upper confidence limit:

  expression: 7.82+tinv(.975,10.3)*sqrt((13.752)**2/10+(8.0818)**2/50)

  value: 17.7993

A 95% confidence interval on the difference between the mean IQ of the children treated with the new drug and the mean IQ of the untreated children is (−2.1593, 17.7993). In other words, it is estimated with 95% confidence that the mean IQ of children treated with the new drug is between 2.1593 points less than and 17.7993 points greater than the mean IQ of the untreated children.

Example 5.2.5 and Example 5.2.6
See Output 5.3. There are no outliers.

5.3 Inference on the Mean and Standard Deviation from a Population of Differences

The paired *t* test is appropriate to use when examining the difference between numerical values that are paired in a meaningful way. The paired *t* test is often used in situations where measurements are made before and after some activity. Also, much research is done with twins, simultaneous measurements on a single individual, and pairs of similar but unrelated subjects.

Inference is based on the differences between paired values x_1 and x_2: $d = x_1 - x_2$. The subscripts indicate the order of subtraction, which is determined with the Task Roles options in the *t* Test task.

- A *population of pairs* is a pairing of two populations of data values. The values in the two populations correspond to persons or objects that are paired.
  - The data values are represented by x_1 and x_2.
  - The mean μ_1 and variance σ_1^2 correspond to the population of x_1 values. The mean μ_2 and variance σ_2^2 correspond to the population of x_2 values.
- A *sample of pairs* is a collection of pairs of data values taken from a population of pairs.
  - The sample for the paired *t* test is *n* pairs of values — x_1 and x_2 — in two columns.
  - Statistics from the two columns have the same subscripts.

Population	Sample Mean	Sample Standard Deviation	Sample Variance
1	$\overline{x}_1$	s_1	s_1^2
2	$\overline{x}_2$	s_2	s_2^2

There is a *population of differences* $d = x_1 - x_2$ that is associated with the population pairs. It is assumed that the population of differences is normally distributed. Nevertheless, the Central Limit Theorem applies to the paired t test in the same way it applies to the one-sample t test.

- The mean difference is represented by μ_d. Its relationship to the means of the paired populations is straightforward: $\mu_d = \mu_1 - \mu_2$.

- The population variance is represented by σ_d^2. Its relationship to the variances of the paired populations is not so straightforward: $\sigma_d^2 = \sigma_1^2 - 2\rho\sigma_1\sigma_2 + \sigma_2^2$.

   o The value ρ is the population correlation coefficient: a measure of the strength of the relationship between the paired values in a population of pairs. See Chapter 7, "Correlation and Regression."

   o σ_d^2 is reduced when $\rho > 0$. This positive correlation occurs when the larger and smaller values in one population tend to be paired with the larger and smaller values, respectively, of the other population.

   o Persons or objects are paired with the objective of creating positively correlated values. This results in reducing the variation among differences.

The mean and variance of a *sample of differences* are analogous.

- The mean difference is represented by $\bar{d}$. It is equal to the difference of the means in the sample of pairs: $\bar{d} = \bar{x}_1 - \bar{x}_2$.

- The variance of the sample of differences is represented by s_d^2. It is equal to $s_d^2 = s_1^2 - 2rs_1s_2 + s_2^2$.

   o The value r is the sample correlation coefficient: a measure of the strength of the relationship between the paired values in a sample of pairs. See Chapter 7, "Correlation and Regression."

   o s_d^2 is reduced when $r > 0$. This positive correlation occurs when the larger and smaller values in one sample tend to be paired with the larger and smaller values, respectively, of the other sample.

   o A reduced s_d^2 results in better inference on μ_d. The test statistic is more likely to detect a false H_0 and the confidence interval is more precise.

5.3.1 Hypothesis Test on the Mean Difference

5.3.1.1 Null and Alternative Hypotheses

The paired t test is applied to hypotheses on the mean in a population of differences. This mean is denoted by μ_d and the comparison number in the hypotheses is denoted by δ_0.

$H_0 : \mu_d = \delta_0$	$H_0 : \mu_d \leq \delta_0$	$H_0 : \mu_d \geq \delta_0$
$H_1 : \mu_d \neq \delta_0$	$H_1 : \mu_d > \delta_0$	$H_1 : \mu_d < \delta_0$

Since the mean difference is equal to the difference of the means in the paired populations — $\mu_d = \mu_1 - \mu_2$ — the following hypotheses are equivalent.

$H_0 : \mu_1 - \mu_2 = \delta_0$	$H_0 : \mu_1 - \mu_2 \leq \delta_0$	$H_0 : \mu_1 - \mu_2 \geq \delta_0$
$H_1 : \mu_1 - \mu_2 \neq \delta_0$	$H_1 : \mu_1 - \mu_2 > \delta_0$	$H_1 : \mu_1 - \mu_2 < \delta_0$

5.3.1.2 Test Statistic

Technically, the paired t test is the one-sample t test applied to a sample of differences. Except for notation, the test statistic is the same t value as discussed in Section 4.3.

$$t \text{ Value} = \frac{\overline{d} - \delta_0}{\left(\dfrac{s_d}{\sqrt{n}} \right)}$$

5.3.1.3 *p*-Value

The p-value is a measure of the likelihood that the sample comes from a population where H_0 is true. Smaller values indicate less likelihood. That is, the more the data agrees with H_1 — the more $\overline{d}$ is different than, greater than, or less than δ_0 — the smaller the p-value.

In terms of the paired t test, the p-value is the probability that a random sample from a population of differences with mean δ_0 would produce a t value at or beyond the current value. If the p-value is small, it is unlikely that the current sample comes from a population with mean δ_0.

The technical definition of the p-value depends on the alternative hypothesis H_1. See Table 5.9. The random variable T represents a future value of the test statistic and follows the t distribution with $n - 1$ degrees of freedom.

Pr > |t| identifies the p-value in the paired t test output.

- The test of the hypotheses $H_0 : \mu_d = \delta_0$ versus $H_1 : \mu_d \neq \delta_0$ is a two-sided test. See the first graph in Table 5.9. *Pr > |t| is the p-value for a two-sided test.*

- The tests of $H_0 : \mu_d \leq \delta_0$ versus $H_1 : \mu_d > \delta_0$ and $H_0 : \mu_d \geq \delta_0$ versus $H_1 : \mu_d < \delta_0$ are one-sided tests. See the second and third graphs in Table 5.9. *The p-values for one-sided tests are computed from the Pr > |t| value.* See Table 5.9.

SAS code expressions are included in Table 5.9 to aid in the discussion. The p-value is computed using an expression in the "Detailed Solutions" section of "Example 5.3: Comparing Paired Measurements." In the expressions, t value and $n - 1$ represent numbers.

Table 5.9 *p*-Values for Paired *t* Test

Hypotheses	Gray areas correspond to probability statements and are examples.
$H_0 : \mu_d = \delta_0$ $H_1 : \mu_d \neq \delta_0$	 $p\text{-value} = 2P\big(T \geq |t \text{ Value}|\big)$	Task output: Pr > |t| SAS code expression: 2*(1-probt(abs(*t* Value),*n* − 1))
$H_0 : \mu_d \leq \delta_0$ $H_1 : \mu_d > \delta_0$	 $p\text{-value} = P\big(T \geq t \text{ Value}\big)$	Computed from task output: • 0.5(Pr > |t|), if *t* Value > 0 • 1 − 0.5(Pr > |t|), if *t* Value ≤ 0 SAS code expression: 1-probt(*t* Value,*n* − 1)
$H_0 : \mu_d \geq \delta_0$ $H_1 : \mu_d < \delta_0$	 $p\text{-value} = P\big(T \leq t \text{ Value}\big)$	Computed from task output: 1 − 0.5(Pr > |t|), if *t* Value ≥ 0 0.5(Pr > |t|), if *t* Value < 0 SAS code expression: probt(*t* Value,*n* − 1)

5.3.1.4 Decision and Conclusions

The formal decision and concluding sentence do not change from the one-sample tests discussed in Chapter 4, "Inferences from One Sample." The concluding observation depends on the particular statistics involved in the test.

If the *p*-value is small, the data agrees with H_1. If the *p*-value is less than the significance level, the risk of making a Type I error is acceptable. Therefore, the *p*-value decision rule is the following:

If the *p*-value < α, reject H_0. Otherwise, do not reject H_0.

Since a hypothesis test begins with the assumption that H_0 is true, concluding a hypothesis test requires one of the following formal statements.

- Reject H_0.
- Do not reject H_0.

When the claim is equivalent to the null hypothesis, the concluding sentence uses the word *reject*. The concluding sentence becomes an expanded version of the formal decision.

When the claim is equivalent to the alternative hypothesis, the concluding sentence uses the word *support*. If the data supports the rejection of H_0, the data supports H_1. If the data does not support rejection of H_0, the data cannot support H_1.

Table 5.10 Concluding Sentences

Formal Statistical Decision	Claim stated as H_0	Claim stated as H_1
Reject H_0.	There is sufficient evidence to reject the claim that ... (claim in words).	There is sufficient evidence to support the claim that ... (claim in words).
Do not reject H_0.	There is not sufficient evidence to reject the claim that ... (claim in words).	There is not sufficient evidence to support the claim that ... (claim in words).

Table 5.11 Concluding Observations

Reject H_0.	The mean of the sample of differences is significantly different/greater/less than δ_0.
Do not reject H_0.	The mean of the sample of differences is not significantly different/greater/less than δ_0.

5.3.2 Estimation of the Mean Difference

The point estimate of the mean of a population of differences μ_d is the mean of a sample of differences $\bar{d}$. Since $\bar{d} = \bar{x}_1 - \bar{x}_2$, the difference $\bar{x}_1 - \bar{x}_2$ is also a point estimate of μ_d.

The confidence interval is based on the t distribution. A critical value for a t distribution is denoted by t_q, where q is between 0 and 1. The critical value t_q is a value on the number line that marks the right q proportion of the distribution. For a fixed q, there is a different t_q value for each degrees-of-freedom value. Using SAS code, $t_q = \text{tinv}(1-q, df)$. In the expression, $1-q$ and df (the degrees-of-freedom value) represent numbers.

For a sample from a normally distributed population of differences, a $(1-\alpha)100\%$ confidence interval on the mean μ_d is:

$$\left(\bar{d} - t_{\alpha/2} \frac{s_d}{\sqrt{n}}, \bar{d} + t_{\alpha/2} \frac{s_d}{\sqrt{n}} \right)$$

The degrees-of-freedom value associated with the critical value is $n-1$.

5.3.3 Estimation of the Variance and Standard Deviation of the Differences

The point estimate of the population variance σ_d^2 is the sample variance s_d^2. The point estimate of the population standard deviation σ_d are the sample standard deviation s_d.

The confidence intervals for the standard deviation and variance are based on the chi-squared (χ^2) distribution. A critical value for a chi-squared distribution is denoted by c_q, where q is between 0 and 1. The critical value c_q is a value on the number line that marks the right q proportion of the distribution. For a fixed q, there is a different c_q value for each degrees-of-freedom value. Using SAS code, $c_q = \text{cinv}(1-q,\text{df})$. In the expression, $1-q$ and df (the degrees-of-freedom value) represent numbers.

For a sample from a normally distributed population of differences, a $(1-\alpha)100\%$ confidence interval on the variance σ_d^2 is:

$$\left(\frac{(n-1)s_d^2}{c_{\alpha/2}}, \frac{(n-1)s_d^2}{c_{1-\alpha/2}} \right)$$

The degrees-of-freedom value associated with the critical values is $n-1$. A $(1-\alpha)100\%$ confidence interval on the standard deviation σ_d is:

$$\left(s_d \sqrt{\frac{n-1}{c_{\alpha/2}}}, s_d \sqrt{\frac{n-1}{c_{1-\alpha/2}}} \right)$$

The confidence interval above is referred to as equal tailed because the area in either distribution tail is $\alpha/2$. The critical values $c_{1-\alpha/2}$ and $c_{\alpha/2}$ might not result in the shortest—most precise—confidence interval. A task option produces uniformly most powerful unbiased (UMPU) confidence intervals. The formulas are the same except for the critical value notation. The critical values $c_{1-\alpha/2}$ and $c_{\alpha/2}$ are replaced by c_{lower} and c_{upper}, the closest critical values that have $(1-\alpha)100\%$ of the distribution between them.

5.3.4 Summary of the Hypothesis Test and Confidence Intervals

5.3.4.1 Hypothesis Test

Plan the experiment.

$$H_0 : \mu_d = \delta_0 \qquad H_0 : \mu_d \leq \delta_0 \qquad H_0 : \mu_d \geq \delta_0 \qquad \left.\vphantom{\begin{array}{c} a \\ b \end{array}}\right\} \text{Task requires } \delta_0.$$
$$H_1 : \mu_d \neq \delta_0 \qquad H_1 : \mu_d > \delta_0 \qquad H_1 : \mu_d < \delta_0$$

The significance level is α.

Task computes the statistics.

T-Tests			
Difference	**DF**	**t Value**	**Pr > |t|**
variable1 - variable2	degrees of freedom $= n-1$	$t \text{ Value} = \dfrac{\bar{d} - \delta_0}{\left(\dfrac{s_d}{\sqrt{n}}\right)}$	p-value for $H_0 : \mu_d = \delta_0$ $H_1 : \mu_d \neq \delta_0$

Determine the *p*-value.

Hypotheses	
$H_0 : \mu_d = \delta_0$ $H_1 : \mu_d \neq \delta_0$	$p\text{-value} = \left(\Pr > \|t\| \right)$
$H_0 : \mu_d \leq \delta_0$ $H_1 : \mu_d > \delta_0$	$p\text{-value} = \begin{cases} 0.5\left(\Pr > \|t\|\right), \text{ if } t \text{ Value} > 0 \\ 1 - 0.5\left(\Pr > \|t\|\right), \text{ if } t \text{ Value} \leq 0 \end{cases}$
$H_0 : \mu_d \geq \delta_0$ $H_1 : \mu_d < \delta_0$	$p\text{-value} = \begin{cases} 1 - 0.5\left(\Pr > \|t\|\right), \text{ if } t \text{ Value} \geq 0 \\ 0.5\left(\Pr > \|t\|\right), \text{ if } t \text{ Value} < 0 \end{cases}$

Apply the results.

If the *p-value* < α, reject H_0. Otherwise, do not reject H_0.

- Reject H_0. There is sufficient evidence to reject/support the claim that ... (claim in words). The sample mean difference is significantly different/greater/less than δ_0.

- Do not reject H_0. There is not sufficient evidence to reject/support the claim that ...(claim in words). The sample mean difference is not significantly different/greater/less than δ_0.

5.3.4.2 Confidence Interval on the Mean

CL stands for *confidence limit* in the task output:

Lower CL Mean	Mean	Upper CL Mean
$\bar{d} - t_{\alpha/2}\dfrac{s_d}{\sqrt{n}}$	$\bar{d}$	$\bar{d} + t_{\alpha/2}\dfrac{s_d}{\sqrt{n}}$

5.3.4.3 Confidence Intervals on the Standard Deviation

CL stands for *confidence limit* in the task output:

Lower CL Std Dev	UMPU Lower CL Std Dev	Std Dev	UMPU Upper CL Std Dev	Upper CL Std Dev
$s_d\sqrt{\dfrac{n-1}{c_{\alpha/2}}}$	$s_d\sqrt{\dfrac{n-1}{c_{\text{upper}}}}$	s_d	$s_d\sqrt{\dfrac{n-1}{c_{\text{lower}}}}$	$s_d\sqrt{\dfrac{n-1}{c_{1-\alpha/2}}}$

5.3.5 Example 5.3: Comparing Paired Measurements

This illustrates inference on a population of differences. The requested analysis includes a hypothesis test, confidence intervals, and a box-and-whisker plot.

- The hypothesis test and confidence intervals are worked out in the Detailed Solutions section below.

- The Paired *t* Test task is discussed in "Instructions for the Paired *t* Test."

- Complete results are in "Task Output, Interpretation, and Analysis" for Example 5.3.

5.3.5.1 General Education Assessment

A university assesses the quality of its general education program by testing each student's intellectual skills before their first general education course and then after completion of the program. The following data represents the results from 22 randomly selected students. Pre are the scores from the pre-general education test and Post are the scores from the post-general education test. The Pre and Post test scores are paired by student.

Student	1	2	3	4	5	6	7	8	9	10	11
Pre	14	24	19	25	20	21	15	16	38	21	16
Post	30	29	40	42	24	38	46	42	75	34	31

Student	12	13	14	15	16	17	18	19	20	21	22
Pre	23	15	25	15	16	13	37	8	42	17	28
Post	38	28	63	16	44	35	70	9	51	40	43

Example 5.3.1

Test the claim that, for all students, the mean difference between the post- and pre-general education test scores is positive. Let $\alpha = 0.05$.

Example 5.3.2

Estimate the mean difference between the post- and pre-general education test scores of all students. Construct a 95% confidence interval for this mean difference.

Example 5.3.3

Estimate the standard deviation of the differences between post- and pre-general education test scores of all students. Construct a 95% equal-tailed confidence interval for this standard deviation.

Example 5.3.4

Construct a box-and-whisker plot of the differences. Are there any outliers?

The results are in the Ex05_03 data set, which is shown below.

	Pre	Post
1	14	30
2	24	29
3	19	40
4	25	42
5	20	24
6	21	38
7	15	46
8	16	42
9	38	75
10	21	34
11	16	31
12	23	38
13	15	28
14	25	63
15	15	16
16	16	44
17	13	35
18	37	70
19	8	9
20	42	51
21	17	40
22	28	43

5.3.5.2 Detailed Solutions

The "difference between post-general education test scores and pre-general education test scores" is the measurement of interest. That is Post − Pre. See Table 5.12.

The Query Builder is used to create the differences. The Summary Tables task is applied to those differences. See Output 5.4.

Table 5.12 Post Minus Pre Differences

Student	1	2	3	4	5	6	7	8	9	10	11
d = Post − Pre	16	5	21	17	4	17	31	26	37	13	15

Student	12	13	14	15	16	17	18	19	20	21	22
d = Post − Pre	15	13	38	1	28	22	33	1	9	23	15

Output 5.4 Summary Tables Output for Example 5.3

	N	Mean	StdDev
d	22	18.181818182	10.856801088

Example 5.3.1

The claim is "the mean difference between post-general education test scores and pre-general education test scores would be positive if all students were tested."

The numerical comparison is "the mean difference … would be positive". This is "$\mu_d > 0$".

Plan the task.

$H_0 : \mu_d \leq 0$

$H_1 : \mu_d > 0$

$\alpha = 0.05$

Compute the statistics.

$$t \text{ Value} = \frac{\bar{d} - \delta_0}{\left(\frac{s_d}{\sqrt{n}}\right)} = \frac{18.181818182 - 0}{\left(\frac{10.856801088}{\sqrt{22}}\right)} = 7.855$$

The degrees of freedom for the one-sample t test is $n - 1$. For Example 5.3, degrees of freedom = 21. Referring to Table 5.9:

p-value = $P(T > 7.855)$ = 1-probt(7.855,21) = 0.000000055 < 0.0001

Apply the results.

Since p-value < 0.05, reject H_0. There is sufficient evidence to support the claim that, for all students, the mean difference between the post- and pre-general education test scores is positive. The sample mean difference, $\bar{d} = 18.18$, is significantly greater than 0.

Example 5.3.2

The estimate of the population mean is $\bar{d} = 18.18$.

The degrees of freedom for the confidence interval on the mean is $n - 1$. For Example 5.3, degrees of freedom = 21.

$$t_{0.025} = \text{tinv}(.975, 21) = 2.0796$$

A 95% confidence interval on the population mean:

$$\left(\bar{d} - t_{.025} \frac{s_d}{\sqrt{n}}, \bar{d} + t_{.025} \frac{s_d}{\sqrt{n}} \right)$$

$$\left(18.181818182 - 2.0796 \frac{10.856801088}{\sqrt{22}}, 18.181818182 + 2.0796 \frac{10.856801088}{\sqrt{22}} \right)$$

$$(13.3682, 22.9954)$$

Example 5.3.3

The estimate of the population standard deviation is $s_d = 10.856801088$.

The degrees of freedom for the confidence interval on the standard deviation is $n - 1$. For Example 5.3, degrees of freedom = 21.

$$c_{0.975} = \text{cinv}(.025, 21) = 10.2829 \quad c_{0.025} = \text{cinv}(.975, 21) = 35.4789$$

A 95% confidence interval on the population standard deviation:

$$\left(s_d \sqrt{\frac{n-1}{c_{.025}}}, s_d \sqrt{\frac{n-1}{c_{.975}}} \right)$$

$$\left(10.856801088 \sqrt{\frac{22-1}{35.4789}}, 10.856801088 \sqrt{\frac{22-1}{10.2829}} \right)$$

$$(8.3527, 15.5151)$$

5.3.6 Instructions for the Paired *t* Test

Open the *t* Test task in one of the following ways:

- From the menu bar, select **Analyze ▶ ANOVA ▶ t Test**.
- On the **Task by Category** tab of the **Task List**, go to the **ANOVA** section and click **t Test**.
- On the **Task by Name** tab of the **Task List**, double click **t Test**.

The *t* Test task has five of major groups of options: *t* Test Type, Task Roles, Analysis, Plots, and Titles. Titles are discussed in general in Chapter 1, "Introduction to SAS Enterprise Guide." The Titles options control the titles and the footnotes in the task output.

5.3.6.1 *t* Test type

Select **Paired** for the paired *t* test. See Figure 5.6. The one-sample *t* test is discussed in Chapter 4, "Inferences from One Sample," and the two-sample *t* test is discussed in Section 5.2.

Figure 5.6 *t* Test Type in the *t* Test Task for Example 5.3

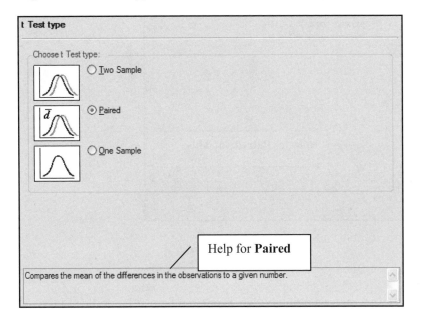

5.3.6.2 Task Roles

Click **Task Roles** on the selection pane to open this group of options. A variable is assigned to a role by dragging its name from **Variables to assign** to a role in **Task Roles**. See Figure 5.7. A variable can be removed from a role by dragging it back to **Variables to assign**. The right and left arrows and the resulting pop-up menus can also be used.

- **Paired variables**: Analysis is performed on the values resulting from the row-wise subtraction of the two variables. The order that the variables are listed here is the order of subtraction. See Figure 5.7.

The roles Group analysis by, Frequency count, and Relative weight are discussed in general in Chapter 1, "Introduction to SAS Enterprise Guide."

In Figure 5.7, the data is in the Ex05_03 data set. The variables Post and Pre are assigned to the Paired variables role. The analysis is on the values resulting from the row-wise subtraction Post − Pre.

Figure 5.7 Task Roles in the *t* Test Task for Example 5.3

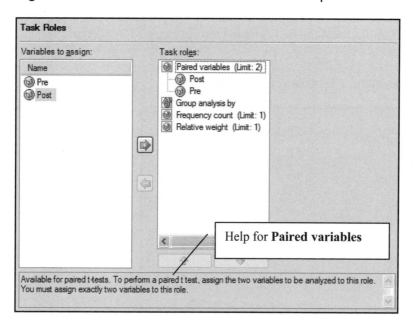

5.3.6.3   Analysis

- The hypothesis test comparison number δ_0 is entered here at Ho =. See Figure 5.8 at the top.

- The task reports the *p*-value for the two-sided test $H_0 : \mu_d = \delta_0$ versus $H_1 : \mu_d \neq \delta_0$ at Pr > |t|. The *p*-values for one-sided tests ($H_0 : \mu_d \leq \delta_0$ versus $H_1 : \mu_d > \delta_0$, $H_0 : \mu_d \geq \delta_0$ versus $H_1 : \mu_d < \delta_0$) are computed from the Pr > |t| value. See Table 5.9.

- A confidence interval on the mean μ_d is automatically part of the output. Its Confidence level is determined here.

- Equal-tailed and UMPU confidence intervals on the standard deviation σ_d are requested here. Their confidence levels are the same as for the confidence interval on the mean.

The options selected in Figure 5.8 requests are a test of $H_0 : \mu_d = 0$ versus $H_1 : \mu_d \neq 0$, a 95% confidence interval on the mean μ_d, and a 95% equal-tailed confidence interval on the standard deviation σ_d.

Since Example 5.3 tests $H_0 : \mu_d \leq 0$ versus $H_1 : \mu_d > 0$, the correct *p*-value is computed from the Pr > |t| value in the analysis section of "Task Output, Interpretation, and Analysis for Example 5.3."

5.3.6.4 Plots

The plots with the paired *t* test are based on the sample of differences.

The box-and-whisker plot is selected in Figure 5.8 at the bottom. The paired *t* test assumes that the differences come from a normally distributed population. Ideally, the sample is not skewed and has no outliers.

Figure 5.8 Analysis Options (Top); Plots Options (Bottom)

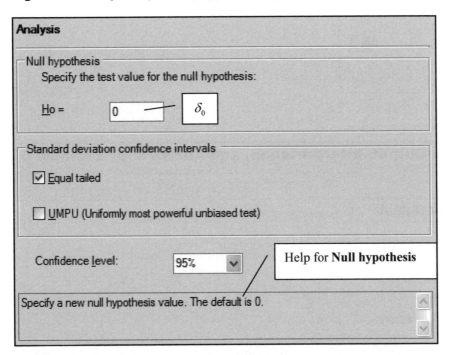

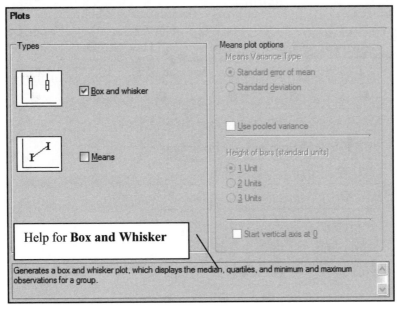

5.3.6.5   When Finished

When finished assigning variables to roles and selecting options, click **Run**. The task adds a *t* Test icon and one or more output icons to the process flow diagram. See Figure 5.9.

Figure 5.9 Example 5.3 Data, Task, and Output Icons on the Process Flow Diagram

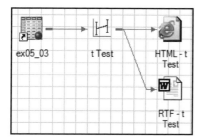

5.3.7   Task Output, Interpretation, and Analysis for Example 5.3

5.3.7.1   Task Output

Output 5.5   Paired *t* Test Output for Example 5.3

t Test

The TTEST Procedure

Statistics						
Difference	N	Lower CL Mean	Mean	Upper CL Mean	Lower CL Std Dev	Std Dev	Upper CL Std Dev
Post - Pre	22	13.368	18.182	22.995	8.3527	10.857	15.515
❶		❷	❸	❹	❺	❻	❼

Std Err	Minimum	Maximum
2.3147	1	38
❽		

T-Tests			
Difference	DF	t Value	Pr > |t|
Post - Pre	21	7.86	<.0001
	❾	❿	⓫

Box Plot

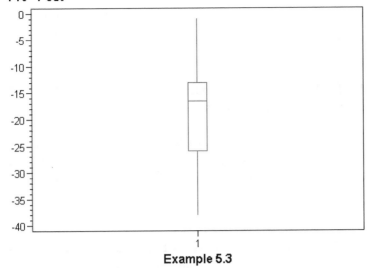

Example 5.3

Comment

- The Statistics table in Output 5.4 has been edited so that it fits within the margins.
- For the box-and-whisker plot, the background is changed to white and the horizontal axis label has been changed from _const to Example 5.3.

5.3.7.2 Interpretation

❶ The **Difference** being analyzed is **Post - Pre**.

❷ Lower 95% confidence limit for the population mean: $\bar{d} - t_{0.025} \dfrac{s_d}{\sqrt{n}}$

❸ Sample mean $\bar{d}$

❹ Upper 95% confidence limit for the population mean: $\bar{d} + t_{0.025} \dfrac{s_d}{\sqrt{n}}$

❺ Lower 95% confidence limit for the population standard deviation: $s_d \sqrt{\dfrac{n-1}{c_{0.025}}}$

❻ Sample standard deviation s_d

❼ Upper 95% confidence limit for the population standard deviation: $s_d \sqrt{\dfrac{n-1}{c_{0.975}}}$

❽ Estimate of the standard error of the mean: $s_d / \sqrt{n}$

❾ degrees of freedom: $n - 1$

❿ t Statistic $= \dfrac{\bar{d} - 0}{\left(\dfrac{s_d}{\sqrt{n}}\right)}$

⓫ p-value for test of the hypotheses $H_0 : \mu_d = 0$ versus $H_1 : \mu_d \neq 0$

5.3.7.3 Analysis

Example 5.3.1

$$H_0 : \mu_d \leq 0$$
$$H_1 : \mu_d > 0$$

Since t value > 0, the p-value for the test of the hypotheses $H_0 : \mu_d \leq 0$ versus $H_1 : \mu_d > 0$ is less than $0.5(0.0001) = 0.00005$. See ❿ and ⓫ in Output 5.4.

Since the p-value < 0.05, reject H_0. There is sufficient evidence to support the claim that, for all students, the mean difference between the post- and pre-general education test scores is positive. The sample mean difference, $\bar{d} = 18.18$, is significantly greater than 0.

Example 5.3.2

See ❷, ❸ and ❹ in Output 5.4. An estimate of the mean difference between the post- and pre-general education test scores of all students is 18.182 points. A 95% confidence interval on the mean difference between the post- and pre-general education test scores of all students is (13.368, 22.995). In other words, the university is 95% confident that, on average, post-general education test scores are between 13.368 and 22.995 points higher than the pre-general education test scores.

Example 5.3.3

See ❺, ❻ and ❼ in Output 5.4. An estimate of the standard deviation of the differences between post- and pre-general education test scores of all students is 10.857. A 95% equal-tailed confidence interval for the standard deviation of the differences between post- and pre-general education test scores of all students is (8.3527, 15.515).

Example 5.3.4

See Output 5.4. There are no outliers.

5.3.8 Example 5.4: Comparing Differences to a Value

Example 5.3 shows that there is a positive difference, on average, between post-general education test scores and pre-general education test scores.

For this example, test the claim that, for all students, the mean difference between the post- and pre-general education test scores is more than 15 points. Let $\alpha = 0.05$.

    a.   Determine H_0 and H_1.

    b.   Determine the p-value.

    c.   State the formal decision, the concluding sentence, and the concluding observation.

This example again uses the Ex05_03 data set shown in Example 5.3.

The task is opened from the process flow diagram. See Figure 5.9. The Analysis options are selected and the new hypothesis test comparison number $\delta_0 = 15$ is entered at Ho =.

The output is the same except for the t tests table.

5.3.9 Output, Interpretation, and Analysis for Example 5.4

5.3.9.1 Output

Output 5.6 Paired *t* Test for Example 5.4

t Test

The TTEST Procedure

Statistics							
Difference	**N**	**Lower CL Mean**	**Mean**	**Upper CL Mean**	**Lower CL Std Dev**	**Std Dev**	**Upper CL Std Dev**
Post - Pre	22	13.368	18.182	22.995	8.3527	10.857	15.515

❶   ❷

Std Err	**Minimum**	**Maximum**
2.3147	1	38

T-Tests			
Difference	**DF**	**t Value**	**Pr > |t|**
Post - Pre	21	1.37	0.1837

❸

5.3.9.2 Interpretation

❶ Confidence interval on μ_d

❷ Confidence interval on σ_d

❸ *p*-value for test of the hypotheses $H_0 : \mu_d = 15$ versus $H_1 : \mu_d \neq 15$

5.3.9.3 Analysis

$H_0 : \mu_d \leq 15$

$H_1 : \mu_d > 15$

Since *t* value > 0, the *p*-value for the test of the hypotheses $H_0 : \mu_d \leq 15$ versus $H_1 : \mu_d > 15$ is $0.5(0.1837) = 0.09185$. See ❸ in Output 5.4.

Since the *p-value* ≥ 0.05, do not reject H_0. There is not sufficient evidence to support the claim that, for all students, the mean difference between the post- and pre-general education test scores is more than 15 points. The sample mean difference, $\bar{d} = 18.182$, is not significantly greater than 15.

5.4 Inference on the Medians of Two Independent Populations

The Wilcoxon Rank-Sum Test and the Median Test are used to compare the medians of two independent populations, θ_1 and θ_2. Two populations are independent when the values in one population are not being paired with the values in the other population. Furthermore, samples are taken from one population without any reference to the other population.

These tests are nonparametric analogs to the two-sample *t*-test for means, which is discussed in Section 5.2. Here, the underlying populations are not assumed to be normally distributed. The Wilcoxon Rank-Sum Test and the Median Test have different assumptions about the populations.

The tests are often considered when the combination of an insufficiently large sample size and a lack of normality in the data—generally outliers and skewness—cause the two-sample *t*-test to be ineffective.

Input is a column of numerical data values—the dependent variable—and a column of classification values—the independent variable. The dependent variable contains two samples. The sample membership of each value is identified by the corresponding value in the independent variable.

The subscripts 1 and 2 correspond to the groups that occur first and second in the data set.

5.4.1 Hypothesis Tests on Two Medians

The following are the three pairs of null and alternative hypotheses comparing θ_1 and θ_2.

$H_0 : \theta_1 = \theta_2$	$H_0 : \theta_1 \leq \theta_2$	$H_0 : \theta_1 \geq \theta_2$
$H_1 : \theta_1 \neq \theta_2$	$H_1 : \theta_1 > \theta_2$	$H_1 : \theta_1 < \theta_2$

5.4.1.1 Wilcoxon Rank-Sum Test

The Wilcoxon Rank-Sum Test assumes that each sample is from a continuous population and that the shapes of the two population distributions are the same.

The test is based on the ranks of the values in the combined samples. Using ranks instead of the actual values reduces the effect of outliers.

- n_1 and n_2 are the numbers of values in the first and second sample.

- All $n_1 + n_2$ observations are ranked smallest to largest without regard to sample membership. Average ranks are used in case of ties.

  o The sum of all ranks is $\dfrac{(n_1 + n_2)(n_1 + n_2 + 1)}{2}$.

  o The mean of all ranks is $\dfrac{(n_1 + n_2 + 1)}{2}$.

- T_1 and T_2 are the sums of the ranks of the first and second samples.

  o $T_1 + T_2 = \dfrac{(n_1 + n_2)(n_1 + n_2 + 1)}{2}$

- $\dfrac{T_1}{n_1}$ and $\dfrac{T_2}{n_2}$ are the means of the ranks of the first and second samples.

  Under H_0, it is assumed that $\theta_1 = \theta_2$. In which case, T_1/n_1 and T_2/n_2 are expected to be equal. If $T_1/n_1 = T_2/n_2$, then $T_1/n_1 = T_2/n_2 = (n_1 + n_2 + 1)/2$.

- T_1 is expected to be $n_1(n_1 + n_2 + 1)/2$.

- T_2 is expected to be $n_2(n_1 + n_2 + 1)/2$.

  Depending on the sample sizes, the test statistic is a measure of the difference between T_1 and its expected value or T_2 and it expected value.

  The test statistic is:

$$Z \text{ Statistic} = \begin{cases} \dfrac{T_1 - \dfrac{n_1(n_1 + n_2 + 1)}{2} \pm 0.5}{\sqrt{\dfrac{n_1 n_2}{n_1 + n_2} s_R^2}} & , \text{if } n_1 \leq n_2 \\[4em] \dfrac{T_2 - \dfrac{n_2(n_1 + n_2 + 1)}{2} \pm 0.5}{\sqrt{\dfrac{n_1 n_2}{n_1 + n_2} s_R^2}} & , \text{if } n_1 > n_2 \end{cases}$$

The continuity correction 0.5 is added if the preceding difference is less than 0. It is subtracted if the preceding difference is greater than 0. The statistic s_R^2 is the variance of all ranks.

The definitions of the *p*-values are in Table 5.13. The random variable Z represents a future value of the test statistic and follows the standard normal distribution.

Table 5.13 *p*-Values for Wilcoxon Rank-Sum Test *Z* Statistic

Hypotheses	p-value =	Compute Dialog Expression
$H_0: \theta_1 = \theta_2$ $H_1: \theta_1 \neq \theta_2$	$2P\big(Z \geq |Z \text{ Statistic}|\big)$	$2*(1 - \text{probnorm}(\text{abs}(Z \text{ Statistic})))$
$H_0: \theta_1 \leq \theta_2$ $H_1: \theta_1 > \theta_2$	$P\big(Z \geq Z \text{ Statistic}\big)$	$1 - \text{probnorm}(Z \text{ Statistic})$
$H_0: \theta_1 \geq \theta_2$ $H_1: \theta_1 < \theta_2$	$P\big(Z \leq Z \text{ Statistic}\big)$	$\text{probnorm}(Z \text{ Statistic})$

5.4.1.2   Median Test

The Median Test only assumes that each sample is from a continuous population. The test is based on proportions of values being above the overall sample median. The effect of outliers is eliminated.

- n_1 and n_2 are the numbers of values in the first and second sample.

- $\tilde{x}$ is the median of all $n_1 + n_2$ values.

- T_1 and T_2 are the numbers of values above $\tilde{x}$ in the first and second samples.

- $\dfrac{T_1}{n_1}$ and $\dfrac{T_2}{n_2}$ are the proportions of values above $\tilde{x}$ in the first and second samples.

- $\dfrac{T_1 + T_2}{n_1 + n_2}$ is the proportion of all $n_1 + n_2$ values above $\tilde{x}$.

  In theory, $(T_1 + T_2)/(n_1 + n_2)$ is expected to equal 0.5 when $n_1 + n_2$ is an even number and to equal $0.5(n_1 + n_2 - 1)/(n_1 + n_2)$ when $n_1 + n_2$ is an odd number. The actual proportions might be lower when multiple values in the combined sample equal $\tilde{x}$.

  Under H_0, it is assumed that $\theta_1 = \theta_2$. The statistic $\tilde{x}$ is the estimate of the common population median. The sample proportions T_1/n_1 and T_2/n_2 are expected to equal $(T_1 + T_2)/(n_1 + n_2)$.

- T_1 is expected to be $n_1(T_1 + T_2)/(n_1 + n_2)$.

- T_2 is expected to be $n_2(T_1 + T_2)/(n_1 + n_2)$.

  Depending on the sample sizes, the test statistic is a measure of the difference between T_1 and its expected value or T_2 and it expected value.

The test statistic is:

$$Z \text{ Statistic} = \begin{cases} \dfrac{T_1 - \dfrac{n_1\left(T_1 + T_2\right)}{\left(n_1 + n_2\right)}}{\sqrt{\left(\dfrac{n_1 n_2}{n_1 + n_2 - 1}\right)\left(\dfrac{T_1 + T_2}{n_1 + n_2}\right)\left(1 - \dfrac{T_1 + T_2}{n_1 + n_2}\right)}}, \text{if } n_1 \le n_2 \\[4ex] \dfrac{T_2 - \dfrac{n_2\left(T_1 + T_2\right)}{\left(n_1 + n_2\right)}}{\sqrt{\left(\dfrac{n_1 n_2}{n_1 + n_2 - 1}\right)\left(\dfrac{T_1 + T_2}{n_1 + n_2}\right)\left(1 - \dfrac{T_1 + T_2}{n_1 + n_2}\right)}}, \text{if } n_1 > n_2 \end{cases}$$

The definitions of the p-values are same as in Table 5.13.

5.4.1.3   Decision and Conclusions

The formal decision and concluding sentence do not change from the one-sample tests discussed in Chapter 4, "Inferences from One Sample." The concluding observation depends on the particular statistics involved in the test.

If the p-value is small, the data agrees with H_1. If the p-value is less than the significance level, the risk of making a Type I error is acceptable. Therefore, the p-value decision rule is the following.

If the p-value $< \alpha$, reject H_0. Otherwise, do not reject H_0.

Since a hypothesis test begins with the assumption that H_0 is true, concluding a hypothesis test requires one of the following formal statements.

- Reject H_0.
- Do not reject H_0.

When the claim is equivalent to the null hypothesis, the concluding sentence uses the word *reject*. The concluding sentence becomes an expanded version of the formal decision.

When the claim is equivalent to the alternative hypothesis, the concluding sentence uses the word *support*. If the data supports the rejection of H_0, the data supports H_1. If the data does not support rejection of H_0, the data cannot support H_1.

Table 5.14 Concluding Sentences

Formal Statistical Decision	Claim stated as H_0	Claim stated as H_1
Reject H_0.	There is sufficient evidence to reject the claim that ... (claim in words).	There is sufficient evidence to support the claim that ... (claim in words).
Do not reject H_0.	There is not sufficient evidence to reject the claim that ... (claim in words).	There is not sufficient evidence to support the claim that ... (claim in words).

Table 5.15 Concluding Observations

Reject H_0.	Sample median 1 is significantly different/greater/less than sample median 2.
Do not reject H_0.	Sample median 1 is not significantly different/greater/less than sample median 2.

5.4.2 Summary of the Wilcoxon Rank-Sum Test

Plan the experiment.

$$H_0 : \theta_1 = \theta_2 \qquad H_0 : \theta_1 \leq \theta_2 \qquad H_0 : \theta_1 \geq \theta_2$$
$$H_1 : \theta_1 \neq \theta_2 \qquad H_1 : \theta_1 > \theta_2 \qquad H_1 : \theta_1 < \theta_2$$

The significance level is α.

Task computes the statistics.

Wilcoxon Scores (Rank Sums) for Variable *Dependent* Classified by Variable *Independent*					
Independent	N	Sum of Scores	Expected Under H0	Std Dev Under H0	Mean Score
value occurring first	n_1	T_1	$\dfrac{n_1(n_1 + n_2 + 1)}{2}$	$\sqrt{\dfrac{n_1 n_2}{n_1 + n_2} s_R^2}$	$\dfrac{T_1}{n_1}$
value occurring second	n_2	T_2	$\dfrac{n_2(n_1 + n_2 + 1)}{2}$	$\sqrt{\dfrac{n_1 n_2}{n_1 + n_2} s_R^2}$	$\dfrac{T_2}{n_2}$
Average scores were used for ties.					

Wilcoxon Two-Sample Test	
Statistic	T_1 if $n_1 \leq n_2$ and T_2 if $n_1 > n_2$
Normal Approximation	
Z	Z Statistic
One-Sided Pr > Z	*p*-value for one-sided tests. See below.
Two-Sided Pr > |Z|	*p*-value for $H_0 : \theta_1 = \theta_2$ versus $H_1 : \theta_1 \neq \theta_2$
Z includes a continuity correction of 0.5.	

Determine the *p*-value for a one-sided test.

Hypotheses	*p*-value
$H_0 : \theta_1 \leq \theta_2$ $H_1 : \theta_1 > \theta_2$	If Sum of Scores $\geq$ Expected Under H₀, *p*-value = One - Sided Pr Otherwise, *p*-value = 1 − One - Sided Pr
$H_0 : \theta_1 \geq \theta_2$ $H_1 : \theta_1 < \theta_2$	If Sum of Scores $\leq$ Expected Under H₀, *p*-value = One - Sided Pr Otherwise, *p*-value = 1 − One - Sided Pr

Apply the results.

If the *p*-value $\leq \alpha$, reject H_0. Otherwise, do not reject H_0.

- Reject H_0. There is sufficient evidence to reject/support the claim that ... (complete claim). Sample median 1 is significantly different/greater/less than sample median 2.

- Do not reject H_0. There is not sufficient evidence to reject/support the claim that ...(complete claim). Sample median 1 is not significantly different/greater/less than sample median 2.

5.4.3 Summary of the Two-Sample Median Test

Plan the experiment.

$H_0 : \theta_1 = \theta_2$ $\quad H_0 : \theta_1 \leq \theta_2$ $\quad H_0 : \theta_1 \geq \theta_2$

$H_1 : \theta_1 \neq \theta_2$ $\quad H_1 : \theta_1 > \theta_2$ $\quad H_1 : \theta_1 < \theta_2$

The significance level is α.

Task computes the statistics.

Median Scores (Number of Points Above Median) for Variable *Dependent* Classified by Variable *Independent*						
Independent	N	Sum of Scores	Expected Under H0		Std Dev Under H0	Mean Score
value occurring first	n_1	T_1	$\dfrac{n_1(T_1+T)}{n_1+n_2}$	$\sqrt{\left(\dfrac{n_1 n_2}{n_1+n_2-1}\right)\left(\dfrac{T_1+T_2}{n_1+n_2}\right)\left(1-\dfrac{T_1+T_2}{n_1+n_2}\right)}$	$\dfrac{T_1}{n_1}$
value occurring second	n_2	T_2	$\dfrac{n_2(T_1+T)}{n_1+n_2}$	$\sqrt{\left(\dfrac{n_1 n_2}{n_1+n_2-1}\right)\left(\dfrac{T_1+T_2}{n_1+n_2}\right)\left(1-\dfrac{T_1+T_2}{n_1+n_2}\right)}$	$\dfrac{T_2}{n_2}$
Average scores were used for ties.						

Median Two-Sample Test	
Statistic	T_1 if $n_1 \leq n_2$ and T_2 if $n_1 > n_2$
Z	Z Statistic
One-Sided Pr > Z	p-value for one-sided tests. See below.
Two-Sided Pr > |Z|	p-value for $H_0 : \theta_1 = \theta_2$ versus $H_1 : \theta_1 \neq \theta_2$

Determine the *p*-value for a one-sided test.

Hypotheses	p-value	
$H_0 : \theta_1 \leq \theta_2$	If Sum of Scores $\geq$ Expected Under H0, p-value = One - Sided Pr	
$H_1 : \theta_1 > \theta_2$	Otherwise, p-value $= 1 -$ One - Sided Pr	
$H_0 : \theta_1 \geq \theta_2$	If Sum of Scores $\leq$ Expected Under H0, p-value = One - Sided Pr	
$H_1 : \theta_1 < \theta_2$	Otherwise, p-value $= 1 -$ One - Sided Pr	

Apply the results.

If the *p*-value $\leq \alpha$, reject H_0. Otherwise, do not reject H_0.

- Reject H_0. There is sufficient evidence to reject/support the claim that ... (complete claim). Sample median 1 is significantly different/greater/less than sample median 2.

- Do not reject H_0. There is not sufficient evidence to reject/support the claim that ...(complete claim). Sample median 1 is not significantly different/greater/less than sample median 2.

5.4.4 Example 5.5: Tests on Two Medians

This illustrates inference on the medians of two populations.

- The hypothesis test and confidence intervals are worked out in the Detailed Solutions section below.

- The Nonparametric One-way ANOVA task is discussed in "Instructions for Tests on Two Medians."

- Complete results are in "Task Output, Interpretation, and Analysis" for Example 5.5.

5.4.4.1 Parts Production

On Example 5.1, the Old River Castings Company tests the claim that parts #12 and #237 generate the same percentage of scrap, on average. The two-sample t test results in p-value $<$ 0.0001. The claim is rejected.

Consider a situation where the data contains a severe outlier. Suppose that on the first day that part #12 is produced, the percentage of scrap is 75 and not 4. The data is below with the new value **75** in bold.

Part #12					Part #237				
75	5	4	4	4	20	15	18	16	19
10	6	6	9	9					
7	8	5	7	6					
3									

The data for Ex05_05 is shown below.

	PctScrap	PartNo
1	20	237
2	75	12
3	5	12
4	4	12
5	15	237
6	4	12
7	4	12
8	10	12
9	6	12
10	6	12
11	9	12
12	9	12
13	7	12
14	8	12
15	5	12
16	7	12
17	18	237
18	16	237
19	6	12
20	19	237
21	3	12

ex05_05 (read-only)

The Two-Sample *t*-test for Means is applied to Ex05_05. Part of the output is below. With the outlier in the data, the claim is not rejected.

Output 5.7 *t* Tests Table and Box Plot for ex05_05 Using the Two-Sample *t* Test for Means

T-Tests					
Variable	**Method**	**Variances**	**DF**	**t Value**	**Pr > |t|**
PctScrap	**Pooled**	Equal	19	-0.90	0.3800
PctScrap	**Satterthwaite**	Unequal	16.3	-1.60	0.1281

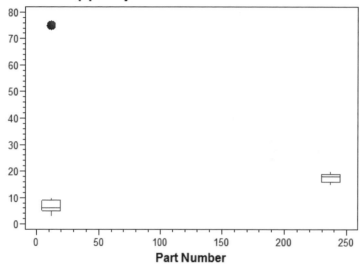

Of the two classification values in the independent variable **PartNo**, 237 appears first and then 12. Therefore, sample statistics associated with parts #237 and #12 appear first and second, respectively, in the Nonparametric One-Way ANOVA output.

Also, the example tests the following hypotheses where subscripts 1 and 2 correspond to parts #237 and #12, respectively.

$$H_0 : \theta_1 = \theta_2$$
$$H_1 : \theta_1 \neq \theta_2$$

Example 5.5.1
Use the Wilcoxon Rank-Sum Test to test the claim that the median percentages of scrap generated by parts #237 and #12 are the same. Let $\alpha = 0.05$.

Example 5.5.2
Use the Median Test to test the claim that the median percentages of scrap generated by parts #237 and #12 are the same. Let $\alpha = 0.05$.

5.4.4.2   Detailed Solutions

Example 5.5.1

Plan the task.

$H_0 : \theta_1 = \theta_2$

$H_1 : \theta_1 \neq \theta_2$

$\alpha = 0.05$

Compute the statistics.

The data from Example 5.5 is in Table 5.16. Rows associated with PartNo = 237 are identified with asterisks. The ranks of the PctScrap data are in the ranks column.

- The rank of 1 is assigned to the smallest observation: observation 21 with PctScrap = 3.

- The second smallest PctScrap value is 4 at observations 4, 6, and 7. These observations are associated with ranks 2, 3 and 4. Because of the tie, they are given the average rank of $(2+3+4)/3 = 9/3 = 3$.

- The mean of all ranks is $(n_1 + n_2 + 1)/2 = (5 + 16 + 1)/2 = 11$.

- The variance of the ranks is $s_R^2 = 38.225$.

Table 5.16 Data from Example 5.5 with Ranks

	Observation	PctScrap	PartNo	ranks
*	1	20	237	20
	2	75	12	21
	3	5	12	5.5
	4	4	12	3
*	5	15	237	16
	6	4	12	3
	7	4	12	3
	8	10	12	15
	9	6	12	8
	10	6	12	8
	11	9	12	13.5
	12	9	12	13.5
	13	7	12	10.5
	14	8	12	12
	15	5	12	5.5
	16	7	12	10.5
*	17	18	237	18
*	18	16	237	17
	19	6	12	8
*	20	19	237	19
	21	3	12	1

PartNo $= 237$	$n_1 = 5$
	$T_1 = 20 + 16 + 18 + 17 + 19 = 90$
	$\dfrac{T_1}{n_1} = \dfrac{90}{5} = 18$
PartNo $= 12$	$n_2 = 16$
	$T_2 = 21 + 5.5 + \ldots + 8 + 1 = 141$
	$\dfrac{T_2}{n_2} = \dfrac{141}{16} = 8.8125$

The nonparametric sample statistics are summarized in the Wilcoxon scores table:

<table>
<tr><th colspan="6">Wilcoxon Scores (Rank Sums) for Variable PctScrap
Classified by Variable PartNo</th></tr>
<tr><th>PartNo</th><th>N</th><th>Sum of
Scores</th><th>Expected
Under H0</th><th>Std Dev
Under H0</th><th>Mean
Score</th></tr>
<tr><td>237</td><td>5</td><td>90</td><td>$\dfrac{5(21+1)}{2} = 55$</td><td>$\sqrt{\dfrac{5\cdot 16}{21}(38.225)} = 12.0673$</td><td>$\dfrac{90}{5} = 18$</td></tr>
<tr><td>12</td><td>16</td><td>141</td><td>$\dfrac{16(21+1)}{2} = 176$</td><td>$\sqrt{\dfrac{5\cdot 16}{21}(38.225)} = 12.0673$</td><td>$\dfrac{141}{16} = 8.8125$</td></tr>
</table>

Since $n_1 < n_2$, Z Statistic $= \dfrac{T_1 - \dfrac{n_1(n_1+n_2+1)}{2} \pm 0.5}{\sqrt{\dfrac{n_1 n_2}{n_1+n_2} s_R^2}} = \dfrac{90 - \dfrac{5(5+16+1)}{2} - 0.5}{\sqrt{\dfrac{5\cdot 16}{21}(38.225)}} = 2.85897$.

p-value $= 2P(Z \geq 2.9004) = 2*(1 - \text{probnorm}(2.9004)) = 0.0037$

Apply the results.

Since the p-value < 0.05, reject H_0. There is sufficient evidence to reject the claim that the median percentages of scrap generated by parts #237 and #12 are the same. Sample median for the #237 parts is significantly different than sample median for the #12 parts.

Example 5.5.2

Plan the task.

$H_0 : \theta_1 = \theta_2$

$H_1 : \theta_1 \neq \theta_2$

$\alpha = 0.05$

Compute the statistics.

The data from Example 5.5 is in Table 5.17. Observations for PartNo = 237 are shaded.

- The overall median of the PctScrap data is $\tilde{x} = 7$.

In the scores column, scores = 1; if PctScrap > $\tilde{x} = 7$, scores = 0 otherwise.

Table 5.17 Data from Example 5.5 with Scores

Observation	PctScrap	PartNo	scores
1	20	237	1
2	75	12	1
3	5	12	0
4	4	12	0
5	15	237	1
6	4	12	0
7	4	12	0
8	10	12	1
9	6	12	0
10	6	12	0
11	9	12	1
12	9	12	1
13	7	12	0
14	8	12	1
15	5	12	0
16	7	12	0
17	18	237	1
18	16	237	1
19	6	12	0
20	19	237	1
21	3	12	0

PartNo = 237	$n_1 = 5$
	$T_1 = 5$
	$\dfrac{T_1}{n_1} = \dfrac{5}{5} = 1$
PartNo = 12	$n_2 = 16$
	$T_2 = 5$
	$\dfrac{T_2}{n_2} = \dfrac{5}{16} = 0.3125$

The proportion of all observations above $\tilde{x} = 7$ is $(T_1 + T_2)/(n_1 + n_2) = (5 + 5)/(5 + 16) = 0.4762$

The nonparametric sample statistics are summarized in the Median scores table:

Median Scores (Number of Points Above Median) for Variable PctScrap Classified by Variable PartNo					
PartNo	N	Sum of Scores	Expected Under H0	Std Dev Under H0	Mean Score
237	5	5	$\dfrac{(10)5}{21} = 2.38$	$\sqrt{\left(\dfrac{10}{21}\right)\left(1-\dfrac{10}{21}\right)\left(\dfrac{5\cdot16}{21-1}\right)} = 0.998866$	$\dfrac{5}{5} = 1$
12	16	5	$\dfrac{(10)16}{21} = 7.62$	$\sqrt{\left(\dfrac{10}{21}\right)\left(1-\dfrac{10}{21}\right)\left(\dfrac{5\cdot16}{21-1}\right)} = 0.998866$	$\dfrac{5}{16} = 0.3125$

Since $n_1 < n_2$,

$$Z \text{ Statistic} = \frac{T_1 - \dfrac{n_1(T_1 + T_2)}{(n_1 + n_2)}}{\sqrt{\left(\dfrac{T_1 + T_2}{n_1 + n_2}\right)\left(1 - \dfrac{T_1 + T_2}{n_1 + n_2}\right)\left(\dfrac{n_1 n_2}{n_1 + n_2 - 1}\right)}} = \frac{5 - \dfrac{5(5+5)}{5+16}}{\sqrt{\left(\dfrac{10}{21}\right)\left(1 - \dfrac{10}{21}\right)\left(\dfrac{5\cdot16}{21-1}\right)}} = 2.62202.$$

$p\text{-value} = 2P(Z \ge 2.6220) = 2*(1 - \text{probnorm}(2.6220)) = 0.0087$

Apply the results.

Since the p-value < 0.05, reject H_0. There is sufficient evidence to reject the claim that the median percentages of scrap generated by parts #237 and #12 are the same. Sample median for the #237 parts is significantly different than sample median for the #12 parts.

5.4.5 Instructions for Tests on Two Medians

Open the Nonparametric One-Way ANOVA task in one of the following ways:

- From the menu bar, select **Analyze ▶ ANOVA ▶ Nonparametric One-Way ANOVA**.
- On the **Task by Category** tab of the **Task List**, go to the **ANOVA** section and click **Nonparametric One-Way ANOVA**.
- On the **Task by Name** tab of the **Task List**, double-click **Nonparametric One-Way ANOVA**.

The Nonparametric One-Way ANOVA task has five groups of options: Task Roles, Analysis, Exact p-values, Results, and Titles. Exact p-values are not discussed in this book. The Results put the task results in data sets. The Titles options control the titles and the footnotes in the output. Titles are discussed in general in Chapter 1, "Introduction to SAS Enterprise Guide."

5.4.5.1 Task Roles

Click **Task Roles** on the selection pane to open this group of options. A variable is assigned to a role by dragging its name from **Variables to assign** to a role in **Task Roles**. See Figure 5.10.

A variable can be removed from a role by dragging it back to **Variables to assign**. The right and left arrows and the resulting pop-up menus can also be used.

- **Dependent variables**: Statistics are computed for each variable in this role. The order that the variables are listed here is the order that they are listed in the output.

- **Independent variable**: This variable contains the classification values that identify sample membership.

The roles Group analysis by and Frequency count are discussed in Chapter 1, "Introduction to SAS Enterprise Guide."

In Figure 5.10, the data is in the Ex05_05 data set. The variable PctScrap is assigned to the Dependent variables role. The variable PartNo is assigned to the Independent variable role.

Figure 5.10 Task Roles in the Nonparametric One-Way ANOVA Task for Example 5.5

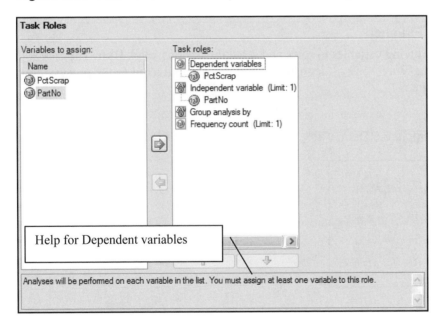

5.4.5.2 Analysis

In Figure 5.11, **Wilcoxon** and **Median** are checked.

Figure 5.11 Analysis Options in the Nonparametric One-Way ANOVA Task for Example 5.5

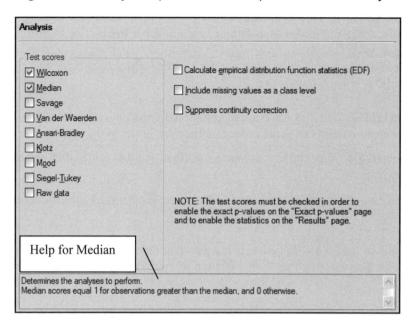

5.4.5.3 When Finished

When finished assigning variables to roles and selecting options, click **Run**. The task adds a Nonparametric One-Way ANOVA icon and one or more output icons to the process flow diagram. See Figure 5.12.

Figure 5.12 Example 5.5 Data, Task, and Output Icons on the Process Flow Diagram

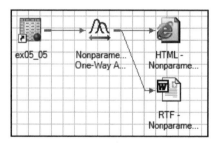

5.4.6 Task Output, Interpretation, and Analysis for Example 5.5: Wilcoxon Rank-Sum Test and the Median Test

5.4.6.1 Task Output: Wilcoxon Rank-Sum Test

The Wilcoxon Rank-Sum Test is in Output 5.8. The Median Test is in Output 5.9.

Output 5.8 Wilcoxon Rank-Sum Test for Example 5.5

Nonparametric One-Way ANOVA

The NPAR1WAY Procedure

Wilcoxon Scores (Rank Sums) for Variable PctScrap Classified by Variable PartNo					
PartNo	N	Sum of Scores	Expected Under H0	Std Dev Under H0	Mean Score
237	5	90.0	55.0	12.067272	18.00000
12	16	141.0	176.0	12.067272	8.81250
Average scores were used for ties.					

Wilcoxon Two-Sample Test		
Statistic	90.0000	❶
Normal Approximation		
Z	2.8590	❷
One-Sided Pr > Z	0.0021	
Two-Sided Pr > |Z|	0.0043	❸
t Approximation		❹
One-Sided Pr > Z	0.0049	
Two-Sided Pr > |Z|	0.0097	
Z includes a continuity correction of 0.5.		

Kruskal-Wallis Test		❺
Chi-Square	8.4124	
DF	1	
Pr > Chi-Square	0.0037	

5.4.6.2 Interpretation

❶ T_1 since $n_1 < n_2$

❷ Z Statistic

❸ *p*-value of the Wilcoxon Rank-Sum Test for $H_0 : \theta_1 = \theta_2$ versus $H_1 : \theta_1 \neq \theta_2$

❹ p-values computed from the t distribution with $n_1 + n_2 - 1$ degrees of freedom

❺ The Kruskal-Wallis test is a nonparametric analog to the one-way analysis of variance. $H_0 : \theta_1 = \theta_2$ versus $H_1 : \theta_1 \neq \theta_2$ is tested here. The Kruskal-Wallis is discussed in Section 6.4.

5.4.6.3 The Median Test

Output 5.9 Two-Sample Median Test for Example 5.5

Nonparametric One-Way ANOVA

The NPAR1WAY Procedure

Median Scores (Number of Points Above Median) for Variable PctScrap Classified by Variable PartNo					
PartNo	**N**	**Sum of Scores**	**Expected Under H0**	**Std Dev Under H0**	**Mean Score**
237	5	5.0	2.380952	0.998866	1.00000
12	16	5.0	7.619048	0.998866	0.31250
Average scores were used for ties.					

Median Two-Sample Test		
Statistic	5.0000	❶
Z	2.6220	❷
One-Sided Pr > Z	0.0044	
Two-Sided Pr > |Z|	0.0087	❸

Median One-Way Analysis		❹
Chi-Square	6.8750	
DF	1	
Pr > Chi-Square	0.0087	

5.4.6.4 Interpretation

❶ T_1 since $n_1 < n_2$

❷ Z Statistic

❸ p-value of the median two-sample test for $H_0 : \theta_1 = \theta_2$ versus $H_1 : \theta_1 \neq \theta_2$

❹ The median one-way test is a nonparametric analog to the one-way analysis of variance. $H_0 : \theta_1 = \theta_2$ versus $H_1 : \theta_1 \neq \theta_2$ is tested here. This is the Median Test discussed in Section 6.4.

5.4.6.5 Analysis

Example 5.5.1

$H_0 : \theta_1 = \theta_2$

$H_1 : \theta_1 \neq \theta_2$

$\alpha = 0.05$

The *p*-value of the Wilcoxon Rank-Sum Test is 0.0043. See ❸ in Output 5.8.

Reject H_0. There is sufficient evidence to reject the claim that the median percentages of scrap generated by parts #237 and #12 are the same. Sample median for the #237 parts is significantly different than sample median for the #12 parts.

Example 5.5.2

$H_0 : \theta_1 = \theta_2$

$H_1 : \theta_1 \neq \theta_2$

$\alpha = 0.05$

The *p*-value of the Median Test is 0.0087. See ❸ in Output 5.9.

Reject H_0. There is sufficient evidence to reject the claim that the median percentages of scrap generated by parts #237 and #12 are the same. Sample median for the #237 parts is significantly different than sample median for the #12 parts.

5.5 Inference on the Median Difference in a Population of Pairs

Inference on the median difference in a population of pairs, θ_d, is done in two steps.

- First, the Query Builder computes the differences in the sample of paired values: $d = x_1 - x_2$. The subscripts indicate the order of subtraction.

- Second, the Sign Test and the Wilcoxon Signed Rank Test are applied to the sample of differences.
  - These tests are discussed in Section 4.5, "Inference on a Population Median."
  - The Distributions task is used for both tests. See "Instructions for Applying the Distributions Task for Nonparametric Tests" in Section 4.6.
  - The results are analogs to the two-sample *t* test discussed in Section 5.3.

5.5.1 Nonparametric Tests and Estimation Applied to Paired Data

5.5.1.1 Hypothesis Tests

Plan the experiment.

$$\left.\begin{array}{lll} H_0 : \theta_d = \theta_0 & H_0 : \theta_d \le \theta_0 & H_0 : \theta_d \ge \theta_0 \\ H_1 : \theta_d \ne \theta_0 & H_1 : \theta_d > \theta_0 & H_1 : \theta_d < \theta_0 \end{array}\right\} \text{Task requires } \theta_0.$$

The significance level is α.

Task computes the statistics.

Tests for Location: Mu0=θ_0				
Test		**Statistic**		**p Value**
Student's t	t	$t = (\bar{d} - \theta_0)/(s_d/\sqrt{n})$	Pr > |t|	*p*-value for $H_0 : \mu_d = \theta_0$ versus $H_1 : \mu_d \ne \theta_0$
Sign	M	$M = n^+ - n_t/2$	Pr >= |M|	*p*-value for $H_0 : \theta_d = \theta_0$ versus $H_1 : \theta_d \ne \theta_0$
Signed Rank	S	$S = \sum r^+ - n_t(n_t + 1)/4$	Pr >= |S|	*p*-value for $H_0 : \theta_d = \theta_0$ versus $H_1 : \theta_d \ne \theta_0$

Determine the *p*-value.

Hypotheses	
$H_0 : \mu_d$ or $\theta_d = \theta_0$ $H_1 : \mu_d$ or $\theta_d \ne \theta_0$	$p\text{-value} = \text{p Value}$
$H_0 : \mu_d$ or $\theta_d \le \theta_0$ $H_1 : \mu_d$ or $\theta_d > \theta_0$	$p\text{-value} = \begin{cases} 0.5(\text{p Value}), & \text{if Statistic} > 0 \\ 1 - 0.5(\text{p Value}), & \text{if Statistic} \le 0 \end{cases}$
$H_0 : \mu_d$ or $\theta_d \ge \theta_0$ $H_1 : \mu_d$ or $\theta_d < \theta_0$	$p\text{-value} = \begin{cases} 1 - 0.5(\text{p Value}), & \text{if Statistic} \ge 0 \\ 0.5(\text{p Value}), & \text{if Statistic} < 0 \end{cases}$

Apply the results.

If the *p*-value $< \alpha$, reject H_0. Otherwise, do not reject H_0.

- Reject H_0. There is sufficient evidence to reject/support the claim that ... (claim in words). The sample mean/median difference is significantly different/greater/less than θ_0.

- Do not reject H_0. There is not sufficient evidence to reject/support the claim that ...(claim in words). The sample mean/median difference is not significantly different/greater/less than θ_0.

5.5.1.2 Confidence Interval on the Median

LCL and **UCL** stand for *lower confidence limit* and *upper confidence limit* in the task output.

		(1-α)100% Confidence Limits Distribution Free		Order Statistics		
Quantile	**Estimate**			**LCL Rank**	**UCL Rank**	**Coverage**
50% Median	$\tilde{d}$	$d_{(k+1)}$	$d_{(n-k)}$	k	$n-k$	$1-2P(Y \le k)$

5.5.2 Example 5.6: Nonparametric Inference on Paired Measurements

In Example 5.3, 22 pairs of observations are used to test the claim that there is a positive difference, on average, between a student's post-general education test score and their pre-general education test score. The two-sample paired *t* test for means on the variables Post and Pre results in a *p*-value < 0.0001 and support for the claim.

Consider a situation where the data contains a severe outlier. Suppose the Pre score for student #2 is incorrectly entered as 240 instead of 24. The data is below, where the incorrectly entered value is identified as 240, and in the Ex05_06 data set.

Student	1	2	3	4	5	6	7	8	9	10	11
Pre	14	**240**	19	25	20	21	15	16	38	21	16
Post	30	29	40	42	24	38	46	42	85	34	31

Student	12	13	14	15	16	17	18	19	20	21	22
Pre	23	15	25	15	16	13	37	8	42	17	28
Post	38	28	63	16	44	35	70	9	51	40	43

Example 5.6.1
Use the Sign Test to test the claim that the median of all post- and pre-test score differences is positive. Let $\alpha = 0.05$.

Example 5.6.2
Estimate the median of all post- and pre-test score differences. Construct a 95% confidence interval.

Example 5.6.3
Use the Wilcoxon Signed Rank Test to test the claim that the median of all post- and pre-test score differences is positive. Let $\alpha = 0.05$.

Example 5.6.4
Construct a histogram and a box-and-whisker plot.

Example 5.6.5

Use the one-sample *t* test to test the claim that the mean of all post- and pre-test score differences is positive. Let $\alpha = 0.05$.

5.5.2.1 Applying the Query Builder

The **ex05_06** table is opened in the project. Its icon is right clicked and **Filter and Query** is selected from the pop-up menu.

4. When the Query Builder opens, **Pre** and **Post** are dragged from the left to the **Select Data** tab.

5. The ▦ **Computed Columns** button is clicked on the Query Builder. This opens the Computed Columns window.

6. **New** is selected. From the pop-up menu, **Build Expression** is selected.

7. The **Advanced Expression Editor** window opens.

    The desired expression is:

    EX05_06.Post - EX05_06.Pre

    On the **Data** tab, EX05_06 is selected by default in the **Available Variables** box. Double-clicking **Post** in the **Variable Values** box produces EX05_06.Post in the **Expression Text** box. The subtraction sign is added. Then EX05_06.Pre is added.

8. Clicking **OK** on the Advanced Expression Editor window returns to **Computed Columns**.

9. The default name **Calculation1** is changed to **Difference**.

10. **Close** is clicked to return to the Query Builder window.

11. **Run** is clicked. Figure 5.13 shows the output table with **Pre**, **Post**, and **Difference**.

Figure 5.13 Query Output for Example 5.6

	Pre	Post	Difference
1	14	30	16
2	240	29	-211
3	19	40	21
4	25	42	17
5	20	24	4
6	21	38	17
7	15	46	31
8	16	42	26
9	38	75	37
10	21	34	13
11	16	31	15
12	23	38	15
13	15	28	13
14	25	63	38
15	15	16	1
16	16	44	28
17	13	35	22
18	37	70	33
19	8	9	1
20	42	51	9
21	17	40	23
22	28	43	15

QUERY_FOR_EX05_06_0000 (read-only)

5.6 Task Output, Interpretation, and Analysis for Example 5.6

The Distribution task is applied to the Difference variable. See "Instructions for Applying the Distributions Task for Nonparametric Tests" in Section 4.5.

5.6.1.1 Task Output

Output 5.10 Distribution Analysis Output for Example 5.6

Distribution analysis of: Difference

The UNIVARIATE Procedure
Variable: Difference

Basic Statistical Measures			
Location		**Variability**	
Mean	8.36364	**Std Deviation**	50.09757
❶ **Median**	16.50000	**Variance**	2510
Mode	15.00000	**Range**	249.00000
		Interquartile Range	13.00000

❷

Tests for Location: Mu0=0				
Test		**Statistic**	**p Value**	
❸ **Student's t**	t	0.783051	Pr > |t|	0.4423
❹ **Sign**	M	10	Pr >= |M|	<.0001
❺ **Signed Rank**	S	104.5	Pr >= |S|	<.0001

Quantiles (Definition 5)						
				Order Statistics		
Quantile	**Estimate**	**95% Confidence Limits Distribution Free**		**LCL Rank**	**UCL Rank**	**Coverage**
100% Max	38.0					
❻ **99%**	38.0	.	.	.	.	.
95%	37.0	33	38	20	22	58.16
90%	33.0	28	38	18	22	83.94
75% Q3	26.0	17	37	13	21	95.56
❼ **50% Median**	16.5	13	26	7	17	96.53
25% Q1	13.0	1	15	2	10	95.56
10%	1.0	-211	9	1	5	83.94
5%	1.0	-211	1	1	3	58.16
❻ **1%**	-211.0	.	.	.	.	.
0% Min	-211.0					

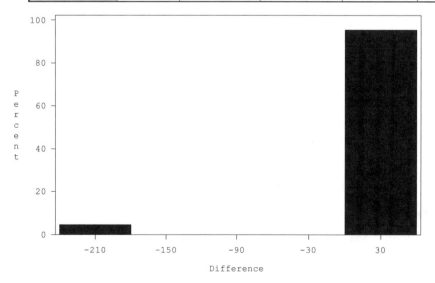

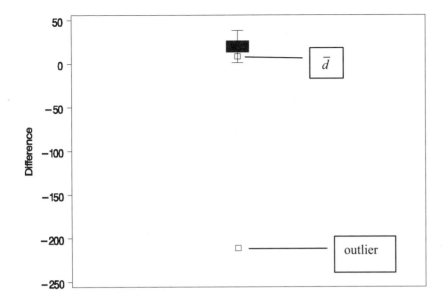

Comment

The box-and-whisker plot produced by the Distribution Analysis task identifies the sample mean $\bar{d}$. In the graph above, $\bar{d}$ is a black box and the outlier is a blue box.

5.6.1.2   Interpretation

❶ Sample median $\tilde{d}$

❷ The hypotheses for Student's one sample t test are $H_0 : \mu_d = 0$ versus $H_1 : \mu_d \neq 0$. The hypotheses for the Sign Test and the Signed Rank Test are $H_0 : \theta_d = 0$ versus $H_1 : \theta_d \neq 0$.

❸ Results of the Student's one sample t test

❹ Results of the Sign Test

❺ Results of the Signed Rank Test

❻ Symmetric confidence limits do not exist in this sample for the 99th and 1st quantile.

❼ Inference on θ_d: The estimate is $\tilde{d} = 16.5$. An approximately 95% confidence interval is $[13, 26)$ based on the ranks of the lower and upper confidence limits: $\left[x_{(7)}, x_{(17)} \right)$. The actual probability associated with the confidence interval is 96.53%.

5.6.1.3   Analysis

Example 5.6.1

$H_0 : \theta_d \leq 0$

$H_1 : \theta_d > 0$

$\alpha = 0.05$

At ❹ in Output 5.10, $M > 0$. The p-value for the Sign Test is less than $0.5(0.0001) = 0.00005$.

Reject H_0. There is sufficient evidence to support the claim that the median of all post- and pre-test score differences is positive. The sample median difference is significantly greater than 0.

Example 5.6.2

An approximately 95% confidence interval is $[13, 26)$. See ❼ in Output 5.10.

Example 5.6.3

$H_0 : \theta_d \leq 0$

$H_1 : \theta_d > 0$

$\alpha = 0.05$

At ❺ in Output 5.10, $S > 0$. The p-value for the Signed Rank Test is less than $0.5(0.0001) = 0.00005$.

Reject H_0. There is sufficient evidence to support the claim that the median of all post- and pre-test score differences is positive. The sample median difference is significantly greater than 0.

Example 5.6.4

The histogram and the box-and-whisker plot are in Output 5.10.

Example 5.6.5

$H_0 : \mu_d \leq 0$

$H_1 : \mu_d > 0$

$\alpha = 0.05$

At ❸ in Output 5.10, $t > 0$. The p-value for the one-sample t test is $0.5(0.4423) = 0.22115$.

Do not reject H_0. There is not sufficient evidence to support the claim that the mean of all post- and pre-test score differences is positive. The sample mean difference is not significantly greater than 0.

Analysis of Variance

6.1 Connection to Chapter 5

This chapter extends the discussion of inference from two to multiple samples. In Chapter 5, "Inferences from Two Samples," the pooled *t* test compares two population means while assuming that the underlying population variances are equal. See below on the left. In this chapter, the one-way analysis of variance compares multiple population means while assuming that the underlying population variances are equal. See below on the right.

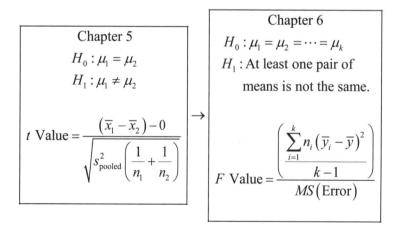

- The letter *y* comes into use as a variable. It is the *dependent* variable. The letter *x* reappears later as an *independent* variable.

- There are multiple samples. Each sample has the standard statistics.

Sample Size	Sample Mean	Sample Standard Deviation	Sample Variance
n_1	$\overline{y}_1$	s_1	s_1^2
n_2	$\overline{y}_2$	s_2	s_2^2
$\vdots$	$\vdots$	$\vdots$	$\vdots$
n_k	$\overline{y}_k$	s_k	s_k^2

- The pooled sample variance s_{pooled}^2 becomes the Mean Square Error $MS(\text{Error})$ in a straightforward manner. Each is the estimate of the common population variance.

6.2 One-Way Analysis of Variance

The One-Way ANOVA task compares the means of populations described by a single *factor*.

- A factor is a general property that exists in multiple forms, at least potentially, among all people or objects being studied. The multiple forms are called *factor levels*.

  - In a study with a single factor, *treatment* and factor level are used interchangeably.

  - Therapy for people suffering from headaches is an example of a factor. An experiment might include only a few specific factor levels, such as no therapy, aspirin, and a new drug.

- A *response* is an observed numerical data value. There is a population of potential responses for each level.

- The *one-way analysis of variance* (ANOVA) is a test of whether the populations corresponding to specific levels of a single factor have the same mean.

- If it is concluded that the means are not the same, then there are *multiple-comparison tests* to identify the differences between means.

The input for the One-Way ANOVA task is a variable of responses and a variable of classification values. These are the *dependent variable* and *independent variable*, respectively.

- The dependent variable contains a sample from each population.

- The rows of the independent variable identify the sample memberships of the responses.

6.2.1 Notation

In the one-way ANOVA, a sample of responses is randomly selected from each population. Let k represent the number of populations in the test. A response is represented by y_{ij}:

- The i subscript identifies the response as being in the sample from population i, where $i = 1,\ldots,k$. These subscripts are assigned according to the sorting order of the classification values.

- The j subscript identifies the response in a list of sample values. The j subscript might be $j = 1,\ldots,n_i$, where n_i is the number of responses in the sample from population i.

The data is *balanced* if the samples have the same number of responses: $n_1 = n_2 = \ldots = n_k$. Otherwise, the data is *unbalanced*.

The statistics for each sample have a single *i* subscript.

Population	Sample Size	Sample Mean	Sample Standard Deviation	Sample Variance
1	n_1	$\bar{y}_1$	s_1	s_1^2
2	n_2	$\bar{y}_2$	s_2	s_2^2
$\vdots$	$\vdots$	$\vdots$	$\vdots$	$\vdots$
k	n_k	$\bar{y}_k$	s_k	s_k^2

- There are a total of $n_.$ responses: $n_. = n_1 + n_2 + \ldots + n_k = \sum_{i=1}^{k} n_i$. (The dot notation is used extensively in Section 6.3. A dot in a subscript location indicates the sum of all such values with that subscript.)

- The mean and variance of all the responses are written without subscripts:

  o Overall sample mean: $\bar{y} = \dfrac{\sum_{i=1}^{k} \sum_{j=1}^{n_i} y_{ij}}{n_.} = \dfrac{n_1 \bar{y}_1 + n_2 \bar{y}_2 + \cdots + n_k \bar{y}_k}{n_.}$

  o Overall sample variance:

  $$s^2 = \dfrac{\sum_{i=1}^{k} \sum_{j=1}^{n_i} (y_{ij} - \bar{y})^2}{n_. - 1} = \dfrac{(n_1 - 1)s_1^2 + (n_2 - 1)s_2^2 + \cdots + (n_k - 1)s_k^2}{n_. - 1}$$

6.2.2 Population Model for the One-Way ANOVA

The random variable *Y* assigns a number to each person or object of interest. The population model for the one-way ANOVA assumes that for population i, $i = 1, \ldots, k$:

$$Y = \mu_i + \varepsilon$$

- μ_i is one of the *k* population means, $i = 1, \ldots, k$.

- ε is also a random variable. It is called an *error*. The errors ε of each population are assumed to be normally distributed with mean 0 and the unknown variance σ^2. The variance is assumed to be the same for each population.

- The values in population i are assumed to be normally distributed with mean μ_i and variance σ^2.

The population means can be further expressed as:

$$\mu_i = \mu + \tau_i$$

- μ is the mean response over all k populations.

- τ_i is a *factor effect* or, in the one-way model, *treatment effect*.

    o   The model assumes that the τ_i values are constants and $\sum_{i=1}^{k} \tau_i = 0$.

    o   The effect τ_i is the difference between the mean of population i and the overall mean μ: $\tau_i = \mu_i - \mu$.

Figure 6.1 represents three population means where τ_i, $i = 1, 2, 3$ is the vertical distance from the line at μ.

Figure 6.1 Example of Population Means

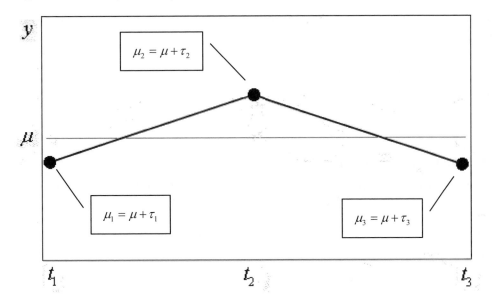

6.2.3 Hypothesis Tests Based on the ANOVA Table

6.2.3.1   Null and Alternative Hypotheses

The null hypothesis tested by the ANOVA table states that all the population means are equal:
$H_0 : \mu_1 = \mu_2 = \ldots = \mu_k$.

The alternative hypothesis is not $\mu_1 \neq \mu_2 \neq \ldots \neq \mu_k$. With just three means, there are a number of ways for $\mu_1 = \mu_2 = \mu_3$ to be false:

- All three means are different ($\mu_1 \neq \mu_2$ and $\mu_1 \neq \mu_3$ and $\mu_2 \neq \mu_3$).

- A pair of means is equal and different from the third ($\mu_1 = \mu_2 \neq \mu_3$, $\mu_1 = \mu_3 \neq \mu_2$, $\mu_1 \neq \mu_2 = \mu_3$).

The expression $\mu_1 \neq \mu_2 \neq \mu_3$ does include the alternatives $\mu_1 = \mu_2 \neq \mu_3$ and $\mu_1 \neq \mu_2 = \mu_3$.

The alternative hypothesis simply states that at least two means are not equal.

The null and alternative hypotheses are:

$H_0 : \mu_1 = \mu_2 = \ldots = \mu_k$
$H_1 :$ At least two means are not equal.

There are equivalent null and alternative hypotheses stated in terms of the factor effects: If $\mu_1 = \mu_2 = \ldots = \mu_k$, then $\mu_i = \mu$ for each population. Therefore, $\mu_i - \mu = \tau_i = 0$ for each population. The equivalent hypotheses are:

$H_0 : \tau_1 = \tau_2 = \ldots = \tau_k = 0$
$H_1 :$ At least one $\tau_i \neq 0$

6.2.3.2 Analysis of Variance Table

Both the hypotheses on the population means and the hypotheses on the factor effects are tested using an analysis of variance (ANOVA) table. The results of both tests are the same.

The components of an ANOVA table are sums of squares, degrees of freedom, mean squares, F values, and p-values.

Sums of Squares

The analysis of variance table is based on a decomposition—or analysis—of the variance of all responses. The numerator of s^2 is equal to the sum of the squared within-sample deviations plus a weighted sum of the squared between-sample deviations:

$$\sum_{i=1}^{k}\sum_{j=1}^{n_i}\left(y_{ij} - \overline{y}\right)^2 = \sum_{i=1}^{k}\sum_{j=1}^{n_i}\left(y_{ij} - \overline{y}_i\right)^2 + \sum_{i=1}^{k}n_i\left(\overline{y}_i - \overline{y}\right)^2$$

This is called a decomposition of the sum of squares. It is represented by the following notation:

$SS(\text{Total}) = SS(\text{Error}) + SS(\text{Model})$

- $SS(\text{Total})$—the numerator of s^2—is the Corrected Total Sum of Squares.

- $SS(\text{Error})$—the sum of the squared within-sample deviations—is the Error Sum of Squares or the Sum-of-Squares Error.

○ The *SS*(Error) is a measure of the random variation in the responses. Random variation is present because the samples are randomly selected from their populations.

- *SS*(Model)—the weighted sum of the squared between-sample deviations—is the Model Sum of Squares. The test of $H_0 : \mu_1 = \mu_2 = \ldots = \mu_k$ is based on the *SS*(Model).

  ○ The *SS*(Model) is a measure of the variation in the sample means due to both the differences in the population means and the random variation in the responses.

  ○ When $H_0 : \mu_1 = \mu_2 = \ldots = \mu_k$ is true, there are no differences in the population means. *SS*(Model) measures only random variation.

  ○ Each sample mean $\overline{y}_i$ estimates its population mean, which is μ when H_0 is true.

  ○ The overall mean $\overline{y}$ always estimates μ.

  ○ The difference $\overline{y}_i - \overline{y}$ estimates 0. Any nonzero value is due to random variation only.

  ○ Consequently, the terms of $SS(\text{Model}) = \sum_{i=1}^{k} n_i (\overline{y}_i - \overline{y})^2$ are determined only by random variation.

  ○ When $H_0 : \mu_1 = \mu_2 = \ldots = \mu_k$ is not true, at least two of the population means are not equal. Consequently, at least two means do not equal the overall mean μ. *SS*(Model) measures nonzero differences in population means plus random variation:

  ○ Each sample mean $\overline{y}_i$ estimates its population mean μ_i.

  ○ The overall mean $\overline{y}$ always estimates μ.

  ○ The difference $\overline{y}_i - \overline{y}$ estimates $\mu_i - \mu$, which is not 0 for at least two population means. Deviations from $\mu_i - \mu$ are due to the random variation in the responses.

  ○ All the terms of $SS(\text{Model}) = \sum_{i=1}^{k} n_i (\overline{y}_i - \overline{y})^2$ are the result of random variation but at least two are also the result of nonzero differences in the population means.

The estimate of τ_i is $\hat{\tau}_i = \overline{y}_i - \overline{y}$. This results in the *SS*(Model) becoming the Treatment Sum of Squares, *SS*(Treatment):

$$SS(\text{Model}) = \sum_{i=1}^{k} n_i (\overline{y}_i - \overline{y})^2 = \sum_{i=1}^{k} n_i (\hat{\tau}_i)^2 = SS(\text{Treatment}).$$

The *SS*(Treatment) is a measure of how much the estimates of the factor effects differ from zero. The test of $H_0 : \tau_1 = \tau_2 = \ldots = \tau_k = 0$ is based on the *SS*(Treatment).

- When $H_0 : \tau_1 = \tau_2 = \ldots = \tau_k = 0$ is true, any nonzero $\hat{\tau}_i$ is due to random variation. In which case, *SS*(Treatment) only measures random variation.

- When $H_0 : \tau_1 = \tau_2 = \ldots = \tau_k = 0$ is not true, at least two of the factor effects are not 0. In which case, *SS*(Treatment) measures nonzero effects plus random variation.

Degrees of Freedom

There are $n_. - 1$ degrees of freedom associated with the overall sample. This is the denominator of s^2. With k being the number of populations being studied:

$$n_. - 1 = (n_. - k) + (k - 1)$$

- $n_. - 1$ are the degrees of freedom associated with the SS(Total).

- $n_. - k$ are the degrees of freedom associated with the SS(Error).

- $k - 1$ are the degrees of freedom associated with the SS(Model) and the SS(Treatment).

Mean Squares

A mean square is a measure of variation that takes into account the number of responses and/or the number of populations. A mean square is created by dividing a sum of squares by the associated degrees of freedom.

- The Model Mean Square is a measure of the variation in the sample means. The variation is due to any differences in the population means and the random selection of the responses.

$$MS(\text{Model}) = \frac{SS(\text{Model})}{k - 1}$$

- The Treatment Mean Square is a measure of how much the estimates of the factor effects differ from zero. Differences are due to any nonzero factor effects and the random variation in the responses.

$$MS(\text{Treatment}) = \frac{SS(\text{Treatment})}{k - 1}$$

- The Error Mean Square, or Mean Square Error, is a measure of the random variation in the responses.

$$MS(\text{Error}) = \frac{SS(\text{Error})}{n_. - k}$$

The MS(Error) is an estimate of σ^2, the common population variance.

Test Statistics: *F* Values

The following is the test statistic for $H_0 : \mu_1 = \mu_2 = \ldots = \mu_k$ versus $H_1 :$ At least two means are not equal.

$$F \text{ Value} = \frac{MS(\text{Model})}{MS(\text{Error})}$$

If H_0 is true, both the MS(Model) and the MS(Error) would measure only random variation. It is expected that:

- $MS(\text{Model}) = MS(\text{Error})$

- $F \text{ Value } = \dfrac{MS(\text{Model})}{MS(\text{Error})} = 1$

The situation is the same for the hypotheses based on factor effects. The following is the test statistic for $H_0 : \tau_1 = \tau_2 = \ldots = \tau_k = 0$ versus H_1 : At least one $\tau_i \neq 0$.

$$F \text{ Value } = \frac{MS(\text{Treatment})}{MS(\text{Error})}$$

If H_0 is true, both the MS(Treatment) and the MS(Error) would measure only random variation. It is expected that:

- $MS(\text{Treatment}) = MS(\text{Error})$

- $F \text{ Value } = \dfrac{MS(\text{Treatment})}{MS(\text{Error})} = 1$

p-Values

The *p-value* is a measure of the likelihood that the samples come from populations where H_0 is true. Smaller values indicate less likelihood. That is, the more the data agrees with H_1—the more $MS(\text{Model})/MS(\text{Error})$ or $MS(\text{Treatment})/MS(\text{Error})$ is greater than 1—the smaller the *p*-value.

- In terms of $H_0 : \mu_1 = \mu_2 = \ldots = \mu_k$, the *p*-value is the probability that random samples from k independent populations with equal means would produce an F value at or beyond the current value. If the *p*-value is small, it is unlikely that the current samples come from populations with equal means.
- In terms of $H_0 : \tau_1 = \tau_2 = \ldots = \tau_k = 0$, the *p*-value is the probability that random samples from k independent populations with zero factor effects would produce an F value at or beyond the current value. If the *p*-value is small, it is unlikely that the current samples come from populations with zero factor effects.

$MS(\text{Model})/MS(\text{Error})$ and $MS(\text{Treatment})/MS(\text{Error})$ are equal and result in the same *p*-value.

Table 6.1 has the technical definition of the *p*-value. The random variable F represents a future value of the test statistic and follows an F distribution. The F distribution depends on two degrees-of-freedom values: the numerator degrees of freedom and the denominator degrees of freedom. For the one-way analysis of variance, these are $k - 1$ and $n_{.} - k$, respectively.

In the SAS code expression, F value, $k - 1$, and $n_{.} - k$ represent numbers. The SAS code expression is included to aid in the discussion. The *p*-value is computed using the expression in the "Detailed Solutions" sections of "Example 6.1: One-Way ANOVA with Balanced Data" and "Example 6.2: One-Way ANOVA with Unbalanced Data."

Table 6.1 *p*-Value for the One-Way ANOVA

Hypotheses	Gray area corresponds to the probability statement and is an example.	
$H_0 : \mu_1 = \mu_2 = \ldots = \mu_k$ $H_1 :$ At least two means are not equal. $H_0 : \tau_1 = \tau_2 = \ldots = \tau_k = 0$ $H_1 :$ At least one $\tau_i \neq 0$	 $p\text{-value} = P(F \geq F \text{ Value})$	Task output: Pr > F SAS code expression: 1-probf(*F* Value, $k-1$, $n_. - k$)

ANOVA Table

The sums of squares, the degrees of freedom (df), the mean squares, the *F* values, and the *p*-values are all organized by the ANOVA table.

The hypotheses on the population means are tested on the Model line of the ANOVA table.

The hypotheses on the factor effects are tested below on a line identified by the name of the independent variable.

$H_0 : \mu_1 = \mu_2 = \ldots = \mu_k$
$H_1 :$ At least two means are not equal.

Source	Df	Sum of Squares	Mean Square	F Value	Pr > F
Model	$k-1$	$SS(\text{Model})$	$\dfrac{SS(\text{Model})}{k-1}$	$\dfrac{MS(\text{Model})}{MS(\text{Error})}$	*p*-value
Error	$n_. - k$	$SS(\text{Error})$	$\dfrac{SS(\text{Error})}{n_. - k}$		
Corrected Total	$n_. - 1$	$SS(\text{Total})$			

Source	Df	ANOVA SS	Mean Square	F Value	Pr > F
Independent Variable	$k-1$	$SS(\text{Treatment})$	$\dfrac{SS(\text{Treatment})}{k-1}$	$\dfrac{MS(\text{Treatment})}{MS(\text{Error})}$	*p*-value

$H_0 : \tau_1 = \tau_2 = \ldots = \tau_k = 0$
$H_1 :$ At least one $\tau_i \neq 0$

6.2.3.3   Decision and Conclusions

The formal decision and concluding sentence do not change from the one-sample tests discussed in Chapter 4, "Inferences from One Sample." The concluding observation depends on the particular statistics involved in the test.

If the p-value is small, the data agrees with H_1. If the p-value is less than the significance level, the risk of making a Type I error is acceptable. Therefore, the p-value decision rule is the following:

If the p-value $< \alpha$, reject H_0. Otherwise, do not reject H_0.

Since a hypothesis test begins with the assumption that H_0 is true, concluding a hypothesis test requires one of the following formal statements:

- Reject H_0.
- Do not reject H_0.

When the claim is equivalent to the null hypothesis, the concluding sentence uses the word *reject*. The concluding sentence becomes an expanded version of the formal decision.

When the claim is equivalent to the alternative hypothesis, the concluding sentence uses the word *support*. If the data supports the rejection of H_0, the data supports H_1. If the data does not support rejection of H_0, the data cannot support H_1.

Table 6.2 Concluding Sentences

Formal Statistical Decision	Claim stated as H_0	Claim stated as H_1
Reject H_0.	There is sufficient evidence to reject the claim that ... (claim in words).	There is sufficient evidence to support the claim that ... (claim in words).
Do not reject H_0.	There is not sufficient evidence to reject the claim that ... (claim in words).	There is not sufficient evidence to support the claim that ... (claim in words).

Table 6.3 Concluding Observations

$H_0 : \mu_1 = \mu_2 = \ldots = \mu_k$ versus H_1 : At least two means are not equal.	
Reject H_0.	At least two sample means are significantly different.
Do not reject H_0.	None of the sample means are significantly different.
$H_0 : \tau_1 = \tau_2 = \ldots = \tau_k = 0$ versus H_1 : At least one τ_i is not 0.	
Reject H_0.	At least two of the factor-effect estimates are significantly different from zero.
Do not reject H_0.	None of the factor-effect estimates are significantly different than zero.

6.2.4 Additional Statistics Included with the ANOVA Table

Coefficient of Determination, R^2

The Coefficient of Determination, denoted by R^2, is the proportion of the variation in the responses that is explained by the model. In terms of the One-Way ANOVA:

- R^2 is the proportion of variation in the responses associated with the between-sample variation. It is the proportion of variation explained by the differences among the k sample means.

- The remaining proportion, $1 - R^2$, is associated with the within-sample variation.

The Coefficient of Determination compares the $SS(\text{Model})$ to the $SS(\text{Total})$:

$$R^2 = \frac{SS(\text{Model})}{SS(\text{Total})}$$

Since $SS(\text{Total}) = SS(\text{Error}) + SS(\text{Model})$, R^2 is also equal to $1 - \dfrac{SS(\text{Error})}{SS(\text{Total})}$:

$$R^2 = \frac{SS(\text{Model})}{SS(\text{Total})} = \frac{SS(\text{Total}) - SS(\text{Error})}{SS(\text{Total})} = 1 - \frac{SS(\text{Error})}{SS(\text{Total})}$$

The F value from the ANOVA table can be expressed in terms of R^2:

$$F \text{ value} = \left(\frac{n_. - k}{k - 1} \right) \frac{R^2}{1 - R^2}$$

Mean of the Responses

The overall mean of the responses is $\bar{y} = \dfrac{\sum\limits_{i=1}^{k}\sum\limits_{j=1}^{n_i} y_{ij}}{n_.} = \dfrac{n_1\bar{y}_1 + n_2\bar{y}_2 + \cdots + n_k\bar{y}_k}{n_.}$.

Root MSE

The $\sqrt{MS(\text{Error})}$ is a measure of the random variation in the responses. It is an estimate of σ, the common population standard deviation.

Coefficient of Variation

The Coefficient of Variation measures the random variation in the responses as a percentage of the overall mean:

$$100\frac{\sqrt{MS(\text{Error})}}{\bar{y}}$$

6.2.5 Summary of the Hypothesis Test

Plan the experiment.

The hypotheses on the means and the hypotheses on the effects are tested at ❶ and ❷ in the tables below. In the one-way ANOVA, these pairs of hypotheses are equivalent and the statistical results are the same.

❶ $H_0 : \mu_1 = \mu_2 = \ldots = \mu_k$

     H_1 : At least two means are not equal.

❷ $H_0 : \tau_1 = \tau_2 = \ldots = \tau_k = 0$

     H_1 : At least one $\tau_i \neq 0$

The significance level is α.

Task computes the statistics.

Source	DF	Sum of Squares	Mean Square	F Value	Pr > F	
Model	$k-1$	$SS(\text{Model})$	$MS(\text{Model}) = \dfrac{SS(\text{Model})}{k-1}$	$\dfrac{MS(\text{Model})}{MS(\text{Error})}$	p-value	❶
Error	$n_. - k$	$SS(\text{Error})$	$MS(\text{Error}) = \dfrac{SS(\text{Error})}{n_. - k}$			
Corrected Total	$n_. - 1$	$SS(\text{Total})$				

R-Square	Coeff Var	Root MSE	*dependent variable* Mean
$\dfrac{SS(\text{Model})}{SS(\text{Error})}$	$100\dfrac{\sqrt{MS(\text{Error})}}{\overline{y}}$	$\sqrt{MS(\text{Error})}$	$\overline{y}$

Source	DF	Anova SS	Mean Square	F Value	Pr > F	
independent variable	$k-1$	$SS(\text{Treatment})$	$MS(\text{Treatment}) = \dfrac{SS(\text{Treatment})}{k-1}$	$\dfrac{MS(\text{Treatment})}{MS(\text{Error})}$	*p*-value	❷

Apply the results.

If the *p*-value $< \alpha$, reject H_0. Otherwise, do not reject H_0.

- Reject H_0. There is sufficient evidence to reject/support the claim that ... (claim in words). At least two sample means are significantly different.

- Do not reject H_0. There is not sufficient evidence to reject/support the claim that ... (claim in words). None of the sample means are significantly different.

6.2.6 Multiple-Comparison Test

If $H_0 : \mu_1 = \mu_2 = \ldots = \mu_k$ is rejected, then the next step is to apply a multiple-comparison test to determine which pairs of means are not equal. A multiple-comparison test uses confidence intervals to examine all possible differences among the *k* population means.

Consider a confidence interval on $\mu_1 - \mu_2$, for example.

- If the confidence interval contains 0, then $\mu_1 - \mu_2 = 0$ is one of the possibilities consistent with the data. In that case, there is not sufficient evidence to reject the $\mu_1 = \mu_2$ component of $H_0 : \mu_1 = \mu_2 = \ldots = \mu_k$.

- If the confidence interval does not contain 0, then the evidence supports a conclusion that $\mu_1 - \mu_2 \neq 0$, or equivalently, $\mu_1 \neq \mu_2$.

The confidence intervals used in multiple-comparison tests are called *comparisons*.

- If a comparison contains 0, the sample means are said to be *not significantly different*.

- If a comparison does not contain 0, the sample means are said to be *significantly different*.

6.2.6.1 Fisher's LSD Multiple-Comparison Test

The comparisons in Fisher's LSD (Least Significant Difference) are based on the two-sample confidence interval discussed in Section 5.2. To compare μ_h and μ_i $(1 \leq h, i \leq k)$, a $100(1-\alpha)\%$ confidence interval on $\mu_h - \mu_i$ is constructed:

$$\left(\left(\bar{y}_h - \bar{y}_i\right) - t_{\alpha/2}\sqrt{MS\left(\text{Error}\right)}\sqrt{\frac{1}{n_h} + \frac{1}{n_i}},\left(\bar{y}_h - \bar{y}_i\right) + t_{\alpha/2}\sqrt{MS\left(\text{Error}\right)}\sqrt{\frac{1}{n_h} + \frac{1}{n_i}}\right)$$

The $t_{\alpha/2}$ critical value comes from the t distribution with $n. - k$ degrees of freedom. Using SAS code, $t_{\alpha/2} = \text{tinv}(1 - \alpha/2, n. - k)$, with $1 - \alpha/2$ and $n. - k$ representing numbers.

The estimate of $\mu_h - \mu_i$ is $\bar{y}_h - \bar{y}_i$. The expression that is added and subtracted to $\bar{y}_h - \bar{y}_i$ is called the *margin of error*. The *LSD* in Fisher's LSD refers to the margin of error:

$$LSD = t_{\alpha/2}\sqrt{MS\left(\text{Error}\right)}\sqrt{\frac{1}{n_h} + \frac{1}{n_i}}$$

If the absolute value of the difference between two sample means is less than the *LSD*, the comparison contains 0. That is, if $\left|\bar{y}_h - \bar{y}_i\right| < LSD$, then:

$$-LSD < \bar{y}_h - \bar{y}_i < LSD$$
$$-\left(\bar{y}_h - \bar{y}_i\right) - LSD < 0 < -\left(\bar{y}_h - \bar{y}_i\right) + LSD$$
$$\left(\bar{y}_h - \bar{y}_i\right) + LSD > 0 > \left(\bar{y}_h - \bar{y}_i\right) - LSD$$
$$\left(\bar{y}_h - \bar{y}_i\right) - LSD < 0 < \left(\bar{y}_h - \bar{y}_i\right) + LSD$$

This is how the *LSD* gets its name. The absolute value of the difference between two sample means must be equal to at least the *LSD* for the comparison not to contain 0—or equivalently, for the sample means to be significantly different. The *LSD* is the *least* value for the *difference* between the two-sample means to be *significant*. It is the *least significant difference*.

The Fisher's LSD comparison is almost the same as the two-sample pooled confidence interval discussed in Section 5.2. The only difference is that the comparison uses $\sqrt{MS\left(\text{Error}\right)}$ and the confidence interval uses $s_{\text{pooled}} = \sqrt{s_{\text{pooled}}^2}$. However, the Error Mean Square $MS\left(\text{Error}\right)$ is a straightforward generalization of pooled variance s_{pooled}^2:

- s_{pooled}^2 is computed for $k = 2$ samples. $s_{\text{pooled}}^2 = \dfrac{\left(n_1 - 1\right)s_1^2 + \left(n_2 - 1\right)s_2^2}{n_1 + n_2 - 2}$

- $MS\left(\text{Error}\right)$ is computed $k \geq 2$ samples.

$$MS\left(\text{Error}\right) = \frac{\sum\limits_{i=1}^{k}\sum\limits_{j=1}^{n_i}\left(y_{ij} - \bar{y}_i\right)^2}{n. - k} = \frac{\left(n_1 - 1\right)s_1^2 + \cdots + \left(n_k - 1\right)s_k^2}{n_1 + \cdots + n_k - k}$$

Both are weighted averages of the sample variances. When $k = 2$, $MS\left(\text{Error}\right) = s_{\text{pooled}}^2$. Both are estimates of σ^2.

6.2.6.2 Output for a Multiple-Comparison Test

The results of multiple-comparison tests are in *lines format* when the data is balanced and in *confidence interval format* when the data is unbalanced.

Lines Format

- The sample means are listed vertically, largest to smallest.

- Means that are not *significantly different* are connected with the same letter.

As an example of the line format, Fisher's LSD is applied to the means of the following five groups. Since the data is balanced, the *LSD* is the same for all comparisons. Assume $LSD = 4$. The results in lines format are in Table 6.4.

Group G1: $\overline{y}_1 = 71, n_1 = 8$

Group G2: $\overline{y}_2 = 83, n_2 = 8$

Group G3: $\overline{y}_3 = 65, n_3 = 8$

Group G4: $\overline{y}_4 = 80, n_4 = 8$

Group G5: $\overline{y}_5 = 72, n_5 = 8$

Table 6.4 Example of Lines Format

Means with the same letter are not significantly different.			
t Grouping	Mean	N	Group
A	83	10	G2
A			
A	80	10	G4
B	72	10	G5
B			
B	71	10	G1
	65	10	G3

The letters A and B are connection symbols and have no other meaning.

- The means for G2 and G4—connected by As—are not significantly different.

- The means for G5 and G1—connected by Bs—are not significantly different.

- All other differences between means are significant.

In word processor text, lines format is written with the sample means listed horizontally, smallest to largest, and means that are not significantly different are connected with lines.

$$\overline{y_3} = 65 \quad \overline{y_1} = 71 \quad \overline{y_5} = 72 \quad \overline{y_4} = 80 \quad \overline{y_2} = 83$$
$$\text{G3} \qquad \text{G1} \qquad \text{G5} \qquad \text{G4} \qquad \text{G2}$$

Confidence Interval Format

- All possible comparisons are shown. For k groups, there are $k(k-1)$ possible comparisons.
- Significantly different means are identified by ***.

Confidence intervals are used for unbalanced data because unbalanced data results in different margins of error—different *LSD* values for Fisher's LSD. One might see the following impossibility. Assume that A, B, and C are sample means and that they are ordered $A < B < C$.

- A and C are not significantly different: $|A - C| < LSD$.

- But A and B are significantly different: $LSD < |A - B|$.

This is not compatible with the lines format.

A situation in which close means are significantly different and more distant means are not can occur when the differences in sample sizes are relatively large. As an example, Fisher's LSD is applied to the means of the following three groups. Since the data is unbalanced, the *LSD* is not the same for all comparisons.

Group S1: $\overline{y_1} = 21.0, n_1 = 8$
Group S2: $\overline{y_2} = 24.0, n_2 = 100$
Group S3: $\overline{y_3} = 24.5, n_3 = 8$

The results in confidence interval format are in Table 6.5. In general, there are k groups of $k - 1$ comparisons. In this example, there are three groups of two comparisons.

- The first group lists all the comparisons where the largest sample mean is first in subtraction order. The comparisons are listed in decreasing order of the remaining means. In this example, S3 is the largest mean. The other means in decreasing order are S2 and S1. The comparisons in the first group are S3 − S2 and then S3 − S1.
- The second (third, …) group lists all the comparisons where the second (third, …) largest mean is first in subtraction order. The comparisons are listed in decreasing order of the remaining means.
  - In this example, S2 is the second largest mean. The other means in decreasing order are S3 and S1. The comparisons in the second group are S2 − S3 and then S2 − S1.
  - S1 is the smallest (third largest) mean. The other means in decreasing order are S3 and S2. The comparisons in the last group are S1 − S3 and then S1 − S2.

Table 6.5 Example of Confidence Interval Format

	Comparison	Difference Between Means	95% Confidence Limits		
1st group	S3 - S2	0.5	-2.439	3.439	
	S3 - S1	3.5	-0.500	7.500	
2nd group	S2 - S3	-0.5	-3.439	2.439	
	S2 - S1	3.0	0.061	5.539	***
3rd group	S1 - S3	-3.5	-7.500	0.500	
	S1 - S2	-3.0	-5.539	-0.061	***

Comparisons significant at the 0.05 level are indicated by ***.

Above:

- S3 has the largest sample mean. It is not significantly different from either of the other two means.

- S2 is the second largest sample mean. It is significantly different from S1.

The largest and smallest means are not significantly different with $|S3 - S1| = 3.5$. But the second largest and the smallest means are significantly different with $|S2 - S1| = 3.0$. These seemingly contradictory results are due to the relatively large differences in the sample sizes.

6.2.7 Example 6.1: One-Way ANOVA with Balanced Data

This example illustrates inference on four population means based on balanced data. The requested analysis includes a hypothesis test on the equality of the means, R^2, and Fisher's LSD multiple-comparison test, sample statistics, box-and-whisker plots, and a means plot.

- The hypothesis test, R^2, and Fisher's LSD are worked out in the "Detailed Solutions" section below.

- The One-Way ANOVA task is discussed in "Instructions for the One-Way ANOVA Task."

- Complete results are in "Task Output, Interpretation, and Analysis for Example 6.1."

6.2.7.1 Physical Activity Counseling

Forty-eight women participate in a study that examines the effectiveness of certain interventions in increasing physical activity (based on "Effects of Physical Activity Counseling in Primary Care," by The Writing Group for the Activity Counseling Trial Research Group, *Journal of the American Medical Association*, Vol. 286, No. 6, pp. 677-687). The women are between 35 and 45 years old. They are considered inactive since their daily energy expenditure (DEE) is at most 35 kcal/kg/day. Each woman is randomly assigned to one of four groups.

- The Advice group receives advice and educational material from a physician.

- The Assistance group receives the same as the Advice group plus one meeting with a health educator. The meeting involves counseling and an individualized plan.

- The Counseling group receives the same as the Assistance group plus continuing contact with a health educator. The contact involves monthly calls, mail-back cards, and weekly classes.

- The Control group receives no intervention.

After six months, the DEE for each woman is measured. All the results are below. The data is balanced.

Advice			Assistance			Counseling			Control		
33.85	33.61	32.62	35.78	34.07	33.34	34.08	34.43	33.92	30.93	32.39	28.95
33.52	31.61	33.75	34.80	33.10	32.61	34.91	35.78	33.24	32.85	31.33	32.07
32.78	31.68	31.44	32.96	32.70	33.88	35.04	35.51	33.56	31.19	32.57	32.39
31.65	32.90	33.47	32.92	35.39	33.39	34.47	35.16	34.50	31.60	34.25	31.50

Example 6.1.1
Test the claim that the mean DEE is the same for all patients receiving advice, assistance, counseling, and no intervention. Let $\alpha = 0.05$.

Example 6.1.2
Determine and interpret the Coefficient of Determination (R^2).

Example 6.1.3
If the claim in Example 6.1.1 is rejected, apply Fisher's LSD multiple-comparison test with a 95% confidence level. Answer the following questions.

- Which group has the highest mean DEE? What groups, if any, have means that are not significantly different from the highest?

- Which group has the lowest mean DEE? What groups, if any, have means that are not significantly different from the lowest?

Example 6.1.4
Determine the following statistics for the overall sample and then broken down by group: number of responses, mean, standard deviation, and variance.

Example 6.1.5
Construct box-and-whisker plots of the data. Are there any outliers?

Example 6.1.6
Construct a means plot.

The results are in the Ex06_01 data set, which is shown below.

	DEE	Group
1	33.85	Advice
2	33.61	Advice
3	32.62	Advice
4	33.52	Advice
5	31.61	Advice
6	33.75	Advice
7	32.78	Advice
8	31.68	Advice
9	31.44	Advice
10	31.65	Advice
11	32.9	Advice
12	33.47	Advice
13	35.78	Assistance
14	34.07	Assistance
15	33.34	Assistance
16	34.8	Assistance

- DEE is the dependent variable containing the responses.
- Group is the independent variable containing the classification values. The classification values in sorting order are Advice, Assistance, Control, and Counseling.

Subscripts 1, 2, 3, and 4 refer to Advice, Assistance, Control, and Counseling, respectively.

- μ_1 is the mean DEE score for all inactive women between 35 and 45 years old after receiving the advice intervention.
- μ_2 ... the assistance intervention.
- μ_3 ... no intervention.
- μ_4 ... the counseling intervention.

The hypotheses to be tested are:

$H_0 : \mu_1 = \mu_2 = \mu_3 = \mu_4$

$H_1 :$ At least two means are not equal.

6.2.7.2 Detailed Solutions

For convenience, the statistics requested in Example 6.1.4 are below in Output 6.1. They are also part of Output 6.2 shown in "Task Output, Interpretation, and Analysis for Example 6.1."

Output 6.1 Summary Tables Output for Example 6.1

Means and Descriptive Statistics

Intervention Group	Mean of DEE	Std. Dev. of DEE	Variance of DEE	Number Nonmissing of DEE
	33.2175	1.4352974338	2.06008	48
Advice	32.74	0.927881262	0.86096	12
Assistance	33.745	1.064608336	1.13339	12
Control	31.835	1.2811465036	1.64134	12
Counseling	34.55	0.7695098794	0.59215	12

Comment

"Intervention Group" is the label of the Group variable. The statistics in the first row are based on all the responses.

Example 6.1.1

Plan the task.

$H_0 : \mu_1 = \mu_2 = \mu_3 = \mu_4$

$H_1 :$ At least two means are not equal.

$\alpha = 0.05$

Compute the statistics.

$$SS(\text{Model}) = \sum_{i=1}^{k} n_i (\overline{y}_i - \overline{y})^2$$

$$= (12)(32.74 - 33.2175)^2 + (12)(33.745 - 33.2175)^2 + (12)(31.835 - 33.2175)^2$$

$$+ (12)(34.55 - 33.2175)^2$$

$$= 50.3175$$

$$SS(\text{Error}) = \sum_{i=1}^{k} \sum_{j=1}^{n_i} (y_{ij} - \overline{y}_i)^2$$

$$= \sum_{i=1}^{k} (n_i - 1) s_i^2$$

$$= (11)(0.86096) + (11)(1.13339) + (11)(1.64134) + (11)(0.59215)$$

$$= 46.5062$$

$$SS(\text{Total}) = SS(\text{Error}) + SS(\text{Model})$$

$$= 50.3175 + 46.5062$$

$$= 96.8237$$

Source	Df	Sum of Squares	Mean Square	*F* Value	Pr > F
Model	3	50.3175	16.7725	15.8680	0.00000039
Error	44	46.5062	1.0570		
Corrected Total	47	96.8237			

Referring to Table 6.1:

$$\text{p-value} = P\left(F > 15.8680\right) = 1 - \text{probf}(15.87, 3, 44) = 0.00000039$$

Apply the results.

Since the *p*-value < 0.05, reject H_0. There is sufficient evidence to reject the claim that the mean DEE is the same for patients receiving advice, assistance, counseling, and no intervention. At least two of the sample means are significantly different.

Example 6.1.2

Coefficient of Determination:

$$R^2 = \frac{SS(\text{Model})}{SS(\text{Total})} = \frac{50.3175}{96.8237} = 0.5197$$

Approximately 52% of the variation in daily energy expenditures is explained by the differences among the intervention group means.

Example 6.1.3

Since $H_0 : \mu_1 = \mu_2 = \mu_3 = \mu_4$ is rejected, the next step is to uncover the differences. Using Fisher's LSD multiple-comparison test, two population means are believed to be different if their respective sample means are greater than $LSD = t_{\alpha/2}\sqrt{MS(\text{Error})}\sqrt{\dfrac{1}{n_h} + \dfrac{1}{n_i}}$. The significance level is $\alpha = 0.05$.

The critical value is $t_{.025} = \text{tinv}(.975, 44) = 2.01537$.

$$LSD = (2.01537)\sqrt{1.0570}\sqrt{\frac{1}{12} + \frac{1}{12}} = 0.8459$$

The only difference with an absolute value less than the LSD is between the Assistance and the Counseling group: $\left|\bar{x}_2 - \bar{x}_4\right| = \left|33.745 - 34.55\right| = \left|-0.805\right| = 0.805$. Since the data is balanced, the results are presented in lines format.

$$\overline{\bar{x}_3 = 31.835 \quad \bar{x}_1 = 32.74 \quad \bar{x}_2 = 33.745 \quad \bar{x}_4 = 34.55}$$

       Control   Advice   Assistance   Counseling

- The Counseling group has the highest mean DEE. The mean DEE for the Assistance group is not significantly different.

- The Control group has the lowest mean DEE. All other groups are significantly higher.

6.2.8 Instructions for the One-Way ANOVA Task

The analysis requested in Example 6.1 is listed in Table 6.6. The first two items are always part of the output. The remaining are options. The figures in this section are for the analysis of Example 6.1.

Table 6.6 Analysis Requested in Example 6.1

Requested Analysis	Whether always part of output
ANOVA tests of the equality of the population means	Always part of the One-Way ANOVA output
Coefficient of Determination R^2	Always part of the One-Way ANOVA output
Fisher's LSD multiple comparison test	Option: Means > Comparison
Breakdown statistics	Option: Means > Breakdown
Box-and-whisker plots of the data	Option: Plots
Means plot	Option: Plots

Open the One-Way ANOVA task in one of the following ways:

- From the menu bar, select **Analyze ▶ ANOVA ▶ One-Way ANOVA**.
- On the **Task by Category** tab of the **Task List**, go to the **ANOVA** section and click **One-Way ANOVA**.
- On the **Task by Name** tab of the **Task List**, double-click **One-Way ANOVA**.

The One-Way ANOVA task has six groups of options: Task Roles, Tests, Means, Plots, Results, and Titles. Welch's variance-weighted ANOVA and the tests for equal variance in Tests are not discussed in this book. The Results options put the task results in data sets. The Titles options control the titles and the footnotes in the output. Titles are discussed in general in Chapter 1, "Introduction to SAS Enterprise Guide."

6.2.8.1 Task Roles

A variable is assigned to role by dragging it from **Variables to Assign** to one of the **Task roles**. A variable might be removed from a role by dragging it back to **Variables to Assign**. Also, the arrows might be used.

- Dependent variables are variables of responses. There is one dependent variable per analysis. Multiple dependent variables produce multiple analyses.
- The Independent variable is a variable of classification values.

The Group analysis by role is discussed in general in Chapter 1, "Introduction to SAS Enterprise Guide."

In Figure 6.2, DEE is assigned to the Dependent variables role and Group is assigned to the Independent variable role.

Figure 6.2 Task Roles in One-Way ANOVA

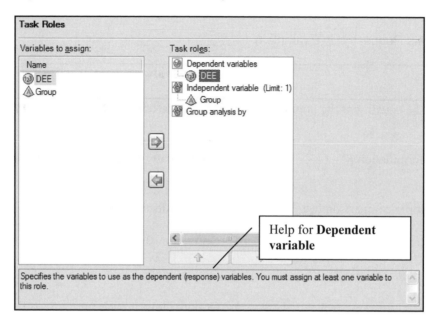

6.2.8.2 Tests

In the "Population Model for the One-Way ANOVA" section, it is assumed that each normally distributed population of responses has the same variance σ^2. Tests of this assumption of equal variances can be requested on this tab. Welch's variance-weighted ANOVA tests $H_0 : \mu_1 = \mu_2 = \ldots = \mu_k$ without using the assumption of equal variances. These options are not applied here.

6.2.8.3 Means

- Selecting **Comparison** shows the list of multiple-comparison tests. At the top in Figure 6.3, **Fisher's least significant-difference test** is selected. That test is discussed in the "Multiple-Comparisons Test" section. Other tests are discussed in the "More Multiple-Comparisons Tests" section.

The **Confidence level** can be typed in the box or selected from the drop-down menu. At the top in Figure 6.3, **95%** (the default) is selected.

- Selecting **Breakdown** shows a list of statistics. The output will include the selected statistics for the overall sample and the individual samples. At the bottom in Figure 6.3, the **Mean**, **Standard deviation**, **Variance**, and **Number of observations** are selected.

Figure 6.3 Mean > Comparison Options (Top), Mean > Breakdown Options (Bottom)

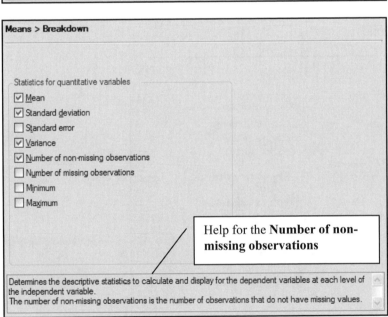

6.2.8.4   Plots

Box-and-whisker plots and a means plot can be selected here.

- Box-and-whisker plots are discussed in Section 3.5. The One-Way ANOVA task assumes that the responses come from normally distributed populations. Ideally, each sample is bell-shaped with no outliers. An outlier is an unusually large or small value relative to the rest of the sample. Outliers are individually identified in the box-and-whisker plot.

The task is most reliable when the data comes from normally distributed populations. Nevertheless, it does a good job as long as there are no severe outliers. Severe outliers can cause incorrect results, especially Type II Errors. A Type II Error occurs when the null hypothesis is not rejected when it is actually false. If the data contains severe outliers, a nonparametric test should be considered.

- The means plot represents each sample with a vertical line centered at the sample mean. The sample means are connected. The result is a convenient way to compare the means and the standard deviations. For the default means plot, the length of the vertical line from its center is one standard deviation. In the One-Way ANOVA task, a vertical line is drawn from $\overline{y}_i - s_i$ to $\overline{y}_i + s_i$ for each sample, $i = 1, \ldots, k$. See the representation below.

In Figure 6.4, both plots are selected. None of the default Means Plot options is changed.

Figure 6.4 Plots Options

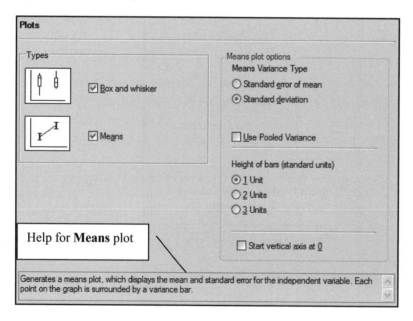

6.2.8.5 When Finished

When finished adding variables to roles and selecting options, click **Run**. The task adds a One-Way ANOVA icon and one or more output icons to the process flow diagram. See Figure 6.5. The resulting output is at Output 6.2.

Figure 6.5 Example 6.1 Data, Task, and Output Icons on the Process Flow Diagram

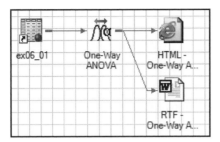

6.2.9 Task Output, Interpretation, and Analysis for Example 6.1

6.2.9.1 Task Output

Output 6.2 One-Way ANOVA Output for Example 6.1

One-Way Analysis of Variance
Results

The ANOVA Procedure

Class Level Information		
Class	**Levels**	**Values**
Group	4	Advice Assistance Control Counseling

❶

Number of Observations Read	48
Number of Observations Used	48

❷

Dependent Variable: DEE   Daily Energy Expenditure ❸

Source	DF	Sum of Squares	Mean Square	F Value	Pr > F
Model	3	50.31750000	16.77250000	15.87	<.0001
Error	44	46.50620000	1.05695909		
Corrected Total	47	96.82370000			

❹

R-Square	Coeff Var	Root MSE	DEE Mean
0.519682	3.095011	1.028085	33.21750

❺

Source	DF	Anova SS	Mean Square	F Value	Pr > F
Group	3	50.31750000	16.77250000	15.87	<.0001

❻

t Tests (LSD) for DEE ❼

NOTE: This test controls the Type I comparison-wise error rate, not the experiment-wise ❽
error rate.

Alpha	0.05 ❾
Error Degrees of Freedom	44 ❿
Error Mean Square	1.056959 ⓫
Critical Value of t	2.01537 ⓬
Least Significant Difference	0.8459 ⓭

Means with the same letter are not significantly different.			
t Grouping	Mean	N	Group
A	34.5500	12	Counseling
A			
A	33.7450	12	Assistance
B	32.7400	12	Advice
C	31.8350	12	Control

⓮ ⓯

Means and Descriptive Statistics

Intervention Group	Mean of DEE	Std. Dev. of DEE	Variance of DEE	Number Non-missing of DEE
	33.2175	1.4352974338	2.06008	48
Advice	32.74	0.927881262	0.86096	12
Assistance	33.745	1.064608336	1.13339	12
Control	31.835	1.2811465036	1.64134	12
Counseling	34.55	0.7695098794	0.59215	12

Box Plot of DEE by Group ⑰

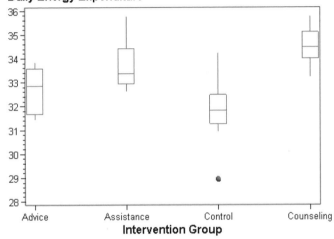

Means Plot of DEE by Group ⑱

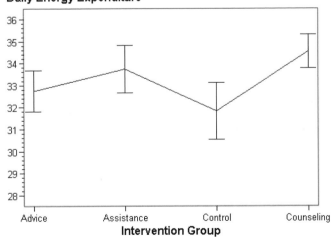

6.2.9.2 Interpretation

❶ Independent variable is Group and $k = 4$. Classification values in sorting order are: Advice, Assistance, Control, and Counseling.

❷ $n_. = 48$.

❸ Dependent variable is DEE. Its variable label is "Daily Energy Expenditure".

❹ ANOVA table

❺ Coefficient of Determination $R^2 = 0.519682$

❻ Test of hypotheses on factor effects. It has the same values and is interpreted in the same way as the Model row in the ANOVA table.

❼ Beginning of Fisher's LSD multiple-comparison test

❽ See the section on "More Multiple-Comparison Tests" for the discussion of comparison-wise and experiment-wise errors.

❾ $\alpha = 0.05$

❿ degrees of freedom $= n_. - k = 48 - 4 = 44$

⓫ $MS(\text{Error}) = 1.056959$

⓬ $t_{.025} = 2.01537$

⓭ $LSD = 0.8459$. Sample means are not connected—are significantly different—if the absolute value of their difference is at least 0.8459.

⓮ The Counseling group has the highest sample mean. The sample mean for the Assistance group is not significantly different.

⓯ The Control group has the lowest sample mean. All other groups are significantly higher.

⓰ The requested statistics

⓱ Box-and-whisker plot.

⓲ Means plot

6.2.9.3 Analysis

Example 6.1.1

$H_0 : \mu_1 = \mu_2 = \mu_3 = \mu_4$

$H_1 :$ At least two means are not equal.

p-value $< .0001$. See ❹ & ❻ in Output 6.2.

Since the p-value < 0.05, reject H_0. There is sufficient evidence to reject the claim that the mean DEE is the same for all patients receiving advice, assistance, counseling, and no intervention. At least two sample means are significantly different.

Example 6.1.2

Coefficient of Determination $R^2 = 0.519682$. See ❺ in Output 6.2.

Approximately 52% of the variation in daily energy expenditures is explained by the differences among the intervention group means.

Example 6.1.3

- The Counseling group has the highest sample mean. The sample mean for the Assistance group is not significantly different. See ⓮ in Output 6.2.

- The Control group has the lowest sample mean. All other groups are significantly higher. See ⓯ in Output 6.2.

Example 6.1.4

See ⓰ in Output 6.2. The top row of statistics is from the overall sample.

Example 6.1.5

See ⓱ in Output 6.2. The Control group has an outlier, DEE = 28.95. In Enterprise Guide, that information is shown when the cursor is placed above the circle that identifies the outlier. There is no reason to believe that the outlier is an error. In any case, it has not had a great impact on the results.

Example 6.1.6

See ⓲ in Output 6.2.

6.2.10 Example 6.2: One-Way ANOVA with Unbalanced Data

This example illustrates inference on three population means based on unbalanced data. The requested analysis includes a hypothesis test on the equality of the means, R^2, Fisher's LSD multiple-comparison test, sample statistics, box-and-whisker plots, and a means plot.

6.2.10.1 Employee Attitude toward Work

A company asks 24 randomly selected employees at three branch offices—Central, North, and South—to complete a standardized psychological questionnaire. Among other things, the questionnaire measures attitude toward tasks and responsibilities. The company wants to know if attitudes toward tasks and responsibilities differ at the three branch offices.

The results are below. The data is unbalanced. The results are also part of the Attitude data set seen following. The Attitude data set is in the Appendix. The task and responsibility Attitude scores are in the Work variable. The Central, North, and South classification values are in Location. The other variables in the Attitude data set are hidden. Work is the dependent variable and Location is the independent variable.

Central	North	South
49	52	56
51	51	57
53	52	51
50	51	57
54	59	58
47	51	57
48	58	59
	51	55
		56

attitude (read-only)

	Location	Work
1	South	56
2	Central	49
3	South	57
4	North	52
5	South	51
6	North	51
7	South	57
8	Central	51
9	Central	53
10	South	58
11	South	57
12	South	59
13	North	52
14	Central	50
15	North	51
16	Central	54
17	North	59
18	Central	47
19	South	55
20	South	56
21	North	51
22	Central	48
23	North	58
24	North	51

Example 6.2.1

Test the claim that the mean task-and-responsibility scores are the same at the three branch offices. Let $\alpha = 0.05$.

Example 6.2.2

Determine and interpret the Coefficient of Determination (R^2).

Example 6.2.3

If the claim in Example 6.2.1 is rejected, apply Fisher's LSD multiple-comparison test with $\alpha = 0.05$. Answer the following questions.

- Which branch office has the sample with the highest mean task-and-responsibility score? Which other samples, if any, have means that are not significantly different from the highest?

- Which branch office has the sample with the lowest mean task-and-responsibility score? Which other samples, if any, have means that are not significantly different from the lowest?

Example 6.2.4

Determine the following statistics for the overall sample and then broken down by location: number of responses, mean, standard deviation, minimum and maximum.

Example 6.2.5

Construct box-and-whisker plots of the data. Are there any outliers?

Example 6.2.6

Construct a means plot. Subscripts 1, 2, and 3 refer to Central, North, and South, respectively.

- μ_1 is the mean task-and-responsibility score for all employees at the Central branch office.

- μ_2 ... at the North branch office.

- μ_3 ... at the South branch office.

The hypotheses to be tested are:

$H_0 : \mu_1 = \mu_2 = \mu_3$

$H_1 :$ At least two means are not equal.

6.2.10.2 Detailed Solutions

The sample sizes, means, and standard deviations below are from the Means and Descriptive Statistics table in Output 6.3. There are a few slight differences between the following results and Output 6.3. This is due to rounding.

Example 6.2.1

Plan the task.

$H_0 : \mu_1 = \mu_2 = \mu_3$

$H_1 :$ At least two means are not equal.

$\alpha = 0.05$

Compute the statistics.

$$SS(\text{Model}) = \sum_{i=1}^{k} n_i (\bar{y}_i - \bar{y})^2$$

$$= (7)(50.28571 - 53.45833)^2 + (8)(53.125 - 53.45833)^2$$
$$+ (9)(56.22222 - 53.45833)^2$$
$$= 140.09929$$

$$SS(\text{Error}) = \sum_{i=1}^{k} \sum_{j=1}^{n_i} (y_{ij} - \bar{y}_i)^2 = \sum_{i=1}^{k} (n_i - 1)(s_i)^2$$

$$= (6)(2.56348)^2 + (7)(3.356763)^2 + (8)(2.279132)^2$$
$$= 159.85912$$

$$SS(\text{Total}) = SS(\text{Error}) + SS(\text{Model})$$
$$= 159.85912 + 140.09929$$
$$= 299.95841$$

Source	Df	Sum of Squares	Mean Square	F Value	Pr > F
Model	2	140.09929	70.0496	9.20211	0.00135
Error	21	159.85912	7.61234		
Corrected Total	23	299.95841			

Referring to Table 6.1:

$$p\text{-value} = P(F > 9.20211) = 1 - \text{probf}(9.20211, 2, 21) = 0.00135$$

Apply the results.

Since the p-value < 0.05, reject H_0. There is sufficient evidence to reject the claim that the mean task-and-responsibility scores are the same at the three branch offices. At least two of the sample means are significantly different.

Example 6.2.2
Coefficient of Determination:

$$R^2 = \frac{SS(\text{Model})}{SS(\text{Total})} = \frac{140.09929}{299.95841} = 0.4671$$

Approximately 47% of the variation in task-and-responsibility scores is explained by the differences among the branch office means.

Example 6.2.3

Since $H_0 : \mu_1 = \mu_2 = \mu_3$ is rejected, the next step is to uncover the differences. Using Fisher's LSD multiple-comparison test, two population means are believed to be different if their respective sample means are greater than $LSD = t_{\alpha/2}\sqrt{MS(\text{Error})}\sqrt{\dfrac{1}{n_h} + \dfrac{1}{n_i}}$. The significance level is $\alpha = 0.05$ and the critical value is $t_{.025} = \text{tinv}(.975, 21) = 2.07961$.

Because the sample sizes are not the same, the confidence interval format is used. Significantly different means are identified by ***.

	Difference Between Means	**95% Confidence Limits**	
South-North	$56.222 - 53.125 = 3.097$	$3.097 \pm 2.07961\sqrt{7.61234}\sqrt{\dfrac{1}{9} + \dfrac{1}{8}} \to (0.309, 5.885)$	***
South-Central	$56.222 - 50.286 = 5.936$	$5.936 \pm 2.07961\sqrt{7.61234}\sqrt{\dfrac{1}{9} + \dfrac{1}{7}} \to (3.044, 8.828)$	***
North-South	$53.125 - 56.222 = -3.097$	$-3.097 \pm 2.07961\sqrt{7.61234}\sqrt{\dfrac{1}{8} + \dfrac{1}{9}} \to (-5.885, -0.309)$	***
North-Central	$53.125 - 50.286 = 2.839$	$2.839 \pm 2.07961\sqrt{7.61234}\sqrt{\dfrac{1}{8} + \dfrac{1}{7}} \to (-0.131, 5.809)$	
Central-South	$50.286 - 56.222 = -5.936$	$-6.222 \pm 2.07961\sqrt{7.61234}\sqrt{\dfrac{1}{7} + \dfrac{1}{9}} \to (-8.828, -3.044)$	***
Central-North	$50.286 - 53.125 = -2.839$	$-3.125 \pm 2.07961\sqrt{7.61234}\sqrt{\dfrac{1}{7} + \dfrac{1}{8}} \to (-5.809, 0.131)$	

- The sample from the South branch office has the highest mean score. The samples from the other offices have means significantly different from the highest.

- The sample from the Central branch office has the lowest mean score. The sample from the South branch office has a mean significantly different from the lowest. The sample from the North branch office has a mean not significantly different from the lowest.

6.2.11 Task Output, Interpretation, and Analysis for Example 6.2

6.2.11.1 Task Output

Output 6.3 One-Way ANOVA Output for Example 6.2

One-Way Analysis of Variance
Results

The ANOVA Procedure

Class Level Information		
Class	**Levels**	**Values**
Location	3	Central North South

❶

Number of Observations Read	24
Number of Observations Used	24

❷

Dependent Variable: Work   Work ❸

Source	DF	Sum of Squares	Mean Square	F Value	Pr > F
Model	2	140.0992063	70.0496032	9.20	0.0013
Error	21	159.8591270	7.6123394		
Corrected Total	23	299.9583333			

❹

R-Square	Coeff Var	Root MSE	Work Mean
0.467062	5.161116	2.759047	53.45833

❺

Source	DF	Anova SS	Mean Square	F Value	Pr > F
Location	2	140.0992063	70.0496032	9.20	0.0013

❻

t Tests (LSD) for Work ❼

NOTE: This test controls the Type I comparison-wise error rate, not the experiment-wise error rate. ❽

Alpha	0.05	❾
Error Degrees of Freedom	21	❿
Error Mean Square	7.612339	⓫
Critical Value of t	2.07961	⓬

Comparisons significant at the 0.05 level are indicated by ***.				
Location Comparison	**Difference Between Means**	**95% Confidence Limits**		
South - North	3.097	0.309	5.885	***
South - Central	5.937	3.045	8.828	***
North - South	-3.097	-5.885	-0.309	***
North - Central	2.839	-0.130	5.809	
Central - South	-5.937	-8.828	-3.045	***
Central - North	-2.839	-5.809	0.130	

⓭ { South - North, South - Central

⓮ { Central - South, Central - North

Means and Descriptive Statistics ⓯

Location of Branch Office	Mean of Work	Std. Dev. of Work	Number Non-missing of Work	Minimum of Work	Maximum of Work
	53.45833	3.611325	24	47	59
Central	50.28571	2.56348	7	47	54
North	53.125	3.356763	8	51	59
South	56.22222	2.279132	9	51	59

Box Plot of Work by Location ⓰

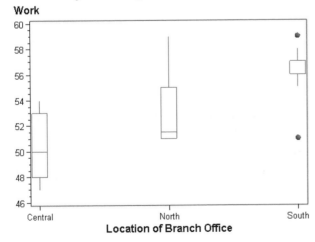

Means Plot of Work by Location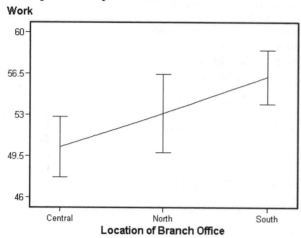

6.2.11.2 Interpretation

❶ Independent variable is Location and $k = 3$. Classification values in sorting order are Central, North, and South.

❷ $n_. = 24$.

❸ Dependent variable is Work. Its variable label is Work.

❹ ANOVA table

❺ Coefficient of Determination $R^2 = 0.467062$

❻ Test of hypotheses on factor effects. It has the same values and is interpreted in the same way as the Model row in the ANOVA table.

❼ Beginning of Fisher's LSD multiple-comparison test

❽ See the section on "More Multiple-Comparison Tests" for the discussion of comparison-wise and experiment-wise errors.

❾ $\alpha = 0.05$

❿ degrees of freedom $= n_. - k = 24 - 3 = 21$

⓫ $MS(\text{Error}) = 7.612339$

⓬ $t_{.025} = 2.07961$

⓭ The South branch office has the highest sample mean. The sample means for the North and Central branch offices are significantly different.

⓮ The Central branch office has the lowest sample mean. The sample mean for the South branch office is significantly different. The sample mean for the North branch office is not significantly different.

⓯ The requested statistics

⓰ Box-and-whisker plot

⓱ Means plot

6.2.11.3 Analysis

Example 6.2.1

$H_0 : \mu_1 = \mu_2 = \mu_3$

$H_1 :$ At least two means are not equal.

*p-v*alue = 0.0013. See ❹ & ❻ in Output 6.3.

Since the *p*-value < 0.05, reject H_0. There is sufficient evidence to reject the claim that the mean task-and-responsibility scores are the same at the three branch offices. At least two of the sample means are significantly different.

Example 6.2.2

Coefficient of Determination R^2 = 0.467062. See ❺ in Output 6.3.

Approximately 47% of the variation in task-and-responsibility scores is explained by the differences among the branch office means.

Example 6.2.3

- The sample from the South branch office has the highest mean score. The samples from the other offices have means significantly different from the highest. See ⓭ in Output 6.3.

- The sample from the Central branch office has the lowest mean score. The sample from the South branch office has a mean significantly different from the lowest. The sample from the North branch office has a mean not significantly different from the lowest. See ⓮ in Output 6.3.

Example 6.2.4

See ⓯ in Output 6.3. The top row of statistics is from the overall sample.

Example 6.2.5

See ⓰ in Output 6.3. The South has two outliers, Work = 51 and Work = 59. In Enterprise Guide, that information is shown when the cursor is placed above the circle that identifies the outlier. There is no reason to believe that the outliers are errors. In any case, they have not had a great impact on the results.

Example 6.2.6

See ⓲ in Output 6.3.

6.2.12 More Multiple-Comparison Tests

Fisher's LSD multiple-comparison test, which is introduced earlier in "Multiple-Comparison Tests," develops from the two-sample pooled confidence interval. This makes it easy to apply and interpret. But its confidence level only applies to individual comparisons, not to the group of comparisons as a whole.

The following statement warns of the problem in the output for Examples 6.1 and 6.2. See ❽ in Output 6.2 and ❽ in Output 6.3.

NOTE: This test controls the Type I comparison-wise error rate, not the experiment-wise error rate.

6.2.12.1 Type I Error Rates

A Type I error is a false positive. In the context of multiple-comparison tests, it is a comparison showing a significant difference when the underlying population means are equal.

- Type I comparison-wise error rate (CER)
    - CER is the likelihood that *a single specific comparison* gives a false positive result.
    - A comparison based on a $100(1-\alpha)\%$ confidence interval has a CER of α.

- Type I experiment-wise error rate (EER)
    - EER is the likelihood that *one or more comparisons* give false positive results.
    - The EER can be as large as $\left(\dfrac{k(k-1)}{2}\right)$ CER where k is the number of means in the experiment.

The previous statement concerning the potential size of an EER comes from probability where $P(E_1 \text{ or } \ldots \text{ or } E_{m-1} \text{ or } E_m) \leq P(E_1) + \cdots + P(E_{m-1}) + P(E_m)$ for any events E_i, $i = 1, \ldots, m$. The justification is in the following steps:

$$P(E_1 \text{ or } E_2) = P(E_1) + P(E_2) - P(E_1 \text{ and } E_2) \leq P(E_1) + P(E_2)$$

$$P(E_1 \text{ or } E_2 \text{ or } E_3) = P((E_1 \text{ or } E_2) \text{ or } E_3) \leq P(E_1 \text{ or } E_2) + P(E_3) \leq P(E_1) + P(E_2) + P(E_3)$$

$$\vdots$$

$$P(E_1 \text{ or } \ldots \text{ or } E_{m-1} \text{ or } E_m) = P((E_1 \text{ or } \ldots \text{ or } E_{m-1}) \text{ or } E_m)$$

$$\leq P(E_1 \text{ or } \ldots \text{ or } E_{m-1}) + P(E_m)$$

$$\leq P(E_1) + \cdots + P(E_{m-1}) + P(E_m)$$

Applied to multiple comparison tests, E_i is the event that a Type I error occurs with i^{th} comparison. In terms of a future experiment, $P(E_i) = \text{CER}$. Then $(E_1 \text{ or } \ldots \text{ or } E_{m-1} \text{ or } E_m)$ is the event that at least one Type I error occurs among the m comparisons. In terms of a future experiment, EER $= P(E_1 \text{ or } \ldots \text{ or } E_{m-1} \text{ or } E_m) \leq P(E_1) + \cdots + P(E_{m-1}) + P(E_m) = m \cdot \text{CER}$.

Where each pair among k means is tested, the number of comparisons is expressed in terms of *combinations of k things taken 2 at a time*:

$$m = \binom{k}{2} = \frac{k!}{(k-2)!2!} = \frac{k(k-1)}{2}$$

The $100(1-\alpha)\%$ confidence level associated with Fisher's LSD in Figure 6.3 is applied to the individual comparisons. For each comparison, the CER is α. For Fisher's LSD, the EER can be as large as $(k(k-1)/2)\alpha$.

In Example 6.1 and Output 6.2, the confidence level is 95% and $\alpha = 0.05$. Therefore, if μ_1 and μ_2 (the population means associated with the Advice and Assistance groups) are equal, there is only a 5% chance that two corresponding sample means would be significantly different. In Output 6.2, the sample means $\bar{y}_1$ and $\bar{y}_2$ are shown to be significantly different. The conclusion is that the population means μ_1 and μ_2 are different because of the small likelihood that populations with equal means would produce significantly different sample means.

But in Example 6.1, there are $\binom{4}{2} = 6$ comparisons for inferences on:

$$\mu_1 - \mu_2 \quad \mu_1 - \mu_3 \quad \mu_1 - \mu_4 \quad \mu_2 - \mu_3 \quad \mu_2 - \mu_4 \quad \mu_3 - \mu_4$$

The EER could be as large as $6\alpha = 6(0.05) = 0.30$. There could be as much as a 30% chance that at least one of the significant differences shown in Output 6.2 is in error. This is considerable doubt.

Three popular methods for controlling the EER are discussed next.

6.2.12.2 Bonferroni *t* Test

In the Bonferroni *t* test, α refers to the maximum EER. The Bonferroni approach is to reduce the CER of the individual Fisher's LSD comparison so that the EER is at most α.

In an experiment involving four populations, there are six possible comparisons. See the discussion immediately above. For $\alpha = 0.05$, the Bonferroni *t* test sets the CER to $\alpha/6 = 0.05/6 = 0.0083$. The EER is then is at most $6 \cdot \text{CER} = 6(\alpha/6) = \alpha = 0.05$. The Bonferroni *t* test would be based on six 99.17% confidence intervals.

The price paid for a lower EER is wider confidence intervals. This results in a higher Type II error rate. A Type II error is a false negative. In the context of multiple-comparison tests, it is a comparison showing no significant difference when the underlying population means are unequal.

Technical Details

- The Bonferroni t test sets the CER to $\alpha \Big/ \binom{k}{2}$, where k is the number of population means

  being studied. The binomial coefficient $\binom{k}{2} = \dfrac{k(k-1)}{2}$ is the number of possible

  comparisons. The EER for the Bonferroni t test is at most

$$\binom{k}{2} \cdot \text{CER} = \binom{k}{2}\left(\alpha \Big/ \binom{k}{2}\right) = \alpha .$$

- The Bonferroni t test is based on $100\left(1 - \alpha \Big/ \binom{k}{2}\right)\%$ confidence intervals being applied

  to all the differences being studied: $\mu_h - \mu_i$ $(1 \le h, i \le k)$. The Bonferroni confidence
  interval is

$$\left((\overline{y}_h - \overline{y}_i) - t_* \sqrt{MS(\text{Error})}\sqrt{\frac{1}{n_h} + \frac{1}{n_i}}, (\overline{y}_h - \overline{y}_i) + t_* \sqrt{MS(\text{Error})}\sqrt{\frac{1}{n_h} + \frac{1}{n_i}} \right)$$

  where $* = \alpha \Big/ \left[2\binom{k}{2} \right]$.

- The t_* critical value comes from the t distribution with $n_. - k$ degrees of freedom.

- In the output, the margin of error is called the minimum significant difference:

$$t_* \sqrt{MS(\text{Error})}\sqrt{\frac{1}{n_h} + \frac{1}{n_i}}$$

6.2.12.3 Tukey' s Studentized Range Test (HSD)

The HSD stands for "honest significant difference." In Tukey's studentized range test, also called Tukey's HSD, the EER is honestly α. The EER for the Bonferroni t test can be less than α.

The confidence intervals based on the studentized range distribution are not as wide as those produced by the Bonferroni t test. This results in a lower Type II error rate.

Tukey's studentized range test, while still controlling the EER, is more likely to detect differences between population means than the Bonferroni t test.

Technical Details

- The Tukey's studentized range test is based on $100(1 - \alpha)\%$ confidence intervals being
  applied to all the differences being studied: $\mu_h - \mu_i$ $(1 \le h, i \le k)$. Tukey's studentized
  range test confidence interval is:

$$\left((\overline{y}_h - \overline{y}_i) - \frac{q_\alpha}{\sqrt{2}} \sqrt{MS(\text{Error})}\sqrt{\frac{1}{n_h} + \frac{1}{n_i}}, (\overline{y}_h - \overline{y}_i) + \frac{q_\alpha}{\sqrt{2}} \sqrt{MS(\text{Error})}\sqrt{\frac{1}{n_h} + \frac{1}{n_i}} \right)$$

- The q_α critical value comes from the studentized range distribution with k and $n_. - k$ degrees of freedom. Using SAS code, $q_\alpha = \text{probmc('range',.,} 1 - \alpha, n_. - k, k)$, with $1 - \alpha$, $n_. - k$, and k representing numbers.

- In the output, the margin of error is called the minimum significant difference:

$$\frac{q_\alpha}{\sqrt{2}} \sqrt{MS(\text{Error})} \sqrt{\frac{1}{n_h} + \frac{1}{n_i}}$$

6.2.12.4 Ryan-Einot-Gabriel-Welsch Multiple-Range Test

The Ryan-Einot-Gabriel-Welsch Multiple-Range Test (REGWQ) is a refinement of Tukey's studentized range test.

- With the REGWQ, α refers to the maximum EER.

- The REGWQ has a lower Type II error rate than either the Bonferroni *t* test or Tukey's studentized range test. It is more likely to detect differences between population means than either test.

- A limitation is that REGWQ should be applied only to balanced data.

Technical Details

The REGWQ and Tukey's studentized range test are both based on the studentized range distribution. Tukey's test uses one value in determining significant difference. The REGWQ uses multiple values, which are called critical ranges.

The largest critical range is applied to the pair of sample means that are farthest apart. This is because a Type I error is most likely to occur with that pair of means. This largest critical range is actually the margin of error for Tukey's test. Sample means that are less far apart are compared to smaller critical ranges.

For any two sample means, let p be the number of ordered means, inclusive, between the smaller mean and the larger mean. If two means are next to one another in order, then $p = 2$. If there is one mean between a pair, then $p = 3$; two means between a pair, $p = 4$; etc. If the pair consists of the smallest mean and largest mean, then $p = k$ where k is the number of populations being studied.

- The REGWQ critical range is applied to all the differences being studied: $\mu_h - \mu_i$ ($1 \le h, i \le k$). The REGWQ critical range is

$$\frac{q_*}{\sqrt{2}} \sqrt{MS(\text{Error})} \sqrt{\frac{2}{n}}$$

where n is the common sample size and $* = \begin{cases} 1 - (1-\alpha)^{p/k} & \text{for } p < k - 1 \\ \alpha & \text{for } p \ge k - 1 \end{cases}$.

- The q_* critical value comes from the studentized range distribution with p and $n_. - k$ degrees of freedom. Using SAS code, $q_* = \text{probmc('range',.,}1-(1-\alpha)^{p/k}, n_.-k, p)$ and $q_* = \text{probmc('range',.,}1-\alpha, n_.-k, p)$, with $1-(1-\alpha)^{p/k}$, $1-\alpha$, $n_.-k$, and p representing numbers.

6.2.13 Example 6.3: Multiple-Comparison Tests with Balanced Data

Additional multiple-comparison tests are applied to Example 6.1.

Example 6.3.1
Apply the Bonferroni t test with $\alpha = 0.05$.

Example 6.3.2
Apply Tukey's studentized range test with $\alpha = 0.05$.

Example 6.3.3
Apply the REGWQ multiple-range test with $\alpha = 0.05$.

For each problem, answer the following questions:

> Which group has the highest mean DEE? What groups, if any, have means that are not significantly different from the highest?

> Which group has the lowest mean DEE? What groups, if any, have means that are not significantly different from the lowest?

The data in Example 6.1 is balanced, with the common sample size $n = 12$. Multiple-comparison test output is in lines format.

There are $k = 4$ population means. The total number of responses is $n_. = 48$. From Output 6.2, $MS(\text{Error}) = 1.05695909$.

6.2.13.1 Example 6.3.1: Bonferroni t test

- The subscript for the critical value is $* = 0.05 / \left[2\binom{4}{2} \right] = 0.05/[2(6)] = 0.0041667$. The critical value is $t_* = t_{0.0041667} = \text{tinv}(.9958333, 44) = 2.76281$.

- The minimum significant difference is $(2.76281)\sqrt{1.05695909}\sqrt{\frac{1}{12}+\frac{1}{12}} = 1.15959$. The sample means $\bar{y}_h$ and $\bar{y}_i$ are significantly different if $|\bar{y}_h - \bar{y}_i| \geq 1.15959$.

Output 6.4 Bonferroni *t* Test Applied to Example 6.3

Bonferroni (Dunn) t Tests for DEE   ❶

NOTE: This test controls the Type I experiment-wise error rate, but it generally has a higher
Type II error rate than REGWQ.

Alpha	0.05	❷
Error Degrees of Freedom	44	❸
Error Mean Square	1.056959	❹
Critical Value of t	2.76281	❺
Minimum Significant Difference	1.1596	❻

Means with the same letter are not significantly different.				
Bon Grouping		**Mean**	**N**	**Group**
	A	34.5500	12	Counseling
	A			
B	A	33.7450	12	Assistance
B				
B	C	32.7400	12	Advice
	C			
	C	31.8350	12	Control

❼ (bracketing Counseling / A–A–A / Assistance)

❽ (bracketing Advice / C–C–C / Control)

Interpretation

❶ Beginning of the Bonferroni *t* test

❷ $\alpha = 0.05$. With respect to the Bonferroni *t* test, α is the maximum value for the EER.

❸ degrees of freedom = $n_. - k$

❹ *MS*(Error)

❺ t_*

❻ Margin of error for the Bonferroni *t* test

❼ The Counseling group has the highest sample mean. The sample mean for the Assistance group is not significantly different. See ❼ in Output 6.4.

❽ The Control group has the lowest sample mean. The sample mean for the Advice group is not significantly different. See ❽ in Output 6.4.

Here, the Bonferroni *t* test finds three differences to be not significant: Counseling and Assistance, Assistance and Advice, and Advice and Control. In Output 6.2, Fisher's LSD found only Counseling and Assistance to be not significant.

The Bonferroni *t* test is said to be a *conservative* multiple-comparison test, while Fisher's LSD is said to be *liberal*. The next two procedures are designed to create a less conservative test while still controlling the experiment-wise error rate.

6.2.13.2 Example 6.3.2: Tukey's Studentized Range Test

- The critical value is $q_{.05} = \text{probmc}('\text{range}',.,.95,44,4) = 3.77596$.

- The minimum significant difference is $\dfrac{3.77596}{\sqrt{2}}\sqrt{1.05696}\sqrt{\dfrac{1}{12}+\dfrac{1}{12}} = 1.1206$. The sample

  means $\overline{y}_h$ and $\overline{y}_i$ are significantly different if $\left|\overline{y}_h - \overline{y}_i\right| \geq 1.1206$.

Output 6.5 Tukey's Studentized Range Test Applied to Example 6.3

Tukey's Studentized Range (HSD) Test for DEE ❶

NOTE: This test controls the Type I experiment-wise error rate, but it generally has a higher Type II error rate than REGWQ.

Alpha	0.05	❷
Error Degrees of Freedom	44	❸
Error Mean Square	1.056959	❹
Critical Value of Studentized Range	3.77596	❺
Minimum Significant Difference	1.1206	❻

Means with the same letter are not significantly different.					
Tukey Grouping		**Mean**	**N**	**Group**	
	A	34.5500	12	Counseling	⎫
	A				⎬ ❼
B	A	33.7450	12	Assistance	⎭
B					
B	C	32.7400	12	Advice	⎫
	C				⎬ ❽
	C	31.8350	12	Control	⎭

Interpretation

❶ Beginning of Tukey's studentized range test

❷ $\alpha = 0.05$. With respect to the Tukey's studentized range test, α is the EER.

❸ degrees of freedom $= n_{\boldsymbol{\cdot}} - k$

❹ $MS(\text{Error})$

❺ $q_{.05}$

❻ Margin of error for Tukey's studentized range test

❼ The Counseling group has the highest sample mean. The sample mean for the Assistance group is not significantly different. See ❼ in Output 6.5.

❽ The Control group has the lowest sample mean. The sample mean for the Advice group is not significantly different. See ❽ in Output 6.5.

The outcomes above are the same as in Output 6.4 where the Bonferroni *t* test is used. Nevertheless, the minimum significant difference here is 1.1206 and in Output 6.4 it is 1.1596. In this example, Tukey's studentized range test is slightly less conservative than the Bonferroni *t* test. When there are more populations in the experiment, the Bonferroni is increasingly more conservative relative to Tukey's test.

6.2.13.3 Example 6.3.3: REGWQ

- For $p = 2$, the critical value is $q_* = \text{probmc}('range',.,1-(.95)**(2/4), 44, 2) = 3.27437$. The critical range is $\dfrac{3.27437}{\sqrt{2}}\sqrt{1.05696}\sqrt{\dfrac{2}{12}} = 0.97178$.

- For $p = 3$, the critical value is $q_* = \text{probmc}('range',.,.95, 44, 3) = 3.43015$. The critical range is $\dfrac{3.43015}{\sqrt{2}}\sqrt{1.05696}\sqrt{\dfrac{2}{12}} = 1.01801$.

- For $p = 4$, the critical value is $q_* = \text{probmc}('range',.,.95, 44, 4) = 3.77596$. The critical range is $\dfrac{3.77596}{\sqrt{2}}\sqrt{1.05696}\sqrt{\dfrac{2}{12}} = 1.2064$.

Output 6.6 REGWQ Applied to Example 6.3

Ryan-Einot-Gabriel-Welsch Multiple Range Test for DEE ❶

NOTE: This test controls the Type I experiment-wise error rate.

Alpha	0.05	❷
Error Degrees of Freedom	44	❸
Error Mean Square	1.056959	❹

Number of Means	2	3	4	
Critical Range	0.9717755	1.0180094	1.1206389	❺

Means with the same letter are not significantly different.			
REGWQ Grouping	**Mean**	**N**	**Group**
A	34.5500	12	Counseling
A			
A	33.7450	12	Assistance
C	32.7400	12	Advice
C			
C	31.8350	12	Control

Interpretation

❶ Beginning of the REGWQ multiple-range test

❷ $\alpha = 0.05$. With the REGWQ, α refers to the maximum EER.

❸ degrees of freedom = $n_. - k$

❹ *MS*(Error)

❺ Critical ranges

❻ The Counseling group has the highest sample mean. The sample mean for the Assistance group is not significantly different.

❼ The Control group has the lowest sample mean. The sample mean for the Advice group is not significantly different.

Here, the REGWQ test finds two differences to be not significant: between Counseling and Assistance and between Advice and Control. Fewer differences are significant here than in Output 6.2 where the liberal Fisher's LSD is applied. More differences are significant here than in Output 6.4 where the conservative Bonferroni *t* test is applied.

6.2.14 Example 6.4: Multiple-Comparison Tests with Unbalanced Data

Additional multiple-comparison tests are applied to Example 6.2.

Example 6.4.1

Apply the Bonferroni *t* test with $\alpha = 0.05$.

Example 6.4.2

Apply Tukey's studentized range test with $\alpha = 0.05$.

For each problem, answer the following questions:

> Which branch office has the sample with the highest mean task-and-responsibility score? Which other samples, if any, have means that are not significantly different from the highest?

Which branch office has the sample with the lowest mean task-and-responsibility score? Which other samples, if any, have means that are not significantly different from the lowest?

The data in Example 6.2 is not balanced. Multiple-comparison test output is in confidence interval format.

There are $k = 3$ population means. The total number of responses is $n_. = 24$. From Output 6.3, $MS(\text{Error}) = 7.6123394$.

6.2.14.1 Example 6.4.1: Bonferroni *t* Test

- The subscript for the critical value is $* = 0.05\Big/\left[2\binom{3}{2}\right] = 0.05/[2(3)] = 0.008333$. The critical value is $t_* = t_{0.008333} = \text{tinv}(.9916667, 21) = 2.60135$.

- Significantly different means are identified by ***.

	Difference Between Means	Simultaneous 95% Confidence Limits	
South-North	$56.222 - 53.125 = 3.097$	$3.097 \pm 2.60135\sqrt{7.61234}\sqrt{\dfrac{1}{9} + \dfrac{1}{8}} \rightarrow (-0.3905, 6.5845)$	
South-Central	$56.222 - 50.286 = 5.936$	$5.936 \pm 2.60135\sqrt{7.61234}\sqrt{\dfrac{1}{9} + \dfrac{1}{7}} \rightarrow (2.3190, 9.5530)$	***
North-South	$53.125 - 56.222 = -3.097$	$-3.097 \pm 2.60135\sqrt{7.61234}\sqrt{\dfrac{1}{8} + \dfrac{1}{9}} \rightarrow (-6.5845, 0.3905)$	
North-Central	$53.125 - 50.286 = 2.839$	$2.839 \pm 2.60135\sqrt{7.61234}\sqrt{\dfrac{1}{8} + \dfrac{1}{7}} \rightarrow (-0.8756, 6.5536)$	
Central-South	$50.286 - 56.222 = -5.936$	$-6.222 \pm 2.60135\sqrt{7.61234}\sqrt{\dfrac{1}{7} + \dfrac{1}{9}} \rightarrow (-9.5530, -2.3190)$	
Central-North	$50.286 - 53.125 = -2.839$	$-3.125 \pm 2.60135\sqrt{7.61234}\sqrt{\dfrac{1}{7} + \dfrac{1}{8}} \rightarrow (-6.5536, 0.8756)$	

Output 6.7 Bonferroni *t* Test Applied to Example 6.4

Bonferroni (Dunn) t Tests for Work ❶

NOTE: This test controls the Type I experiment-wise error rate, but it generally has a higher Type II error rate than Tukey's for all pair-wise comparisons.

Alpha	0.05	❷
Error Degrees of Freedom	21	❸
Error Mean Square	7.612339	❹
Critical Value of t	2.60135	❺

Comparisons significant at the 0.05 level are indicated by ***.				
Location Comparison	Difference Between Means	Simultaneous 95% Confidence Limits		
South - North	3.097	-0.390	6.585	
South - Central	5.937	2.320	9.554	***
North - South	-3.097	-6.585	0.390	
North - Central	2.839	-0.875	6.554	
Central - South	-5.937	-9.554	-2.320	***
Central - North	-2.839	-6.554	0.875	

❻ { South - North, South - Central }

❼ { Central - South, Central - North }

Interpretation

❶ Beginning of the Bonferroni *t* test

❷ $\alpha = 0.05$. With respect to the Bonferroni *t* test, α is the maximum value for the EER.

❸ degrees of freedom = $n_. - k$

❹ MS(Error)

❺ t_*

❻ The South branch office has the highest sample mean. The sample mean for the North branch office is not significantly different.

❼ The Central branch office has the lowest sample mean. The sample mean for the North branch office is not significantly different.

6.2.14.2 Example 6.4.2: Tukey's Studentized Range Test

- The critical value is $q_{.05} = \text{probmc}('range',.,.95, 41, 3) = 3.56463$.

- Significantly different means are identified by ***.

	Difference Between Means	**Simultaneous 95% Confidence Levels**	
South-North	$56.222 - 53.125 = 3.097$	$3.097 \pm \dfrac{3.56463}{\sqrt{2}}\sqrt{7.61234}\sqrt{\dfrac{1}{9}+\dfrac{1}{8}} \to (-0.2822, 6.4762)$	
South-Central	$56.222 - 50.286 = 5.936$	$5.936 \pm \dfrac{3.56463}{\sqrt{2}}\sqrt{7.61234}\sqrt{\dfrac{1}{9}+\dfrac{1}{7}} \to (2.4313, 9.4407)$	***
North-South	$53.125 - 56.222 = -3.097$	$-3.097 \pm \dfrac{3.56463}{\sqrt{2}}\sqrt{7.61234}\sqrt{\dfrac{1}{8}+\dfrac{1}{9}} \to (-6.4762, 0.2822)$	
North-Central	$53.125 - 50.286 = 2.839$	$2.839 \pm \dfrac{3.56463}{\sqrt{2}}\sqrt{7.61234}\sqrt{\dfrac{1}{8}+\dfrac{1}{7}} \to (-0.7602, 6.4382)$	
Central-South	$50.286 - 56.222 = -5.936$	$-6.222 \pm \dfrac{3.56463}{\sqrt{2}}\sqrt{7.61234}\sqrt{\dfrac{1}{7}+\dfrac{1}{9}} \to (-9.4407, -2.4313)$	***
Central-North	$50.286 - 53.125 = -2.839$	$-3.125 \pm \dfrac{3.56463}{\sqrt{2}}\sqrt{7.61234}\sqrt{\dfrac{1}{7}+\dfrac{1}{8}} \to (-6.4382, 0.7602)$	

Output 6.8 Tukey's Studentized Range Test Applied to Example 6.4

Tukey's Studentized Range (HSD) Test for Work ❶

NOTE: This test controls the Type I experiment-wise error rate.

Alpha	0.05	❷
Error Degrees of Freedom	21	❸
Error Mean Square	7.612339	❹
Critical Value of Studentized Range	3.56463	❺

	Comparisons significant at the 0.05 level are indicated by ***.			
Location Comparison	**Difference Between Means**	**Simultaneous 95% Confidence Limits**		
South - North	3.097	-0.282	6.476	
South - Central	5.937	2.432	9.441	***
North - South	-3.097	-6.476	0.282	
North - Central	2.839	-0.760	6.439	
Central - South	-5.937	-9.441	-2.432	***
Central - North	-2.839	-6.439	0.760	

❻ { South - North, South - Central }

❼ { Central - South, Central - North }

Interpretation

❶ Beginning of Tukey's studentized range test

❷ $\alpha = 0.05$. With respect to the Tukey's studentized range test, α is the EER.

❸ degrees of freedom = $n_\cdot - k$

❹ $MS(\text{Error})$

❺ $q_{.05}$

❻ The South branch office has the highest sample mean. The sample mean for the North branch office is not significantly different.

❼ The Central branch office has the lowest sample mean. The sample mean for the North branch office is not significantly different.

The outcomes above are the same as in Output 6.7 where the Bonferroni *t* test is used. Nevertheless, the confidence intervals are narrower here than in Output 6.7. This results in Tukey's studentized range test having a lower Type II error rate than the Bonferroni *t* test. Tukey's studentized range test is more likely to detect differences between population means.

6.2.15 Recommendations for Multiple-Comparison Tests

- Fisher's LSD is not recommended. Fisher's LSD is a good place to begin studying multiple-comparison tests. But there's the possibility of a high Type I experiment-wise error rate (EER).

- The Bonferroni *t* test is not the best procedure. However, it is a good place to examine the strategy for controlling the EER.

- For unbalanced data, Tukey's studentized range test is recommended. Tukey's studentized range test has greater power than the Bonferroni *t* test. That is, it is more likely to detect differences between population means.

- For balanced data, the Ryan-Einot-Gabriel-Welsch Multiple-Range Test is recommended. The REGWQ Multiple-Range Test has greater power than Tukey's studentized range test.

6.3 Factorial Analysis of Variance

Factorial analysis of variance compares the means of populations described by two or more *crossed* factors.

- Factors are crossed when all possible combinations of factor levels are present in the study. In the case of two factors, every level of one factor is associated with every level of the second factor.

- Each of these combinations—with one level from each factor in the study—is a *treatment*.

- There is a population of potential responses associated with each treatment.

The Linear Models task is used for factorial ANOVA. The input is a variable of responses and two or more variables of classification values. These are the *dependent variable* and *independent variables*.

- The dependent variable contains a sample of responses from each population.
- The independent variables represent the factors in the study. The rows of the independent variables identify the treatments and the respective samples.

In Example 6.5, two factors might influence the quality of life of headache patients:

> A clinical trial investigates the effectiveness of a new drug for the treatment of headaches. The new drug is administered at two dosages: 5 milligrams and 10 milligrams. Female and male patients are randomly assigned to receive the drug at either a 5-milligram or a 10-milligram dosage.

> After one month, the patients complete a quality-of-life (QOL) questionnaire. The QOL scores are on a 100-point scale. The standardized mean score is 50. Higher scores indicate a better quality of life.

The two factors are the dosage of the new drug—with levels 5 milligrams and 10 milligrams—and the sex of the patient—with levels female and male. The factors are crossed.

The outcome being studied is quality of life. The response is the QOL score produced by the questionnaire. There is a population of potential QOL scores associated with each of the four treatments:

female patients taking the new drug at the 5-milligram dosage	male patients taking the new drug at the 5-milligram dosage
female patients taking the new drug at the 10-milligram dosage	male patients taking the new drug at the 10-milligram dosage

A two-way factorial ANOVA examines how crossed factors affect responses:

- First, there is a test of whether the factors have any effect at all. In terms of Example 6.5, are there any differences among the four dosage-gender treatments?
- If so, interaction is considered. Do females and males respond differently to the two dosages?
- If interaction is not present, the effects of the individual factors are examined. Do patients on the two dosages respond differently, regardless of gender? Do females and males respond differently, regardless of dosage?
- If interaction is present, the responses associated with the treatments are compared. Which dosage-gender treatment has the best response? Which has the worst response?

6.3.1 Notation

Three subscripts are required for a two-way factorial analysis of variance. An individual response is represented by the variable y_{ijk}. Let A and B represent the two independent variables.

- The subscripts i and j identify the response as being in the sample associated with i^{th} level of A and j^{th} level of B.
    - $i = 1,\ldots,a$ where a is the number of A levels and $j = 1,\ldots,b$ where b is the number of B levels.
    - Also, i^{th} and j^{th} are variable representations of 1st, 2nd, 3rd, 4th, etc.
- The k subscript identifies the response from the sample list. Here, $k = 1,\ldots,n_{ij}$, where n_{ij} is the sample size associated with i^{th} level of A and j^{th} level of B.

If the sample sizes are all the same, the data is *balanced*. Otherwise, the data is *unbalanced*.

In a two-way factorial analysis of variance, the number of treatments is equal to ab. In the balanced case, the total number of responses is equal to abn, where n is the common sample size in the balanced data set.

The dot notation is needed here. Dots in subscript locations indicate the sum of all such values with those subscripts. When used with a mean, dots indicate both summing and averaging. As examples:

- $y_{12\bullet} = \sum_{k=1}^{n_{12}} y_{12k}$ and $\bar{y}_{12\bullet} = \dfrac{y_{12\bullet}}{n_{12}}$

- $y_{1\bullet\bullet} = \sum_{j=1}^{b}\sum_{k=1}^{n_{1j}} y_{1jk}$, $n_{1\bullet} = \sum_{j=1}^{b} n_{1j}$, and $\bar{y}_{1\bullet\bullet} = \dfrac{y_{1\bullet\bullet}}{n_{1\bullet}}$

- $y_{\bullet\bullet\bullet} = \sum_{i=1}^{a}\sum_{j=1}^{b}\sum_{k=1}^{n_{ij}} y_{ijk}$, $n_{\bullet\bullet} = \sum_{i=1}^{a}\sum_{j=1}^{b} n_{ij}$, and $\bar{y}_{\bullet\bullet\bullet} = \dfrac{y_{\bullet\bullet\bullet}}{n_{\bullet\bullet}}$

Treatment Means

$\bar{y}_{ij\bullet}$ is the mean of the sample associated with treatment formed by the ith level of A and the jth level of B: $\bar{y}_{ij\bullet} = y_{ij\bullet}/n_{ij} = \left.\sum_{k=1}^{n_{ij}} y_{ijk}\right/ n_{ij}$.

Factor-Level Means

- $\bar{y}_{i\bullet\bullet}$ is the mean of all the responses associated with the ith level of A:

    $\bar{y}_{i\bullet\bullet} = y_{i\bullet\bullet}/n_{i\bullet} = \left.\sum_{j=1}^{b}\sum_{k=1}^{n_{ij}} y_{ijk}\right/ n_{i\bullet}$

- $\bar{y}_{\bullet j\bullet}$ is the mean of all the responses associated with the jth level of B:

    $\bar{y}_{\bullet j\bullet} = y_{\bullet j\bullet}/n_{\bullet j} = \left.\sum_{i=1}^{a}\sum_{k=1}^{n_{ij}} y_{ijk}\right/ n_{\bullet j}$

Overall Mean

$\overline{y}_{...}$ is the mean of all the responses: $\overline{y}_{...} = y_{...}/n_{..} = \sum\limits_{i=1}^{a}\sum\limits_{j=1}^{b}\sum\limits_{k=1}^{n_{ij}} y_{ijk} \Big/ n_{..}$

The means can be organized in the following manner:

		B			
		$j=1$	$j=2$ ...	$j=b$	
	$i=1$	$\overline{y}_{11.}$	$\overline{y}_{12.}$ ...	$\overline{y}_{1b.}$	$\overline{y}_{1..}$
A	$i=2$	$\overline{y}_{21.}$	$\overline{y}_{22.}$ ...	$\overline{y}_{2b.}$	$\overline{y}_{2..}$
	$\vdots$	$\vdots$	$\vdots$ $\ddots$	$\vdots$	$\vdots$
	$i=a$	$\overline{y}_{a1.}$	$\overline{y}_{a2.}$ ...	$\overline{y}_{ab.}$	$\overline{y}_{a..}$
		$\overline{y}_{.1.}$	$\overline{y}_{.2.}$ ...	$\overline{y}_{.b.}$	$\overline{y}_{...}$

6.3.2 Population Model for the Two-way Factorial ANOVA

The random variable Y assigns a number to each person or object of interest. There are two factors, A and B. Factor A has a levels and factor B has b levels. Both a and b are at least 2. There is a population of numerical values associated with the treatment formed by the ith level of A and the jth level of B, where $i=1,...,a$ and $j=1,...,b$. There are ab populations.

The population model for the two-way factorial ANOVA assumes that for the population associated with the ith level of A and the jth level of B:

$$Y = \mu_{ij} + \varepsilon$$

- μ_{ij} is the mean of the population associated with the ith level of A and the jth level of B.

- ε is also a random variable. It is called an *error*. The errors ε of each population are assumed to be normally distributed with mean 0 and the unknown variance σ^2. The variance is assumed to be the same for each population.

- The values in the population associated with the ith level of A and the jth level of B are assumed to be normally distributed with mean μ_{ij} and variance σ^2.

The factorial ANOVA investigates how the factors contribute to the values of the population means. The model expresses each population mean as the sum of the overall mean, main effects, and an interaction effect:

population mean = overall mean + main effects + interaction effect

There is a main effect term for each factor. In the two-factor model, there is a single interaction term. All the terms are assumed to be fixed unknown constants.

$$\mu_{ij} = \mu + \alpha_i + \beta_j + (\alpha\beta)_{ij}$$

- μ is the *overall mean* of the *ab* populations.

- α_i is the *main effect* associated with the ith level of A.

  - It is the average contribution associated with the ith level of A.

  - In terms of means, it is the difference between the mean of the combined populations associated with the ith level of A and μ.

  - That is, $\alpha_i = \mu_{i\cdot} - \mu$, where $\mu_{i\cdot} = \sum_{j=1}^{b} \mu_{ij} \Big/ b$ is the mean of the combined populations associated with the ith level of A. The mean $\mu_{i\cdot}$ is referred to as a *factor A population mean*.

  - The model assumes $\sum_{i=1}^{a} \alpha_i = 0$.

- β_j is the *main effect* associated with j^{th} level of B.

  - It is the average contribution associated with the jth level of B.

  - In terms of means, it is the difference between the mean of the combined populations associated with the jth level of B and μ.

  - That is, $\beta_j = \mu_{\cdot j} - \mu$, where $\mu_{\cdot j} = \sum_{i=1}^{a} \mu_{ij} \Big/ a$ is the mean of the combined populations associated with the jth level of B. The mean $\mu_{\cdot j}$ is referred to as a *factor B population mean*.

  - The model assumes $\sum_{j=1}^{b} \beta_j = 0$.

- $(\alpha\beta)_{ij}$ is the A*B *interaction effect* associated with the treatment that includes the ith level of A and the jth level of B.

  - It is the contribution beyond the overall mean and the main effects that is associated with the treatment that includes the ith level of A and the jth level of B.

  - It is the difference between the *treatment-population mean* μ_{ij} and the sum of the overall mean and the main effects.

  - That is, $(\alpha\beta)_{ij} = \mu_{ij} - (\mu + \alpha_i + \beta_j)$.

  - The model assumes $\sum_{i=1}^{a} (\alpha\beta)_{ij} = 0$ and $\sum_{j=1}^{b} (\alpha\beta)_{ij} = 0$.

6.3.3 Interaction

The influences of A at each level of B can be expressed as a one-way ANOVA model. When there is no interaction, the model is essentially the same at each level of B. When there is interaction, the model is not the same at each level of B.

6.3.3.1 Absence of Interaction

Interaction is absent when all $(\alpha\beta)_{ij} = 0$.

- For level j of factor B, the treatment means associated with factor A are $\mu_{ij} = \mu + \alpha_i + \beta_j$, $i = 1,\ldots,a$.

- This becomes a one-way ANOVA model of A: $\mu_{ij} = (\mu + \beta_j) + \alpha_i = \mu_{.j} + \alpha_i$.

- The mean changes with j but the treatment effects α_i remain the same.

- The influences of A are the same at each level of B. For example, if α_1 is the largest A effect, μ_{1j} is the largest mean at each level j.

If there is no interaction and $\alpha_1 = \alpha_2 = \ldots = \alpha_a = 0$, A is not an important factor in the variation of the responses.

6.3.3.2 Presence of Interaction

Interaction is present when some or all $(\alpha\beta)_{ij} \neq 0$.

- For level j of factor B, the treatment means associated with factor **A** are
$\mu_{ij} = \mu + \alpha_i + \beta_j + (\alpha\beta)_{ij}$, $i = 1,\ldots,a$.

- This becomes a one-way ANOVA model of A: $\mu_{ij} = (\mu + \beta_j) + \alpha_i + (\alpha\beta)_{ij} = \mu_{.j} + \tau_{ij}$
where $\tau_{ij} = \alpha_i + (\alpha\beta)_{ij}$.

- Both the mean and the treatment effects τ_{ij} change with j.

- The influences of A are not the same at each level of B. For example, μ_{1j} depends on both α_1 and $(\alpha\beta)_{1j}$. Even if α_1 is the largest A effect, μ_{1j} might not be the largest mean at each level j.

If there is interaction and $\alpha_1 = \alpha_2 = \ldots = \alpha_a = 0$, A might still be an important factor in the variation of the responses. A might be an important factor at some levels of B and not others.

6.3.3.3 Example

Figure 6.6 shows a case where interaction is absent, and Figure 6.7 shows a case where interaction is present. In both cases, the underlying model has two crossed factors, A and B. Each factor has two levels: a_1 and a_2 for A, b_1 and b_2 for B. The treatments and the associated population means are shown below. In both figures:

		B	
		b_1	b_2
A	a_1	(a_1, b_1) μ_{11}	(a_1, b_2) μ_{12}
	a_2	(a_2, b_1) μ_{21}	(a_2, b_2) μ_{22}

- The numerical response axis (y) is the vertical axis. The value of the overall mean μ is marked on the vertical axis and identified with a dotted line.

- The levels of factor A are marked on the horizontal axis. Means associated with levels of factor B are connected.

- The four population means are identified with filled circles.

In Figure 6.6, there is no interaction: $(\alpha\beta)_{11} = (\alpha\beta)_{12} = (\alpha\beta)_{21} = (\alpha\beta)_{22} = 0$.

With no interaction, the influence of A is the same at each level of B. At each level of B in Figure 6.6, there is the same negative impact at a_1 and the same positive impact at a_2.

The difference between the means is the same at each level of B. This results in parallel lines.

- At b_1: $\mu_{11} - \mu_{21} = (\mu + \alpha_1 + \beta_1) - (\mu + \alpha_2 + \beta_1) = \alpha_1 - \alpha_2$

- At b_2: $\mu_{12} - \mu_{22} = (\mu + \alpha_1 + \beta_2) - (\mu + \alpha_2 + \beta_2) = \alpha_1 - \alpha_2$

Figure 6.6 Example of Population Means Where There Is No Interaction

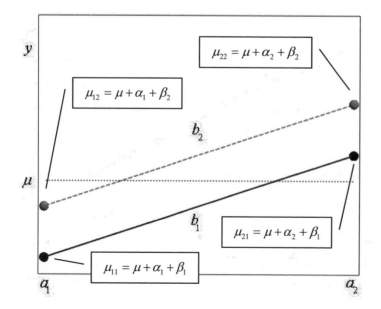

In Figure 6.7, there is interaction. The means are the result of adding the following interaction terms to the means in Figure 6.7:

$$(\alpha\beta)_{11} = \alpha_2 \quad (\alpha\beta)_{12} = \alpha_1$$

$$(\alpha\beta)_{21} = \alpha_1 \quad (\alpha\beta)_{22} = \alpha_2$$

Recall from the constraints on the main effects that $\alpha_1 + \alpha_2 = 0$.

$$
\begin{aligned}
\mu_{11} &= \mu + \alpha_1 + \beta_1 + (\alpha\beta)_{11} & \mu_{12} &= \mu + \alpha_1 + \beta_2 + (\alpha\beta)_{12} \\
&= \mu + \alpha_1 + \beta_1 + \alpha_2 & &= \mu + \alpha_1 + \beta_2 + \alpha_1 \\
&= \mu + \beta_1 & &= \mu + 2\alpha_1 + \beta_2
\end{aligned}
$$

$$
\begin{aligned}
\mu_{21} &= \mu + \alpha_2 + \beta_1 + (\alpha\beta)_{21} & \mu_{22} &= \mu + \alpha_2 + \beta_2 + (\alpha\beta)_{22} \\
&= \mu + \alpha_2 + \beta_1 + \alpha_1 & &= \mu + \alpha_2 + \beta_2 + \alpha_2 \\
&= \mu + \beta_1 & &= \mu + 2\alpha_2 + \beta_2
\end{aligned}
$$

With interaction, the influence of A is not the same at each level of B.

- At b_1: $\mu_{11} = \mu + \beta_1$ and $\mu_{21} = \mu + \beta_1$. The interaction terms have eliminated A as a factor. At b_1, the A main effects are 0.
- At b_2: $\mu_{12} = \mu + 2\alpha_1 + \beta_2$ and $\mu_{22} = \mu + 2\alpha_2 + \beta_2$. The interaction terms have increased the influence of A. At b_2, the A main effects are $2\alpha_1$ and $2\alpha_2$.

Figure 6.7 Example of Population Means Where Interaction Is Present

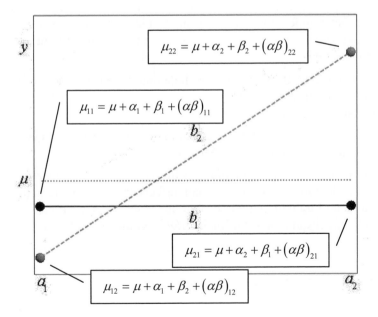

6.3.4 Hypothesis Tests Based on the ANOVA Table

6.3.4.1 Null and Alternative Hypotheses: Full Model, Interaction Effects, and Main Effects

Test of the Full Model

The first hypothesis test determines if there are any differences among the treatment-population means.

$H_0 : \mu_{11} = \mu_{12} = \ldots = \mu_{ab}$

$H_1 :$ At least two means are not equal.

- If the null hypothesis is not rejected, then one cannot conclude that there are any differences among the treatment-population means. Influence of the factors on the responses does not appear to differ among treatments. The analysis ends at this point.

- If the null hypothesis is rejected, then one can conclude that there are at least some differences among the treatment-population means. The analysis continues with the goal of understanding the nature of these differences. The next step is to consider the test of interaction effects.

Test of the Interaction Effects

The null and alternative hypotheses are:

$H_0 : (\alpha\beta)_{11} = (\alpha\beta)_{12} = \ldots = (\alpha\beta)_{ab} = 0$

$H_1 :$ At least one interaction effect is not 0.

- If the null hypothesis is not rejected, then one cannot conclude that there is interaction. The influences of one factor appear to be the same at each level of the second factor. Only the main effects appear to be making contributions to the treatment-population means. The next step is to consider the tests of main effects.

- If the null hypothesis is rejected, then one can conclude that there is interaction. The influences of one factor appear to differ among the levels of the second factor. Interaction effects appear to be making contributions to the treatment-population means.
  - The next step is to examine the treatment-population means using least squares means. See the section on "Least-Squares Means."
  - When interaction appears to be present, the tests of main effects are generally ignored. These tests determine whether the main effects are 0. With interaction, the main effects of a factor might effectively be 0 at one level of a second factor and not 0 at another level. Any result of a test of main effects would be misleading.

Tests of the Main Effects

The null and alternative hypotheses on the A main effects are:

$H_0 : \alpha_1 = \alpha_2 = \ldots = \alpha_a = 0$

$H_1 :$ At least one *A* main effect is not 0.

Since $\alpha_i = \mu_{i.} - \mu$, the following are equivalent:

$$\alpha_1 = \alpha_2 = \ldots = \alpha_a = 0$$

$$\mu_{1.} - \mu = \mu_{2.} - \mu = \ldots = \mu_{a.} - \mu = 0$$

$$\mu_{1.} = \mu_{2.} = \ldots = \mu_{a.} = \mu$$

Therefore, the hypotheses on A main effects are equivalent to the following hypotheses on the factor A population means:

$H_0 : \mu_{1.} = \mu_{2.} = \ldots = \mu_{a.}$

H_1 : At least two means are not equal.

Similarly, there are two equivalent pairs of hypotheses for factor B:

$H_0 : \beta_1 = \beta_2 = \ldots = \beta_b = 0$ $H_0 : \mu_{.1} = \mu_{.2} = \ldots = \mu_{.b}$

H_1 : At least one B main effect is not 0. H_1 : At least two means are not equal.

For each test of main effects:

- If the null hypothesis is not rejected, then one cannot conclude that there are any differences among these factor-population means. Influence on the responses does not appear to differ among the levels of this factor. The analysis of this factor ends at this point.

- If the null hypothesis is rejected, then one can conclude that there is a difference between at least two of these factor-population means. Influence on the responses does appear to differ among the levels of this factor. The next step is to examine the possible differences.

6.3.4.2   Analysis of Variance Table

An ANOVA table produces the statistics to test the foregoing hypotheses. The details are below.

Model, Error, and Total Sums of Squares

The sums of squares break down essentially in the same way as with the one-way ANOVA.

$$\sum_{i=1}^{a}\sum_{j=1}^{b}\sum_{k=1}^{n_{ij}}\left(y_{ijk} - \overline{y}_{...}\right)^2 = \sum_{i=1}^{a}\sum_{j=1}^{b}\sum_{k=1}^{n_{ij}}\left(y_{ijk} - \overline{y}_{ij.}\right)^2 + \sum_{i=1}^{a}\sum_{j=1}^{b}n_{ij}\left(\overline{y}_{ij.} - \overline{y}_{...}\right)^2$$

$$SS(Total) = SS(Error) + SS(Model)$$

- SS(Total) (the numerator of the overall sample variance $s^2 = \dfrac{\displaystyle\sum_{i=1}^{a}\sum_{j=1}^{b}\sum_{k=1}^{n_{ij}}\left(y_{ijk} - \overline{y}_{...}\right)^2}{n_{..} - 1}$) is the

  Corrected Total Sum of Squares.

- *SS*(Error) (the sum of the squared within-sample deviations) is the Error Sum of Squares or the Sum-of-Squares Error.
  - The *SS*(Error) is a measure of the random variation in the responses. Random variation is present because the samples are randomly selected from their populations.

- *SS*(Model) (the weighted sum of the squared between-sample deviations) is the Model Sum of Squares.
  - The *SS*(Model) is a measure of the variation in the sample means $\bar{y}_{ij}$. due to both the differences in the population means μ_{ij} and the random variation in the responses.

  - When $H_0 : \mu_{11} = \mu_{12} = \ldots = \mu_{ab}$ is true, there are no differences in the population means. *SS*(Model) measures only random variation:
    - Each sample mean $\bar{y}_{ij}$. estimates its population mean, which is μ when H_0 is true.

    - The overall sample mean $\bar{y}_{...}$ always estimates μ.

    - The difference $\bar{y}_{ij}$. $- \bar{y}_{...}$ estimates 0. Any nonzero value is due to random variation only.

    - Consequently, the terms of $SS(Model) = \sum_{i=1}^{a} \sum_{j=1}^{b} n_{ij} \left(\bar{y}_{ij}. - \bar{y}_{...} \right)^2$ are determined only by random variation.

  - When $H_0 : \mu_{11} = \mu_{12} = \ldots = \mu_{ab}$ is not true, at least two of the population means are not equal and, consequently, do not equal the overall mean μ. *SS*(Model) measures nonzero differences in population means plus random variation:
    - Each sample mean $\bar{y}_{ij}$. estimates its population mean μ_{ij}.

    - The overall sample mean $\bar{y}_{...}$ always estimates μ.

    - The difference $\bar{y}_{ij}$. $- \bar{y}_{...}$ estimates $\mu_{ij} - \mu$, which is not 0 for at least two population means. Deviations from $\mu_{ij} - \mu$ are due to the random variation in the responses.

    - All the terms of $SS(Model) = \sum_{i=1}^{a} \sum_{j=1}^{b} n_{ij} \left(\bar{y}_{ij}. - \bar{y}_{...} \right)^2$ are the result of random variation but at least two are also the result of nonzero differences in the population means.

Sums of Squares for Effects with Balanced Data

When the data is balanced, the sums of squares for effects develop from the *SS*(Model) in a straightforward manner. Let $n_{ij} = n$ for all treatment samples. The *SS*(Model) breaks down into sums of squares for main effects and interaction effects.

$$n\sum_{i=1}^{a} \sum_{j=1}^{b} \left(\bar{y}_{ij}. - \bar{y}_{...} \right)^2 = bn\sum_{i=1}^{a} \left(\bar{y}_{i..} - \bar{y}_{...} \right)^2 + an\sum_{j=1}^{b} \left(\bar{y}_{.j.} - \bar{y}_{...} \right)^2 + n\sum_{i=1}^{a} \sum_{j=1}^{b} \left(\bar{y}_{ij}. - \bar{y}_{i..} - \bar{y}_{.j.} + \bar{y}_{...} \right)^2$$

$$SS(Model) = SS(A) + SS(B) + SS(A*B)$$

- $SS(A)$ is the Factor A Sum of Squares. It is a measure of the variation in the factor-sample means $\bar{y}_{i..}$ due to both the factor A main effects α_i and the random variation in the responses.

  - $\bar{y}_{i..} - \bar{y}_{...}$ is the estimate of α_i. The notation is $\hat{\alpha}_i = \bar{y}_{i..} - \bar{y}_{...}$. Therefore, $SS(A) = bn\sum_{i=1}^{a}\left(\hat{\alpha}_i\right)^2$. $SS(A)$ becomes a measure of how much the estimates of the factor A main effects differ from zero.

  - When $H_0 : \alpha_1 = \alpha_2 = \ldots = \alpha_a = 0$ is true, any nonzero $\hat{\alpha}_i$ is due to random variation. In which case, $SS(A)$ only measures random variation.

  - When $H_0 : \alpha_1 = \alpha_2 = \ldots = \alpha_a = 0$ is not true, at least two of the factor A main effects are not 0. In which case, $SS(A)$ measures the variation due to nonzero main effects plus random variation.

- $SS(B)$ is the Factor B Sum of Squares. It is a measure of the variation in the factor-sample means $\bar{y}_{.j.}$ due to both the factor B main effects β_j and the random variation in the responses.

  - $\bar{y}_{.j.} - \bar{y}_{...}$ is the estimate of β_j. The notation is $\hat{\beta}_j = \bar{y}_{.j.} - \bar{y}_{...}$. Therefore, $SS(B) = an\sum_{j=1}^{b}\left(\hat{\beta}_j\right)^2$. $SS(B)$ becomes a measure of how much the estimates of the factor B main effects differ from zero.

  - When $H_0 : \beta_1 = \beta_2 = \ldots = \beta_b = 0$ is true, any nonzero $\hat{\beta}_j$ is due to random variation. In which case, $SS(B)$ only measures random variation.

  - When $H_0 : \beta_1 = \beta_2 = \ldots = \beta_b = 0$ is not true, at least two of the factor B main effects are not 0. In which case, $SS(B)$ measures the variation due to nonzero main effects plus random variation.

- $SS(A*B)$ is the Interaction Sum of Squares. It is a measure of the variation in the treatment-sample means $\bar{y}_{ij.}$ due to both the A*B interaction effects $(\alpha\beta)_{ij}$ and the random variation in the responses.

  - $\bar{y}_{ij.} - \left(\bar{y}_{...} + \hat{\alpha}_i + \hat{\beta}_j\right) = \bar{y}_{ij.} - \bar{y}_{i..} - \bar{y}_{.j.} + \bar{y}_{...}$ is the estimate of $(\alpha\beta)_{ij}$. The notation is $\widehat{(\alpha\beta)}_{ij} = \bar{y}_{ij.} - \bar{y}_{i..} - \bar{y}_{.j.} + \bar{y}_{...}$. Therefore, $SS(A*B) = n\sum_{i=1}^{a}\sum_{j=1}^{b}\left(\widehat{(\alpha\beta)}_{ij}\right)^2$. $SS(A*B)$ becomes a measure of how much the estimates of the A*B interaction effects differ from zero.

  - When $H_0 : (\alpha\beta)_{11} = (\alpha\beta)_{12} = \ldots = (\alpha\beta)_{ab} = 0$ is true, any nonzero $\widehat{(\alpha\beta)}_{ij}$ is due to random variation. In which case, $SS(A*B)$ only measures random variation.

  - When $H_0 : (\alpha\beta)_{11} = (\alpha\beta)_{12} = \ldots = (\alpha\beta)_{ab} = 0$ is not true, at least two of the A*B interaction effects are not 0. In which case, $SS(A*B)$ measures the variation due to nonzero interaction effects plus random variation.

A General View of Sums of Squares

The *linear model* provides expressions of the sums of squares that do not depend on whether the data is balanced or not. The linear model is a general approach where all the treatment means in a population model are expressed by a single expression, the *linear model function*.

- The linear model function contains all the parameters that define the means, although some of the parameters might be included indirectly. The function is a sum with one parameter in each term.

- The parameters are coefficients of quantitative variables.
  - The quantitative variables determine which parameters are present for a particular population mean.
  - All variables in a linear model are quantitative variables.

The linear model function for the two-way factorial analysis of variance is:

$$\mu_{ij} = \mu x_0 + \alpha_1 x_1 + \cdots + \alpha_{a-1} x_{a-1} + \beta_1 w_1 + \cdots + \beta_{b-1} w_{b-1} + (\alpha\beta)_{11} z_{11} + \cdots + (\alpha\beta)_{a-1,b-1} z_{a-1,b-1}$$

- The parameters are: $\mu, \alpha_1, \ldots, \alpha_a, \beta_1, \ldots, \beta_b, (\alpha\beta)_{11}, \ldots, (\alpha\beta)_{a,b}$.

- The parameters $\alpha_a, \beta_b, (\alpha\beta)_{1b}, \ldots, (\alpha\beta)_{a-1,b}, (\alpha\beta)_{a1}, \ldots, (\alpha\beta)_{a,b}$ are included indirectly. They are functions of other parameters:

  - $\alpha_a = -\alpha_1 - \cdots - \alpha_{a-1}$ since $\sum_{i=1}^{a} \alpha_i = 0$ and $\beta_b = -\beta_1 - \cdots - \beta_{b-1}$ since $\sum_{j=1}^{b} \beta_j = 0$.

  - $(\alpha\beta)_{ib} = -(\alpha\beta)_{i1} - \cdots - (\alpha\beta)_{i,b-1}$ since $\sum_{j=1}^{b} (\alpha\beta)_{ij} = 0$ and

    $(\alpha\beta)_{aj} = -(\alpha\beta)_{1j} - \cdots - (\alpha\beta)_{a-1,j}$ since $\sum_{i=1}^{a} (\alpha\beta)_{ij} = 0$.

The quantitative variables are $x_0, x_1, \ldots, x_{a-1}, w_1, \ldots, w_{b-1}, z_{11}, \ldots, z_{a-1,b-1}$. They determine which parameters are present with the following values. See Table 6.7.

- 1 if its parameter coefficient is in the model.

- 0 if its parameter coefficient and the indirectly included parameter are not in the model.
  - −1 if the indirectly included parameter is in the model.

Table 6.7 Quantitative Variables for the Two-Factor ANOVA

For μ:	For $\alpha_1,\ldots,\alpha_a$:	For $\beta_1,\ldots,\beta_b$:	For $(\alpha\beta)_{11},\ldots,(\alpha\beta)_{a,b}$:
$x_0 = 1$ always	$x_1,\ldots,x_{a-1}$ where • $x_i = 1$ if α_i is in the model • $x_i = 0$ if α_i and α_a are not in the model • $x_i = -1$ if α_a is in the model	$w_1,\ldots,w_{b-1}$ where • $w_j = 1$ if β_j is in the model • $w_j = 0$ if β_j and β_b are not in the model • $w_j = -1$ if β_b is in the model	$z_{11},z_{12},\ldots,z_{21},\ldots,z_{a-1,b-1}$ where $z_{ij} = x_i w_j$

Consider the two-way factorial design where factor A has two levels ($a = 2$) and factor B has three levels ($b = 3$). The linear model function is:

$$\mu_{ij} = \mu x_0 + \alpha_1 x_1 + \beta_1 w_1 + \beta_2 w_2 + (\alpha\beta)_{11} z_{11} + (\alpha\beta)_{12} z_{12}$$

The quantitative variables $x_0, x_1, w_1, w_2, z_{11}, z_{12}$ produce the appropriate parameters for each mean:

$$\mu_{11} = \mu + \alpha_1 + \beta_1 + (\alpha\beta)_{11} = \mu \cdot 1 + \alpha_1 \cdot 1 + \beta_1 \cdot 1 + \beta_2 \cdot 0 + (\alpha\beta)_{11} \cdot 1 + (\alpha\beta)_{12} \cdot 0$$
$$\mu_{12} = \mu + \alpha_1 + \beta_2 + (\alpha\beta)_{12} = \mu \cdot 1 + \alpha_1 \cdot 1 + \beta_1 \cdot 0 + \beta_2 \cdot 1 + (\alpha\beta)_{11} \cdot 0 + (\alpha\beta)_{12} \cdot 1$$
$$\mu_{13} = \mu + \alpha_1 + \beta_3 + (\alpha\beta)_{13} = \mu \cdot 1 + \alpha_1 \cdot 1 + \beta_1(-1) + \beta_2(-1) + (\alpha\beta)_{11}(-1) + (\alpha\beta)_{12}(-1)$$
$$\mu_{21} = \mu + \alpha_2 + \beta_1 + (\alpha\beta)_{21} = \mu \cdot 1 + \alpha_1(-1) + \beta_1 \cdot 1 + \beta_2 \cdot 0 + (\alpha\beta)_{11}(-1) + (\alpha\beta)_{12} \cdot 0$$
$$\mu_{22} = \mu + \alpha_2 + \beta_2 + (\alpha\beta)_{22} = \mu \cdot 1 + \alpha_1(-1) + \beta_1 \cdot 0 + \beta_2 \cdot 1 + (\alpha\beta)_{11} \cdot 0 + (\alpha\beta)_{12}(-1)$$
$$\mu_{23} = \mu + \alpha_1 + \beta_3 + (\alpha\beta)_{23} = \mu \cdot 1 + \alpha_1(-1) + \beta_1(-1) + \beta_2(-1) + (\alpha\beta)_{11} \cdot 1 + (\alpha\beta)_{12} \cdot 1$$

x_0	x_1	w_1	w_2	z_{11}	z_{12}
1	1	1	0	1	0
1	1	0	1	0	1
1	1	-1	-1	-1	-1
1	-1	1	0	-1	0
1	-1	0	1	0	-1
1	-1	-1	-1	1	1

Sample for a Linear Model

An individual response y_{ijk} is associated with its treatment mean μ_{ij} through the quantitative variables. The table in Figure 6.8 represents a data set for a sample described by a linear model. The sample is for the two-way factorial design with two levels for factor A and three levels for factor B.

The responses y_{ijk} and the quantitative variables $x_0, x_1, w_1, w_2, z_{11}, z_{12}$ become in a data set. Here, they are expressed as y, x0, x1, w1, w2, z11, and z12.

Figure 6.8 Data Set for a Linear Model

y	x0	x1	w1	w2	z11	z12
y_{111}	1	1	1	0	1	0
y_{112}	1	1	1	0	1	0
$\vdots$	$\vdots$	$\vdots$	$\vdots$	$\vdots$	$\vdots$	$\vdots$
$y_{11n_{11}}$	1	1	1	0	1	0
y_{121}	1	1	0	1	0	1
y_{122}	1	1	0	1	0	1
$\vdots$	$\vdots$	$\vdots$	$\vdots$	$\vdots$	$\vdots$	$\vdots$
$y_{12n_{12}}$	1	1	0	1	0	1
y_{131}	1	1	−1	−1	−1	−1
y_{132}	1	1	−1	−1	−1	−1
$\vdots$	$\vdots$	$\vdots$	$\vdots$	$\vdots$	$\vdots$	$\vdots$
$y_{13n_{13}}$	1	1	−1	−1	−1	−1
y_{211}	1	−1	1	0	−1	0
y_{212}	1	−1	1	0	−1	0
$\vdots$	$\vdots$	$\vdots$	$\vdots$	$\vdots$	$\vdots$	$\vdots$
$y_{21n_{21}}$	1	−1	1	0	−1	0
y_{221}	1	−1	0	1	0	−1
y_{222}	1	−1	0	1	0	−1
$\vdots$	$\vdots$	$\vdots$	$\vdots$	$\vdots$	$\vdots$	$\vdots$
$y_{22n_{22}}$	1	−1	0	1	0	−1
y_{231}	1	−1	−1	−1	1	1
y_{232}	1	−1	−1	−1	1	1
$\vdots$	$\vdots$	$\vdots$	$\vdots$	$\vdots$	$\vdots$	$\vdots$
$y_{23n_{23}}$	1	−1	−1	−1	1	1

Least Squares Estimation

The estimates of the parameters are those values that are closest to the responses y_{ijk} in the sense of *least squares*. The estimates of the parameters in the linear function

$\mu_{ij} = \mu x_0 + \alpha_1 x_1 + \beta_1 w_1 + \beta_2 w_2 + (\alpha\beta)_{11} z_{11} + (\alpha\beta)_{12} z_{12}$ are those values that minimize the sum of the squared differences:

$$\sum_{i=1}^{a}\sum_{j=1}^{b}\sum_{k=1}^{n_{ij}}\left(y_{ijk} - \hat{\mu}_{ij}\right)^2 =$$

$$\sum_{i=1}^{a}\sum_{j=1}^{b}\sum_{k=1}^{n_{ij}}\left(y_{ijk} - \left(\hat{\mu}x_0 + \hat{\alpha}_1 x_1 + \hat{\beta}_1 w_1 + \hat{\beta}_2 w_2 + \widehat{(\alpha\beta)}_{11} z_{11} + \widehat{(\alpha\beta)}_{12} z_{12}\right)\right)^2$$

The hat notation ^ means "estimate of."

$$\hat{\mu}_{ij} = \overline{y}_{ij}$$

- This results in *SS(Total)*, *SS(Error)*, and *SS(Model)* being the same and having the same interpretation as in the balanced case.
- The test of the null hypothesis $H_0 : \mu_{11} = \mu_{12} = \ldots = \mu_{ab}$ is the same as in the balanced case.

The estimates of the other parameters are discussed in the "Least-Squares Means" section. Analysis of this design can be done with the Linear Models task or the Linear Regression task.

Sums of Squares for Effects

With a linear model, the sum of squares for an effect is the difference between the Error Sum of Squares for the model with the effect being absent—the *reduced model*—and the Error Sum of Squares for the full model. In general, when the data is not balanced,

$$SS(A) + SS(B) + SS(A*B) \neq SS(Model).$$

SS(A) is the difference between the Error Sum of Squares associated with the reduced model for $H_0 : \alpha_1 = \alpha_2 = 0$ and the Error Sum of Squares associated with the full model.

$$SS(A) = SS\left(\text{Reduced Model Error for } H_0 : \alpha_1 = \alpha_2 = 0\right) - SS\left(\text{Full Model Error}\right)$$

$$SS(A) = \sum_{i=1}^{a}\sum_{j=1}^{b}\sum_{k=1}^{n_{ij}}\left(y_{ijk} - \hat{\mu}_{0,ij}\right)^2 - \sum_{i=1}^{a}\sum_{j=1}^{b}\sum_{k=1}^{n_{ij}}\left(y_{ijk} - \overline{y}_{ij.}\right)^2$$

- Above, $\hat{\mu}_{0,ij}$ is the estimate of μ_{ij} given H_0. For $H_0 : \alpha_1 = \alpha_2 = 0$,

  $\hat{\mu}_{0,ij} = \hat{\mu}_0 x_0 + \hat{\beta}_{0,1} w_1 + \hat{\beta}_{0,2} w_2 + \widehat{(\alpha\beta)}_{0,11} z_{11} + \widehat{(\alpha\beta)}_{0,12} z_{12}$. In general, all the estimates would be different from those obtained with the full model.

- The reduced model Error Sum of Squares and estimates are produced by applying the Linear Models task with the responses and all quantitative variables except x_1. As a practical matter, x0 is always in both models, and it is not listed below. In terms of Figure 6.8:

  $$SS(A) = SS\left(\text{Error with } w1, w2, z11, z12\right) - SS\left(\text{Error with } x1, w1, w2, z11, z12\right)$$

- When $H_0 : \alpha_1 = \alpha_2 = 0$ is true, x_1 plays no role in determining which parameters are present in the model. Including x_1 in the full model reduces the Error Sum of Squares but the amount of the reduction is due to random variation. In which case, *SS(A)* measures only random variation.

- When $H_0 : \alpha_1 = \alpha_2 = 0$ is not true, x_1 does play a role in determining which parameters are present. The reduction in the Error Sum of Squares is due both to variation being explained by the A main effects and to random variation. In which case, *SS(A)* measures the variation due to nonzero main effects plus random variation.

$SS(B)$ is the difference between the Error Sum of Squares associated with the reduced model for $H_0 : \beta_1 = \beta_2 = \beta_3 = 0$ and Error Sum of Squares associated with the full model.

$$SS(B) = SS\left(\text{Reduced Model Error for } H_0 : \beta_1 = \beta_2 = \beta_3 = 0\right) - SS\left(\text{Full Model Error}\right)$$

$$SS(B) = \sum_{i=1}^{a}\sum_{j=1}^{b}\sum_{k=1}^{n_{ij}}\left(y_{ijk} - \hat{\mu}_{0,ij}\right)^2 - \sum_{i=1}^{a}\sum_{j=1}^{b}\sum_{k=1}^{n_{ij}}\left(y_{ijk} - \bar{y}_{ij\bullet}\right)^2$$

- Above, $\hat{\mu}_{0,ij}$ is the estimate of μ_{ij} given H_0. For $H_0 : \beta_1 = \beta_2 = \beta_3 = 0$,

  $\hat{\mu}_{0,ij} = \hat{\mu}_0 x_0 + \hat{\alpha}_{0,1} x_1 + \widehat{(\alpha\beta)}_{0,11} z_{11} + \widehat{(\alpha\beta)}_{0,12} z_{12}$. In general, all the estimates would be different than those obtained with the full model.

- The reduced model Error Sum of Squares and estimates are produced by applying the Linear Models task with the responses and all quantitative variables but w_1 and w_2. In terms of Figure 6.8:

  $$SS(B) = SS\left(\text{Error with x1, z11, z12}\right) - SS\left(\text{Error with x1, w1, w2, z11, z12}\right)$$

- When $H_0 : \beta_1 = \beta_2 = \beta_3 = 0$ is true, w_1 and w_2 play no role in determining which parameters are present for each μ_{ij}. Including w_1 and w_2 in the full model reduces the Error Sum of Squares but the amount of the reduction is due to random variation. In that case, $SS(B)$ measures only random variation.

- When $H_0 : \beta_1 = \beta_2 = \beta_3 = 0$ is not true, w_1 and w_2 do play a role in determining which parameters are present for each μ_{ij}. The reduction in the Error Sum of Squares is due both to variation being explained by the B main effects and to random variation. In that case, $SS(B)$ measures the variation due to nonzero main effects plus random variation.

$SS(A*B)$ is the difference between the Error Sum of Squares associated with the reduced model for $H_0 : \text{all } (\alpha\beta)_{ij} = 0$ and Error Sum of Squares associated with the full model.

$$SS(A*B) = SS\left(\text{Reduced Model Error for } H_0 : \text{all } (\alpha\beta)_{ij} = 0\right) - SS\left(\text{Full Model Error}\right)$$

$$SS(A*B) = \sum_{i=1}^{a}\sum_{j=1}^{b}\sum_{k=1}^{n_{ij}}\left(y_{ijk} - \hat{\mu}_{0,ij}\right)^2 - \sum_{i=1}^{a}\sum_{j=1}^{b}\sum_{k=1}^{n_{ij}}\left(y_{ijk} - \bar{y}_{ij\bullet}\right)^2$$

- Above, $\hat{\mu}_{0,ij}$ is the estimate of μ_{ij} given H_0. For $H_0 : \text{all } (\alpha\beta)_{ij} = 0$,

  $\hat{\mu}_{0,ij} = \hat{\mu}_0 x_0 + \hat{\alpha}_{0,1} x_1 + \hat{\beta}_{0,1} w_1 + \hat{\beta}_{0,2} w_2$. In general, all the estimates would be different than those obtained with the full model.

- The reduced model Error Sum of Squares and estimates are produced by applying the Linear Models task with the responses and all quantitative variables but z_{11} and z_{12}. In terms of Figure 6.8:

  $$SS(A*B) = SS\left(\text{Error with x1, w1, w2}\right) - SS\left(\text{Error with x1, w1, w2, z11, z12}\right)$$

- When H_0 : all $(\alpha\beta)_{ij} = 0$ is true, z_{11} and z_{12} play no role in determining which parameters are present for each μ_{ij}. Including z_{11} and z_{12} in the full model reduces the Error Sum of Squares, but the amount of the reduction is due to random variation. In that case, $SS(A*B)$ measures only random variation.

- When H_0 : all $(\alpha\beta)_{ij} = 0$ is not true, z_{11} and z_{12} do play a role in determining which parameters are present for each μ_{ij}. The reduction in the Error Sum of Squares is due both to variation being explained by the A*B interaction effects and to random variation. In that case, $SS(A*B)$ measures the variation due to nonzero interaction effects plus random variation.

Degrees of Freedom

There are $n_{..} - 1$ degrees of freedom associated with the overall sample. This is the denominator of s^2. With ab being the number of populations being studied:

$$n_{..} - 1 = (n_{..} - ab) + (ab - 1)$$

- $n_{..} - 1$ are the degrees of freedom associated with the SS(Total).

- $n_{..} - ab$ are the degrees of freedom associated with the SS(Error).

- $ab - 1$ are the degrees of freedom associated with the SS(Model).

The SS(Model) degrees of freedom break down further:

$$ab - 1 = (a - 1) + (b - 1) + ((a - 1)(b - 1))$$

- $a - 1$ are the degrees of freedom associated with the $SS(A)$.

- $b - 1$ are the degrees of freedom associated with the $SS(B)$.

- $(a - 1)(b - 1)$ are the degrees of freedom associated with the $SS(A*B)$.

Mean Squares

The mean squares are the sums of squares that have been adjusted for the number of treatment-populations, effects, or responses involved. A mean square is equal to a sum of squares divided by the associated degrees of freedom.

The Model Mean Square and the mean squares for the effects each have an expected value equal to σ^2 when H_0 is true. The Error Mean Square has an expected value equal to σ^2 whether or not H_0 is true. The Error Mean Square is an estimate of σ^2.

- Model Mean Square: $MS(Model) = \dfrac{SS(Model)}{ab - 1}$

- Mean Square for Factor A: $MS(A) = \dfrac{SS(A)}{a - 1}$

- Mean Square for Factor B: $MS(B) = \dfrac{SS(B)}{b - 1}$

- Mean Square for A*B interaction: $MS(A*B) = \dfrac{SS(A*B)}{(a-1)(b-1)}$

- Error Mean Square, or Mean Square Error: $MS(Error) = \dfrac{SS(Error)}{n_{..} - ab}$

Test Statistics

The test statistics are:

Test	Hypotheses	Test Statistic
• Full Model	$H_0 : \mu_{11} = \mu_{12} = \ldots = \mu_{ab}$ $H_1 :$ At least two means are not equal.	F Value $= \dfrac{MS(Model)}{MS(Error)}$
• Main Effects	$\begin{cases} H_0 : \alpha_1 = \alpha_2 = \ldots = \alpha_a = 0 \\ H_1 : \text{At least one A main effect is not 0.} \\ \overline{} \\ H_0 : \mu_{1.} = \mu_{2.} = \ldots = \mu_{a.} \\ H_1 : \text{At least two means are not equal.} \end{cases}$	F Value $= \dfrac{MS(A)}{MS(Error)}$
	$\begin{cases} H_0 : \beta_1 = \beta_2 = \ldots = \beta_b = 0 \\ H_1 : \text{At least one B main effect is not 0.} \\ \overline{} \\ H_0 : \mu_{.1} = \mu_{.2} = \ldots = \mu_{.b} \\ H_1 : \text{At least two means are not equal.} \end{cases}$	F Value $= \dfrac{MS(B)}{MS(Error)}$
• Interaction Effects	$H_0 : (\alpha\beta)_{11} = (\alpha\beta)_{12} = \ldots = (\alpha\beta)_{ab} = 0$ $H_1 :$ At least one interaction effect is not 0.	F Value $= \dfrac{MS(A*B)}{MS(Error)}$

- For each test, when H_0 is true, the numerator mean square measures only random variation. The MS(Error) measures only random variation in any case.

- For each test, when H_0 is true, the numerator mean square and the MS(Error) are measuring the same thing. It is expected that the F value = 1.

p-Value

For each test, the *p-value* is a measure of the likelihood that the samples come from populations where H_0 is true. Smaller values indicate less likelihood. That is, the more the data agrees with H_1 (the more the F value is greater than 1) the smaller the *p*-value.

- In terms of the test of the full model, the *p*-value is the probability that random samples from *ab* independent populations with equal means would produce an F value at or beyond the current value. If the *p*-value is small, it is unlikely that the current samples come from populations with equal means.

- In terms of the test of interaction effects, the *p*-value is the probability that random samples from *ab* independent populations with interaction effects equal to 0 would produce an *F* value at or beyond the current value. If the *p*-value is small, it is unlikely that the current samples come from populations with interaction effects equal to 0.

- In terms of the test of main effects, the *p*-value is the probability that random samples from *a* (or *b*) independent populations with A (or B) main effects equal to 0 would produce an *F* value at or beyond the current value. If the *p*-value is small, it is unlikely that the current samples come from populations with A (or B) main effects equal to 0.

For each test, $p\text{-value} = P(F \geq F \text{ value})$. The random variable *F* represents a future value of the test statistic and follows an *F* distribution. Figure 6.9 shows an example of the *F* distribution with the gray area corresponding to the probability statement.

Figure 6.9 Example of the *F* Distribution with Gray Area Representing the *p*-Value

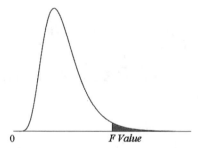

The *F* distribution depends on two degrees-of-freedom values: the numerator degrees of freedom and the denominator degrees of freedom. The numerator degrees of freedom are the degrees of freedom associated with the numerator mean square. The denominator degrees of freedom are the degrees of freedom associated with the *MS*(Error), $n_{..} - ab$.

In the SAS code, the expressions within the parentheses represent numbers.

Table 6.8 *p*-Value for the Factorial ANOVA

Hypotheses	In the task output, all *p*-values are in a variable headed by: Pr > F
$H_0: \mu_{11} = \mu_{12} = \ldots = \mu_{ab}$ H_1: At least two means are not equal.	Row header this test: Model SAS code for *p*-value: 1-probf(F Value, $ab - 1$, $n_{..} - ab$)
$H_0: \alpha_1 = \alpha_2 = \ldots = \alpha_a = 0$ H_1: At least one A main effect is not 0. ------- $H_0: \mu_{1.} = \mu_{2.} = \ldots = \mu_{a.}$ H_1: At least two means are not equal.	Row header this test: 1st Factor (A, for example) SAS code for *p*-value: 1-probf(F Value, $a - 1$, $n_{..} - ab$)
$H_0: \beta_1 = \beta_2 = \ldots = \beta_b = 0$ H_1: At least one B main effect is not 0. ------- $H_0: \mu_{.1} = \mu_{.2} = \ldots = \mu_{.b}$ H_1: At least two means are not equal.	Row header this test: 2nd Factor (B, for example) SAS code for *p*-value: 1-probf(F Value, $b - 1$, $n_{..} - ab$)
$H_0: (\alpha\beta)_{11} = (\alpha\beta)_{12} = \ldots = (\alpha\beta)_{ab} = 0$ H_1: At least one interaction effect is not 0.	Row header this test: 1st Factor*2nd Factor (A*B, for example) SAS code for *p*-value: 1-probf(F Value, $(a-1)(b-1)$, $n_{..} - ab$)

ANOVA Table

The ANOVA table organizes all the necessary statistics: sums of squares, degrees of freedom, mean squares, *F* values, and the *p*-values.

Unless changed in the Linear Models task, the output contains three tables listing sums of squares.

- One table lists *SS*(Model), *SS*(Error), and *SS*(Total) along with the corresponding statistics.

- Two tables list *SS*(*A*), *SS*(*B*), and *SS*(*A*B*) along with the corresponding statistics.

  - The first table contains a Type I SS (Sum of Squares) variable. Type I sums of squares have not been discussed here and that table is not shown below. These sums of squares are dependent on the how the independent variables are listed.

  - The second table contains a Type III SS (Sum of Squares) variable. This is the sum of squares discussed earlier in the subsections "Sums of Squares for Effects with Balanced Data" and "A General View of Sums of Squares." This table is included below. These sums of squares are not dependent on the how the independent variables are listed.

Source	Df	Sum of Squares	Mean Square	F Value	Pr > F
Model	$ab-1$	$SS(Model)$	$\dfrac{SS(Model)}{ab-1}$	$\dfrac{MS(Model)}{MS(Error)}$	p-value
Error	$n_{..}-ab$	$SS(Error)$	$\dfrac{SS(Error)}{n_{..}-ab}$		
Corrected Total	$n_{..}-1$	$SS(Total)$			

Source	Df	Type III SS	Mean Square	F Value	Pr > F
A	$a-1$	$SS(A)$	$\dfrac{SS(A)}{a-1}$	$\dfrac{MS(A)}{MS(Error)}$	p-value
B	$b-1$	$SS(B)$	$\dfrac{SS(B)}{b-1}$	$\dfrac{MS(B)}{MS(Error)}$	p-value
A*B	$(a-1)(b-1)$	$SS(A*B)$	$\dfrac{SS(A*B)}{(a-1)(b-1)}$	$\dfrac{MS(A*B)}{MS(Error)}$	p-value

6.3.4.3 Decision and Conclusions

The formal decisions and concluding sentences do not change from the one-sample tests discussed in Chapter 4, "Inferences from One Sample." The concluding observations depend on the particular statistics involved in the test.

If the *p*-value is small, the data agrees with H_1. If the *p*-value is less than the significance level, the risk of making a Type I error is acceptable. Therefore, the *p*-value decision rule is the following:

If the *p*-value $< \alpha$, reject H_0. Otherwise, do not reject H_0.

Since a hypothesis test begins with the assumption that H_0 is true, concluding a hypothesis test requires one of the following formal statements:

- Reject H_0.
- Do not reject H_0.

When the claim is equivalent to the null hypothesis, the concluding sentence uses the word *reject*. The concluding sentence becomes an expanded version of the formal decision.

When the claim is equivalent to the alternative hypothesis, the concluding sentence uses the word *support*. If the data supports the rejection of H_0, the data supports H_1. If the data does not support rejection of H_0, the data cannot support H_1.

Table 6.9 Concluding Sentences

Formal Statistical Decision	Claim stated as H_0	Claim stated as H_1
Reject H_0.	There is sufficient evidence to reject the claim that ... (claim in words).	There is sufficient evidence to support the claim that ... (claim in words).
Do not reject H_0.	There is not sufficient evidence to reject the claim that ... (claim in words).	There is not sufficient evidence to support the claim that ... (claim in words).

Table 6.10 Concluding Observations

Test of the Full Model	
Reject H_0.	At least two treatment-sample means are significantly different.
Do not reject H_0.	None of the treatment-sample means is significantly different.
Test of Main Effects	
Reject H_0.	At least two factor-A (or B) sample means are significantly different.
Do not reject H_0.	None of the factor-A (or B) sample means is significantly different.
Test of Interaction Effects	
Reject H_0.	There is significant interaction.
Do not reject H_0.	There is no significant interaction.

6.3.5 Summary of the Hypothesis Tests

Plan the experiment.

The circled numbers associate the hypotheses with the appropriate statistics.

❶
$$H_0 : \mu_{11} = \mu_{12} = \ldots = \mu_{ab}$$
$$H_1 : \text{At least two means are not equal.}$$

❷
$$\begin{cases} H_0 : \alpha_1 = \alpha_2 = \ldots = \alpha_a = 0 \\ H_1 : \text{At least one } A \text{ main effect is not 0.} \\ \hline H_0 : \mu_{1.} = \mu_{2.} = \ldots = \mu_{a.} \\ H_1 : \text{At least two means are not equal.} \end{cases}$$

❸
$$\begin{cases} H_0 : \beta_1 = \beta_2 = \ldots = \beta_b = 0 \\ H_1 : \text{At least one B main effect is not 0.} \\ \hline H_0 : \mu_{.1} = \mu_{.2} = \ldots = \mu_{.b} \\ H_1 : \text{At least two means are not equal.} \end{cases}$$

❹
$$H_0 : (\alpha\beta)_{11} = (\alpha\beta)_{12} = \ldots = (\alpha\beta)_{ab} = 0$$
$$H_1 : \text{At least one interaction effect is not 0.}$$

For each test, the significance level is α.

Task computes the statistics.

Source	DF	Sum of Squares	Mean Square	F Value	Pr > F	
Model	$ab - 1$	SS(Model)	$MS(Model) = \dfrac{SS(Model)}{ab - 1}$	$\dfrac{MS(Model)}{MS(Error)}$	p-value	❶
Error	$n_{..} - ab$	SS(Error)	$MS(Error) = \dfrac{SS(Error)}{n_T - ab}$			
Corrected Total	$n_{..} - 1$	SS(Total)				

R-Square	Coeff Var	Root MSE	*dependent variable* Mean
$\dfrac{SS(Model)}{SS(Error)}$	$100 \dfrac{\sqrt{MS(Error)}}{\overline{y}_{...}}$	$\sqrt{MS(Error)}$	$\overline{y}_{...}$

Source	DF	Type III SS	Mean Square	F Value	Pr > F	
1ˢᵗ factor	$a - 1$	SS(A)	$MS(A) = \dfrac{SS(A)}{a - 1}$	$\dfrac{MS(A)}{MS(Error)}$	p-value	❷
2ⁿᵈ factor	$b - 1$	SS(B)	$MS(B) = \dfrac{SS(B)}{b - 1}$	$\dfrac{MS(B)}{MS(Error)}$	p-value	❸
1ˢᵗ factor *2ⁿᵈ factor	$(a-1)(b-1)$	SS(A*B)	$MS(A*B) = \dfrac{SS(A*B)}{(a-1)(b-1)}$	$\dfrac{MS(A*B)}{MS(Error)}$	p-value	❹

Apply the results.

- For each test: If the p-value $< \alpha$, reject H_0. Otherwise, do not reject H_0.
- See Tables 6.8 and 6.9 for the concluding sentences and observations.

6.3.6 Least-Squares Means

An arithmetic mean is the common average: the sum of responses divided by the number of responses being summed. (Arithmetic is pronounced "ar-ith-'me-tic as an adjective.) Arithmetic means are called means in Section 6.2. The more precise name is used here to distinguish them from least squares means.

When the data is balanced, arithmetic means and least-squares means are the same.

When the data is unbalanced, factor-sample means computed as arithmetic means become weighted averages of treatment-sample means.

$$\overline{y}_{i\bullet\bullet} = \frac{\displaystyle\sum_{j=1}^{b}\sum_{k=1}^{n_{ij}} y_{ijk}}{n_{i\bullet}} = \frac{\displaystyle\sum_{j=1}^{b} n_{ij}\overline{y}_{ij\bullet}}{n_{i\bullet}} \qquad \overline{y}_{\bullet j\bullet} = \frac{\displaystyle\sum_{i=1}^{a}\sum_{k=1}^{n_{ij}} y_{ijk}}{n_{\bullet j}} = \frac{\displaystyle\sum_{i=1}^{a} n_{ij}\overline{y}_{ij\bullet}}{n_{\bullet j}} .$$

This characteristic makes arithmetic means less desirable estimates of the factor-population means $\mu_{i\bullet}$ and $\mu_{\bullet j}$. Treatments with larger sample sizes would have greater influence on the estimate.

Least squares means are common averages of the treatment-sample means. Because each treatment is treated equally, the least-squares means are the better estimates of the factor-population means $\mu_{i\bullet}$ and $\mu_{\bullet j}$. In this section, the hat notation $\hat{\mu}_{i\bullet}$, for example, indicates an estimate and a least-squares mean.

- The least-squares estimate of $\mu_{i\bullet}$ is $\hat{\mu}_{i\bullet} = \dfrac{\overline{y}_{i1} + \overline{y}_{i2} + \cdots + \overline{y}_{ib}}{b} = \dfrac{\displaystyle\sum_{j=1}^{b}\overline{y}_{ij}}{b}$.

- The least-squares estimate of $\mu_{\bullet j}$ is $\hat{\mu}_{\bullet j} = \dfrac{\overline{y}_{1j} + \overline{y}_{2j} + \cdots + \overline{y}_{aj}}{a} = \dfrac{\displaystyle\sum_{i=1}^{a}\overline{y}_{ij}}{a}$.

The least-squares estimate of μ_{ij} is the treatment-sample mean: $\hat{\mu}_{ij} = \overline{y}_{ij}$.

Least squares means are used to estimate the parameters that define the treatment-population mean $\mu_{ij} = \mu + \alpha_i + \beta_j + (\alpha\beta)_{ij}$:

$$\hat{\mu} = \frac{\displaystyle\sum_{i=1}^{a}\sum_{j=1}^{b}\overline{y}_{ij\bullet}}{ab}$$

$$\hat{\alpha}_i = \hat{\mu}_{i\bullet} - \hat{\mu}$$

$$\hat{\beta}_j = \hat{\mu}_{\bullet j} - \hat{\mu}$$

$$\widehat{(\alpha\beta)}_{ij} = \overline{y}_{ij\bullet} - \left(\hat{\mu} + \hat{\alpha}_i + \hat{\beta}_j \right)$$

Example 6.6 analyzes the influence that the factors Location and Gender have on scores measuring attitude toward Work. In terms of notation:

- 1 as the first subscript refers to the Central branch office.
- 1 or 2 as the second subscript refers to female or male employees.

In the sample from the Central branch office, $n_{11} = 5$ scores are from female employees and $n_{12} = 2$ scores are from male employees.

The arithmetic and least-squares means of the seven scores are:

- $\bar{y}_{1\cdot\cdot} = \dfrac{y_{1\cdot\cdot}}{n_{1\cdot}} = \dfrac{y_{11\cdot} + y_{12\cdot}}{n_{11} + n_{12}} = \dfrac{n_{11}\bar{y}_{11\cdot} + n_{12}\bar{y}_{12\cdot}}{n_{11} + n_{12}} = \dfrac{5\bar{y}_{11\cdot} + 2\bar{y}_{12\cdot}}{7} = \dfrac{5}{7}\bar{y}_{11\cdot} + \dfrac{2}{7}\bar{y}_{12\cdot} = \dfrac{5}{7}(51.4) + \dfrac{2}{7}(46.5) = 50$

- $\hat{\mu}_{1\cdot} = \dfrac{\bar{y}_{11\cdot} + \bar{y}_{12\cdot}}{2} = \dfrac{51.4 + 46.5}{2} = 48.95$

The arithmetic mean gives $\bar{y}_{11\cdot}$ two and a half times more weight than $\bar{y}_{12\cdot}$. The least-squares estimate gives the treatment-sample means equal weight. Unless the unequal weights are a planned part of the study, the least-squares estimate is preferred.

6.3.6.1   Multiple-Comparison Tests Based on Least-Squares Means

Multiple-comparison tests based on least-squares means can take the form of hypothesis tests and confidence intervals.

Hypothesis Tests

All pairs of factor-population means and treatment-population means can be tested for equality. Only p-values are reported. Table 6.11 has the least-squares tests for the two-way factorial ANOVA.

Table 6.11 Least-Squares Means Hypothesis Tests for Two-Way Factorial Design

Factor A population means
$H_0 : \mu_{h\cdot} - \mu_{i\cdot} = 0$
$H_1 : \mu_{\cdot j} - \mu_{i\cdot} \neq 0$
$t\ \text{Value} = \dfrac{\hat{\mu}_{h\cdot} - \hat{\mu}_{i\cdot}}{\sqrt{\dfrac{MSE(Error)}{b^2}}\sqrt{\displaystyle\sum_{j=1}^{b}\dfrac{1}{n_{hj}} + \sum_{j=1}^{b}\dfrac{1}{n_{ij}}}}$
$p\text{-value} = \begin{cases} \textbf{No Adjustment (Fisher's LSD)} \\ P\big(T \geq \lvert t\ \text{Value}\rvert\big) = 2*(1\text{-probt}(\text{abs}(t\ \text{Value}), n_{\cdot\cdot} - ab)) \\[4pt] \hline \textbf{Bonferroni} \\ \dbinom{a}{2} P\big(T \geq \lvert t\ \text{Value}\rvert\big) = a*(a-1)*(1\text{-probt}(\text{abs}(t\ \text{Value}), n_{\cdot\cdot} - ab)) \\[4pt] \hline \textbf{Tukey} \\ P\big(Q \geq \sqrt{2}\lvert t\ \text{Value}\rvert\big) = 1\text{-probmc}('range', \text{sqrt}(2)*\text{abs}(t\ \text{Value}), ., n_{\cdot\cdot} - ab, a) \end{cases}$

Factor B population means

$H_0 : \mu_{\cdot j} - \mu_{\cdot l} = 0$

$H_1 : \mu_{\cdot j} - \mu_{\cdot l} \neq 0$

$$t \text{ Value} = \frac{\hat{\mu}_{\cdot j} - \hat{\mu}_{\cdot l}}{\sqrt{\dfrac{MSE(Error)}{a^2}} \sqrt{\displaystyle\sum_{i=1}^{a} \frac{1}{n_{ij}} + \sum_{i=1}^{a} \frac{1}{n_{il}}}}$$

$p\text{-value} = \begin{cases} \textbf{No Adjustment (Fisher's LSD)} \\ P(T \geq |t \text{ Value}|) = 2*(1\text{-probt(abs}(t \text{ Value}), n_{\cdot\cdot} - ab)) \\[2mm] \hline \textbf{Bonferroni} \\ \dbinom{b}{2} P(T \geq |t \text{ Value}|) = b*(b-1)*(1\text{-probt(abs}(t \text{ Value}), n_{\cdot\cdot} - ab)) \\[2mm] \hline \textbf{Tukey} \\ P(Q \geq \sqrt{2}|t \text{ Value}|) = 1\text{-probmc('range',sqrt(2)*abs}(t \text{ Value}), ., n_{\cdot\cdot} - ab, b) \end{cases}$

Treatment population means

$H_0 : \mu_{ij} - \mu_{hl} = 0$

$H_1 : \mu_{ij} - \mu_{hl} \neq 0$

$$t \text{ Value} = \frac{\bar{y}_{ij\cdot} - \bar{y}_{hl\cdot}}{\sqrt{MSE(Error)} \sqrt{\dfrac{1}{n_{ij}} + \dfrac{1}{n_{hl}}}}$$

$p\text{-value} = \begin{cases} \textbf{No Adjustment (Fisher's LSD)} \\ P(T \geq |t \text{ Value}|) = 2*(1\text{-probt(abs}(t \text{ Value}), n_{\cdot\cdot} - ab)) \\[2mm] \hline \textbf{Bonferroni} \\ \dbinom{ab}{2} P(T \geq |t \text{ Value}|) = ab*(ab-1)*(1\text{-probt(abs}(t \text{ Value}), n_{\cdot\cdot} - ab)) \\[2mm] \hline \textbf{Tukey} \\ P(Q \geq \sqrt{2}|t \text{ Value}|) = 1\text{-probmc('range',sqrt(2)*abs}(t \text{ Value}), ., n_{\cdot\cdot} - ab, ab) \end{cases}$

In Table 6.11, the random variable T represents a future value of the t value. It follows the t distribution with $n_{\cdot\cdot} - ab$ degrees of freedom. The random variable Q represents a future value of $\sqrt{2}(t \text{ Value})$. It follows the studentized range distribution with $n_{\cdot\cdot} - ab$ degrees of freedom, along with a, b, and ab parameters, respectively, for the three cases involving the Tukey adjustment.

- If the p-value $< \alpha$, reject H_0.
  - There is sufficient evidence to conclude that the two factor-population means or treatment-population means are different.
  - The two factor-sample means or treatment-sample means are significantly different.

- If the *p*-value $\geq \alpha$, do not reject H_0.

  There is not sufficient evidence to conclude that the two factor-population means or treatment-population means are different.

- The two factor-sample means or treatment-sample means are not significantly different.

The *p*-values can be adjusted to control the Type I experiment-wise error rate (EER). The EER is the likelihood that one or more tests show a significant difference when the corresponding population means are equal. Table 6.11 illustrates the Bonferroni and Tukey adjustments. No adjustment results in a two-sample *t* test that is equivalent to Fisher's LSD.

Confidence Intervals

Confidence intervals on the difference of factor-population means or treatment-population also test the hypotheses in Table 6.11.

Below are the confidence intervals for the two-way factorial ANOVA. The formulas for the margins of error are in Table 6.12.

- Factor A: $\left(\hat{\mu}_{h\bullet} - \hat{\mu}_{i\bullet} \right) \pm$ Margin of Error

- Factor B: $\left(\hat{\mu}_{\bullet j} - \hat{\mu}_{\bullet l} \right) \pm$ Margin of Error

    - Treatment-population means: $\left(\overline{y}_{hj\bullet} - \overline{y}_{il\bullet} \right) \pm$ Margin of Error

The margin of error controls the Type I experiment-wise error rate (EER). The EER is the likelihood that one or more confidence intervals show a significant difference when the corresponding population means are equal.

Table 6.12 Margins of Error for Confidence Intervals Using Least-Squares Means

Multiple - comparison test	Margin of error for confidence interval on μ_h - μ_i
Fisher's LSD	$t_{\alpha/2} \sqrt{\dfrac{MSE\left(Error\right)}{b^2}} \sqrt{\sum\limits_{j=1}^{b} \dfrac{1}{n_{hj}} + \sum\limits_{j=1}^{b} \dfrac{1}{n_{ij}}}$
Bonferroni *t*-test	$t_{*} \sqrt{\dfrac{MSE\left(Error\right)}{b^2}} \sqrt{\sum\limits_{j=1}^{b} \dfrac{1}{n_{hj}} + \sum\limits_{j=1}^{b} \dfrac{1}{n_{ij}}}$ with $* = \alpha \left/ \left[2 \binom{a}{2} \right] \right.$
Tukey's HSD	$\dfrac{q_{\alpha}}{\sqrt{2}} \sqrt{\dfrac{MSE\left(Error\right)}{b^2}} \sqrt{\sum\limits_{j=1}^{b} \dfrac{1}{n_{hj}} + \sum\limits_{j=1}^{b} \dfrac{1}{n_{ij}}}$

Multiple - comparison test	Margin of error for confidence interval on $\mu_{\cdot j} - \mu_{\cdot i}$
Fisher's LSD	$t_{\alpha/2}\sqrt{\dfrac{MSE(Error)}{a^2}}\sqrt{\displaystyle\sum_{i=1}^{a}\frac{1}{n_{ij}}+\sum_{i=1}^{a}\frac{1}{n_{il}}}$
Bonferroni t-test	$t_{*}\sqrt{\dfrac{MSE(Error)}{a^2}}\sqrt{\displaystyle\sum_{i=1}^{a}\frac{1}{n_{ij}}+\sum_{i=1}^{a}\frac{1}{n_{il}}}$ with $*=\alpha\left/\left[2\binom{b}{2}\right]\right.$
Tukey's HSD	$\dfrac{q_{\alpha}}{\sqrt{2}}\sqrt{\dfrac{MSE(Error)}{a^2}}\sqrt{\displaystyle\sum_{i=1}^{a}\frac{1}{n_{ij}}+\sum_{i=1}^{a}\frac{1}{n_{il}}}$

Multiple - comparison test	Margin of error for confidence interval on $\mu_{ij} - \mu_{hl}$
Fisher's LSD	$t_{\alpha/2}\sqrt{MS(Error)}\sqrt{\dfrac{1}{n_{ij}}+\dfrac{1}{n_{hl}}}$
Bonferroni t-test	$t_{*}\sqrt{MS(Error)}\sqrt{\dfrac{1}{n_{ij}}+\dfrac{1}{n_{hl}}}$ with $*=\alpha\left/\left[2\binom{ab}{2}\right]\right.$
Tukey's HSD	$\dfrac{q_{\alpha}}{\sqrt{2}}\sqrt{MS(Error)}\sqrt{\dfrac{1}{n_{ij}}+\dfrac{1}{n_{hl}}}$

In Table 6.12, $t_{\alpha/2}$ and t_{*} are critical values from the t distribution with $n_{\cdot\cdot}-ab$ degrees of freedom. Also, q_{α} is a critical value from the studentized range distribution with $n_{\cdot\cdot}-ab$ degrees of freedom, along with a, b, and ab parameters, respectively, for the three cases involving the Tukey adjustment.

- If a confidence interval does not contain 0:
  - The data is consistent with the conclusion that the two means are different.
  - The two factor-sample means or treatment-sample means are significantly different.
- If a confidence interval contains 0:
  - The data is consistent with the conclusion that the two means are equal.
  - The two factor-sample means or treatment-sample means are not significantly different.

6.3.7 Multiple-Comparison Tests Based on Arithmetic Means

The use of arithmetic means is somewhat limited in factorial analysis of variance:

- Arithmetic means are used only to perform multiple-comparison tests on factor-population means.
- Arithmetic means should be used only with balanced data.

Comparisons based on arithmetic means are straightforward extensions of the multiple-comparison tests discussed in Section 6.2.

- For factor A, one concludes that $\mu_{h.} - \mu_{i.} \neq 0$, when $\left| \bar{y}_{h..} - \bar{y}_{i..} \right| \geq$ Margin of Error.

- For factor B, one concludes that $\mu_{.j} - \mu_{.l} \neq 0$, when $\left| \bar{y}_{.j.} - \bar{y}_{.l.} \right| \geq$ Margin of Error.

The form of the margin of error depends on the multiple-comparison test. See Table 6.13. Because they are used with balance data, the comparisons are presented in lines format. See "Output for a Multiple-Comparison Test" in Section 6.2.

Table 6.13 Minimum Significant Difference for Arithmetic Multiple-Comparison Tests

Multiple - Comparison test	Minimum Significant Difference for Test on $\alpha_h - \alpha_i$
Fisher's LSD	$t_{\alpha/2} \sqrt{MS(Error)} \sqrt{\dfrac{2}{bn}}$
Bonferroni t-Test	$t_* \sqrt{MS(Error)} \sqrt{\dfrac{2}{bn}}$ with $* = \alpha \bigg/ \left[2 \binom{a}{2} \right]$
Tukey's HSD	$\dfrac{q_\alpha}{\sqrt{2}} \sqrt{MS(Error)} \sqrt{\dfrac{2}{bn}}$
REGWQ Multiple Range Test	$\dfrac{q_*}{\sqrt{2}} \sqrt{MS(Error)} \sqrt{\dfrac{2}{bn}}$ with $* = \begin{cases} 1 - (1-\alpha)^{p/a} & \text{for } p < a - 1 \\ \alpha & \text{for } p \geq a - 1 \end{cases}$
For minimum significant difference on tests of $\beta_j - \beta_l$, interchange a and b.	

In Table 6.13, $t_{\alpha/2}$ and t_* are critical values from the t distribution with $n_{..} - ab$ degrees of freedom. Also, q_α and q_* are critical values from the studentized range distribution with $ab(n-1)$ and a (or b) degrees of freedom.

6.3.8 Example 6.5: Two-Way ANOVA with Balanced Data

This example illustrates two-way factorial analysis of variance with balanced data. Least-squares means are also illustrated.

- The hypothesis tests and comparisons using least-squares means are worked out in the "Detailed Solutions" section below.

- Requesting a two-way factorial ANOVA with the Linear Models task is discussed in "Instructions for the Two-way Factorial ANOVA Using the Linear Models Task."

- Complete results are in "Task Output, Interpretation, and Analysis" for Example 6.5.

6.3.8.1   Investigating a New Headache Drug

The effectiveness of a new drug for the treatment of headaches is investigated in a clinical trial. The new drug is administered at two dosages: 5 milligrams and 10 milligrams. These are denoted as N05 and N10, respectively. The superficial properties of the medications are identical. Female and male patients are randomly assigned to receive one of the two new dosages. After one month, the patients complete a quality-of-life (QOL) questionnaire. The QOL scores are on a 100-point scale. The standardized mean score is 50. Higher scores indicate a better quality of life. The results of the clinical trial are below.

QOL		\multicolumn{8}{c}{Treatment}														
		\multicolumn{8}{c}{N05}							\multicolumn{8}{c}{N10}							
Sex	F	49	42	25	70	46	56	62	42	62	62	59	75	64	76	73	59
	M	50	46	69	72	70	47	63	58	61	52	65	54	58	55	61	58

Use the Linear Models task to apply a two-way factorial analysis of variance to this data.

Example 6.5.1
Test the claim that the mean responses are the same for all populations associated with the treatments. Let $\alpha = 0.05$. If the claim is not rejected, the analysis is complete.

Example 6.5.2
If the mean responses in Example 6.5.1 are not all equal, test the claim that there is no interaction between the types of treatment and sex. Let $\alpha = 0.05$.

Example 6.5.3
If there is significant interaction, determine which treatment-sex combination has the highest mean quality-of-life score. Use the Tukey-adjusted least-squares means to determine which other combinations, if any, have means that are not significantly different from the highest.

Example 6.5.4
If there is no significant interaction, test the claim that the mean quality-of-life score is the same for both new dosages. Let $\alpha = 0.05$.

Example 6.5.5
If there is no significant interaction, test the claim that the mean quality-of-life score is the same for females and males. Let $\alpha = 0.05$.

Example 6.5.6
Construct main effects plots and a two-way effects plot.

The results are a subset of the Headache data set in the Appendix. Only rows with the Treatment values N05 and N10 are included.

The Query Builder applies the filter headache.Treatment IN('N05', 'N10'). See Figure 6.10.

Figure 6.10 Edit Filter Window for Example 6.5

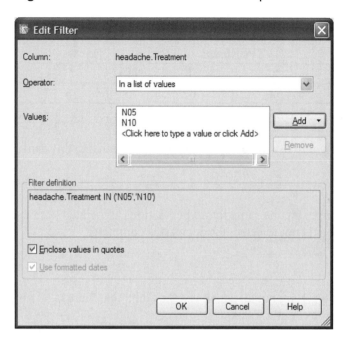

Only the variables Treatment, Sex, and QOL are selected for output. The result is the QUERY_FOR_HEADACHE_0000 data set below.

- QOL is the dependent variable.
- Treatment and Sex are classification variables. The levels of Treatment are N05 and N10. The levels of Sex are F and M.

Let Treatment be factor A and Sex be factor B.

- The subscripts $i = 1$ and 2 refer to the Treatment levels N05 and N10, respectively.
- The subscripts $j = 1$ and 2 refer to the Sex levels F and M, respectively.

The two-way factorial model is appropriate for this example. The factors Treatment and Sex are crossed. Treatment*Sex interaction might be present.

	Treatment	Sex	QOL
	QUERY_FOR_HEADACHE_0000 (read-only)		
1	N10	F	59
2	N05	F	42
3	N10	M	52
4	N10	F	59
5	N10	M	55
6	N10	F	73
7	N05	M	72
8	N10	M	61
9	N05	F	25
10	N05	M	46
11	N10	F	62
12	N10	M	61
13	N10	M	58
14	N10	M	54
15	N05	M	69
16	N05	M	63
17	N10	M	65
18	N05	F	49
19	N05	M	47
20	N10	F	62
21	N05	F	70
22	N10	F	76
23	N10	F	64
24	N05	F	62
25	N05	F	56
26	N05	F	42
27	N10	F	75
28	N05	M	50
29	N05	F	46
30	N05	M	70
31	N05	M	58
32	N10	M	58

This example involves four population means: $\mu_{ij} = \mu + \alpha_i + \beta_j + (\alpha\beta)_{ij}$.

- $\mu_{11} = \mu + \alpha_1 + \beta_1 + (\alpha\beta)_{11}$ is the mean response for all female patients who take the new drug at the 5-milligram dosage.

- $\mu_{12} = \mu + \alpha_1 + \beta_2 + (\alpha\beta)_{12}$ is the mean response for all male patients who take the new drug at the 5-milligram dosage.

- $\mu_{21} = \mu + \alpha_2 + \beta_1 + (\alpha\beta)_{21}$ is the mean response for all female patients who take the new drug at the 10-milligram dosage.

- $\mu_{22} = \mu + \alpha_2 + \beta_2 + (\alpha\beta)_{22}$ is the mean response for all male patients who take the new drug at the 10-milligram dosage.

Treatment main effects are α_i: the difference between the mean score of all patients who use the N05 or N10 dosage ($\mu_{i.}$) and the mean score of all patients who use either new dosage (μ).

Sex main effects are β_j: the difference between the mean score of female or male patients who use either new dosage ($\mu_{.j}$) and the mean score of all patients who use either new dosage (μ).

Treatment*Sex interaction effects are $(\alpha\beta)_{ij}$:

- $(\alpha\beta)_{11}$ is the difference between the mean score of female patients who use dosage N05 (μ_{11}) and the overall mean plus the N05 main effect and the female main effect ($\mu + \alpha_1 + \beta_1$).

- $(\alpha\beta)_{12}$ is the difference between the mean scores of all male patients using dosage N05 (μ_{12}) and the overall mean plus the N05 main effect and the male main effect ($\mu + \alpha_1 + \beta_2$).

- $(\alpha\beta)_{21}$ is the difference between the mean score of female patients who use dosage N10 (μ_{21}) and the overall mean plus the N10 main effect and the female main effect ($\mu + \alpha_2 + \beta_1$).

- $(\alpha\beta)_{22}$ is the difference between the mean scores of all male patients using dosage N10 (μ_{22}) and the overall mean plus the N10 main effect and the male main effect ($\mu + \alpha_2 + \beta_2$).

6.3.8.2   Detailed Solutions

The statistics below have been computed with the Summary Tables task. "Quality of Life" is the label of the QOL variable.

Output 6.9 Summary Tables Output for Example 6.5

Summary Tables

			N	Mean	Var
Quality of Life	**Treatment**	**Sex**			
	N05	**F**	8	49	191.71428571
		M	8	59.375	114.26785714
	N10	**F**	8	66.25	51.928571429
		M	8	58	18.285714286
Quality of Life		**Treatment**			
		N05	16	54.1875	171.49583333
		N10	16	62.125	50.916666667
Quality of Life		**Sex**			
		F	16	57.625	193.05
		M	16	58.6875	62.3625
Quality of Life			32	58.15625	123.87802419

Example 6.5.1

Plan the task.

$H_0 : \mu_{11} = \mu_{12} = \mu_{21} = \mu_{22}$

$H_1 :$ At least two means are not equal.

$\alpha = 0.05$

Compute the statistics.

$$SS(Model) = \sum_{i=1}^{2} \sum_{j=1}^{2} n_{ij} \left(\overline{y}_{ij\cdot} - \overline{y}_{\cdots} \right)^2$$

$$= (8)(49 - 58.15625)^2 + (8)(59.375 - 58.15625)^2$$
$$+ (8)(66.25 - 58.15625)^2 + (8)(58 - 58.15625)^2$$
$$= 1206.84375$$

$$SS(Total) = (n_{\cdot\cdot} - 1)s^2, \text{ where } s^2 \text{ is the overall sample variance}$$
$$= (32 - 1)(123.87802419)$$
$$= 3840.218750$$

$$SS(Error) = SS(Total) - SS(Model)$$
$$= 3840.218750 - 1206.843750$$
$$= 2633.375$$

Source	DF	Sum of Squares	Mean Square	F Value	Pr > F
Model	3	1206.843750	402.28125	4.27735	0.013198
Error	28	2633.375	94.049107		
Corrected Total	31	3840.218750			

Referring to Table 6.8:

$$p\text{-value} = P(F > 4.27735) = 1 - \text{probf}(4.27735, 3, 28) = 0.013198$$

Apply the results.

Since the p-value < 0.05, reject H_0. There is sufficient evidence to reject the claim that the mean responses are the same for all populations associated with the treatments. At least two of the treatment-sample means are significantly different.

The section of the ANOVA table containing the statistics for the effects is constructed next:

Treatment: $\hat{\alpha}_1 = \bar{y}_{1..} - \bar{y}_{...} = 54.1875 - 58.15625 = -3.96875$

$\hat{\alpha}_2 = \bar{y}_{2..} - \bar{y}_{...} = 62.125 - 58.15625 = 3.96875$

$SS(\text{Treatment}) = bn\sum_{i=1}^{2}(\hat{\alpha}_i)^2 = (2)(8)(-3.96875)^2 + (2)(8)(3.96875)^2 = 504.03125$

Sex: $\hat{\beta}_1 = \bar{y}_{.1.} - \bar{y}_{...} = 57.625 - 58.15625 = -0.53125$

$\hat{\beta}_2 = \bar{y}_{.2.} - \bar{y}_{...} = 58.6875 - 58.15625 = 0.53125$

$SS(\text{Sex}) = an\sum_{j=1}^{2}(\hat{\beta}_j)^2 = (2)(8)(-0.53125)^2 + (2)(8)(0.53125)^2 = 9.03125$

Treatment * Sex: $\widehat{(\alpha\beta)}_{11} = \bar{y}_{11.} - \bar{y}_{1..} - \bar{y}_{.1.} + \bar{y}_{...} = 49 - 54.1875 - 57.625 + 58.15625 = -4.65625$

$\widehat{(\alpha\beta)}_{12} = \bar{y}_{12.} - \bar{y}_{1..} - \bar{y}_{.2.} + \bar{y}_{...} = 59.375 - 54.1875 - 58.6875 + 58.15625 = 4.65625$

$\widehat{(\alpha\beta)}_{21} = \bar{y}_{21.} - \bar{y}_{2..} - \bar{y}_{.1.} + \bar{y}_{...} = 66.25 - 62.125 - 57.625 + 58.15625 = 4.65625$

$\widehat{(\alpha\beta)}_{22} = \bar{y}_{22.} - \bar{y}_{2..} - \bar{y}_{.2.} + \bar{y}_{...} = 58 - 62.125 - 58.6875 + 58.15625 = -4.65625$

$SS(\text{Treatment*Sex}) = n\sum_{i=1}^{2}\sum_{j=1}^{2}\left(\widehat{(\alpha\beta)}_{ij}\right)^2$

$= 8(-4.65625)^2 + 8(4.65625)^2 + 8(4.65625)^2 + 8(-4.65625)^2$

$= 693.78125$

Source	DF	Type III SS	Mean Square	*F* Value	Pr > F
Treatment	1	504.03125	504.03125	5.36223	0.02812
Sex	1	9.03125	9.03125	0.09603	0.75894
Treatment*Sex	1	693.78125	693.78125	7.37680	0.01119

Referring to Table 6.8:

$p\text{-value} = P(F > 5.36223) = 1 - \text{probf}(5.36223, 1, 28) = 0.02812$

$p\text{-value} = P(F > 0.09603) = 1 - \text{probf}(0.09603, 1, 28) = 0.75894$

$p\text{-value} = P(F > 7.37680) = 1 - \text{probf}(7.37680, 1, 28) = 0.01119$

Example 6.5.2

Plan the task.

$H_0 : (\alpha\beta)_{11} = (\alpha\beta)_{12} = (\alpha\beta)_{21} = (\alpha\beta)_{22} = 0$

H_1: At least one interaction effect is not 0.

Compute the statistics.

See the Treatment*Sex test above.

Apply the results.

Since the p-value < 0.05, reject H_0. There is sufficient evidence to reject the claim that there is no interaction between the types of treatment and sex. There is significant interaction.

Example 6.5.3

Female patients taking the new drug at 10 milligrams have the highest treatment-sample mean with $\bar{y}_{21} = 66.25$. The mean response of the male patients taking the new drug at 5 milligrams ($\bar{y}_{12} = 59.375$) and the mean response the male patients taking the new drug at 10 milligrams ($\bar{y}_{22} = 58$) are both not significantly different from the highest treatment-sample mean. Below are the comparisons using Tukey-adjusted least-squares means:

N10-F versus N05-M

$$H_0 : \mu_{21} - \mu_{12} = 0$$
$$H_1 : \mu_{21} - \mu_{12} \neq 0$$

$$t \text{ Value} = \frac{\bar{y}_{21\cdot} - \bar{y}_{12\cdot}}{\sqrt{MSE(Error)}\sqrt{\frac{1}{n}+\frac{1}{n}}} = \frac{66.25 - 59.375}{\sqrt{94.049107}\sqrt{\frac{1}{8}+\frac{1}{8}}} = 1.41783$$

$$p\text{-value} = P\left(Q \geq \sqrt{2}|t \text{ Value}|\right)$$
$$= 1\text{-probmc('range',sqrt(2)*abs(1.41783),.,28,4)}$$
$$= 0.49915$$

N10-F versus N10-M

$$H_0 : \mu_{21} - \mu_{22} = 0$$
$$H_1 : \mu_{21} - \mu_{22} \neq 0$$

$$t \text{ Value} = \frac{\bar{y}_{21\cdot} - \bar{y}_{22\cdot}}{\sqrt{MSE(Error)}\sqrt{\frac{1}{n}+\frac{1}{n}}} = \frac{66.25 - 58}{\sqrt{94.049107}\sqrt{\frac{1}{8}+\frac{1}{8}}} = 1.70140$$

$$p\text{-value} = P\left(Q \geq \sqrt{2}|t \text{ Value}|\right)$$
$$= 1\text{-probmc('range',sqrt(2)*abs(1.70140),.,28,4)}$$
$$= 0.34190$$

N10-F versus N05-F

$$H_0 : \mu_{21} - \mu_{11} = 0$$

$$H_1 : \mu_{21} - \mu_{11} \neq 0$$

$$t\ \text{Value} = \frac{\bar{y}_{21\cdot} - \bar{y}_{11\cdot}}{\sqrt{MSE\left(Error\right)}\sqrt{\dfrac{1}{n} + \dfrac{1}{n}}} = \frac{66.25 - 49}{\sqrt{94.049107}\sqrt{\dfrac{1}{8} + \dfrac{1}{8}}} = 3.55747$$

$$p\text{-value} = P\left(Q \geq \sqrt{2}\,\lvert t\ \text{Value}\rvert\right)$$

$$= 1 - \text{probmc}(\text{'range'},\text{sqrt}(2)*\text{abs}(3.55747),.,28,4)$$

$$= 0.00701$$

6.3.9 Instructions for the Two-way Factorial ANOVA Using the Linear Models Task

The Linear Models task is capable of executing any number of designs. Here it is applied to the two-way factorial analysis of variance. The figures in this section are for the analysis of Example 6.5.

Open the Linear Models task in one of the following ways:

- From the menu bar, select **Analyze ▶ ANOVA ▶ Linear Models**.

- On the **Task by Category** tab of the **Task List**, go to the **ANOVA** section and click **Linear Models**.

- On the **Task by Name** tab of the **Task List**, double-click **Linear Models**.

The Linear Models task has eight groups of options: Task Roles, Model, Model Options, Advanced Options, Post Hoc Tests, Plots, Predictions, and Titles.

The Advance Model Options are not discussed in this book. Predictions are discussed in Chapter 7, "Correlation and Regression." Titles are discussed in general in Chapter 1, "Introduction to SAS Enterprise Guide." The Titles options control output titles and the footnotes.

6.3.9.1 Task Roles

A variable is assigned to a role by dragging it from **Variables to Assign** to one of the **Task Roles**. A variable can be removed from a role by dragging it back to **Variables to Assign**. Also, the arrows can be used. See Figure 6.11.

- Dependent variables are the variables of responses. There is one dependent variable per analysis. Multiple dependent variables produce multiple analyses.

- Quantitative variables are not used in factorial analysis of variance. The use of quantitative variables as independent variables is discussed in Chapter 7, "Correlation and Regression."

- Classification variables are the independent variables for factorial analysis of variance.

The roles Group analysis by, Frequency count, Relative weight are discussed in Chapter 1, "Introduction to SAS Enterprise Guide."

In Figure 6.11, QOL is assigned to the Dependent variables role. Treatment and Sex are assigned to the Classification variables role.

Figure 6.11 Task Roles in Linear Models

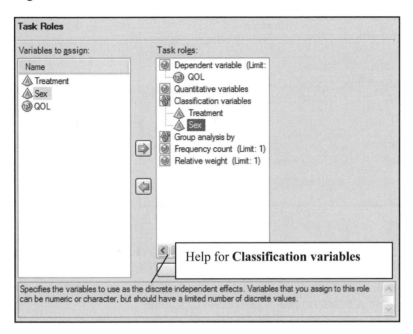

6.3.9.2　Model

Many statistical designs can be created with the Model options. Creating a factorial model requires two steps:

1. Hold down the **Ctrl** button on the keyboard while selecting the independent variables in the **Class and quantitative variables** box.

2. Click **Factorial**.

The resulting model has a main effect for each independent variable and all possible interactions. The **Effects** box lists the independent variables and all possible crossed variables.

It might be desirable to have fewer than all possible interactions in a model. The maximum number of interacting factors—crossed variables—can be adjusted in the Degrees field. For Degrees to be active, there must be more than two independent variables.

In Figure 6.12, the model includes Sex and Treatment main effects and a Sex*Treatment interaction effect.

Figure 6.12 Model Creation Options in Linear Models

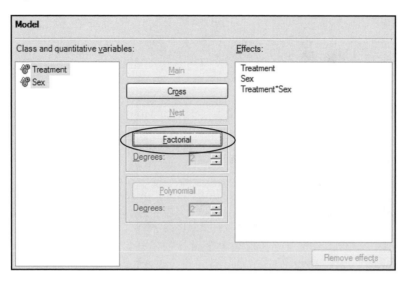

6.3.9.3   Model Options

By default, the Type I and Type III sums of squares are checked. No changes are needed here. The analysis discussed here is based on the Type III sum of squares.

Figure 6.13 Model Options in Linear Models

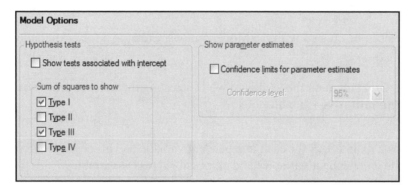

6.3.9.4   Post Hoc Tests > Least Squares

Least-squares means are appropriate for comparisons on both main effects and interaction effects. These means are also appropriate for both balanced and unbalanced data. The options for least squares tests are shown in Figure 6.15.

To request tests with least squares means:

    1.   Click **Add**. The options list appears in the **Options for means tests** box.

2. At **Class effects to use**:

   a. Use the drop-down menu to change **False** to **True** for each desired comparison.

   b. The selected effects are shown in the **Effects to estimate** box. In Figure 6.14, **Treatment* Sex** is selected.

3. At **Comparisons**:

   a. For **Show p-values for differences**, select **All pairwise differences**.

   b. For **Adjustment method for comparison**, select a method computing *p*-values. In Figure 6.14, **Tukey** is selected.

4. Confidence intervals are not requested here. At **Confidence limits, Show confidence limits** remains at **False**.

5. The **Covariates** section is relevant only when the Quantitative variables role has been assigned. The section is not relevant here.

Figure 6.14 Least Squares Options for Post Hoc Tests in Linear Models

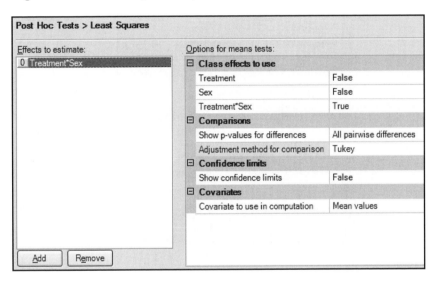

6.3.9.5 Post Hoc Tests > Arithmetic

Arithmetic means are appropriate for comparisons of main effects when the data is balanced. The options for arithmetic tests are shown in Figure 6.16.

To request tests with arithmetic means:

1. Click **Add**. The options list appears in the **Options for means tests** box.

2. At **Class effects to use**:

   a. Use the drop-down menu to change **False** to **True** for each desired comparison.

   b. The selected effects are shown in the **Effects to estimate** box. In Figure 6.15, **Sex** and **Treatment** are selected.

3. At **Comparisons**: For **Comparison method**, select a multiple-comparison test. In Figure 6.15, the **Ryan-Einot-Gabriel-Welsch multiple-range test** is selected.

4. The default selections remain for the **Error mean square** section.

5. The Means options control the output.

   a. At **Show means for**, select **All model variables**. This refers to the dependent variable and to any variables assigned to the **Quantitative variables** role.

   b. At **Join nonsignificant subsets**, select **True**.

   c. At **Sort means in descending order**, select **True**.

6. No options in the **Confidence intervals** section are requested here.

7. **Homogeneity of variance** section is not applied here.

Figure 6.15 Arithmetic Options for Post Hoc Tests in Linear Models

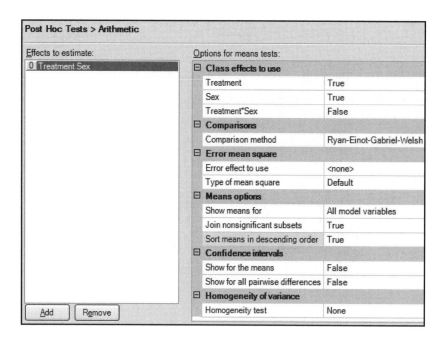

6.3.9.6   Plots > Means

The Linear Models task produces means plots for main effects and for two-way effects. The options for the means plots are shown in Figure 6.15.

Means Plots for Main Effects

When **Dependent means for main effects** is checked, a plot of the factor-level means is created for each variable assigned to the Classification variables role.

- The plot represents each factor-level sample with a vertical line centered at the sample mean. For a basic means plot for main effects, the length of the vertical line from its center is one standard error.

- The classification values are listed along the horizontal axis in the sorting of the classification values.

- The sample means are connected.

The vertical lines are represented below. In the expressions, $s_{i\cdot\cdot}$ is the standard deviation of all responses at the i level of A and $s_{\cdot j\cdot}$ is the standard deviation of all responses at the j level of B.

$$\bar{y}_{i\cdot\cdot} + \frac{s_{i\cdot\cdot}}{\sqrt{n_{i\cdot}}}$$

$$|$$

Factor A: $\bar{y}_{i\cdot\cdot}$ $(i=1,\ldots,a)$

$$|$$

$$\bar{y}_{i\cdot\cdot} - \frac{s_{i\cdot\cdot}}{\sqrt{n_{i\cdot}}}$$

$$\bar{y}_{\cdot j\cdot} + \frac{s_{\cdot j\cdot}}{\sqrt{n_{\cdot j}}}$$

$$|$$

Factor B: $\bar{y}_{\cdot j\cdot}$ $(j=1,\ldots,b)$

$$|$$

$$\bar{y}_{\cdot j\cdot} - \frac{s_{\cdot j\cdot}}{\sqrt{n_{\cdot j}}}$$

Means Plots for Two-Way Effects

When **Dependent means for two-way effects** is checked, a means plot is created for each of the two-way effects requested with the Model options.

- The plot represents each two-factor sample with a vertical line centered at the sample mean. For a basic means plot for two-way effects, the length of the vertical line from its center is one standard error.

- The classification values from the variable whose name comes first in sorting order are listed along the horizontal axis.

- The sample means associated with each level from the variable whose name comes second in sorting order are connected.

The vertical lines are represented below. In the expressions, $s_{ij\cdot}$ is the standard deviation of the two-factor sample associated with i^{th} level of A and j^{th} level of B.

$$\bar{y}_{ij\cdot} + \frac{s_{ij\cdot}}{\sqrt{n}}$$

$$|$$

Two-Way Effects: $\bar{y}_{ij\cdot}$ $(i=1,\ldots,a \text{ and } j=1,\ldots,b)$

$$|$$

$$\bar{y}_{ij\cdot} - \frac{s_{ij\cdot}}{\sqrt{n}}$$

To request means plots:

1. Check **Dependent means for main effects** for a means plot for each variable assigned to the Classification variables role.

2. Check **Dependent means for two-way effects** for a means plot for each of the two-way effects requested with the **Model** options.

3. **Predicted means** should be selected. These are least-squares means, which are equal to **Observed means**—arithmetic means—when the data is balanced.

4. It is recommended that vertical bars represent one standard error from the mean. At **Height of standard error bars, 1** is recommended.

In Figure 6.16, three plots are requested. The plots are listed in the **Summary of requested plots** box beneath **Means (3 plots)**. The first two illustrate main effects. The third illustrates two-way effects.

Figure 6.16 Means Options for Plots in Linear Models

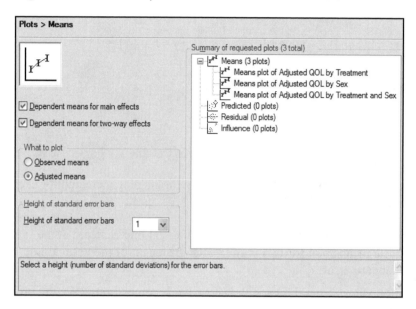

6.3.9.7   When Finished

When finished adding variables to roles and selecting options, click **Run**. The task adds a Linear Models icon and one or more output icons to the process flow diagram. See Figure 6.17. The resulting output is at Output 6.10.

Figure 6.17 Example 6.5 Data, Task, and Output Icons on the Process Flow Diagram

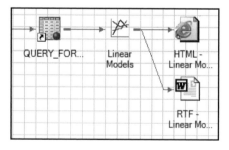

6.3.10 Task Output, Interpretation, and Analysis for Example 6.5

6.3.10.1 Task Output

Output 6.10 Linear Models Output for Example 6.5

The GLM Procedure

Class Level Information		
Class	**Levels**	**Values**
Treatment	2	N05 N10
Sex	2	F M

❶

Number of Observations Read	32
Number of Observations Used	32

❷

Dependent Variable: QOL   Quality of Life   ❸

Source	DF	Sum of Squares	Mean Square	F Value	Pr > F
Model	3	1206.843750	402.281250	4.28	0.0132
Error	28	2633.375000	94.049107		
Corrected Total	31	3840.218750			

❹

R-Square	Coeff Var	Root MSE	QOL Mean
0.314264	16.67558	9.697892	58.15625

❺ ❻

Source	DF	Type I SS	Mean Square	F Value	Pr > F
Sex	1	9.0312500	9.0312500	0.10	0.7589
Treatment	1	504.0312500	504.0312500	5.36	0.0282
Treatment*Sex	1	693.7812500	693.7812500	7.38	0.0112

Source	DF	Type III SS	Mean Square	F Value	Pr > F
Sex	1	9.0312500	9.0312500	0.10	0.7589
Treatment	1	504.0312500	504.0312500	5.36	0.0282
Treatment*Sex	1	693.7812500	693.7812500	7.38	0.0112

❼

Least Squares Means ❽
Adjustment for Multiple Comparisons: Tukey

Treatment	Sex	QOL LSMEAN	LSMEAN Number
N05	F	49.0000000	1
N05	M	59.3750000	2
N10	F	66.2500000	3 ❾
N10	M	58.0000000	4

Least Squares Means for effect Treatment*Sex Pr > |t| for H0: LSMean(i)=LSMean(j) Dependent Variable: QOL				
i/j	1	2	3	4
1		0.1655	0.0070	0.2695
2	0.1655		0.4991	0.9919
3	0.0070	0.4991		0.3419 ❿
4	0.2695	0.9919	0.3419	

❿

Ryan-Einot-Gabriel-Welsch Multiple Range Test for QOL ⓫

NOTE: This test controls the Type I experiment-wise error rate.

Alpha	0.05
Error Degrees of Freedom	28
Error Mean Square	94.04911

Number of Means	2
Critical Range	7.0234454

Means with the same letter are not significantly different.			
REGWQ Grouping	Mean	N	Sex
A	58.688	16	M
A			
A	57.625	16	F

Ryan-Einot-Gabriel-Welsch Multiple Range Test for QOL ⑫

NOTE: This test controls the Type I experiment-wise error
rate.

Alpha	0.05
Error Degrees of Freedom	28
Error Mean Square	94.04911

Number of Means	2
Critical Range	7.0234454

Means with the same letter are not significantly different.			
REGWQ Grouping	Mean	N	Treatment
A	62.125	16	N10
B	54.188	16	N05

Means plot of QOL by Sex ⑬

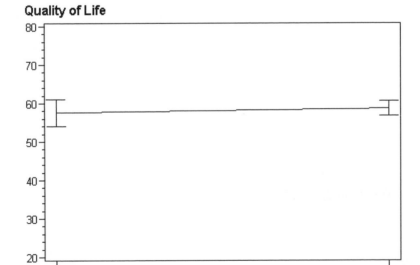

Means plot of QOL by Treatment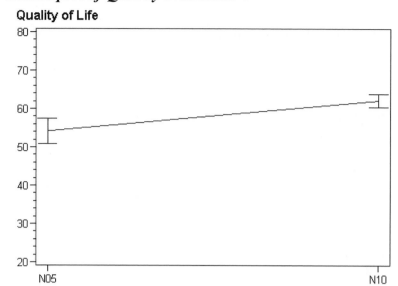

Means plot of QOL by Sex and Treatment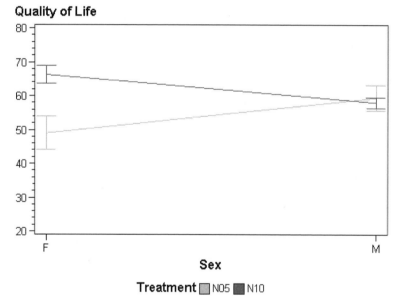

6.3.10.2 Interpretation

❶ Independent variables are: Treatment with $a = 2$ and levels N05 and N10, Sex with $b = 2$ and levels F and M.

❷ $n_{..} = 32$

❸ Dependent variable is QOL. Its variable label is "Quality of Life".

❹ ANOVA table for the test of the full model

❺ Coefficient of Determination $R^2 = 0.314264$

❻ $\bar{y}_{...} = 58.15625$

❼ p-values for the tests of the Sex and Treatment main effects and the Treatment* Sex interaction effect

❽ Beginning of the least squares means output. The Tukey method is used to adjust the p-values.

❾ The N10-F treatment has the highest mean at 66.25.

❿ Row and column with the p-values for the three pair-wise comparisons involving the N10-F treatment mean. The row and column have the same values.

⓫ Beginning of the REGW multiple range test for the Sex main effects. Since there is significant interaction, this output is not used in the analysis.

⓬ Beginning of the REGW multiple range test for the Treatment main effects. Since there is significant interaction, this output is not used in the analysis.

⓭ Means plot for the Sex main effects. Because there is significant interaction, this plot can be misleading.

⓮ Means plot for the Treatment main effects. Because there is significant interaction, this plot can be misleading.

⓯ Means plot for the Sex*Treatment two-way effects.

6.3.10.3 Analysis

Example 6.5.1
$H_0 : \mu_{11} = \mu_{12} = \mu_{21} = \mu_{22}$

H_1 : At least two means are not equal.

p-value = 0.0132. See ❹ in Output 6.10.

Since the p-value < 0.05, reject H_0. There is sufficient evidence to reject the claim that the mean responses are the same for all populations associated with the treatments. At least two treatment-sample means are significantly different.

Example 6.5.2
$H_0 : (\alpha\beta)_{11} = (\alpha\beta)_{12} = (\alpha\beta)_{21} = (\alpha\beta)_{22} = 0$

H_1 : At least one interaction effect is not 0.

p-value = 0. 0112. See ❼ in Output 6.10.

Since the p-value < 0.05, reject H_0. There is sufficient evidence to reject the claim that there is no interaction between the types of treatment and sex. There is significant interaction.

Example 6.5.3
Females taking the N10 dosage have the highest mean quality-of-life score. See ❾ in Output 6.10.

The mean scores for males taking the N05 dosage and males taking the N10 dosage are not significantly different from the mean score for females taking the N10 dosage. See ❿ in Output 6.10.

Example 6.5.4

This question is skipped because there is significant interaction. (With a p-value = 0.0282 for Treatment, one could conclude that the mean quality-of-life scores are not the same for the two new dosages. This is the case for females but not for males. The interaction is seen in the two-way effects graph in Output 6.10.)

Example 6.5.5

This question is skipped because there is significant interaction. (With a p-value = 0.7589 for Sex, one could conclude that the mean quality-of-life score is the same for females and males. Based on the least-squares analysis of the treatment means, this is the case. Mean scores for females and males are not significantly different for the N05 dosage and for the N10 dosage.)

Example 6.5.6

See Output 6.10.

6.3.11 Example 6.6: Two-Way ANOVA with Unbalanced Data

6.3.11.1 Employee Attitude toward Work

A company randomly selects 24 male and female employees to complete a standardized psychological questionnaire. Among other things, the questionnaire measures an employee's attitude toward their tasks and responsibilities. The employees are located at three branch offices: Central, North, and South. The data is below.

Work		Gender								
		Female					Male			
Location	Central	49	51	53	50	54	47	48		
	North	52	51	52	51	59	51	58	51	
	South	56	57	51	57	58	57	59	55	56

Use the Linear Models task to apply a two-way factorial analysis of variance to this data.

Example 6.6.1

Test the claim that the mean responses are the same for all populations associated with the treatments. Let $\alpha = 0.05$. If the claim is not rejected, the analysis is complete.

Example 6.6.2

If the mean responses in Example 6.6.1 are not all equal, test the claim that there is no interaction between location and gender. Let $\alpha = 0.05$.

Example 6.6.3

If there is significant interaction, use the Tukey-adjusted least-squares means to determine which combination of gender and location has the highest mean. What other combinations, if any, have means that are not significantly different from the highest?

Example 6.6.4

If there is no significant interaction, test the claim that the mean work attitude score is the same for females and males. Let $\alpha = 0.05$. If the claim is rejected, use the least-squares means to determine whether females or males have the higher mean score.

Example 6.6.5

If there is no significant interaction, test the claim that the mean work attitude score is the same at all locations. Let $\alpha = 0.05$. If the claim is rejected, use the Tukey-adjusted least-squares means to determine which location has the highest mean score. What locations, if any, have means that are not significantly different from the highest?

Example 6.6.6

Construct main effects plots and a two-way effects plot.

The data is in the Attitude data set below. Variables other than Work, Gender, and Location are hidden.

	Location	Gender	Work
1	South	F	56
2	Central	F	49
3	South	F	57
4	North	F	52
5	South	M	51
6	North	M	51
7	South	M	57
8	Central	F	51
9	Central	F	53
10	South	F	58
11	South	M	57
12	South	F	59
13	North	M	52
14	Central	F	50
15	North	M	51
16	Central	F	54
17	North	F	59
18	Central	M	47
19	South	M	55
20	South	F	56
21	North	F	51
22	Central	M	48
23	North	F	58
24	North	F	51

- Work is the dependent variable.
- Gender and Location are classification variables. The levels of Gender are F and M. The levels of Location are Central, North, and South.

Let Gender be factor A and Location be factor B.

- The subscripts $i = 1$ and 2 refer to the Gender levels F and M, respectively.
- The subscripts $j = 1$, 2, and 3 refer to the Location levels Central, North, and South, respectively.

The two-way factorial model is appropriate for this example. The factors Gender and Location are crossed. Gender*Location interaction might be present.

This example involves six population means: $\mu_{ij} = \mu + \alpha_i + \beta_j + (\alpha\beta)_{ij}$.

Gender main effects are α_i: the difference between the mean score of female or male employees from all locations ($\mu_{i.}$) and the mean score of all employees from all locations (μ).

Location main effects are β_j: the difference between the mean score of all employees from the Central, North, or South location ($\mu_{.j}$) and the mean score of all employees from all locations (μ).

Gender*Location interaction effects are $(\alpha\beta)_{ij}$:

- $(\alpha\beta)_{11}$ is the difference between the mean score of female employees from the Central office (μ_{11}) and the overall mean plus the female main effect and the Central office main effect ($\mu + \alpha_1 + \beta_1$).

- $(\alpha\beta)_{12}$ is the difference between the mean scores of female employees from the North office (μ_{12}) and the overall mean plus the female main effect and the North office main effect ($\mu + \alpha_1 + \beta_2$).

- $(\alpha\beta)_{13}$ is the difference between the mean scores of female employees from the South office (μ_{13}) and the overall mean plus the female main effect and the South office main effect ($\mu + \alpha_1 + \beta_3$).

- $(\alpha\beta)_{11}$ is the difference between the mean score of male employees from the Central office (μ_{21}) and the overall mean plus the male main effect and the Central office main effect ($\mu + \alpha_2 + \beta_1$).

- $(\alpha\beta)_{12}$ is the difference between the mean scores of male employees from the North office (μ_{22}) and the overall mean plus the male main effect and the North office main effect ($\mu + \alpha_2 + \beta_2$).

- $(\alpha\beta)_{13}$ is the difference between the mean scores of male employees from the South office (μ_{23}) and the overall mean plus the male main effect and the South office main effect ($\mu + \alpha_2 + \beta_3$).

6.3.11.2 Detailed Solutions

For the purposes of this section, the data is put in the form shown earlier in Figure 6.8. It is stored as data set Ex06_06 and presented below.

	work	x1	w1	w2	z11	z12
1	49	1	1	0	1	0
2	51	1	1	0	1	0
3	53	1	1	0	1	0
4	50	1	1	0	1	0
5	54	1	1	0	1	0
6	52	1	0	1	0	1
7	59	1	0	1	0	1
8	51	1	0	1	0	1
9	58	1	0	1	0	1
10	51	1	0	1	0	1
11	56	1	-1	-1	-1	-1
12	57	1	-1	-1	-1	-1
13	58	1	-1	-1	-1	-1
14	59	1	-1	-1	-1	-1
15	56	1	-1	-1	-1	-1
16	47	-1	1	0	-1	0
17	48	-1	1	0	-1	0
18	51	-1	0	1	0	-1
19	52	-1	0	1	0	-1
20	51	-1	0	1	0	-1
21	51	-1	-1	-1	1	1
22	57	-1	-1	-1	1	1
23	57	-1	-1	-1	1	1
24	55	-1	-1	-1	1	1

The Linear Models task is applied to Ex06_06. The dependent variable is work. The independent quantitative variables are x1, w1, w2, z12, and z12. This is the full model. All parameters in the model $\mu_{ij} = \mu + \alpha_i + \beta_j + (\alpha\beta)_{ij}$ are included.

The table in Example 6.6.1 is from the task output. The results would be the same if the steps for computing the full model ANOVA table in the "Detailed Solutions" section of Example 6.5 were followed.

Example 6.6.1

Plan the task.

$H_0 : \mu_{11} = \mu_{12} = \mu_{13} = \mu_{21} = \mu_{22} = \mu_{23}$

$H_1 :$ At least two means are not equal.

Compute the statistics.

Source	DF	Sum of Squares	Mean Square	F Value	Pr > F
Model	5	187.9916667	37.5983333	6.04	0.0019
Error	18	111.9666667	6.2203704		
Corrected Total	23	299.9583333			

Apply the results.

Since the p-value < 0.05, reject H_0. There is sufficient evidence to reject the claim that the mean responses are the same for all populations associated with the treatments. At least two of the treatment-sample means are significantly different.

The section of the ANOVA table containing the statistics for the effects is constructed next. The Error Sum of Squares for each of the three reduced models is the result of applying Linear Models to that model.

Gender:

$$
\begin{aligned}
SS(\text{Gender}) &= SS(\text{Reduced Model Error for } H_0 : \alpha_1 = \alpha_2 = 0) - SS(\text{Full Model Error}) \\
&= SS(\text{Error with w1, w2, z11, z12}) - SS(\text{Error with x1, w1, w2, z11, z12}) \\
&= 159.72970 - 111.96667 \\
&= 47.76303
\end{aligned}
$$

Location:

$$
\begin{aligned}
SS(\text{Gender}) &= SS(\text{Reduced Model Error for } H_0 : \beta_1 = \beta_2 = \beta_3 = 0) - SS(\text{Full Model Error}) \\
&= SS(\text{Error with x1, z11, z12}) - SS(\text{Error with x1, w1, w2, z11, z12}) \\
&= 268.43303 - 111.96667 \\
&= 156.46636
\end{aligned}
$$

Location * Gender:

$$
\begin{aligned}
SS(\text{Location*Gender}) &= SS\left(\text{Reduced Model Error for } H_0 : (\alpha\beta)_{ij} = 0\right) - SS(\text{Full Model Error}) \\
&= SS(\text{Error with x1, w1, w2}) - SS(\text{Error with x1, w1, w2, z11, z12}) \\
&= 114.47971 - 111.96667 \\
&= 2.51304
\end{aligned}
$$

Source	DF	Type III SS	Mean Square	F Value	Pr > F
Gender	1	47.76303	47.76303	7.67849	0.01259
Location	2	156.46636	78.23318	12.57693	0.00038
Location*Sex	2	2.51304	1.25652	0.20200	0.81892

Referring to Table 6.8:

$$p\text{-value} = P(F > 7.67849) = 1\text{-probf}(7.67849, 1, 18) = 0.01259$$
$$p\text{-value} = P(F > 12.57693) = 1\text{-probf}(12.57693, 2, 18) = 0.00038$$
$$p\text{-value} = P(F > 0.20200) = 1\text{-probf}(0.20200, 2, 18) = 0.81892$$

Example 6.6.2

Plan the task.

$$H_0 : (\alpha\beta)_{11} = (\alpha\beta)_{12} = (\alpha\beta)_{13} = (\alpha\beta)_{21} = (\alpha\beta)_{22} = (\alpha\beta)_{23} = 0$$

H_1 : At least one interaction effect is not 0.

Compute the statistics.

p-value = 0.81892. See the Gender*Location test above.

Apply the results.

Since the *p*-value > 0.05, fail to reject H_0. There is not sufficient evidence to reject the claim that there is no interaction between the types of gender and location. There is no significant interaction.

- Example 6.6.3 is skipped because there is no significant interaction.
- The statistics below have been computed with the Summary Tables task. "Location of Office" is the label of the Location variable. These statistics are needed below.

	Work					
	Location of Office					
	Central		**North**		**South**	
	N	Mean	N	Mean	N	Mean
Gender						
F	5	51.4	5	54.2	5	57.2
M	2	47.5	3	51.333333333	4	55

Example 6.6.4

Plan the task.

$H_0 : \alpha_1 = \alpha_2 = 0$

$H_1 :$ At least one Gender main effect is not 0.

Compute the statistics.

p-value = 0.01259. See the Gender test above.

Apply the results.

Since the *p*-value < 0.05, reject H_0. There is sufficient evidence to reject the claim that the mean work attitude score is the same for females and males. The mean scores for the females and the males are significantly different.

The least squares means for females and males are below. Females have the higher score.

$\hat{\mu}_{1.} = \frac{1}{3}(51.4 + 54.2 + 57.2) = 54.266666667$

$\hat{\mu}_{2.} = \frac{1}{3}(47.5 + 51.333333333 + 55) = 51.277777778$

The comparison test using a Tukey-adjusted *p*-value has the same result as the ANOVA test.

$$H_0 : \mu_{1.} - \mu_{2.} = 0$$
$$H_1 : \mu_{1.} - \mu_{2.} \neq 0$$

$$t \text{ Value} = \frac{\hat{\mu}_{1.} - \hat{\mu}_{2.}}{\sqrt{\dfrac{MSE(Error)}{b^2}}\sqrt{\displaystyle\sum_{j=1}^{b}\frac{1}{n_{1j}} + \sum_{j=1}^{b}\frac{1}{n_{2j}}}} = \frac{54.266666667 - 51.277777778}{\sqrt{\dfrac{6.22037}{3^2}}\sqrt{\left(\dfrac{1}{5}+\dfrac{1}{5}+\dfrac{1}{5}\right)+\left(\dfrac{1}{2}+\dfrac{1}{3}+\dfrac{1}{4}\right)}} = 2.771008$$

$$p\text{-value} = P\left(Q \geq \sqrt{2}\,|t \text{ Value}|\right)$$
$$= 1\text{-probmc('range',sqrt(2)*abs(2.771008),.,18,2)}$$
$$= 0.012594$$

Example 6.6.5

Plan the task.

$$H_0 : \beta_1 = \beta_2 = \beta_3 = 0$$
$$H_1 : \text{At least one Location main effect is not 0.}$$

Compute the statistics.

p-value = 0.00038. See the Location test above.

Apply the results.

Since the *p*-value < 0.05, reject H_0. There is sufficient evidence to reject the claim that the mean work attitude score is the same at all locations. At least two of the location mean scores are significantly different.

The least-squares means for the Central, North, and South locations are below. The South location has the highest mean score.

$$\hat{\mu}_{.1} = \frac{1}{2}(51.4 + 47.5) = 49.45$$

$$\hat{\mu}_{.2} = \frac{1}{2}(54.2 + 51.333333333) = 52.766666667$$

$$\hat{\mu}_{.3} = \frac{1}{2}(57.2 + 55) = 56.1$$

Next are the comparison tests using Tukey-adjusted *p*-values. The Central and North locations have means that are significantly less than the highest mean. (The Central and North locations have means that are not significantly different from each other.)

$$H_0 : \mu_{\cdot 1} - \mu_{\cdot 2} = 0$$
$$H_1 : \mu_{\cdot 1} - \mu_{\cdot 2} \neq 0$$

$$t \text{ Value} = \frac{\hat{\mu}_{\cdot 1} - \hat{\mu}_{\cdot 2}}{\sqrt{\dfrac{MSE(Error)}{a^2}}\sqrt{\displaystyle\sum_{i=1}^{a}\frac{1}{n_{i1}} + \sum_{i=1}^{a}\frac{1}{n_{i2}}}} = \frac{49.45 - 52.766666667}{\sqrt{\dfrac{6.22037}{2^2}}\sqrt{\left(\dfrac{1}{5}+\dfrac{1}{2}\right)+\left(\dfrac{1}{5}+\dfrac{1}{3}\right)}} = -2.39488$$

$$p\text{-value} = P\left(Q \geq \sqrt{2}\left|t \text{ Value}\right|\right)$$
$$= 1\text{-probmc('range',sqrt(2)*abs(-2.39488),.,18,3)}$$
$$= 0.06801$$

$$H_0 : \mu_{\cdot 1} - \mu_{\cdot 3} = 0$$
$$H_1 : \mu_{\cdot 1} - \mu_{\cdot 3} \neq 0$$

$$t \text{ Value} = \frac{\hat{\mu}_{\cdot 1} - \hat{\mu}_{\cdot 3}}{\sqrt{\dfrac{MSE(Error)}{a^2}}\sqrt{\displaystyle\sum_{i=1}^{a}\frac{1}{n_{i1}} + \sum_{i=1}^{a}\frac{1}{n_{i3}}}} = \frac{49.45 - 56.1}{\sqrt{\dfrac{6.22037}{2^2}}\sqrt{\left(\dfrac{1}{5}+\dfrac{1}{2}\right)+\left(\dfrac{1}{5}+\dfrac{1}{4}\right)}} = -4.97273$$

$$p\text{-value} = P\left(Q \geq \sqrt{2}\left|t \text{ Value}\right|\right)$$
$$= 1\text{-probmc('range',sqrt(2)*abs(-4.97273),.,18,3)}$$
$$= 0.00028$$

$$H_0 : \mu_{\cdot 2} - \mu_{\cdot 3} = 0$$
$$H_1 : \mu_{\cdot 2} - \mu_{\cdot 3} \neq 0$$

$$t \text{ Value} = \frac{\hat{\mu}_{\cdot 2} - \hat{\mu}_{\cdot 3}}{\sqrt{\dfrac{MSE(Error)}{a^2}}\sqrt{\displaystyle\sum_{i=1}^{a}\frac{1}{n_{i2}} + \sum_{i=1}^{a}\frac{1}{n_{i3}}}} = \frac{52.766666667 - 56.1}{\sqrt{\dfrac{6.22037}{2^2}}\sqrt{\left(\dfrac{1}{3}+\dfrac{1}{5}\right)+\left(\dfrac{1}{4}+\dfrac{1}{5}\right)}} = -2.69557$$

$$p\text{-value} = P\left(Q \geq \sqrt{2}\left|t \text{ Value}\right|\right)$$
$$= 1\text{-probmc('range',sqrt(2)*abs(-2.69557),.,18,3)}$$
$$= 0.03750$$

6.3.11.3 Linear Models Task

- **Task Roles**:
  - QOL is assigned to the Dependent variables role.
  - The Treatment and Sex role is assigned to the Classification variables role.
- **Model**: The model includes Gender and Location main effects and a Gender*Location interaction effect.
- **Post Hoc Tests > Least Squares:**
  - Comparisons for Gender, Location, and Gender*Location are selected.
  - **All pairwise differences** is selected.
  - **Tukey** adjustment is selected.
- **Plots > Means**: Plots for main effects and two-way effects are selected.

6.3.12 Task Output, Interpretation, and Analysis for Example 6.6

6.3.12.1 Output

Output 6.11 Linear Models Output for Example 6.6

The GLM Procedure

Class Level Information		
Class	**Levels**	**Values**
Gender	2	F M
Location	3	Central North South

❶

Number of Observations Read	24
Number of Observations Used	24

❷

Dependent Variable: Work   Work ❸

Source	DF	Sum of Squares	Mean Square	F Value	Pr > F
Model	5	187.9916667	37.5983333	6.04	0.0019
Error	18	111.9666667	6.2203704		
Corrected Total	23	299.9583333			

❹

R-Square	Coeff Var	Root MSE	Work Mean
0.626726	4.665441	2.494067	53.45833

❺   ❻

Source	DF	Type I SS	Mean Square	F Value	Pr > F
Gender	1	26.1361111	26.1361111	4.20	0.0552
Location	2	159.3425095	79.6712547	12.81	0.0003
Gender*Location	2	2.5130461	1.2565230	0.20	0.8189

Source	DF	Type III SS	Mean Square	F Value	Pr > F
Gender	1	47.7630363	47.7630363	7.68	0.0126
Location	2	156.4663674	78.2331837	12.58	0.0004
Gender*Location	2	2.5130461	1.2565230	0.20	0.8189

❼

Least-Squares Means ❽
Adjustment for Multiple Comparisons: Tukey-Kramer

	Gender	Work LSMEAN	H0:LSMean1=LSMean2 Pr > |t|	
❾	F	54.2666667	0.0126	❿
	M	51.2777778		

Location	Work LSMEAN	LSMEAN Number	
Central	49.4500000	1	
North	52.7666667	2	
South	56.1000000	3	⓫

Least Squares Means for effect Location **Pr > |t| for H0: LSMean(i)=LSMean(j)** **Dependent Variable: Work**			
i/j	1	2	3
1		0.0680	0.0003
2	0.0680		0.0375
3	0.0003	0.0375	

⓬

⓬

Gender	Location	Work LSMEAN	LSMEAN Number
F	Central	51.4000000	1
F	North	54.2000000	2
F	South	57.2000000	3
M	Central	47.5000000	4
M	North	51.3333333	5
M	South	55.0000000	6

⓭

\multicolumn{7}{l}{**Least Squares Means for effect Gender*Location**}						
\multicolumn{7}{l}{**Pr > |t| for H0: LSMean(i)=LSMean(j)**}						
\multicolumn{7}{l}{**Dependent Variable: Work**}						
i/j	**1**	**2**	**3**	**4**	**5**	**6**
1		0.5043	0.0181	0.4505	1.0000	0.3063
2	0.5043		0.4322	0.0469	0.6245	0.9964
3	0.0181	0.4322		0.0023	0.0459	0.7734
4	0.4505	0.0469	0.0023		0.5585	0.0277
5	1.0000	0.6245	0.0459	0.5585		0.4196
6	0.3063	0.9964	0.7734	0.0277	0.4196	

Means plot of Work by Gender ⓮

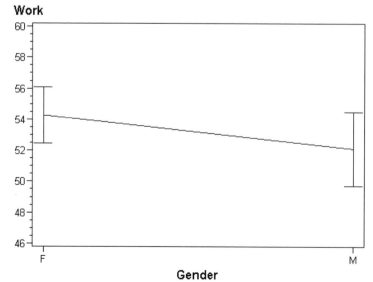

Means plot of Work by Location ⓯

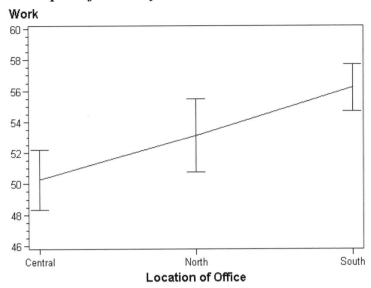

Means plot of Work by Gender and Location ⓰

6.3.12.2 Interpretation

❶ Independent variables are: Gender with $a = 2$ and levels F and M, Location with $b = 3$, and levels Central, North, and South.

❷ $n_{..} = 24$

❸ Dependent variable is Work. Its variable label is also Work.

❹ ANOVA table for the test of the full model

❺ Coefficient of Determination $R^2 = 0.626726$

❻ $\bar{y}_{...} = 53.45833$

❼ *p*-values for the tests of the Gender and Location main effects and the Gender*Location interaction effect

❽ Beginning of the least-squares means output. The Tukey method is used to adjust the *p*-values. The name Tukey-Kramer is used when the data is unbalanced.

❾ The females have the highest mean at 54.2666667.

❿ *p*-values for the least squares comparison of the Gender means.

⓫ Among the three locations, the South location has the highest mean at 56.1.

⓬ Row and variable with the *p*-values for the three pair-wise comparisons involving the South mean. Row and variable have the same values.

⓭ Least-squares output for treatment means.

⓮ Means plot for the Gender main effects.

⓯ Means plot for the Location main effects.

⓰ Means plot for the Gender*Location two-way effects.

6.3.12.3 Analysis

Example 6.6.1

$H_0 : \mu_{11} = \mu_{12} = \mu_{13} = \mu_{21} = \mu_{22} = \mu_{23}$

H_1 : At least two means are not equal.

p-value = 0.0019. See ❹ in Output 6.11.

Since the *p*-value < 0.05, reject H_0. There is sufficient evidence to reject the claim that the mean responses are the same for all populations associated with the treatments. At least two of the treatment-sample means are significantly different.

Example 6.6.2

$H_0 : (\alpha\beta)_{11} = (\alpha\beta)_{12} = (\alpha\beta)_{13} = (\alpha\beta)_{21} = (\alpha\beta)_{22} = (\alpha\beta)_{23} = 0$

H_1 : At least one interaction effect is not 0.

p-value = 0. 8189. See ❼ in Output 6.11.

Since the *p*-value > 0.05, fail to reject H_0. There is not sufficient evidence to reject the claim that there is no interaction between the types of gender and location. There is no significant interaction.

Example 6.6.3

There is no significant interaction.

Example 6.6.4

$H_0 : \alpha_1 = \alpha_2 = 0$

H_1 : At least one Gender main effect is not 0.

p-value = 0. 0126. See ❼ in Output 6.11.

Since the *p*-value < 0.05, reject H_0. There is sufficient evidence to reject the claim that the mean work attitude score is the same for females and males. The mean scores for the females and the males are significantly different.

Females have the higher mean score. See ❾ in Output 6.11.

Example 6.6.5

$H_0 : \beta_1 = \beta_2 = \beta_3 = 0$

$H_1 :$ At least one Location main effect is not 0.

p-value = 0. 0004. See ❼ in Output 6.11.

Since the *p*-value < 0.05, reject H_0. There is sufficient evidence to reject the claim that the mean work attitude score is the same at all locations. At least two of the location mean scores are significantly different.

The South location has the highest mean score. See ⓫ in Output 6.11. The mean score for the South location is significantly higher than the mean scores for the Central and North locations. See ⓬ in Output 6.11.

Example 6.6.6
See Output 6.11.

6.3.13 Three-Factor ANOVA

The three-factor ANOVA is a straightforward extension of the two-factor ANOVA.

6.3.13.1 Population Model

Let A represent a factor with *a* levels, B represent a factor with *b* levels, and C represent a factor with *c* levels. The model for the three-factor factorial analysis of variance has *abc* populations of responses. Each response *y* is equal to its population mean plus its deviation from the mean:

$y = \mu_{ijk} + \varepsilon$, where $i = 1,\ldots,a$, $j = 1,\ldots,b$, and $k = 1,\ldots,c$.

- μ_{ijk} is the mean of the population associated with the treatment formed by the ith level of A, the jth level of B, and the kth level of C.
- The responses in each population are assumed to be normally distributed with mean μ_{ijk} and unknown variance σ^2. The variance is assumed to be the same for each population.
- ε is the deviation from the mean. As a consequence of the previous bullet, the errors ($y - \mu_{ijk}$) of each population are assumed to be normally distributed with mean 0 and the variance σ^2.

The factorial ANOVA investigates how the factors contribute to the values of the population means. The three-factor model expresses each population mean as the sum of the overall mean, the main effects, the two-factor interaction effects, and that a three-way interaction effect. All the terms are assumed to be fixed unknown constants.

$$\mu_{ijk} = \mu + \alpha_i + \beta_j + \gamma_k + (\alpha\beta)_{ij} + (\alpha\gamma)_{ik} + (\beta\gamma)_{jk} + (\alpha\beta\gamma)_{ijk}$$

- μ is the *overall mean* of the abc populations.

- α_i, β_j, and γ_k represent the main effects for factors A, B, and C, respectively. The model assumes that the effects are fixed values and that the sum of the main effects for each factor equals 0.

- $(\alpha\beta)_{ij}$, $(\alpha\gamma)_{ik}$, and $(\beta\gamma)_{jk}$ represent the effects for the two-factor interactions A*B, A*C, and B*C, respectively. The model assumes that the effects are fixed values and, for the effects of each two-factor interaction, the sum over either subscript equals 0.

- $(\alpha\beta\gamma)_{ijk}$ represents the effects for the three-factor interaction A*B*C. The model assumes that the effects are fixed values and the sum of the effects over any subscript equals 0.

6.3.13.2 Null and Alternative Hypotheses

Test of the Full Model
The first hypothesis test determines if there are any differences among the population means.

$H_0 : \mu_{111} = \mu_{112} = \ldots = \mu_{abc}$
$H_1 :$ At least two means are not equal.

- If the null hypothesis is not rejected, the tests on the interactions and the main effects will not result in rejected null hypotheses.

- If the null hypothesis is rejected, the next step is to consider the test of the three-way interaction effects.

Test of the Three-Way Interaction Effects
$H_0 : (\alpha\beta\gamma)_{111} = (\alpha\beta\gamma)_{112} = \ldots = (\alpha\beta\gamma)_{abc} = 0$
$H_1 :$ At least one interaction effect is not 0.

- If the null hypothesis is not rejected, the next step is to consider the tests of the two-way interaction effects.

- If the null hypothesis is rejected, the next step is to examine the treatment means using least-squares means.

Tests of the Two-Way Interaction Effects

$H_0 : (\alpha\beta)_{11} = (\alpha\beta)_{12} = \ldots = (\alpha\beta)_{ab} = 0$

H_1 : At least one interaction effect is not 0.

$H_0 : (\alpha\gamma)_{11} = (\alpha\gamma)_{12} = \ldots = (\alpha\gamma)_{ac} = 0$

H_1 : At least one interaction effect is not 0.

$H_0 : (\beta\gamma)_{11} = (\beta\gamma)_{12} = \ldots = (\beta\gamma)_{bc} = 0$

H_1 : At least one interaction effect is not 0.

- If all three null hypotheses are not rejected, the next step is to consider the tests of the main effects of the three factors.
- If any of the three null hypotheses are rejected, the next step is to:
  - Examine the two-factor means associated with the factors involved in significant interaction.
  - Consider the tests of the main effects of any factor not involved in any significant interaction.

Tests of the Main Effects

$H_0 : \alpha_1 = \alpha_2 = \ldots = \alpha_a = 0$

H_1 : At least one A main effect is not 0.

$H_0 : \beta_1 = \beta_2 = \ldots = \beta_b = 0$

H_1 : At least one B main effect is not 0.

$H_0 : \gamma_1 = \gamma_2 = \ldots = \gamma_c = 0$

H_1 : At least one C main effect is not 0.

- If a null hypothesis is not rejected, then one cannot conclude that there are any differences among these factor-level means. The analysis of this factor ends at this point.
- If a null hypothesis is rejected, the next step is to examine the possible differences with multiple-comparison tests.

6.3.14 Example 6.7: Three-Way ANOVA

6.3.14.1 Investigating a New Headache Drug

A clinical trial is designed to investigate the effectiveness of a new drug for the treatment of headaches.

In the trial, the new drug is administered at two dosages: 5 milligrams and 10 milligrams. These are denoted as N05 and N10, respectively. The new drug is compared to a standard drug therapy (ST) and a placebo (PL). The superficial properties of the treatments are identical.

Patients are randomly assigned to receive one of the four treatments. A patient's sex and severity of disability is recorded. The severity is recorded as mild, moderate, or severe.

After one month, the patients complete a quality-of-life (QOL) questionnaire. The QOL scores are on a 100-point scale. The standardized mean score is 50. Higher scores indicate a better quality of life.

Example 6.7.1

Test the claim that the mean responses are the same for all populations associated with the treatments. Let $\alpha = 0.05$. If the claim is not rejected, the analysis is complete.

Example 6.7.2

If the mean responses in Example 6.7.1 are not all equal, test the claim that there is no three-way interaction between treatment, sex, and baseline severity. Let $\alpha = 0.05$. If there is interaction, use the Tukey-adjusted least-squares means to determine which treatment-sex-baseline combination has the highest mean quality-of-life score. What combinations, if any, have means that are not significantly different from the highest?

Example 6.7.3

If there is no three-way interaction, test the claim that there is no significant two-way interaction:

- Between treatment and sex. Let $\alpha = 0.05$. If there is interaction, use the Tukey-adjusted least-squares means to determine which treatment-sex combination has the highest mean quality-of-life score. What combinations, if any, have means that are not significantly different from the highest?

- Between treatment and baseline severity. Let $\alpha = 0.05$. If there is interaction, use the Tukey-adjusted least-squares means to determine which treatment-baseline combination has the highest mean quality-of-life score. What combinations, if any, have means that are not significantly different from the highest?

- Between sex and baseline severity. Let $\alpha = 0.05$. If there is interaction, use the Tukey-adjusted least-squares means to determine which sex-baseline combination has the highest mean quality-of-life score. What combinations, if any, have means that are not significantly different from the highest?

Example 6.7.4

For any factor not involved in a significant interaction, test the claim that the mean quality-of-life score is the same at all its levels. Let $\alpha = 0.05$. If the claim is rejected, use the Tukey-adjusted least-squares means to determine which level has the highest mean quality-of-life score. What levels, if any, have means that are not significantly different from the highest?

Example 6.7.5

Construct main effects plots and a two-way effects plot.

The results are below. This is the Headache data set from Appendix. Variables that are not part of this example are hidden.

	Treatment	Sex	QOL	Baseline
	headache (read-only)			
1	N10	F	59	Severe
2	N05	F	42	Severe
3	ST	F	36	Moderate
4	N10	M	52	Severe
5	N10	F	59	Severe
6	ST	M	65	Mild
7	N10	M	55	Moderate
8	PL	M	37	Mild
9	N10	F	73	Mild
10	PL	F	28	Moderate
11	N05	M	72	Moderate
12	ST	M	47	Moderate
13	ST	F	33	Severe
14	ST	F	44	Moderate
15	N10	M	61	Mild

The quality-of-life responses are in the QOL variable, the dependent variable. The treatment classification values N05, N10, PL, and ST are in the independent variable Treatment. The F and M values are in the independent variable Sex. The mild, moderate, and severe disability levels are in the Baseline independent variable.

- QOL is the dependent variable.
- Treatment, Sex, and Baseline are classification variables.

Let Treatment be factor A, Sex be factor B, and Baseline factor C.

- The subscripts $i = 1, 2, 3,$ and 4 refer to the Treatment levels N05, N10, PL, and ST, respectively.
- The subscripts $j = 1$ and 2 refer to the Sex levels F and M, respectively.
- The subscripts $k = 1, 2,$ and 3 refer to the Baseline levels Mild, Moderate, and Severe, respectively.

The three-factor factorial model is appropriate for this example. All three factors are crossed and interaction might be present.

There are $4 \times 2 \times 3 = 24$ population means:

$$\mu_{ijk} = \mu + \alpha_i + \beta_j + \gamma_k + (\alpha\beta)_{ij} + (\alpha\gamma)_{ik} + (\beta\gamma)_{jk} + (\alpha\beta\gamma)_{ijk} .$$

Main Effects	**Two-Factor Interaction Effects**	**Three-Factor Interaction Effects**
Treatment α_i	Treatment*Sex $(\alpha\beta)_{ij}$	Treatment*Sex*Baseline $(\alpha\beta\gamma)_{ijk}$
Sex β_j	Treatment*Baseline $(\alpha\gamma)_{ik}$	
Baseline γ_k	Sex*Baseline $(\beta\gamma)_{jk}$	

6.3.14.2 Linear Models Task

- **Task Roles**:
  - ○ QOL is assigned to the Dependent variables role.
  - ○ Treatment, Sex, and Baseline are assigned to the Classification variables role.
- **Model**: **Factorial** is selected. The order of the effects and the order of the variables in effects do not matter.
  - ○ Baseline, Sex, and Treatment are main effects.
  - ○ Baseline*Sex, Baseline*Treatment, Sex*Treatment, and Baseline*Sex*Treatment are interaction effects.
- **Post Hoc Tests > Least Squares:**
  - ○ Comparisons for all effects are selected.
  - ○ **All pairwise differences** is selected.
  - ○ **Tukey** adjustment is selected.
- **Plots > Means**: Plots for main effects and two-way effects are selected.

6.3.15 Task Output, Interpretation, and Analysis for Example 6.7

6.3.15.1 Task Output

- The table with the Type I Sum of Squares is not shown.
- Only least squares output for Baseline means and Treatment*Sex means are shown.
- Only means plots for Baseline means and Treatment*Sex means are shown.

Output 6.12 Linear Models Output for Example 6.7

The GLM Procedure

Class Level Information		
Class	**Levels**	**Values**
Treatment	4	N05 N10 PL ST
Sex	2	F M
Baseline	3	Mild Moderate Severe

❶

Number of Observations Read	52
Number of Observations Used	52

❷

Dependent Variable: QOL   Quality of Life ❸

Source	DF	Sum of Squares	Mean Square	F Value	Pr > F	
Model	23	9654.33974	419.75390	8.41	<.0001	❹
Error	28	1398.33333	49.94048			
Corrected Total	51	11052.67308				

R-Square	Coeff Var	Root MSE	QOL Mean
0.873485	13.91430	7.066858	50.78846

❺   ❻

Source	DF	Type III SS	Mean Square	F Value	Pr > F	
Baseline	2	1945.190160	972.595080	19.48	<.0001	
Sex	1	94.815735	94.815735	1.90	0.1792	❼
Treatment	3	4959.249777	1653.083259	33.10	<.0001	
Sex*Baseline	2	75.165955	37.582977	0.75	0.4805	
Treatment*Baseline	6	172.220098	28.703350	0.57	0.7470	❽
Treatment*Sex	3	701.160980	233.720327	4.68	0.0090	
Treatme*Sex*Baseline	6	332.097220	55.349537	1.11	0.3825	❾

Least Squares Means ❿
Adjustment for Multiple Comparisons: Tukey-Kramer

Location	QOL LSMEAN	LSMEAN Number	
Mild	57.3541667	1	⓫
Moderate	47.2083333	2	
Severe	39.7708333	3	

Least Squares Means for effect Baseline Pr > |t| for H0: LSMean(i)=LSMean(j) Dependent Variable: QOL			
i/j	1	2	3
1		0.0011	<.0001
2	0.0011		0.0190
3	<.0001	0.0190	

⑫

⑫

Treatment	Sex	QOL LSMEAN	LSMEAN Number
N05	F	50.8888889	1
N05	M	57.9444444	2
N10	F	65.4444444	3
N10	M	57.4444444	4
PL	F	30.6666667	5
PL	M	32.0000000	6
ST	F	39.5000000	7
ST	M	51.0000000	8

⑬

Least Squares Means for effect Treatment*Sex Pr > |t| for H0: LSMean(i)=LSMean(j) Dependent Variable: QOL								
i/j	1	2	3	4	5	6	7	8
1		0.5239	0.0078	0.6114	0.0025	0.0054	0.0978	1.0000
2	0.5239		0.4483	1.0000	<.0001	<.0001	0.0011	0.7493
3	0.0078	0.4483		0.3689	<.0001	<.0001	<.0001	0.0449
4	0.6114	1.0000	0.3689		<.0001	0.0001	0.0016	0.8112
5	0.0025	<.0001	<.0001	<.0001		1.0000	0.5779	0.0096
6	0.0054	<.0001	<.0001	0.0001	1.0000		0.7510	0.0182
7	0.0978	0.0011	<.0001	0.0016	0.5779	0.7510		0.2278
8	1.0000	0.7493	0.0449	0.8112	0.0096	0.0182	0.2278	

⑭

⑭

Means plot of QOL by Baseline ⓑ

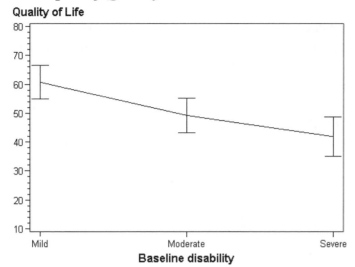

Means plot of QOL by Sex and Treatment ⓰

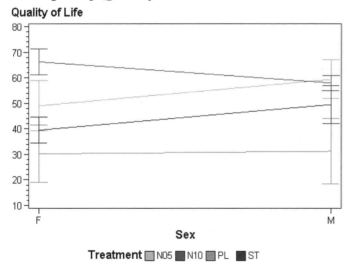

6.3.15.2 Interpretation

❶ Independent variables are: Treatment with $a = 4$ and levels N05, N10, PL, and ST; Sex with $b = 2$ and levels F and M; Baseline with $c = 3$ and levels Mild, Moderate, and Severe.

❷ $n_{...} = 52$

❸ Dependent variable is QOL. Its variable label is "Quality of Life."

❹ ANOVA table for the test of the full model

❺ Coefficient of Determination $R^2 = 0.873485$

❻ $\bar{y}_{...} = 50.78846$

❼ p-values for the tests of the main effects Baseline, Sex, and Treatment

❽   *p*-values for the tests of two-factor interaction: Sex*Baseline, Treatment*Baseline, and Treatment*Sex

❾   *p*-value for the test of the three-factor interaction: Treatment*Sex*Baseline

❿   Beginning of the least-squares means output. The Tukey method is used to adjust the *p*-values. The name Tukey-Kramer is used when the data is unbalanced.

⓫   Among the Baseline levels, Mild has the highest mean at 57.3541667.

⓬   Row and variable with the *p*-values for the three pair-wise comparisons involving the Mild mean. Row and variable have the same values.

⓭   Among the eight Treatment*Sex means, the N10-F mean is highest at 65.4444444.

⓮   Row and variable with the *p*-values for the three pair-wise comparisons involving the N10-F mean. Row and variable have the same values.

⓯   Means plot for the Baseline main effects.

⓰   Means plot for the Treatment*Sex two-way effects.

6.3.15.3 Analysis

Example 6.7.1

$H_0 : \mu_{111} = \mu_{112} = \cdots = \mu_{423}$

H_1 : At least two means are not equal.

p-value < 0.0001. See ❹ in Output 6.12.

Since the *p*-value < 0.05, reject H_0. There is sufficient evidence to reject the claim that the mean responses are the same for all populations associated with the treatments. At least two of the treatment-sample means are significantly different.

Example 6.7.2

$H_0 : (\alpha\beta\gamma)_{111} = (\alpha\beta\gamma)_{112} = \cdots = (\alpha\beta\gamma)_{423} = 0$

H_1 : At least one interaction effect is not 0.

p-value = 0. 0.3825. See ❾ in Output 6.12.

Since the *p*-value > 0.05, fail to reject H_0. There is not sufficient evidence to reject the claim that there is no three-way interaction between treatment, sex, and baseline severity. There is no significant three-way interaction.

Example 6.7.3a

$H_0 : (\alpha\beta)_{11} = (\alpha\beta)_{12} = \cdots = (\alpha\beta)_{42} = 0$

H_1 : At least one interaction effect is not 0.

p-value = 0.0090. See ❽ in Output 6.12.

Since the *p*-value < 0.05, reject H_0. There is sufficient evidence to reject the claim that there is no significant two-way interaction between treatment and sex. There is significant two-way interaction between treatment and sex.

The N10-F mean is highest at 65.4444444. See ⓭ in Output 6.12. The N05-M and the N10-M means are not significantly different from the N10-F mean. See ⓮ in Output 6.12.

Example 6.7.3b

$$H_0 : (\alpha\gamma)_{11} = (\alpha\gamma)_{12} = \cdots = (\alpha\gamma)_{43} = 0$$

H_1 : At least one interaction effect is not 0.

p-value = 0.7470. See ❽ in Output 6.12.

Since the p-value > 0.05, fail to reject H_0. There is not sufficient evidence to reject the claim that there is no significant two-way interaction between treatment and baseline severity. There is no significant two-way interaction between treatment and baseline severity.

Example 6.7.3c

$$H_0 : (\beta\gamma)_{111} = (\beta\gamma)_{112} = \cdots = (\beta\gamma)_{23} = 0$$

H_1 : At least one interaction effect is not 0.

p-value = 0.4805. See ❽ in Output 6.12.

Since the p-value > 0.05, fail to reject H_0. There is not sufficient evidence to reject the claim that there is no significant two-way interaction between sex and baseline severity. There is no significant two-way interaction between sex and baseline severity.

Example 6.6.4

$$H_0 : \gamma_1 = \gamma_2 = \gamma_3 = 0$$

H_1 : At least one Baseline main effect is not 0.

p-value < 0.0001. See ❼ in Output 6.12.

Since the p-value < 0.05, reject H_0. There is sufficient evidence to reject the claim that the mean quality-of-life score is the same for all baseline levels. At least two of the baseline means are significantly different.

Patients with a mild baseline severity have the highest mean 57.3541667. See ⓫ in Output 6.12. Patients in the other two groups have means that are significantly lower. See ⓬ in Output 6.12.

Example 6.7.5

See Output 6.12.

6.4 Nonparametric One-Way Analysis of Variance

The nonparametric one-way analysis of variance (Nonparametric One-Way ANOVA) task is used to determine whether two or more populations have the same median responses. In terms of statistical notation, the null hypothesis asserts that $\theta_1 = \theta_2 = \cdots = \theta_k$, where k is the number of populations being studied.

Two nonparametric tests are presented here: the Kruskal-Wallis Test and the Median One-Way ANOVA. Both tests are analogs to the One-Way ANOVA discussed in Section 6.2. Also, both tests are extensions of the two-sample tests discussed in Section 5.4. The Kruskal-Wallis Test is an extension of the Wilcoxon Rank-Sum Test. The Median One-Way ANOVA is an extension of the Median Two-Sample Test.

The tests are often considered when the combination of an insufficiently large sample size and a lack of normality in the data—generally outliers and skewness—cause the one-way analysis of variance to be ineffective.

The subscripts $1, 2, ..., k$ correspond to the groups that appear 1st, 2nd, ..., k^{th} (last) in the data set. Output order and the subscript order are the same. The sample statistics produced by the Nonparametric One-Way ANOVA task are listed in the order that the groups appear in the data.

Input is a column of numerical data values—the dependent variable—and a column of classification values—the independent variable. The dependent variable contains k samples. The sample membership of each value is identified by the corresponding value in the independent variable.

6.4.1 Hypothesis Tests on Population Medians

The Nonparametric One-Way ANOVA tests the null hypothesis that k population medians are equal against the alternative hypothesis that at least one pair of medians is not equal.

$H_0 : \theta_1 = \theta_2 = \cdots = \theta_k$

H_1 : At least one pair of medians is not equal.

6.4.1.1 Kruskal-Wallis Test

The Kruskal-Wallis Test assumes that each sample is from a continuous population and that the shapes of the population distributions are the same.

The test is based on the ranks of the values in the combined samples. Using ranks instead of the actual values reduces the effect of outliers.

- Let n_i be the number of values in the sample i where $i = 1, 2, ..., k$.

- Let $n_.$ be the total number of values, $n_. = n_1 + n_2 + ... + n_k$.

- All $n_.$ values are ranked smallest to largest without regard to sample membership. Average ranks are used in case of ties.

  - The sum of all ranks is $\dfrac{n_.(n_. + 1)}{2}$.

  - The mean of all rank is $\dfrac{(n_. + 1)}{2}$.

- T_i and $\dfrac{T_i}{n_i}$ are the sum and mean, respectively, of the ranks in sample i.

Under H_0, it is assumed that the population medians are equal, $\theta_1 = \theta_2 = \cdots = \theta_k$. In which case, all T_i/n_i are expected to be equal. Furthermore, it is expected that $T_i/n_i = (n_. + 1)/2$ for each sample. Therefore, each T_i is expected to be $n_i(n_. + 1)/2$.

The test statistic is a measure of the difference between the sums of the sample ranks T_i and their expected values. The test statistic is:

$$\text{Chi-Square} = \frac{\sum_{i=1}^{k} \frac{1}{n_i}\left(T_i - \frac{n_i(n_. + 1)}{2}\right)^2}{s_R^2}, \text{ where } s_R^2 \text{ is the variance of all ranks.}$$

The definition of the chi square p-value is in Table 6.14. The random variable Q represents a future value of the test statistic and follows the chi-square distribution with $k-1$ degrees of freedom.

Table 6.14 *p*-Values for Kruskal-Wallis Chi-Square Statistic

Hypotheses	*p* - value =	Expression
$H_0 : \theta_1 = \theta_2 = \cdots = \theta_k$ H_1 : At least one pair of medians are not equal.	$P(Q \geq \text{Chi-Square})$	1 - probchi(Chi-Square, $k-1$)

6.4.1.2 Median One-Way ANOVA

The Median One-Way ANOVA assumes only that each sample is from a continuous population. The test is based on proportions of values being above the overall sample median. The effect of outliers is eliminated.

- Let n_i be the number of value in sample i where $i = 1, 2, \ldots, k$.
- Let $n_.$ be the total number of values, $n_. = n_1 + n_2 + \ldots + n_k$.
- Let the overall median of all $n_.$ values be $\hat{\theta}$.
- T_i and $\frac{T_i}{n_i}$ are the number and proportion, respectively, of values above $\hat{\theta}$ in sample i.
- Let $T_.$ be the total number of values above $\hat{\theta}$, $T_. = T_1 + T_2 + \ldots + T_k$. $T_./n_.$ is the proportion of values above $\hat{\theta}$.

In theory, $T_./n_.$ is expected to equal 0.5 when $n_.$ is an even number and to equal $0.5(n_. - 1)/n_.$ when $n_.$ is an odd number. The actual proportions might be lower when multiple values in the combined sample equal $\hat{\theta}$.

Under H_0, it is assumed that $\theta_1 = \theta_2 = \cdots = \theta_k$. The statistic $\hat{\theta}$ is the estimate of the common population median. In which case, all T_i/n_i are expected to be equal. Furthermore, it is expected that $T_i/n_i = T./n.$ for each sample. Therefore, each T_i is expected to be $n_i T./n.$.

The test statistic is a measure of the difference between the sums T_i and their expected values. The test statistic is:

$$\text{Chi-Square} = \frac{\sum_{i=1}^{k} \dfrac{1}{n_i}\left(T_i - \dfrac{n_i T.}{n.}\right)^2}{\left(\dfrac{n.}{n. - 1}\right)\left(\dfrac{T.}{n.}\right)\left(1 - \dfrac{T.}{n.}\right)}$$

The definitions of the *p*-values are same as in Table 6.14.

6.4.1.3   Decision and Conclusions

The formal decision and concluding sentence do not change from the one-sample tests discussed in Chapter 4, "Inferences from One Sample." The concluding observation depends on the particular statistics involved in the test.

- If the *p*-value is small, the data agrees with H_1. If the *p*-value is less than the significance level, the risk of making a Type I error is acceptable. Therefore, the *p*-value decision rule is the following:

    If the *p*-value $< \alpha$, reject H_0. Otherwise, do not reject H_0.

    Since a hypothesis test begins with the assumption that H_0 is true, concluding a hypothesis test requires one of the following formal statements:

    - Reject H_0.
    - Do not reject H_0.

- When the claim is equivalent to the null hypothesis, the concluding sentence uses the word *reject*. The concluding sentence becomes an expanded version of the formal decision.

    When the claim is equivalent to the alternative hypothesis, the concluding sentence uses the word *support*. If the data supports the rejection of H_0, the data supports H_1. If the data does not support rejection of H_0, the data cannot support H_1.

Table 6.15 Concluding Sentences

Formal Statistical Decision	Claim stated as H_0	Claim stated as H_1
Reject H_0.	There is sufficient evidence to reject the claim that ... (claim in words).	There is sufficient evidence to support the claim that ... (claim in words).
Do not reject H_0.	There is not sufficient evidence to reject the claim that ... (claim in words).	There is not sufficient evidence to support the claim that ... (claim in words).

Table 6.16 Concluding Observations

Reject H_0.	At least two sample medians are significantly different.
Do not reject H_0.	None of the sample medians is significantly different.

6.4.2 Summary of the Kruskal-Wallis Test

Plan the experiment.

$H_0 : \theta_1 = \theta_2 = \cdots = \theta_k$

$H_1 :$ At least one pair of medians are not equal.

The significance level is α.

Task computes the statistics.

<table>
<tr><th colspan="7">Wilcoxon Scores (Rank Sums) for Variable Dependent
Classified by Variable Independent</th></tr>
<tr><th>Independent</th><th>N</th><th>Sum of
Scores</th><th>Expected
Under H0</th><th>Std Dev
Under H0</th><th>Mean
Score</th></tr>
<tr><td>value occurring first</td><td>n_1</td><td>T_1</td><td>$\dfrac{n_1(n_.+1)}{2}$</td><td>$\sqrt{\dfrac{n_1(n_.-n_1)}{n_.}s_R^2}$</td><td>$\dfrac{T_1}{n_1}$</td></tr>
<tr><td>value occurring second</td><td>n_2</td><td>T_2</td><td>$\dfrac{n_2(n_.+1)}{2}$</td><td>$\sqrt{\dfrac{n_2(n_.-n_2)}{n_.}s_R^2}$</td><td>$\dfrac{T_2}{n_2}$</td></tr>
<tr><td>⋮</td><td>⋮</td><td>⋮</td><td>⋮</td><td>⋮</td><td>⋮</td></tr>
<tr><td>value occurring last</td><td>n_k</td><td>T_k</td><td>$\dfrac{n_k(n_.+1)}{2}$</td><td>$\sqrt{\dfrac{n_k(n_.-n_k)}{n_.}s_R^2}$</td><td>$\dfrac{T_k}{n_k}$</td></tr>
<tr><td colspan="6" align="center">Average scores were used for ties.</td></tr>
</table>

<table>
<tr><th colspan="2">Kruskal-Wallis Test</th></tr>
<tr><td>Chi-Square</td><td>$\dfrac{\sum\limits_{i=1}^{k}\dfrac{1}{n_i}\left(T_i-\dfrac{n_i(n_.+1)}{2}\right)^2}{s_R^2}$</td></tr>
<tr><td>DF</td><td>$k-1$</td></tr>
<tr><td>Pr > Chi-Square</td><td>p-value</td></tr>
</table>

Apply the results.

If the p-value $\le \alpha$, reject H_0. Otherwise, do not reject H_0.

- Reject H_0. There is sufficient evidence to reject/support the claim that ... (complete claim). At least two sample medians are significantly different.

- Do not reject H_0. There is not sufficient evidence to reject/support the claim that ...(complete claim). None of the sample medians is significantly different.

6.4.3 Summary of the Median One-Way ANOVA

Plan the experiment.

$H_0 : \theta_1 = \theta_2 = \cdots = \theta_k$

$H_1 :$ At least one pair of medians are not equal.

The significance level is α.

Task computes the statistics.

Median Scores (Number of Points Above Median) for Variable *Dependent* Classified by Variable *Independent*					
Independent	N	Sum of Scores	Expected Under H0	Std Dev Under H0	Mean Score
value occurring first	n_1	T_1	$\dfrac{n_1 T_.}{n_.}$	$\sqrt{n_1\left(\dfrac{n_.-n_1}{n_.-1}\right)\left(\dfrac{T_.}{n_.}\right)\left(1-\dfrac{T_.}{n_.}\right)}$	$\dfrac{T_1}{n_1}$
value occurring second	n_2	T_2	$\dfrac{n_2 T_.}{n_.}$	$\sqrt{n_2\left(\dfrac{n_.-n_1}{n_.-1}\right)\left(\dfrac{T_.}{n_.}\right)\left(1-\dfrac{T_.}{n_.}\right)}$	$\dfrac{T_2}{n_2}$
$\vdots$	$\vdots$	$\vdots$	$\vdots$	$\vdots$	$\vdots$
value occurring last	n_k	T_k	$\dfrac{n_k T_.}{n_.}$	$\sqrt{n_k\left(\dfrac{n_.-n_1}{n_.-1}\right)\left(\dfrac{T_.}{n_.}\right)\left(1-\dfrac{T_.}{n_.}\right)}$	$\dfrac{T_k}{n_k}$
Average scores were used for ties.					

Median One-Way Analysis	
Chi-Square	$\dfrac{\displaystyle\sum_{i=1}^{k}\dfrac{1}{n_i}\left(T_i-\dfrac{n_i T_.}{n_.}\right)^2}{\left(\dfrac{n_.}{n_.-1}\right)\left(\dfrac{T_.}{n_.}\right)\left(1-\dfrac{T_.}{n_.}\right)}$
DF	$k-1$
Pr > Chi-Square	p-value

Apply the results.

If the *p*-value $\leq \alpha$, reject H_0. Otherwise, do not reject H_0.

- Reject H_0. There is sufficient evidence to reject/support the claim that ... (complete claim). At least two sample medians are significantly different.

- Do not reject H_0. There is not sufficient evidence to reject/support the claim that ...(complete claim). None of the sample medians are significantly different.

6.4.4 Example 6.8: Nonparametric One-Way ANOVA

This example illustrates inference on four population medians. The requested analysis includes the Kruskal-Wallis Test and the Median One-Way ANOVA.

- Both tests are worked out in the "Detailed Solutions" section below.

- The Nonparametric One-Way ANOVA task is discussed in "Instructions for Nonparametric One-Way ANOVA."

- Complete results are in "Task Output, Interpretation, and Analysis for Example 6.8."

In Example 6.8, forty-eight women participate in a study that examines the effectiveness of certain interventions in increasing physical activity. The One-Way ANOVA task is used to test the claim that the mean daily energy expenditure (DEE) is the same for patients receiving advice, assistance, counseling, and no intervention. The claim is rejected with p-value < 0.0001.

Consider a situation where the data contains an outlier. Suppose that observation 47 is 44.83 instead of 34.25. The data is below and the new value 44.83 is in bold.

Advice			Assistance			Counseling			Control		
33.85	33.61	32.62	35.78	34.07	33.34	34.08	34.43	33.92	30.93	32.39	28.95
33.52	31.61	33.75	34.80	33.10	32.61	34.91	35.78	33.24	32.85	31.33	32.07
32.78	31.68	31.44	32.96	32.70	33.88	35.04	35.51	33.56	31.19	32.57	32.39
31.65	32.90	33.47	32.92	35.39	33.39	34.47	35.16	34.50	31.60	**44.83**	31.50

The One-Way ANOVA task is applied to data. The ANOVA table and box-and-whisker plots are below. With the outlier in the data, the claim is not rejected.

Output 6.13 ANOVA Table and Box-and-Whisker Plots from the One-Way ANOVA Task

Source	DF	Sum of Squares	Mean Square	F Value	Pr > F
Model	3	28.0598250	9.3532750	2.06	0.1199
Error	44	200.2159667	4.5503629		
Corrected Total	47	228.2757917			

Daily Energy Expenditure

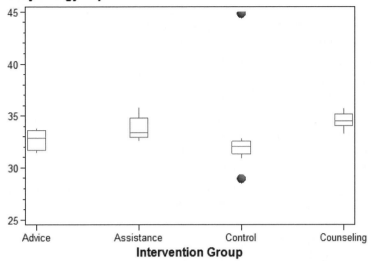

In the Ex06_08 data set, the four classification values in the independent variable Group appear in the following order: Advice, Assistance, Counseling, and Control. The corresponding sample statistics appear in the same order in the Nonparametric One-Way ANOVA output.

In addition, subscripts 1, 2, 3, and 4 correspond to Advice, Assistance, Counseling, and Control, respectively.

$H_0 : \theta_1 = \theta_2 = \theta_3 = \theta_4$

$H_1 :$ At least one pair of medians are not equal.

Example 6.8.1
Use the Kruskal-Wallis Test to test the claim that the DEE medians are the same for patients receiving advice, assistance, counseling, and no intervention. Let $\alpha = 0.05$.

Example 6.8.2
Use the Median One-Way ANOVA to test the claim that the DEE medians are the same for patients receiving advice, assistance, counseling, and no intervention. Let $\alpha = 0.05$.

6.4.4.1   Detailed Solutions

Example 6.8.1
The complete claim is that "the median DEE is the same for patients receiving advice, assistance, counseling, and no intervention." The Kruskal-Wallis Test is applied here.

Table 6.16 Data from Example 6.8 with Ranks

Advice		Assistance		Counseling		Control	
DEE	ranks	DEE	ranks	DEE	ranks	DEE	ranks
33.85	32	35.78	46.5	34.08	36	30.93	2
33.61	30	34.07	35	34.43	37	32.39	12.5
32.62	16	33.34	25	33.92	34	28.95	1
33.52	28	34.8	40	34.91	41	32.85	19
31.61	8	33.1	23	35.78	46.5	31.33	4
33.75	31	32.61	15	33.24	24	32.07	11
32.78	18	32.96	22	35.04	42	31.19	3
31.68	10	32.7	17	35.51	45	32.57	14
31.44	5	33.88	33	33.56	29	32.39	12.5
31.65	9	32.92	21	34.47	38	31.6	7
32.9	20	35.39	44	35.16	43	44.83	48
33.47	27	33.39	26	34.5	39	31.5	6

Plan the task.

$H_0 : \theta_1 = \theta_2 = \theta_3 = \theta_4$

H_1 : At least one pair of medians are not equal.

$\alpha = 0.05$

Compute the statistics.

The data from Example 6.4 is in Table 6.16. The ranks of the DEE data are in ranks.

Below are statistics on the sample ranks:

Advice	Assistance	Counseling	Control
$n_1 = 12$	$n_2 = 12$	$n_3 = 12$	$n_4 = 12$
$T_1 = 234$	$T_2 = 347.5$	$T_3 = 454.5$	$T_4 = 140$
$\dfrac{T_1}{n_1} = 19.5$	$\dfrac{T_2}{n_2} = 28.9583$	$\dfrac{T_3}{n_3} = 37.875$	$\dfrac{T_4}{n_4} = 11.6667$

The mean and variance of all ranks are $\dfrac{(n. + 1)}{2} = \dfrac{48 + 1}{2} = 24.5$ and $s_R^2 = 195.9787$.

The nonparametric sample statistics are summarized in the Wilcoxon scores table below.

Wilcoxon Scores (Rank Sums) for Variable DEE

Classified by Variable Group

PartNo	N	Sum of Scores	Expected Under H0	Std Dev Under H0	Mean Score
Advice	12	234	$\dfrac{12(48+1)}{2}=294$	$\sqrt{\dfrac{12\cdot 36}{48}(195.9787)}=41.9977$	$\dfrac{234}{12}=19.5$
Assistance	12	347.5	$\dfrac{12(48+1)}{2}=294$	$\sqrt{\dfrac{12\cdot 36}{48}(195.9787)}=41.9977$	$\dfrac{347.5}{12}=28.9583$
Counseling	12	140	$\dfrac{12(48+1)}{2}=294$	$\sqrt{\dfrac{12\cdot 36}{48}(195.9787)}=41.9977$	$\dfrac{140}{12}=11.6667$
Control	12	454.5	$\dfrac{12(48+1)}{2}=294$	$\sqrt{\dfrac{12\cdot 36}{48}(195.9787)}=41.9977$	$\dfrac{454.5}{12}=37.875$

$$\text{Chi-Square}=\frac{\sum_{i=1}^{k}n_i\left(\dfrac{T_i}{n_i}-\dfrac{n_.+1}{2}\right)^2}{s_R^2}$$

$$=\left(12(19.5-24.5)^2+12(28.9583-24.5)^2+12(37.875-24.5)^2+12(11.6667-24.5)^2\right)\big/195.9787$$

$$=23.786$$

$$p\text{-value}=P(Q\geq 23.786)=1\text{-probnorm}(23.786,3)=0.000028<0.0001$$

Apply the results.

Since p-value < 0.05, reject H_0. There is sufficient evidence to reject the claim that the median DEE is the same for patients receiving advice, assistance, counseling, and no intervention. At least two sample medians are significantly different.

Example 6.8.2

The complete claim is "the median DEE is the same for patients receiving advice, assistance, counseling, and no intervention." The Median One-Way ANOVA is applied here.

Plan the task.

$H_0 : \theta_1 = \theta_2 = \theta_3 = \theta_4$

$H_1 :$ At least one pair of medians are not equal.

$\alpha = 0.05$

Compute the statistics.

The data from Example 6.8 is in Table 6.17.

- The overall median of the DEE data is $\hat{\theta}=33.29$.

- In the scores column: scores $= 1$, if DEE $> \hat{\theta}=33.29$; otherwise, scores $= 0$.

Table 6.17 Data from Example 6.8 with Scores

Advice		Assistance		Counseling		Control	
DEE	**scores**	**DEE**	**scores**	**DEE**	**scores**	**DEE**	**scores**
33.85	1	35.78	1	34.08	1	30.93	0
33.61	1	34.07	1	34.43	1	32.39	0
32.62	0	33.34	1	33.92	1	28.95	0
33.52	1	34.8	1	34.91	1	32.85	0
31.61	0	33.1	0	35.78	1	31.33	0
33.75	1	32.61	0	33.24	0	32.07	0
32.78	0	32.96	0	35.04	1	31.19	0
31.68	0	32.7	0	35.51	1	32.57	0
31.44	0	33.88	1	33.56	1	32.39	0
31.65	0	32.92	0	34.47	1	31.6	0
32.9	0	35.39	1	35.16	1	44.83	1
33.47	1	33.39	1	34.5	1	31.5	0

Below are the sample statistics:

Advice	Assistance	Counseling	Control
$n_1 = 12$	$n_2 = 12$	$n_3 = 12$	$n_4 = 12$
$T_1 = 5$	$T_2 = 7$	$T_3 = 11$	$T_4 = 1$
$\dfrac{T_1}{n_1} = 0.41667$	$\dfrac{T_2}{n_2} = 0.58333$	$\dfrac{T_3}{n_3} = 0.91667$	$\dfrac{T_4}{n_4} = 0.08333$

- The proportion of all values above $\hat{\theta} = 33.29$ is $\dfrac{T_.}{n_.} = \dfrac{5+7+11+1}{48} = 0.5$

- The nonparametric sample statistics are summarized in the Median scores table below.

Median Scores (Number of Points Above Median) for Variable DEE

Classified by Variable Group

PartNo	N	Sum of Scores	Expected Under H0	Std Dev Under H0	Mean Score
Advice	12	5	$\dfrac{12(24)}{48} = 6$	$\sqrt{12\left(\dfrac{36}{47}\right)(0.5)(0.5)} = 1.51587$	$\dfrac{5}{12} = 0.41667$
Assistance	12	7	$\dfrac{12(24)}{48} = 6$	$\sqrt{12\left(\dfrac{36}{47}\right)(0.5)(0.5)} = 1.51587$	$\dfrac{7}{12} = 0.58333$
Counseling	12	11	$\dfrac{12(24)}{48} = 6$	$\sqrt{12\left(\dfrac{36}{47}\right)(0.5)(0.5)} = 1.51587$	$\dfrac{11}{12} = 0.91667$
Control	12	1	$\dfrac{12(24)}{48} = 6$	$\sqrt{12\left(\dfrac{36}{47}\right)(0.5)(0.5)} = 1.51587$	$\dfrac{1}{12} = 0.08333$

$$\text{Chi-Square} = \frac{\sum_{i=1}^{k} n_i \left(\frac{T_i}{n_i} - \frac{T_.}{n_.} \right)^2}{\left(\frac{n_.}{n_. - 1} \right)\left(\frac{T_.}{n_.} \right)\left(1 - \frac{T_.}{n_.} \right)}$$

$$= \left(12(0.41667 - 0.5)^2 + 12(0.58333 - 0.5)^2 + 12(0.91667 - 0.5)^2 + 12(0.08333 - 0.5)^2 \right) \Big/ \left(\left(\frac{48}{47} \right)(0.5)(0.5) \right)$$

$$= 16.972$$

$$p\text{-value} = P(Q \geq 16.972) = 1\text{-probnorm}(16.972, 3) = 0.0007$$

Apply the results.

Since p-value < 0.05, reject H_0. There is sufficient evidence to reject the claim that the median DEE is the same for patients receiving advice, assistance, counseling, and no intervention. At least two sample medians are significantly different.

6.4.5 Instructions for Nonparametric One-Way ANOVA

Open the Nonparametric One-Way ANOVA task in one of the following ways:

- From the menu bar, select **Analyze ▶ ANOVA ▶ Nonparametric One-Way ANOVA**.

- On the **Task by Category** tab of the **Task List**, go to the **ANOVA** section and click **Nonparametric One-Way ANOVA**.

- On the **Task by Name** tab of the **Task List**, double-click **Nonparametric One-Way ANOVA**.

The Nonparametric One-Way ANOVA task has five groups of options: Task Roles, Analysis, Exact p-values, Results, and Titles. Exact p-values are not discussed in this book. The Results put the task results in data sets. Titles are discussed in general in Chapter 1, "Introduction to SAS Enterprise Guide." The Titles options control the titles and the footnotes in the output.

6.4.5.1 Task Roles

Click **Task Roles** on the selection pane to open this group of options. A variable is assigned to a role by dragging its name from **Variables to assign** to a role in **Task Roles**. See Figure 6.18. A variable can be removed from a role by dragging it back to **Variables to assign**. The right and left arrows and the resulting pop-up menus can also be used.

- **Dependent variables**: Statistics are computed for each variable in this role. The order that the variables are listed here is the order that they are listed in the output. See Figure 6.18.

- **Independent variable**: This variable contains the classification values that identify sample membership. See Figure 6.18.

The Group analysis by and Frequency count roles are discussed in general in Chapter 1, "Introduction to SAS Enterprise Guide."

In Figure 6.18, the data is in the Ex06_08 data set. The variable DEE is assigned to the Dependent variables role. The variable Group is assigned to the Independent variable role.

Figure 6.18 Task Roles in the Nonparametric One-Way ANOVA Task for Example 6.8

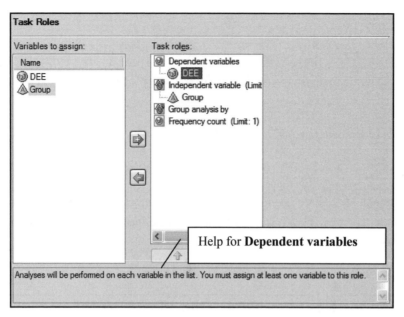

6.4.5.2 Analysis

In Figure 6.19, **Wilcoxon** and **Median** are checked.

Figure 6.19 Analysis Options in the Nonparametric One-Way ANOVA Task for Example 6.8

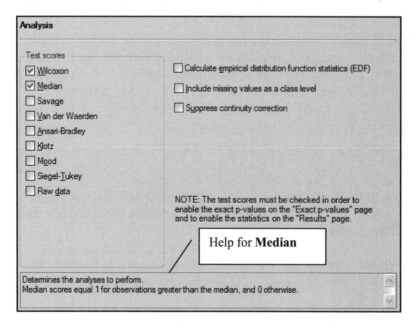

6.4.5.3 When Finished

When finished assigning variables to roles and selecting options, click **Run**. The task adds a Nonparametric One-Way ANOVA icon and one or more output icons to the process flow diagram. See Figure 6.20.

Figure 6.20 Example 6.8 Data, Task, and Output Icons on the Process Flow Diagram

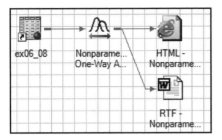

6.4.6 Task Output, Interpretation, and Analysis for Example 6.8

6.4.6.1   Task Output

The Kruskal-Wallis Test is in Output 6.14. The Median One-Way ANOVA is in Output 6.15.

Output 6.14 Kruskal-Wallis Test for Example 6.8

Nonparametric One-Way ANOVA

The NPAR1WAY Procedure

Wilcoxon Scores (Rank Sums) for Variable DEE Classified by Variable Group					
Group	N	Sum of Scores	Expected Under H0	Std Dev Under H0	Mean Score
Advice	12	234.00	294.0	41.997720	19.500000
Assistance	12	347.50	294.0	41.997720	28.958333
Counseling	12	454.50	294.0	41.997720	37.875000
Control	12	140.00	294.0	41.997720	11.666667
Average scores were used for ties.					

Kruskal-Wallis Test		
Chi-Square	23.7860	
DF	3	❶
Pr > Chi-Square	<.0001	❷

6.4.6.2   Interpretation

❶ Degrees of freedom $k - 1 = 4 - 1 = 3$

❷ *p*-value

Output 6.15 Median One-Way ANOVA for Example 6.8

Nonparametric One-Way ANOVA

The NPAR1WAY Procedure

Median Scores (Number of Points Above Median) for Variable DEE Classified by Variable Group					
Group	N	Sum of Scores	Expected Under H0	Std Dev Under H0	Mean Score
Advice	12	5.0	6.0	1.515873	0.416667
Assistance	12	7.0	6.0	1.515873	0.583333
Counseling	12	11.0	6.0	1.515873	0.916667
Control	12	1.0	6.0	1.515873	0.083333
Average scores were used for ties.					

Median One-Way Analysis		
Chi-Square	16.9722	
DF	3	❶
Pr > Chi-Square	0.0007	❷

6.4.6.3 Interpretation

❶ Degrees of freedom $k - 1 = 4 - 1 = 3$

❷ p-value

6.4.6.4 Analysis

Example 6.8.1

$H_0 : \theta_1 = \theta_2 = \theta_3 = \theta_4$

H_1 : At least one pair of medians are not equal.

$\alpha = 0.05$

The p-value of the Kruskal-Wallis Test is less than 0.0001. See ❷ in Output 6.14.

Reject H_0. There is sufficient evidence to reject the claim that the DEE medians are the same for patients receiving advice, assistance, counseling, and no intervention. At least two sample medians are significantly different.

Example 6.8.2

$H_0 : \theta_1 = \theta_2 = \theta_3 = \theta_4$

$H_1 :$ At least one pair of medians are not equal.

$\alpha = 0.05$

The *p*-value of the Median One-Way ANOVA is 0.0007. See ❷ in Output 6.15.

Reject H_0. There is sufficient evidence to reject the claim that the DEE medians are the same for patients receiving advice, assistance, counseling, and no intervention. At least two sample medians are significantly different.

Correlation and Regression

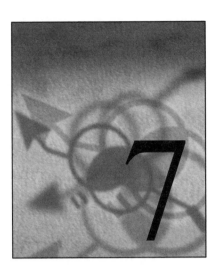

7.1 Correlation

Correlation analysis is used to examine the relationship between two numeric variables, such as x and y below. Each pair of values (x_i, y_i), $i = 1, \ldots, n$, comes from one person or object. In an application, it does not matter which variable is x or y. The roles are the same.

x	**y**
x_1	y_1
x_2	y_2
$\vdots$	$\vdots$
x_i	y_i
$\vdots$	$\vdots$
x_n	y_n

The basic question is whether there is a positive or negative relationship between the variables.

- In this context, positive means that the smaller x values tend to be paired with smaller y values and larger x values tend to be paired with larger y values.

- Negative means the smaller x values tend to be paired with larger y values and larger x values tend to be paired with smaller y values.

A sample of pairs $(x_1, y_1), (x_2, y_2), \ldots, (x_n, y_n)$ can be represented by a *scatter plot*. Each pair becomes a *data point* on the plot. See Figure 7.1. There is a positive relationship among the data points.

Figure 7.1 Scatter Plot of Data Points

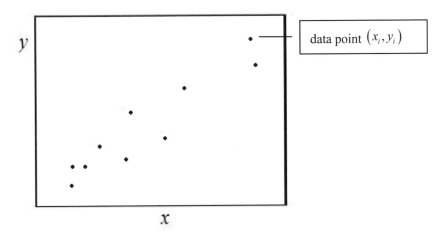

data point (x_i, y_i)

- A *correlation coefficient* is a measure of the strength of the relationship between x and y.

- The sample means, standard deviations, and variances have the following notation.

Mean	Standard Deviation	Variance
$\overline{x}$	s_x	s_x^2
$\overline{y}$	s_y	s_y^2

7.1.1 Pearson Correlation Coefficient

The *Pearson correlation coefficient*, represented by r, is a measure of the strength of the *linear* (line-like) *relationship* between two numeric variables. It is the sum of the products of the x deviations and the y deviations divided by $n-1$, s_x, and s_y.

$$r = \frac{\sum_{i=1}^{n}(x_i - \overline{x})(y_i - \overline{y})}{(n-1)s_x s_y}$$

An important property is:

$$-1 \le r \le 1$$

How the Pearson correlation coefficient measures *linearity*, or line-like behavior, can be seen in a plot of the paired deviations $(x_i - \overline{x}, y_i - \overline{y})$. See Figure 7.2. The pattern of the paired deviations in Figure 7.2 is identical to the pattern of the original data points (x_i, y_i) in Figure 7.1. The paired deviations are centered at the origin $(0,0)$, and the original data points are centered at $(\overline{x}, \overline{y})$.

- If the product of a pair of deviations is positive, $(x_i - \overline{x})(y_i - \overline{y}) > 0$, then the corresponding point $(x_i - \overline{x}, y_i - \overline{y})$ is in either Quadrant I or Quadrant III. See Figure 7.2.

- If $\sum_{i=1}^{n}(x_i - \overline{x})(y_i - \overline{y}) > 0$, then generally most of the points $(x_i - \overline{x}, y_i - \overline{y})$ are in either Quadrant I or Quadrant III. This creates a line-like pattern. On average, the points $(x_i - \overline{x}, y_i - \overline{y})$—and therefore, the original data points (x_i, y_i)—are following a line with positive slope.

- If the product of a pair of deviations is negative, $(x_i - \overline{x})(y_i - \overline{y}) < 0$, then the corresponding point $(x_i - \overline{x}, y_i - \overline{y})$ is in either Quadrant II or Quadrant IV. See Figure 7.2.

- If $\sum_{i=1}^{n}(x_i - \overline{x})(y_i - \overline{y}) < 0$, then generally most of the points $(x_i - \overline{x}, y_i - \overline{y})$ are in either Quadrant II or Quadrant IV. This creates a line-like pattern. On average, the points $(x_i - \overline{x}, y_i - \overline{y})$—and therefore, the original data points (x_i, y_i)—are following a line with negative slope.

Division by $n-1$, s_x, and s_y results in a value between -1 and 1. This helps in interpretation.

Figure 7.2 Scatter Plot of Paired Deviations

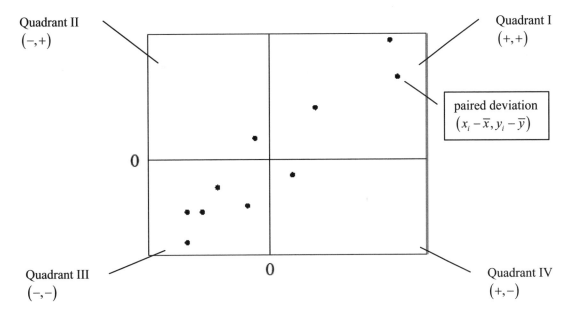

Figure 7.3 illustrates of a range of Pearson correlation coefficients.

- In (a) and (d), the points fall exactly on unseen straight lines. The lines describe all the variation in the points. In (a), $r = -1$. In (d), $r = 1$.

- In (b), the points follow, on average, an unseen straight line with negative slope. The line describes some of the variation in the points. Here, $r = -0.5$.

- In (c), the points follow, on average, an unseen straight line with positive slope. The line describes a large part of the variation in the points. Here, $r = 0.9$.

- In (e), the points follow, on average, an unseen horizontal line. This is a line with zero slope and no x term. There is no linear relationship between the x values and the y values. Here, $r = 0$.

- In (f), the points follow an unseen nonlinear curve. There is a relationship between the x values and the y values, but it is not linear. Here, $r = 0$.

Figure 7.3 Scatter Plots of Samples Illustrating a Range of Pearson Correlation Coefficients

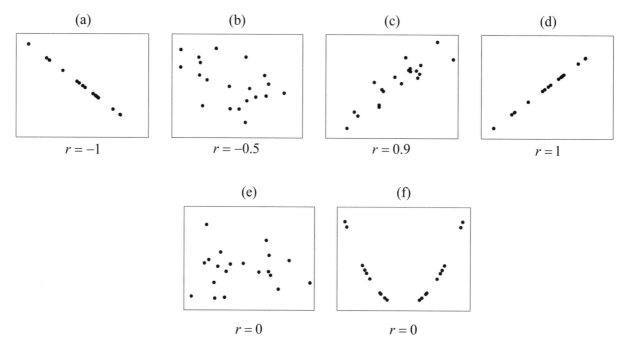

Positive linear correlation is present in the data when $r > 0$ and r is significantly different from 0. Significance is a result of the hypothesis test discussed in the "Hypothesis Test" section. With positive correlation, smaller x values tend to be paired with smaller y values, and larger x values tend to be paired with larger y values. The closer r is to 1, the stronger this tendency.

Negative linear correlation is present in the data when $r < 0$ and r is significantly different from 0. In this case, smaller x values tend to be paired with larger y values and larger x values tend to be paired with smaller y values. The closer r is to -1, the stronger this tendency.

Linear correlation is absent in the data when r is not significantly different from 0. In this case, both smaller and larger x values tend to be paired with smaller y values and with larger y values.

7.1.1.1   Population Model

There is a pair of random variables (X, Y) in correlation analysis. Recall that a random variable is a function that assigns a number to each person or object of interest. The pair (X, Y) assigns a pair of numbers to each person or object of interest.

The population correlation coefficient ρ, a lowercase Greek *rho*, quantifies the strength of the linear relationship between X and Y. That is, ρ quantifies the tendency of the assigned pairs to follow a straight line. Its properties are similar to those of r.

- $-1 \leq \rho \leq 1$

- Positive linear correlation is present in the population when $\rho > 0$: Smaller x values tend to be paired with smaller y values, and larger x values tend to be paired with larger y values. The closer ρ is to 1, the stronger this tendency.

- Negative linear correlation is present in the population when $\rho < 0$: Smaller x values tend to be paired with larger y values, and larger x values tend to be paired with smaller y values. The closer ρ is to -1, the stronger this tendency.

- Linear correlation is absent in the population when $\rho = 0$: Both smaller and larger x values tend to be paired with smaller y values and with larger y values.

The estimate of ρ is r. In terms of notation, $\hat{\rho} = r$.

The population of (x, y) pairs is described by a bivariate normal probability distribution. Both the x values and the y values follow normal probability distributions. The joint distribution is governed by ρ.

Figure 7.4 shows two bivariate normal probability distributions. The height of the surface above the xy-plane indicates the relative occurrence of the (x, y) pairs in the population.

- In Figure 7.4 (a), $\rho = 0.9$. The (x, y) pairs are mostly close to a line with positive slope. A sample from this population would be similar to that shown in Figure 7.3 (c).

- In Figure 7.4 (b), $\rho = -0.5$. The (x, y) pairs are spread out from a line with negative slope. A sample from this population would be similar to that shown in Figure 7.3 (b).

Figure 7.4 Bivariate Normal Probability Distribution with (a) $\rho = 0.9$ and (b) $\rho = -0.5$

(a)   (b)

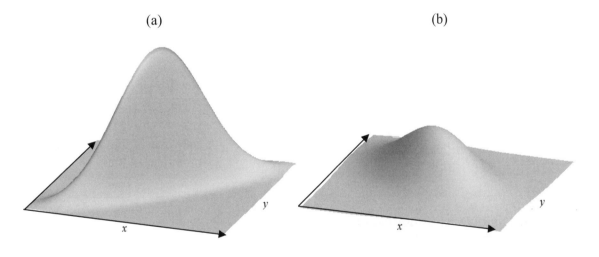

7.1.1.2 Hypothesis Test

The Correlations task tests the following null and alternative hypotheses:

$H_0 : \rho = 0$

$H_1 : \rho \neq 0$

The theory is based on the assumption that the sample of n data-value pairs is randomly selected from a population that follows a bivariate normal distribution. The resulting test statistic follows the Student's t distribution with $n-2$ degrees of freedom.

$$t \text{ Value} = \frac{r-0}{\sqrt{\dfrac{1-r^2}{n-2}}}$$

In terms of $H_0 : \rho = 0$, the p-value is the probability that a random sample from a population where there is no linear correlation between the paired values would produce a t value at or beyond the current value. If the p-value is small, it is unlikely that the current sample comes from a population where there is no linear correlation between the paired values.

The technical definition of the p-value is in Table 7.1. The random variable T represents a future value of the test statistic and follows the t distribution with $n-2$ degrees of freedom. In the SAS code expression, t value and $n-2$ represent numbers. The SAS code expression is included to aid in the discussion. The p-value is computed using the expression in the "Detailed Solutions" section of "Example 7.1: Pearson Correlation Coefficients."

Table 7.1 p-Value for Hypothesis Test on the Population Correlation Coefficient

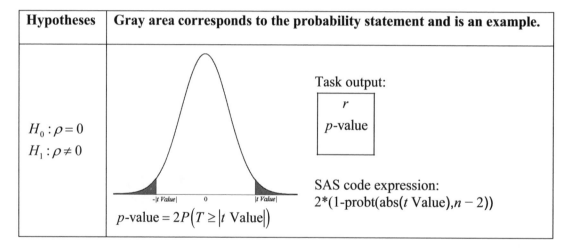

Hypotheses	Gray area corresponds to the probability statement and is an example.
$H_0 : \rho = 0$ $H_1 : \rho \neq 0$	$p\text{-value} = 2P\left(T \geq |t \text{ Value}|\right)$ Task output: r p-value SAS code expression: $2*(1\text{-probt}(\text{abs}(t \text{ Value}),n-2))$

Decision and Conclusions

The formal decision and concluding sentence do not change from the one-sample tests discussed in Chapter 4, "Inferences from One Sample." The concluding observation depends on the particular statistics involved in the test.

If the p-value is small, the data agrees with H_1. If the p-value is less than the significance level, the risk of making a Type I error is acceptable. Therefore, the p-value decision rule is the following:

If the p-value $< \alpha$, reject H_0. Otherwise, do not reject H_0.

Since a hypothesis test begins with the assumption that H_0 is true, concluding a hypothesis test requires one of the following formal statements:

- Reject H_0.

- Do not reject H_0.

When the claim is equivalent to the null hypothesis, the concluding sentence uses the word *reject*. The concluding sentence becomes an expanded version of the formal decision.

When the claim is equivalent to the alternative hypothesis, the concluding sentence uses the word *support*. If the data supports the rejection of H_0, the data supports H_1. If the data does not support the rejection of H_0, the data cannot support H_1.

Table 7.2 Concluding Sentences

Formal Statistical Decision	Claim stated as H_0	Claim stated as H_1
Reject H_0.	There is sufficient evidence to reject the claim that ... (claim in words).	There is sufficient evidence to support the claim that ... (claim in words).
Do not reject H_0.	There is not sufficient evidence to reject the claim that ... (claim in words).	There is not sufficient evidence to support the claim that ... (claim in words).

Table 7.3 Concluding Observations

	$r < 0$	$r > 0$
Reject H_0.	There is a significant negative linear correlation between the variables.	There is a significant positive linear correlation between the variables.
Do not reject H_0.	There is no significant linear correlation between the variables.	

7.1.1.3 Pearson Partial Correlation Coefficient

A sample *partial correlation coefficient* is a measure of the strength of a relationship between paired numerical variables that controls the effect of one or more other variables.

The Pearson partial correlation coefficient is the combination of the Pearson correlation coefficient and linear regression, which is discussed in the next two sections. The Pearson partial correlation coefficient of the variables w and y that controls the effect of the variable x is represented by $r_{wy \cdot x}$. Specifically, $r_{wy \cdot x}$ is the Pearson correlation coefficient of the pairs $\left(w_i - \hat{w}_i, y_i - \hat{y}_i \right), i = 1, \ldots, n$.

- $w_i - \hat{w}_i$ are the residuals formed by the regression function $\hat{w}_i$ with w being the dependent variable and x being the explanatory variable. In other words, they are the w values with the linear effect of x removed.

- $y_i - \hat{y}_i$ are the residuals formed by the regression function $\hat{y}_i$ with y being the dependent variable and x being the explanatory variable. In other words, they are the y values with the linear effect of x removed.

$$r_{wy \cdot x} = \frac{\sum\limits_{i=1}^{n} \left(w_i - \hat{w}_i \right)\left(y_i - \hat{y}_i \right)}{(n-1)\left(s_{w - \hat{w}} \right)\left(s_{y - \hat{y}} \right)}$$

This can be expressed in terms of the w-y, w-x, y-x Pearson correlation coefficients: r_{wy}, r_{wx}, and r_{yx}.

$$r_{wy \cdot x} = \frac{r_{wy} - r_{wx} r_{yx}}{\sqrt{1 - r_{wx}^2} \sqrt{1 - r_{yx}^2}}$$

The scatter plots in Figure 7.5 are of two variables before and after controlling the effect of a third variable. In the first plot, $r_{wy} = 0.95120$. In the second plot, $r_{wy \cdot x} = 0.65427$. Here, the relationship between w and x is not as strong with the effect of x being controlled. The data for these plots is analyzed in "Example 7.3: Partial Correlation Coefficients."

Figure 7.5 Scatter Plots of *w* and *x* before and after Controlling the Effect of *x*

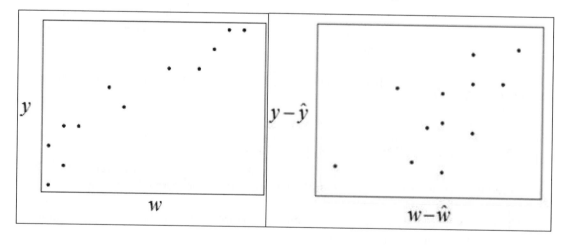

The hypothesis test on the population partial correlation coefficient $\rho_{wy\bullet x}$ is analogous to the test on ρ. The null and alternative hypotheses are:

$$H_0 : \rho_{wy\bullet x} = 0$$
$$H_1 : \rho_{wy\bullet x} \neq 0$$

The test statistic follows the Student's t distribution with $n-3$ degrees of freedom:

$$t \text{ Value} = \frac{r_{wy\bullet x} - 0}{\sqrt{\dfrac{1 - r_{wy\bullet x}^2}{n-3}}}$$

7.1.2 Spearman Correlation Coefficient

The *Spearman correlation coefficient* is a measure of the strength of the *monotonic relationship* in a sample of pairs. A monotonic relationship exists when one variable tends to increase or decrease with respect to the other variable. A linear relationship is a type of monotonic relationship.

The Spearman correlation coefficient is the Pearson correlation coefficient applied to the ranks of the data. It is represented by r_s.

$$r_s = \frac{\sum_{i=1}^{n}\left(r(x_i) - \frac{n+1}{2}\right)\left(r(y_i) - \frac{n+1}{2}\right)}{(n-1)s_{r(x)}s_{r(y)}}$$

- $r(x_i)$: the rank of x_i
- $r(y_i)$: the rank of y_i

- $s_{r(x)}$: the standard deviation of the ranks of x_i
- $s_{r(y)}$: the standard deviation of the ranks of y_i

Ranks correspond to the positions data would have if sorted from smallest to largest. Tied values are given average ranks, called *midranks*. The mean of the ranks is $(n+1)/2$. For example:

- 45, 68, 33, 53, 70 have ranks 2, 4, 1, 3, 5. The mean of the ranks is 3.
- 45, 68, 33, 45, 70 have ranks 2.5, 4, 1, 2.5, 5. The mean of these ranks is 3.

The Spearman correlation coefficient is less sensitive to outlying pairs than the Pearson. Data points based on ranks keep much of the original pattern but limit the effects of outliers. See Figure 7.6.

- (a) shows a scatter plot of a sample. There are no outliers and no points unusually far from the other data points. The statistics r_s and r are below the scatter plot. The two values are close.

- (b) shows a scatter plot of the data points based on the ranks of the data. Technically, r_s is the Pearson correlation coefficient of the data points in (b).

- The scatter plots are similar. This is reflected in r_s and r being similar. The r statistic is preferred because it is based on the original data.

Figure 7.6 (a) Scatter Plot of Data, (b) Scatter Plot Based on Ranks

(a)   (b)

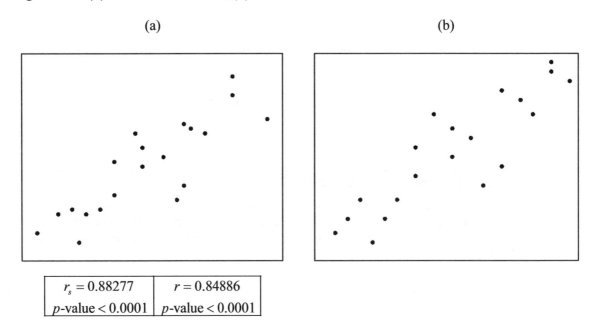

$r_s = 0.88277$	$r = 0.84886$
p-value < 0.0001	p-value < 0.0001

The sample plotted in Figure 7.7 (a) contains an outlier.

- With $r = 0.05417$ and the p-value $= 0.8206$, the interpretation is that there is no significant linear correlation in the sample. However, the outlier has increased the standard deviations s_x and s_y so much that they mask the correlation that does exist.

- The outlier still exists among the data points based on ranks in (b), but its impact is much smaller. With $r_s = 0.57143$ and the p-value $= 0.0085$, there is a significant increasing relationship between the paired values in the sample.

Figure 7.7 (a) Scatter Plot of Data with Outlier, (b) Scatter Plot Based on Ranks

(a)   (b)

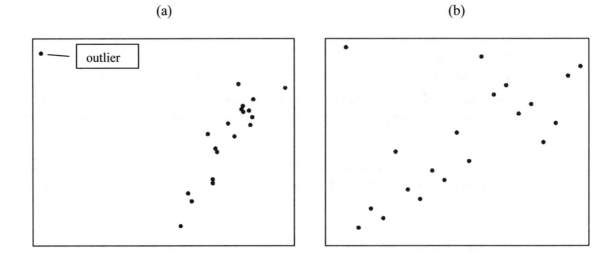

$\theta = 0.57143$	$r = 0.05417$
p-value = 0.0085	*p*-value = 0.8206

An increasing relationship is present in the data when $\theta > 0$ and θ is significantly different from 0. Significance is a result of the test discussed in "Hypothesis Test with the Spearman Correlation Coefficient." See Table 7.4. With an increasing relationship, smaller *x* values tend to be paired with smaller *y* values and larger *x* values with larger *y* values. The closer θ is to 1, the stronger this tendency.

A decreasing relationship is present in the data when $\theta < 0$ and θ is significantly different from 0. In this case, smaller *x* values tend to be paired with larger *y* values and larger *x* values with smaller *y* values. The closer r_s is to -1, the stronger this tendency.

No monotonic relationship is present in the data when r_s is not significantly different from 0. In this case, both smaller and larger *x* values tend to be paired with smaller *y* values and with larger *y* values.

7.1.2.1 Hypothesis Test with the Spearman Correlation Coefficient

This is a test on whether there is a monotonic relationship between the paired random variables X and Y. It is a nonparametric test: it is not a test regarding a parameter. The null and alternative hypotheses are:

H_0 : There is no monotonic relationship between X and Y.

H_1 : There is a monotonic relationship between X and Y.

The same form of the *t* value is used with both the Spearman and Pearson correlation coefficients:

$$t \text{ value} = \frac{\theta - 0}{\sqrt{\dfrac{1 - \theta^2}{n - 2}}}$$

In terms of H_0, the *p*-value is the probability that a random sample from a population where there is no monotonic relationship between the paired values would produce a *t* value at or beyond the current value. If the *p*-value is small, it is unlikely that the current sample comes from a population where there is no monotonic relationship between the paired values.

The technical definition of the *p*-value is in Table 7.4. The random variable T represents a future value of the test statistic and follows the *t* distribution with $n - 2$ degrees of freedom. In the SAS code expression, the *t* value and $n - 2$ represent numbers. The SAS code expression is included to aid in the discussion. The *p*-value is computed using the expression in the "Detailed Solutions" section of "Example 7.2: Spearman Correlation Coefficients."

Table 7.4 *p*-Value for Hypothesis Test with the Spearman Correlation Coefficient

Hypotheses	Gray area corresponds to the probability statement and is an example.
H_0 : There is no ... relationship .... H_1 : There is ... relationship	 $p\text{-value} = 2P\left(T \geq \lvert t \text{ Value}\rvert\right)$ Task output: r_s p-value SAS code expression: 2*(1-probt(abs(*t* Value),*n* − 2))

Decision and Conclusions

The formal decision and concluding sentence do not change from the one-sample tests discussed in Chapter 4, "Inferences from One Sample." The concluding observation depends on the particular statistics involved in the test.

If the *p*-value is small, the data agrees with H_1. If the *p*-value is less than the significance level, the risk of making a Type I error is acceptable. Therefore, the *p*-value decision rule is the following:

If the *p-value* < α, reject H_0. Otherwise, do not reject H_0.

Since a hypothesis test begins with the assumption that H_0 is true, concluding a hypothesis test requires one of the following formal statements:

- Reject H_0.
- Do not reject H_0.

When the claim is equivalent to the null hypothesis, the concluding sentence uses the word *reject*. The concluding sentence becomes an expanded version of the formal decision.

When the claim is equivalent to the alternative hypothesis, the concluding sentence uses the word *support*. If the data supports the rejection of H_0, the data supports H_1. If the data does not support the rejection of H_0, the data cannot support H_1.

Table 7.5 Concluding Sentences

Formal Statistical Decision	Claim stated as H_0	Claim stated as H_1
Reject H_0.	There is sufficient evidence to reject the claim that ... (claim in words).	There is sufficient evidence to support the claim that ... (claim in words).
Do not reject H_0.	There is not sufficient evidence to reject the claim that ... (claim in words).	There is not sufficient evidence to support the claim that ... (claim in words).

Table 7.6 Concluding Observations

	$\theta < 0$	$\theta > 0$
Reject H_0.	There is a significant decreasing relationship between variables.	There is a significant increasing relationship between the variables.
Do not reject H_0.	There is no significant increasing or decreasing relationship between the variables.	

7.1.2.2 Spearman Partial Correlation Coefficient

The Spearman partial correlation coefficient is the Pearson partial correlation coefficient applied to the ranks of the data. The Spearman partial correlation coefficient (of the variables w and y) that controls the effect of the variable x is represented by $\theta_{wy \cdot x}$. It is computed with the w-y, w-x, y-x Spearman correlation coefficients: θ_{wy}, θ_{wx}, and θ_{yx}.

$$\left(r_s\right)_{wy \cdot x} = \frac{\theta_{wy} - \theta_{wx}\theta_{yx}}{\sqrt{1-\theta_{wx}^2}\sqrt{1-\theta_{yx}^2}}$$

The hypothesis test on the population partial correlation coefficient $\theta_{wy \cdot x}$ is analogous to the test on θ. The null and alternative hypotheses are:

H_0 : There is no monotonic relationship between W and Y when the effect X is controlled.

H_1 : There is a monotonic relationship between W and Y when the effect X is controlled.

The test statistic follows the Student's t distribution with $n-3$ degrees of freedom:

$$t\ \text{Value} = \frac{\theta_{wy \cdot x} - 0}{\sqrt{\dfrac{1-\theta_{wy \cdot x}^2}{n-3}}}$$

7.1.3 Example 7.1: Pearson Correlation Coefficients

Example 7.1 applies the Pearson correlation coefficient as a descriptive statistic and as a basis for inference on the population correlation coefficient. The requested analysis includes a number of Pearson correlation coefficients, hypothesis tests, and scatter plots.

- The correlation coefficients and the hypothesis tests are worked out in the "Detailed Solutions" section.
- The Correlations task is discussed in "Instructions for Correlation Analysis."
- Complete results are in "Task Output, Interpretation, and Analysis for Example 7.1."

7.1.3.1   Student Data

The table below contains the midterm and final exam scores for 10 students who have been randomly selected from a particular course. The table also contains the number of times absent and the commute time in minutes for each student.

Student	Midterm	Final	Absent	Commute
1	64	63	5	10
2	64	68	5	20
3	66	68	4	5
4	68	72	3	50
5	72	69	5	5
6	73	80	3	10
7	78	74	2	10
8	81	85	3	20
9	91	96	2	25
10	92	90	3	60

These values are in the Ex07_01 data set. The variable names are as shown in the table: Midterm, Final, Absent, and Commute.

Example 7.1.1

Determine the Pearson correlation coefficient for the following pairs of measurements:

- midterm and final exam scores
- final exam score and numbers of absences
- final exam scores and commute times

Example 7.1.2

Test the claim that, among all students who take this particular course, there is a linear correlation between the midterm exam score and the final exam score. Let $\alpha = 0.05$.

Example 7.1.3

Test the claim that, among all students who take this particular course, there is a linear correlation between the final exam score and the number of absences. Let $\alpha = 0.05$.

Example 7.1.4

Test the claim that, among all students who take this particular course, there is a linear correlation between the final exam score and the commute time. Let $\alpha = 0.05$.

Example 7.1.5

Construct scatter plots for the midterm and final exam scores; the final exam scores and the numbers of absences; and the final exam scores and commute times.

7.1.3.2 Detailed Solutions

The Correlations task output has a table containing the sample sizes, means, and standard deviations. For convenience, the table from the output for Example 7.1 is in Output 7.1. It is also part of Output 7.2 in "Task Output, Interpretation, and Analysis for Example 7.1."

Output 7.1 Simple Statistics Table for Example 7.1

Simple Statistics							
Variable	**N**	**Mean**	**Std Dev**	**Sum**	**Minimum**	**Maximum**	**Label**
Midterm	10	74.90000	10.40780	749.00000	64.00000	92.00000	Midterm
Final	10	76.50000	10.83462	765.00000	63.00000	96.00000	Final
Absent	10	3.50000	1.17851	35.00000	2.00000	5.00000	Absent
Commute	10	21.50000	19.01023	215.00000	5.00000	60.00000	Commute

Example 7.1.1

For the Midterm and Final scores:

$$n = 10 \quad \bar{x} = 74.9 \quad s_x = 10.40780$$
$$\bar{y} = 76.5 \quad s_y = 10.83462$$

$$r = \frac{\sum_{i=1}^{n}(x_i - \bar{x})(y_i - \bar{y})}{(n-1)s_x s_y}$$
$$= \frac{950.5}{(10-1)(10.40780)(10.83462)}$$
$$= 0.93656$$

Midterm	Final	$x_i - \bar{x}$	$y_i - \bar{y}$	$(x_i - \bar{x})(y_i - \bar{y})$
64	63	−10.9	−13.5	147.15
64	68	−10.9	−8.5	92.65
66	68	−8.9	−8.5	75.65
68	72	−6.9	−4.5	31.05
72	69	−2.9	−7.5	21.75
73	80	−1.9	3.5	−6.65
78	74	3.1	−2.5	−7.75
81	85	6.1	8.5	51.85
91	96	16.1	19.5	313.95
92	90	17.1	13.5	230.85
			$\sum(x_i - \bar{x})(y_i - \bar{y}) = 950.5$	

Final	Absent	$x_i - \bar{x}$	$y_i - \bar{y}$	$(x_i - \bar{x})(y_i - \bar{y})$
63	5	−13.5	1.5	−20.25
68	5	−8.5	1.5	−12.75
68	4	−8.5	0.5	−4.25
72	3	−4.5	−0.5	2.25
69	5	−7.5	1.5	−11.25
80	3	3.5	−0.5	−1.75
74	2	−2.5	−1.5	3.75
85	3	8.5	−0.5	−4.25
96	2	19.5	−1.5	−29.25
90	3	13.5	−0.5	−6.75
			$\sum(x_i - \bar{x})(y_i - \bar{y}) = -84.5$	

For the Final and Absent scores:

$$n = 10 \quad \bar{x} = 76.5 \quad s_x = 10.83462$$
$$\bar{y} = 3.5 \quad s_y = 1.17851$$

$$
\begin{aligned}
r &= \frac{\sum_{i=1}^{n}(x_i - \bar{x})(y_i - \bar{y})}{(n-1)s_x s_y} \\
&= \frac{-84.5}{(10-1)(10.83462)(1.17851)} \\
&= -0.73530
\end{aligned}
$$

For the Final and Commute scores:

$$n = 10 \quad \bar{x} = 76.5 \quad s_x = 10.83462$$
$$\bar{y} = 21.5 \quad s_y = 19.01023$$

$$r = \frac{\sum\limits_{i=1}^{n}(x_i - \bar{x})(y_i - \bar{y})}{(n-1)s_x s_y}$$

$$= \frac{867.5}{(10-1)(10.83462)(19.01023)}$$

$$= 0.46798$$

Final	Commute	$x_i - \bar{x}$	$y_i - \bar{y}$	$(x_i - \bar{x})(y_i - \bar{y})$
63	10	−13.5	−11.5	155.25
68	20	−8.5	−1.5	12.75
68	5	−8.5	−16.5	140.25
72	50	−4.5	28.5	−128.25
69	5	−7.5	−16.5	123.75
80	10	3.5	−11.5	−40.25
74	10	−2.5	−11.5	28.75
85	20	8.5	−1.5	−12.75
96	25	19.5	3.5	68.25
90	60	13.5	38.5	519.75
$\sum (x_i - \bar{x})(y_i - \bar{y}) = 867.5$				

Example 7.1.2

Plan the task.

$H_0 : \rho = 0$

$H_1 : \rho \neq 0$

$\alpha = 0.05$

Compute the statistics.

$$t \text{ Statistic} = \frac{r - 0}{\sqrt{\dfrac{1 - r^2}{n-2}}} = \frac{0.93656}{\sqrt{\dfrac{1 - (0.93656)^2}{(10-2)}}} = 7.5576$$

Since 7.5576 is positive, the absolute value function can be dropped:

$p\text{-value} = 2\,P(T \geq 7.5576) = 2*(1\text{-probt}(7.5576,8)) = 0.000066 < 0.0001$

Apply the results.

Since the *p*-value < 0.05, reject H_0. There is sufficient evidence to support the claim that, among all students who take this particular course, there is a linear correlation between the midterm exam score and the final exam score. There is a significant positive correlation between the midterm and the final exam scores in the sample.

Example 7.1.3

Plan the task.

$H_0 : \rho = 0$

$H_1 : \rho \neq 0$

$\alpha = 0.05$

Compute the statistics.

$$t\text{ Statistic} = \frac{r-0}{\sqrt{\dfrac{1-r^2}{n-2}}} = \frac{-0.73530}{\sqrt{\dfrac{1-(-0.73530)^2}{(10-2)}}} = -3.0686$$

$p\text{-value} = 2P\left(T \geq |-3.0686|\right) = 2*(1\text{-probt(abs(-3.0686),8))} = 0.015381$

Apply the results.

Since the p-value < 0.05, reject H_0. There is sufficient evidence to support the claim that, among all students who take this particular course, there is a linear correlation between the final exam score and the number of absences. There is a significant negative correlation between the final exam scores and the numbers of absences in the sample.

Example 7.1.4

Plan the task.

$H_0 : \rho = 0$

$H_1 : \rho \neq 0$

$\alpha = 0.05$

Compute the statistics.

$$t\text{ Statistic} = \frac{r-0}{\sqrt{\dfrac{1-r^2}{n-2}}} = \frac{0.46798}{\sqrt{\dfrac{1-(0.46798)^2}{(10-2)}}} = 1.4978$$

Since 1.4978 is positive, the absolute value function can be dropped:

$p\text{-value} = 2P\left(T \geq 1.4978\right) = 2*(1\text{-probt(abs(1.5671),8))} = 0.172562$

Apply the results.

Since the p-value > 0.05, do not reject H_0. There is not sufficient evidence to support the claim that, among all students who take this particular course, there is a linear correlation between the final exam score and the commute time. There is no significant correlation between the final exam scores and the commute times in the sample.

7.1.4 Instructions for Correlation Analysis

The analysis requested in Example 7.1 is listed in Table 7.7. The first two items appear unless they are deselected. Plots are options. The Correlations task is applied to the Ex07_01 data set.

Table 7.7 Analysis Requested in Example 7.1

Requested Analysis		Whether always part of output
Example 7.1.1	Pearson correlation coefficient	Default selection on **Options**
Example 7.1.2, Example 7.1.3, Example 7.1.4	Hypothesis test on population correlation coefficient	*p*-value reported with the Pearson correlation coefficient
Example 7.1.5	Scatter plots	Option on **Results**

To open the Correlations task, do one of the following:

- From the menu bar, select **Analyze ▶ Multivariate ▶ Correlations**.
- On the **Task by Category** tab of the **Task List**, go to the **Multivariate** section and click **Correlations**.
- On the **Task by Name** tab of the **Task List**, double-click **Correlations**.

The Correlations task has five groups of options: Task Roles, Options, Results, Data Output, and Titles. The Output Data options put the task results in data sets. The Titles options control the titles and the footnotes in the task output. Titles are discussed in general in Chapter 1, "Introduction to SAS Enterprise Guide."

7.1.4.1 Task Roles

A variable is assigned to a role by dragging it from **Variables to assign** to one of the **Task roles**. A variable can be removed from a role by dragging it back to **Variables to assign**. Also, the arrows can be used.

- Analysis variables are the columns of data values.
- If one or more variables are in the Correlate with role, the Analysis variables are paired only with the Correlate with variables.
- If one or more variables are in the Partial variables role, partial correlation coefficients are computed with the variables in the Partial variables role being controlled.

The roles Group analysis by, Frequency count, and Relative weight are discussed in Section 1.3.

In Figure 7.8, all variables are assigned to the Analysis variables role. A correlation coefficient is produced for each pair. The correlations requested in Example 7.1 appear with other correlations in the output.

Because all the correlations requested in Example 7.1 involve Final, another approach would be to assign Midterm, Absent, and Commute to Analysis variables and Final to Correlate with. Only the requested correlations would be in the output.

Figure 7.8 Task Roles in the Correlations Task

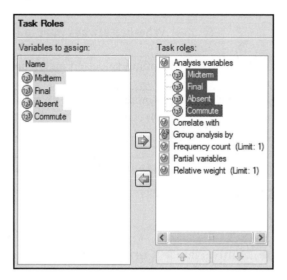

7.1.4.2 Options

Pearson is the default selection. See Figure 7.9. The Spearman correlation coefficient is applied in Example 7.2.

Figure 7.9 Options in the Correlations Task

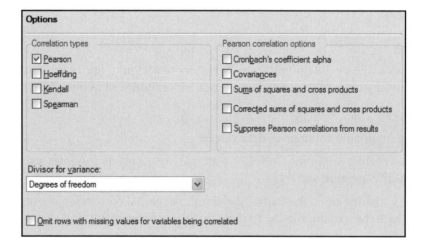

7.1.4.3 Results

Create a scatter plot for each correlation pair is checked in Figure 7.10. A report on the amount of output is at Summary of correlations to calculate.

Figure 7.10 Results Options

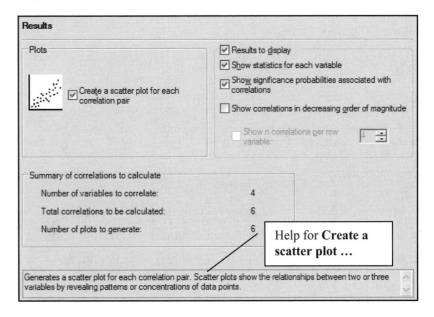

7.1.4.4   When Finished

When you are finished adding variables to roles and selecting options, click **Run**. The task adds a Correlations icon and one or more output icons to the process flow diagram. See Figure 7.11. The results for Example 7.1 are in Output 7.2.

Figure 7.11 Example 7.1 Data, Task, and Output Icons on the Process Flow Diagram

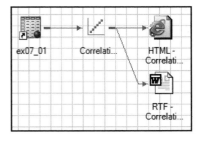

7.1.5 Task Output, Interpretation, and Analysis for Example 7.1

Output 7.2 contains the Correlations output for Example 7.1. The original output contains six scatter plots. Only the three that are requested in Example 7.1 are shown here.

7.1.5.1   Task Output

Output 7.2 Correlations Output for Example 7.1

Correlation Analysis

The CORR Procedure

4 Variables:	Midterm Final Absent Commute

Simple Statistics							
Variable	**N**	**Mean**	**Std Dev**	**Sum**	**Minimum**	**Maximum**	**Label**
Midterm	10	74.90000	10.40780	749.00000	64.00000	92.00000	Midterm
Final	10	76.50000	10.83462	765.00000	63.00000	96.00000	Final
Absent	10	3.50000	1.17851	35.00000	2.00000	5.00000	Absent
Commute	10	21.50000	19.01023	215.00000	5.00000	60.00000	Commute

❶
❷
❸

Pearson Correlation Coefficients, N = 10 Prob > |r| under H0: Rho=0				
	Midterm	**Final**	**Absent**	**Commute**
Midterm	1.00000 ❹	0.93656	-0.70205	0.46695
		5 <.0001	0.0236	0.1736
Final	0.9365 ❺	1.00000	-0.73530	0.46798
	<.0001		6 0.0154	7 0.1726
Absent	-0.70205	-0.73530	1.00000	-0.33477
	0.0236	❻ 0.0154		0.3444
Commute	0.46695	0.46798	-0.33477	1.00000
	0.1736	❼ 0.1726	0.3444	

Scatter plot of Midterm by Final ❽

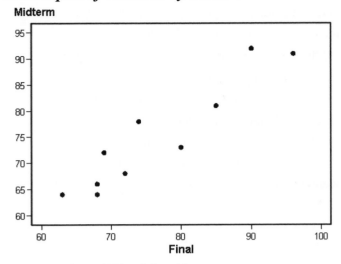

Scatter plot of Final by Absent ❾

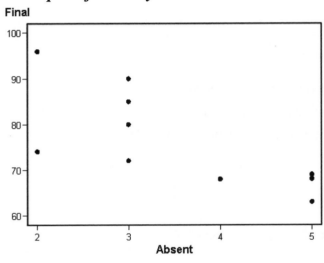

Scatter plot of Final by Commute ❿

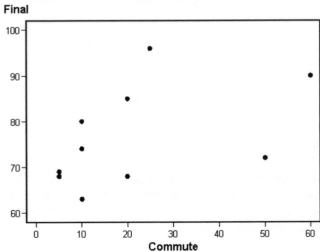

7.1.5.2   Interpretation

❶&❷   indicate how the results are read:

The top number is the Pearson correlation coefficient r.

The second number is the p-value of the hypothesis test on $H_0 : \rho = 0$.

❸   Each pair of variables involves $n = 10$ pairs of values.

❹   The correlation coefficient of a variable with itself is always 1.

❺   For Midterm and Final, $r = 0.93656$ and the p-value < 0.0001.

❻   For Final and Absent, $r = -0.73530$ and the p-value $= 0.0154$.

❼   For Final and Commute, $r = 0.46798$ and the p-value $= 0.1726$.

❽   Scatter plot for Midterm and Final

❾   Scatter plot for Final and Absent

❿   Scatter plot for Final and Commute

7.1.5.3   Analysis

Example 7.1.1

The Pearson correlation coefficients

* midterm and final exam scores: 0.93656. See ❺ in Output 7.2.

* final exam score and number of absences: −0.73530. See ❻ in Output 7.2.

* final exam score and commute time: 0.46798. See ❼ in Output 7.2.

Example 7.1.2

$H_0 : \rho = 0$

$H_1 : \rho \neq 0$

p-value $< .0001$. See ❺ in Output 7.2.

Since the p-value < 0.05, reject H_0. There is sufficient evidence to support the claim that, among all students who take this particular course, there is a linear correlation between the midterm exam score and the final exam score. There is a significant positive correlation between the midterm and the final exam scores in the sample.

Example 7.1.3

$H_0 : \rho = 0$

$H_1 : \rho \neq 0$

p-value $= 0.0154$. See ❻ in Output 7.2.

Since the p-value < 0.05, reject H_0. There is sufficient evidence to support the claim that, among all students who take this particular course, there is a linear correlation between the final exam score and the number of absences. There is a significant negative correlation between the final exam scores and the numbers of absences in the sample.

Example 7.1.4

$H_0 : \rho = 0$

$H_1 : \rho \neq 0$

p-value = 0.1726. See ❼ in Output 7.2.

Since the p-value > 0.05, do not reject H_0. There is not sufficient evidence to support the claim that, among all students who take this particular course, there is a linear correlation between the final exam score and the commute time. There is no significant correlation between the final exam scores and the commute times in the sample.

Example 7.1.5
See ❽, ❾, and ❿ in Output 7.2.

7.1.6 Example 7.2: Spearman Correlation Coefficients

Example 7.2 applies the Spearman correlation coefficient as a descriptive statistic and as a basis for inference on the population of paired values. The requested analysis includes a number of Spearman and Pearson correlation coefficients, hypothesis tests, and scatter plots. The Spearman correlation coefficients and the hypothesis tests are worked out in the "Detailed Solutions" section.

7.1.6.1   Student Data with Outlier

Student	Midterm	Final	Absent
1	64	63	5
2	64	68	5
3	66	68	4
4	68	72	3
5	72	69	5
6	73	80	3
7	78	74	2
8	81	85	3
9	91	96	2
10	92	90	3
11	94	72	25

Note that an eleventh student has been added to the data in Example 7.1.

These values are in the Ex07_02 data set. The variable names are as shown in the table: Midterm, Final, and Absent.

Example 7.2.1
Determine the Spearman and Pearson correlation coefficients for the following pairs of measurements:

    a. midterm and final exam scores

    b. final exam score and numbers of absences

Example 7.2.2
Use the Spearman correlation coefficient to test the claim that, among all students who take this particular course, there is a monotonic relationship between the midterm exam score and the final exam score. Let $\alpha = 0.05$.

Example 7.2.3
Use the Spearman correlation coefficient to test the claim that, among all students who take this particular course, there is a monotonic relationship between the final exam score and the number of absences. Let $\alpha = 0.05$.

Example 7.2.4
Construct a scatter plot for the midterm and final exam scores and a scatter plot for the final exam scores and the numbers of absences. On each plot, identify the data point associated with the eleventh student.

7.1.6.2   Detailed Solutions

Example 7.2.1
For the Midterm and Final scores:

Midterm x	Final y	$r(x)$	$r(y)$	$r(x)-\dfrac{n+1}{2}$	$r(y)-\dfrac{n+1}{2}$	$\left(r(x)-\dfrac{n+1}{2}\right)^2$	$\left(r(y)-\dfrac{n+1}{2}\right)^2$	$\left(r(x)-\dfrac{n+1}{2}\right)\left(r(y)-\dfrac{n+1}{2}\right)$
64	63	1.5	1	-4.5	-5	20.25	25	22.5
64	68	1.5	2.5	-4.5	-3.5	20.25	12.25	15.75
66	68	3	2.5	-3	-3.5	9	12.25	10.5
68	72	4	5.5	-2	-0.5	4	0.25	1
72	69	5	4	-1	-2	1	4	2
73	80	6	8	0	2	0	4	0
78	74	7	7	1	1	1	1	1
81	85	8	9	2	3	4	9	6
91	96	9	11	3	5	9	25	15
92	90	10	10	4	4	16	16	16
94	72	11	5.5	5	-0.5	25	0.25	-2.5
sums:		66	66	0	0	109.5	109	87.25

$$n = 11 \quad s_{rx} = \sqrt{\dfrac{\sum\limits_{i=1}^{n}\left(r(x_i) - \dfrac{n+1}{2}\right)}{n-1}} = \sqrt{\dfrac{109.5}{10}} = 3.30908$$

$$s_{ry} = \sqrt{\dfrac{\sum\limits_{i=1}^{n}\left(r(y_i) - \dfrac{n+1}{2}\right)}{n-1}} = \sqrt{\dfrac{109}{10}} = 3.30151$$

$$\theta = \dfrac{\sum\limits_{i=1}^{n}\left(r(x_i) - \dfrac{n+1}{2}\right)\left(r(y_i) - \dfrac{n+1}{2}\right)}{(n-1)s_{rx}s_{ry}}$$

$$= \dfrac{87.25}{(11-1)(3.30908)(3.30151)}$$

$$= 0.79863$$

For the Final and Absent scores:

Final x	Absent y	$r(x)$	$r(y)$	$r(x) - \dfrac{n+1}{2}$	$r(y) - \dfrac{n+1}{2}$	$\left(r(x) - \dfrac{n+1}{2}\right)^2$	$\left(r(y) - \dfrac{n+1}{2}\right)^2$	$\left(r(x) - \dfrac{n+1}{2}\right)\left(r(y) - \dfrac{n+1}{2}\right)$
63	5	1	9	-5	3	25	9	-15
68	5	2.5	9	-3.5	3	12.25	9	-10.5
68	4	2.5	7	-3.5	1	12.25	1	-3.5
72	3	5.5	4.5	-0.5	-1.5	0.25	2.25	0.75
69	5	4	9	-2	3	4	9	-6
80	3	8	4.5	2	-1.5	4	2.25	-3
74	2	7	1.5	1	-4.5	1	20.25	-4.5
85	3	9	4.5	3	-1.5	9	2.25	-4.5
96	2	11	1.5	5	-4.5	25	20.25	-22.5
90	3	10	4.5	4	-1.5	16	2.25	-6
72	25	5.5	11	-0.5	5	0.25	25	-2.5
sums:		66	66	0	0	109	102.5	-77.25

$$n = 11 \quad s_{rx} = \sqrt{\dfrac{\sum\limits_{i=1}^{n}\left(r(x_i) - \dfrac{n+1}{2}\right)}{n-1}} = \sqrt{\dfrac{109}{10}} = 3.30151$$

$$s_{ry} = \sqrt{\dfrac{\sum\limits_{i=1}^{n}\left(r(y_i) - \dfrac{n+1}{2}\right)}{n-1}} = \sqrt{\dfrac{102.5}{10}} = 3.20156$$

$$\theta = \frac{\sum_{i=1}^{n}\left(r(x_i)-\frac{n+1}{2}\right)\left(r(y_i)-\frac{n+1}{2}\right)}{(n-1)s_{rx}s_{ry}}$$

$$= \frac{-77.25}{(11-1)(3.30151)(3.20156)}$$

$$= -0.73084$$

Example 7.2.2

Plan the task.

H_0 : There is no monotonic relationship between the midterm exam score and the final exam score.

H_1 : There is a monotonic relationship between the midterm exam score and the final exam score.

Compute the statistics.

$$t \text{ Statistic} = \frac{\theta-0}{\sqrt{\frac{1-\theta^2}{n-2}}} = \frac{0.79863}{\sqrt{\frac{1-(0.79863)^2}{(11-2)}}} = 3.9811$$

Since 3.9811 is positive, the absolute value function can be dropped:

$$p\text{-value} = 2P(T \geq 3.9811) = 2*(1-\text{probt}(3.9811,9)) = 0.0032$$

Apply the results.

Since the *p*-value < 0.05, reject H_0. There is sufficient evidence to support the claim that, among all students who take this particular course, there is a monotonic relationship between the midterm exam score and the final exam score. There is a significant increasing relationship between the midterm and the final exam scores in the sample.

Example 7.2.3

Plan the task.

H_0 : There is no monotonic relationship between the final exam score and the number of absences.

H_1 : There is a monotonic relationship between the final exam score and the number of absences.

Compute the statistics.

$$t \text{ Statistic} = \frac{\theta - 0}{\sqrt{\dfrac{1 - \theta^2}{n - 2}}} = \frac{-0.73084}{\sqrt{\dfrac{1 - (-0.73084)^2}{(10 - 2)}}} = -3.2123$$

$$p\text{-value} = 2P\big(T \geq |-3.2123|\big) = 2*(1 - \text{probt}(\text{abs}(-3.2123), 8)) = 0.01062$$

Apply the results.

Since the *p*-value < 0.05, reject H_0. There is sufficient evidence to support the claim that, among all students who take this particular course, there is a monotonic relationship between the final exam score and the number of absences. There is a significant decreasing relationship between the final exam scores and the numbers of absences in the sample.

7.1.6.3 Correlations Task

The following task selections are different from Example 7.1:

- The active data is Ex07_02.
- Task Roles
  - Midterm and Absent are assigned to Analysis variables.
  - Final is assigned to Correlate with.
- Options: Both Pearson and Spearman are selected.

7.1.7 Task Output, Interpretation, and Analysis for Example 7.2

7.1.7.1 Task output

Output 7.3 Correlations Output for Example 7.2

Correlation Analysis

The CORR Procedure

1 With Variables:	Final
2 Variables:	Midterm Absent

Simple Statistics						
Variable	N	Mean	Std Dev	Median	Minimum	Maximum
Final	11	76.09091	10.36778	72.00000	63.00000	96.00000
Midterm	11	76.63636	11.43042	73.00000	64.00000	94.00000
Absent	11	5.45455	6.57820	3.00000	2.00000	25.00000

❶
❷ | Pearson Correlation Coefficients, N = 11 ❸ | | |
Prob > |r| under H0: Rho=0		
	Midterm	**Absent**
Final	0.73612	-0.25286
	❹ 0.0098	❺ 0.4531

❻
❼ | Spearman Correlation Coefficients, N = 11 | | |
Prob > |r| under H0: Rho=0		
	Midterm	**Absent**
Final	0.79863	-0.73084
	❽ 0.0032	❾ 0.0106

Scatter plot of Midterm by Final ❿

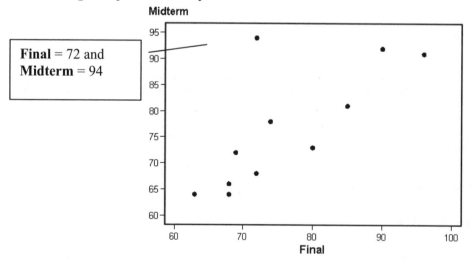

Final = 72 and
Midterm = 94

Scatter plot of Final by Absent ⓫

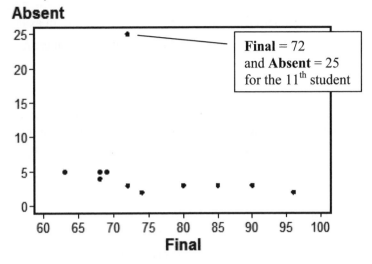

7.1.7.2   Interpretation

❶&❷   indicate how the results are read:

The top number is the Pearson correlation coefficient r.

The second number is the p-value of the hypothesis test on $H_0 : \rho = 0$.

❸   Each pair of variables involves $n = 11$ pairs of values.

❹   For Midterm and Final, $r = 0.73612$ and the p-value = 0.0098.

❺   For Final and Absent, $r = -0.25286$ and the p-value = 0.4531.

❻&❼   indicate how the results are read:

The top number is the Spearman correlation coefficient θ.

The second number is the p-value of the hypothesis test.

❽   For Midterm and Final, $\theta = 0.79863$ and the p-value = 0.0032.

❾   For Final and Absent, $\theta = -0.73084$ and the p-value = 0.0106.

❿   Scatter plot for Midterm and Final

⓫   Scatter plot for Final and Absent

7.1.7.3   Analysis

Example 7.2.1

	Spearman correlation coefficients	Pearson correlation coefficients
midterm and final exam scores	$\theta = 0.79863$ See ❽ in Output 7.3.	$r = 0.73612$ See ❹ in Output 7.3.
final exam score and number of absences	$\theta = -0.73084$ See ❾ in Output 7.3.	$r = -0.25286$ See ❺ in Output 7.3.

Example 7.2.2

H_0: There is no monotonic relationship between the midterm exam score and the final exam score.

H_1: There is a monotonic relationship between the midterm exam score and the final exam score.

p-value = 0.0032. See ❽ in Output 7.3.

Since the p-value < 0.05, reject H_0. There is sufficient evidence to support the claim that, among all students who take this particular course, there is a monotonic relationship between the midterm exam score and the final exam score. There is a significant increasing relationship between the midterm and the final exam scores in the sample.

Example 7.2.3

H_0: There is no monotonic relationship between the final exam score and the number of absences.

H_1: There is a monotonic relationship between the final exam score and the number of absences.

p-value = 0.0106. See ❾ in Output 7.3.

Since the p-value < 0.05, reject H_0. There is sufficient evidence to support the claim that, among all students who take this particular course, there is a monotonic relationship between the final exam score and the number of absences. There is a significant decreasing relationship between the final exam scores and the numbers of absences in the sample.

Example 7.2.4

See ❿ and ⓫ in Output 7.3.

7.1.8 Example 7.3: Partial Correlation Coefficients

7.1.8.1 Reading Assessment, Homework, and Age

In a particular school district, reading assessment tests are given to students in three age groups: 9, 13, and 17. The scores are standardized so that comparisons can be made between groups. Four students from each group are randomly selected. The typical number of pages read daily in class and homework is determined for each student. The results are below.

These values are in the Ex07_03 data set. The variable names are as shown in the table: age, score, and pages.

Student	age	score	pages
1	9	55	20
2	9	56	21
3	9	57	23
4	9	57	22
5	13	53	15
6	13	55	18
7	13	52	12
8	13	54	14
9	17	50	11
10	17	49	10
11	17	51	10
12	17	52	11

Example 7.3.1

Determine the Pearson and Spearman correlation coefficients for the following pairs of measurements:

- age and reading assessment score
- age and number of pages read
- reading assessment score and number of pages read

Example 7.3.1

Determine the Pearson and Spearman partial correlation coefficient for the reading assessment score and the number of pages read with the effect of age being controlled.

7.1.8.2   Detailed Solutions

Example 7.3.1

The Correlations output for the Pearson and Spearman correlation coefficients follows.

Output 7.4 Simple Statistics Table for Example 7.1

<table>
<thead>
<tr><th colspan="4" align="center">**Pearson Correlation Coefficients, N = 12**
Prob > |r| under H0: Rho=0</th></tr>
<tr><th></th><th align="right">age</th><th align="right">score</th><th align="right">pages</th></tr>
</thead>
<tbody>
<tr><td>**age**
student age</td><td align="right">1.00000</td><td align="right">-0.91537
<.0001</td><td align="right">-0.94513
<.0001</td></tr>
<tr><td>**score**
reading assessment score</td><td align="right">-0.91537
<.0001</td><td align="right">1.00000</td><td align="right">0.95120
<.0001</td></tr>
<tr><td>**pages**
average daily reading in class and homework</td><td align="right">-0.94513
<.0001</td><td align="right">0.95120
<.0001</td><td align="right">1.00000</td></tr>
</tbody>
</table>

<table>
<thead>
<tr><th colspan="4" align="center">**Spearman Correlation Coefficients, N = 12**
Prob > |r| under H0: Rho=0</th></tr>
<tr><th></th><th align="right">age</th><th align="right">score</th><th align="right">pages</th></tr>
</thead>
<tbody>
<tr><td>**age**
student age</td><td align="right">1.00000</td><td align="right">-0.92138
<.0001</td><td align="right">-0.94943
<.0001</td></tr>
<tr><td>**score**
reading assessment score</td><td align="right">-0.92138
<.0001</td><td align="right">1.00000</td><td align="right">0.96826
<.0001</td></tr>
<tr><td>**pages**
average daily reading in class and homework</td><td align="right">-0.94943
<.0001</td><td align="right">0.96826
<.0001</td><td align="right">1.00000</td></tr>
</tbody>
</table>

Example 7.3.2

$$r_{score,pages \cdot age} = \frac{r_{score,pages} - r_{age,score}r_{age,pages}}{\sqrt{1 - r_{age,score}^2}\sqrt{1 - r_{age,pages}^2}} = \frac{(0.95120) - (-0.91537)(-0.94513)}{\sqrt{1 - (-0.91537)^2}\sqrt{1 - (-0.94513)^2}} = 0.65426$$

$$\theta_{score,pages \cdot age} = \frac{\theta_{score,pages} - \theta_{age,score}\theta_{age,pages}}{\sqrt{1 - \theta_{age,score}^2}\sqrt{1 - \theta_{age,pages}^2}} = \frac{(0.96826) - (-0.92138)(-0.94943)}{\sqrt{1 - (-0.92138)^2}\sqrt{1 - (-0.94943)^2}} = 0.76598$$

7.1.8.3 Correlations Task

- The active data is Ex07_03.
- Task Roles
  - Score and pages are assigned to Analysis variables.
  - Age is assigned to Partial variables.
- Options: Both Pearson and Spearman are selected.

7.1.9 Task Output and Interpretation for Example 7.3

7.1.9.1 Task Output

Output 7.5 Correlations Output for Example 7.3.2

Correlation Analysis

The CORR Procedure

1 Partial Variables:	age
2 Variables:	score pages

Simple Statistics								
Variable	N	Mean	Std Dev	Median	Minimum	Maximum	Partial Variance	Partial Std Dev
age	12	13.00000	3.41121	13.00000	9.00000	17.00000		
score	12	53.41667	2.67848	53.50000	49.00000	57.00000	1.27917	1.13100
pages	12	15.58333	4.96274	14.50000	10.00000	23.00000	2.89167	1.70049

❶   ❷

Label
student age
reading assessment score
average daily reading in class and homework

Pearson Partial Correlation Coefficients, N = 12 Prob > |r| under H0: Partial Rho=0		
	score	pages
score reading assessment score	1.00000	❸ 0.65427 0.0290
pages average daily reading in class and homework	❸ 0.65427 0.0290	1.00000

Spearman Partial Correlation Coefficients, N = 12 Prob > |r| under H0: Partial Rho=0		
	score	**pages**
score reading assessment score	1.00000	❹ 0.76595 0.0060
pages average daily reading in class and homework	❹ 0.76595 0.0060	1.00000

7.1.9.2 Interpretation

❶ The partial variance is equal to the Error Mean Square, *MS*(Error), in the linear regression analysis of variance table with the controlled variable(s) as the explanatory variable(s). For simple linear regression with score as the dependent variable and age as the explanatory variable, *MS*(Error) = 1.27917. With pages as the dependent variable and age as the explanatory variable, *MS*(Error) = 2.89167.

❷ The partial standard deviation is $\sqrt{MS\left(\text{Error}\right)}$.

❸ The Pearson partial correlation coefficient for the reading assessment score and the number of pages read with the effect of age being controlled is 0.65427.

❹ The Spearman partial correlation coefficient for the reading assessment score and the number of pages read with the effect of age being controlled is 0.76595.

7.2 Simple Linear Regression

Both simple linear regression and the Pearson correlation coefficient are used to examine the linear relationship between two numeric variables, such as x and y below. Each pair of values $\left(x_i, y_i\right)$, $i = 1,\ldots,n$, comes from one person or object.

x	y
x_1	y_1
x_2	y_2
$\vdots$	$\vdots$
x_i	y_i
$\vdots$	$\vdots$
x_n	y_n

Unlike the Pearson correlation coefficient, the roles of the two variables in simple linear regression are not the same.

- The values in one variable are assumed to be fixed and known before the other variable is determined.
  - This variable is the *independent*, *explanatory*, or *predictor* variable.
  - These values are generally denoted with *x*.

- The values of the other variable are assumed to have been obtained through random selection.
  - This variable is the *dependent* or *response* variable.
  - The values are generally denoted with *y*.

It is assumed that each (x_i, y_i) pair contains a y_i value that has been randomly selected from persons or objects that are known to correspond to the value x_i.

Simple linear regression estimates the mean response at each *x* value using a straight line. The line is called the *sample regression line*. See Figure 7.12.

Figure 7.12 Sample Regression Line and Sample of Data Points

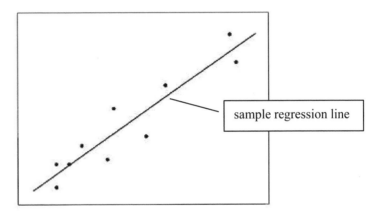

7.2.1 The Name: Simple ... Linear ... Regression

- *Simple* means that there is a single explanatory variable. Multiple linear regression involves two or more explanatory variables and a single response variable. See Section 7.3.

- *Linear* describes a type of relationship between the explanatory variable and the means of the responses. In simple linear regression, the relationship between the fixed *x* values and the means of the corresponding populations of *y* values are described by a straight line. See Figure 7.13.

- *Regression.* In the late 19th century, Sir Francis Galton observed in a study on peas that daughters of tall plants tended to be shorter than their parents and daughters of short plants tended to be taller. He noted that the range of heights did not become greater from generation to generation. Heights tended to "revert" or "regress" to a mean. Galton's mathematical description of this tendency is the precursor of modern statistical regression.

7.2.2 Population Model for Simple Linear Regression

The random variable *Y* assigns a number to each person or object of interest. Additionally, there are *n* fixed numbers: $x_1, \ldots, x_n$. There is a population of assigned numbers for each x_i.

The population model for simple linear regression assumes that for the population associated with x_i:

$$Y = \mu_i + \varepsilon$$

- μ_i is the mean of the population associated with x_i.

- ε is also a random variable. It is called an *error*. The errors ε of each population are assumed to be normally distributed with mean 0 and the unknown variance σ^2. The variance is assumed to be the same for each population.

- The values in the population associated with x_i are assumed to be normally distributed with mean μ_i and variance σ^2.

The population means are expressed with the *simple linear regression function*:

$$\mu = \beta_0 + \beta_1 x$$

- In this function, x is the explanatory variable.
  - It is the generalization in the theory of the explanatory variable x, the data set column.
  - The explanatory variable x represents the numbers in an interval that contains the values from the explanatory variable x: $x_1, \ldots, x_n$.

- For x_i, $\mu_i = \beta_0 + \beta_1 x_i$.

- Both β_0 and β_1 are unknown constants.
  - β_0 is the y-intercept. When $x = 0$, $\mu = \beta_0$. The line crosses the y-axis at the point $(0, \beta_0)$. The y-intercept is a mathematical fact, but it generally plays no role in the analysis.
  - β_1 is the slope of the line. When x increases by 1, μ changes by β_1.

In Figure 7.13, the line $\mu = \beta_0 + \beta_1 x$ has positive slope. Therefore, $\beta_1 > 0$. The population means increase as x increases. The result is that the explanatory variable is useful in predicting the responses.

Figure 7.13 Regression Function in Simple Linear Regression

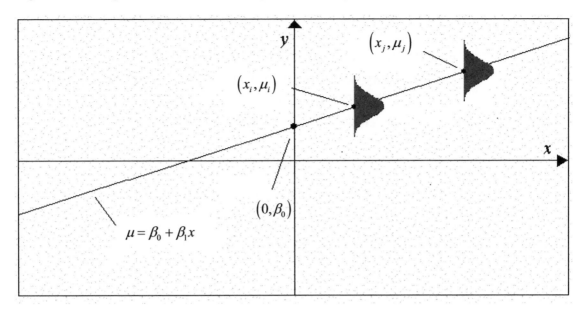

In Figure 7.14, the line is horizontal. The slope parameter is zero, $\beta_1 = 0$, and $\mu = \beta_0$ for all x. The population means do not change as x changes. The explanatory variable would not be useful in predicting the responses.

Figure 7.14 Population Means Not Dependent on the Explanatory Variable

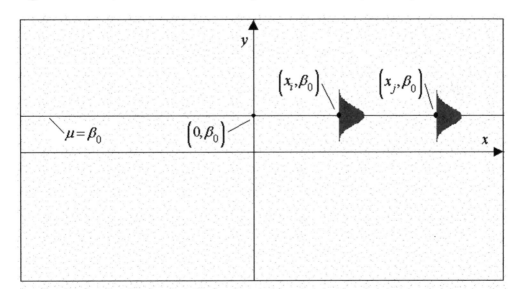

7.2.3 Sample Regression Line

A sample consists of n pairs of values: $(x_1, y_1), (x_2, y_2), \ldots, (x_n, y_n)$. Each pair becomes a data point in a scatter plot. Simple linear regression determines the best sample regression line to pass through the middle of the sample data points. See Figure 7.15.

The *sample regression function* is the equation of the sample regression line: $\hat{y} = b_0 + b_1 x$.

- As with the simple linear regression function $\mu = \beta_0 + \beta_1 x$, x is the explanatory variable.
    - It is the generalization of the explanatory variable x, the data set column.
    - The explanatory variable x represents the numbers in an interval that contains the values from the explanatory variable x: $x_1, \ldots, x_n$.
- b_1 is the slope. If x increases by 1, $\hat{y}$ changes by b_1.

    - $b_1 = r \dfrac{s_y}{s_x}$, where r is the Pearson correlation coefficient discussed in Section 7.2, and s_x and s_y are the standard deviations of the x and y values.

    - b_1 is an estimate of β_1. In notational terms, $b_1 = \hat{\beta}_1$.
- b_0 is the y-intercept. When $x = 0$, $\hat{y} = b_0$.

    - $b_0 = \bar{y} - b_1 \bar{x}$, where $\bar{x}$ and $\bar{y}$ are the means of the x and y values.

    - b_0 is an estimate of β_0. In notational terms, $b_0 = \hat{\beta}_0$.
- $\hat{y}_i = b_0 + b_1 x_i$ is the *fitted value* given x_i. It is the estimate of μ_i.

Figure 7.15 Sample Regression Line and Sample of Data Points

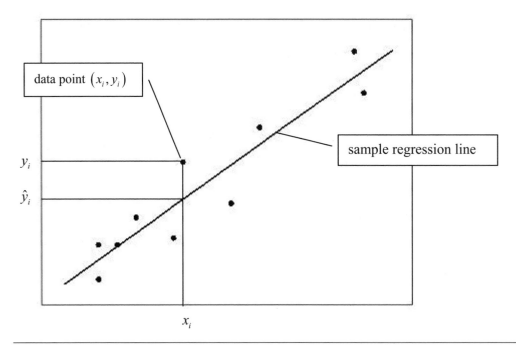

7.2.3.1 Least Squares

The sample regression line is fit to the data using a technique called *least squares*. The technique determines the line that minimizes the squared distance between the observed values y_i and the fitted values $\hat{y}_i = b_0 + b_1 x_i$. That is, for all numbers c and d, b_0 and b_1 are the values such that:

$$\sum_{i=1}^{n}\left(y_i - \hat{y}_i\right)^2 = \sum_{i=1}^{n}\left(y_i - \left(b_0 + b_1 x_i\right)\right)^2 \le \sum_{i=1}^{n}\left(y_i - \left(c + dx_i\right)\right)^2$$

Details

The following verifies that $\sum_{i=1}^{n}\left(y_i - \left(c + dx_i\right)\right)^2$ is minimized when $d = r\, s_y / s_x$ and $c = \bar{y} - b_1\bar{x}$.

$$\sum_{i=1}^{n}\left(y_i - \left(c + dx_i\right)\right)^2$$

$$= \sum_{i=1}^{n}\left(y_i - \bar{y} + \bar{y} - c - dx_i - d\bar{x} + d\bar{x}\right)^2 \quad \text{(Drop parentheses. Subtract and add } \bar{y} \text{ and } d\bar{x}.\text{)}$$

$$= \sum_{i=1}^{n}\left(\left(y_i - \bar{y}\right) - \left(c - \bar{y} + d\bar{x}\right) - d\left(x_i - \bar{x}\right)\right)^2 \quad \text{(Regroup and factor.)}$$

$$= \sum_{i=1}^{n}\left(y_i - \bar{y}\right)^2 - \left(c - \bar{y} + d\bar{x}\right)\sum_{i=1}^{n}\left(y_i - \bar{y}\right) - d\sum_{i=1}^{n}\left(x_i - \bar{x}\right)\left(y_i - \bar{y}\right) \quad \text{(Expand and sum.)}$$

$$\quad - \left(c - \bar{y} + d\bar{x}\right)\sum_{i=1}^{n}\left(y_i - \bar{y}\right) + n\left(c - \bar{y} + d\bar{x}\right)^2 + \left(c - \bar{y} + d\bar{x}\right)d\sum_{i=1}^{n}\left(x_i - \bar{x}\right)$$

$$\quad - d\sum_{i=1}^{n}\left(x_i - \bar{x}\right)\left(y_i - \bar{y}\right) + \left(c - \bar{y} + d\bar{x}\right)d\sum_{i=1}^{n}\left(x_i - \bar{x}\right) + d^2\sum_{i=1}^{n}\left(x_i - \bar{x}\right)^2$$

$$= (n-1)s_y^2 - 0 - d(n-1)s_x s_y r \quad \text{(Substitute. See * below.)}$$

$$\quad -0 + n\left(c - \bar{y} + d\bar{x}\right)^2 + 0$$

$$\quad - d(n-1)s_x s_y r + 0 + d^2(n-1)s_x^2$$

$$= (n-1)s_y^2 + n\left(c - \bar{y} + d\bar{x}\right)^2 - 2d(n-1)s_x s_y r + d^2(n-1)s_x^2 \quad \text{(Simplify)}$$

$$= (n-1)s_y^2 + n\left(c - \bar{y} + d\bar{x}\right)^2 - 2d(n-1)s_x s_y r + d^2(n-1)s_x^2 - (n-1)s_y^2 r^2 + (n-1)s_y^2 r^2 \quad \text{(Subtract and add } (n-1)s_y^2 r^2.\text{)}$$

$$= (n-1)s_y^2\left(1 - r^2\right) + n\left(c - \bar{y} + d\bar{x}\right)^2 + (n-1)s_y^2 r^2 - 2d(n-1)s_x s_y r + d^2(n-1)s_x^2 \quad \text{(Factor and regroup.)}$$

$$= (n-1)s_y^2\left(1 - r^2\right) + n\left(c - \bar{y} + d\bar{x}\right)^2 + (n-1)\left(s_y r - ds_x\right)^2 \quad \text{(Factor)}$$

Therefore, $\sum_{i=1}^{n} \left(y_i - \left(c + dx_i \right) \right)^2 = (n-1)s_y^2 \left(1 - r^2 \right) + n \left(c - \bar{y} + d\bar{x} \right)^2 + (n-1) \left(s_y r - ds_x \right)^2$. This is

minimized when $n \left(c - \bar{y} + d\bar{x} \right)^2 = 0$ and $(n-1) \left(s_y r - ds_x \right)^2 = 0$. These are 0 when c and d are:

$$(n-1) \left(s_y r - ds_x \right)^2 = 0 \qquad\qquad n \left(c - \bar{y} + d\bar{x} \right)^2 = 0$$
$$s_y r - ds_x = 0 \qquad\qquad c - \bar{y} + d\bar{x} = 0$$
$$ds_x = s_y r \qquad\qquad c = \bar{y} - d\bar{x}$$
$$d = \frac{s_y r}{s_x} = r \frac{s_y}{s_x}$$

The line with slope $b_1 = r \dfrac{s_y}{s_x}$ and y-intercept $b_0 = \bar{y} - b_1 \bar{x}$ best fits the data.

In the Analysis of Variance Table section:

$$SS(\text{Error}) = \sum_{i=1}^{n} \left(y_i - \hat{y}_i \right)^2 = \sum_{i=1}^{n} \left(y_i - \left(b_0 + b_1 x_i \right) \right)^2 = (n-1)s_y^2 \left(1 - r^2 \right)$$

* In the substitution step:

- $(n-1)s_y^2$ is substituted for $\sum_{i=1}^{n} \left(y_i - \bar{y} \right)^2$ since $s_y^2 = \dfrac{\sum_{i=1}^{n} \left(y_i - \bar{y} \right)^2}{n-1}$

- $(n-1)s_x^2$ is substituted for $\sum_{i=1}^{n} \left(x_i - \bar{x} \right)^2$ since $s_y^2 = \dfrac{\sum_{i=1}^{n} \left(x_i - \bar{x} \right)^2}{n-1}$

- $(n-1)s_x s_y r$ is substituted for $\sum_{i=1}^{n} \left(x_i - \bar{x} \right) \left(y_i - \bar{y} \right)$ since $r = \dfrac{\sum_{i=1}^{n} \left(x_i - \bar{x} \right) \left(y_i - \bar{y} \right)}{(n-1)s_x s_y}$

- $\sum_{i=1}^{n} \left(y_i - \bar{y} \right) = 0$ because $\bar{y} = \dfrac{\sum_{i=1}^{n} y_i}{n}$, $\;n\bar{y} = \sum_{i=1}^{n} y_i$, $\;0 = \sum_{i=1}^{n} y_i - n\bar{y}$, $\;0 = \sum_{i=1}^{n} \left(y_i - \bar{y} \right)$

- $\sum_{i=1}^{n} \left(x_i - \bar{x} \right) = 0$ because $\bar{x} = \dfrac{\sum_{i=1}^{n} x_i}{n}$, $\;n\bar{x} = \sum_{i=1}^{n} x_i$, $\;0 = \sum_{i=1}^{n} x_i - n\bar{x}$, $\;0 = \sum_{i=1}^{n} \left(x_i - \bar{x} \right)$

7.2.4 Test of the Simple Linear Regression Model

The test of the population model for simple linear regression is based on an analysis of variance (ANOVA) table. The null and alternative hypotheses are:

$$H_0 : \beta_1 = 0$$
$$H_1 : \beta_1 \neq 0$$

- If $\beta_1 = 0$, then $\mu = \beta_0$. The means of the populations do not change with x.

- If $\beta_1 \neq 0$, then $\mu = \beta_0 + \beta_1 x$. The means of the populations do change with x.

7.2.4.1 Analysis of Variance Table

The components of an ANOVA table are sums of squares, degrees of freedom, mean squares, F value and p-value.

The role of an analysis of variance table is to analyze the deviations of the responses from the mean, $y_i - \overline{y}$. In linear regression, each deviation is broken into two parts:

$$\left(y_i - \overline{y} \right) = \left(y_i - \hat{y}_i \right) + \left(\hat{y}_i - \overline{y} \right)$$

$$\begin{pmatrix} \text{deviation from} \\ \text{the mean} \end{pmatrix} = \begin{pmatrix} \text{deviation from} \\ \text{the regression line} \end{pmatrix} + \begin{pmatrix} \text{effect of the} \\ \text{explanatory variable} \end{pmatrix}$$

This is shown graphically in Figure 7.16.

Figure 7.16 Breakdown of $y_i - \overline{y}$

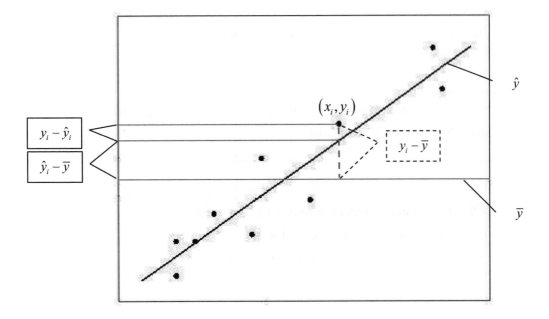

Sums of Squares

The breakdown in the deviation from the mean results in the following sums of squares.

$$\sum_{i=1}^{n}\left(y_i - \bar{y}\right)^2 = \sum_{i=1}^{n}\left(y_i - \hat{y}_i\right)^2 + \sum_{i=1}^{n}\left(\hat{y}_i - \bar{y}\right)^2$$

$$SS(\text{Total}) = SS(\text{Error}) + SS(\text{Model})$$

- $SS(\text{Total})$ (the numerator of s_y^2) is the Corrected Total Sum of Squares.

- $SS(\text{Error})$ (the sum of the squared deviations from the sample regression line) is the Error Sum of Squares or the Sum-of-Squares Error.

  - The $SS(\text{Error})$ is a measure of the random variation. Random variation is present because the responses are randomly selected from their populations.

  - In Least Squares section, it is shown that $SS(\text{Error}) = (n-1)s_y^2(1-r^2)$.

- $SS(\text{Model})$ (the sum of the squared differences between the fitted values $\hat{y}_i$ and the mean of the responses $\bar{y}$) is the Model Sum of Squares.

  - The $SS(\text{Model})$ is a measure of the variation in the responses due to both a linear relationship and the random variation in the responses. The $SS(\text{Model})$ measures the variation through the statistic b_1:

  - $$SS(\text{Model}) = \sum_{i=1}^{n}\left(\hat{y}_i - \bar{y}\right)^2 = \sum_{i=1}^{n}\left(b_0 + b_1 x_i - \bar{y}\right)^2 = \sum_{i=1}^{n}\left(\bar{y} - b_1\bar{x} + b_1 x_i - \bar{y}\right)^2$$
    $$= \sum_{i=1}^{n}\left(b_1 x_i - b_1\bar{x}\right)^2 = \left(b_1\right)^2 \sum_{i=1}^{n}\left(x_i - \bar{x}\right)^2 = \left(b_1\right)^2\left[(n-1)s_x^2\right]$$

    - When $H_0 : \beta_1 = 0$ is true, b_1 estimates 0. Any nonzero value is due to random variation only. In that case, $SS(\text{Model})$ measures only random variation.

    - When $H_1 : \beta_1 \neq 0$ is true, $SS(\text{Model})$ measures a nonzero β_1 plus random variation.

Degrees of Freedom

There are $n-1$ degrees of freedom associated with the overall sample. This is the denominator of s_y^2. With one explanatory variable in the model:

$$n-1 = (n-2) + (1)$$

- $n-1$ are the degrees of freedom associated with the $SS(\text{Total})$.
- $n-2$ are the degrees of freedom associated with the $SS(\text{Error})$.
- 1 is the degree of freedom associated with the $SS(\text{Model})$.

Mean Squares

The mean squares are the sums of squares adjusted for the number of parameters in the model and/or the number of responses. A mean square is equal to a sum of squares divided by the associated degrees of freedom.

- The Model Mean Square is a measure of the variation in the responses explained by the sample regression function. The variation is due to a possibly nonzero population slope parameter and the random selection of the responses.

$$MS(\text{Model}) = \frac{SS(\text{Model})}{1}$$

- The Error Mean Square, or Mean Square Error, is a measure of the random variation in the responses.

$$MS(\text{Error}) = \frac{SS(\text{Error})}{n-2}$$

The MS(Error) is an estimate of σ^2, the common population variance.

F Value

The following is the test statistic for $H_0 : \beta_1 = 0$ versus $H_1 : \beta_1 \neq 0$.

$$F \text{ Value } = \frac{MS(\text{Model})}{MS(\text{Error})}$$

If H_0 is true, both the MS(Model) and the MS(Error) would measure only random variation. It is expected that:

- $MS(\text{Model}) = MS(\text{Error})$

- $F \text{ Value } = \frac{MS(\text{Model})}{MS(\text{Error})} = 1$

p-Values

The *p*-value is a measure of the likelihood that the samples come from populations where H_0 is true. Smaller values indicate less likelihood. That is, the more the data agrees with H_1 (the more $MS(\text{Model})/MS(\text{Error})$ is greater than 1) the smaller the *p*-value.

The *p*-value is the probability that randomly selected responses from populations with means that are not dependent on a linear regression function of the explanatory variable would produce an *F* value at or beyond the current value. If the *p*-value is small, it is unlikely that the means are not dependent on a linear regression function of the explanatory variable.

Table 7.8 has the technical definition of the *p*-value. The random variable *F* represents a future value of the test statistic and follows an *F* distribution. The *F* distribution depends on two degrees-of-freedom values: the numerator degrees of freedom and the denominator degrees of freedom. For simple linear regression, these are 1 and $n - 2$, respectively.

In the SAS code expression, F value and $n - 2$ represent numbers. The SAS code expression is included to aid in the discussion. The p-value is computed using the expression in the "Detailed Solutions" section of "Example 7.4: Simple Linear Regression."

Table 7.8 p-Value for the Test of the Simple Linear Regression Model

Hypotheses	Gray area corresponds to the probability statement and is an example.
$H_0 : \beta_1 = 0$ $H_1 : \beta_1 \neq 0$	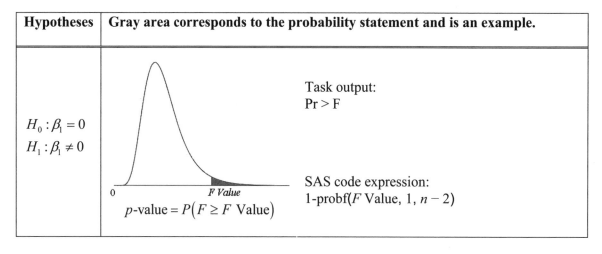 Task output: Pr > F SAS code expression: 1-probf(F Value, 1, $n - 2$)

ANOVA Table

The sums of squares, the degrees of freedom (Df), the mean squares, the F value, and the p-value are all organized by the ANOVA table.

Source	Df	Sum of Squares	Mean Square	F Value	$Pr > F$
Model	1	$SS(\text{Model})$	$\dfrac{SS(\text{Model})}{1}$	$\dfrac{MS(\text{Model})}{MS(\text{Error})}$	p-value
Error	$n - 2$	$SS(\text{Error})$	$\dfrac{SS(\text{Error})}{n - 2}$		
Corrected Total	$n - 1$	$SS(\text{Total})$			

Decision and Conclusions

The formal decision and concluding sentence do not change from the one-sample tests discussed in Chapter 4, "Inferences from One Sample." The concluding observation depends on the particular statistics involved in the test.

If the p-value is small, the data agrees with H_1. If the p-value is less than the significance level, the risk of making a Type I error is acceptable. Therefore, the p-value decision rule is the following.

If the p-value $< \alpha$, reject H_0. Otherwise, do not reject H_0.

Since a hypothesis test begins with the assumption that H_0 is true, concluding a hypothesis test requires one of the following formal statements:

- Reject H_0.
- Do not reject H_0.

When the claim is equivalent to the null hypothesis, the concluding sentence uses the word *reject*. The concluding sentence becomes an expanded version of the formal decision.

When the claim is equivalent to the alternative hypothesis, the concluding sentence uses the word *support*. If the data supports the rejection of H_0, the data supports H_1. If the data does not support rejection of H_0, the data cannot support H_1.

Table 7.9 Concluding Sentences

Formal Statistical Decision	Claim stated as H_0	Claim stated as H_1
Reject H_0.	There is sufficient evidence to reject the claim that ... (claim in words).	There is sufficient evidence to support the claim that ... (claim in words).
Do not reject H_0.	There is not sufficient evidence to reject the claim that ... (claim in words).	There is not sufficient evidence to support the claim that ... (claim in words).

Table 7.10 Concluding Observations

Reject H_0.	The explanatory variable explains a significant amount of the variation in the responses.
Do not reject H_0.	The explanatory variable does not explain a significant amount of the variation in the responses.

7.2.5 Tests and Confidence Intervals on the Model Parameters

7.2.5.1 Intercept Parameter

- The estimate of β_0 is $b_0 = \overline{y} - b_1 \overline{x}$.
- The estimator b_0 follows a normal distribution with mean β_0 and variance $\sigma^2 \left(\dfrac{1}{n} + \dfrac{\overline{x}^2}{(n-1)s_x^2} \right)$. The standard deviation of an estimator is called the standard error.

- The standard error of b_0 is $\sqrt{\sigma^2 \left(\dfrac{1}{n} + \dfrac{\bar{x}^2}{(n-1)s_x^2} \right)}$.

- The *MS*(Error) is an estimate of σ^2. The estimate of the standard error of b_0 is $se(b_0) =$
$\sqrt{MS\,(\text{Error}) \left(\dfrac{1}{n} + \dfrac{\bar{x}^2}{(n-1)s_x^2} \right)}$.

The hypotheses regarding the *y*-intercept of the simple linear regression function are $H_0 : \beta_0 = 0$ versus $H_1 : \beta_0 \neq 0$. The following is the test statistic. It follows the *t* distribution with $n - 2$ degrees of freedom.

$$t \text{ Value} = \frac{b_0 - 0}{\sqrt{MS\,(\text{Error}) \left(\dfrac{1}{n} + \dfrac{\bar{x}^2}{(n-1)s_x^2} \right)}}$$

The following is a $100(1 - \alpha)\%$ confidence interval on β_0. The $t_{\alpha/2}$ critical value comes from the *t* distribution with $n - 2$ degrees of freedom.

$$b_0 \pm t_{\alpha/2} \sqrt{MS\,(\text{Error}) \left(\dfrac{1}{n} + \dfrac{\bar{x}^2}{(n-1)s_x^2} \right)}$$

7.2.5.2 Slope Parameter

- The estimate of β_1 is $b_1 = r \dfrac{s_y}{s_x}$.

- The estimator b_1 follows a normal distribution with mean β_1 and variance $\dfrac{\sigma^2}{(n-1)s_x^2}$.

  Therefore, the standard error of b_1 is $\sqrt{\dfrac{\sigma^2}{(n-1)s_x^2}}$.

- The estimate of the standard error of b_1 is $se(b_1) = \sqrt{\dfrac{MS\,(\text{Error})}{(n-1)s_x^2}}$.

In simple linear regression, the hypotheses on the model and the hypotheses on the slope parameter are the same:

$H_0 : \beta_1 = 0$
$H_1 : \beta_1 \neq 0$

The following is the test statistic. It follows the *t* distribution with $n - 2$ degrees of freedom.

$$t \text{ Value} = \frac{b_1 - 0}{\sqrt{\dfrac{MS(\text{Error})}{(n-1)s_x^2}}}$$

This test produces a result that is equivalent to the test of the model in the analysis of variance table. Specifically, this *t* value squared is equal to the *F* value of the analysis of variance table.

$$(t \text{ Value})^2 = \left(\frac{b_1 - 0}{\sqrt{\dfrac{MS(\text{Error})}{(n-1)s_x^2}}} \right)^2 = \frac{(b_1)^2}{\left(\dfrac{MS(\text{Error})}{(n-1)s_x^2} \right)} = \frac{(n-1)s_x^2 (b_1)^2}{MS(\text{Error})} = \frac{MS(\text{Model})}{MS(\text{Error})} = F \text{ value}$$

The following is a $100(1 - \alpha)\%$ confidence interval on β_1. The $t_{\alpha/2}$ critical value comes from the *t* distribution with $n - 2$ degrees of freedom.

$$b_1 \pm t_{\alpha/2} \sqrt{\frac{MS(\text{Error})}{(n-1)s_x^2}}$$

p-Values

The *p*-value is a measure of the likelihood that the samples come from populations where H_0 is true. Smaller values indicate less likelihood. That is, the more the data agrees with H_1 (the more a *t* Value is different from 0) the smaller the *p*-value.

In terms of $H_0 : \beta_0 = 0$, the *p*-value is the probability that randomly selected responses from populations with means determined by a simple linear regression function with 0 *y*-intercept would produce a *t* value at or beyond the current value. If the *p*-value is small, it is unlikely that the simple linear regression function has 0 *y*-intercept.

In terms of $H_0 : \beta_1 = 0$, the *p*-value is the probability that randomly selected responses from populations with means that are not dependent on a linear regression function of the explanatory variable would produce a *t* value at or beyond the current value. If the *p*-value is small, it is unlikely that the means are not dependent on a linear regression function of the explanatory variable.

Table 7.11 has the technical definition of the *p*-value. The random variable *T* represents a future value of the test statistic and follows a *t* distribution with $n - 2$ degrees of freedom.

In the SAS code expression, *t* value and $n - 2$ represent numbers. The SAS code expression is included to aid in the discussion. The *p*-value is computed using the expression in the "Detailed Solutions" section of "Example 7.4: Simple Linear Regression."

Table 7.11 *p*-Value for the Tests Based on Parameter Estimates

Hypotheses	Gray area corresponds to the probability statement and is an example.
$H_0 : \beta_0 = 0$ $H_1 : \beta_0 \neq 0$	Task output: Pr > |t|
$H_0 : \beta_1 = 0$ $H_1 : \beta_1 \neq 0$	SAS code expression: 2*(1-probt(abs(*t* Value),*n* − 2))

$p\text{-value} = 2P\big(T \geq |t \text{ Value}|\big)$

Parameter Estimates

The parameter estimates output is below the analysis of variance table.

Parameter Estimates

Variable	Df	Parameter Estimate	Standard Error	t Value	Pr > |t|
Intercept	1	b_0	$se(b_0)$	$\dfrac{b_0}{se(b_0)}$	*p*-value
explanatory variable	1	b_1	$se(b_1)$	$\dfrac{b_1}{se(b_1)}$	*p*-value

Decision and Conclusions

The formal decision and concluding sentence do not change from the one-sample tests discussed in Chapter 4, "Inferences from One Sample." The concluding observation depends on the particular statistics involved in the test.

If the *p*-value is small, the data agrees with H_1. If the *p*-value is less than the significance level, the risk of making a Type I error is acceptable. Therefore, the *p*-value decision rule is the following:

> If the *p*-value < α, reject H_0. Otherwise, do not reject H_0.

Since a hypothesis test begins with the assumption that H_0 is true, concluding a hypothesis test requires one of the following formal statements:

- Reject H_0.
- Do not reject H_0.

When the claim is equivalent to the null hypothesis, the concluding sentence uses the word *reject*. The concluding sentence becomes an expanded version of the formal decision.

When the claim is equivalent to the alternative hypothesis, the concluding sentence uses the word *support*. If the data supports the rejection of H_0, the data supports H_1. If the data does not support the rejection of H_0, the data cannot support H_1.

Table 7.12 Concluding Sentences

Formal Statistical Decision	Claim stated as H_0	Claim stated as H_1
Reject H_0.	There is sufficient evidence to reject the claim that ... (claim in words).	There is sufficient evidence to support the claim that ... (claim in words).
Do not reject H_0.	There is not sufficient evidence to reject the claim that ... (claim in words).	There is not sufficient evidence to support the claim that ... (claim in words).

Table 7.13 Concluding Observations

$H_0 : \beta_0 = 0$ versus $H_1 : \beta_0 \neq 0$	
Reject H_0.	The y-intercept of the sample regression line is significantly different from 0.
Do not reject H_0.	The sample regression line y-intercept is not significantly different from 0.
$H_0 : \beta_1 = 0$ versus $H_1 : \beta_1 \neq 0$	
Reject H_0.	The slope of the sample regression line is significantly different from 0. The explanatory variable explains a significant amount of the variation in the responses.
Do not reject H_0.	The slope of the sample regression line is not significantly different from 0. The explanatory variable does not explain a significant amount of the variation in the responses.

7.2.6 Simple Linear Regression and Correlation

The tests on the slope parameter and population correlation coefficient are equivalent. The hypotheses are:

$$H_0 : \beta_1 = 0 \qquad H_0 : \rho = 0$$
$$H_1 : \beta_1 \neq 0 \qquad H_1 : \rho \neq 0$$

Below, the test statistic for the hypotheses on β_1 is the first expression on the left, and the test statistic for the hypotheses on ρ is on the right.

$$t \text{ Value} = \frac{b_1 - 0}{\sqrt{\dfrac{MS(\text{Error})}{(n-1)s_x^2}}} = \frac{r \dfrac{s_y}{s_x} - 0}{\sqrt{\dfrac{\left((n-1)s_y^2\left(1-r^2\right)\right)\big/(n-2)}{(n-1)s_x^2}}} = \frac{r-0}{\left(\dfrac{s_x}{s_y}\right)\sqrt{\dfrac{\left(s_y^2\left(1-r^2\right)\right)\big/(n-2)}{s_x^2}}} = \frac{r-0}{\sqrt{\dfrac{1-r^2}{n-2}}}$$

7.2.7 Additional Statistics Included with the ANOVA Table

7.2.7.1 Coefficient of Determination and Adjusted Coefficient of Determination

The Coefficient of Determination, denoted by R^2, measures the reduction in the variation of the responses due to fitting the model to the data. Here, the model is the simple linear regression function which is estimated by $\hat{y} = b_0 + b_1 x$.

Consider Figure 7.17 where graph (a) shows a scatter plot and a sample regression line.

- In graph (b), the scatter plot has been rotated in three dimensions so that one is looking down the plane through the y axis.
  - One sees the variation of the responses y_i, $i = 1,\ldots,n$, along the y axis and without regard for the x_i values.
  - This variation is measured by the $SS(\text{Total})$.

- In graph (c), the scatter plot has been rotated in three dimensions so that one is looking down the sample regression line $\hat{y} = b_0 + b_1 x$.
  - One sees the variation of the residuals $y_i - \hat{y}_i$ without regard for the x_i values.
  - This variation is measured by the $SS(\text{Error})$.

The difference in variation is measured by $SS(\text{Total}) - SS(\text{Error})$. Division by $SS(\text{Total})$ results in R^2.

$$R^2 = \frac{SS(\text{Total}) - SS(\text{Error})}{SS(\text{Total})} = 1 - \frac{SS(\text{Error})}{SS(\text{Total})}$$

Figure 7.17 (a) Scatter Plot with Regression Line, (b) Dispersion of Responses, (c) Dispersion of Residuals

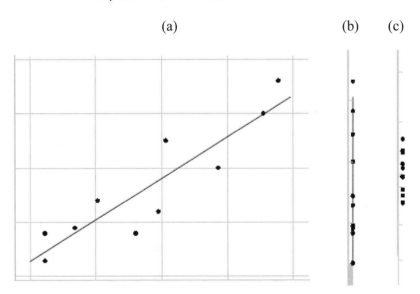

(a)   (b)   (c)

- $0 \leq R^2 \leq 1$, with larger values indicating greater reduction in the variation of the responses due to fitting the model to the data.

- Since $SS(\text{Total}) - SS(\text{Error}) = SS(\text{Model})$:

  - $$R^2 = \frac{SS(\text{Model})}{SS(\text{Total})}$$

  - R^2 is also interpreted as the proportion of variation in the responses explained by the model.

- The F value from the ANOVA table can be expressed in terms of R^2:

  $$F \text{ value} = (n-2)\frac{R^2}{1-R^2}$$

- In simple linear regression, $R^2 = (r)^2$ where r is the Pearson correlation coefficient of the response and explanatory variables.

The Adjusted Coefficient of Determination (adj-R^2) makes degrees-of-freedom adjustments. The interpretation of adj-R^2 is the same as the interpretation of R^2. It becomes more important in multiple linear regression, which is discussed in Section 7.3.

$$\text{adj-}R^2 = 1 - \frac{\left(\dfrac{SS(\text{Error})}{n-2}\right)}{\left(\dfrac{SS(\text{Total})}{n-1}\right)} = 1 - \frac{MS(\text{Error})}{s_y^2}$$

7.2.7.2   Other Statistics

- Root MSE: The $\sqrt{MS(\text{Error})}$ is a measure of the random variation in the responses. It is an estimate of σ, the common population standard deviation.

- Dependent Mean: This is the mean of the responses $\bar{y}$.

- Coefficient of Variation: The Coefficient of Variation measures the random variation in the responses as a percentage of the overall mean: $100\dfrac{\sqrt{MS(\text{Error})}}{\bar{y}}$.

7.2.8 Summary of Hypothesis Tests

Plan the task.

The circled numbers associate the hypotheses with the appropriate statistics.

❶ & ❸ $H_0 : \beta_1 = 0$ ❷ $H_0 : \beta_0 = 0$

           $H_1 : \beta_1 \neq 0$ $H_1 : \beta_0 \neq 0$

For each test, the significance level is α.

Compute the statistics.

Analysis of Variance					
Source	**DF**	**Sum of Squares**	**Mean Square**	**F Value**	**Pr > F**
Model	1	$SS(\text{Model})$	$MS(\text{Model}) = SS(\text{Model})$	$\dfrac{MS(\text{Model})}{MS(\text{Error})}$	p-value ❶
Error	$n - 2$	$SS(\text{Error})$	$MS(\text{Error}) = \dfrac{SS(\text{Error})}{n-2}$		
Corrected Total	$n - 1$	$SS(\text{Total})$			

Root MSE	$\sqrt{MS(\text{Error})}$	**R-Square**	R^2
Dependent Mean	$\bar{y}$	**Adj R-Sq**	adj-R^2
Coeff Var	$100\dfrac{\sqrt{MS(\text{Error})}}{\bar{y}}$		

Parameter Estimates						
Variable	**DF**	**Parameter Estimate**	**Standard Error**	**t Value**	**Pr > |t|**	
Intercept	1	b_0	$se(b_0)$	$\dfrac{b_0}{se(b_0)}$	*p*-value	❷
explanatory variable	1	b_1	$se(b_1)$	$\dfrac{b_1}{se(b_1)}$	*p*-value	❸

Apply the results.

For each test: If the *p*-value $< \alpha$, reject H_0. Otherwise, do not reject H_0.

See Tables 7.12 and 7.13 for the concluding sentences and observations.

7.2.9 Estimation of a Mean Response for a Given x

The mean of a population of responses is determined by the linear regression function $\mu = \beta_0 + \beta_1 x$. When the explanatory variable has value x_k, the mean is $\mu_k = \beta_0 + \beta_1 x_k$. The value x_k may or may not be in the data set.

- The point estimate of μ_k is $\hat{y}_k = b_0 + b_1 x_k$.

- The population associated with the $\hat{y}_k$ statistic follows a normal distribution with mean

  $\beta_0 + \beta_1 x_k$ and variance $\sigma^2 \left(\dfrac{1}{n} + \dfrac{\left(x_k - \overline{x}\right)^2}{(n-1)s_x^2} \right)$.

With $\sqrt{MS\left(Error\right)}$ estimating σ, a $100(1 - \alpha)\%$ confidence interval on μ_k is:

$$\hat{y} \pm t_{\alpha/2} \sqrt{MS\left(Error\right)} \sqrt{\frac{1}{n} + \frac{\left(x_k - \overline{x}\right)^2}{(n-1)s_x^2}}$$

The $t_{\alpha/2}$ critical value comes from the *t* distribution with $n - 2$ degrees of freedom.

The point estimates and confidence limits can be included in the output and as variables in an output data set.

- The output column or data set variable name for the point estimates is the prefix predicted_ combined with the name of the dependent variable. The variable label is Predicted Value of *dependent_variable*.

- The output column or data set variable name for the lower limits is the prefix lclm_ combined with the name of the dependent variable. The variable label is Lower Bound of __% C.I. for Mean.

- The output column or data set variable name for the upper limits is the prefix uclm_ combined with the name of the dependent variable. The variable label is Upper Bound of __% C.I. for Mean.

7.2.10 Prediction of a New Response for a Given x

A new response is predicted in the sense that an interval is constructed that will, with a given confidence level, contain a future response. For an explanatory value x_k, the interval is based on a normal distribution with mean and variance:

$$\mu_k = \beta_0 + \beta_1 x_k \text{ and } \sigma^2 \left(1 + \frac{1}{n} + \frac{(x_k - \overline{x})^2}{(n-1)s_x^2} \right)$$

- $\mu_k = \beta_0 + \beta_1 x_k$ is estimated by $\hat{y}_k = b_0 + b_1 x_k$.

- The variance takes into account the variance of the population of potential responses (σ^2) and the variance of the statistic $\hat{y}_k = b_0 + b_1 x_k$ — $\sigma^2 \left(\frac{1}{n} + \frac{(x_k - \overline{x})^2}{(n-1)s_x^2} \right)$:

$$\sigma^2 + \sigma^2 \left(\frac{1}{n} + \frac{(x_k - \overline{x})^2}{(n-1)s_x^2} \right) = \sigma^2 \left(1 + \frac{1}{n} + \frac{(x_k - \overline{x})^2}{(n-1)s_x^2} \right)$$

With $\sqrt{MS(\text{Error})}$ estimating σ, a $100(1 - \alpha)\%$ *prediction interval* is:

$$\hat{y}_k \pm t_{\alpha/2} \sqrt{MS(\text{Error})} \sqrt{1 + \frac{1}{n} + \frac{(x_k - \overline{x})^2}{(n-1)s_x^2}}$$

The $t_{\alpha/2}$ critical value comes from the t distribution with $n - 2$ degrees of freedom.

The prediction limits can be included in the output and as variables in an output data set.

- The output column or data set variable name for the lower limits is the prefix lcl_ combined with the name of the dependent variable. The variable label is Lower Bound of __% C.I. (Individual Pred).

- The output column or data set variable name for the upper limits is the prefix ucl_ combined with the name of the dependent variable. The variable label is Upper Bound of __% C.I. (Individual Pred).

7.2.11 Example 7.4: Simple Linear Regression

Example 7.4 applies the material covered in Section 7.2.

- All topics except the scatter plot are addressed in the "Detailed Solutions" section.

- The Linear Regression task is introduced in "Instructions for Simple Linear Regression."

- Complete results are in "Task Output, Interpretation, and Analysis for Example 7.4."

7.2.11.1 Value of Homework

The responses are from 10 randomly selected students taking a particular course. The goal is to use homework scores to explain final exam scores. Homework is the explanatory variable x and Final is the dependent variable y.

Student	Homework	Final
1	47	63
2	59	68
3	47	68
4	62	72
5	51	69
6	70	80
7	54	74
8	63	85
9	78	96
10	76	90

These values are in the Ex07_04 data set.

Example 7.4.1
Determine the sample regression equation.

Example 7.4.2
Use the analysis of variance table to test the claim that, among all students that take this particular course, homework scores are useful in explaining final exam scores. Let $\alpha = 0.05$.

Example 7.4.3
Test $H_0 : \beta_0 = 0$ versus $H_0 : \beta_0 \neq 0$. Let $\alpha = 0.05$.

Example 7.4.4
Use the parameter t test to test $H_0 : \beta_1 = 0$ versus $H_0 : \beta_1 \neq 0$. Let $\alpha = 0.05$.

Example 7.4.5
Determine and interpret the Coefficient of Determination (R^2).

Example 7.4.6
Compute a 95% confidence interval on β_0.

Example 7.4.7
Compute a 95% confidence interval on β_1.

Example 7.4.8
Estimate the mean final exam scores for students who have homework scores 45, 55, 65, and 75. Construct 95% confidence intervals on the mean final exam scores.

Example 7.4.9
Construct 95% prediction intervals on the final exam scores for the next students who have homework scores 45, 55, 65, and 75.

Example 7.4.10
Obtain a scatter plot of the data that includes the sample regression line and 95% confidence limits on the mean final exam scores.

Example 7.4.11
Include the fitted values, confidence intervals on mean responses, and prediction intervals in an output data set. Use the List Data task to show the results. Allow the variable labels to be the column headings.

7.2.11.2 Adding New *x* Values

Example 7.4 asks for estimates, confidence limits, and prediction limits for Homework scores 45, 55, 65, and 75. None of these values is in the table. They need to be added to the original table or they need to be put in a new data set.

In Figure 7.18 (a), four new rows are added to Ex07_04 and the resulting data set is saved as Ex07_04_with_new_rows. The new values are added to the Homework column. The corresponding rows in the Final column are left as missing values.

In Figure 7.18 (b), the four new Homework values are in a separate data set, Ex07_04_more_x. There is no Final column.

Figure 7.18 (a) Original Table with New Rows, (b) Values in Separate Data Set

(a)

	Homework	Final
ex07_04_with_new_rows (read-only)		
1	47	63
2	59	68
3	47	68
4	62	72
5	51	69
6	70	80
7	54	74
8	63	85
9	78	96
10	76	90
11	45	.
12	55	.
13	65	.
14	75	.

(b)

	Homework
ex07_04_more_x (read-only)	
1	45
2	55
3	65
4	75

When new values are in a separate file, a copy of the file should be exported to the SASUSER library. This results in easier access when working with the Predictions option in the Linear Regression task. For example, to export Ex07_04_more_x to the SASUSER library:

- The Ex07_04_more_x data set is opened from a Windows folder.

- Its icon is right-clicked. **Export ▶ Export ex07_04_more_x** is selected from the pop-up menu.

- The Export ex07_04_more_x (Process Flow) To windows appears and SAS Servers is selected.

- The Export window appears. Navigate to the SASUSER library by **Servers ▶ Local ▶ Libraries ▶ SASUSER**.

- Click **Save**.

7.2.11.3 Detailed Solutions

The solutions begin with Correlations output.

Output 7.6 Correlation Task Output for Example 7.4

Correlation Analysis
The CORR Procedure

2 Variables:	Homework Final

Simple Statistics						
Variable	**N**	**Mean**	**Std Dev**	**Sum**	**Minimum**	**Maximum**
Homework	10	60.70000	11.27485	607.00000	47.00000	78.00000
Final	10	76.50000	10.83462	765.00000	63.00000	96.00000

Pearson Correlation Coefficients, N = 10 **Prob > |r| under H0: Rho=0**		
	Final	**Homework**
Homework	1.00000	0.90547 0.0003
Final	0.90547 0.0003	1.00000

Example 7.4.1

$$b_1 = r\frac{s_y}{s_x} = (0.90547)\frac{10.83462}{11.27485} = 0.87012 \quad b_0 = \bar{y} - b_1\bar{x} = 76.5 - (0.87012 \cdot 60.7) = 23.68372$$

The equation for the sample regression line is $\hat{y} = 23.68372 + 0.87012x$.

Example 7.4.2

In Example 7.4.2, the complete claim is "among all students that take this particular course, homework scores are useful in explaining final exam scores." Such explanation is possible when the mean final exam score is a mathematical function of the homework score. In terms of simple linear regression, that function is $\mu = \beta_0 + \beta_1 x$. The claim is $\beta_1 \neq 0$.

Plan the task.

$H_0 : \beta_1 = 0$

$H_1 : \beta_1 \neq 0$

$\alpha = 0.05$

Compute the statistics.

$$SS(Model) = \sum_{i=1}^{n} (\hat{y}_i - \bar{y})^2$$

$$= (b_1)^2 \left[(n-1) s_x^2 \right]$$

$$= (0.87012)^2 \left[9(11.27485)^2 \right]$$

$$= 866.20833$$

$$SS(Error) = \sum_{i=1}^{n} (y_i - \hat{y}_i)^2$$

$$= (n-1) s_y^2 (1 - r^2)$$

$$= 9(10.83462)^2 (1 - 0.90547^2)$$

$$= 190.30125$$

$$SS(Total) = SS(Error) + SS(Model)$$

$$= 190.30125 + 866.20833$$

$$= 1056.50958$$

Source	Df	Sum of Squares	Mean Square	F Value	Pr > F
Model	1	866.20833	866.20833	36.41419	0.000311
Error	8	190.30125	23.78766		
Corrected Total	9	1056.50958			

For Pr > F, p-value $= P(F \geq 36.41419) = 1 - \text{probf}(36.41419, 1, 8) = 0.000311$

Apply the results.

Since the p-value $= 0.000311$, reject H_0. There is sufficient evidence to support the claim that, among all students that take this particular course, homework scores are useful in explaining final exam scores. The sample regression line does explain a significant amount of the variation in the final exam scores.

Example 7.4.3

Plan the task.

$H_0 : \beta_0 = 0$

$H_1 : \beta_0 \neq 0$

$\alpha = 0.05$

Compute the statistics.

$$t \text{ Value} = \frac{b_0}{\sqrt{MS(Error)\left(\frac{1}{n} + \frac{\overline{x}^2}{(n-1)s_x^2}\right)}} = \frac{23.68394}{\sqrt{(23.78766)\left(\frac{1}{10} + \frac{(60.7)^2}{9(11.27485)^2}\right)}} = 2.6649$$

For Pr > |t|, p-value $= 2P(T \geq |2.6649|) = 2*(1\text{-probt}(abs(2.6649),8)) = 0.028587$

Apply the results.

Since the p-value < 0.05, reject H_0. The y-intercept of the sample regression line is significantly different from 0.

Example 7.4.4

Plan the task.

$H_0 : \beta_1 = 0$

$H_1 : \beta_1 \neq 0$

$\alpha = 0.05$

Compute the statistics.

$$t \text{ Value} = \frac{b_1}{\sqrt{\frac{MS(Error)}{(n-1)s_x^2}}} = \frac{0.87012}{\sqrt{\frac{23.78766}{9(11.27485)^2}}} = 6.0350$$

For Pr > |t|, p-value $= 2P(T \geq |6.0350|) = 2*(1 - \text{probt}(abs(6.0350),8)) = 0.000311$

Apply the results.

Since the p-value < 0.05, reject H_0. The slope of the sample regression line is significantly different from 0.

Example 7.4.5
Coefficient of Determination:

$$R^2 = \frac{SS(Model)}{SS(Total)} = \frac{866.20833}{1056.50958} = 0.81988$$

The model has reduced the variation in the responses by approximately 82%.

Approximately 82% of the variation in the final exam scores is explained by the homework scores.

Example 7.4.6
A 95% confidence interval on β_0 is:

$$b_0 \pm t_{.025}\sqrt{MS(Error)\left(\frac{1}{n}+\frac{\overline{x}^2}{(n-1)s_x^2}\right)} \text{ with } t_{.025} = \text{tinv}(.975,8) = 2.306004$$

$$23.68394 \pm 2.306004\sqrt{(23.78766)\left(\frac{1}{10}+\frac{(60.7)^2}{9(11.27485)^2}\right)}$$

$$23.68394 \pm 20.49429$$

$$(3.18965, 44.17823)$$

Example 7.4.7
A 95% confidence interval on β_1 is:

$$b_1 \pm t_{.025}\sqrt{\frac{MS(Error)}{(n-1)s_x^2}} \text{ with } t_{.025} = \text{tinv}(.975,8) = 2.306004$$

$$23.68394 \pm 2.306004\sqrt{\frac{23.78766}{9(11.27485)^2}}$$

$$0.87012 \pm 0.33251$$

$$(0.53761, 1.20263)$$

Example 7.4.8
The estimate of the mean final exam score for students with a homework score of 75 is 88.94:

$$\hat{y} = 23.68395 + 0.87012x = 23.68395 + 0.87012(75) = 88.94295$$

A 95% confidence interval on the mean final exam score for students with a homework score of 75 is:

$$\hat{y} \pm t_{.025}\sqrt{MS\left(Error\right)}\sqrt{\frac{1}{n}+\frac{\left(x_k-\overline{x}\right)^2}{\left(n-1\right)s_x^2}} \quad \text{with } t_{.025}=\text{tinv}(.975,8)=2.306004$$

$$88.94295 \pm 2.306004\sqrt{23.78766}\sqrt{\frac{1}{10}+\frac{\left(75-60.7\right)^2}{9\left(11.27485\right)^2}}$$

$$88.94295 \pm 5.93788$$

$$\left(83.00507, 94.88083\right)$$

Based on the data, one can be 95% confident that the mean final exam score is between 83.01 and 94.88 for students with a homework score of 75.

Example 7.4.9

A 95% prediction interval for final exam score for the next student with a homework score of 75 is:

$$\hat{y} \pm t_{.025}\sqrt{MS\left(Error\right)}\sqrt{1+\frac{1}{n}+\frac{\left(x_k-\overline{x}\right)^2}{\left(n-1\right)s_x^2}} \quad \text{with } t_{.025}=\text{tinv}(.975,8)=2.306004$$

$$88.94295 \pm 2.306004\sqrt{23.78766}\sqrt{1+\frac{1}{10}+\frac{\left(75-60.7\right)^2}{9\left(11.27485\right)^2}}$$

$$88.94295 \pm 12.71821$$

$$\left(76.22474, 101.66116\right)$$

Based on the data, one can be 95% confident that the next student with a homework score of 75 will score between 76.22 and 101.66 on their final exam. Assuming 100 possible points and integer scores, that would be at least 77.

7.2.12 Instructions for Simple Linear Regression

The analysis requested in Example 7.4 is listed in Table 7.14. The Linear Regression task is applied to the Ex07_04 data set.

Table 7.14 Analysis Requested in Example 7.4

Requested Analysis		Whether always part of output
Example 7.3.1	Sample regression equation.	Always part of the Linear Regression output
Example 7.3.2	ANOVA test of the model	Always part of the Linear Regression output
Example 7.3.3, Example 7.3.4	Tests on the parameters in the regression function	Always part of the Linear Regression output
Example 7.3.5	Coefficient of Determination R^2	Always part of the Linear Regression output
Example 7.3.6, Example 7.3.7	Confidence intervals on the parameters in the regression function	Option on **Statistics**
Example 7.3.8	Estimate of the mean response at given values of the explanatory variable, along with confidence intervals	Option on **Predictions**
Example 7.3.9	Prediction intervals	Option on **Predictions**
Example 7.3.10	Scatter plot with confidence intervals	Option on **Plots** > **Predicted**

To open the Linear Regression task, do either of the following:

- From the menu bar, select **Analyze ▶ Linear ▶ Regression**.
- On the **Task by Category** tab of the **Task List**, go to the **Regression** section and click **Linear**.
- On the **Task by Name** tab of the **Task List**, double-click **Linear**.

The Linear Regression task has six groups of options: Task Roles, Model, Statistics, Plots, Predictions, and Titles. Titles options are discussed in general in Chapter 1, "Introduction to SAS Enterprise Guide." These Titles options control the titles and the footnotes in the task output.

7.2.12.1 Task Roles

A variable is assigned to a role by dragging it from **Variables to assign** to one of the **Task Roles**. A variable may be removed from a role by dragging it back to **Variables to assign**. Also, the arrows can be used.

- **Dependent variable** is the *y* response variable.

- **Explanatory variables** are *x* variables. There is only one explanatory variable in simple linear regression. Models with multiple explanatory variables are discussed in Section 7.3.

The roles Group analysis by, Frequency count, and Relative weight are discussed in Section 1.3.

In Figure 7.19, Final is assigned to the Dependent variable role and Homework is assigned to the Explanatory variables role.

Figure 7.19 Task Roles in Linear Regression

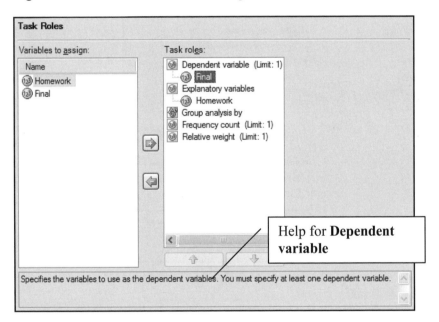

7.2.12.2 Model

Model options are discussed in Section 7.3. The options are used in multiple linear regression to select the best explanatory variables for the model. The default selection is appropriate for simple linear regression: the Model selection method is Full model fitted (no selection).

7.2.12.3 Statistics

Confidence intervals on the parameters in the regression function are requested here. In Figure 7.20:

- Confidence limits for parameter estimates is checked.
- Confidence level is set to 95%. The confidence level can be selected from the drop-down menu or typed in.

The Confidence level here also determines the confidence level for any confidence intervals on mean responses and the prediction level for any prediction intervals. These confidence and prediction intervals are requested at Predictions.

Figure 7.20 Statistics Options in Linear Regression

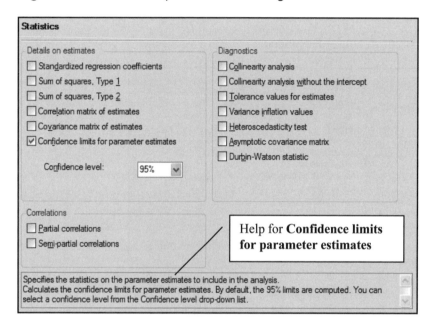

7.2.12.4 Plots > Predicted

In Figure 7.21, Observed vs Independents and Confidence limits are selected.

Checking **Observed vs Independents** produces a scatter plot that includes the sample regression line. Selecting **Confidence limits** produces curves showing upper and lower 95% confidence limits on the mean responses. Selecting **Prediction limits** produces curves showing upper and lower 95% prediction limits.

Figure 7.21 Plots > Predicted Options in Linear Regression

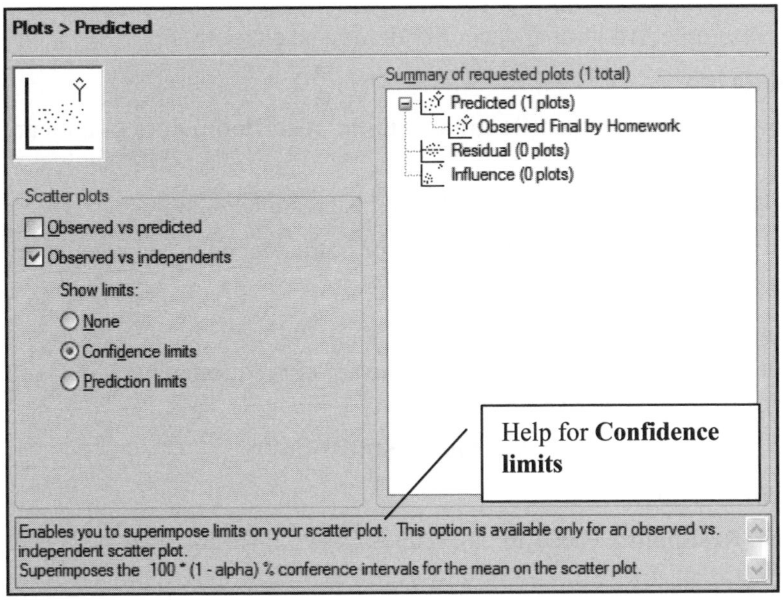

7.2.12.5 Predictions

The statistics sought here are fitted values, confidence intervals on mean responses, and prediction intervals.

- **Data to predict** box
  - **Original sample** is checked in Figure 7.22. This results in statistics being computed for each row of the active data set.
    - The active data set is Ex07_04. Statistics are computed for each of the 10 rows.
    - If the active data set was the Ex07_04_with_new_rows in Figure 7.18, statistics would be computed for each of the 14 rows. The last 4 rows, the rows without values for the dependent variable, would not be included in computing any statistics in the ANOVA table or parameter tests.
  - **Additional data** is checked in Figure 7.22. This allows an additional data set to be added to the analysis. For convenience here, copies of data sets with additional data should be in the SASUSER library. See "Adding New x Values" in "Example 7.4: Simple Linear Regression."
    - Click **Browse** to select the data set.
      - The Open window appears. The **Look in** box should contain **SASUSER**. If not, it can be navigated to by **Servers ▶ Local ▶ Libraries ▶ SASUSER**.
      - Select the data set and click **Open**. In Figure 7.22, the additional data is in SASUSER.EX07_04_MORE_X, which is the data set Ex07_04_more_x in the SASUSER library.
    - Statistics are computed for each of the 4 rows. The added 4 rows, rows without values for the dependent variable, are not included in computing any statistics in the ANOVA table or parameter tests.
    - If a row in the added data set has values for both the explanatory and the dependent variable, that observation is included in computing the statistics in the

ANOVA table and parameter tests. If a row contains only a value for the dependent variable, it is ignored.

- Original sample, Additional data or both may be checked.

- **Save output data** box
  - This box becomes active when **Original sample**, **Additional data** or both are checked.
  - **Predictions** is checked by default. A data set is created containing:
    - The original sample, the additional data or both, depending on what is selected in the **Data to predict** box
    - Fitted values
    - If requested, **Diagnostic statistics**. These are not requested here. Diagnostic statistics are discussed in Section 7.3.
    - Statistics discussed next in **Additional Statistics**.

- **Additional Statistics** box
  - If requested, **Residuals**. These are not requested here. Residual analysis is discussed in Section 7.3.
  - **Prediction limits** is checked in Figure 7.22. Confidence limits on mean responses and prediction limits are included in:
    - the task results if **Show predictions** is checked
    - the output data set if **Predictions** is checked
  - The default confidence level and prediction level is 95%. It can be changed at **Confidence level** with the Statistics options. **Confidence limits for parameter estimates** must be checked for **Confidence level** to be active. The levels for the parameters, mean responses, and predictions are the same.

- **Display output** box
  - **Display output** is checked by default. This might be deselected if the task were being used just to produce an output data set.
  - **Show predictions** is checked in Figure 7.22. This includes the requested predictions in the task results.

Figure 7.22 Predictions Options in Linear Regression

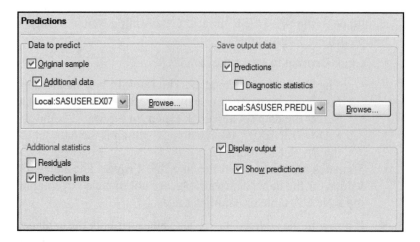

7.2.12.6 When Finished

When finished adding variables to roles and selecting options, click **Run**. The task adds a **Linear** icon, an icon for the additional data, and one or more output icons to the process flow diagram. See Figure 7.23. The results for Example 7.4 are in Output 7.7.

Figure 7.23 Example 7.4 Data, Task, and Output Icons on the Process Flow Diagram

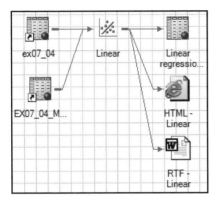

7.2.13 Task Output, Interpretation, and Analysis for Example 7.4

7.2.13.1 Task Output

Output 7.7 contains the Linear Regression results for Example 7.4. Output 7.8 contains a listing of the output data set requested in Figure 7.22. The column headings in Output 7.8 are the variable labels.

Output 7.7 Simple Linear Regression for Example 7.4

Linear Regression Results

The REG Procedure
Model: Linear_Regression_Model
Dependent Variable: Final ❶

Number of Observations Read	14
Number of Observations Used	10
Number of Observations with Missing Values	4

❷

Analysis of Variance					
Source	DF	Sum of Squares	Mean Square	F Value	Pr > F
Model	1	866.20073	866.20073	36.41	0.0003
Error	8	190.29927	23.78741		
Corrected Total	9	1056.50000			

❸

Root MSE	4.87723	R-Square	0.8199
Dependent Mean	76.50000	Adj R-Sq	0.7974
Coeff Var	6.37547		

❹

Parameter Estimates							
Variable	DF	Parameter Estimate	Standard Error	t Value	Pr > |t|	95% Confidence Limits	
Intercept	1	❺ 23.68394	8.88731	2.66	❼ 0.0286	3.18976	44.17813
Homework	1	❻ 0.87012	0.14419	6.03	❽ 0.0003	0.53761	1.20262

❾ ❿

Observed Final by Homework ⓫

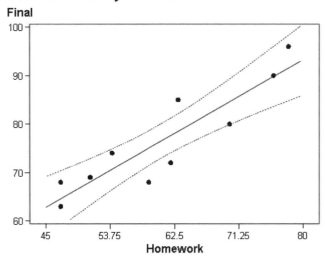

Regression Analysis Predictions

⑫	⑬	⑭	⑮	⑯	⑰
Final	predicted_ Final	lcl_ Final	lclm_ Final	ucl_ Final	uclm_ Final
63	64.5794	51.9345	58.8001	77.224	70.3587
68	75.0208	63.2114	71.4196	86.830	78.6220
68	64.5794	51.9345	58.8001	77.224	70.3587
72	77.6312	65.8274	74.0484	89.435	81.2139
69	68.0599	55.8310	63.2586	80.289	72.8611
80	84.5921	72.3976	79.8791	96.787	89.3050
74	70.6702	58.6658	66.4735	82.675	74.8669
85	78.5013	66.6806	74.8634	90.322	82.1392
96	91.5530	78.4293	84.7899	104.677	98.3161
90	89.8128	76.9666	83.6055	102.659	96.0201
.	62.8392	49.9398	56.5224	75.739	69.1559
.	71.5403	59.5932	67.5103	83.488	75.5704
.	80.2415	68.3593	76.4083	92.124	84.0747
.	88.9427	76.2245	83.0048	101.661	94.8805

Output 7.8 Output for Example 7.4.11

Report Listing

	⑱	⑫	⑬	⑮	⑰	⑭	⑯
Row number	Homework	Final	Predicted Value of Final	Lower Bound of 95% C.I. for Mean	Upper Bound of 95% C.I. for Mean	Lower Bound of 95% C.I.(Individual Pred)	Upper Bound of 95% C.I.(Individual Pred)
1	47	63	64.5794	58.8001	70.3587	51.9345	77.224
2	59	68	75.0208	71.4196	78.6220	63.2114	86.830
3	47	68	64.5794	58.8001	70.3587	51.9345	77.224
4	62	72	77.6312	74.0484	81.2139	65.8274	89.435
5	51	69	68.0599	63.2586	72.8611	55.8310	80.289
6	70	80	84.5921	79.8791	89.3050	72.3976	96.787
7	54	74	70.6702	66.4735	74.8669	58.6658	82.675
8	63	85	78.5013	74.8634	82.1392	66.6806	90.322
9	78	96	91.5530	84.7899	98.3161	78.4293	104.677
10	76	90	89.8128	83.6055	96.0201	76.9666	102.659

Report Listing

	⑱	⑫	⑬	⑮	⑰	⑭	⑯
Row number	Homework	Final	Predicted Value of Final	Lower Bound of 95% C.I. for Mean	Upper Bound of 95% C.I. for Mean	Lower Bound of 95% C.I.(Individual Pred)	Upper Bound of 95% C.I.(Individual Pred)
11	45	.	62.8392	56.5224	69.1559	49.9398	75.739
12	55	.	71.5403	67.5103	75.5704	59.5932	83.488
13	65	.	80.2415	76.4083	84.0747	68.3593	92.124
14	75	.	88.9427	83.0048	94.8805	76.2245	101.661

7.2.13.2 Interpretation

❶ Dependent variable is Final.

❷ $n = 10$ (14 observations read: 10 from Ex07_04 and 4 from Ex07_04_more_x. The 10 observations from Ex07_04 had values for the explanatory variable and for the dependent variable. The 4 observations from Ex07_04_more_x did not have values for the dependent variable.)

❸ ANOVA table

❹ Coefficient of Determination R^2

❺ b_0

❻ b_1

❼ p-value for the test of $H_0 : \beta_0 = 0$ versus $H_1 : \beta_0 \neq 0$

❽ p-value for the test of $H_0 : \beta_1 = 0$ versus $H_1 : \beta_1 \neq 0$

❾ 95% confidence interval on β_0

❿ 95% confidence interval on β_1

⓫ scatter plot of data with sample regression line and curves identifying 95% confidence limits on mean responses

⑫ dependent variable Final

⑬ fitted values $\hat{y}_i = b_0 + b_1 x_i$

⑭ lcl are lower confidence limits on future responses. These are the lower prediction limits.

⑮ lclm are lower confidence limits on the mean responses.

⑯ ucl are upper confidence limits on future responses. These are the upper prediction limits.

⑰ uclm are upper confidence limits on the mean responses.

⑱ explanatory variable Homework

7.2.13.3 Analysis

Example 7.4.1

$\hat{y} = 23.68394 + 0.87012x$
See ❺&❻ in Output 7.7.

Example 7.4.2
$H_0 : \beta_1 = 0$
$H_1 : \beta_1 \neq 0$

p-value = 0.0003. See ❸ in Output 7.7.

Since the *p*-value < 0.05, reject H_0. There is sufficient evidence to support the claim that, among all students who take this particular course, homework scores are useful in explaining final exam scores. The sample regression line explains a significant amount of the variation in the final exam scores.

Example 7.4.3
$H_0 : \beta_0 = 0$
$H_1 : \beta_0 \neq 0$

p-value = 0.0286. See ❼ in Output 7.7.

Since the *p*-value < 0.05, reject H_0. The *y*-intercept of the sample regression line is significantly different from 0.

Example 7.4.4
$H_0 : \beta_1 = 0$
$H_1 : \beta_1 \neq 0$

p-value = 0.0003. See ❽ in Output 7.7.

Since the *p*-value < 0.05, reject H_0. The slope of the sample regression line is significantly different from 0.

Example 7.4.5
$R^2 = 0.8199$

See ❹ in Output 7.7. The model has reduced the variation in the responses by approximately 82%.

Approximately 82% of the variation in the final exam scores is explained by the homework scores.

Example 7.4.6
A 95% confidence interval on β_0 is $(3.18976, 44.17813)$. See ❾ in Output 7.7.

Example 7.4.7
A 95% confidence interval on β_1 is $(0.53761, 1.20262)$. See ❿ in Output 7.7. On average, final exam scores increase from 0.5 to 1.2 points when homework scores increase by 1 point.

Example 7.4.8
See rows 11 through 14 in columns identified by ⓭, ⓯, and ⓱ in Outputs 7.7 and 7.8.

- For students who have a 45 homework score, the mean final exam score is estimated to be 62.8392. A 95% confidence interval on the mean is $(56.5224, 69.1559)$.

- For students who have a 55 homework score, the mean final exam score is estimated to be 71.5403. A 95% confidence interval on the mean is $(67.5103, 75.5704)$.

- For students who have a 65 homework score, the mean final exam score is estimated to be 80.2415. A 95% confidence interval on the mean is $(76.4083, 84.0747)$.

- For students who have a 75 homework score, the mean final exam score is estimated to be 88.9427. A 95% confidence interval on the mean is $(83.0048, 94.8805)$.

Example 7.4.9
See rows 11 through 14 in columns identified by ⓮ and ⓰ in Outputs 7.7 and 7.8.

- For a student who has a 45 homework score, a 95% prediction interval is $(49.9398, 75.739)$.

- For a student who has a 55 homework score, a 95% prediction interval is $(59.5932, 83.488)$.

- For a student who has a 65 homework score, a 95% prediction interval is $(68.3593, 92.124)$.

- For a student who has a 75 homework score, a 95% prediction interval is $(76.2245, 101.661)$.

Example 7.4.10
See ⓫ in Output 7.7.

7.3 Multiple Linear Regression

Multiple linear regression extends simple linear regression from one to multiple explanatory variables. The table below shows three explanatory variables and a response variable:

x1	x2	x3	y
x_{11}	x_{12}	x_{13}	y_1
x_{21}	x_{22}	x_{23}	y_2
$\vdots$	$\vdots$	$\vdots$	$\vdots$
x_{i1}	x_{i2}	x_{i3}	y_i
$\vdots$	$\vdots$	$\vdots$	$\vdots$
x_{n1}	x_{n2}	x_{n3}	y_n

- The columns x1, x2, and x3 are the independent, explanatory, or predictor variables.
- y is the dependent or response variable.

The values in the explanatory variables are assumed to be fixed and known before the response variable is determined. The values in the response variable are a randomly obtained sample.

It is assumed that each row $\left(x_{i1}, x_{i2}, x_{i3}, y_i\right)$, $i = 1, \ldots, n$, contains a y_i value that has been randomly selected from persons or objects that are known to correspond to the values x_{i1}, x_{i2}, and x_{i3}.

7.3.1 Notation

In the multiple linear regression, the number of explanatory variables is represented by $p-1$. When the y-intercept is added, the multiple linear regression function has p terms. The data values have the following notation:

x1	x2	$\cdots$	xj	$\cdots$	xp_1	y
x_{11}	x_{12}	$\cdots$	x_{1j}	$\cdots$	$x_{1,p-1}$	y_1
x_{21}	x_{22}	$\cdots$	x_{2j}	$\cdots$	$x_{2,p-1}$	y_2
$\vdots$	$\vdots$				$\vdots$	$\vdots$
x_{i1}	x_{i2}	$\cdots$	x_{ij}	$\cdots$	$x_{i,p-1}$	y_i
$\vdots$	$\vdots$				$\vdots$	$\vdots$
x_{n1}	x_{n2}	$\cdots$	x_{nj}	$\cdots$	$x_{n,p-1}$	y_n

The first subscript, $i = 1, \ldots, n$, identifies rows. The second subscript, $j = 1, \ldots, p-1$, identifies explanatory variables.

The means associated with the variables are: $\overline{x}_1, \overline{x}_2, \ldots, \overline{x}_{p-1}, \overline{y}$.

7.3.2 Population Model for Multiple Linear Regression

The random variable Y assigns a number to each person or object of interest. Additionally, there are n rows of $p-1$ fixed numbers: $x_{i1},\ldots,x_{i,p-1}$. There is a population of assigned numbers for each row $x_{i1},\ldots,x_{i,p-1}$.

The population model for multiple linear regression assumes that for the population associated with row $x_{i1},\ldots,x_{i,p-1}$:

$$Y = \mu_i + \varepsilon$$

- μ_i is the mean of the population associated with row $x_{i1},\ldots,x_{i,p-1}$.

- ε is also a random variable. It is called an *error*. The errors ε of each population are assumed to be normally distributed with mean 0 and the unknown variance σ^2. The variance is assumed to be the same for each population.

- The values in the population associated with row $x_{i1},\ldots,x_{i,p-1}$ are assumed to be normally distributed with mean μ_i and variance σ^2.

The population means are expressed as the *multiple linear regression function*:

$$\mu = \beta_0 + \beta_1 x_1 + \beta_2 x_2 + \cdots + \beta_{p-1} x_{p-1}$$

- In this function, $x_1, x_2, \ldots, x_{p-1}$ are the explanatory variables.

  o The explanatory variable x_j is the generalization in the theory of the explanatory variable xj, a data set column.

  o The explanatory variable x_j represents the numbers in an interval that contains the values from the explanatory variable xj: $x_{1j},\ldots,x_{nj}$.

- For the row $x_{i1},\ldots,x_{i,p-1}$, $\mu_i = \beta_0 + \beta_1 x_{i1} + \beta_2 x_{i2} + \cdots + \beta_{p-1} x_{i,p-1}$

- $\beta_0, \beta_1, \beta_2, \ldots, \beta_{p-1}$ are unknown constants.

  o β_0 is the *y*-intercept. The *y*-intercept is a mathematical fact, but it generally plays no role in the analysis. If $x_1 = \ldots = x_{p-1} = 0$, $\mu = \beta_0$.

  o β_j, with $j = 1, 2, \ldots, p-1$, is a *partial regression coefficient*.

    ▪ "Partial" because each explanatory variable has only a partial effect on the mean.

    ▪ When x_j increases by 1, μ changes by β_j.

7.3.2.1   Linear

The known constants are *linear with respect to the* μ. In simple linear regression, the population means are defined by the equation of a line: $\mu = \beta_0 + \beta_1 x$. Each mean is equal to a constant plus a multiple of a known value. In multiple linear regression, each mean is equal to a constant plus multiples of known values: $\mu = \beta_0 + \beta_1 x_1 + \beta_2 x_2 + \cdots + \beta_{p-1} x_{p-1}$. The result is no longer a line in two dimensions. But it is considered linear because the basic form of the equation is the same.

No explanatory variable should be linear with respect to other explanatory variables. That is, no explanatory variable should be equal to a constant plus multiples of other explanatory variables. This would not add information to the model. The statistical results would not be desirable.

An explanatory variable can be a nonlinear function of other explanatory variables. For example, $\mu = \beta_0 + \beta_1 x + \beta_2 x^2$ is a perfectly good multiple linear regression function. The variables x and x^2 are not linear with respect to one another. That is, $x^2 \neq mx + b$ in general. They are linear with respect to μ: $\mu = \beta_0 + \beta_1 x + \beta_2 x^2$ is $\mu_i = \beta_0 + \beta_1 x_1 + \beta_2 x_2$ with $x_1 = x$ and $x_2 = x^2$.

7.3.3 Sample Regression Equation

The multiple linear regression function, $\mu = \beta_0 + \beta_1 x_1 + \beta_2 x_2 + \cdots + \beta_{p-1} x_{p-1}$, is estimated by the *sample regression equation*:

$$\hat{y} = b_0 + b_1 x_1 + b_2 x_2 + \cdots + b_{p-1} x_{p-1}$$

- As in the multiple linear regression function, $x_1, x_2, \ldots, x_{p-1}$ are the explanatory variables.

  - The explanatory variable x_j is the generalization of the explanatory variable xj, a data set column.

  - The explanatory variable x_j represents the numbers in an interval that contains the values from the explanatory variable xj: $x_{1j}, \ldots, x_{nj}$.

- $b_0, b_1, \ldots, b_{p-1}$ are statistics determined using a technique called least squares. Least squares is discussed shortly.

  - b_0 is an estimate of β_0. In notational terms, $\hat{\beta}_0 = b_0$. b_0 is the y-intercept. If $x_1 = x_2 = \ldots = x_{p-1} = 0$, $\hat{y} = b_0$. The y-intercept is a mathematical fact, but it generally plays no role in the analysis.

  - b_j, with $j = 1, 2, \ldots, p-1$, is an estimate of the partial regression coefficient β_j. In notational terms, $\hat{\beta}_j = b_j$. If x_j increases by 1, $\hat{y}$ changes by b_j.

- $\hat{y}_i = b_0 + b_1 x_{i1} + b_2 x_{i2} + \cdots + b_{p-1} x_{i,p-1}$ is the *fitted value* given $x_{i1}, x_{i2}, \ldots, x_{i,p-1}$. It is the estimate of μ_i.

7.3.3.1 Least Squares

The sample regression equation is fit to the data using a technique called *least squares*. The technique determines the values of $b_0, b_1, \ldots, b_{p-1}$ that produce the smallest squared distance between the observed values y_i and the fitted values $\hat{y}_i = b_0 + b_1 x_{i1} + b_2 x_{i2} + \cdots + b_{p-1} x_{i,p-1}$. That is, $b_0, b_1, \ldots, b_{p-1}$ are the values such that

$$\sum_{i=1}^{n} (y_i - \hat{y}_i)^2 = \sum_{i=1}^{n} \left(y_i - \left(b_0 + b_1 x_{i1} + \ldots + b_{p-1} x_{i,p-1} \right) \right)^2 \le \sum_{i=1}^{n} \left(y_i - \left(d_0 + d_1 x_{i1} + \ldots + d_{p-1} x_{i,p-1} \right) \right)^2$$

for all numbers $d_0, d_1, \ldots, d_{p-1}$.

Details

Linear algebra provides a convenient way to examine least squares for multiple regression.

- The $p-1$ explanatory variables and a column of ones for the y-intercept become the *design matrix* X.
- The response variable becomes the *response vector* y.

x_{11}	x_{12}	$\cdots$	$x_{1,p-1}$	y_1
x_{21}	x_{22}	$\cdots$	$x_{2,p-1}$	y_2
$\vdots$	$\vdots$		$\vdots$	$\vdots$
x_{i1}	x_{i2}	$\cdots$	$x_{i,p-1}$	y_i
$\vdots$	$\vdots$		$\vdots$	$\vdots$
x_{n1}	x_{n2}	$\cdots$	$x_{n,p-1}$	y_n

$$\rightarrow \quad \mathrm{X} = \begin{bmatrix} 1 & x_{11} & x_{12} & \cdots & x_{1,p-1} \\ 1 & x_{21} & x_{22} & \cdots & x_{2,p-1} \\ \vdots & \vdots & \vdots & & \vdots \\ 1 & x_{i1} & x_{i2} & \cdots & x_{i,p-1} \\ \vdots & \vdots & \vdots & & \vdots \\ 1 & x_{n1} & x_{n2} & \cdots & x_{n,p-1} \end{bmatrix} \quad \mathrm{y} = \begin{bmatrix} y_1 \\ y_2 \\ \vdots \\ y_i \\ \vdots \\ y_n \end{bmatrix}$$

The vector of the least-squares regression coefficients is:

$$\begin{bmatrix} b_0 \\ b_1 \\ \vdots \\ b_{p-1} \end{bmatrix} = \mathrm{b} = \left(\mathrm{X'X} \right)^{-1} \mathrm{X'y}$$

The following verifies that $\sum_{i=1}^{n} \left(y_i - \left(d_0 + d_1 x_{i1} + \ldots + d_{p-1} x_{i,p-1} \right) \right)^2$ is minimized when $d_0 = b_0$, $d_1 = b_1$, $\ldots, d_{p-1} = b_{p-1}$.

$$\sum_{i=1}^{n}\left(y_{i}-\left(d_{0}+d_{1}x_{i1}+\ldots+d_{p-1}x_{i,p-1}\right)\right)^{2}$$

$$=\left(\mathrm{y\text{-}Xd}\right)'\left(\mathrm{y\text{-}Xd}\right)\qquad\left(\text{where } \mathrm{d}=\begin{bmatrix}d_{0}\\d_{1}\\\vdots\\d_{p-1}\end{bmatrix}\right)$$

$$=\left(\mathrm{y\text{-}X}\left(X'X\right)^{-1}X'y+X\left(X'X\right)^{-1}X'y\text{-}Xd\right)'\left(\mathrm{y\text{-}X}\left(X'X\right)^{-1}X'y+X\left(X'X\right)^{-1}X'y\text{-}Xd\right)$$

$$=\left(\left(\mathrm{I\text{-}X}\left(X'X\right)^{-1}X'\right)y+X\left(\left(X'X\right)^{-1}X'y\text{-}d\right)\right)'\left(\left(\mathrm{I\text{-}X}\left(X'X\right)^{-1}X'\right)y+X\left(\left(X'X\right)^{-1}X'y\text{-}d\right)\right)$$

$\left(\,\mathrm{I}\text{ is the identity matrix: 1's along the diagonal and 0's elsewhere.}\right)$

$$\left(\left(\mathrm{I\text{-}X}\left(X'X\right)^{-1}X'\right)y+X\left(\left(X'X\right)^{-1}X'y\text{-}d\right)\right)$$

$$=\mathrm{y}'\left(\mathrm{I\text{-}X}\left(X'X\right)^{-1}X'\right)y+\left(\left(X'X\right)^{-1}X'y\text{-}d\right)'X'X\left(\left(X'X\right)^{-1}X'y\text{-}d\right)$$

Therefore, $\sum_{i=1}^{n}\left(y_{i}-\left(d_{0}+d_{1}x_{i1}+\ldots+d_{p-1}x_{i,p-1}\right)\right)^{2}$ minimizes when:

$$\left(\left(X'X\right)^{-1}X'y\text{-}d\right)'X'X\left(\left(X'X\right)^{-1}X'y\text{-}d\right)=0$$

The product $X'X$ is positive definite. That is, for any vector w not equal to all 0s ($w \ne 0$), $w'X'Xw>0$. If $w'X'Xw = 0$, then $w=0$.

Since $X'X$ is positive definite:

$$\left(X'X\right)^{-1}X'y\text{-}d=0$$
$$d=\left(X'X\right)^{-1}X'y$$

The least-squares expression is minimized when $d=b=\left(X'X\right)^{-1}X'y$.

7.3.3.2 Plotting Responses versus Fitted Values

Plotting the responses y_{i} against the fitted values $\hat{y}_{i}$ shows how well the fitted values actually do in explaining the responses in the sample. The closer the points are to the identity line, the better the sample regression equation fits the data. For points on the identity line, $\hat{y}_{i} = y_{i}$. See Figure 7.24.

Figure 7.24 Plot of Fitted-Observed Pairs with Identity Line

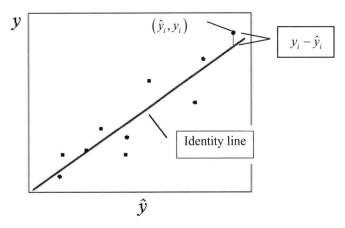

- The closeness of the point $(\hat{y}_i, y_i)$ to the identity line is measured by the vertical difference $y_i - \hat{y}_i$. See Figure 7.24. This is the *deviation* of the response from the fitted value.

- The sum of the squared deviations is the Sum of Squares Error, $SS(Error) =$
$$\sum_{i=1}^{n} (y_i - \hat{y}_i)^2.$$

  - The common population variance σ^2 is estimated by $\hat{\sigma}^2 = SS(Error)/(n - p)$, which is called the Mean Square Error. The estimate of σ is $\hat{\sigma} = \sqrt{SS(Error)/(n - p)}$.

  - Both $\hat{\sigma}^2$ and $\hat{\sigma}$ are measures of how well the sample regression equation fits the data. Smaller values indicate a better fit.

7.3.4 Test of the Multiple Linear Regression Model

The question to be answered is whether the means μ_i associated with the rows $x_{i1}, x_{i2}, \ldots, x_{i,p-1}$ depend on a multiple linear regression function $\mu = \beta_0 + \beta_1 x_1 + \beta_2 x_2 + \cdots + \beta_{p-1} x_{p-1}$.

- If $\beta_1 = \beta_2 = \cdots = \beta_{p-1} = 0$, then $\mu = \beta_0$. That is, the means of the populations do not depend on a multiple linear regression function of the explanatory variables $x_1, x_2, \ldots, x_{p-1}$.

- If at least one of the parameters $\beta_0, \beta_1, \ldots, \beta_{p-1}$ is not 0, then the means of the populations do depend on a multiple linear regression function that includes at least one of the explanatory variables $x_1, x_2, \ldots, x_{p-1}$.

The null and alternative hypotheses are:

$H_0 : \beta_1 = \ldots = \beta_{p-1} = 0$

$H_1 :$ At least one of the parameters $\beta_1, \ldots, \beta_{p-1}$ is not 0.

The test of the multiple linear regression model is based on an analysis of variance (ANOVA) table.

7.3.4.1 Analysis of Variance Table

The components of an ANOVA table are sums of squares, degrees of freedom, mean squares, F value, and p-value.

The role of an analysis of variance table is to examine the deviations of the responses from the mean, $y_i - \overline{y}$. In linear regression, each deviation is broken down into two parts:

$$\left(y_i - \overline{y}\right) = \left(y_i - \hat{y}_i\right) + \left(\hat{y}_i - \overline{y}\right)$$

$$\begin{pmatrix} \text{deviation from} \\ \text{the mean} \end{pmatrix} = \begin{pmatrix} \text{deviation from} \\ \text{the fitted value} \end{pmatrix} + \begin{pmatrix} \text{effect of the} \\ \text{explanatory variables} \end{pmatrix}$$

This is shown graphically in Figure 7.25.

Figure 7.25 Breakdown of $y_i - \overline{y}$

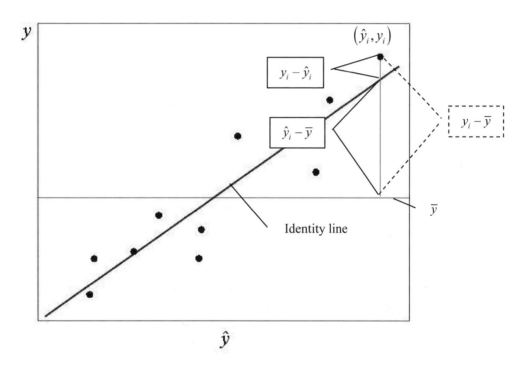

Sums of Squares

The breakdown in the deviation from the mean results in the following sums of squares breakdown:

$$\sum_{i=1}^{n}\left(y_i - \overline{y}\right)^2 = \sum_{i=1}^{n}\left(y_i - \hat{y}_i\right)^2 + \sum_{i=1}^{n}\left(\hat{y}_i - \overline{y}\right)^2$$

$$SS(\text{Total}) = SS(\text{Error}) + SS(\text{Model})$$

- $SS(\text{Total})$ (the numerator of s_y^2) is the Corrected Total Sum of Squares.

- SS(Error) (the sum of the squared deviations from the fitted values) is the Error Sum of Squares or the Sum-of-Squares Error.

  o The SS(Error) is a measure of the random variation. Random variation is present because the responses are randomly selected from their populations.

- SS(Model) (the sum of the squared differences between the fitted values $\hat{y}_i$ and the mean of the responses $\bar{y}$) is the Model Sum of Squares.

  o The SS(Model) is a measure of the variation in the responses due to both the multiple linear regression function and the random variation in the responses.

  o The SS(Model) measures the variation through the statistics $b_1, \ldots, b_{p-1}$. The following uses the fact that $b_0 = \bar{y} - b_1 \bar{x}_1 - \cdots - b_{p-1} \bar{x}_{p-1}$:

$$SS(\text{Model}) = \sum_{i=1}^{n} (\hat{y}_i - \bar{y})^2 = \sum_{i=1}^{n} (b_0 + b_1 x_{1i} + \ldots + b_{p-1} x_{p-1,i} - \bar{y})^2$$

$$= \sum_{i=1}^{n} (b_1 (x_{1i} - \bar{x}_1) + \ldots + b_{p-1} (x_{p-1,i} - \bar{x}_{p-1}))^2$$

- When $H_0 : \beta_1 = \cdots = \beta_{p-1} = 0$ is true, each of the statistics $b_1, \ldots, b_{p-1}$ estimates 0. Nonzero values are due to random variation only. In which case, SS(Model) measures only random variation.

- When $H_0 : \beta_1 = \cdots = \beta_{p-1} = 0$ is not true, SS(Model) measures the nonzero values of the parameters $\beta_0, \beta_1, \ldots, \beta_{p-1}$ plus random variation.

Degrees of Freedom

There are $n-1$ degrees of freedom associated with the overall sample. This is the denominator of s_y^2. With there being $p-1$ explanatory variable in the model:

$$n-1 = (n-p) + (p-1)$$

- $n-1$ are the degrees of freedom associated with the SS(Total).
- $n-p$ are the degrees of freedom associated with the SS(Error).
- $p-1$ is the degree of freedom associated with the SS(Model).

Mean Squares

The mean squares are the sums of squares adjusted for the number of parameters in the model and/or the number of responses. A mean square is equal to a sum of squares divided by the associated degrees of freedom.

- The Model Mean Square is a measure of the variation in the responses explained by the sample regression function. The variation is due to possibly nonzero population partial regression coefficients and the random selection of the responses.

$$MS(\text{Model}) = \frac{SS(\text{Model})}{p-1}$$

- The Error Mean Square, or Mean Square Error, is a measure of the random variation in the responses.

$$MS(\text{Error}) = \frac{SS(\text{Error})}{n - p}$$

The $MS(\text{Error})$ is an estimate of σ^2, the common population variance.

F Value

The test statistic for the hypotheses

$$H_0 : \beta_1 = \ldots = \beta_{p-1} = 0$$

H_1 : At least one of the parameters $\beta_1, \ldots, \beta_{p-1}$ is not 0.

is:

$$F \text{ Value } = \frac{MS(\text{Model})}{MS(\text{Error})}$$

If H_0 is true, both the $MS(\text{Model})$ and the $MS(\text{Error})$ would measure only random variation. It is expected that:

- $MS(\text{Model}) = MS(\text{Error})$

- $F \text{ Value } = \dfrac{MS(\text{Model})}{MS(\text{Error})} = 1$

Sums of Squares in Matrix Form

It is first necessary to present the vector of fitted values $\hat{\mathbf{y}}$ and vector of means $\bar{\mathbf{y}}$.

- $$\hat{\mathbf{y}} = \begin{bmatrix} \hat{y}_1 \\ \vdots \\ \hat{y}_i \\ \vdots \\ \hat{y}_n \end{bmatrix} = \begin{bmatrix} b_0 + b_1 x_{11} + \cdots + b_{p-1} x_{1,p-1} \\ \vdots \\ b_0 + b_1 x_{i1} + \cdots + b_{p-1} x_{i,p-1} \\ \vdots \\ b_0 + b_1 x_{n1} + \cdots + b_{p-1} x_{n,p-1} \end{bmatrix} = \begin{bmatrix} 1 & x_{11} & \cdots & x_{1,p-1} \\ \vdots & \vdots & & \vdots \\ 1 & x_{i1} & \cdots & x_{i,p-1} \\ \vdots & \vdots & & \vdots \\ 1 & x_{n1} & \cdots & x_{n,p-1} \end{bmatrix} \begin{bmatrix} b_0 \\ b_1 \\ \vdots \\ b_{p-1} \end{bmatrix} = \mathbf{Xb} = \mathbf{X}(\mathbf{X}'\mathbf{X})^{-1}\mathbf{X}'\mathbf{y}$$

- $$\bar{\mathbf{y}} = \begin{bmatrix} \bar{y} \\ \vdots \\ \bar{y} \\ \vdots \\ \bar{y} \end{bmatrix}^{n \times 1} = \left(\frac{1}{n}\right) \begin{bmatrix} 1 & 1 & \cdots & 1 \\ \vdots & \vdots & & \vdots \\ 1 & 1 & \cdots & 1 \\ \vdots & \vdots & & \vdots \\ 1 & 1 & \cdots & 1 \end{bmatrix}^{n \times n} \begin{bmatrix} y_1 \\ \vdots \\ y_i \\ \vdots \\ y_n \end{bmatrix} = \mathbf{1}(\mathbf{1}'\mathbf{1})^{-1}\mathbf{1}'\mathbf{y}, \text{ where } \mathbf{1} = \begin{bmatrix} 1 \\ \vdots \\ 1 \\ \vdots \\ 1 \end{bmatrix}^{n \times 1}$$

In matrix form, the sums of squares are:

$$SS(\text{Total}) = \sum_{i=1}^{n}(y_i - \bar{y})^2 = (\text{y-}\bar{\text{y}})'(\text{y-}\bar{\text{y}}) = \text{y}'\left(\text{I-1}(1'1)^{-1}1'\right)\text{y}$$

$$SS(\text{Error}) = \sum_{i=1}^{n}(y_i - \hat{y}_i)^2 = (\text{y-}\hat{\text{y}})'(\text{y-}\hat{\text{y}}) = \text{y}'\left(\text{I-X}(X'X)^{-1}X'\right)\text{y}$$

$$SS(\text{Model}) = \sum_{i=1}^{n}(\hat{y}_i - \bar{y})^2 = (\hat{\text{y}}\text{-}\bar{\text{y}})'(\hat{\text{y}}\text{-}\bar{\text{y}}) = \text{y}'\left(X(X'X)^{-1}X'\text{-1}(1'1)^{-1}1'\right)\text{y}$$

p-Values

The p-value is a measure of the likelihood that the samples come from populations where H_0 is true. Smaller values indicate less likelihood. That is, the more the data agrees with H_1 (the more $MS(\text{Model})/MS(\text{Error})$ is greater than 1) the smaller the p-value.

The p-value is the probability that randomly selected responses from populations with means that are not dependent on a linear regression function of the explanatory variables would produce an F value at or beyond the current value. If the p-value is small, it is unlikely that the means are not dependent on a linear regression function of the explanatory variables.

Table 7.15 has the technical definition of the p-value. The random variable F represents a future value of the test statistic and follows an F distribution. The F distribution depends on two degrees-of-freedom values: the numerator degrees of freedom and the denominator degrees of freedom. For multiple linear regression, these are $p-1$ and $n-p$, respectively.

In the SAS code expression, F value, $p-1$, and $n-p$ represent numbers. The SAS code expression is included to aid in the discussion. The p-value is computed using the expression in the "Detailed Solutions" section of "Example 7.5: Multiple Linear Regression."

Table 7.15 p-Value for the Test of the Multiple Linear Regression Model

Hypotheses	Gray area corresponds to the probability statement and is an example.	
$H_0: \beta_1 = \ldots = \beta_{p-1} = 0$ $H_1:$ At least one of the parameters $\beta_1, \ldots, \beta_{p-1}$ is not 0.	 p-value $= P(F \geq F \text{ Value})$	Task output: Pr > F SAS code expression: 1-probf(F Value, $p-1$, $n-p$)

ANOVA Table

The sums of squares, the degrees of freedom (Df), the mean squares, the F value, and the p-value are all organized by the ANOVA table.

Source	Df	Sum of Squares	Mean Square	F Value	Pr > F
Model	$p-1$	$SS(\text{Model})$	$\dfrac{SS(\text{Model})}{p-1}$	$\dfrac{MS(\text{Model})}{MS(\text{Error})}$	p-value
Error	$n-p$	$SS(\text{Error})$	$\dfrac{SS(\text{Error})}{n-p}$		
Corrected Total	$n-1$	$SS(\text{Total})$			

7.3.4.2   Decision and Conclusions

The formal decision and concluding sentence do not change from the one-sample tests discussed in Chapter 4, "Inferences from One Sample." The concluding observation depends on the particular statistics involved in the test.

If the p-value is small, the data agrees with H_1. If the p-value is less than the significance level, the risk of making a Type I error is acceptable. Therefore, the p-value decision rule is the following:

If the p-value $< \alpha$, reject H_0. Otherwise, do not reject H_0.

Since a hypothesis test begins with the assumption that H_0 is true, concluding a hypothesis test requires one of the following formal statements:

- Reject H_0.
- Do not reject H_0.

When the claim is equivalent to the null hypothesis, the concluding sentence uses the word *reject*. The concluding sentence becomes an expanded version of the formal decision.

When the claim is equivalent to the alternative hypothesis, the concluding sentence uses the word *support*. If the data supports the rejection of H_0, the data supports H_1. If the data does not support the rejection of H_0, the data cannot support H_1.

Table 7.16 Concluding Sentences

Formal Statistical Decision	Claim stated as H_0	Claim stated as H_1
Reject H_0.	There is sufficient evidence to reject the claim that ... (claim in words).	There is sufficient evidence to support the claim that ... (claim in words).
Do not reject H_0.	There is not sufficient evidence to reject the claim that ... (claim in words).	There is not sufficient evidence to support the claim that ... (claim in words).

Table 7.17 Concluding Observations

Reject H_0.	The sample regression equation explains a significant amount of the variation in the responses.
Do not reject H_0.	The sample regression equation does not explain a significant amount of the variation in the responses.

7.3.5 Tests and Confidence Intervals on Model Parameters

The estimates of parameters $\beta_0, \beta_1, \ldots, \beta_{p-1}$ are the statistics $b_0, b_1, \ldots, b_{p-1}$ where:

$$\begin{bmatrix} b_0 \\ b_1 \\ \vdots \\ b_{p-1} \end{bmatrix} = b = \left(X'X \right)^{-1} X'y$$

- The variances of $b_0, b_1, \ldots, b_{p-1}$ are along the diagonal of $\sigma^2 \left(X'X \right)^{-1}$.

- The variance of the statistic b_j, $j = 0, \ldots, p-1$, is the product of σ^2 and the value at position $j+1$ along the diagonal of $\left(X'X \right)^{-1}$.

- The standard deviation of an estimator is called the *standard error*. The estimates of the standard errors of $b_0, b_1, \ldots, b_{p-1}$ are the square roots of the values along the diagonal of $MS\left(\text{Error}\right)\left(X'X \right)^{-1}$.

- The estimate of the standard error of b_j, denoted by $se\left(b_j\right)$, is the square root of the product of $MS\left(\text{Error}\right)$ and the value at position $j+1$ along the diagonal of $\left(X'X \right)^{-1}$.

The hypotheses on β_j, $j = 0, \ldots, p-1$, are:

$$H_0 : \beta_j = 0$$
$$H_1 : \beta_j \neq 0$$

The test statistic is named a *t* value. It follows the *t* distribution with $n - p$ degrees of freedom.

$$t \text{ Value} = \frac{b_j - 0}{se(b_j)}$$

A 100(1 − α)% confidence interval on β_j is $b_j \pm t_{\alpha/2} se(b_j)$. The $t_{\alpha/2}$ critical value comes from the *t* distribution with $n - p$ degrees of freedom.

If $H_0 : \beta_1 = \ldots = \beta_{p-1} = 0$ is rejected, the next step is to identify the explanatory variables that determine the populations means.

- When $H_0 : \beta_j = 0$ is true, then the mean response does not depend on x_j.
$$\mu = \beta_0 + \ldots + \beta_{j-1} x_{j-1} + 0 x_j + \beta_{j+1} x_{j+1} + \ldots$$
$$= \beta_0 + \ldots + \beta_{j-1} x_{j-1} + \beta_{j+1} x_{j+1} + \ldots$$

  The variable x_j plays no role in determining the population means.

- When $H_1 : \beta_j \neq 0$ is true, then the population means do depend, at least partially, on the explanatory variable x_j. The explanatory variable x_j is useful in explaining the response.

The *t* value is a measure of the additional contribution made by x_j to the model's explanatory ability:

$$(t \text{ Value})^2 = \left(\frac{b_j - 0}{se(b_j)} \right)^2 = \frac{SS(\text{Model})_{p-1} - SS(\text{Model})_{p-2}}{MS(\text{Error})_{p-1}}$$

- $SS(\text{Model})_{p-1}$ and $MS(\text{Error})_{p-1}$ are based on all $p-1$ explanatory variables.

- $SS(\text{Model})_{p-2}$ is based on the all explanatory variables except x_j.

- $SS(\text{Model})_{p-1} - SS(\text{Model})_{p-2}$ is the additional contribution made by x_j.

7.3.5.1   Decision and Conclusions

The formal decision and concluding sentence do not change from the one-sample tests discussed in Chapter 4, "Inferences from One Sample." The concluding observation depends on the particular statistics involved in the test.

If the p-value is small, the data agrees with H_1. If the p-value is less than the significance level, the risk of making a Type I error is acceptable. Therefore, the p-value decision rule is the following:

If the p-value $< \alpha$, reject H_0. Otherwise, do not reject H_0.

Since a hypothesis test begins with the assumption that H_0 is true, concluding a hypothesis test requires one of the following formal statements:

- Reject H_0.

- Do not reject H_0.

When the claim is equivalent to the null hypothesis, the concluding sentence uses the word *reject*. The concluding sentence becomes an expanded version of the formal decision.

When the claim is equivalent to the alternative hypothesis, the concluding sentence uses the word *support*. If the data supports the rejection of H_0, the data supports H_1. If the data does not support the rejection of H_0, the data cannot support H_1.

Table 7.18 Concluding Sentences

Formal Statistical Decision	Claim stated as H_0	Claim stated as H_1
Reject H_0.	There is sufficient evidence to reject the claim that ... (claim in words).	There is sufficient evidence to support the claim that ... (claim in words).
Do not reject H_0.	There is not sufficient evidence to reject the claim that ... (claim in words).	There is not sufficient evidence to support the claim that ... (claim in words).

Table 7.19 Concluding Observations

$H_0 : \beta_0 = 0$ versus $H_1 : \beta_0 \neq 0$	
Reject H_0.	The y-intercept of the sample regression equation is significantly different from 0.
Do not reject H_0.	The y-intercept of the sample regression equation is not significantly different from 0.
$H_0 : \beta_j = 0$ versus $H_1 : \beta_j \neq 0$;, $j = 1, \ldots, p\text{-}1$	
Reject H_0.	The explanatory variable x_j explains a significant amount of the variation in the responses.
Do not reject H_0.	The explanatory variable x_j does not explain a significant amount of the variation in the responses.

7.3.6 Coefficients of Determination

The Coefficient of Determination, denoted by R^2, measures the reduction in the variation of the responses due to fitting the model to the data. Here, the model is the multiple linear regression function which is estimated by $\hat{y} = b_0 + b_1 x_1 + b_2 x_2 + \cdots + b_{p-1} x_{p-1}$.

Consider Figure 7.26 where graph (a) shows a plot of responses versus fitted values.

- In graph (b), the plot has been rotated in three dimensions so that one is looking down the plane through the vertical axis.
   - One sees the variation of the responses y_i, $i = 1, \ldots, n$, along the vertical axis and without regard for the fitted values $\hat{y}_i$.
   - This variation is measured by the $SS(\text{Total})$.

- In graph (c), the plot has been rotated in three dimensions so that one is looking down the identity line.
   - One sees the variation of the residuals $y_i - \hat{y}_i$ without regard for the fitted values $\hat{y}_i$.
   - This variation is measured by the $SS(\text{Error})$.

The difference in variation is measured by $SS(\text{Total}) - SS(\text{Error})$. Division by $SS(\text{Total})$ results in R^2.

$$R^2 = \frac{SS(\text{Total}) - SS(\text{Error})}{SS(\text{Total})} = 1 - \frac{SS(\text{Error})}{SS(\text{Total})}$$

Figure 7.26 (a) Plot of $(\hat{y}_i, y_i)$ Pairs, (b) Dispersion of Responses, (c) Dispersion of Residuals

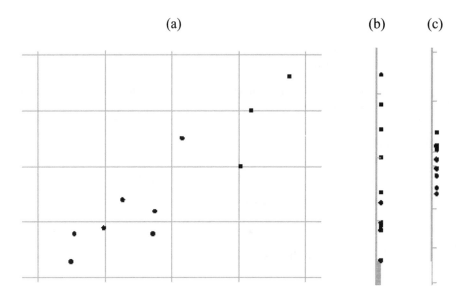

(a)   (b)   (c)

- $0 \le R^2 \le 1$, with larger values indicating greater reduction in the variation of the responses due to fitting the model to the data.

- Since $SS(\text{Total}) - SS(\text{Error}) = SS(\text{Model})$:

  - $R^2 = \dfrac{SS(\text{Model})}{SS(\text{Total})}$

  - R^2 is also interpreted as the proportion of variation in the responses explained by the model.

- The F value from the ANOVA table can be expressed in terms of R^2:

$$F \text{ value} = \left(\frac{n-p}{p-1}\right)\frac{R^2}{1-R^2}$$

The Adjusted Coefficient of Determination, adj-R^2, makes degrees-of-freedom adjustments. The interpretation of adj-R^2 is the same as the interpretation of R^2.

$$\text{adj-}R^2 = 1 - \frac{\left(\dfrac{SS(\text{Error})}{n-p}\right)}{\left(\dfrac{SS(\text{Total})}{n-1}\right)} = 1 - \frac{MS(\text{Error})}{s_y^2}$$

- Adding an explanatory variable to the model always increases R^2, even when the additional variable contains no information.

- The adj-R^2 takes into account the number of explanatory variables. Adding another explanatory variable increases the adj-R^2 only if the new variable contributes something to the model's ability to explain. Adding an explanatory variable may decrease the adj-R^2 if the addition variable contributes little or nothing.

7.3.7 Summary of Hypothesis Tests

Plan the task.

The circled numbers associate the hypotheses with the appropriate statistics.

❶ $\qquad H_0 : \beta_1 = \ldots = \beta_{p-1} = 0$

$\qquad H_1 :$ At least one of the parameters $\beta_1, \ldots, \beta_{p-1}$ is not 0.

❷ $\qquad H_0 : \beta_0 = 0$

$\qquad H_1 : \beta_0 \neq 0$

❸ $\qquad H_0 : \beta_j = 0$, $j = 1, \ldots, p-1$

$\qquad H_1 : \beta_j \neq 0$

For each test, the significance level is α.

Compute the statistics.

Analysis of Variance						
Source	**DF**	**Sum of Squares**	**Mean Square**	**F Value**	**Pr > F**	
Model	$p-1$	$SS(\text{Model})$	$MS(\text{Model}) = \dfrac{SS(\text{Model})}{p-1}$	$\dfrac{MS(\text{Model})}{MS(\text{Error})}$	p-value	❶
Error	$n-p$	$SS(\text{Error})$	$MS(\text{Error}) = \dfrac{SS(\text{Error})}{n-p}$			
Corrected Total	$n-1$	$SS(\text{Total})$				

Root MSE	$\sqrt{MS(\text{Error})}$	**R-Square**	R^2
Dependent Mean	$\overline{y}$	**Adj R-Sq**	adj-R^2
Coeff Var	$100 \dfrac{\sqrt{MS(\text{Error})}}{\overline{y}}$		

Parameter Estimates						
Variable	**DF**	**Parameter Estimate**	**Standard Error**	**t Value**	**Pr > |t|**	
Intercept	1	b_0	$se(b_0)$	$\dfrac{b_0}{se(b_0)}$	p-value	❷
explanatory variable	1	b_1	$se(b_1)$	$\dfrac{b_1}{se(b_1)}$	p-value	
⋮	⋮	⋮	⋮	⋮	⋮	❸
explanatory variable	1	b_{p-1}	$se(b_{p-1})$	$\dfrac{b_{p-1}}{se(b_{p-1})}$	p-value	

Apply the results.

For each test: If the *p-value* < α, reject H_0. Otherwise, do not reject H_0.

See Tables 7.18 and 7.19 for the concluding sentences and observations.

7.3.8 Estimation of a Mean Response for Given x Values

The mean of a population of responses is determined by the linear regression function $\mu = \beta_0 + \beta_1 x_1 + \beta_2 x_2 + \cdots + \beta_{p-1} x_{p-1}$. When the explanatory variables have values $x_{k1}, x_{k2}, \ldots, x_{k,p-1}$, the mean is:

$$\mu_k = \beta_0 + \beta_1 x_{k1} + \beta_2 x_{k2} + \cdots + \beta_{p-1} x_{k,p-1}$$

The values $x_{k1}, x_{k2}, \ldots, x_{k,p-1}$ may or may not be a row from the data set.

- The point estimate of μ_k is $\hat{y}_k = b_0 + b_1 x_{k1} + b_2 x_{k2} + \cdots + b_{p-1} x_{k,p-1}$.

- The population associated with the $\hat{y}_k$ statistic follows a normal distribution with mean $\mu_k = \beta_0 + \beta_1 x_{k1} + \beta_2 x_{k2} + \cdots + \beta_{p-1} x_{k,p-1}$ and variance $\sigma^2 x_k (X'X)^{-1} x_k'$, where $x_k = (1, x_{k1}, x_{k2}, \ldots, x_{k,p-1})$.

With $\sqrt{MS(\text{Error})}$ estimating σ, a $100(1 - \alpha)$% *confidence interval* on μ_k is:

$$\hat{y}_k \pm t_{\alpha/2} \sqrt{MS(\text{Error})} \sqrt{x_k (X'X)^{-1} x_k'}$$

- The $t_{\alpha/2}$ critical value comes from the *t* distribution with $n - p$ degrees of freedom.

- $\sigma\sqrt{x_k\left(X'X\right)^{-1}x_k'}$ is the standard error of the estimate $\hat{y}_k$. The estimate of the standard error is $\sqrt{MS\left(\text{Error}\right)}\sqrt{x_k\left(X'X\right)^{-1}x_k'}$.

The point estimates and confidence limits can be included in the output and as variables in an output data set. The standard error estimates can be included as a variable in an output data set.

- The output column or data set variable name for the point estimates is the prefix predicted_ combined with the name of the dependent variable. The variable label is Predicted Value of *dependent_variable.*

- The output column or data set variable name for the lower limits is the prefix lclm_ combined with the name of the dependent variable. The variable label is Lower Bound of __% C.I. for Mean.

- The output column or data set variable name for the upper limits is the prefix uclm_ combined with the name of the dependent variable. The variable label is Upper Bound of __% C.I. for Mean.

- The variable name for the standard error estimates is the prefix stdp_ combined with the name of the dependent variable. The variable label is Standard Error of Mean Predicted Value.

7.3.9 Prediction of a New Response for Given x Values

A new response is predicted in the sense that an interval is constructed that will, with a given confidence level, contain a future response. For explanatory values $x_{k1}, x_{k2}, \ldots, x_{k,\,p-1}$, the interval is based on a normal distribution with mean and variance:

$$\mu_k = \beta_0 + \beta_1 x_{k1} + \beta_2 x_{k2} + \cdots + \beta_{p-1} x_{k,p-1}$$

and

$$\sigma^2\left(1+x_k\left(X'X\right)^{-1}x_k'\right), \text{ where } x_k = \left(1, x_{k1}, x_{k2}, \ldots, x_{k,\,p-1}\right)$$

- μ_k is estimated by $\hat{y}_k = b_0 + b_1 x_{k1} + b_2 x_{k2} + \cdots + b_{p-1} x_{k,p-1}$.

- The variance takes into account the variance of the population of potential responses (σ^2) and the variance of the statistic $\hat{y}_k$ $(\sigma^2 x_k\left(X'X\right)^{-1}x_k')$:

$$\sigma^2 + \sigma^2 x_k\left(X'X\right)^{-1}x_k' = \sigma^2\left(1+x_k\left(X'X\right)^{-1}x_k'\right)$$

With $\sqrt{MS\left(\text{Error}\right)}$ estimating σ, a $100(1-\alpha)$% *prediction interval* is:

$$\hat{y}_k \pm t_{\alpha/2}\sqrt{MS\left(\text{Error}\right)}\sqrt{1+x_k\left(X'X\right)^{-1}x_k'}$$

- The $t_{\alpha/2}$ critical value comes from the t distribution with $n-p$ degrees of freedom.

- $\sigma\sqrt{1+x_k\left(X'X\right)^{-1}x_k'}$ is the standard error of a new response. The estimate of the standard error is $\sqrt{MS\left(\text{Error}\right)}\sqrt{1+x_k\left(X'X\right)^{-1}x_k'}$.

The prediction limits can be included in the output and as variables in an output data set. The standard error estimates can be included as a variable in an output data set.

- The output column or data set variable name for the lower limits is the prefix lcl_ combined with the name of the dependent variable. The variable label is Lower Bound of __% C.I. (Individual Pred).

- The output column or data set variable name for the upper limits is the prefix ucl_ combined with the name of the dependent variable. The variable label is Upper Bound of __% C.I. (Individual Pred).

- The variable name for the standard error estimates is the prefix stdi_ combined with the name of the dependent variable. The variable label is Standard Error of Individual Prediction.

7.3.10 Regression Diagnostics

An inadequate model or a single disproportionately influential observation may result in unreliable estimates and hypothesis test errors. Regression diagnostics identify these problems.

- Plots of *ordinary residuals* versus the explanatory variables help to identify functions that are not in the model. These plots are requested on the Plots > Residual options of the Linear Regression task.

- The *leverage* statistics identify outlying rows of the explanatory variable. These rows can result in unreliable estimates. Plots of leverage values are requested on the Plots > Influence options. Leverage values are part of the output data set when **Diagnostic** statistics is checked on the Predictions options.

- *Studentized residuals* identify outlying responses that can cause Type II errors (not rejecting H_0 when H_0 is false) in the tests of the model and the parameters. Plots of studentized residuals are requested on the Plots > Residual options. Studentized residuals are part of the task results and part of the output data set when **Residuals** is checked on the Predictions options.

- *DFFITS* (difference of fits) and *Cook's distance* identify outliers that cause significant changes to the sample regression equation when added or deleted. Such changes indicate unreliable estimation. Plots of DFFITS values are requested on the Plots > Influence options. DFFITS and Cook's distance values are part of the output data set when **Diagnostic statistics** is checked on the Predictions options.

- *VIF* (variance inflation factor) values identify highly correlated explanatory variables. Such high correlation results in Type II Errors and unreliable estimation. VIF is selected on the Statistics options.

7.3.10.1 Hat Matrix

A value that is used later in this section is h_{ii} : the ith diagonal value of the hat matrix, $i = 1, \ldots, n$.

- The *hat matrix* is $X(X'X)^{-1} X'$. It gets its name from its role in producing $\hat{y}$ (y-hat) the vector of fitted values: $X(X'X)^{-1} X'y = \hat{y}$.

- In terms of the h notation: $\begin{bmatrix} h_{11} & h_{12} & \cdots & & h_{1n} \\ h_{21} & h_{22} & \cdots & & \vdots \\ \vdots & \vdots & h_{33} & & \\ & & & \ddots & \\ h_{n1} & \cdots & & & h_{nn} \end{bmatrix}$

- Also, $h_{ii} = x_i'(X'X)^{-1} x_i$ where $x_i' = \begin{bmatrix} 1 & x_{i1} & x_{i2} & \cdots & x_{i,p-1} \end{bmatrix}$ is the ith row of X .

7.3.10.2 Ordinary Residuals and Model Adequacy

Ordinary residuals are the deviations from the fitted values: $y_i - \hat{y}_i$, $i = 1, \ldots, n$. The sum of the residuals is 0: $\sum_{i=1}^{n}(y_i - \hat{y}_i) = 0$. This makes the residual mean equal to 0.

A plot of the ordinary residuals $y_i - \hat{y}_i$ against the values of an explanatory variable helps to determine if the current model adequately describes the relationship between the response means and that explanatory variable:

- The variation of the residuals is the variation of the responses not explained by the explanatory variables.
- If the response means depend on a function of one or more explanatory variables that is not included in the model, that function influences the variation of the residuals.
- When the residuals are plotted against the values of an explanatory variable, the nonrandom pattern of the functional relationship may be seen.
- If it is seen, one or more explanatory variables can be added to explain this variation.

In Figure 7.27 (a), the regression function adequately describes the relationship between the response means and the *x* values. The points are randomly distributed on either side of the horizontal line at 0.

In Figure 7.27 (b), the regression function does not adequately describe the relationship between the response means and the *x* values. The points show that the residuals contain an x^2 component. A new explanatory variable with x^2 values should be added.

Figure 7.27 (a) Random Pattern of Residuals, (b) Nonrandom Pattern of Residuals

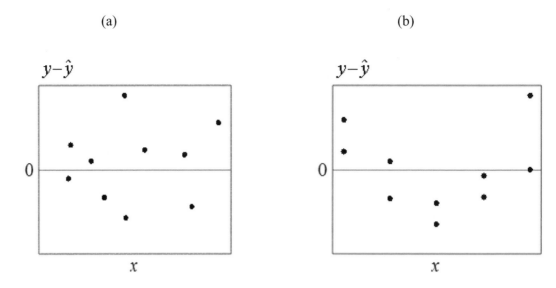

The ordinary residuals can be included in the output and as a variable in an output data set.

- The output column or data set variable name is the prefix residual_ combined with the name of the dependent variable.
- The variable label is Residual.

7.3.10.3 Leverage and Outlying Rows of Explanatory Values

The h_{ii} values play a direct role in regression diagnostics. The h_{ii} statistic is the *leverage* of $x_i' = \begin{bmatrix} 1 & x_{i1} & x_{i2} & \cdots & x_{i,p-1} \end{bmatrix}$, the ith row of X. Large leverage values identify rows that are outliers with respect to the other rows. Outlying rows can have a disproportionate influence in determining the sample regression equation. The result could be unreliable estimates.

The h_{ii} statistic is based on the distance between the ith row $x_i' = \begin{bmatrix} 1 & x_{i1} & x_{i2} & \cdots & x_{i,p-1} \end{bmatrix}$ and the "average row," which is the *centroid* $\bar{x}' = \begin{bmatrix} 1 & \bar{x}_1 & \bar{x}_2 & \cdots & \bar{x}_{p-1} \end{bmatrix}$. The actual distance is $\sqrt{h_{ii} - \dfrac{1}{n}}$ where the distance is defined by the following:

$$dist\left(x_i', \bar{x}'\right) = \sqrt{\left(x_i - \bar{x}\right)'\left(X'X\right)^{-1}\left(x_i - \bar{x}\right)} = \sqrt{x_i'\left(X'X\right)^{-1}x_i - \frac{1}{n}} = \sqrt{h_{ii} - \frac{1}{n}}$$

The sum of the h_{ii} values is always p, the number of explanatory variables plus the intercept. The mean of the h_{ii} values is p/n. Rows with leverage values $h_{ii} > 2\dfrac{p}{n}$ are considered to be unusually far from the centroid. That is, they are outliers with respect to the other rows. This criterion is suggested by Belsley, Kuh, and Welsch (1980).

Rows with leverage values $h_{ii} > 2\dfrac{p}{n}$ are considered outliers.

An outlying row of explanatory values is generally only a problem if it is part of an unusually influential observation. See "DFFITS, Cook's Distance, and Influential Observations."

The leverage values can be included as a variable in an output data set.

- The variable name is the prefix h_ combined with the name of the dependent variable.
- The variable label is Leverage.

7.3.10.4 Studentized Deleted Residuals and Outlying Responses

An *outlying response* y_i is unusually far from its fitted value $\hat{y}_i$ or, equivalently, has an unusually large residual $y_i - \hat{y}_i$. An outlying response disproportionately increases the

$MS(\text{Error}) = \sum_{i=1}^{n}(y_i - \hat{y}_i)^2 \Big/ (n-p)$. This may cause Type II errors (not rejecting H_0 when H_0 is false) in the tests of the model and the parameters.

The variance of $y_i - \hat{y}_i$ is $\sigma^2(1 - h_{ii})$. Since the variances differ from one residual to another, a common number cannot be used to identify outliers. It is necessary to studentize (standardize) by dividing by the estimate of $\sqrt{\sigma^2(1 - h_{ii})}$, the standard error of the residual. $MS(\text{Error})$ estimates σ^2. The *studentized residuals* or *standardized residuals* are:

$$student_i = \frac{y_i - \hat{y}_i}{\sqrt{MS(\text{Error})(1 - h_{ii})}}$$

However, studentized residuals have an important flaw. A single large $y_i - \hat{y}_i$ causes a large $MS(\text{Error})$ in the denominator of all studentized residuals. This could reduce the studentized residuals to the point that an outlier avoids detection.

A solution is to eliminate the current observation from the calculation of its fitted value $\hat{y}_i$ and the $MS(\text{Error})$. In the following, (i) in the subscript indicates that the ith observation has been deleted from the calculations.

- $\hat{y}_{i(i)}$ is the fitted value for the explanatory values $x_{i1},\ldots,x_{i,p-1}$ but without observation $(x_{i1},\ldots,x_{i,p-1},y_i)$ included in the calculations.
- $MS(\text{Error})_{(i)}$ is the Mean Square Error based on all observations but $(x_{i1},\ldots,x_{i,p-1},y_i)$.

$$MS(\text{Error})_{(i)} = \sum_{l \neq i}(y_l - \hat{y}_{l(i)})^2 \Big/ (n-1-p)$$

This results in the studentized deleted residuals or studentized residuals without current observation:

$$rstudent_i = \frac{y_i - \hat{y}_{i(i)}}{\sqrt{\dfrac{MS(\text{Error})_{(i)}}{1 - h_{ii}}}}$$

These residuals are excellent tools for identifying outliers.

Studentized deleted residuals follow the t distribution with $n - p - 1$ degrees of freedom. Absolute values greater than 2.5 rarely occur by chance. Using this value to identify outliers is suggested by Freund and Littell (1991).

> A response is an outlier if its studentized deleted residual has an absolute value greater than 2.5.
>
> An outlying response is generally only a problem if it is part of an unusually influential observation. See "DFFITS, Cook's Distance, and Influential Observations."

The studentized residuals and the studentized deleted residuals can be included in the output and as variables in an output data set. The estimates of the residual standard errors can be included as a variable in an output data set.

- The output column or variable name for the studentized residuals is the prefix student_ combined with the name of the dependent variable. Its label is Studentized Residual.

- The output column or variable name for the studentized deleted residuals is the prefix rstudent_ combined with the name of the dependent variable. Its label is Studentized Residual without Current Obs.

- The variable name for the standard error estimates is the prefix stdr_ combined with the name of the dependent variable. The variable label is Standard Error of Residual.

7.3.10.5 DFFITS, Cook's Distance, and Influential Observations

An *influential observation* is an outlier that causes significant changes to the sample regression equation if added or deleted. The observation may have an outlying row of explanatory values, an outlying response, or both. An influential observation results in unreliable estimates.

DFFITS stands for DiFference of FITS. A DFFITS statistic for the ith observation measures the difference in fitted values computed with and without the current observation: $\hat{y}_i - \hat{y}_{i(i)}$. The (i) in the subscript indicates that the ith observation has been deleted from the calculations. See the discussion of the deleted observation above in "Studentized Deleted Residuals and Outlying Responses." The difference is standardized by an estimate of the standard deviation of $\hat{y}_i$.

$$DFFITS_i = \frac{\hat{y}_i - \hat{y}_{i(i)}}{\sqrt{MS(\text{Error})_{(i)}\, h_{ii}}}$$

The following criterion is suggested in the "Influence Diagnostics" section of "The REG Procedure" chapter of the *SAS/STAT User's Guide in SAS OnlineDoc.*

An observation has unusually high influence if
$\left| DFFITS_i \right| > 2$.

Another measure of influence is Cook's Distance. It measures how much impact adding or deleting an observation has on all the fitted values. Cook's Distance is based on the differences $\hat{y}_l - \hat{y}_{l(i)}$, $l = 1,\ldots,n$ and the ith observation deleted.

$$D_i = \frac{\sum_{l=1}^{n}\left(\hat{y}_l - \hat{y}_{l(i)}\right)^2}{p\left(MS\left(\text{Error}\right)\right)}$$

Cook's Distance is also written in terms of the impact that adding or deleting an observation has on the estimates of parameters $\beta_0, \beta_1, \ldots, \beta_{p-1}$:

$$D_i = \frac{\left(\text{b-b}_{(i)}\right)' X'X \left(\text{b-b}_{(i)}\right)}{pMS\left(\text{Error}\right)}$$

Both $\text{b} = \begin{bmatrix} b_0 \\ b_1 \\ \vdots \\ b_{p-1} \end{bmatrix}$ and $\text{b}_{(i)} = \begin{bmatrix} b_{0(i)} \\ b_{1(i)} \\ \vdots \\ b_{p-1(i)} \end{bmatrix}$ are vectors of least-squares regression coefficients. The first is

based on all n observations. The second is based on all but the ith observation.

The F distribution with p and $n - p$ degrees of freedom is used to identify observations with unusually high influence. This is suggested by Kutner, Nachtsheim, and Neter (2004). Let $F_{0.50}$ represent the 50th percentile or median of the F distribution. In terms of SAS code, this is finv(.5,p, $n - p$) where p and $n - p$ represent numbers.

An observation has unusually high influence if $D_i \geq F_{0.50}$.

Table 7.20 shows $F_{0.50}$ for various numerator degrees of freedom and denominator degrees of freedom (ddf).

Observations with unusually high influence should be investigated.

- High influence observations may involve incorrect values. If possible, corrections should be made. If not, observations with errors should be deleted.

- High influence observations without errors should not be deleted. They may identify unforeseen aspects of the study. One might consider robust regression. The ROBUSTREG procedure becomes available with SAS 9.1. Discussion of robust regression is beyond the scope of this text.

The DFFITS and Cook's Distance values can be included as variables in an output data set.

- The variable name for the DFFITS values is the prefix dffits_ combined with the name of the dependent variable. Its label is Standard Influence on Predicted Value.

- The variable name for the Cook's Distance values is the prefix cookd_ combined with the name of the dependent variable. Its label is Cook's D Influence Statistic.

Table 7.20 $F_{0.50}$ for $p = 2,\ldots,15$ and $n - p = 2,3,\ldots,15$ and $20,25,\ldots,125$

ddf	numerator degrees of freedom													
	p													
$n{-}p$	2	3	4	5	6	7	8	9	10	11	12	13	14	15
2	1.000	1.135	1.207	1.252	1.282	1.305	1.321	1.334	1.345	1.354	1.361	1.367	1.372	1.377
3	0.881	1.000	1.063	1.102	1.129	1.148	1.163	1.174	1.183	1.191	1.197	1.203	1.207	1.211
4	0.828	0.941	1.000	1.037	1.062	1.080	1.093	1.104	1.113	1.120	1.126	1.131	1.135	1.139
5	0.799	0.907	0.965	1.000	1.024	1.041	1.055	1.065	1.073	1.080	1.085	1.090	1.094	1.098
6	0.780	0.886	0.942	0.977	1.000	1.017	1.030	1.040	1.048	1.054	1.060	1.065	1.069	1.072
7	0.767	0.871	0.926	0.960	0.983	1.000	1.013	1.022	1.030	1.037	1.042	1.047	1.051	1.054
8	0.757	0.860	0.915	0.948	0.971	0.988	1.000	1.010	1.018	1.024	1.029	1.034	1.038	1.041
9	0.749	0.852	0.906	0.939	0.962	0.978	0.990	1.000	1.008	1.014	1.019	1.024	1.028	1.031
10	0.743	0.845	0.899	0.932	0.954	0.971	0.983	0.992	1.000	1.006	1.012	1.016	1.020	1.023
11	0.739	0.840	0.893	0.926	0.948	0.964	0.977	0.986	0.994	1.000	1.005	1.010	1.013	1.017
12	0.735	0.835	0.888	0.921	0.943	0.959	0.972	0.981	0.989	0.995	1.000	1.004	1.008	1.012
13	0.731	0.832	0.885	0.917	0.939	0.955	0.967	0.977	0.984	0.990	0.996	1.000	1.004	1.007
14	0.729	0.828	0.881	0.914	0.936	0.952	0.964	0.973	0.981	0.987	0.992	0.996	1.000	1.003
15	0.726	0.826	0.878	0.911	0.933	0.949	0.960	0.970	0.977	0.983	0.989	0.993	0.997	1.000
20	0.718	0.816	0.868	0.900	0.922	0.938	0.950	0.959	0.966	0.972	0.977	0.982	0.985	0.989
25	0.713	0.811	0.862	0.894	0.916	0.931	0.943	0.952	0.960	0.966	0.971	0.975	0.979	0.982
30	0.709	0.807	0.858	0.890	0.912	0.927	0.939	0.948	0.955	0.961	0.966	0.971	0.974	0.978
35	0.707	0.804	0.856	0.887	0.909	0.924	0.936	0.945	0.952	0.958	0.963	0.968	0.971	0.974
40	0.705	0.802	0.854	0.885	0.907	0.922	0.934	0.943	0.950	0.956	0.961	0.965	0.969	0.972
45	0.704	0.801	0.852	0.883	0.905	0.920	0.932	0.941	0.948	0.954	0.959	0.963	0.967	0.970
50	0.703	0.800	0.851	0.882	0.903	0.919	0.930	0.940	0.947	0.953	0.958	0.962	0.966	0.969

ddf	numerator degrees of freedom														
	p														
$n-p$	2	3	4	5	6	7	8	9	10	11	12	13	14	15
55	0.702	0.799	0.850	0.881	0.902	0.918	0.929	0.938	0.946	0.952	0.957	0.961	0.965	0.968
60	0.701	0.798	0.849	0.880	0.901	0.917	0.928	0.937	0.945	0.951	0.956	0.960	0.964	0.967
65	0.701	0.797	0.848	0.879	0.901	0.916	0.928	0.937	0.944	0.950	0.955	0.959	0.963	0.966
70	0.700	0.796	0.847	0.879	0.900	0.915	0.927	0.936	0.943	0.949	0.954	0.958	0.962	0.965
75	0.700	0.796	0.847	0.878	0.899	0.915	0.926	0.935	0.943	0.949	0.954	0.958	0.961	0.965
80	0.699	0.795	0.846	0.878	0.899	0.914	0.926	0.935	0.942	0.948	0.953	0.957	0.961	0.964
85	0.699	0.795	0.846	0.877	0.898	0.914	0.925	0.934	0.942	0.948	0.953	0.957	0.960	0.963
90	0.699	0.795	0.846	0.877	0.898	0.913	0.925	0.934	0.941	0.947	0.952	0.956	0.960	0.963
95	0.698	0.794	0.845	0.877	0.898	0.913	0.925	0.934	0.941	0.947	0.952	0.956	0.960	0.963
100	0.698	0.794	0.845	0.876	0.897	0.913	0.924	0.933	0.940	0.946	0.951	0.956	0.959	0.962
105	0.698	0.794	0.845	0.876	0.897	0.912	0.924	0.933	0.940	0.946	0.951	0.955	0.959	0.962
110	0.698	0.794	0.844	0.876	0.897	0.912	0.924	0.933	0.940	0.946	0.951	0.955	0.959	0.962
115	0.697	0.793	0.844	0.875	0.897	0.912	0.923	0.932	0.940	0.946	0.951	0.955	0.958	0.962
120	0.697	0.793	0.844	0.875	0.896	0.912	0.923	0.932	0.939	0.945	0.950	0.955	0.958	0.961
125	0.697	0.793	0.844	0.875	0.896	0.911	0.923	0.932	0.939	0.945	0.950	0.954	0.958	0.961

7.3.10.6 VIF and Multicollinearity

Multicollinearity exists when two or more explanatory variables are correlated. When explanatory variables are highly correlated, they contain very similar information on the variation of the response means.

- Such variables often cannot explain a significant amount of the variation beyond that provided by the other correlated variables.
- When correlated variables are in the model, none of them can be significant even though each may be significant without the other correlated variables in the model.

Multicollinearity is measured by the variance inflation factor (VIF). For the explanatory variable x_j, $j = 1, \ldots, p-1$, the VIF is:

$$VIF_j = \frac{1}{\left(1 - R_j^2\right)}$$

where R_j^2 is the coefficient of determination with x_j being the dependent variable against the other $p-2$ explanatory variables

Table 7.21 lists pairs of VIF_j and R_j^2 values. See also Figure 7.28.

Table 7.21 VIF_j and R_j^2 Pairs for $VIF_j = 1,\ldots,16$

VIF_j	1	2	3	4	5	6	7	8	9	10	11	12	13	14	15	16
R_j^2	0	0.50	0.67	0.75	0.80	0.83	0.86	0.88	0.89	0.90	0.91	0.92	0.92	0.93	0.93	0.94

Figure 7.28 Graph of Corresponding VIF_j and R_j^2 Values for $0 \leq VIF_j \leq 30$

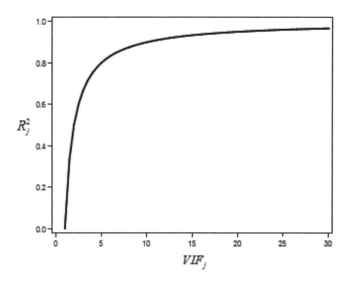

The correlation of x_j to the other explanatory variables inflates the variance of the estimate b_k by a factor of VIF_j. An inflated variance results in the reduced significance of the corresponding hypothesis test. The following criterion is suggested by Freund and Littell (1991):

> Explanatory variable x_j may be involved in excessive multicollinearity if VIF_j is relatively large and the corresponding *p*-value is large.

> Multicollinearity often exists when the model *p*-value is small, all the explanatory variables have larger *p*-values, and some explanatory variables have relatively large VIF values.

Remedial measures for multicollinearity include the following:

- One or more of the correlated variables may be dropped from the analysis. The remaining variable or variables may then become significant.

- Explanatory variables of the form x and x^2 are often highly correlated. The centered variable $x - \bar{x}$ and its square $(x - \bar{x})^2$ are generally not highly correlated. See "Centering Variables with the Standardize Data Task," which is next.

- One might consider ridge regression, which is an option of the REG procedure. Discussion of ridge regression is beyond the scope of this text.

7.3.10.7 Centering Variables with the Standardize Data Task

To *center* a variable is to subtract the variable mean from each value. Below, variables x1 and $x2$ are centered. The new variables are stnd_x1 and stnd_x2 .

x1	x2
x_{11}	x_{12}
x_{21}	x_{22}
$\vdots$	$\vdots$
x_{i1}	x_{i2}
$\vdots$	$\vdots$
x_{n1}	x_{n2}

$\rightarrow$

stnd_x1	stnd_x2
$x_{11} - \overline{x}_1$	$x_{12} - \overline{x}_2$
$x_{21} - \overline{x}_1$	$x_{22} - \overline{x}_2$
$\vdots$	$\vdots$
$x_{i1} - \overline{x}_1$	$x_{i2} - \overline{x}_2$
$\vdots$	$\vdots$
$x_{n1} - \overline{x}_1$	$x_{n2} - \overline{x}_2$

The resulting variable is centered at 0. That is, the mean of the new values is 0:

$$\frac{\sum_{i=1}^{n}\left(x_{ij} - \overline{x}_j\right)}{n} = \frac{\sum_{i=1}^{n} x_{ij} - \sum_{i=1}^{n} \overline{x}_j}{n} = \frac{n\overline{x}_j - n\overline{x}_j}{n} = 0$$

A variable is centered by requesting the Standardize Data task to transform the variable so that its mean is 0. The task opens in one of the following ways:

- From the menu bar, select **Analyze ▶ Data ▶ Standardize Data**.
- On the **Task by Category** tab of the **Task List**, go to the **Data** section and click **Standardize Data**.
- On the Task by Name tab of the Task List, double-click Standardize Data.

Standardize Data options
- Task Roles
  - Analysis variables are the variables to be centered, or, more generally, standardized.
  - Group analysis by, Frequency count, and Relative weight are discussed in Section 1.2.2.

- **Standardize**
  - The Standardize Data task can transform variables to a given mean and a given standard deviation. Centering requires a new mean equal to 0 and the standard deviation to be unchanged. This is done in Figure 7.29.
  - At **Standardize to**:
    - **New mean** is checked and **0** is in the entry box.
    - **New standard deviation** is not checked.

Figure 7.29 Standardize Options in the Standardize Data Task

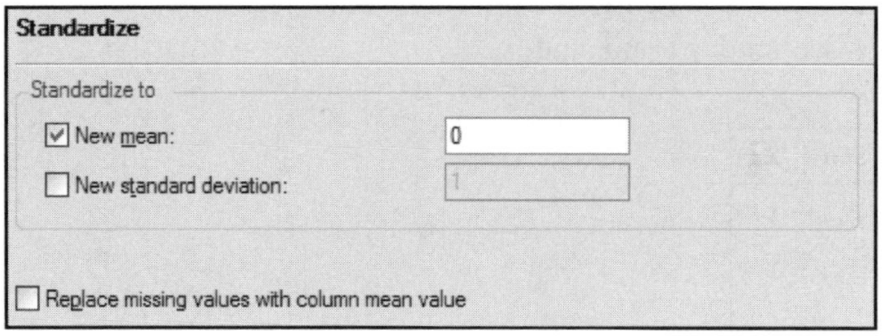

- **Results**
  - The output of the Standardize Data task is a SAS data set.
    - If **Add new standardized variables** is selected, the data set contains:
      - □ The original variables of the input data set
      - □ A new variable for each listed in **Analysis variables**. The name is the stnd_ prefix with the name of the original variable.
    - If **Replace existing variables** is selected, the data set contains:
      - □ The same number of variables and the same names as the input data
      - □ The values of the variables listed in **Analysis variables** have been replaced by the transformed values.
      - □ Variables not listed in **Analysis variables** are unchanged.
- The name and location of the output data set is at **Location to save the output data**. The name can be changed in the entry box. Click **Browse** to navigate to a new location.

7.3.11 Example 7.5: Multiple Linear Regression

Example 7.5 applies the material covered so far in Section 7.3.

- All topics but the scatter plots are addressed in the "Detailed Solutions" section.

- The Linear Regression task is discussed in "Instructions for Multiple Linear Regression."

- Complete results are in "Task Output, Interpretation, and Analysis for Example 7.5."

7.3.11.1 Value of Homework and Cost of Commuting

The responses are from 10 randomly selected students taking a particular course. The goal is to determine if homework scores and commuting times are important in explaining final exam scores. Homework and Commute are the explanatory variables x1 and x2. Final is the dependent variable y.

Student	Homework	Commute	Final
1	47	10	63
2	59	20	68
3	47	5	68
4	62	50	72
5	51	5	69
6	70	10	80
7	54	10	74
8	63	20	85
9	78	25	96
10	76	60	90

These values are in the Ex07_05 data set.

Example 7.5.1
Determine the sample regression equation.

Example 7.5.2
Test the claim that, among all students that take this particular course, homework scores, commuting times, or both are useful in explaining final exam scores. Let $\alpha = 0.05$.

Example 7.5.3
Determine and interpret the Coefficient of Determination (R^2) and the Adjusted Coefficient of Determination (adj-R^2).

Example 7.5.4
Test the claim that, among all students that take this particular course, homework scores are useful in explaining final exam scores. Let $\alpha = 0.05$.

Example 7.5.5
Compute a 95% confidence interval on the change in final exam score means associated with a 1 point increase in homework score.

Example 7.5.6
Test the claim that, among all students that take this particular course, commuting times are useful in explaining final exam scores. Let $\alpha = 0.05$.

Example 7.5.7
Compute a 95% confidence interval on the change in final exam score means associated with a 1-minute increase in commuting time.

Example 7.5.8
Check for multicollinearity using the VIF statistics.

Example 7.5.9
Estimate the mean final exam scores for students who have, respectively, homework scores and commuting times: 65 and 10, 65 and 45. Construct 95% confidence intervals on the mean final exam scores.

Example 7.5.10
Construct 95% prediction intervals on the final exam scores of the next students who have, respectively, homework scores and commuting times: 65 and 10, 65 and 45.

Example 7.5.11
Include the fitted values, the confidence intervals, and the prediction intervals in an output data set.

Example 7.5.12
Obtain a scatter plot of the responses versus the fitted values.

Example 7.5.13
Obtain a scatter plot of the ordinary residuals against each of the explanatory variables. Check for model adequacy.

Example 7.5.14
Check for any outlying responses, outlying explanatory rows, and unusually influential observations:

   a. Use plots of the studentized deleted residuals, leverage values, and the DFFITS values against fitted values.

   b. Include studentized deleted residuals and diagnostic statistics (leverage, DFFITS, Cook's Distance) in the output data set.

Example 7.5.15
Use the List Data task to show the output data set. Use variable names as column headings.

7.3.11.2 Adding New *X* Values
Example 7.5 asks for estimates, confidence limits, and prediction limits for two pairs of Homework and Commute scores: 65 and 10, 65 and 45. But neither of these pairs are in the table. They need to be added to the original table, or they need to be put in a new data set.

In Figure 7.30 (a), two new rows are added to Ex07_05, and the resulting data set is saved as Ex07_05_with_new_rows. The new values are added to the Homework and Commute columns. The corresponding rows in the Final column are left as missing values.

In Figure 7.30 (b), the two new Homework and Commute values are in a separate data set, Ex07_05_more_x. There is no Final column.

Figure 7.30 (a) Original Table with New Rows, (b) New Values in Separate Data Set

(a)

(b)

ex07_05_with_new_rows (read-only)

	Homework	Commute	Final
1	47	10	63
2	59	20	68
3	47	5	68
4	62	50	72
5	51	5	69
6	70	10	80
7	54	10	74
8	63	20	85
9	78	25	96
10	76	60	90
11	65	10	.
12	65	45	.

ex07_05_more_x (read-only)

	Homework	Commute
1	65	10
2	65	45

Estimates, confidence limits, and prediction limits are requested on the Predictions options of the Linear Regression task. See the Predictions section of "Instructions for Multiple Linear Regression."

When new values are in a separate file, a copy of the file should be exported to the SASUSER library. This results in easier access when working with the Predictions option in the Linear Regression task. For example, to export Ex07_05_more_x to the SASUSER library:

- Ex07_05_more_x is opened from a Windows folder.

- Its icon is right-clicked. **Export ▶ Export ex07_05_more_x** is selected from the pop-up menu.

- The Export ex07_05_more_x (Process Flow) To windows appears and SAS Servers is selected.

- The **Export** window appears. Navigate to the SASUSER library by **Servers ▶ Local ▶ Libraries ▶ SASUSER**.

- Click **Save**.

7.3.11.3 Detailed Solutions

The least squares b_0, b_1, b_2 for the sample regression equation are obtained using the linear algebra tools described earlier. Other results that are used later are also computed now.

The computations have been done using SAS/IML software. The code is provided in "SAS Code for Example 4.1 and Example 7.5" in the Appendix.

For Example 7.5, the design matrix X and response vector y would be:

$$X = \begin{pmatrix} 1 & 47 & 10 \\ 1 & 59 & 20 \\ 1 & 47 & 5 \\ 1 & 62 & 50 \\ 1 & 51 & 5 \\ 1 & 70 & 10 \\ 1 & 54 & 10 \\ 1 & 63 & 20 \\ 1 & 78 & 25 \\ 1 & 76 & 60 \end{pmatrix} \quad y = \begin{pmatrix} 63 \\ 68 \\ 68 \\ 72 \\ 69 \\ 80 \\ 74 \\ 85 \\ 96 \\ 90 \end{pmatrix}$$

- The statistics b_0, b_1, b_2 are: $b = \begin{bmatrix} b_0 \\ b_1 \\ b_2 \end{bmatrix} = (X'X)^{-1} X'y = \begin{bmatrix} 19.961925 \\ 0.9627199 \\ -0.088327 \end{bmatrix}$

- $(X'X)^{-1} = \begin{bmatrix} 4.2105462 & -0.075201 & 0.0211233 \\ -0.075201 & 0.001425 & -0.000526 \\ 0.0211233 & -0.000526 & 0.0005013 \end{bmatrix}$

- The diagonal elements of the hat matrix $X(X'X)^{-1} X'$:

$$\begin{bmatrix} h_{11} & h_{22} & h_{33} & h_{44} & h_{55} & h_{66} & h_{77} & h_{88} & h_{99} & h_{10,10} \end{bmatrix} =$$
$$\begin{bmatrix} 0.268160 & 0.102566 & 0.266339 & 0.470625 & 0.202327 & 0.40196 & 0.149277 & 0.112293 & 0.468998 & 0.557455 \end{bmatrix}$$

Example 7.5.1
The sample regression equation is: $\hat{y} = 19.961925 + 0.9627199 x_1 - 0.088327 x_2$

Example 7.5.2
In Example 7.4.2, the complete claim is "among all students that take this particular course, homework scores, commuting times, or both are useful in explaining final exam scores." Such explanation is possible when the mean final exam score is a mathematical function of at least one of the measurements. In terms of multiple linear regression, that function is $\mu = \beta_0 + \beta_1 x_1 + \beta_2 x_2$. The claim is $\beta_1 \neq 0$ or $\beta_2 \neq 0$.

Plan the task.

$H_0 : \beta_1 = \beta_2 = 0$

$H_1 : \beta_1 \neq 0$ or $\beta_2 \neq 0$

$\alpha = 0.05$

Compute the statistics.

SAS/IML software is used in creating the following table. The code is provided in "SAS Code for Example 4.1 and Example 7.5" in the Appendix.

	x_1	x_2	y	$\hat{y}$	$\hat{y} - \bar{y}$	$y - \hat{y}$	$(\hat{y} - \bar{y})^2$	$(y - \hat{y})^2$
1	47	10	63	64.326494	−12.17351	−1.326494	148.19425	1.7595863
2	59	20	68	74.995866	−1.504134	−6.995866	2.2624186	48.942143
3	47	5	68	64.768127	−11.73187	3.2318726	137.63683	10.445
4	62	50	72	75.234225	−1.265775	−3.234225	1.6021854	10.460214
5	51	5	69	68.619007	−7.880993	0.3809929	62.110049	0.1451556
6	70	10	80	86.469052	9.9690521	−6.469052	99.382	41.848635
7	54	10	74	71.065533	−5.434467	2.9344666	29.533427	8.6110941
8	63	20	85	78.846746	2.3467458	6.1532542	5.507216	37.862537
9	78	25	96	92.845911	16.345911	3.1540888	267.18881	9.9482763
10	76	60	90	87.829037	11.329037	2.1709626	128.34709	4.7130787
							881.76428 $SS(Model)$	174.73572 $SS(Error)$

Source	Df	Sum of Squares	Mean Square	F Value	Pr > F
Model	2	881.76428	440.88214	17.66196	0.001840
Error	7	174.73572	24.96225		
Corrected Total	9	1056.5			

For Pr > F, p-value $= P(F \geq 17.66196) = 1\text{-probf}(17.66196, 2,7) = 0.001840$

Apply the results.

Since the p-value $= 0.001840$, reject H_0. There is sufficient evidence to support the claim that among all students that take this particular course, homework scores, commuting times, or both are useful in explaining final exam scores. The sample regression equation explains a significant amount of the variation in the final exam scores.

Example 7.5.3
Coefficient of Determination:

$$R^2 = \frac{SS(\text{Model})}{SS(\text{Total})} = \frac{881.76428}{1056.5} = 0.8346$$

The model has reduced the variation in the responses by approximately 83%.

Using the coefficient of determination, approximately 83% of variation in the final exam scores is explained by the homework scores and commute times.

Adjusted Coefficient of Determination:

$$\text{adj-}R^2 = 1 - \frac{\left(\dfrac{SS(\text{Error})}{n-p}\right)}{\left(\dfrac{SS(\text{Total})}{n-1}\right)} = 1 - \frac{\left(\dfrac{174.73572}{7}\right)}{\left(\dfrac{1056.5}{9}\right)} = 1 - \frac{24.96225}{117.38889} = 0.78735$$

Using the adjusted coefficient of determination, approximately 79% of variation in the final exam scores is explained by the homework scores and commute times.

Example 7.5.4

In Example 7.4.5, the complete claim is "among all students that take this particular course, homework scores are useful in explaining final exam scores." Such explanation is possible when the mean final exam score is a mathematical function of at least the homework score. In terms of multiple linear regression, that function is $\mu = \beta_0 + \beta_1 x_1$ or $\mu = \beta_0 + \beta_1 x_1 + \beta_2 x_2$. The claim is $\beta_1 \neq 0$.

Plan the task.

$H_0 : \beta_1 = 0$

$H_1 : \beta_1 \neq 0$

$\alpha = 0.05$

Compute the statistics.

The estimate of the standard error of b_1, denoted by $se(b_1)$, is the square root of the product of $MS(\text{Error})$ and the 2nd value along the diagonal of $(\text{X}'\text{X})^{-1}$: $se(b_1) = \sqrt{(24.96225)(0.001425)}$ $= 0.188603$.

$$t\ \text{Value} = \frac{b_1}{se(b_1)} = \frac{0.9627199}{0.188603} = 5.10448$$

For $\text{Pr} > |t|$, $p\text{-value} = 2P(T \geq |5.10448|) = 2*(1 - \text{probt}(\text{abs}(5.10448), 7)) = 0.001393$

Apply the results.

Since the p-value $= 0.001393$, reject H_0. There is sufficient evidence to support the claim that, among all students that take this particular course, homework scores are useful in explaining final exam scores. Homework scores explain a significant amount of the variation in the final exam scores.

Example 7.5.5

"The change in final exam score means associated with a 1-point increase in homework score" is β_1. At 95% confidence interval on β_1 is:

$$b_1 \pm t_{0.025} se(b_1)$$

$0.9627199 \pm (2.364624)(0.188603)$ where $t_{.025} = \text{tinv}(.975,7) = 2.364624$

$(0.516745, 1.408695)$

Example 7.5.6

In Example 7.5.7, the complete claim is "among all students that take this particular course, commuting times are useful in explaining final exam scores." Such an explanation is possible when the mean final exam score is a mathematical function of at least the commuting time. In terms of multiple linear regression, that function is $\mu = \beta_0 + \beta_2 x_2$ or $\mu = \beta_0 + \beta_1 x_1 + \beta_2 x_2$. The claim is $\beta_2 \neq 0$.

Plan the task.

$H_0 : \beta_2 = 0$

$H_1 : \beta_2 \neq 0$

$\alpha = 0.05$

Compute the statistics.

The estimate of the standard error of b_2, denoted by $se(b_2)$, is the square root of the product of $MS(\text{Error})$ and the 3ʳᵈ value along the diagonal of $(X'X)^{-1}$: $se(b_2) = \sqrt{(24.96225)(0.0005013)}$
$= 0.111864$.

$$t \text{ Value} = \frac{b_2}{se(b_2)} = \frac{-0.088327}{0.111864} = -0.789593$$

For Pr > |t|, p-value $= 2P\left(T \geq \left|-0.789593\right|\right) = 2*(1 - \text{probt}(\text{abs}(-0.789593), 7)) = 0.455674$

Apply the results.

Since the p-value $= 0.455674$, do not reject H_0. There is not sufficient evidence to support the claim that, among all students that take this particular course, commuting times are useful in explaining final exam scores. Commuting times do not explain a significant amount of the variation in the final exam scores.

Example 7.5.7

"The change in final exam score means associated with a 1-minute increase in commuting time" is β_2. At 95% confidence interval on β_2 is:

$$b_2 \pm t_{0.025} se(b_2)$$
$$-0.088327 \pm (2.364624)(0.111864) \text{ where } t_{.025} = \text{tinv}(.975,7) = 2.364624$$
$$(-0.352843, 0.176189)$$

Example 7.5.8

Linear regression is applied with x_1 being the dependent variable and x_2 being the explanatory variable. The coefficient of determination is $R_1^2 = 0.3867$. The VIF statistic for x_1 is:

$$VIF_1 = \frac{1}{1 - R_1^2} = \frac{1}{1 - 0.3867} = 1.63052$$

Similarly, linear regression is applied with x_2 being the dependent variable and x_1 being the explanatory variable. The coefficient of determination is $R_2^2 = 0.3867$. The VIF statistic for x_2 is:

$$VIF_2 = \frac{1}{1 - R_2^2} = \frac{1}{1 - 0.3867} = 1.63052$$

There is no excessive multicollinearity. The VIF statistics are not large. One of the explanatory variables is strongly significant.

Example 7.5.9

The estimate of the mean final exam score for students with a homework score of 65 and a commute time of 10 minutes is 81.66:

$$\hat{y} = 19.961925 + 0.9627199x_1 - 0.088327x_2 = 19.961925 + 0.9627199(65) - 0.088327(10) = 81.655449$$

A 95% confidence interval on the mean final exam score for students with a homework score of 65 and a commute time of 10 minutes:

$$\hat{y} \pm t_{.025} \sqrt{MS(\text{Error})} \sqrt{x_k (X'X)^{-1} x'_k} \text{ with } t_{.025} = \text{tinv}(.975,7) = 2.364624$$

$$81.655449 \pm 2.364624\sqrt{24.96225} \sqrt{\begin{bmatrix} 1 & 65 & 10 \end{bmatrix}(X'X)^{-1}\begin{bmatrix} 1 \\ 65 \\ 10 \end{bmatrix}}$$

$$81.655449 \pm 2.364624\sqrt{24.96225}\sqrt{0.2446191}$$

$$(75.812271, 87.498627)$$

Based on the data, one can be 95% confident that the mean final exam score is between 75.81 and 87.50 for students with a homework score of 65 and a commute time of 10 minutes.

The matrix multiplication above has been done using SAS/IML software. The code is provided in "SAS Code for Example 4.1 and Example 7.5" in the Appendix.

Example 7.5.10
A 95% prediction interval for final exam score for the next student with a homework score of 65 and a commute time of 10 minutes:

$$\hat{y} \pm t_{.025} \sqrt{MS(\text{Error})} \sqrt{1 + x_k (X'X)^{-1} x'_k} \text{ with } t_{.025} = \text{tinv}(.975, 7) = 2.364624$$

$$81.655449 \pm 2.364624 \sqrt{24.96225} \sqrt{1 + \begin{bmatrix} 1 & 65 & 10 \end{bmatrix} (X'X)^{-1} \begin{bmatrix} 1 \\ 65 \\ 10 \end{bmatrix}}$$

$$81.655449 \pm 2.364624 \sqrt{24.96225} \sqrt{1.2446191}$$

$$(68.475243, 94.835655)$$

Based on the data, one can be 95% confident that the next student with a homework score of 65 and a commute time of 10 minutes will score between 68.48 and 94.84 on their final exam. Assuming integer scores, that score would be between 69 and 94.

The matrix multiplication above has been done using SAS/IML software. The code is provided in "SAS Code for Example 4.1 and Example 7.5" in the Appendix.

Example 7.5.14
The *leverage* statistics for the 10 observations are :

$$\begin{bmatrix} h_{11} & h_{22} & h_{33} & h_{44} & h_{55} & h_{66} & h_{77} & h_{88} & h_{99} & h_{10,10} \end{bmatrix} =$$

$$\begin{bmatrix} 0.268160 & 0.102566 & 0.266339 & 0.470625 & 0.202327 & 0.40196 & 0.149277 & 0.112293 & 0.468998 & 0.557455 \end{bmatrix}$$

None of the values is greater than $2\frac{p}{n} = 2\frac{3}{10} = 0.6$. None of the rows of explanatory values is an outlier.

Here, the studentized deleted residual, DFFITS, and Cook's distance are computed just for the first observation.

Linear regression is applied to the explanatory variables and dependent variable on the right.

	x_1	x_2	y	$\hat{y}_{(1)}$
1	47	10	.	64.812547
2	59	20	68	75.214753
3	47	5	68	65.241172
4	62	50	72	75.457865
5	51	5	69	68.994325
6	70	10	80	86.393171
7	54	10	74	71.380563
8	63	20	85	78.967905
9	78	25	96	92.613600
10	76	60	90	87.736646

- Since y is missing for the first observation, the statistics are computed using rows 2 through 9.

- The resulting Mean Square Error is $MS(\text{Error})_{(1)} = 28.72190$.

- Fitted values are requested for all 10 rows.

- $\hat{y}_{(1)}$ is the column of fitted values computed without observation 1.

The $\hat{y}$ values below (the fitted values based on all 10 observations) come from the solution for Example 7.5.2.

	x_1	x_2	y	$\hat{y}$	$\hat{y}_{(1)}$	$\hat{y} - \hat{y}_{(1)}$	$\left(\hat{y} - \hat{y}_{(1)}\right)^2$
1	47	10	63	64.326494	64.812547	-0.486053	0.236248
2	59	20	68	74.995866	75.214753	-0.218887	0.047911
3	47	5	68	64.768127	65.241172	-0.473045	0.223772
4	62	50	72	75.234225	75.457865	-0.223639	0.050015
5	51	5	69	68.619007	68.994325	-0.375317	0.140863
6	70	10	80	86.469052	86.393171	0.075881	0.005758
7	54	10	74	71.065533	71.380563	-0.315030	0.099244
8	63	20	85	78.846746	78.967905	-0.121159	0.014679
9	78	25	96	92.845911	92.613600	0.232312	0.053969
10	76	60	90	87.829037	87.736646	0.092391	0.008536

$$\sum_{l=1}^{10}\left(\hat{y}_l - \hat{y}_{l(1)}\right)^2 = 0.880994$$

The studentized deleted residual for observation 1
is: $\dfrac{y_1 - \hat{y}_{1(1)}}{\sqrt{\dfrac{MS(\text{Error})_{(1)}}{1 - h_{11}}}} = \dfrac{63 - 64.812547}{\sqrt{\dfrac{28.72190}{1 - 0.268160}}} = -0.289328$

Its absolute value is not greater than 2.5. This response is not an outlier.

The *DFFITS statistic for observation 1* is:

$$DFFITS_1 = \frac{\hat{y}_1 - \hat{y}_{1(1)}}{\sqrt{MS(\text{Error})_{(1)} h_{11}}} = \frac{64.326494 - 64.812547}{\sqrt{(28.72190)(0.268160)}} = -0.175138$$

Its absolute value is not greater than 2. This observation does not have unusually high influence.

Cook's distance for observation 1 is: $D_1 = \dfrac{\sum\limits_{l=1}^{10}\left(\hat{y}_l - \hat{y}_{l(1)}\right)^2}{p\left(MS(\text{Error})\right)} = \dfrac{0.880994}{3(24.96225)} = 0.011764$

From Table 7.20, $F_{0.50}$ is 0.871 for $p = 3$ and $n - p = 7$. Cook's distance for observation 1 is smaller, so this observation does not have unusually high influence.

7.3.12 Instructions for Multiple Linear Regression

The analysis requested in Example 7.5 is listed in Table 7.22. The Linear Regression task is applied to the Ex07_05 data set.

Table 7.22 Analysis Requested in Example 7.5

Requested Analysis		Whether Always Part of Output
Example 7.5.1	Sample regression equation.	Always part of the Linear Regression output
Example 7.5.2	ANOVA test of the model	Always part of the Linear Regression output
Example 7.5.3	Coefficient of Determination R^2, Adjusted Coefficient of Determination adj-R^2	Always part of the Linear Regression output
Example 7.5.4, Example 7.5.6	Tests on the parameters in the regression function	Always part of the Linear Regression output
Example 7.5.5, Example 7.5.7	Confidence intervals on the parameters in the regression function	Option on **Statistics**
Example 7.5.8	VIF statistics	Option on **Statistics**
Example 7.5.9	Estimate of the mean response at given values of the explanatory variable, along with confidence intervals	Option on **Predictions**
Example 7.5.10	Prediction intervals	Option on **Predictions**
Example 7.5.11	Fitted values, confidence intervals, and prediction intervals in an	Option on **Predictions**

Requested Analysis		Whether Always Part of Output
	output data set	
Example 7.5.12	Scatter plot of responses against fitted values	Option on **Plots > Predicted**
Example 7.5.13	Scatter plot of ordinary residuals against explanatory variables	Option on **Plots > Residual**
Example 7.5.14	Plots of the leverage statistics and the DFFITS statistics against the fitted values	Options on **Plots > Influence**
Example 7.5.14	Leverage statistics, studentized deleted residuals, DFFITS statistics, Cook's distance statistics in an output data set	Options on **Predictions**

To open the Linear Regression task, choose one of the following:

- From the menu bar, select **Analyze ▶ Linear ▶ Regression**.

- On the **Task by Category** tab of the **Task List**, go to the **Regression** section and click **Linear**.

- On the **Task by Name** tab of the **Task List**, double-click **Linear**.

The Linear Regression task has six groups of options: Task Roles, Model, Statistics, Plots, Predictions, and Titles. Titles options are discussed in general in Chapter 1, "Introduction to SAS Enterprise Guide." These Titles options control the titles and the footnotes in the task output.

7.3.12.1 Task Roles

A variable is assigned to a role by dragging it from **Variables to assign** to one of the **Task Roles**. A variable may be removed from a role by dragging it back to **Variables to assign**. Also, the arrows may be used.

- **Dependent variable** is the y response variable.

- **Explanatory variables** are x variables.

- The **Group analysis by** variable groups the rows of data. There is a separate analysis for each group.

In Figure 7.31, Final is assigned to the Dependent variable role. Homework and Commute are assigned to the Explanatory variables role.

Figure 7.31 Task Roles in Linear Regression

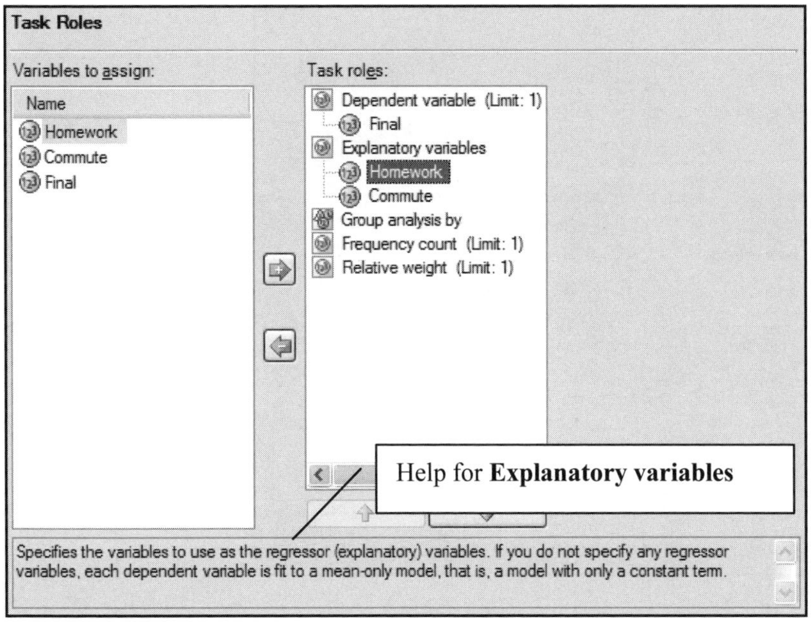

7.3.12.2 Model

The Model options are discussed later in the "Model Selection" section. These options are used to select the best subset of explanatory variables for the model. The default selection is appropriate for Example 7.5: the Model selection method is **Full model fitted (no selection)**.

7.3.12.3 Statistics

Confidence intervals on the parameters in the regression function and VIF values are requested here. In Figure 7.32:

- **Confidence limits for parameter estimates** is checked. Confidence level is set to 95%. The confidence level can be selected from the drop-down menu or typed.

  The Confidence level here determines the confidence level for any confidence intervals on mean responses and the prediction level for any prediction intervals. These confidence and prediction intervals are requested on the Predictions options.

- Variance inflation values is checked.

Figure 7.32 Statistics Options in Linear Regression

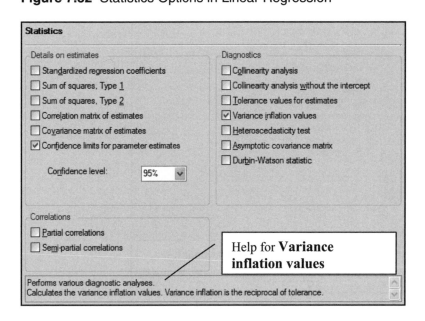

7.3.12.4 Plots

- Plots > Predicted options. See top of Figure 7.33.

  o **Observed vs predicted** is checked. This produces a scatter plot of $(\hat{y}_i, y_i)$ pairs.

- Plots > Residual options. See second in Figure 7.33.

  o **Studentized vs predicted Y** is checked. This produces a scatter plot of $(\hat{y}_i, rstudent_i)$ pairs.

  o **Ordinary vs Independents** is checked. This produces a scatter plot of $(x_{ij}, y_i - \hat{y}_i)$ pairs for each explanatory variable x_j.

- Plots > Influence options. See bottom of Figure 7.33.

  o **DFFITS vs predicted Y** is checked. This produces a scatter plot of $(\hat{y}_i, DFFITS_i)$ pairs.

  o **Leverage vs predicted Y** is checked. This produces a scatter plot of $(\hat{y}_i, h_{ii})$ pairs.

Figure 7.33 (Top) Plots > Predicted, (Second) Plots > Residual,
(Bottom) Plots > Influence

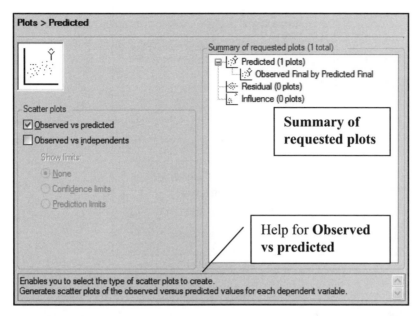

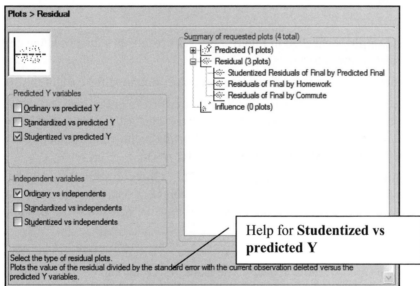

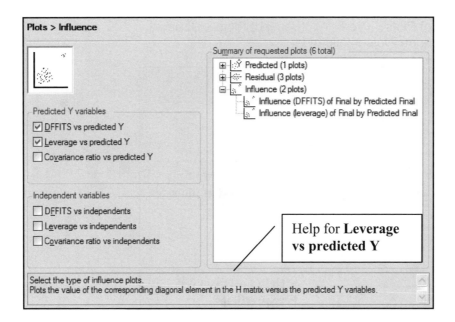

7.3.12.5 Predictions

- **Data to predict** box
  - ○ **Original sample** is checked in Figure 7.34. This results in statistics being computed for each row of the active data set.
    - ▪ The active data set is Ex07_05. Statistics are computed for each of the 10 rows.
    - ▪ If the active data set was Ex07_05_with_new_rows in Figure 7.30, statistics would be computed for each of the 14 rows. The last 4 rows do not have values for the dependent variable. They would not be included in computing any statistics in the ANOVA table or parameter tests.
  - ○ **Additional data** is checked in Figure 7.34. This allows an additional data set to be added to the analysis. For convenience here, copies of data sets with additional data should be in the SASUSER library. See "Adding New X Values" in "Example 7.5: Multiple Linear Regression."
    - ▪ Click **Browse** to select the data set.
      - □ The Open window appears. The **Look in** box should contain **SASUSER**. If not, it can be navigated to by **Servers ▶ Local ▶ Libraries ▶ SASUSER**.
      - □ Select the data set and click **Open**. In Figure 7.33, the additional data is in SASUSER.EX07_05_MORE_X, which is the data set Ex07_05_more_x in the SASUSER library.
    - ▪ Statistics are computed for each of the 2 rows. The added 2 rows, rows without values for the dependent variable, are not included in computing any statistics in the ANOVA table or parameter tests.
    - ▪ If a row in the added data set has values for both the explanatory and the dependent variable, that observation is included in computing the statistics in the ANOVA table and parameter tests. If a row contains only a value for the dependent variable, it is ignored.
    - ▪ **Original sample**, **Additional data**, or both may be checked.

- **Save output data** box. This box becomes active when **Original sample**, **Additional data**, or both are checked.
  - o **Predictions** is checked by default. A data set is created containing:
    - ▪ The original sample, the additional data or both, depending on what is selected in the **Data to predict** box
    - ▪ Fitted values
    - ▪ Diagnostic statistics, if requested. These statistics include leverage, DFFITS, and Cook's distance. **Diagnostic statistics** is checked in Figure 7.34.
    - ▪ Additional requested statistics. See next bullet.
- **Additional Statistics** box
  - o **Residuals** is checked in Figure 7.34. These include ordinary residuals, studentized residuals, and studentized deleted residuals.
  - o **Prediction limits** is checked in Figure 7.34. Confidence limits on mean responses and prediction limits are included in:
    - ▪ the task results if **Show predictions** is checked
    - ▪ the output data set if **Predictions** is checked
  - o The default confidence level and prediction level is 95%. It can be changed at **Confidence level** on the Predictions options. **Confidence limits for parameter estimates** must be checked for **Confidence level** to be active. The levels for the parameters, mean responses, and predictions are the same.
- **Display output** box
  - o **Display output** is checked by default. This might be deselected if the task were being used just to produce an output data set.
  - o **Show predictions** is checked in Figure 7.34. This includes the requested predictions in the task results.

Figure 7.34 Predictions Options in Linear Regression

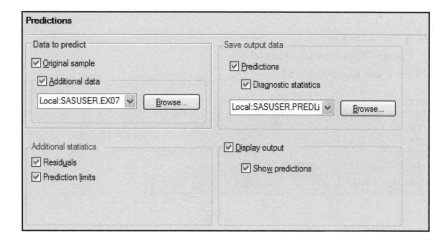

7.3.12.6 When Finished

When finished adding variables to roles and selecting options, click **Run**. The task adds a **Linear** icon, an icon for the additional data set, and one or more output icons to the process flow diagram. See Figure 7.35. The results for Example 7.5 are in Output 7.9 and Output 7.10.

Figure 7.35 Example 7.5 Data, Task, and Output Icons on a Process Flow Diagram

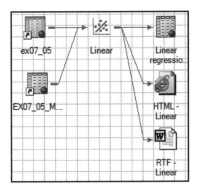

7.3.13 Task Output, Interpretation, and Analysis for Example 7.5

7.3.13.1 Task Output

- Output 7.9 contains the Linear Regression results for Example 7.5.
- Output 7.10 lists the output data set requested in Figure 7.34. The column headings are the variable names.

Output 7.9 Multiple Linear Regression for Example 7.5

Linear Regression Results

The REG Procedure
Model: Linear_Regression_Model
Dependent Variable: Final ❶

Number of Observations Read	12
Number of Observations Used	10
Number of Observations with Missing Values	2

❷

Analysis of Variance					
Source	DF	Sum of Squares	Mean Square	F Value	Pr > F
Model	2	881.76428	440.88214	17.66	0.0018
Error	7	174.73572	24.96225		
Corrected Total	9	1056.50000			

❸

Root MSE	4.99622	R-Square	0.8346
Dependent Mean	76.50000	Adj R-Sq	0.7874
Coeff Var	6.53101		

❹

Parameter Estimates								
Variable	DF	Parameter Estimate	Standard Error	t Value	Pr > |t|	Variance Inflation	95% Confidence Limits	
Intercept	1	19.96192 ❺	10.25206	1.95	0.0926 ❽	0	-4.28034	44.20419 ⓭
Homework	1	0.96272 ❻	0.18861	5.10	0.0014 ❾	1.63039 ⓫	0.51674	1.40870 ⓮
Commute	1	-0.08833 ❼	0.11186	-0.79	0.4557 ❿	1.63039 ⓬	-0.35284	0.17618 ⓯

Regression Analysis Plots
Observed Final by Predicted Final ⓰

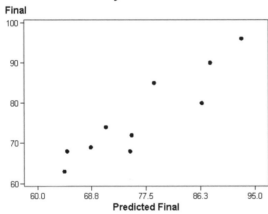

Studentized Residuals of Final by Predicted Final ⓱

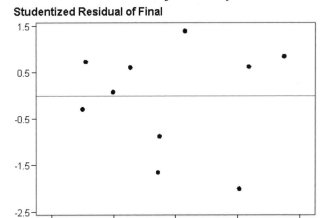

Residuals of Final by Homework ⓲

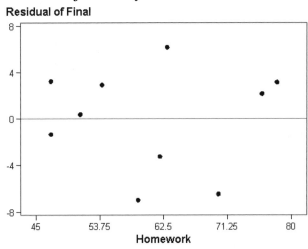

Residuals of Final by Commute ⓳

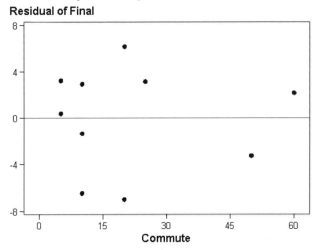

Influence (DFFITS) of Final by Predicted Final ⑳

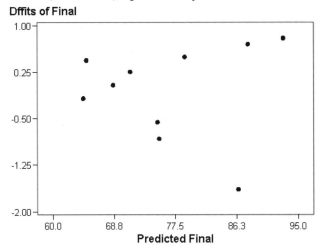

Influence (leverage) of Final by Predicted Final ㉑

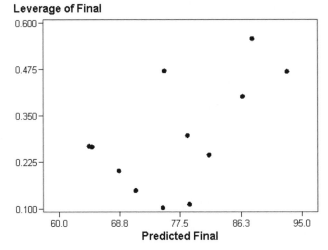

Regression Analysis Predictions

㉒ Final	㉓ predicted_Final	㉔ residual_Final	㉕ student_Final	㉖ rstudent_Final
63	64.3265	-1.32649	-0.31035	-0.28933
68	74.9959	-6.99587	-1.47808	-1.64992
68	64.7681	3.23187	0.75520	0.72953
72	75.2342	-3.23423	-0.88971	-0.87464
69	68.6190	0.38099	0.08538	0.07909
80	86.4691	-6.46905	-1.67430	-2.00196
74	71.0655	2.93447	0.63679	0.60740
85	78.8467	6.15325	1.30716	1.39194
96	92.8459	3.15409	0.86633	0.84886
90	87.8290	2.17096	0.65318	0.62404
.	81.6555	.	.	.
.	78.5640	.	.	.

㉗ lcl_Final	㉘ lclm_Final	㉙ ucl_Final	㉚ uclm_Final
51.0222	58.2086	77.631	70.444
62.5906	71.2123	87.401	78.779
51.4734	58.6711	78.063	70.865
60.9072	67.1294	89.561	83.339
55.6647	63.3049	81.573	73.933
72.4805	78.9788	100.458	93.959
58.4002	66.5010	83.731	75.630
66.3869	74.8878	91.307	82.806
78.5268	84.7551	107.165	100.937
73.0852	79.0082	102.573	96.650
68.4752	75.8123	94.836	87.499
65.1095	72.1259	92.019	85.002

Output 7.10 Listing for Example 7.5.15

Report Listing

Row number	Home work ㉛	Commute ㉜	Final ㉒	predicted _Final ㉓	stdp_ Final ㉝	lclm_ Final ㉘	uclm_ Final ㉚	lcl_ Final ㉗	ucl_ Final ㉙
1	47	10	63	64.3265	2.58725	58.2086	70.444	51.0222	77.631
2	59	20	68	74.9959	1.60009	71.2123	78.779	62.5906	87.401
3	47	5	68	64.7681	2.57845	58.6711	70.865	51.4734	78.063
4	62	50	72	75.2342	3.42751	67.1294	83.339	60.9072	89.561
5	51	5	69	68.6190	2.24734	63.3049	73.933	55.6647	81.573
6	70	10	80	86.4691	3.16762	78.9788	93.959	72.4805	100.458
7	54	10	74	71.0655	1.93036	66.5010	75.630	58.4002	83.731
8	63	20	85	78.8467	1.67424	74.8878	82.806	66.3869	91.307
9	78	25	96	92.8459	3.42159	84.7551	100.937	78.5268	107.165
10	76	60	90	87.8290	3.73033	79.0082	96.650	73.0852	102.573
11	65	10	.	81.6555	2.47108	75.8123	87.499	68.4752	94.836
12	65	45	.	78.5640	2.72266	72.1259	85.002	65.1095	92.019

Row number	residual _Final ㉔	stdr_ Final ㉞	student_ Final ㉕	cookd_ Final ㉟	h_ Final ㊱	rstudent _Final ㉖	dffits_ Final ㊲	stdi_ Final ㊳
1	-1.32649	4.27415	-0.31035	0.01176	0.26816	-0.28933	-0.17514	5.62638
2	-6.99587	4.73307	-1.47808	0.08323	0.10257	-1.64992	-0.55778	5.24619
3	3.23187	4.27947	0.75520	0.06902	0.26634	0.72953	0.43956	5.62234
4	-3.23423	3.63516	-0.88971	0.23458	0.47063	-0.87464	-0.82468	6.05889
5	0.38099	4.46225	0.08538	0.00062	0.20233	0.07909	0.03983	5.47839
6	-6.46905	3.86373	-1.67430	0.62806	0.40196	-2.00196	-1.64127	5.91575
7	2.93447	4.60825	0.63679	0.02372	0.14928	0.60740	0.25444	5.35617
8	6.15325	4.70735	1.30716	0.07205	0.11229	1.39194	0.49506	5.26928
9	3.15409	3.64074	0.86633	0.22096	0.46900	0.84886	0.79777	6.05553
10	2.17096	3.32369	0.65318	0.17914	0.55746	0.62404	0.70039	6.23519
11	.	.	.	.	0.24462	.	.	5.57391
12	.	.	.	.	0.29696	.	.	5.68992

7.3.13.2 Interpretation

❶ Dependent variable is Final.

❷ $n = 10$ (12 observations read: 10 from Ex07_05 and 2 from Ex07_05_more_x. The 10 observations from Ex07_04 had values for the two explanatory variables and for the dependent variable. The 2 observations from Ex07_05_more_x did not have values for the dependent variable.)

❸ ANOVA table

❹ Coefficient of Determination R^2 and Adjusted Coefficient of Determination adj-R^2

❺ b_0

❻ b_1

❼ b_2

❽ p-value for the test of $H_0 : \beta_0 = 0$ versus $H_1 : \beta_0 \neq 0$

❾ p-value for the test of $H_0 : \beta_1 = 0$ versus $H_1 : \beta_1 \neq 0$

❿ p-value for the test of $H_0 : \beta_2 = 0$ versus $H_1 : \beta_2 \neq 0$

⑪ VIF_1

⑫ VIF_2

⑬ 95% confidence interval on β_0

⑭ 95% confidence interval on β_1

⑮ 95% confidence interval on β_2

⑯ scatter plot of responses y_i versus fitted values $\hat{y}_i$

⑰ scatter plot of studentized deleted residuals $rstudent_i$ versus fitted values $\hat{y}_i$

⑱ scatter plot of ordinary residuals $y_i - \hat{y}_i$ versus values of x_1 (Homework)

⑲ scatter plot of ordinary residuals $y_i - \hat{y}_i$ versus values of x_2 (Commute)

⑳ scatter plot of $DFFITS_i$ versus fitted values $\hat{y}_i$

㉑ scatter plot of leverage values h_{ii} versus fitted values $\hat{y}_i$

㉒ dependent variable Final

㉓ fitted values $\hat{y}_i = b_0 + b_1 x_{i1} + b_2 x_{i2}$

㉔ ordinary residuals $y_i - \hat{y}_i$

㉕ studentized residuals $\left(y_i - \hat{y}_i \right) \Big/ \sqrt{MS\left(\text{Error}\right)\left(1 - h_{ii}\right)}$

㉖ studentized deleted residuals $\left(y_i - \hat{y}_{i(i)} \right) \Big/ \sqrt{MS\left(\text{Error}\right)_{(i)} \Big/ \left(1 - h_{ii}\right)}$

㉗ lower confidence limits on future responses. These are the lower prediction limits.

㉘ lower confidence limits on the mean responses

㉙ upper confidence limits on future responses. These are the upper prediction limits.

㉚ upper confidence limits on the mean responses

㉛ explanatory variable Homework

㉜ explanatory variable Commute

㉝ estimate of the standard error of $\hat{y}_i$

③④ estimate of the standard error of ordinary residual $y_i - \hat{y}_i$

③⑤ Cook's distance $D_i = \sum_{l=1}^{n} \left(\hat{y}_l - \hat{y}_{l(i)}\right)^2 \Big/ \left(p\, MS(\text{Error})\right)$

③⑥ leverage h_{ii}

③⑦ $DFFITS_i = \left(\hat{y}_i - \hat{y}_{i(i)}\right) \Big/ \sqrt{MS(\text{Error})_{(i)}\, h_{ii}}$

③⑧ estimate of the standard error of a new response

7.3.13.3 Analysis

Example 7.5.1

$\hat{y} = 19.96192 + 0.96272x_1 - 0.08833x_2$
See ❺, ❻, & ❼ in Output 7.9.

Example 7.5.2

$H_0 : \beta_1 = \beta_2 = 0$

$H_1 : \beta_1 \neq 0 \text{ or } \beta_2 \neq 0$

p-value = 0.0018. See ❸ in Output 7.9.

Since the p-value < 0.05, reject H_0. There is sufficient evidence to support the claim that among all students that take this particular course, homework scores, commuting times, or both are useful in explaining final exam scores. The sample regression equation explains a significant amount of the variation in the final exam scores.

Example 7.5.3

Coefficient of Determination: $R^2 = 0.8346$. See ❹ in Output 7.9.

The model has reduced the variation in the responses by approximately 83%.

Using the coefficient of determination, approximately 83% of variation in the final exam scores is explained by the homework scores and commute times.

Adjusted Coefficient of Determination: adj-$R^2 = 0.7874$. See ❹ in Output 7.9.

Using the adjusted coefficient of determination, approximately 79% of variation in the final exam scores is explained by the homework scores and commute times.

Example 7.5.4

$H_0 : \beta_1 = 0$

$H_1 : \beta_1 \neq 0$

p-value = 0.0014. See ❾ in Output 7.9.

Since the p-value < 0.05, reject H_0. There is sufficient evidence to support the claim that, among all students that take this particular course, homework scores are useful in explaining final exam scores. Homework scores explain a significant amount of the variation in the final exam scores.

Example 7.5.5

A 95% confidence interval on β_1 is $(0.51674, 1.40870)$. See ⑭ in Output 7.9. On average, final exam scores increase from 0.5 to 1.4 points when homework scores increase by 1 point.

Example 7.5.6

$H_0 : \beta_2 = 0$

$H_1 : \beta_2 \neq 0$

p-value $= 0.4557$. See ⑩ in Output 7.9.

Since the p-value > 0.05, do not reject H_0. There is not sufficient evidence to support the claim that, among all students that take this particular course, commuting times are useful in explaining final exam scores. Commuting times do not explain a significant amount of the variation in the final exam scores.

Example 7.5.7

A 95% confidence interval on β_2 is $(-0.35284, 0.17618)$. See ⑮ in Output 7.9. On average, final exam scores do not change significantly when commuting times increase by 1 minute.

Example 7.5.8

$VIF_1 = 1.63039$ and $VIF_2 = 1.63039$. See ⑪ & ⑫ in Output 7.9.

There is no excessive multicollinearity. The VIF statistics are not large. One of the explanatory variables is strongly significant.

Example 7.5.9

See rows 11 and 12 in columns identified by ㉓, ㉘, and ㉚ in Outputs 7.9 and 7.10.

- For students who have a 65-homework score and a 10-minute commuting time, the mean final exam score is estimated to be 81.6555. A 95% confidence interval on the mean is $(75.8123, 87.499)$.

- For students who have a 65-homework score and a 45-minute commuting time, the mean final exam score is estimated to be 78.5640. A 95% confidence interval on the mean is $(72.1259, 85.002)$.

Example 7.5.10

See rows 11 and 12 in columns identified by ❷❼ and ❷❾ in Outputs 7.9 and 7.10.

- For students who have a 65-homework score and a 10-minute commuting time, a 95% prediction interval is $(68.4752, 94.836)$.

- For students who have a 65-homework score and a 45-minute commuting time, a 95% prediction interval is $(65.1095, 92.019)$.

Example 7.5.11

See Output 7.10.

Example 7.5.12

See ❶❻ in Output 7.9.

Example 7.5.13

- The scatter plot of the ordinary residuals against the Homework values is at ❶❽ in Output 7.9. The points appear to be random.

- The scatter plot of the ordinary residuals against the Commute values is at ❶❾ in Output 7.9. The points appear to be random.

The model appears to adequately describe the relationship between the dependent and explanatory variables.

Example 7.5.14

- Leverage. See ❷❶ in Output 7.9 and ❸❻ in Output 7.10. None of the values is greater than $2\dfrac{p}{n} = 2\dfrac{3}{10} = 0.6$. None of the rows of explanatory values is an outlier.

- Studentized deleted residuals. See ❶❼ and ❷❻ in Output 7.9. See ❷❻ in Output 7.10. None of the values is greater than 2.5. None of the responses is an outlier.

- DFFITS. See ❷⓪ in Output 7.9 and ❸❺ in Output 7.10. None of the values is greater than 2. None of the observations has unusual influence.

- Cook's distance. See ❸❸ in Output 7.10. From Table 7.20, $F_{0.50}$ is 0.871 for $p = 3$ and $n - p = 7$. None of the values is greater than 0.871. None of the observations has unusual influence.

Example 7.5.14

See Output 7.10.

7.3.14 Example 7.6: Regression Diagnostics

This example illustrates:

- The use of a plot of ordinary residuals

- The identification of outliers and highly influential observations

7.3.14.1 Spray Timing in Apple Trees

Apples trees are sprayed to protect them from insects. A study examines how the frequency of spraying relates to the level of protection (based on "Effect of Spray Timing on Efficacy of Avaunt 30WG for Control of Codling Moth, *Cydia pomonella*, in Apple," by R. Zimmerman, *Western Colorado Research Center 2000 Report*). Trees are sprayed every 6, 8, 10, 12, or 14 days during the season. At the end of each season, all apples are removed from each tree and are examined for insect damage.

The results are on the right in the table below: Days are the days between spraying and pct is the percentage of damaged apples. These values are in the Ex07_06 data set.

tree	days	pct
1	6	2.0
2	6	2.5
3	6	1.9
4	6	2.6
5	8	2.6
6	8	3.3
7	8	2.5
8	8	3.4
9	10	3.7
10	10	4.1
11	10	3.6
12	10	4.2
13	12	6.2
14	12	0.0
15	12	6.1
16	12	6.0
17	14	8.2
18	14	9.3
19	14	8.1
20	14	9.4

Example 7.6.1

Analyze the data with days being the explanatory variable and pct being the dependent variable.

1. Determine the sample regression equation.

2. Determine and interpret the Adjusted Coefficient of Determination (adj-R^2).

3. Determine the estimate of σ: $\hat{\sigma} = \sqrt{MS(\text{Error})}$.

4. Obtain a scatter plot of the ordinary residuals against the explanatory variable. Check for model adequacy.

Example 7.6.2

The analysis shows that there is a quadratic (x^2) component to the relationship between days and pct.

    a.   Use the Standardize Data task to center the days values. Add a new variable (stnd_days) for the centered values.

    b.   Create a query of the Standardized Data output data set to compute a new explanatory variable stnd_days2 that is stnd_days squared, stnd_days**2.

Example 7.6.3

Use the query results to analyze the data with days and with stnd_days2 being the explanatory variables and pct being the dependent variable.

    a.   Determine the sample regression equation.

    b.   Determine and interpret the Adjusted Coefficient of Determination (adj-R^2).

    c.   Determine the estimate of σ: $\hat{\sigma} = \sqrt{MS(\text{Error})}$.

    d.   Check for any outlying responses, outlying explanatory rows, and unusually influential observations.

        i.   Use plots of the studentized deleted residuals, leverage values, and the DFFITS values against fitted values.

        ii.   Include studentized deleted residuals and diagnostic statistics (leverage, DFFITS, and Cook's Distance) in an output data set.

Example 7.6.4

The analysis shows that there is a highly influential observation. It is meant to be an error.

    a.   Create a query of the Linear Regression output data set to create a new explanatory variable.

    b.   Create a filter to include observations that do not have unusually high influence, $|DFFITS_i| \leq 2$. The filter would be:

$$\text{WHERE } data\_set\_name.\text{dffits\_pct BETWEEN -2 AND 2}$$

Example 7.6.5

Use the results from the preceding query to analyze the data with days and stnd_days2 being the explanatory variables and pct being the dependent variable.

    a.   Determine the sample regression equation.

    b.   Determine the Adjusted Coefficient of Determination (adj-R^2).

    c.   Determine the estimate of σ: $\hat{\sigma} = \sqrt{MS(\text{Error})}$.

Example 7.6.6

Compare the results in parts b and c in Example 7.6.1, Example 7.6.3, and Example 7.6.5.

The process flow diagram for Example 7.6 is shown in Figure 7.36.

The output for Example 7.6.1 is in Output 7.11. The output for Example 7.6.3 is in Output 7.12 and Output 7.13. The output for Example 7.6.5 is in Output 7.14.

Figure 7.36 Process Flow Diagram for Example 7.6

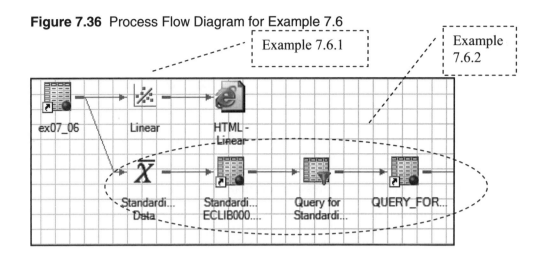

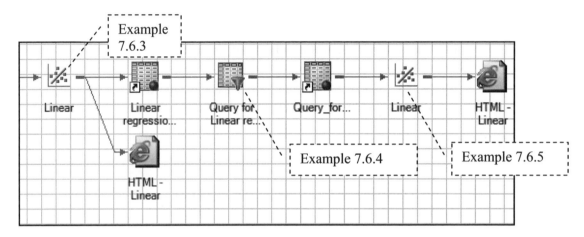

7.3.15 Task Output, Interpretation, and Analysis for Example 7.6

7.3.15.1 Task Output

Output 7.11 Linear Regression for Example 7.6.1

Linear Regression Results

The REG Procedure
Model: Linear_Regression_Model
Dependent Variable: pct

Number of Observations Read	20	
Number of Observations Used	20	❶

Analysis of Variance					
Source	DF	Sum of Squares	Mean Square	F Value	Pr > F
Model	1	85.55625	85.55625	31.64	<.0001
Error	18	48.66925	2.70385		
Corrected Total	19	134.22550			

❷ Root MSE	1.64434	R-Square	0.6374	
Dependent Mean	4.48500	Adj R-Sq	0.6173	❸
Coeff Var	36.66305			

Parameter Estimates					
Variable	DF	Parameter Estimate	Standard Error	t Value	Pr > |t|
Intercept	1	❹ -2.82750	1.35096	-2.09	0.0508
days	1	❺ 0.73125	0.13000	5.63	<.0001

Regression Analysis Plots
Residuals of pct by days ❻

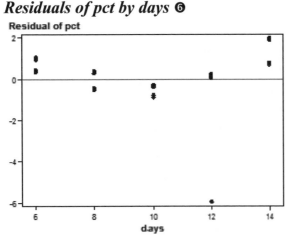

Output 7.12 Linear Regression for Example 7.6.3

Linear Regression Results

The REG Procedure
Model: Linear_Regression_Model
Dependent Variable: pct

Number of Observations Read	20	
Number of Observations Used	20	❼

Analysis of Variance					
Source	DF	Sum of Squares	Mean Square	F Value	Pr > F
Model	2	98.28643	49.14321	23.25	<.0001
Error	17	35.93907	2.11406		
Corrected Total	19	134.22550			

❽	Root MSE	1.45398	R-Square	0.7322	
	Dependent Mean	4.48500	Adj R-Sq	0.7007	❾
	Coeff Var	32.41877			

Parameter Estimates					
Variable	DF	Parameter Estimate	Standard Error	t Value	Pr > |t|
Intercept	1	❿ -3.78107	1.25618	-3.01	0.0079
days	1	⓫ 0.73125	0.11495	6.36	<.0001
stnd_days2	1	⓬ 0.11920	0.04857	2.45	0.0252

Regression Analysis Plots
Studentized Residuals of pct by Predicted pct ⓑ

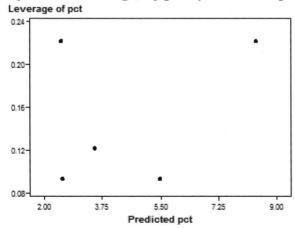

Influence (DFFITS) of pct by Predicted pct ⓪

Influence (leverage) of pct by Predicted pct ⓯

Output 7.13 Listing of the Output Data Set for Example 7.6.3

Report Listing

	⑯	⑰	⑱	⑲	⑳	㉑	㉒	㉓
Row number	days	pct	stnd_ days2	predicted_ pct	stdp_pct	residual_ pct	stdr_pct	student_pct
1	6	2.0	16	2.51357	0.68419	-0.51357	1.28295	-0.40031
2	6	2.5	16	2.51357	0.68419	-0.01357	1.28295	-0.01058
3	6	1.9	16	2.51357	0.68419	-0.61357	1.28295	-0.47825
4	6	2.6	16	2.51357	0.68419	0.08643	1.28295	0.06737
5	8	2.6	4	2.54571	0.44306	0.05429	1.38483	0.03920
6	8	3.3	4	2.54571	0.44306	0.75429	1.38483	0.54468
7	8	2.5	4	2.54571	0.44306	-0.04571	1.38483	-0.03301
8	8	3.4	4	2.54571	0.44306	0.85429	1.38483	0.61689
9	10	3.7	0	3.53143	0.50666	0.16857	1.36285	0.12369
10	10	4.1	0	3.53143	0.50666	0.56857	1.36285	0.41719
11	10	3.6	0	3.53143	0.50666	0.06857	1.36285	0.05031
12	10	4.2	0	3.53143	0.50666	0.66857	1.36285	0.49057
13	12	6.2	4	5.47071	0.44306	0.72929	1.38483	0.52662
14	12	0.0	4	5.47071	0.44306	-5.47071	1.38483	-3.95046
15	12	6.1	4	5.47071	0.44306	0.62929	1.38483	0.45441
16	12	6.0	4	5.47071	0.44306	0.52929	1.38483	0.38220
17	14	8.2	16	8.36357	0.68419	-0.16357	1.28295	-0.12750
18	14	9.3	16	8.36357	0.68419	0.93643	1.28295	0.72991
19	14	8.1	16	8.36357	0.68419	-0.26357	1.28295	-0.20544
20	14	9.4	16	8.36357	0.68419	1.03643	1.28295	0.80785

	㉔	㉕	㉖	㉗	㉘
Row number	cookd_ pct	h_pct	rstudent_ pct	dffits_pct	stdi_pct
1	0.01519	0.22143	-0.3902	-0.20809	1.60692
2	0.00001	0.22143	-0.0103	-0.00547	1.60692
3	0.02168	0.22143	-0.4671	-0.24912	1.60692
4	0.00043	0.22143	0.0654	0.03486	1.60692
5	0.00005	0.09286	0.0380	0.01217	1.51999
6	0.01012	0.09286	0.5331	0.17056	1.51999
7	0.00004	0.09286	-0.0320	-0.01025	1.51999

Row number	㉔ cookd_pct	㉕ h_pct	㉖ rstudent_pct	㉗ dffits_pct	㉘ stdi_pct
8	0.01298	0.09286	0.6053	0.19365	1.51999
9	0.00070	0.12143	0.1201	0.04463	1.53973
10	0.00802	0.12143	0.4068	0.15124	1.53973
11	0.00012	0.12143	0.0488	0.01815	1.53973
12	0.01109	0.12143	0.4793	0.17820	1.53973
13	0.00946	0.09286	0.5151	0.16481	1.51999
14	0.53249	0.09286	-13.3842	-4.28215	1.51999
15	0.00705	0.09286	0.4435	0.14191	1.51999
16	0.00498	0.09286	0.3724	0.11914	1.51999
17	0.00154	0.22143	-0.1237	-0.06599	1.60692
18	0.05051	0.22143	0.7195	0.38369	1.60692
19	0.00400	0.22143	-0.1996	-0.10642	1.60692
20	0.06187	0.22143	0.7992	0.42622	1.60692

Output 7.14 Linear Regression for Example 7.6.5

Linear Regression Results

The REG Procedure
Model: Linear_Regression_Model
Dependent Variable: pct

Number of Observations Read	19
Number of Observations Used	19 ㉘

Analysis of Variance					
Source	**DF**	**Sum of Squares**	**Mean Square**	**F Value**	**Pr > F**
Model	2	110.10479	55.05240	298.91	<.0001
Error	16	2.94679	0.18417		
Corrected Total	18	113.05158			

㉙ **Root MSE**	0.42916	**R-Square**	0.9739	
Dependent Mean	4.72105	**Adj R-Sq**	0.9707	㉚
Coeff Var	9.09024			

Parameter Estimates					
Variable	DF	Parameter Estimate	Standard Error	t Value	Pr > |t|
Intercept	1	㉛ -4.01799	0.37120	-10.82	<.0001
days	1	㉜ 0.80663	0.03439	23.45	<.0001
days2	1	㉝ 0.09227	0.01448	6.37	<.0001

7.3.15.2 Interpretation

❶ $n = 20$ for Example 7.6.1

❷ $\hat{\sigma} = \sqrt{MS(Error)} = 1.64434$ for Example 7.6.1

❸ adj-$R^2 = 0.6173$ for Example 7.6.1

❹ $b_0 = -2.82750$ for Example 7.6.1

❺ $b_1 = 0.73125$ for Example 7.6.1

❻ Curved, nonrandom pattern. This indicates a quadratic (x^2) relationship between the population means and the explanatory variable.

❼ $n = 20$ for Example 7.6.3

❽ $\hat{\sigma} = \sqrt{MS(Error)} = 1.45398$ for Example 7.6.3

❾ adj-$R^2 = 0.7007$ for Example 7.6.3

❿ $b_0 = -3.78107$ for Example 7.6.3

⓫ $b_1 = 0.73125$ for Example 7.6.3

⓬ $b_2 = 0.11920$ for Example 7.6.3

⓭ scatter plot of studentized deleted residuals $rstudent_i$ versus fitted values $\hat{y}_i$ for Example 7.6.3

⓮ scatter plot of $DFFITS_i$ versus fitted values $\hat{y}_i$ for Example 7.6.3

⓯ scatter plot of leverage values h_{ii} versus fitted values $\hat{y}_i$ for Example 7.6.3

⓰ explanatory variable days for Example 7.6.3

⓱ dependent variable pct for Example 7.6.3

⓲ explanatory variable stnd_days2 for Example 7.6.3

⓳ fitted values $\hat{y}_i = b_0 + b_1 x_{i1} + b_2 x_{i2}$ for Example 7.6.3

⓴ estimate of the standard error of $\hat{y}_i$ for Example 7.6.3

㉑ ordinary residuals $y_i - \hat{y}_i$ for Example 7.6.3

㉒ estimate of the standard error of ordinary residual $y_i - \hat{y}_i$ for Example 7.6.3

㉓ studentized residuals $(y_i - \hat{y}_i)/\sqrt{MS(Error)(1 - h_{ii})}$ for Example 7.6.3

㉔ Cook's distance $D_i = \sum_{l=1}^{n}(\hat{y}_l - \hat{y}_{l(i)})^2 / (p\, MS(Error))$ for Example 7.6.3

㉕ leverage h_{ii} for Example 7.6.3

㉖ studentized deleted residuals $\left(y_i - \hat{y}_{i(i)}\right)\Big/\sqrt{MS\left(\text{Error}\right)_{(i)}\big/\left(1 - h_{ii}\right)}$ for Example 7.6.3

㉗ $DFFITS_i = \left(\hat{y}_i - \hat{y}_{i(i)}\right)\Big/\sqrt{MS\left(\text{Error}\right)_{(i)} h_{ii}}$ for Example 7.6.3

㉘ estimate of the standard error of a new response for Example 7.6.3

㉙ $n = 19$ for Example 7.6.5

㉚ $\hat{\sigma} = \sqrt{MS\left(Error\right)} = 0.42916$ for Example 7.6.5

㉛ adj-$R^2 = 0.9707$ for Example 7.6.5

㉜ $b_0 = -4.01799$ for Example 7.6.5

㉝ $b_1 = 0.80663$ for Example 7.6.5

㉞ $b_2 = 0.09227$ for Example 7.6.5

7.3.15.3 Analysis

Example 7.6.1

    a. $\hat{y} = -2.82750 + 0.73125x_1$. See ❹ & ❺ in Output 7.11.

    b. $\hat{\sigma} = \sqrt{MS\left(Error\right)} = 1.64434$. See ❷ in Output 7.11.

    c.   adj-$R^2 = 0.6173$. See ❸ in Output 7.11.

    d.   See ❻ in Output 7.11.

Example 7.6.3

    a. $\hat{y} = -3.78107 + 0.73125x_1 + 0.11920x_2$. See ❿, ⓫, & ⓬ in Output 7.12.

    b. $\hat{\sigma} = \sqrt{MS\left(Error\right)} = 1.45398$. See ❽ in Output 7.12.

    c.   adj-$R^2 = 0.7007$. See ❾ in Output 7.12.

    d.   For plots, see ⓭, ⓮, & ⓯ in Output 7.12. Data set is Output 7.13.

Example 7.6.5

    a. $\hat{y} = -4.01799 + 0.80663x_1 + 0.09227x_2$. See ㉛, ㉜, & ㉝ in Output 7.14.

    b. $\hat{\sigma} = \sqrt{MS\left(Error\right)} = 0.42916$. See ⓴ in Output 7.14.

    c.   adj-$R^2 = 0.9707$. See ㉚ in Output 7.14.

Example 7.6.6

	$\hat{\sigma} = \sqrt{MS\left(Error\right)}$	adj-R^2
Example 7.6.1	1.64431	0.6173
Example 7.6.3	1.45398	0.7007
Example 7.6.5	0.42916	0.9707

- $\hat{\sigma}$ is a measure of the variation not explained by the model. Reduction (improvement) occurs both when stnd_days2 is added to the model in Example 7.6.3 and when the unusually influential observation is eliminated in Example 7.6.5.

- adj-$R^2 = 1 - MS(\text{Error})/s_y^2$. It is the proportion of the variation in the responses that is explained by the model. The adj-R^2 increases (improves) as $\hat{\sigma} = \sqrt{MS(\text{Error})}$ decreases.

7.3.16 Example 7.7: Regression Diagnostics

This examines multicollinearity.

7.3.16.1 Possible Predictors of Young Children Being Overweight

Eighteen mother-son pairs participate in a study investigating possible predictors of fatness in young children (based on "Association between Infant Breastfeeding and Overweight in Young Children," by Hediger et al., *Journal of the American Medical Association*, Vol. 285, No. 19, pp. 2453-2460). A measure of fatness is the body mass index: BMI = (weight in kilograms)/(height in meters)^2. The boys are all five years old and have been breast fed.

The results are below. The possible predictors are breastfeeding duration in months (BD), mother's current weight (mother_weight), and mother's current BMI (mother_BMI). The response variable is the child's current BMI (child_BMI).

observation	BD	mother_weight	mother_BMI	child_BMI
1	5	104	19.2	11.8
2	1	109	20.2	15.5
3	3	126	24.0	13.3
4	1	154	30.3	19.1
5	2	107	19.3	14.5
6	1	141	25.1	16.6
7	1	152	27.7	17.7
8	4	140	24.1	16.9
9	6	157	27.3	16.7
10	1	180	31.1	18.4
11	1	168	28.3	14.7
12	1	134	21.0	17.7
13	10	172	27.9	13.5
14	1	158	24.2	14.4
15	3	177	27.5	16.2
16	10	184	28.7	16.8
17	3	190	27.3	16.9
18	10	216	33.3	18.7

These values are in the Ex07_07 data set.

Example 7.7.1

Analyze the data with BD, mother_weight, and mother_BMI being the explanatory variables and child_BMI being the dependent variable.

5. Test the claim that at least one of the possible predictors is useful in explaining the BMI of a 5-year-old boy. Let $\alpha = 0.05$.

6. Determine the Adjusted Coefficient of Determination (adj-R^2).

7. Test the claim that breastfeeding duration is useful in explaining the BMI of a 5-year-old boy. Let $\alpha = 0.05$.

8. Test the claim that the mother's weight is useful in explaining the BMI of a 5-year-old boy. Let $\alpha = 0.05$.

9. Test the claim that the mother's BMI is useful in explaining the BMI of a 5-year-old boy. Let $\alpha = 0.05$.

10. Check for multicollinearity using the VIF statistics.

Example 7.7.2

Weight and BMI carry much of the same information. Variables based on these measurements would likely be highly correlated. The analysis in Example 7.7.1 shows that mother_weight and mother_BMI are involved in excessive multicollinearity.

11. Analyze the data with BD and mother_weight being the explanatory variables and child_BMI being the dependent variable.

    a. Test the claim that at least one of the possible predictors is useful in explaining the BMI of a 5-year-old boy. Let $\alpha = 0.05$.

    b. Determine the Adjusted Coefficient of Determination (adj-R^2).

    c. Test the claim that breastfeeding duration is useful in explaining the BMI of a 5-year-old boy. Let $\alpha = 0.05$.

    d. Test the claim that the mother's weight is useful in explaining the BMI of a 5-year-old boy. Let $\alpha = 0.05$.

12. Analyze the data with BD and mother_BMI being the explanatory variables and child_BMI being the dependent variable.

    a. Test the claim that at least one of the possible predictors is useful in explaining the BMI of a 5-year-old boy. Let $\alpha = 0.05$.

    b. Determine the Adjusted Coefficient of Determination (adj-R^2).

    c. Test the claim that breastfeeding duration is useful in explaining the BMI of a 5-year-old boy. Let $\alpha = 0.05$.

    d. Test the claim that the mother's BMI is useful in explaining the BMI of a 5-year-old boy. Let $\alpha = 0.05$.

The results for Example 7.7.1, Example 7.7.2.a, and Example 7.7.2.b are in Outputs 7.15, 7.17, and 7.17.

7.3.17 Task Output, Interpretation, and Analysis for Example 7.7

7.3.17.1 Task Output

Output 7.15 Linear Regression for Example 7.7.1

Linear Regression Results

The REG Procedure
Model: Linear_Regression_Model
Dependent Variable: child_BMI

Number of Observations Read	18
Number of Observations Used	18

Analysis of Variance						
Source	DF	Sum of Squares	Mean Square	F Value	Pr > F	
Model	3	31.90647	10.63549	3.97	0.0306	❶
Error	14	37.50464	2.67890			
Corrected Total	17	69.41111				

Root MSE	1.63674	R-Square	0.4597	
Dependent Mean	16.07778	Adj R-Sq	0.3439	❷
Coeff Var	10.18011			

Parameter Estimates							
Variable	DF	Parameter Estimate	Standard Error	t Value		Pr > |t|	Variance Inflation	
Intercept	1	7.80079	2.63612	2.96		0.0104	0	
BD	1	-0.21532	0.13529	-1.59	❸	0.1338	1.28750	❻
mother_weight	1	0.00949	0.03120	0.30	❹	0.7654	5.84055	❼
mother_BMI	1	0.29256	0.22309	1.31	❺	0.2108	5.27258	❽

Output 7.16 Linear Regression for Example 7.7.2.a

Linear Regression Results

The REG Procedure
Model: Linear_Regression_Model
Dependent Variable: child_BMI

Number of Observations Read	18
Number of Observations Used	18

Analysis of Variance					
Source	DF	Sum of Squares	Mean Square	F Value	Pr > F
Model	2	27.29944	13.64972	4.86	0.0236
Error	15	42.11167	2.80744		
Corrected Total	17	69.41111			

❾

Root MSE	1.67554	R-Square	0.3933
Dependent Mean	16.07778	Adj R-Sq	0.3124 ❿
Coeff Var	10.42148		

Parameter Estimates					
Variable	DF	Parameter Estimate	Standard Error	t Value	Pr > |t|
Intercept	1	9.90582	2.14063	4.63	0.0003
BD	1	-0.24312	0.13679	-1.78	0.0958 ⓫
mother_weight	1	0.04574	0.01481	3.09	0.0075 ⓬

Output 7.17 Linear Regression for Example 7.7.2.b

Linear Regression Results

The REG Procedure
Model: Linear_Regression_Model
Dependent Variable: child_BMI

Number of Observations Read	18
Number of Observations Used	18

Analysis of Variance					
Source	DF	Sum of Squares	Mean Square	F Value	Pr > F
Model	2	31.65839	15.82919	6.29	0.0104
Error	15	37.75272	2.51685		
Corrected Total	17	69.41111			

⑬

Root MSE	1.58646	R-Square	0.4561
Dependent Mean	16.07778	Adj R-Sq	0.3836 ⑭
Coeff Var	9.86739		

Parameter Estimates					
Variable	DF	Parameter Estimate	Standard Error	t Value	Pr > |t|
Intercept	1	7.65178	2.51067	3.05	0.0081
BD	1	-0.20109	0.12305	-1.63	0.1230 ⑮
mother_BMI	1	0.35271	0.10027	3.52	0.0031 ⑯

7.3.17.2 Interpretation

❶ ANOVA table for Example 7.7.1

❷ Adjusted Coefficient of Determination adj-R^2 for Example 7.7.1

❸ p-value for the test of $H_0 : \beta_1 = 0$ versus $H_0 : \beta_1 \neq 0$ for Example 7.7.1

❹ p-value for the test of $H_0 : \beta_2 = 0$ versus $H_0 : \beta_2 \neq 0$ for Example 7.7.1

❺ p-value for the test of $H_0 : \beta_3 = 0$ versus $H_0 : \beta_3 \neq 0$ for Example 7.7.1

❻ VIF_1 for Example 7.7.1

❼ VIF_2 for Example 7.7.1

❽ VIF_3 for Example 7.7.1

❾ ANOVA table for Example 7.7.2.a

❿ Adjusted Coefficient of Determination adj-R^2 for Example 7.7.2.a

⓫ p-value for the test of $H_0 : \beta_0 = 0$ versus $H_0 : \beta_0 \neq 0$ for Example 7.7.2.a

⓬ p-value for the test of $H_0 : \beta_1 = 0$ versus $H_0 : \beta_1 \neq 0$ for Example 7.7.2.a

⓭ ANOVA table for Example 7.7.2.b

⓮ Adjusted Coefficient of Determination adj-R^2 for Example 7.7.2.b

⓯ p-value for the test of $H_0 : \beta_0 = 0$ versus $H_0 : \beta_0 \neq 0$ for Example 7.7.2.b

⓰ p-value for the test of $H_0 : \beta_1 = 0$ versus $H_0 : \beta_1 \neq 0$ for Example 7.7.2.b

7.3.17.3 Analysis

Example 7.7.1

a. $H_0 : \beta_1 = \beta_2 = \beta_3 = 0$

H_1 : At least one of the parameters β_1, β_2, or β_3 is not 0.

p-value = 0.0306. See ❶ in Output 7.15.

Since the p-value < 0.05, reject H0. There is sufficient evidence to support the claim that at least one of the possible predictors is useful in explaining the BMI of a 5-year-old boy. The sample regression equation explains a significant amount of the variation in the boys' BMI values.

b. Adjusted Coefficient of Determination: adj-R^2 = 0.3439 . See ❷ in Output 7.15.

c. $H_0 : \beta_1 = 0$

$H_1 : \beta_1 \neq 0$

p-value = 0.1338. See ❸ in Output 7.15.

Since the p-value > 0.05, do not reject H_0. There is not sufficient evidence to support the claim that breastfeeding duration is useful in explaining the BMI of a 5-year-old boy. The breastfeeding duration values do not explain a significant amount of the variation in the boys' BMI values.

d. $H_0 : \beta_2 = 0$

$H_1 : \beta_2 \neq 0$

p-value = 0.7654. See ❹ in Output 7.15.

Since the p-value > 0.05, do not reject H_0. There is not sufficient evidence to support the claim that the mother's weight is useful in explaining the BMI of a 5-year-old boy. The weights of the mothers do not explain a significant amount of the variation in the boys' BMI values.

e. $H_0 : \beta_3 = 0$

$H_1 : \beta_3 \neq 0$

p-value = 0.2108. See ❺ in Output 7.15.

Since the p-value > 0.05, do not reject H_0. There is not sufficient evidence to support the claim that the mother's BMI is useful in explaining the BMI of a 5-year-old boy. The BMI values of the mothers do not explain a significant amount of the variation in the boys' BMI values.

f. There is excessive multicollinearity. The test of the full model is significant but none of the tests of the explanatory variables is significant. The VIF statistics for mother_weight and mother_BMI ($VIF_2 = 5.84055$, $VIF_3 = 5.27258$) are relatively large compared to the VIF statistic for BD ($VIF_1 = 1.28750$). See ❻, ❼, & ❽ in Output 7.15.

Example 7.7.2.a

a. $H_0 : \beta_1 = \beta_2 = 0$

   $H_1 : \beta_1 \neq 0 \text{ or } \beta_2 \neq 0$

   *p-v*alue = 0.0236. See ❾ in Output 7.16.

   Since the *p*-value < 0.05, reject H_0. There is sufficient evidence to support the claim that breastfeeding duration or mother's weight is useful in explaining the BMI of a 5-year-old boy. The sample regression equation explains a significant amount of the variation in the boys' BMI values.

b.   Adjusted Coefficient of Determination: adj-R^2 = 0.3124 . See ❿ in Output 7.16.

c. $H_0 : \beta_1 = 0$

   $H_1 : \beta_1 \neq 0$

   *p-v*alue = 0.0958. See ⓫ in Output 7.16.

   Since the *p*-value > 0.05, do not reject H_0. There is not sufficient evidence to support the claim that breastfeeding duration is useful in explaining the BMI of a 5-year-old boy. The breastfeeding duration values do not explain a significant amount of the variation in the boys' BMI values.

d. $H_0 : \beta_2 = 0$

   $H_1 : \beta_2 \neq 0$

   *p-v*alue = 0.0075. See ⓬ in Output 7.16.

   Since the *p*-value < 0.05, reject H_0. There is sufficient evidence to support the claim that the mother's weight is useful in explaining the BMI of a 5-year-old boy. The weights of the mothers explain a significant amount of the variation in the boys' BMI values.

Example 7.7.2.b

a. $H_0 : \beta_1 = \beta_2 = 0$

   $H_1 : \beta_1 \neq 0 \text{ or } \beta_2 \neq 0$

   *p-v*alue = 0.0104. See ⓭ in Output 7.17.

   Since the *p*-value < 0.05, reject H_0. There is sufficient evidence to support the claim that breastfeeding duration or mother's BMI is useful in explaining the BMI of a 5-year-old boy. The sample regression equation explains a significant amount of the variation in the boys' BMI values.

b.   Adjusted Coefficient of Determination: adj-R^2 = 0.3836 . See ⓮ in Output 7.17.

c. $H_0 : \beta_1 = 0$

   $H_1 : \beta_1 \neq 0$

   *p-v*alue = 0.1230. See ⓯ in Output 7.17.

   Since the p-value > 0.05, do not reject H0. There is not sufficient evidence to support the claim that breastfeeding duration is useful in explaining the BMI of a 5-year-old boy. The breastfeeding duration values do not explain a significant amount of the variation in the boys' BMI values.

d. $H_0 : \beta_2 = 0$

$H_1 : \beta_2 \neq 0$

*p-v*alue = 0.0031. See ⑯ in Output 7.17.

Since the *p*-value < 0.05, reject H_0. There is sufficient evidence to support the claim that the mother's BMI is useful in explaining the BMI of a 5-year-old boy. The BMI values of the mothers explain a significant amount of the variation in the boys' BMI values.

7.3.18 Model Selection

Sometimes a researcher has a large number of explanatory variables, and it is necessary to pare away those variables that are not useful. Model selection methods are designed to do just that.

- *Adj-*R^2 *selection* computes the adj-R^2 for all possible models containing at least one of the explanatory variables. The models are listed in order of highest to lowest adj-R^2.

- *Stepwise selection* automatically enters or removes explanatory variables one at a time until there is a single best model.

The model selected in the stepwise method is "best" according to the rules of that process. Stepwise selection and adj-R^2 selection do not necessarily result in the same "best" model.

The automatic nature of stepwise regression is a concern for some authors. But which method to use really depends on which method works best for the researcher.

In any case, model selection is not the end of the analysis. Not all of the explanatory variables selected may be significant. Regression diagnostics may be required. The completion of model selection is the beginning of all the analysis discussed before this section.

Type II sum of squares is also presented in this section. Stepwise selection uses Type II sum of squares to determine the explanatory variables that enter and are removed from the model.

7.3.18.1 Adj-R^2 Selection: Comparing All Possible Regression Models

In adj-R^2 selection, the adj-R^2 values are computed for all possible models containing at least one of the explanatory variables. There are $2^{p-1} - 1$ such models. In the output, the adj-R^2 values are ordered highest to lowest. See the table below.

Since adj-$R^2 = 1 - MS(Error)/s_y^2$, finding the model with the highest adj-R^2 is equivalent to finding the model with the lowest $\hat{\sigma} = \sqrt{MS(Error)}$.

- adj-R^2 is the proportion of the variation in the responses that is explained by the model.

- $\hat{\sigma}$ is a measure of the variation not explained by the model.

There are no hard and fast rules with adj-R^2 selection. The goal is to reduce the number of models the researcher might examine to a manageable few. Models with similarly high adj-R^2 can reasonably be selected for further analysis.

The output for adj-R^2 selection is described by the following table. The variable m represents the number of explanatory variables in the corresponding model.

Number in Model	Adjusted R-Square	R-Square	Root MSE	Variables in Model
m	largest adj-R^2 among all models	corresponding R^2	corresponding $\sqrt{MS(Error)}$	corresponding variable name(s)
$\vdots$	2nd largest adj-R^2 among all models	$\vdots$	$\vdots$	$\vdots$
$\vdots$	3rd largest adj-R^2 among all models	$\vdots$	$\vdots$	$\vdots$
$\vdots$	$\vdots$	$\vdots$	$\vdots$	$\vdots$

7.3.18.2 Type II Sum of Squares

In regression, a Type II sum of squares measures the reduction of unexplained variation in the responses due to a specific explanatory variable or the intercept. Stepwise selection uses Type II sum of squares to determine which explanatory variables enter and are removed from the model.

As an example, consider a sample with a dependent variable y and explanatory variables x1, x2, and x3. There are n observations: $y_i, x_{i1}, x_{i2}, x_{i3}$, with $i = 1, \ldots, n$.

Let *Type II SS*$(x2)$ represent the Type II sum of squares associated with x2.

- *Type II SS*$(x2)$ is the Error Sum of Squares for the model containing x1 and x3 minus the Error Sum of Squares for the model containing x1, x2, and x3.

- The model containing x1 and x3 is the *reduced model*. The model is reduced by excluding x2. The model containing x1, x2, and x3 is the *full model*.

$$Type\ II\ SS(x2) = SS(\text{Error})^{(R)} - SS(\text{Error})$$

$$= \sum_{i=1}^{n}\left(y_i - \hat{y}_i^{(R)}\right)^2 - \sum_{i=1}^{n}\left(y_i - \hat{y}_i\right)^2$$

$$= \sum_{i=1}^{n}\left(y_i - \left(b_0^{(R)} + b_1^{(R)}x_1 + b_3^{(R)}x_3\right)\right)^2 - \sum_{i=1}^{n}\left(y_i - \left(b_0 + b_1x_1 + b_2x_2 + b_3x_3\right)\right)^2$$

The superscript (R) indicates that the statistic is based on the reduced model. No superscript indicates the statistic is based on the full model. In general, $SS(\text{Error})^{(R)} \geq SS(\text{Error})$, $\hat{y}_i^{(R)} \neq \hat{y}_i$, $b_0^{(R)} \neq b_0$, $b_1^{(R)} \neq b_1$, etc.

7.3.18.3 Stepwise Selection: Finding the Best Model

Stepwise selection automatically enters or removes explanatory variables one at a time until there is a single best multiple regression model. For convenience, the name Best Model refers to that model as it is being created and as it is ultimately presented.

- An explanatory variable enters the Best Model if its *p*-value is less than or equal to the significance level α_{ENTER}. Here, $\alpha_{\text{ENTER}} = 0.15$ is used.

- An explanatory variable is removed from the Best Model if its *p*-value is greater than the significance level α_{STAY}. Here, $\alpha_{\text{STAY}} = 0.15$ is used.

Search for the first variable to enter the Best Model.

The process begins by considering all 1-variable models.

- The Type II sum of squares is computed for each explanatory variable xj:
  $Type\,II\,SS(\text{xj})$.

- An *F* value is computed for each explanatory variable xj:

$$F \text{ value} = \frac{Type\,II\,SS(\text{xj})}{\left(\dfrac{SS(\text{Error})}{n-2}\right)} = \frac{Type\,II\,SS(\text{xj})}{MS(\text{Error})}$$

Each *F* value is assumed to follow the *F* distribution with 1 numerator and $n-2$ denominator degrees of freedom.

- The selection process stops if each of the *p*-values > 0.15 (α_{ENTER}).

- If there at least one *p*-value ≤ 0.15 (α_{ENTER}), the explanatory variable with the smallest *p*-value enters the Best Model.

- The regression output for this variable is displayed in Step 1. See "Stepwise Regression Output."

Check to remove variables.

After each step, the *p*-values of all explanatory variables in the Best Model are checked.

- If a variable has a *p*-value > 0.15 (α_{STAY}), the variable is removed. The regression output for the remaining variables is displayed in a new step. See "Stepwise Regression Output."

- If all the variables have *p*-values ≤ 0.15 (α_{STAY}), the process searches for another variable to enter the Best Model. See below.

Search for another variable to enter the Best Model.

Let *m* be the number of explanatory variables currently in the Best Model.

- If all the original explanatory variables are currently in the Best Model ($m = p - 1$), the process stops.

- If there is at least one variable that is not currently in the Best Model, the process considers all $(m+1)$-variable models containing the m current variables plus a variable not in the Best Model.

- The Type II sum of squares is computed for the added variable in each of the $(m+1)$-variable models being considered. That is, $Type\, II\, SS(xj)$ is computed for each xj not currently in the Best Model.

- An *F* value is computed for each xj not currently in the Best Model:

$$F \text{ value} = \frac{Type\, II\, SS(xj)}{\left(\dfrac{SS(Error)}{n-m-2}\right)} = \frac{Type\, II\, SS(xj)}{MS(Error)}$$

Each *F* value is assumed to follow the *F* distribution with $m+1$ numerator and $n-m-2$ denominator degrees of freedom.

- The selection process stops if either of the following is true:

  o Each of these *F* values have *p*-values > 0.15 (α_{ENTER}).

  o There is at least one *p*-value ≤ 0.15 (α_{ENTER}), but the explanatory variable with the smallest *p*-value was just removed from the Best Model.

- If neither of the previous two conditions is true, the explanatory variable associated with the smallest *p*-value enters the Best Model.

- The regression output for the variables in the Best Model is displayed in a new step. See "Stepwise Regression Output."

- The selection process checks to see if any variables should be removed. See "Check to Remove Variables."

7.3.18.4 Stepwise Regression Output

The following output is presented each time an explanatory variable enters or is removed from the Best Model. It is very similar to the output shown in this section's "Summary of Hypothesis Tests." In the tests of individual parameters, Type II sum of squares are added and *F*-value tests replace t value tests. The tests are equivalent: $F \text{ value} = (t \text{ value})^2$. The interpretations of the *p*-values are the same.

The variable *m* represents the number of explanatory variables currently in the Best Model.

Stepwise Selection: Step ❶

Variable ❷ ❸ : *R-Square =* ❹ *and C(p) =* ❺

Analysis of Variance					
Source	**DF**	**Sum of Squares**	**Mean Square**	**F Value**	**Pr > F**
Model	m	$SS(\text{Model})$	$MS(\text{Model}) = \dfrac{SS(\text{Model})}{m}$	$\dfrac{MS(\text{Model})}{MS(\text{Error})}$	p-value
Error	$n - m - 1$	$SS(\text{Error})$	$MS(\text{Error}) = \dfrac{SS(\text{Error})}{n - m - 1}$		
Corrected Total	$n - 1$	$SS(\text{Total})$			

Variable	**Parameter Estimate**	**Standard Error**	**Type II SS**	**F Value**	**Pr >F**
Intercept	b_0	$se(b_0)$	$Type\ II\ SS(\text{intercept})$	$\dfrac{Type\ II\ SS}{MS(Error)}$	p-value
explanatory variable	b_1	$se(b_1)$	❻	$\dfrac{Type\ II\ SS}{MS(Error)}$	p-value
⋮	⋮	⋮	⋮	⋮	⋮
explanatory variable	b_m	$se(b_m)$	❻	$\dfrac{Type\ II\ SS}{MS(Error)}$	p-value

Bounds on condition number: ❼, ❽

❶ Step number 1, 2, …

❷ Name of explanatory variable to be entered or removed in this step

❸ Either Entered or Removed

❹ R^2 for the Best Model in this step

❺ *Mallows C_p statistic*: This compares the $MS(\text{Error})$ for the subset of m explanatory variables with the $MS(\text{Error})$ for the original set of $p - 1$ explanatory variables. When the ratio of the two is approximately 1, then the C_p is approximately to $m + 1$.

$$C_p = (n - m - 1)\left(\frac{MS(\text{Error: current } m \text{ explanatory variables})}{MS(\text{Error: original } p - 1 \text{ explanatory variables})} - 1 \right) + (m + 1)$$

- If C_p is close to $m + 1$, then the subset of m explanatory variables reduces the unexplained variation about as well as the original set of $p - 1$ explanatory variables.

- If C_p is much larger than $m + 1$, then the subset of m explanatory variables is missing an important explanatory variable from the original set of $p - 1$ explanatory variables.

- Values of C_p less than $m + 1$ are usually still close to $m + 1$ and are due to random variation. Values of C_p much less than $m + 1$ can occur when the number of original explanatory variables is large. Such values would indicate that too many explanatory variables are in the current Best Model.

❻ *Type II SS* (xj) for one of the original explanatory variables

❼,❽ The *condition number* is a measure of multicollinearity among the explanatory variables. The condition number for the explanatory variables in this step is between ❼ and ❽. A condition number greater than 30 indicates the presence of excessive multicollinearity. This value is suggested in Freund and Littell (1991).

The following output is presented at the end of the selection process, after the last explanatory variable has been entered or removed.

Summary of Stepwise Selection								
Step	**Variable Entered**	**Variable Removed**	**Number Vars In**	**Partial R-Square**	**Model R-Square**	**C(p)**	**F Value**	**Pr > F**
1	variable name		m	❿	❹	❺	⓫	⓬
2	variable name here ...	... or here	⋮	⋮	⋮	⋮	⋮	⋮
⋮	⋮	⋮	⋮	⋮	⋮	⋮	⋮	⋮

❿ Change in R^2 :

$$\text{partial } R^2 = \begin{cases} \text{step 1: partial } R^2 = \text{model } R^2 \\ \text{after step 1: partial } R^2 = \text{absolute value of change in } R^2 \text{ from previous step} \end{cases}$$

⓫ F value $= \dfrac{Type\,II\,SS(\mathrm{xj})}{\left(\dfrac{SS(\text{Error})}{n-m-2}\right)} = \dfrac{Type\,II\,SS(\mathrm{xj})}{MS(\text{Error})}$ for entered variables. For removed variables, it

is the F value before the variable was removed.

⓬ p-value corresponding to ⓫

7.3.19 Example 7.8: Model Selection

Student	Midterm	Final	Homework	Absent	Commute
1	64	63	47	5	10
2	64	68	59	5	20
3	66	68	47	4	5
4	68	72	62	3	50
5	72	69	51	5	5
6	73	80	70	3	10
7	78	74	54	2	10
8	81	85	63	3	20
9	91	96	78	2	25
10	92	90	76	3	60

This example illustrates both adj-R^2 selection and stepwise selection.

7.3.19.1 More Student Data

The responses are from 10 randomly selected students taking a particular course. The goal is to pare away explanatory variables that are not useful in explaining final exam scores.

Midterm, Homework, Absent, and Commute are the explanatory variables. Final is the dependent variable.

These values are in the Ex07_08 data set.

The Linear Models task is executed for each of the following.

Example 7.8.1

Apply the adj-R^2 selection method. Include $\sqrt{MS(Error)}$ for each model. What explanatory variables are in the model with the highest adj-R^2?

Example 7.8.2

Apply the stepwise selection method with $\alpha_{ENTER} = 0.15$ and $\alpha_{STAY} = 0.15$. What explanatory variables are in the selected model?

7.3.20 Instructions for Model Selection

The analysis requested in Example 7.8 is listed in Table 7.23. The figures below are from this analysis.

Table 7.23 Analysis Requested in Example 7.8

Requested Analysis		Whether Always Part of Output
Example 7.8.1	adj-R^2 selection including $\sqrt{MS(Error)}$ values	Option on **Model**
Example 7.8.2	Stepwise selection	Option on **Model**

7.3.20.1 Task Roles

Variables are assigned to roles in the same manner as in "Instructions for Multiple Linear Regression."

In Figure 7.37, Final is assigned to a Dependent variables role. Midterm, Homework, Absent, and Commute are assigned to Explanatory variables roles.

7.3.20.2 Model

Model selection methods are requested on the Model options.

- For Example 7.8.1:
  - **Adjusted R-squared selection** is selected in the drop-down menu at **Model selection method** in Figure 7.38 (top).
  - Root MSE is checked at Model fit statistics.
- For Example 7.8.2:
  - **Stepwise selection** is selected in the drop-down menu at **Model selection method** in Figure 7.38 (bottom).
  - The default value at **To enter the model** is $\alpha_{\text{ENTER}} = 0.15$. The default value at **To stay in the model** is $\alpha_{\text{STAY}} = 0.15$.

Figure 7.37 Task Roles in Linear Regression

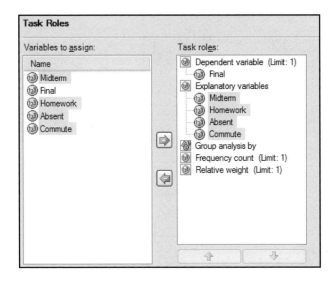

Figure 7.38 Model Options: adj-R^2 Selection Requested (Top), Stepwise Selection Requested (Bottom)

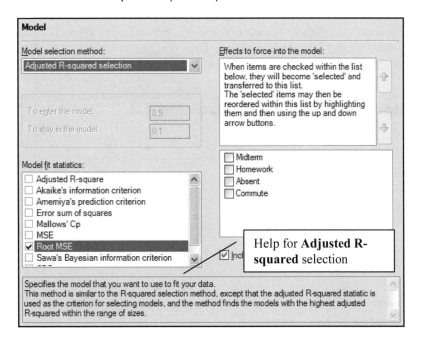

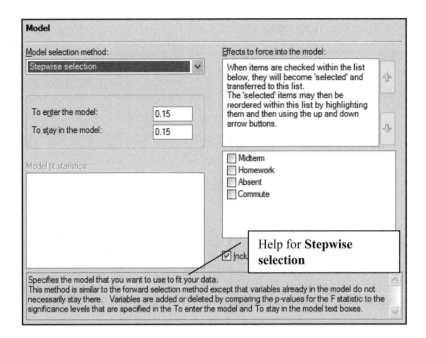

7.3.20.3 When Finished

When you are finished adding variables to roles and selecting options, click **Run**. The task adds a Linear icon and one or more output icons to the process flow diagram. The results for Example 7.8.1 are in Output 7.18. The results for Example 7.8.2 are in Output 7.19.

7.3.21 Task Output and Analysis for Example 7.8

7.3.21.1 Task Output

Output 7.18 adj-R^2 Selection for Example 7.8.1

Linear Regression Results

The REG Procedure
Model: Linear_Regression_Model
Dependent Variable: Final

Adjusted R-Square Selection Method

Number of Observations Read	10
Number of Observations Used	10

Number in Model	Adjusted R-Square	R-Square	Root MSE	Variables in Model
3	0.9496	0.9664	2.43228	Midterm Homework Commute
4	0.9450	0.9694	2.54084	Midterm Homework Absent Commute
2	0.9420	0.9549	2.61042	Midterm Homework
3	0.9383	0.9589	2.69157	Midterm Homework Absent
1	0.8618	0.8772	4.02786	Midterm
2	0.8574	0.8891	4.09149	Midterm Absent
2	0.8436	0.8784	4.28486	Midterm Commute
3	0.8353	0.8902	4.39696	Midterm Absent Commute
2	0.8300	0.8678	4.46706	Homework Absent
3	0.8176	0.8784	4.62752	Homework Absent Commute
1	0.7974	0.8199	4.87723	Homework
2	0.7874	0.8346	4.99622	Homework Commute
1	0.4833	0.5407	7.78845	Absent
2	0.4807	0.5961	7.80780	Absent Commute
1	0.1214	0.2190	10.15580	Commute

Output 7.19 Stepwise Selection for Example 7.8.2

Linear Regression Results

The REG Procedure
Model: Linear_Regression_Model
Dependent Variable: Final

Number of Observations Read	10
Number of Observations Used	10

Stepwise Selection: Step 1

Variable Midterm Entered: R-Square = 0.8772 and C(p) = 14.1041

Analysis of Variance					
Source	DF	Sum of Squares	Mean Square	F Value	Pr > F
Model	1	926.71069	926.71069	57.12	<.0001
Error	8	129.78931	16.22366		
Corrected Total	9	1056.50000			

Variable	Parameter Estimate	Standard Error	Type II SS	F Value	Pr >F
Intercept	3.47461	9.74580	2.06218	0.13	0.7307
Midterm	0.97497	0.12900	926.71069	57.12	<.0001

Bounds on condition number: 1, 1

Stepwise Selection: Step 2

Variable Homework Entered: R-Square = 0.9549 and C(p) = 3.3886

Analysis of Variance					
Source	DF	Sum of Squares	Mean Square	F Value	Pr > F
Model	2	1008.80010	504.40005	74.02	<.0001
Error	7	47.69990	6.81427		
Corrected Total	9	1056.50000			

Variable	Parameter Estimate	Standard Error	Type II SS	F Value	Pr >F
Intercept	4.61538	6.32470	3.62872	0.53	0.4892
Midterm	0.61224	0.13384	142.59937	20.93	0.0026
Homework	0.42880	0.12354	82.08941	12.05	0.0104

Bounds on condition number: 2.5626, 10.25

All variables left in the model are significant at the 0.1500 level.

No other variable met the 0.1500 significance level for entry into the model.

Summary of Stepwise Selection								
Step	Variable Entered	Variable Removed	Number Vars In	Partial R-Square	Model R-Square	C(p)	F Value	Pr > F
1	Midterm		1	0.8772	0.8772	14.1041	57.12	<.0001
2	Homework		2	0.0777	0.9549	3.3886	12.05	0.0104

7.3.21.2 Analysis

Example 7.8.1
Midterm Homework Commute

Example 7.8.2
Midterm Homework

7.4 References

Freund, R.J. and Littell, R.C. (1991), *SAS System for Regression*, Second Edition, Cary, NC: SAS Institute Inc.

Kutner, M. H., Nachtsheim, C. J., and Neter, J. (2004), *Applied Linear Regression Models*, Fourth Edition, New York, NY: McGraw-Hill/Irwin.

Analysis of 2-Way Contingency Tables

8.1 Inference on Two Binomial Proportions from Independent Populations

A *binomial proportion* applies to a situation where every person or object in a population is categorized as either having or not having a given characteristic. The proportion corresponding to the group with the given characteristic is the *binomial* proportion.

This section considers inference on two binomial proportions from independent populations. The populations are independent in that the members of one population are not paired with the members of the other population. Also, sampling in one population does not influence sampling in the other.

Let A represent a characteristic. Let Population 1 and Population 2 represent the populations. If a population is the focus of the study, it should be Population 1.

- p_1 is the proportion of Population 1 that has characteristic A, and $1 - p_1$ is the proportion that does not have characteristic A.

- p_2 is the proportion of Population 2 that has characteristic A, and $1 - p_2$ is the proportion that does not have characteristic A.

This is organized in the following table:

Table 8.1 Populations Model for Inference on Two Binomial Proportions

	A	not A	Total
Population 1	p_1	$1 - p_1$	1
Population 2	p_2	$1 - p_2$	1

The null and alternative hypotheses considered here are:

$$H_0 : p_1 = p_2$$
$$H_1 : p_1 \neq p_2$$

The test is an extension of the asymptotic one-sample test on a proportion discussed in Section 4.5, "Inference on a Population Median."

Fisher's Exact Test is an extension of the exact test discussed in Section 4.5. See Section 8.5. That test is also applied to $H_0 : p_1 \le p_2$ versus $H_1 : p_1 > p_2$ and $H_0 : p_1 \ge p_2$ versus $H_1 : p_1 < p_2$.

The proportions p_1 and p_2 are also referred to as *risks*. This section considers estimation of the *risk difference* $p_1 - p_2$, the *relative risk* p_1/p_2, and the *odds ratio* $\left(p_1/(1-p_1) \right) / \left(p_2/(1-p_2) \right)$.

8.1.1 Data

The data is organized in the following 2×2 *contingency table*. The dot notation represents summation over a subscript.

Table 8.2 Summarized Data for Inference on Two Proportions

	A	not A	Total	
Sample 1	n_{11}	n_{12}	$n_{11} + n_{12} = n_{1.}$	(fixed)
Sample 2	n_{21}	n_{22}	$n_{21} + n_{22} = n_{2.}$	(fixed)
Total	$n_{11} + n_{21} = n_{.1}$ (random)	$n_{12} + n_{22} = n_{.2}$ (random)	$n_{.1} + n_{.2} = n_{1.} + n_{2.} = n_{..}$	

- Samples 1 and 2 come from the Populations 1 and 2.
  - Sample 1 consists of n_{11} persons or objects that have characteristic A and n_{12} persons or objects that do not.
  - Sample 2 consists of n_{21} persons or objects that have characteristic A and n_{22} persons or objects that do not.
  - The locations of the n_{ij} values ($i = 1,2$ and $j = 1,2$) are *cells*. The n_{ij} values are *cell frequencies*.
  - There are 2 rows and 2 columns of cell frequencies. The *size* of this contingency table is 2×2. The row and column of totals are not counted here.
  - All cell frequencies are randomly determined values. They are the result of random selections from populations.
- The size of Sample 1 is $n_{1.}$. The size of Sample 2 is $n_{2.}$. These values are fixed by the investigator.
- The total number in both samples that have characteristic A is $n_{.1}$. The total number that do not is $n_{.2}$. These values are randomly determined. They are the result of random selection.

8.1.1.1 Table Format

The data tables in this section follow the format shown in Table 8.2.

- The samples are summarized along the rows. If a population is the focus of the study, its sample should be Sample 1.
- The frequencies associated with a given characteristic are in the first column.

Table format is not important for a hypothesis test. The results are the same whether the samples are associated with rows or columns and whether the characteristic is in the first or second location.

Table format does matter for other applications.

- Confidence intervals on $p_1 - p_2$ and the relative risk p_1/p_2 assume that Samples 1 and 2 are associated with rows 1 and 2, respectively. Results are computed for the characteristics associated with both columns—for A and not A, in terms of Table 8.2.

- The odds ratio assumes that the frequency associated with the characteristic in the sample of the focus population is either n_{11} or n_{22}. In this section, that frequency is always n_{11}.

To control the table format, see "Table Statistics > Computation Options" in the "Instructions for Table Analysis" section.

8.1.1.2 Variables

The data enters the task as two or three variables. As two variables, there is a pair of values for each person or object in the sample. One value identifies the sample and one value indicates whether the characteristic is present or not. As an example, the variable sample below identifies membership in Sample 1 or Sample 2. The variable characteristic indicates whether the characteristic is present (A) or not (B).

sample	characteristic
1	A
2	A
2	B
2	A
1	B
⋮	⋮

As three variables, the data enters in summarized form. A third variable is added that contains the frequencies with which the respective pairs occur in the sample. As an example, the variables sample and characteristic below contain a unique pair for each table cell. The variable frequency has the respective cell frequencies.

sample	characteristic	frequency
1	A	n_{11}
1	B	n_{12}
2	A	n_{21}
2	B	n_{22}

The pairs do not have to be unique. If a pair is repeated, the sum of the associated frequencies is used. Also, the values do not have to be sorted.

8.1.2 Hypothesis Test on Two Population Proportions

8.1.2.1 Test Statistic

A test statistic for the hypotheses $H_0 : p_1 = p_2$ versus $H_1 : p_1 \neq p_2$ is the Pearson chi-squared (χ^2) statistic. It compares the *observed* cell frequencies n_{ij} with the *expected* cell frequencies E_{ij}. The expected cell frequencies are the values that are expected when the null hypothesis is true. They are generally not integers.

$$\text{chi-square} = \sum_{i=1}^{2} \sum_{j=1}^{2} \frac{\left(n_{ij} - E_{ij}\right)^2}{E_{ij}}$$

In general, an expected cell frequency is equal to the estimate of the population proportion under H_0 times the sample size. Since p_1 and p_2 are equal under H_0, the two samples are combined to produce an estimate of the common proportion. That estimate is represented by $\hat{p}$.

$$\hat{p} = \frac{n_{11} + n_{21}}{n_{1\cdot} + n_{2\cdot}} = \frac{n_{\cdot 1}}{n_{\cdot\cdot}}$$

The four expected cell frequencies are computed in the following way:

$E_{11} = \hat{p} n_{1\cdot} = \dfrac{n_{\cdot 1}}{n_{\cdot\cdot}} n_{1\cdot} = \dfrac{n_{1\cdot} n_{\cdot 1}}{n_{\cdot\cdot}}$	$E_{12} = \left(1 - \hat{p}\right) n_{1\cdot} = \left(1 - \dfrac{n_{\cdot 1}}{n_{\cdot\cdot}}\right) n_{1\cdot} = \dfrac{n_{\cdot 2}}{n_{\cdot\cdot}} n_{1\cdot} = \dfrac{n_{1\cdot} n_{\cdot 2}}{n_{\cdot\cdot}}$
$E_{21} = \hat{p} n_{2\cdot} = \dfrac{n_{\cdot 1}}{n_{\cdot\cdot}} n_{2\cdot} = \dfrac{n_{2\cdot} n_{\cdot 1}}{n_{\cdot\cdot}}$	$E_{22} = \left(1 - \hat{p}\right) n_{2\cdot} = \left(1 - \dfrac{n_{\cdot 1}}{n_{\cdot\cdot}}\right) n_{2\cdot} = \dfrac{n_{\cdot 2}}{n_{\cdot\cdot}} n_{2\cdot} = \dfrac{n_{2\cdot} n_{\cdot 2}}{n_{\cdot\cdot}}$

In any case, $E_{ij} = n_{i\cdot} n_{\cdot j} / n_{\cdot\cdot}$. That is, an expected cell frequency is equal to the respective row total times the respective column total, with the product divided by the overall total.

8.1.2.2 Expected Cell Frequency Rule for 2×2 Tables

With a 2×2 table, the chi-square statistic is appropriate to use only if all four expected cell frequencies are 5 or greater. The chi-square statistic approximately follows the chi-square probability distribution when that condition is met. If this is not the case, one should consider using Fisher's Exact Test. See Section 8.5.

8.1.2.3 Alternate Form of the Test Statistic

Sometimes the hypotheses $H_0 : p_1 = p_2$ versus $H_1 : p_1 \neq p_2$ are tested with the following statistic:

$$z = \frac{(\hat{p}_1 - \hat{p}_2)}{\sqrt{\hat{p}(1 - \hat{p})}\sqrt{\dfrac{1}{n_{1\cdot}} + \dfrac{1}{n_{2\cdot}}}} \quad \text{where } \hat{p}_1 = \frac{n_{11}}{n_{1\cdot}} \text{ and } \hat{p}_2 = \frac{n_{21}}{n_{2\cdot}}$$

It is analogous to the pooled t test for $H_0 : \mu_1 = \mu_2$ versus $H_1 : \mu_1 \neq \mu_2$ discussed in Chapter 5, "Inferences from Two Samples."

$$t \text{ Value} = \frac{(\bar{x}_1 - \bar{x}_2)}{s_{\text{pooled}}\sqrt{\dfrac{1}{n_1} + \dfrac{1}{n_2}}}$$

The dot notation is not used in Chapter 5: $n_1 = n_{1\cdot}$ and $n_2 = n_{2\cdot}$.
The z statistic and the chi-square statistic are equivalent in that

$$\text{chi-square} = \sum_{i=1}^{2}\sum_{j=1}^{2}\frac{\left(n_{ij} - E_{ij}\right)^2}{E_{ij}} = (z)^2.$$

This is shown algebraically here:

$$\text{chi-square} = \sum_{i=1}^{2}\sum_{j=1}^{2}\frac{\left(n_{ij} - E_{ij}\right)^2}{E_{ij}}$$

$$= \frac{\left(n_{11} - \hat{p}n_{1\cdot}\right)^2}{\hat{p}n_{1\cdot}} + \frac{\left(n_{12} - (1-\hat{p})n_{1\cdot}\right)^2}{(1-\hat{p})n_{1\cdot}} + \frac{\left(n_{21} - \hat{p}n_{2\cdot}\right)^2}{\hat{p}n_{2\cdot}} + \frac{\left(n_{22} - (1-\hat{p})n_{2\cdot}\right)^2}{(1-\hat{p})n_{2\cdot}}$$

$$= \frac{\left(n_{11} - \hat{p}n_{1\cdot}\right)^2}{\hat{p}n_{1\cdot}} + \frac{\left((n_{1\cdot} - n_{11}) - (1-\hat{p})n_{1\cdot}\right)^2}{(1-\hat{p})n_{1\cdot}} + \frac{\left(n_{21} - \hat{p}n_{2\cdot}\right)^2}{\hat{p}n_{2\cdot}} + \frac{\left((n_{2\cdot} - n_{21}) - (1-\hat{p})n_{2\cdot}\right)^2}{(1-\hat{p})n_{2\cdot}}$$

$$= \frac{\left(n_{11} - \hat{p}n_{1\cdot}\right)^2}{\hat{p}n_{1\cdot}} + \frac{\left(n_{11} - \hat{p}n_{1\cdot}\right)^2}{(1-\hat{p})n_{1\cdot}} + \frac{\left(n_{21} - \hat{p}n_{2\cdot}\right)^2}{\hat{p}n_{2\cdot}} + \frac{\left(n_{21} - \hat{p}n_{2\cdot}\right)^2}{(1-\hat{p})n_{2\cdot}}$$

$$= \frac{\left(n_{11} - \hat{p}n_{1\cdot}\right)^2}{n_{1\cdot}}\left(\frac{1}{\hat{p}} + \frac{1}{(1-\hat{p})}\right) + \frac{\left(n_{21} - \hat{p}n_{2\cdot}\right)^2}{n_{2\cdot}}\left(\frac{1}{\hat{p}} + \frac{1}{(1-\hat{p})}\right)$$

$$= \left(\frac{\left(n_{11} - \hat{p}n_{1\cdot}\right)^2}{n_{1\cdot}} + \frac{\left(n_{21} - \hat{p}n_{2\cdot}\right)^2}{n_{2\cdot}}\right)\frac{1}{\hat{p}(1-\hat{p})} = \frac{n_{2\cdot}\left(n_{11} - \hat{p}n_{1\cdot}\right)^2 + n_{1\cdot}\left(n_{21} - \hat{p}n_{2\cdot}\right)^2}{n_{1\cdot}n_{2\cdot}\hat{p}(1-\hat{p})}$$

$$= \frac{n_{2\cdot}n_{1\cdot}^2\left(\dfrac{n_{11}}{n_{1\cdot}} - \hat{p}\right)^2 + n_{1\cdot}n_{2\cdot}^2\left(\dfrac{n_{21}}{n_{2\cdot}} - \hat{p}\right)^2}{n_{1\cdot}n_{2\cdot}\hat{p}(1-\hat{p})} = \frac{n_{1\cdot}\left(\hat{p}_1 - \hat{p}\right)^2 + n_{2\cdot}\left(\hat{p}_2 - \hat{p}\right)^2}{\hat{p}(1-\hat{p})}$$

$$= \frac{n_{1\cdot}\left(\hat{p}_1 - \dfrac{n_{1\cdot}\hat{p}_1 + n_{2\cdot}\hat{p}_2}{n_{\cdot\cdot}}\right)^2 + n_{2\cdot}\left(\hat{p}_2 - \dfrac{n_{1\cdot}\hat{p}_1 + n_{2\cdot}\hat{p}_2}{n_{\cdot\cdot}}\right)^2}{\hat{p}(1-\hat{p})}$$

$$= \frac{n_{1\cdot}\left(\dfrac{n_{\cdot\cdot}\hat{p}_1 - n_{1\cdot}\hat{p}_1 - n_{2\cdot}\hat{p}_2}{n_{\cdot\cdot}}\right)^2 + n_{2\cdot}\left(\dfrac{n_{\cdot\cdot}\hat{p}_2 - n_{1\cdot}\hat{p}_1 - n_{2\cdot}\hat{p}_2}{n_{\cdot\cdot}}\right)^2}{\hat{p}(1-\hat{p})}$$

$$= \frac{n_{1\cdot}\left(\dfrac{n_{2\cdot}\hat{p}_1 - n_{2\cdot}\hat{p}_2}{n_{\cdot\cdot}}\right)^2 + n_{2\cdot}\left(\dfrac{n_{1\cdot}\hat{p}_1 - n_{1\cdot}\hat{p}_2}{n_{\cdot\cdot}}\right)^2}{\hat{p}(1-\hat{p})} = \frac{\left(\hat{p}_1 - \hat{p}_2\right)^2\left(\dfrac{n_{1\cdot}n_{2\cdot}^2 + n_{2\cdot}n_{1\cdot}^2}{n_{\cdot\cdot}^2}\right)}{\hat{p}(1-\hat{p})}$$

$$= \frac{\left(\hat{p}_1 - \hat{p}_2\right)^2 \left(\dfrac{n_{1\cdot}n_{2\cdot}}{n_{\cdot\cdot}}\right)\left(\dfrac{n_{2\cdot} + n_{1\cdot}}{n_{\cdot\cdot}}\right)}{\hat{p}\left(1 - \hat{p}\right)} = \frac{\left(\hat{p}_1 - \hat{p}_2\right)^2}{\hat{p}\left(1 - \hat{p}\right)\left(\dfrac{n_{\cdot\cdot}}{n_{1\cdot}n_{2\cdot}}\right)} = \frac{\left(\hat{p}_1 - \hat{p}_2\right)^2}{\hat{p}\left(1 - \hat{p}\right)\left(\dfrac{1}{n_{1\cdot}} + \dfrac{1}{n_{2\cdot}}\right)} = \left(z\right)^2$$

8.1.2.4   *p*-Value

The *p-value* is a measure of the likelihood that the samples comes from populations where H_0 is true. Smaller values indicate less likelihood. That is, the more the data agrees with H_1 (the more the observed cell frequencies n_{ij} differ from the expected cell frequencies E_{ij}) the smaller the *p*-value.

In terms of a test on two binomial proportions, the *p*-value is the probability that random samples from two independent populations with equal proportions would produce a chi-square statistic at or beyond the current value. If the *p*-value is small, it is unlikely that the current samples come from two populations with equal proportions.

The technical definition of the *p*-value is in Table 8.3. The random variable Q represents a future value of the test statistic and follows the chi-square distribution with 1 degree of freedom.

SAS code expressions are included in Table 8.3 to aid in the discussion. The *p*-value is computed using an expression in the "Detailed Solutions" section of "Example 8.1: Inference on Two Binomial Proportions." In the expression, chi-square represents a number.

Table 8.3 *p*-Value for Test of Homogeneity

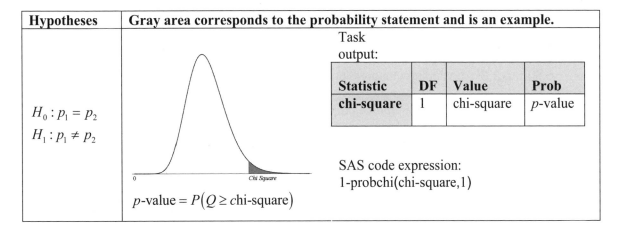

Hypotheses	Gray area corresponds to the probability statement and is an example.
$H_0 : p_1 = p_2$ $H_1 : p_1 \neq p_2$	Task output: 	Statistic	DF	Value	Prob	 	chi-square	1	chi-square	*p*-value	 SAS code expression: 1-probchi(chi-square,1) *p*-value $= P\left(Q \geq chi\text{-square}\right)$

8.1.2.5   Decision and Conclusions

The formal decision and concluding sentence do not change from the one-sample tests discussed in Chapter 4, "Inferences from One Sample." The concluding observation depends on the particular statistics involved in the test.

If the p-value is small, the data agrees with H_1. If the p-value is less than the significance level, the risk of making a Type I error is acceptable. Therefore, the p-value decision rule is the following:

If the p-value $< \alpha$, reject H_0. Otherwise, do not reject H_0.

Since a hypothesis test begins with the assumption that H_0 is true, concluding a hypothesis test requires one of the following formal statements:

- Reject H_0.
- Do not reject H_0.

When the claim is equivalent to the null hypothesis, the concluding sentence uses the word *reject*. The concluding sentence becomes an expanded version of the formal decision.

When the claim is equivalent to the alternative hypothesis, the concluding sentence uses the word *support*. If the data supports the rejection of H_0, the data supports H_1. If the data does not support rejection of H_0, the data cannot support H_1.

Table 8.4 Concluding Sentences

Formal Statistical Decision	Claim stated as H_0	Claim stated as H_1
Reject H_0.	There is sufficient evidence to reject the claim that ... (claim in words).	There is sufficient evidence to support the claim that ... (claim in words).
Do not reject H_0.	There is not sufficient evidence to reject the claim that ... (claim in words).	There is not sufficient evidence to support the claim that ... (claim in words).

Table 8.5 Concluding Observations

Reject H_0.	The sample proportions are significantly different.
Do not reject H_0.	The sample proportions are not significantly different.

8.1.3 Estimation of the Difference in Population Proportions

- The point estimates of the population proportions or the population risks p_1 and p_2 are the sample proportions $\hat{p}_1 = n_{11}/n_{1\cdot}$ and $\hat{p}_2 = n_{21}/n_{2\cdot}$.

- The point estimate of the difference in the population proportions or the risk difference $p_1 - p_2$ is the difference in the sample means $\hat{p}_1 - \hat{p}_2$.

The following is an extension of the asymptotic confidence interval on a population proportion p discussed in Section 4.5, "Inference on a Population Median."

A $100(1-\alpha)\%$ asymptotic confidence interval on $p_1 - p_2$ is:

$$\left(\hat{p}_1 - \hat{p}_2 - z_{\alpha/2}\sqrt{\frac{\hat{p}_1(1-\hat{p}_1)}{n_{1.}} + \frac{\hat{p}_2(1-\hat{p}_2)}{n_{2.}}}, \hat{p}_1 - \hat{p}_2 + z_{\alpha/2}\sqrt{\frac{\hat{p}_1(1-\hat{p}_1)}{n_{1.}} + \frac{\hat{p}_2(1-\hat{p}_2)}{n_{2.}}} \right)$$

The SAS code expression for $z_{\alpha/2}$ (the critical value for the standard normal distribution) is probit($1-\alpha/2$), where $1-\alpha/2$ represents a number.

8.1.4 Relative Risk

The relative risk is the ratio of the population proportions or risks p_1 and p_2:

$$RR = \frac{p_1}{p_2}$$

The relative risk compares the occurrence of a given characteristic in two populations. It is often applied in *prospective* or *cohort* studies involving a risk factor or a potential treatment. Such studies select groups of individuals (cohorts) before the occurrence of a disease.

8.1.4.1 Prospective Study of a Risk Factor

Studies involving a suspected risk factor for a disease have two populations of disease-free individuals. The members of one population have been exposed to the risk factor, and the members of the other population have not. The characteristic being studied is the occurrence of the disease. In terms of Table 8.1, Populations 1 and 2 are the exposed and the unexposed individuals. Characteristic A is the occurrence of the disease.

- p_1 is the proportion of the exposed population that develops the disease. It is the risk (and probability) that an individual in the exposed population develops the disease.

- p_2 is the proportion of the unexposed population that develops the disease. It is the risk (and probability) that an individual in the unexposed population develops the disease.

The relative risk $RR = p_1/p_2$ compares the rates that the disease occurs in the two populations.

- $RR = 1$: Exposure does not change the risk of developing the disease.
- $RR > 1$: Exposure increases the risk of developing the disease.
- $RR < 1$: Exposure decreases the risk of developing the disease.

8.1.4.2 Prospective Study of a Potential Treatment

Studies involving a potential treatment for a disease have two populations of individuals with the disease. The members of one population have been treated and the members of the other population have not. The characteristic being studied is continuation of the disease. In terms of

Table 8.1, Populations 1 and 2 are the treated and the untreated individuals. Characteristic A is the continuation of the disease.

- p_1 is the proportion of a treated population that continues to have the disease. It is the probability that an individual in a treated population continues to have the disease.

- p_2 is the proportion of an untreated population that continues to have the disease. It is the probability that an individual in the untreated population continues to have the disease.

The relative risk $RR = p_1/p_2$ compares the rates at which that recovery occurs in the two populations.

- $RR = 1$: Treatment does not affect the likelihood that recovery occurs.
- $RR > 1$: Treatment increases the likelihood that the disease continues.
- $RR < 1$: Treatment decreases the likelihood that the disease continues.

8.1.4.3   Estimation

The data is organized in the following contingency table. It is an example of the table shown in Table 8.6.

Table 8.6 Contingency Table for Relative Risk Data

	Disease	No Disease	Total
Exposure/Treatment	n_{11}	n_{12}	$n_{1\cdot}$ (fixed)
No Exposure/No Treatment	n_{21}	n_{22}	$n_{2\cdot}$ (fixed)
Total	$n_{\cdot 1}$ (random)	$n_{\cdot 2}$ (random)	$n_{\cdot\cdot}$

The point estimate of the relative risk $RR = p_1/p_2$ is:

$$\widehat{RR} = \frac{\hat{p}_1}{\hat{p}_2} = \frac{n_{11}/n_{1\cdot}}{n_{21}/n_{2\cdot}}$$

A $100(1-\alpha)\%$ confidence interval on $RR = p_1/p_2$ is:

$$\left(\widehat{RR}\, e^{-z_{\alpha/2}\sqrt{v_2}}, \widehat{RR}\, e^{z_{\alpha/2}\sqrt{v_2}} \right) \text{ where } v_2 = \frac{\left(1 - \dfrac{n_{11}}{n_{1\cdot}}\right)}{n_{11}} + \frac{\left(1 - \dfrac{n_{21}}{n_{2\cdot}}\right)}{n_{21}}$$

The point estimate and confidence interval are in the Cohort (Col1 Risk) row of the Estimates of the Relative Risk table. The frequencies associated with the disease are in the first column, and the sample of exposed or treated individuals is summarized in the first row.

If the frequencies associated with the disease are in the second column, the point estimate and confidence interval are in the Cohort (Col2 Risk) row. See Section 8.1.6, "Summary of the Measures of Risk."

8.1.5 Odds Ratio

8.1.5.1   Odds

The *odds* of an event is a measure of the likelihood that the event will occur. It is ratio of the probability that the event will occur and the probability that the event will not occur.

Let A be any event. The odds of A occurring are:

$$\text{odds}(A) = \frac{P(A)}{P(\text{not A})} = \frac{P(A)}{1 - P(A)}$$

- When rolling a fair die with outcomes 1, 2, 3, 4, 5 and 6, the odds of rolling a 1 is 1/5. It is also said that the odds are 1 to 5, the odds are 5 to 1 against, and the odds are 1:5.

- The odds of rolling an even number is $(1/2)/(1/2) = 1$. Also, the odds of rolling an even number are 1 to 1 or 1:1.

The probability that a randomly selected person or object has a given characteristic is equal to the proportion of the population that has the characteristic. In terms of Table 8.1:

- The odds are $p_1/(1 - p_1)$ that a randomly selected member in Population 1 has characteristic A.

- The odds are $p_2/(1 - p_2)$ that a randomly selected member in Population 2 has characteristic A.

8.1.5.2   Odds Ratio

The *odds ratio* of two events is a measure of the likelihood of one event occurring relative to a second event occurring. It is the ratio of the odds for the first event and the odds for the second event. Let A_1 and A_2 denote any two events. The odds ratio of A_1 occurring relative to A_2 is:

$$OR = \frac{\text{odds}(A_1)}{\text{odds}(A_2)} = \frac{\left(\dfrac{P(A_1)}{P(\text{not } A_1)}\right)}{\left(\dfrac{P(A_2)}{P(\text{not } A_2)}\right)} = \frac{\left(\dfrac{P(A_1)}{1 - P(A_1)}\right)}{\left(\dfrac{P(A_2)}{1 - P(A_2)}\right)}$$

The relationship is also expressed as $\text{odds}(A_1) = OR\,\text{odds}(A_2)$.

A fair die with outcomes 1, 2, 3, 4, 5 and 6 is rolled:

- The odds ratio of rolling a 1 or 2 relative to rolling just a 1 is 5/2 or 2.5:

$$\left(\frac{2}{6} \bigg/ \frac{4}{6}\right) \bigg/ \left(\frac{1}{6} \bigg/ \frac{5}{6}\right) = \left(\frac{1}{2}\right) \bigg/ \left(\frac{1}{5}\right) = \frac{5}{2}.$$

- The odds of rolling a 1 or 2 are 2.5 times greater than the odds of rolling just a 1.

In terms of Table 8.1, the odds ratio of characteristic A occurring in Population 1 relative to it occurring in Population 2 is:

$$OR = \frac{p_1/(1-p_1)}{p_2/(1-p_2)}$$

The odds ratio reflects the ratio p_1/p_2, the difference $p_1 - p_2$, and the absolute size of p_1 (through $1 - p_1$). The odds ratio can be written as $OR = \left(p_1/p_2\right)\left(1 + \left(p_1 - p_2\right)/\left(1 - p_1\right)\right)$. Table 8.7 shows different OR values for constant values of RR.

Table 8.7 Comparisons of RR and OR Values

p_1	p_2	RR	OR	p_1	p_2	RR	OR
0.02	0.01	2	2.02	0.01	0.02	0.5	0.49
0.20	0.10	2	2.25	0.10	0.20	0.5	0.44
0.50	0.25	2	3	0.25	0.50	0.5	0.33
0.90	0.45	2	11	0.45	0.90	0.5	0.09

The odds ratio is applied to prospective studies such as those described in the "Relative Risk" section.

It is also applied to *retrospective* or *case-control* studies. Such studies select a group of individuals after the occurrence of a disease and a group of individuals who are disease free. The two groups are the cases and the controls, respectively.

8.1.5.3   Retrospective Study of a Risk Factor

A retrospective study of a suspected risk factor compares a population of individuals that have a particular disease with a disease-free population. The characteristic being studied is exposure to the risk factor. In terms of Table 8.1, Populations 1 and 2 are those that have and do not have the disease. Characteristic A is exposure to the risk factor.

- p_1 is the proportion of those with the disease that have been exposed to the risk factor. For those with the disease, the *odds* of having been exposed to the risk factor are $p_1/(1-p_1)$.

- p_2 is the proportion of those free of the disease that have been exposed to the risk factor. For those free of the disease, the *odds* of having been exposed to the risk factor are $p_2/(1-p_2)$.

The odds ratio of a person with the disease having been exposed to the risk factor relative to a person free of the disease having been exposed to the risk factor is

$$OR = \left(p_1/(1-p_1)\right)/\left(p_2/(1-p_2)\right).$$

- $OR = 1$: Those with the disease have the same odds of having been exposed to the risk factor as those free of the disease.

- $OR > 1$:
  - Those with the disease have greater odds of having been exposed to the risk factor than those free of the disease.
  - The odds that those with the disease have been exposed to the risk factor are *OR* times greater than the odds that those free of disease have been exposed to the risk factor.

- $OR < 1$:
  - Those with the disease have smaller odds of having been exposed to the risk factor than those free of the disease.
  - The odds that those with the disease have been exposed to the risk factor are *OR* of the odds that those free of disease have been exposed to the risk factor.

8.1.5.4   Estimation

The data is organized in the following contingency table. It is an example of the table shown in Table 8.2.

Table 8.8 Contingency Table for Odds Ratio Data

	Exposure	No Exposure	Total	
Disease	n_{11}	n_{12}	$n_{1\cdot}$	(fixed)
No Disease	n_{21}	n_{22}	$n_{2\cdot}$	(fixed)
Total	$n_{\cdot 1}$	$n_{\cdot 2}$	$n_{\cdot\cdot}$	
	(random)	(random)		

The point estimate of the odds ratio $OR = \left(p_1 / (1 - p_1) \right) / \left(p_2 / (1 - p_2) \right)$ is:

$$\widehat{OR} = \frac{\hat{p}_1 / (1 - \hat{p}_1)}{\hat{p}_2 / (1 - \hat{p}_2)} = \frac{\left(\dfrac{n_{11}}{n_{1\bullet}} \right)}{\left(\dfrac{n_{12}}{n_{1\bullet}} \right)} \div \frac{\left(\dfrac{n_{21}}{n_{2\bullet}} \right)}{\left(\dfrac{n_{22}}{n_{2\bullet}} \right)} = \frac{n_{11} n_{22}}{n_{12} n_{21}}$$

A $100(1 - \alpha)\%$ confidence interval on $OR = \left(p_1 / (1 - p_1) \right) / \left(p_2 / (1 - p_2) \right)$ is:

$$\left(\widehat{OR} \, e^{-z_{\alpha/2} \sqrt{v_1}}, \widehat{OR} \, e^{z_{\alpha/2} \sqrt{v_1}} \right) \text{ where } v_1 = \frac{1}{n_{11}} + \frac{1}{n_{12}} + \frac{1}{n_{21}} + \frac{1}{n_{22}}$$

The point estimate and confidence interval are in the Case-Control (Odds Ratio) row of the Estimates of the Relative Risk table. See the next section.

8.1.6 Summary of the Measures of Risk

Estimates of the Relative Risk (Row1/Row2)		
Type of Study	**Value**	**$100(1\text{-}\alpha)\%$ Confidence Limits**
Case-Control (Odds Ratio)	$\widehat{OR} = \dfrac{n_{11} n_{22}}{n_{12} n_{21}}$	$\widehat{OR} \, e^{-z_{\alpha/2} \sqrt{v_1}}$ $\qquad$ $\widehat{OR} \, e^{z_{\alpha/2} \sqrt{v_1}}$
Cohort (Col1 Risk)	$\widehat{RR} = \dfrac{n_{11}/n_{1\bullet}}{n_{21}/n_{2\bullet}}$	$\widehat{RR} \, e^{-z_{\alpha/2} \sqrt{v_2}}$ $\qquad$ $\widehat{RR} \, e^{z_{\alpha/2} \sqrt{v_2}}$
Cohort (Col2 Risk)	$\widehat{RR} = \dfrac{n_{12}/n_{1\bullet}}{n_{22}/n_{2\bullet}}$	$\widehat{RR} \, e^{-z_{\alpha/2} \sqrt{v_3}}$ $\qquad$ $\widehat{RR} \, e^{z_{\alpha/2} \sqrt{v_3}}$

$$v_1 = \frac{1}{n_{11}} + \frac{1}{n_{12}} + \frac{1}{n_{21}} + \frac{1}{n_{22}}, \; v_2 = \frac{\left(1 - \dfrac{n_{11}}{n_{1\bullet}} \right)}{n_{11}} + \frac{\left(1 - \dfrac{n_{21}}{n_{2\bullet}} \right)}{n_{21}}, \; v_3 = \frac{\left(1 - \dfrac{n_{12}}{n_{1\bullet}} \right)}{n_{12}} + \frac{\left(1 - \dfrac{n_{22}}{n_{2\bullet}} \right)}{n_{22}}$$

8.1.7 Example 8.1: Inference on Two Binomial Proportions

8.1.7.1 Asthma in Infants, a Prospective Study

A study investigates how well an intervention program reduces the level of asthma in high-risk infants. Twenty-five infants are included in the intervention program. The control group consists of 24 infants who do not receive the intervention. After a period of time, it is determined whether the infants show signs of probable development of asthma. The results of the study are below.

Group	Signs		Total
	Yes	No	
Program	3	22	25
Control	10	14	24
Total	13	36	49

The data is presented by a stacked bar chart below. See "Instructions for a Stacked Frequency Bar Chart."

Figure 8.1 Example 8.1 Data in Stacked Bar Chart

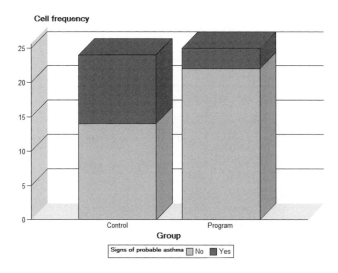

This is a prospective study of a potential treatment for asthma in infants.

- p_1 is the proportion of all infants who receive the intervention and who show signs of probable asthma. Equivalently, it is the risk of showing signs of probable asthma among infants who receive the intervention.

- p_2 is the proportion of all infants who do not receive the intervention and who show signs of probable asthma. Equivalently, it is the risk of showing signs of probable asthma among infants who do not receive the intervention.

The hypotheses being tested here are:

$$H_0 : p_1 = p_2$$
$$H_1 : p_1 \neq p_2$$

Example 8.1.1
Test the claim that the proportion of infants with signs of probable asthma is the same among those who receive the intervention and those who do not. Let $\alpha = 0.05$.

Example 8.1.2
Estimate $p_1 - p_2$ with a 95% confidence interval.

Example 8.1.3
Estimate the relative risk with a 95% confidence interval.

Example 8.1.4
Estimate the odds ratio with a 95% confidence interval.

8.1.7.2 Data
The data can be entered in table form or list form. Data sets Ex08_01_table and Ex08_01_list are shown below:

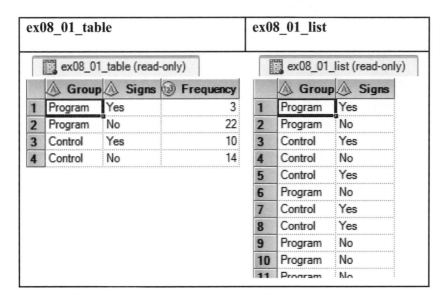

The Group variable has the sample names and the Sign variable has the treatment outcomes.

- In Ex08_01_table, all four possible Group-Sign pairs are listed. The Frequency variable contains the respective cell frequencies.

- In Ex08_01_list, there is a Group-Sign pair for each of the 49 infants in the study.

The data set order (Program occurring before Control in Group and Yes occurring before No in Signs) is consistent with the table format (frequencies for the treated individuals in the first row and frequencies for the disease in the first column). Data set order is selected in the Table Analysis task. See "Table Statistics > Computation Options" in the "Instructions for Table Analysis" section.

8.1.7.3 Detailed Solutions

Example 8.1.1

Plan the task.

$H_0 : p_1 = p_2$

$H_1 : p_1 \neq p_2$

$\alpha = 0.05$.

Compute the statistics.

$$\text{chi-square} = \sum_{i=1}^{2} \sum_{j=1}^{2} \frac{\left(n_{ij} - E_{ij}\right)^2}{E_{ij}}$$

$$= \frac{\left(3 - \frac{25 \cdot 13}{49}\right)^2}{\left(\frac{25 \cdot 13}{49}\right)} + \frac{\left(22 - \frac{25 \cdot 36}{49}\right)^2}{\left(\frac{25 \cdot 36}{49}\right)} + \frac{\left(10 - \frac{24 \cdot 13}{49}\right)^2}{\left(\frac{24 \cdot 13}{49}\right)} + \frac{\left(14 - \frac{24 \cdot 36}{49}\right)^2}{\left(\frac{24 \cdot 36}{49}\right)}$$

$$= \frac{\left(3 - 6.6327\right)^2}{6.6327} + \frac{\left(22 - 18.3673\right)^2}{18.3673} + \frac{\left(10 - 6.3673\right)^2}{6.3673} + \frac{\left(14 - 17.6327\right)^2}{17.6327}$$

$$= 1.9896 + 0.7185 + 2.0725 + 0.7484 = 5.5290$$

$p\text{-value} = P(Q \geq 5.5290) = 1 - \text{probchi}(5.5290, 1) = 0.0187$

Apply results.

Since the p-value < 0.05, there is sufficient evidence to reject the claim that the proportion of infants with signs of probable asthma is the same for those who receive the intervention and for those who do not. The sample proportions are significantly different.

Example 8.1.2

$\hat{p}_1 = \dfrac{3}{25} = 0.12$ and $\hat{p}_2 = \dfrac{10}{24} = 0.417$

$z_{0.025} = \text{probit}(.975) = 1.9600$

A 95% confidence interval on $p_1 - p_2$ is:

$$\left(\hat{p}_1 - \hat{p}_2 - z_{\alpha/2}\sqrt{\frac{\hat{p}_1(1-\hat{p}_1)}{n_{1\cdot}} + \frac{\hat{p}_2(1-\hat{p}_2)}{n_{2\cdot}}}, \hat{p}_1 - \hat{p}_2 + z_{\alpha/2}\sqrt{\frac{\hat{p}_1(1-\hat{p}_1)}{n_{1\cdot}} + \frac{\hat{p}_2(1-\hat{p}_2)}{n_{2\cdot}}} \right)$$

$$\left(0.12 - 0.417 - 1.9600\sqrt{\frac{0.12(0.88)}{25} + \frac{0.417(0.583)}{24}}, 0.12 - 0.417 + 1.9600\sqrt{\frac{0.12(0.88)}{25} + \frac{0.417(0.583)}{24}} \right)$$

$$(-0.297 - 0.235, -0.297 + 0.235)$$

$$(-0.532, -0.062)$$

Example 8.1.3

$$\widehat{RR} = \hat{p}_1/\hat{p}_2 = \left(\frac{3}{25}\right)\Big/\left(\frac{10}{24}\right) = 0.288$$

$$\left(\widehat{RR}\, e^{-1.96\sqrt{v_2}}, \widehat{RR}\, e^{1.96\sqrt{v_2}} \right) \text{ with } v_2 = \frac{\left(1 - \dfrac{n_{11}}{n_{1\cdot}}\right)}{n_{11}} + \frac{\left(1 - \dfrac{n_{21}}{n_{2\cdot}}\right)}{n_{21}} = \frac{\left(1 - \dfrac{3}{25}\right)}{3} + \frac{\left(1 - \dfrac{10}{24}\right)}{10} = 0.351667$$

$$\left(0.288 e^{-1.96\sqrt{0.351667}}, 0.288 e^{1.96\sqrt{0.351667}} \right)$$

$$(0.090, 0.921)$$

Example 8.1.4

$$\widehat{OR} = \frac{n_{11}n_{22}}{n_{12}n_{21}} = \frac{(3)(14)}{(22)(10)} = 0.191$$

$$\left(\widehat{OR}\, e^{-1.96\sqrt{v_1}}, \widehat{OR}\, e^{1.96\sqrt{v_1}} \right) \text{ with } v_1 = \frac{1}{n_{11}} + \frac{1}{n_{12}} + \frac{1}{n_{21}} + \frac{1}{n_{22}} = \frac{1}{3} + \frac{1}{22} + \frac{1}{10} + \frac{1}{14} = 0.550216$$

$$\left(0.191 e^{-1.96\sqrt{0.550216}}, 0.191 e^{1.96\sqrt{0.550216}} \right)$$

$$(0.0446, 0.8174)$$

8.1.8 Instructions for Table Analysis

Open the Table Analysis task in one of the following ways:

- From the menu bar, select **Describe ▶ Table Analysis**.
- On the **Task by Category** tab of the **Task List**, go to the **Describe** section and click **Table Analysis**.
- On the **Task by Name** tab of the **Task List**, double-click **Table Analysis**.

The Table Analysis task has six groups of options: Task Roles, Tables, Cell Statistics, Table Statistics, Results, and Titles. The Results options put the task results in data sets. The Titles options control the titles and the footnotes in the task output. Titles are discussed in general in Chapter 1, "Introduction to SAS Enterprise Guide."

8.1.8.1   Task Roles

Click **Task Roles** on the selection pane to open this group of options. A variable is assigned to a role by dragging its name from **Variables** to **Task Roles**. See Figure 8.2. A variable may be removed from a role by dragging it back to **Variables**. The right and left arrows and the resulting pop-up menus can also be used.

- Frequency count:
  - o This variable lists the frequencies for the cells defined by the respective rows of the Table variables. If a row is repeated, the sum of the associated frequencies is used.
  - o If no variable is assigned to the Frequency count role, a cell frequency is equal to the number of times the corresponding pair is repeated in the two classification variables creating the table.

- Table variables: These are the classification variables that create the contingency tables. Tables are created with the Tables options.

In Figure 8.2, Frequency is assigned to the Frequency Count role. Signs and Group are assigned to the Table variables role.

The Group analysis by role is discussed in Section 1.2.

Figure 8.2 Task Roles in the Table Analysis Task for Example 8.1

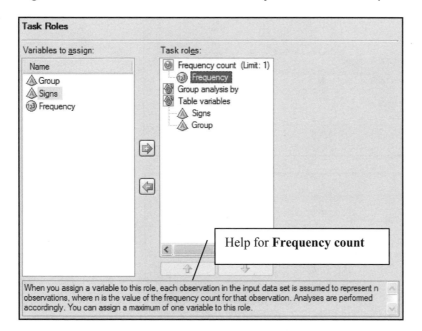

8.1.8.2   Tables

The Table analysis variables are listed in the Variables permitted in table box. In the top window in Figure 8.3, Group and Signs are in that box.

To create a table:

1. Drag two variables to the Preview area on the right.

   The variable on the left defines the rows. The variable on the top defines the columns.

   Variables can be dragged from one position to the other.

   The table is listed in the **Tables to be generated** box.

2. To create another table click **<select to begin defining a new table>**.

3. To delete a table select it from the **Tables to be generated** box and click **Delete**.

   In the bottom window in Figure 8.3, a Group by Signs table is to be created. Group defines the rows and Signs define the columns.

Figure 8.3 Tables Options in the Table Analysis Task for Example 8.1:
The top window appears before a table is defined.
The bottom appears after the Group by Signs table is defined.

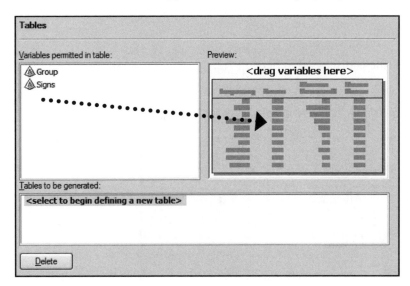

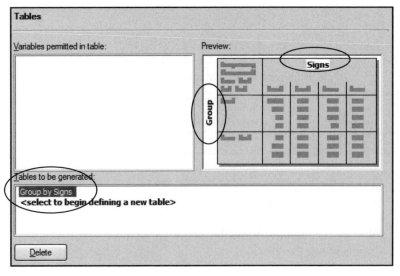

8.1.8.3 Cell Statistics

These are the statistics that can be included in the table cells.

- Cumulative column percentages

- Row percentages: $n_{ij}/n_{i.}$

- Column percentages: $n_{ij}/n_{.j}$

- Cell frequencies: n_{ij}.

- Cell percentages: $n_{ij}/n_{..}$

- Missing value frequencies: Missing values in the Table variables are treated as a category.

- Cell contribution to Pearson chi-square: $\dfrac{\left(n_{ij}-E_{ij}\right)^2}{E_{ij}}$

- Cell frequency deviation from expected: $n_{ij}-E_{ij}$

- Expected cell frequency: E_{ij}

- Percentage of total frequency: Cell percentage relative to total frequency in 3-way analysis and higher.

In Figure 8.4, the following are checked: Row percentages, Cell Frequencies, Cell contribution to Pearson chi-square, Cell frequency deviation from expected, and Expected cell frequency.

Figure 8.4 Cell Statistics in the Table Analysis Task for Example 8.1

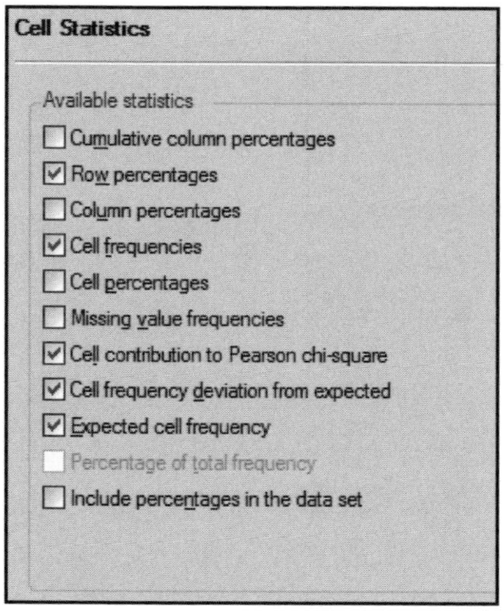

8.1.8.4 Table Statistics > Association

Tests of Association

Checking **Chi-square tests** produces a number of test statistics and *p*-values, including the Pearson chi-square test. It is checked in Figure 8.5.

Fisher's exact test is always part of the output for 2×2 tables.

Measures of Association

Relative differences for 2×2 tables results in estimates and confidence intervals on individual proportions and the difference of proportions.

Relative risk for 2×2 tables results in estimates and confidence intervals on the odds ratio and the relative risk.

Both are checked in Figure 8.5.

Figure 8.5 Options for Tests and Measures of Association in the Table Analysis Task for Example 8.1

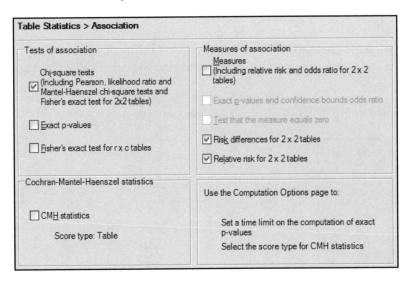

Figure 8.6 Computation Options in the Table Analysis Task for Example 8.1

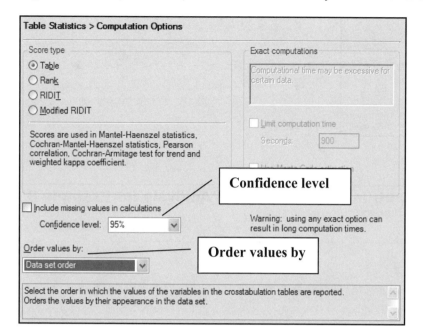

8.1.8.5 Table Statistics > Computation Options

- The Order values by options determine how the rows and columns are ordered. The drop-down menu lists four sorting criteria:

  o Data set order: Row and column values are ordered as they first appear in the data set. This is selected in Figure 8.6.

  o Formatted values: The Create Format task can provide alternate presentation values for data values.

  o Descending frequencies: Row and column values are ordered by their respective totals.

  o Unformatted values: This is the default selection. Rows and columns are in the ascending order of the values as they exist in the data set.

The Confidence level for relative risk and odds ratio confidence intervals is determined here. The default is 95%.

8.1.8.6 When Finished

When finished assigning variables to roles and selecting options, click **Run**. The task adds a Table Analysis icon and one or more output icons to the process flow diagram. See Figure 8.7.

Figure 8.7 Example 8.1 Data, Task, and Output Icons on the Process Flow Diagram

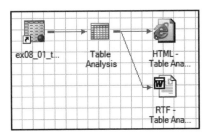

8.1.9 Task Output, Interpretation, and Analysis for Example 8.1

8.1.9.1   Task Output

Output 8.1 Table Analysis for Example 8.1

Table Analysis
Results

The FREQ Procedure

	Table of Group by Signs		
❷	**Group(Group)**	**Signs(Signs of probable asthma)**	
❸	**Frequency** **Expected** **Deviation** **Cell chi-square** **Row Pct**	**Yes**	**No**	**Total**
	Program	3 6.6327 -3.633 1.9896 12.00	22 18.367 3.6327 0.7185 88.00	25
	Control	10 6.3673 3.6327 2.0725 41.67	14 17.633 -3.633 0.7484 58.33	24
Total		13	36	49

❶ (marker at Table of Group by Signs)

Statistics for Table of Group by Signs

Statistic	DF	Value	Prob	
Chi-Square	1	5.5289	0.0187	❹
Likelihood Ratio Chi-Square	1	5.7488	0.0165	
Continuity Adj. Chi-Square	1	4.1116	0.0426	
Mantel-Haenszel Chi-Square	1	5.4161	0.0200	
Phi Coefficient		-0.3359		
Contingency Coefficient		0.3184		
Cramer's V		-0.3359		

Fisher's Exact Test	
Cell (1,1) Frequency (F)	3
Left-sided Pr <= F	0.0203
Right-sided Pr >= F	0.9969
Table Probability (P)	0.0172
Two-sided Pr <= P	0.0255

	Column 1 Risk Estimates						❺
	Risk	**ASE**	**(Asymptotic) 95% Confidence Limits**		**(Exact) 95% Confidence Limits**		
Row 1	0.1200	0.0650	0.0000	0.2474	0.0255	0.3122	❻
Row 2	0.4167	0.1006	0.2194	0.6139	0.2211	0.6336	
Total	0.2653	0.0631	0.1417	0.3889	0.1495	0.4108	
Difference	-0.2967	0.1198	-0.5315	-0.0619			❼
Difference is (Row 1 - Row 2)							

Column 2 Risk Estimates					❽
	Risk	ASE	(Asymptotic) 95% Confidence Limits		(Exact) 95% Confidence Limits	
Row 1	0.8800	0.0650	0.7526	1.0000	0.6878	0.9745
Row 2	0.5833	0.1006	0.3861	0.7806	0.3664	0.7789
Total	0.7347	0.0631	0.6111	0.8583	0.5892	0.8505
Difference	0.2967	0.1198	0.0619	0.5315		

Difference is (Row 1 - Row 2)

Estimates of the Relative Risk (Row1/Row2)				
Type of Study	Value	95% Confidence Limits		
Case-Control (Odds Ratio)	0.1909	0.0446	0.8170	❾
Cohort (Col1 Risk)	0.2880	0.0901	0.9208	❿
Cohort (Col2 Risk)	1.5086	1.0443	2.1792	⓫

Sample Size = 49

8.1.9.2 Interpretation

❶ Table is defined by the Group and Signs variables.

❷ Group is the row variable. Group in parentheses is the variable label.

Signs is the column variable. Signs of probable asthma in parentheses is the variable label.

❸ Contents of table cells:

Frequency is the cell frequency or cell count n_{ij}.

Expected is the expected frequency E_{ij}.

Deviation is $n_{ij} - E_{ij}$.

Cell chi-square is $\dfrac{\left(n_{ij} - E_{ij}\right)^2}{E_{ij}}$.

Row Pct is row percent: $\dfrac{p_{ij}}{p_{\cdot j}}100\%$.

❹ Chi-square test statistic

❺ Estimates of proportions or risks associated with the first column of the table

❻ One-sample estimates. See Section 4.4.2, "Estimation of the Proportion." Total combines the two samples: $\hat{p} = n_{\cdot 1}/n_{\cdot \cdot}$.

❼ Estimation for $p_1 - p_2$. ASE is the asymptotic standard error, $\sqrt{\dfrac{\hat{p}_1(1-\hat{p}_1)}{n_{1\cdot}} + \dfrac{\hat{p}_2(1-\hat{p}_2)}{n_{2\cdot}}}$.

❽ Estimates of proportions or risks associated with the second column of the table

❾ Estimation for the odds ratio

❿ Estimation for the relative risk for the characteristic associated with the first column in the table. $\widehat{RR} = \left(n_{11}/n_{1\cdot}\right)/\left(n_{21}/n_{2\cdot}\right)$

⓫ Estimation for the relative risk for the characteristic associated with the second column in the table. $\widehat{RR} = \left(n_{12}/n_{1\cdot}\right)/\left(n_{22}/n_{2\cdot}\right)$

8.1.9.3 Analysis

Example 8.1.1
$H_0 : p_1 = p_2$
$H_1 : p_1 \neq p_2$

p-value = 0.0187. See ❹ in Output 8.1.

Since the p-value < 0.05, there is sufficient evidence to reject the claim that the proportion of infants with signs of probable asthma is the same for those who receive the intervention as for those who do not. The sample proportions are significantly different.

Example 8.1.2
The estimate of $p_1 - p_2$ is $\hat{p}_1 - \hat{p}_2 = -0.2967$. A 95% confidence interval is (-0.5315, -0.0619). See ❼ in Output 8.1. With 95% confidence, the proportion of signs of probable asthma among infants receiving the intervention is between 0.0619 and 0.5315 less than the proportion among infants not receiving the intervention.

Example 8.1.3
The estimated relative risk is $\widehat{RR} = 0.2880$. A 95% confidence interval is (0.0901, 0.9208). See ❿ in Output 8.1. With 95% confidence, the risk of showing signs of probable asthma among infants receiving the intervention is between 0.0901 and 0.9208 of the risk.

Example 8.1.4

The estimated odds ratio is $\widehat{OR} = 0.1909$. A 95% confidence interval is (0.0446, 0.8170). See ❾ in Output 8.1. With 95% confidence, the odds of showing signs of probable asthma among infants receiving the intervention is between 0.0446 and 0.8170 of the odds among infants not receiving the intervention.

8.1.10 Example 8.2: Inference on Two Binomial Proportions

8.1.10.1 Cancer and Cell Phones, a Retrospective Study

A retrospective study examines the relationship between brain cancer and the use of cellular telephones (based on "Handheld Cellular Telephone Use and Risk of Brain Cancer," by Muscat et al., *Journal of the American Medical Association*, Vol. 284, No. 23, pp. 3001-3007). Forty-seven brain cancer patients and 43 patients with benign conditions take part in the study. Each is asked if they use a handheld cellular telephone on a regular basis. The results are below.

		Regular Use		
		Yes	No	Total
Brain	Yes	7	40	47
Cancer	No	8	35	43
	Total	15	75	90

The data set is in the data set Ex08_02.

	Brain_Cancer	Regular_Use	Count
1	Yes	Yes	7
2	Yes	No	40
3	No	Yes	8
4	No	No	35

ex08_02 (read-only)

Figure 8.8 Example 8.2 Data in Stacked Bar Chart

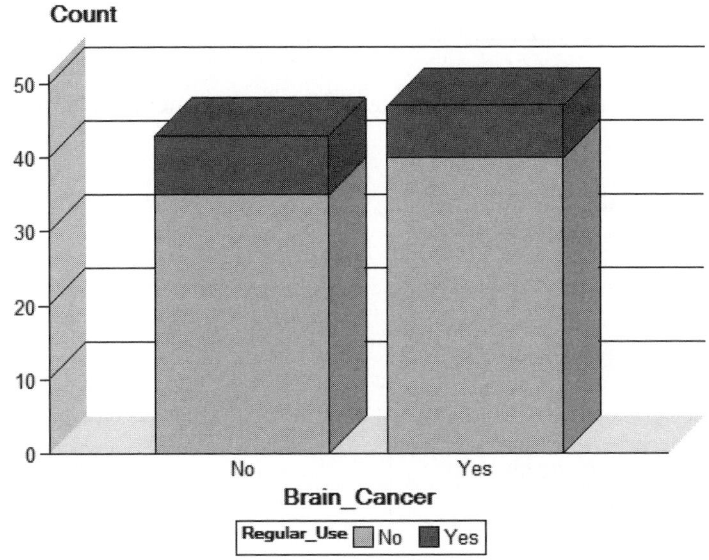

This is a retrospective study of a possible risk factor for brain cancer.

- p_1 is the proportion of regular cell phone users among those with brain cancer.

- p_2 is the proportion of regular cell phone users among those free of brain cancer.

   The hypotheses being tested here are:

   $$H_0 : p_1 = p_2$$
   $$H_1 : p_1 \neq p_2$$

Example 8.2.1
Test the claim that the proportion of regular cell phone users is the same among those with brain cancer and those free of brain cancer. Let $\alpha = 0.05$.

Example 8.2.2
Estimate $p_1 - p_2$ with a 95% confidence interval.

Example 8.2.3
Estimate the odds ratio with a 95% confidence interval.

8.1.11 Task Output, Interpretation, and Analysis for Example 8.2

8.1.11.1 Task Output

The Fisher's Exact Test and the Column 2 Risk Estimates tables are not included below.

Output 8.2 Table Analysis for Example 8.2

Table Analysis
Results

The FREQ Procedure

❶	Table of Brain_Cancer by Regular_Use		
❷	**Brain_Cancer**	**Regular_Use**	
Frequency **Expected** **Deviation** **Cell chi-square** **Row Pct**	**Yes**	**No**	**Total**
Yes	7 7.8333 -0.833 0.0887 14.89	40 39.167 0.8333 0.0177 85.11	47
No	8 7.1667 0.8333 0.0969 18.60	35 35.833 -0.833 0.0194 81.40	43
Total	15	75	90

Statistics for Table of Brain_Cancer by Regular_Use

Statistic	DF	Value	Prob	
Chi-Square	1	0.2227	0.6370	❸
Likelihood Ratio Chi-Square	1	0.2225	0.6372	
Continuity Adj. Chi-Square	1	0.0356	0.8503	
Mantel-Haenszel Chi-Square	1	0.2202	0.6389	
Phi Coefficient		-0.0497		

Statistic	DF	Value	Prob
Contingency Coefficient		0.0497	
Cramer's V		-0.0497	

Column 1 Risk Estimates							
	Risk	**ASE**	**(Asymptotic) 95% Confidence Limits**		**(Exact) 95% Confidence Limits**		❹
Row 1	0.1489	0.0519	0.0472	0.2507	0.0620	0.2831	
Row 2	0.1860	0.0593	0.0697	0.3024	0.0839	0.3340	❺
Total	0.1667	0.0393	0.0897	0.2437	0.0964	0.2600	
Difference	-0.0371	0.0789	-0.1917	0.1174			❻
Difference is (Row 1 - Row 2)							

Estimates of the Relative Risk (Row1/Row2)				
Type of Study	**Value**	**95% Confidence Limits**		
Case-Control (Odds Ratio)	0.7656	0.2520	2.3260	❼
Cohort (Col1 Risk)	0.8005	0.3170	2.0213	
Cohort (Col2 Risk)	1.0456	0.8678	1.2598	

Sample Size = 90

8.1.11.2 Interpretation
❶ Table is defined by the Brain_Cancer and Regular_Use variables.

❷ Brain_Cancer is the row variable. Regular_Use is the column variable.

❸ Chi-square test statistic

❹ Estimates of proportions or risks associated with the first column of the table

❺ One-sample estimates

❻ Estimation for $p_1 - p_2$

❼ Estimation for the odds ratio

8.1.11.3 Analysis

Example 8.2.1

$H_0 : p_1 = p_2$

$H_1 : p_1 \neq p_2$

p-value = 0.6370. See ❸ in Output 8.2.

Since the p-value > 0.05, there is not sufficient evidence to reject the claim that the proportion of regular cell phone users is the same among those with brain cancer and those free of brain cancer. The sample proportions are not significantly different.

Example 8.2.2

The estimate of $p_1 - p_2$ is $\hat{p}_1 - \hat{p}_2 = -0.0371$. A 95% confidence interval is (-0.1917, 0.1174). See ❻ in Output 8.2. With 95% confidence, the proportion of regular cell phone users among those with brain cancer is between 0.1917 less and 0.1174 greater than the proportion among those free of brain cancer.

Example 8.2.3

The estimated odds ratio is not significantly different from 1. A 95% confidence interval on the odds ratio is (0.2520, 2.3260). See ❼ in Output 8.2.

8.1.12   Instructions for a Stacked Frequency Bar Chart

Open the Bar Chart task in one of the following ways:

- From the menu bar, select **Graph ▶ Bar Chart**.
- On the **Task by Category** tab of the **Task List**, go to the Graph section and click **Bar Chart**.
- On the **Task by Name** tab of the **Task List**, double-click **Bar Chart**.

Use the selection pane on the left to navigate through selecting a bar chart, assigning columns to roles, and selecting options. Titles options are discussed in general in Chapter 1, "Introduction to SAS Enterprise Guide." They control the titles and the footnotes in the task output.

8.1.12.1 Bar Chart

The Stacked Vertical Bar is selected in Figure 8.9.

Figure 8.9 Bar Chart Options in the Bar Chart Task for Example 8.1

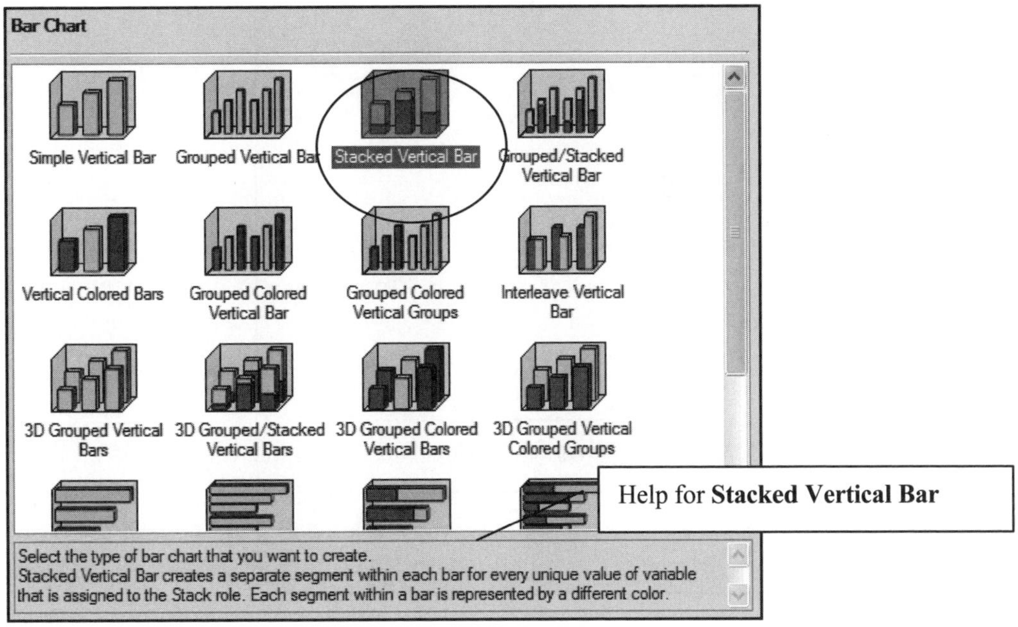

8.1.12.2 Task Roles

Click **Task Roles** on the selection pane to open this group of options. A variable is assigned to a role by dragging its name from **Columns to assign** to a role in **Task roles**. See Figure 8.10. A variable may be removed from a role by dragging it back to **Columns to assign**. The right and left arrows and the resulting pop-up menus can also be used.

- Column to chart: There is a bar for each unique value in the variable that is assigned here.

- Stack: The bars are partitioned by the unique values in the variable that is assigned here. The sizes of the partitions indicate the frequencies associated with the groups identified by the Stack variable.

- Sum of: If a variable is assigned to the Frequency count role in the Table Analysis task, it is assigned here.

The Group analysis by role is discussed in "Common Task Roles" in Chapter 1, "Introduction to SAS Enterprise Guide."

In Figure 8.10, Group is assigned to the Column to chart role; Signs to the Stack role; and Frequencies to the Sum of role.

Figure 8.10 Task Roles in the Bar Chart Task for Example 8.1

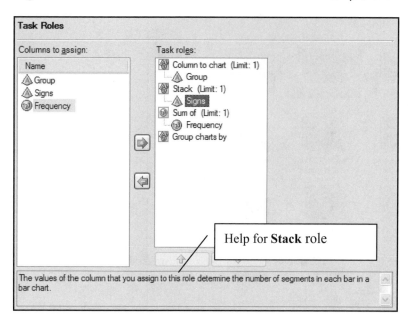

8.1.12.3 Appearance > Bars

If the Column to chart variable is numeric, it is generally necessary to change the Bar options so that there is one bar for each unique data value.

- Check **Specify number of bars**.
- Select **One bar for each unique data value**.

8.1.12.4 Appearance > Advanced

No changes are needed here. Note that if there is a Sum of variable, the Statistic used to calculate bar is Sum. If there is no Sum of variable, the statistic is Frequency.

8.1.12.5 When Finished

When finished assigning variables to roles and selecting options, click **Run**. The task adds a Bar Chart icon and one or more output icons to the process flow diagram. The stack bar chart for Ex08_01_table is in Section 8.1.7, "Example 8.1: Inference on Two Binomial Proportions."

8.2 Test of Homogeneity

The *test of homogeneity* is a test of the equality of respective proportions from independent populations. It is a straightforward extension of the test of equality of two binomial proportions presented in this section. With the test of homogeneity, there can be two or more populations and each population can be divided into two or more categories.

- Population 1, Population 2, ... , and Population r ($r \geq 2$) represent the populations being considered.

- $A_1, A_2, ... , A_c$ ($c \geq 2$) represent the categories dividing every population. These categories are *exhaustive* and *mutually exclusive*. That is, every member of a population is in a category and every member of a population is in only one category.

- p_{ij} ($i = 1, 2, ..., r$ and $j = 1, 2, ... c$) represents the proportion of Population i that is in category A_j.

This is organized in the following table.

Table 8.9 Populations Model for the Test of Homogeneity

	A_1	A_2	...	A_c	Total
Population 1	p_{11}	p_{12}	...	p_{1c}	1
Population 2	p_{21}	p_{22}	...	p_{2c}	1
$\vdots$	$\vdots$	$\vdots$	$\vdots$	$\vdots$	$\vdots$
Population r	p_{r1}	p_{r2}	...	p_{rc}	1

The null hypothesis for the test of homogeneity states that the proportions associated with each category are the same in all populations:

H_0 : The proportions associated with each category are the same in all populations.

H_1 : The proportions associated with each category are not the same in all populations.

The null and alternative hypotheses in terms of p_{ij} are:

$H_0 : p_{1j} = ... = p_{rj}$ for each category

$H_1 : p_{ij} \neq p_{kj}$ for at least one pair of populations in at least one category

8.2.1 Data

The data is organized in the following $r \times c$ contingency table. The dot notation represents summation over a subscript.

Table 8.10 Summarized Data for Inference on Two Proportions

	A_1	A_2	$\cdots$	A_c	Total
Sample 1	n_{11}	n_{12}	$\cdots$	n_{1c}	$n_{11} + \cdots + n_{1c} = n_{1\cdot}$ (fixed)
Sample 2	n_{21}	n_{22}	$\cdots$	n_{2c}	$n_{21} + \cdots + n_{2c} = n_{2\cdot}$ (fixed)
$\vdots$	$\vdots$	$\vdots$	$\vdots$	$\vdots$	$\vdots$
Sample r	n_{r1}	n_{r2}	$\cdots$	n_{rc}	$n_{r1} + \cdots + n_{rc} = n_{r\cdot}$ (fixed)
Total	$n_{11} + \cdots + n_{r1} = n_{\cdot 1}$ (random)	$n_{12} + \cdots + n_{r2} = n_{\cdot 2}$ (random)	$\cdots$	$n_{1c} + \cdots + n_{rc} = n_{\cdot c}$ (random)	$\sum_{j=1}^{c} n_{\cdot j} = \sum_{i=1}^{r} n_{i\cdot} = n_{\cdot\cdot}$

- Sample i comes from the Population i, $i = 1, \ldots, r$.

  - Sample i consists of $n_{i1}, n_{i2}, \ldots, n_{ic}$ persons or objects from categories 1, 2, $\ldots$, c, respectively.

  - There are r rows and c columns of cell frequencies. The *size* of this contingency table is $r \times c$. The row and column of totals are not counted here.

  - All cell frequencies are randomly determined values. They are the result of random selections from populations.

- The size of Sample i is $n_{i\cdot}$. Sample sizes are fixed by the investigator.

- The total number associated with A_j in all samples is $n_{\cdot j}$, $j = 1, \ldots, c$. These values are randomly determined. They are the result of random selection.

8.2.1.1   Table Format

The data tables in this section follow the format shown in Table 8.2. The samples are summarized along the rows.

However, table format is not important for the test of homogeneity. The results are the same whether the samples are associated with rows or columns.

8.2.1.2   Variables

The data enters the task as two or three variables. As two variables, there is a pair of values for each person or object in the sample. The values identify the sample and the category. As an example, the variable sample below identifies membership in Sample 1 or Sample 2. The variable category identifies category A, B, or C.

sample	category
1	A
2	C
2	B
2	A
1	C
⋮	⋮

As three variables, the data enters in summarized form. A third variable is added that contains the frequencies that the respective pairs occur in the sample. As an example, the variables sample and category below contain a unique pair for each table cell. The variable frequency has the respective cell frequencies.

sample	category	frequency
1	A	n_{11}
1	B	n_{12}
1	C	n_{13}
2	A	n_{21}
2	B	n_{22}
2	C	n_{23}

The pairs do not have to be unique. If a pair is repeated, the sum of the associated frequencies is used. Also, the values do not have to be sorted.

8.2.2 Test of Homogeneity

8.2.2.1 Test Statistic

A test statistic for the test of homogeneity is the Pearson chi-squared (χ^2) statistic. It compares the *observed* cell frequencies n_{ij} with the *expected* cell frequencies E_{ij}. The expected cell frequencies are the values that are expected when the null hypothesis is true. They are generally not integers.

$$\text{chi-square} = \sum_{i=1}^{r} \sum_{j=1}^{c} \frac{\left(n_{ij} - E_{ij}\right)^2}{E_{ij}}$$

In general, an expected cell frequency is equal to the estimate of a population proportion under H_0 times the sample size. Under H_0 for the test of homogeneity, the proportions associated with each category are equal to a common value. Let all the proportions associated with category A_j be equal to p_j: $p_{1j} = \ldots = p_{rj} = p_j$. The samples are combined to produce an estimate:

$$\hat{p}_j = \frac{n_{\cdot j}}{n_{\cdot\cdot}}$$

The expected cell frequency for category A_j in Sample i is the column j total times the row i total divided by the overall total:

$$E_{ij} = \hat{p}_j n_{i\cdot} = \frac{n_{\cdot j} n_{i\cdot}}{n_{\cdot\cdot}}$$

8.2.2.2   Expected Cell Frequency Rule

The chi-square statistic approximately follows the chi-square probability distribution. It is appropriate to use if both of the following conditions are met:

- All expected cell frequencies are 1 or more.
- At most 20% of the expected cell frequencies are less than 5.

If these are not met, one may need to consider combining categories. The exact test for larger tables often requires an excessive amount of time.

8.2.2.3   *p*-Value

The *p-value* is a measure of the likelihood that the samples come from populations where H_0 is true. Smaller values indicate less likelihood. That is, the more the data agrees with H_1 (the more the observed cell frequencies n_{ij} differ from the expected cell frequencies E_{ij}) the smaller the *p*-value.

In terms of a test of homogeneity, the *p*-value is the probability that random samples from independent populations with equal category proportions would produce a chi-square statistic at or beyond the current value. If the *p*-value is small, it is unlikely that the current samples come from populations with equal category proportions.

The technical definition of the *p*-value is in Table 8.11. The random variable Q represents a future value of the test statistic and follows the chi-square distribution with $(r-1)(c-1)$ degree of freedom.

SAS code expressions are included in Table 8.11 to aid in the discussion. The *p*-value is computed using an expression in the "Detailed Solutions" section of "Example 8.3: Test of Homogeneity." In the expression, chi-square and $(r-1)(c-1)$ represent numbers.

Table 8.11 *p*-Value for Test of Homogeneity

Hypotheses	Gray area corresponds to the probability statement and is an example.
H_0: The proportions associated with each category are the same in all populations. H_1: The proportions associated with each category are not the same in all populations.	Task output: 	Statistic	DF	Value	Prob
---	---	---	---
chi-square	$(r-1)(c-1)$	chi-square	p-value	 SAS code expression: 1-probchi(chi-square, $(r-1)(c-1)$) *p*-value = $P(Q \geq \text{chi-square})$

8.2.2.4 Decision and Conclusions

The formal decision and concluding sentence do not change from the one-sample tests discussed in Chapter 4, "Inferences from One Sample." The concluding observation depends on the particular statistics involved in the test.

If the *p*-value is small, the data agrees with H_1. If the *p*-value is less than the significance level, the risk of making a Type I error is acceptable. Therefore, the *p*-value decision rule is the following:

If the *p-value* < α, reject H_0. Otherwise, do not reject H_0.

Since a hypothesis test begins with the assumption that H_0 is true, concluding a hypothesis test requires one of the following formal statements:

- Reject H_0.

- Do not reject H_0.

When the claim is equivalent to the null hypothesis, the concluding sentence uses the word *reject*. The concluding sentence becomes an expanded version of the formal decision.

When the claim is equivalent to the alternative hypothesis, the concluding sentence uses the word *support*. If the data supports the rejection of H_0, the data supports H_1. If the data does not support rejection of H_0, the data cannot support H_1.

Table 8.12 Concluding Sentences

Formal Statistical Decision	Claim stated as H_0	Claim stated as H_1
Reject H_0.	There is sufficient evidence to reject the claim that ... (claim in words).	There is sufficient evidence to support the claim that ... (claim in words).
Do not reject H_0.	There is not sufficient evidence to reject the claim that ... (claim in words).	There is not sufficient evidence to support the claim that ... (claim in words).

Table 8.13 Concluding Observations

Reject H_0.	At least two sample proportions within at least one category are significantly different.
Do not reject H_0.	The sample proportions within each category are not significantly different.

8.2.3 Example 8.3: Test of Homogeneity

8.2.3.1 Chewing Tobacco and Dental Caries

The effects of chewing tobacco on dental health are examined using information collected in a large health survey. One of the issues being investigated is whether the likelihood of having dental caries (cavities) is associated with years of tobacco chewing. Fifty men are randomly selected from each of four years-of-use populations. The populations are defined by tobacco chewing for 1 year or less, 2 to 3 years, 4 to 5 years, and 6 years or more. The men are examined for dental caries. The results of the study are below.

	Caries		
Years	yes	no	Total
1-	12	38	50
2-3	18	32	50
4-5	25	25	50
6+	28	22	50
Total	83	117	200

The data is in the data set Ex08_03. The data is presented by a stacked bar chart below in Figure 8.11.

	Years		Caries		Frequency
1	1-		yes		12
2	1-		no		38
3	2-3		yes		18
4	2-3		no		32
5	4-5		yes		25
6	4-5		no		25
7	6+		yes		28
8	6+		no		22

ex08_03 (read-only)

Figure 8.11 Example 8.3 Data in Stacked Bar Chart

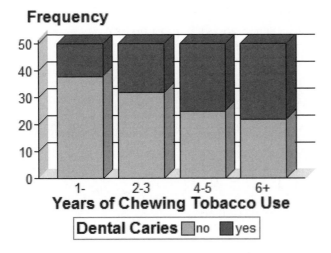

This test of homogeneity involves four populations and two categories. The categories are having and not having dental caries. The row totals are fixed by the investigators. The column totals are randomly determined. The null and alternative hypotheses in symbols and words are:

$H_0 : p_{11} = p_{21} = p_{31} = p_{41}$ and $p_{12} = p_{22} = p_{32} = p_{42}$

$H_1 :$ There is at least one inequality in one of the categories.

$H_0 :$ The proportion of men with dental caries is the same in each years-of-use population.

$H_1 :$ The proportion of men with dental caries is the not same in each years-of-use population.

Example 8.3.

Test the claim that the proportion of men with dental caries is the same in each years-of-use population. Let $\alpha = 0.05$.

8.2.3.2 Detailed Solution

Compute the statistics.

$$\hat{p}_1 = \frac{83}{200} = 0.415 \text{ and } \hat{p}_2 = \frac{117}{200} = 0.585$$

For each cell in the first column, $E_{i1} = (0.415)(50) = 20.75$. For each cell in the second column, $E_{i2} = (0.585)(50) = 29.25$.

$$
\begin{aligned}
\text{chi-square} &= \sum_{i=1}^{4}\sum_{j=1}^{2} \frac{\left(n_{ij} - E_{ij}\right)^2}{E_{ij}} \\
&= \frac{(12-20.75)^2}{(20.75)} + \frac{(38-29.25)^2}{(29.25)} + \frac{(18-20.75)^2}{(20.75)} + \frac{(32-29.25)^2}{(29.25)} \\
&\quad + \frac{(25-20.75)^2}{(20.75)} + \frac{(25-29.25)^2}{(29.25)} + \frac{(28-20.75)^2}{(20.75)} + \frac{(22-29.25)^2}{(29.25)} \\
&= 3.6898 + 2.6175 + 0.3645 + 0.2585 + 0.8705 + 0.6175 + 2.5331 + 1.7970 \\
&= 12.7484
\end{aligned}
$$

The degrees of freedom are $(r-1)(c-1) = (4-1)(2-1) = 3$.

$$p\text{-value} = P(Q \geq 12.7484) = 1 - \text{probchi}(12.7484, 3) = 0.0052$$

Apply results.

Since the p-value < 0.05, there is sufficient evidence to reject the claim that the proportion of men with dental caries is the same in each years-of-use population. At least some of the differences between the years-of-use samples are significant.

8.2.4 Instructions for Table Analysis

Open the Table Analysis task in one of the following ways:

- From the menu bar, select **Describe ▶ Table Analysis**.
- On the **Task by Category** tab of the **Task List**, go to the **Describe** section and click **Table Analysis**.
- On the **Task by Name** tab of the **Task List**, double click **Table Analysis**.

The Table Analysis task has six groups of options: Task Roles, Tables, Cell Statistics, Table Statistics, Results, and Titles. The Results options put the task results in data sets. The Titles options control the titles and the footnotes in the task output. Titles are discussed in general in Chapter 1, "Introduction to SAS Enterprise Guide."

8.2.4.1 Task Roles

Click **Task Roles** on the selection pane to open this group of options. A variable is assigned to a role by dragging its name from **Variables to assign to Task Roles**. See Figure 8.12. A variable may be removed from a role by dragging it back to **Variables to assign**. The right and left arrows and the resulting pop-up menus can also be used.

- Frequency count:
  - o This variable lists the frequencies for the cells defined by the respective rows of the Table variables. If a row is repeated, the sum of the associated frequencies is used.
  - o If no variable is assigned to the Frequency count role, a cell frequency is equal to the number of times the corresponding pair is repeated in the two classification variables creating the table.
- Table variables: These are the classification variables that create the contingency tables. Tables are created with the Tables options.

In Figure 8.12, Frequency is assigned to the Frequency Count role. Caries and Years are assigned to the Table variables role.

The Group analysis by role is discussed in "Common Task Roles" in Chapter 1, "Introduction to SAS Enterprise Guide."

Figure 8.12 Task Roles in the Table Analysis Task for Example 8.3

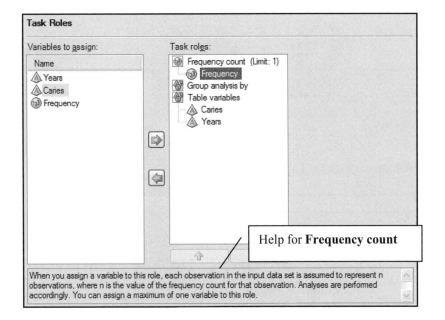

8.2.4.2 Tables

The Table analysis variables are listed in the **Variables permitted in table** box. In the top window in Figure 8.13, Caries and Years are in that box. To create a table:

1. Drag two variables to the Preview area on the right.

   The variable on the left side defines the rows. The variable on the top defines the columns.

   Variables can be dragged from one position to the other.

   The table is listed in the **Tables to be generated** box.

2. To create another table click **<select to begin defining a new table>**.

3. To delete a table select it from **Tables to be generated box** and click **Delete**.

   In the bottom window in Figure 8.13, a Years-by-Caries table is to be created. Years define the rows and Caries define the columns.

Figure 8.13 Tables Options in the Table Analysis Task for Example 8.1: The top window displays before a table is defined. The bottom window displays after the Years-by-Caries is defined.

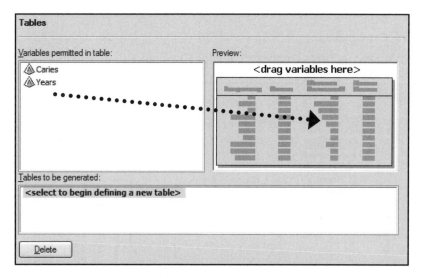

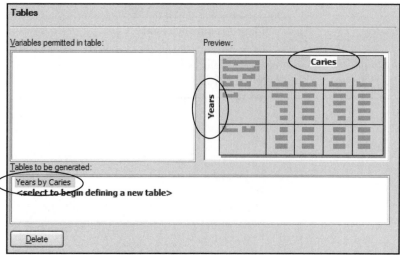

8.2.4.3   Cell Statistics

These are the statistics that can be included in the table cells:

- Cumulative column percentages

- Row percentages: $n_{ij}/n_{i.}$

- Column percentages: $n_{ij}/n_{.j}$

- Cell frequencies: n_{ij}.

- Cell percentages: $n_{ij}/n_{..}$

- Missing value frequencies: Missing values in the Table variables are treated as a category.

- Cell contribution to Pearson chi-square: $\dfrac{\left(n_{ij}-E_{ij}\right)^2}{E_{ij}}$

- Cell frequency deviation from expected: $n_{ij}-E_{ij}$

- Expected cell frequency: E_{ij}

- Percentage of total frequency: Cell percentage relative to total frequency in 3-way analysis and higher.

In Figure 8.14, the following are checked: Row percentages, Cell Frequencies, Cell contribution to Pearson chi-square, Cell frequency deviation from expected, and Expected cell frequency.

Figure 8.14 Cell Statistics in the Table Analysis Task for Example 8.3

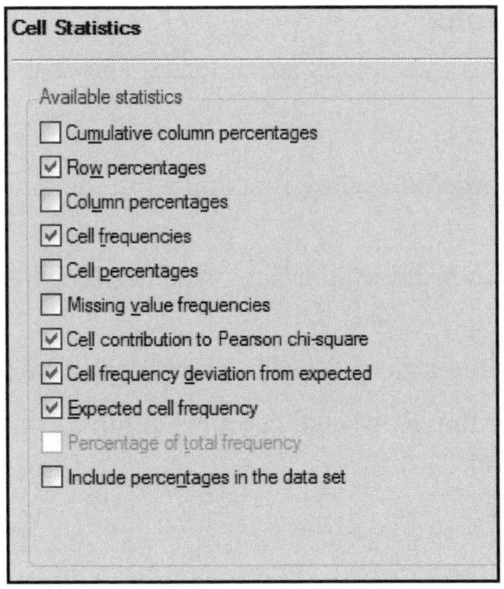

8.2.4.4   Table Statistics > Association

The test of homogeneity is a test of association. Checking **Chi-square tests** produces a number of test statistics and *p*-values, including the Pearson chi-square. It is checked in Figure 8.15.

Figure 8.15   Options for Tests and Measures of Association in the Table Analysis Task for Example 8.3

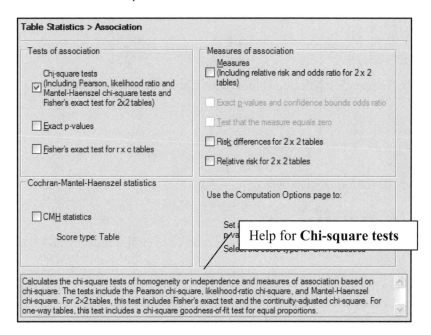

8.2.4.5   Table Statistics > Computation Options

The Order values by options determine how the rows and columns are ordered. The drop-down menu lists four sorting criteria:

- Data set order: Row and column values are ordered as they first appear in the data set. This is selected in Figure 8.16.

- Formatted values: The Create Format task can provide alternate presentation values for data values.

- Descending frequencies: Row and column values are ordered by their respective totals.

- Unformatted values: This is the default selection. Rows and columns are in the ascending order of the values as they exist in the data set.

8.2.4.6 When Finished

When finished assigning variables to roles and selecting options, click **Run**. The task adds a
Table Analysis icon and one or more output icons to the process flow diagram. See Figure 8.17.

Figure 8.16 Computation Options in the Table Analysis Task for Example 8.3

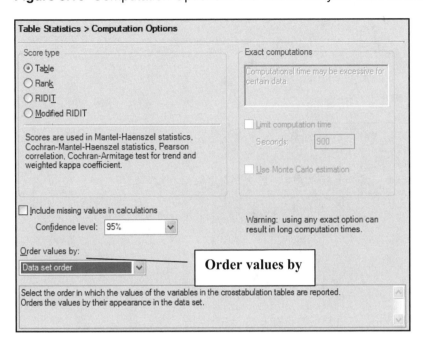

Figure 8.17 Example 8.3 Data, Task, and Output Icons on the Process Flow Diagram

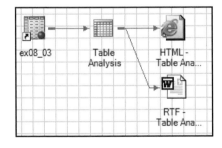

8.2.5 Task Output, Interpretation, and Analysis for Example 8.3

8.2.5.1 Task Output

Output 8.3 Table Analysis for Example 8.3

Table Analysis
Results

The FREQ Procedure

❶	**Table of Years by Caries**		
❷ **Years(Years of Chewing Tobacco Use)**	**Caries(Dental Caries)**		
❸ **Frequency Expected Deviation Cell chi-square Row Pct**	**yes**	**no**	**Total**
1-	12 20.75 -8.75 3.6898 24.00	38 29.25 8.75 2.6175 76.00	50
2-3	18 20.75 -2.75 0.3645 36.00	32 29.25 2.75 0.2585 64.00	50
4-5	25 20.75 4.25 0.8705 50.00	25 29.25 -4.25 0.6175 50.00	50
6+	28 20.75 7.25 2.5331 56.00	22 29.25 -7.25 1.797 44.00	50
Total	83	117	200

Statistics for Table of Years by Caries

Statistic	DF	Value	Prob
chi-square	3	12.7484	0.0052 ❹
Likelihood Ratio chi-square	3	13.0932	0.0044
Mantel-Haenszel chi-square	1	12.3978	0.0004
Phi Coefficient		0.2525	
Contingency Coefficient		0.2448	
Cramer's V		0.2525	

Sample Size = 200

8.2.5.2   Interpretation

❶   Table is defined by the Years and Caries variables.

❷   **Years** is the row variable. Years of Chewing Tobacco Use in parentheses is the variable label.

Caries is the column variable. Dental Caries in parentheses is the variable label.

❸   Contents of table cells:

Frequency is the cell frequency or cell count n_{ij}.

Expected is the expected frequency E_{ij}.

Deviation is $n_{ij} - E_{ij}$.

Cell chi-square is $\dfrac{\left(n_{ij} - E_{ij}\right)^2}{E_{ij}}$.

Row Pct is row percent: $\dfrac{p_{ij}}{p_{\cdot j}}100\%$.

❹   Chi-square test statistic

8.2.5.3   Analysis

H_0 : The proportion of men with dental caries is the same in each years-of-use population.

H_1 : The proportion of men with dental caries is not the same in each years-of-use population.

p-value = 0.0052. See ❹ in Output 8.3.

Since the p-value < 0.05, there is sufficient evidence to reject the claim that the proportion of men with dental caries is the same in each years-of-use population. At least some of the differences between the years-of-use samples are significant.

8.3 Test of Independence

The *test of independence* examines the association between two sets of categories in a single population. Two sets of categories are independent if:

- Roughly speaking, each set does not affect the other.

- More precisely, the distribution of proportions in one set of categories is the same in each category of the other set as it is in the population.

Two sets of categories are not independent or dependent if the distribution of proportions in one set of categories differs among the categories of the other set.

Let $A_1, A_2, \ldots, A_r$ ($r \geq 2$) and $B_1, B_2, \ldots, B_c$ ($c \geq 2$) represent the two sets of categories. Each set of categories is exhaustive and mutually exclusive. That is, every member of the population is in one and only one category of each set.

Let p_{ij} ($i = 1, 2, \ldots, r$ and $j = 1, 2, \ldots c$) represent the proportion of the population in categories A_i and B_j.

This is organized in the following table.

Table 8.14 Population Model for the Test of Independence

	B_1	B_2	$\ldots$	B_c	Total
A_1	p_{11}	p_{12}	$\ldots$	p_{1c}	$p_{11} + \cdots + p_{1c} = p_{1\cdot}$
A_2	p_{21}	p_{22}	$\ldots$	p_{2c}	$p_{21} + \cdots + p_{2c} = p_{2\cdot}$
$\vdots$	$\vdots$	$\vdots$	$\vdots$	$\vdots$	$\vdots$
A_r	p_{r1}	p_{r2}	$\ldots$	p_{rc}	$p_{r1} + \cdots + p_{rc} = p_{r\cdot}$
	$p_{11} + \cdots + p_{r1} = p_{\cdot 1}$	$p_{12} + \cdots + p_{r2} = p_{\cdot 2}$	$\ldots$	$p_{1c} + \cdots + p_{rc} = p_{\cdot c}$	$\sum_{j=1}^{c} p_{\cdot j} = \sum_{i=1}^{r} p_{i\cdot} = 1$

The hypotheses for the test of independence state that the two sets of categories are and are not independent.

H_0 : The two sets of categories are independent.

H_1 : The two sets of categories are not independent.

In terms of proportions, independence means that the proportions of $A_1, A_2, \ldots, A_r$ in each B_j are $p_{1\cdot}, p_{2\cdot}, \ldots, p_{r\cdot}$, respectively. (The role of the sets can be reversed.) Therefore, the proportion of the population in A_i and B_j is $p_{i\cdot}$ of the proportion of the population in B_j. That is, if the sets of categories are independent, $p_{ij} = p_{i\cdot}p_{\cdot j}$. The null and alternative hypotheses in terms of p_{ij} are:

$H_0 : p_{ij} = p_{i\cdot}p_{\cdot j}$ for each *i-j* pair

$H_1 : p_{ij} \neq p_{i\cdot}p_{\cdot j}$ for at least one *i-j* pair

8.3.1 Data

The data is organized in the following $r \times c$ contingency table. The dot notation represents summation over a subscript.

Table 8.15 Summarized Data for the Test of Independence

	B_1	B_2	$\cdots$	B_c	Total
A_1	n_{11}	n_{12}	$\cdots$	n_{1c}	$n_{11} + \cdots + n_{1c} = n_{1.}$ (random)
A_2	n_{21}	n_{22}	$\cdots$	n_{2c}	$n_{21} + \cdots + n_{2c} = n_{2.}$ (random)
$\vdots$	$\vdots$	$\vdots$	$\vdots$	$\vdots$	$\vdots$
A_r	n_{r1}	n_{r2}	$\cdots$	n_{rc}	$n_{r1} + \cdots + n_{rc} = n_{r.}$ (random)
Total	$n_{11} + \cdots + n_{r1} = n_{.1}$ (random)	$n_{12} + \cdots + n_{r2} = n_{.2}$ (random)	$\cdots$	$n_{1c} + \cdots + n_{rc} = n_{.c}$ (random)	$\displaystyle\sum_{j=1}^{c} n_{.j} = \sum_{i=1}^{r} n_{i.} = n_{..}$

There is one sample of $n_{..}$ persons or objects from a population. The sample size is fixed by the investigator.

The row and column totals are randomly determined. They are the result of random selection.

8.3.1.1 Table Format

Table format is not important for the test of independence. The results are the same regardless of which set of categories is associated with the rows or the columns.

8.3.1.2 Variables

The data enters the task as two or three variables. As two variables, there is a pair of values for each person or object in the sample. The values identify a category from each set. As an example, the variable set1 below identifies categories 1 or 2. The variable set2 identifies categories A, B, or C.

set1	set2
1	A
2	C
2	B
2	A
1	C
$\vdots$	$\vdots$

As three variables, the data enters in summarized form. A third variable is added that contains the frequencies with which the respective pairs occur in the sample. As an example, the variables set1 and set2 below contain a unique pair for each table cell. The variable frequency has the respective cell frequencies.

set1	set2	frequency
1	A	n_{11}
1	B	n_{12}
1	C	n_{13}
2	A	n_{21}
2	B	n_{22}
2	C	n_{23}

The pairs do not have to be unique. If a pair is repeated, the sum of the associated frequencies is used. Also, the values do not have to be sorted.

8.3.2 Test of Independence

8.3.2.1 Test Statistic

A test statistic for the test of independence is the Pearson chi-squared (χ^2) statistic. It compares the *observed* cell frequencies n_{ij} with the *expected* cell frequencies E_{ij}. The expected cell frequencies are the values that are expected when the null hypothesis is true. They are generally not integers.

$$\text{chi-square} = \sum_{i=1}^{r} \sum_{j=1}^{c} \frac{\left(n_{ij} - E_{ij}\right)^2}{E_{ij}}$$

In general, an expected cell frequency is equal to the estimate of a population proportion under H_0 times the sample size. Under H_0 for the test of independence, the proportion associated with each cell is $p_{ij} = p_{i.}p_{.j}$. The estimate are $\hat{p}_{i.} = n_{i.}/n_{..}$ and $\hat{p}_{.j} = n_{.j}/n_{..}$.

The expected frequency for the cell associated with categories A_i and B_j is the row i total times the column j total divided by the overall total:

$$E_{ij} = n_{..}\hat{p}_{i.}\hat{p}_{.j} = n_{..} \frac{n_{i.}}{n_{..}} \frac{n_{.j}}{n_{..}} = \frac{n_{i.}n_{.j}}{n_{..}}$$

8.3.2.2 Expected Cell Frequency Rule

The chi-square statistic follows approximately the chi-square probability distribution. It is appropriate to use if both of the following conditions are met:

- All expected cell frequencies are 1 or more.

- At most 20% of the expected cell frequencies are less than 5.

If these are not met, one may need to consider combining categories. The exact test for larger tables often requires an excessive amount of time.

8.3.2.3 *p*-Value

The *p-value* is a measure of the likelihood that the samples come from populations where H_0 is true. Smaller values indicate less likelihood. That is, the more the data agrees with H_1 (the more the observed cell frequencies n_{ij} differ from the expected cell frequencies E_{ij}) the smaller the *p*-value.

In terms of a test of independence, the *p*-value is the probability that a random sample from a population with independent sets of categories would produce a chi-square statistic at or beyond the current value. If the *p*-value is small, it is unlikely that the current sample comes from a population with independent sets of categories.

The technical definition of the *p*-value is in Table 8.16. The random variable Q represents a future value of the test statistic and follows the chi-square distribution with $(r-1)(c-1)$ degrees of freedom.

SAS code expressions are included in Table 8.16 to aid in the discussion. The *p*-value is computed using an expression in the "Detailed Solutions" section of "Example 8.4: Test of Independence." In the expression, chi-square and $(r-1)(c-1)$ represent numbers.

Table 8.16 *p*-Value for Test of Homogeneity

Hypotheses	Gray area corresponds to the probability statement and is an example.			
H_0: the two sets of categories are independent. H_1: the two sets of categories are not independent.	Task output: **Statistic**	**DF**	**Value**	**Prob**
	chi-square	$(r{-}1)(c{-}1)$	chi-square	*p*-value
	$p\text{-value} = P(Q \geq \text{chi-square})$	SAS code expression: 1-probchi(chi-square, $(r{-}1)(c{-}1)$)		

8.3.2.4 Decision and Conclusions

The formal decision and concluding sentence do not change from the one-sample tests discussed in Chapter 4, "Inferences from One Sample." The concluding observation depends on the particular statistics involved in the test.

If the p-value is small, the data agrees with H_1. If the p-value is less than the significance level, the risk of making a Type I error is acceptable. Therefore, the p-value decision rule is the following:

> If the p-value $< \alpha$, reject H_0. Otherwise, do not reject H_0.

Since a hypothesis test begins with the assumption that H_0 is true, concluding a hypothesis test requires one of the following formal statements:

- Reject H_0.
- Do not reject H_0.

When the claim is equivalent to the null hypothesis, the concluding sentence uses the word *reject*. The concluding sentence becomes an expanded version of the formal decision.

When the claim is equivalent to the alternative hypothesis, the concluding sentence uses the word *support*. If the data supports the rejection of H_0, the data supports H_1. If the data does not support the rejection of H_0, the data cannot support H_1.

Table 8.17 Concluding Sentences

Formal Statistical Decision	Claim stated as H_0	Claim stated as H_1
Reject H_0.	There is sufficient evidence to reject the claim that ... (claim in words).	There is sufficient evidence to support the claim that ... (claim in words).
Do not reject H_0.	There is not sufficient evidence to reject the claim that ... (claim in words).	There is not sufficient evidence to support the claim that ... (claim in words).

Table 8.18 Concluding Observations

Reject H_0.	The sample proportions for one set of categories differ significantly among the categories of the other set.
Do not reject H_0.	The sample proportions for one set of categories do not differ significantly among the categories of the other set.

8.3.3 Example 8.4: Test of Independence

8.3.3.1 Gender and Hospitalization

A university health clinic does a study to determine whether a student's gender is a factor in whether a visit to the clinic leads to being admitted to a hospital. The records of 74 students who have visited the clinic in the past four months are randomly selected. The results are below.

Hospital

Gender	No	Yes	Total
Female	32	8	40
Male	18	16	34
Total	50	24	74

The data is in the data set Ex08_04. The data is presented by a stacked bar chart below in Figure 8.18.

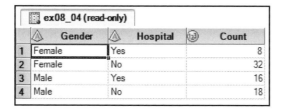

Figure 8.18 Example 8.4 Data in Stacked Bar Chart

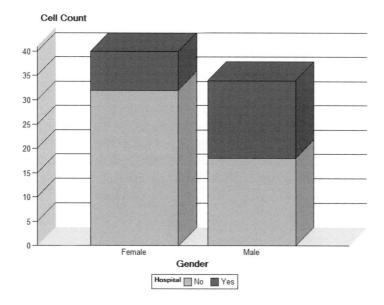

This is an example of a one-population model. The row and column totals are randomly determined. The test of independence is appropriate here.

Example 8.4

Test the claim that gender and hospitalization are independent. Let $\alpha = 0.05$.

8.3.3.2   Detailed Solution

Plan the task.

H_0 : Gender and hospitalization are independent.

H_1 : Gender and hospitalization are not independent.

$\alpha = 0.05$

Compute the statistics.

$$\text{chi-square} = \sum_{i=1}^{2} \sum_{j=1}^{2} \frac{\left(n_{ij} - E_{ij} \right)^2}{E_{ij}}$$

$$= \frac{\left(32 - \frac{(40)(50)}{74} \right)^2}{\left(\frac{(40)(50)}{74} \right)} + \frac{\left(8 - \frac{(40)(24)}{74} \right)^2}{\left(\frac{(40)(24)}{74} \right)} + \frac{\left(18 - \frac{(34)(50)}{74} \right)^2}{\left(\frac{(40)(24)}{74} \right)} + \frac{\left(16 - \frac{(34)(24)}{74} \right)^2}{\left(\frac{(40)(24)}{74} \right)}$$

$$= 0.9150 + 1.9063 + 1.0765 + 2.2427$$

$$= 6.1405$$

The degrees of freedom are $(r-1)(c-1) = (2-1)(2-1) = 1$.

$p\text{-value} = P(Q \geq 6.1405) = 1 - \text{probchi}(6.1405,1) = 0.0132$

Apply results.

Since the p-value < 0.05, there is sufficient evidence to reject the claim that gender and hospitalization are independent. The proportions of females and males that are not hospitalized differ significantly from the proportions of females and males that are hospitalized. Also, the proportions of females that are and are not hospitalized differ significantly from the proportions of males that are and are not hospitalized.

8.3.4 Instructions for Table Analysis

Open the Table Analysis task in one of the following ways:

- From the menu bar, select **Describe ▶ Table Analysis**.

- On the **Task by Category** tab of the **Task List**, go to the **Describe** section and click **Table Analysis**.

- On the **Task by Name** tab of the **Task List**, double-click **Table Analysis**.

Use the selection pane on the left to navigate through assigning data columns to roles and selecting options.

The Table Analysis task has six groups of options: Task Roles, Tables, Cell Statistics, Table Statistics, Results, and Titles. The Results options put the task results in data sets. The Titles options control the titles and the footnotes in the task output. Titles are discussed in general in Chapter 1, "Introduction to SAS Enterprise Guide."

8.3.4.1 Task Roles

Click **Task Roles** on the selection pane to open this group of options. A variable is assigned to a role by dragging its name from **Variables to assign to Task Roles**. See Figure 8.19. A variable may be removed from a role by dragging it back to **Variables to assign**. The right and left arrows and the resulting pop-up menus can also be used.

- Frequency count:
  - This variable lists the frequencies for the cells defined by the respective rows of the Table variables. If a row is repeated, the sum of the associated frequencies is used.
  - If no variable is assigned to the Frequency count role, a cell frequency is equal to the number of times the corresponding pair is repeated in the two classification variables creating the table.

- Table variables: These are the classification variables that create the contingency tables. Tables are created with the Tables options.

In Figure 8.19, Count is assigned to the Frequency Count role. Hospital and Gender are assigned to the Table variables role.

The Group analysis by role is discussed in "Common Task Roles" in Chapter 1, "Introduction to SAS Enterprise Guide."

Figure 8.19 Task Roles in the Table Analysis Task for Example 8.3

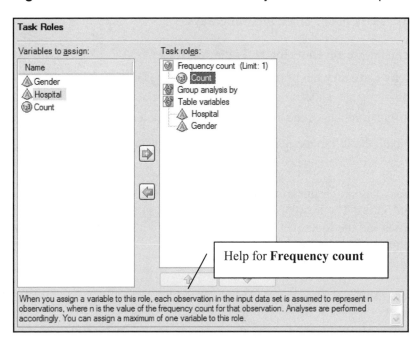

8.3.4.2 Tables

The Table analysis variables are listed in the **Variables permitted in table** box. In the top window in Figure 8.19, Gender and Hospital are in that box. To create a table:

1. Drag two variables to the Preview area on the right.

    The variable on the left side defines the rows. The variable on the top defines the columns.

    Variables can be dragged from one position to the other.

    The table is listed in the **Tables to be generated** box.

2. To create another table click **<select to begin defining a new table>**.

3. To delete a table, select it from the **Tables to be generated** box and click **Delete**.

    In the bottom window in Figure 8.19, a Gender by Hospital table is to be created. Gender defines the rows and Hospital defines the columns.

Figure 8.19 Tables Options in the Table Analysis Task for Example 8.4:
The top window displays before a table is defined.
The bottom displays after Gender by Hospital is defined.

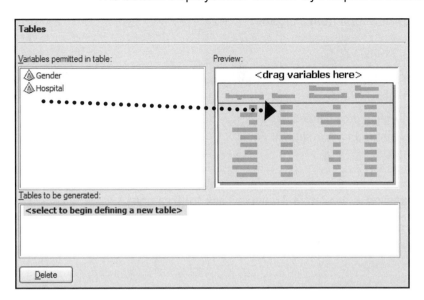

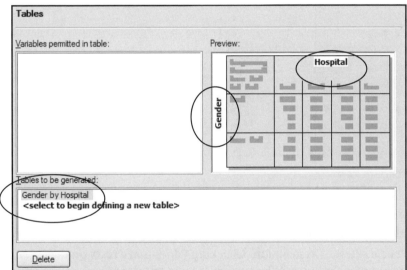

8.3.4.3 Cell Statistics

These are the statistics that can be included in the table cells:

- Cumulative column percentages
- Row percentages: $n_{ij}/n_{i\cdot}$
- Column percentages: $n_{ij}/n_{\cdot j}$
- Cell frequencies: n_{ij}.
- Cell percentages: $n_{ij}/n_{\cdot\cdot}$
- Missing value frequencies: Missing values in the Table variables are treated as a category.

- Cell contribution to Pearson chi-square: $\dfrac{\left(n_{ij} - E_{ij}\right)^2}{E_{ij}}$

- Cell frequency deviation from expected: $n_{ij} - E_{ij}$

- Expected cell frequency: E_{ij}

- Percentage of total frequency: Cell percentage relative to total frequency in 3-way analysis and higher.

In Figure 8.20, the following are checked: Row percentages, Column percentages, Cell Frequencies, Cell contribution to Pearson chi-square, Cell frequency deviation from expected, and Expected cell frequency.

Figure 8.20 Cell Statistics in the Table Analysis Task for Example 8.4

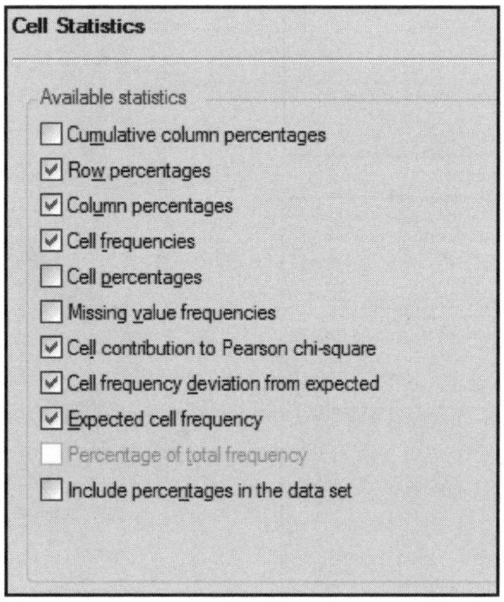

8.3.4.4   Table Statistics > Association

The test of independence is a test of association. Checking **Chi-square tests** produces a number of test statistics and *p*-values, including the Pearson chi-square test. It is checked in Figure 8.21.

Figure 8.21 Options for Tests and Measures of Association in the Table Analysis Task for Example 8.4

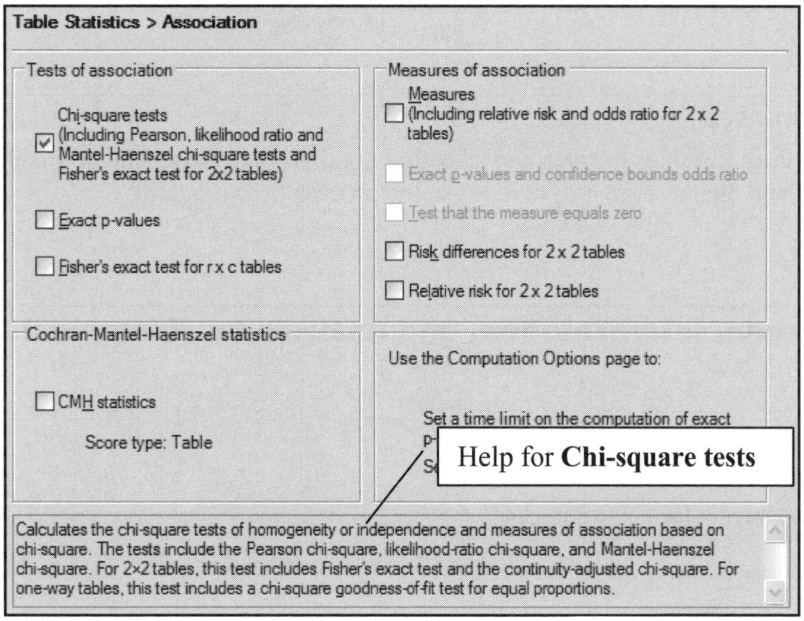

Figure 8.22 Computation Options in the Table Analysis Task for Example 8.3

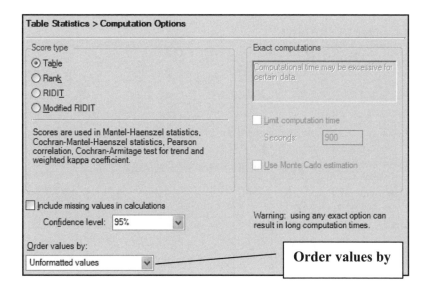

8.3.4.5   Table Statistics > Computation Options

The Order values by options determine how the rows and columns are ordered. The drop-down menu lists four sorting criteria:

- Data set order: Row and column values are ordered as they first appear in the data set.

- Formatted values: The Create Format task can provide alternate presentation values for data values.

- Descending frequencies: Row and column values are ordered by their respective totals.
- Unformatted values: This is the default selection. Rows and columns are in the ascending order of the values as they exist in the data set. This is selected in Figure 8.22.

8.3.4.6　When Finished

When finished assigning variables to roles and selecting options, click **Run**. The task adds a Table Analysis icon and one or more output icons to the process flow diagram.

8.3.5　Task Output, Interpretation, and Analysis for Example 8.4

8.3.5.1　Task Output

Output 8.4 Table Analysis for Example 8.4

Table Analysis
Results

The FREQ Procedure

❶	Table of Gender by Hospital		
❷	Gender	Hospital	
❸	Frequency Expected Deviation Cell chi-square Row Pct Col Pct	No	Yes	Tot al
	Female	32 27.027 4.973 0.915 80.00 64.00	8 12.973 -4.973 1.9063 20.00 33.33	40
	Male	18 22.973 -4.973 1.0765 52.94 36.00	16 11.027 4.973 2.2427 47.06 66.67	34
	Total	50	24	74

Statistics for Table of Gender by Hospital

Statistic	DF	Value	Prob	
chi-square	1	6.1405	0.0132	❹
Likelihood Ratio chi-square	1	6.2043	0.0127	
Continuity Adj. chi-square	1	4.9678	0.0258	
Mantel-Haenszel chi-square	1	6.0576	0.0138	
Phi Coefficient		0.2881		
Contingency Coefficient		0.2768		
Cramer's V		0.2881		

Fisher's Exact Test	
Cell (1,1) Frequency (F)	32
Left-sided Pr <= F	0.9970
Right-sided Pr >= F	0.0127
Table Probability (P)	0.0097
Two-sided Pr <= P	0.0239

Sample Size = 74

8.3.5.2 Interpretation

❶ Table is defined by the Gender and Hospital variables.

❷ Gender is the row variable. Hospital is the column variable.

❸ Contents of table cells:

Frequency is the cell frequency or cell count n_{ij} .

Expected is the expected frequency E_{ij} .

Deviation is $n_{ij} - E_{ij}$.

Cell chi-square is $\dfrac{\left(n_{ij} - E_{ij}\right)^2}{E_{ij}}$.

Row Pct is row percent: $\dfrac{p_{ij}}{p_{\cdot j}}100\%$.

Col Pct is column percent: $\dfrac{p_{ij}}{p_{i\cdot}}100\%$.

❹ Chi-square test statistic

8.3.5.3   Analysis

Example 8.4

H_0 : Gender and hospitalization are independent.

H_1 : Gender and hospitalization are dependent.

p-value = 0.0132. See ❹ in Output 8.4.

Since the p-value < 0.05, there is sufficient evidence to reject the claim that gender and hospitalization are independent.

The proportions of females and males that are not hospitalized differ significantly from the proportions of females and males that are hospitalized. The table below shows just the column percents:

Table of Gender by Hospital			
Gender	Hospital		
Col Pct	No	Yes	Total
Female	64.00	33.33	
Male	36.00	66.67	
Total	50	24	74

Also, the proportions of females that are and are not hospitalized differ significantly from the proportions of males that are and are not hospitalized. The table below shows just the row percents:

Table of Gender by Hospital			
Gender	Hospital		
Row Pct	No	Yes	Total
Female	80.00	20.00	
Male	52.94	47.06	
Total	50	24	74

8.3.6 Example 8.5: Test of Independence

8.3.6.1 Gender and Grade Expectations

A school district does a survey to investigate factors that may affect their students' future performance in college mathematics. Fifty college-bound seniors are randomly selected and agree to take part in the survey. One issue of interest to the investigators is whether females and males view college mathematics with equal confidence. The table below classifies each student by gender (female = 0, male = 1) and expected grade (A = 4, B = 3, C = 2):

	Expected Grade			
Gender	2	3	4	Total
0	2	7	10	19
1	7	12	12	31
Total	9	19	22	50

The Mathpred data set in Appendix 1 contains the results of the survey. The gender values are in the Gender variable and the expected grade values are in the ExpectedGrd variable.

This is an example of a one-population model. The row and column totals are randomly determined. The test of independence is appropriate here.

Example 8.5

Test the claim that gender and hospitalization are independent. Let $\alpha = 0.05$.

8.3.7 Task Output, Interpretation, and Analysis for 8.5

8.3.7.1   Task Output

Output 8.5 Table Analysis for Example 8.5

Table Analysis
Results

The FREQ Procedure

❶	Table of Gender by ExpectedGrd			
❷	Gender(Female =0 Male=1)	ExpectedGrd(A=4, B=3, C=2)		
❸	Frequency Expected Deviation Cell chi-square Row Pct Col Pct	**2**	**3**	**4**	**Total**
	0	2 3.42 -1.42 0.5896 10.53 22.22	7 7.22 -0.22 0.0067 36.84 36.84	10 8.36 1.64 0.3217 52.63 45.45	19
	1	7 5.58 1.42 0.3614 22.58 77.78	12 11.78 0.22 0.0041 38.71 63.16	12 13.64 -1.64 0.1972 38.71 54.55	31
	Total	9	19	22	50

Statistics for Table of Gender by ExpectedGrd

Statistic	DF	Value	Prob	
chi-square	2	1.4807	0.4770	❹
Likelihood Ratio chi-square	2	1.5471	0.4614	
Mantel-Haenszel chi-square	1	1.4102	0.2350	
Phi Coefficient		0.1721		
Contingency Coefficient		0.1696		
Cramer's V		0.1721		

Sample Size = 50

8.3.7.2   Interpretation

❶ Table is defined by the Gender and ExpectedGrd variables.

❷ Gender is the row variable. Female=0 Male=1 in parentheses is the variable label.
ExpectedGrd is the column variable. A=4, B=3, C=2 in parentheses is the variable label.

❸ Contents of table cells:

Frequency is the cell frequency or cell count n_{ij}.

Expected is the expected frequency E_{ij}.

Deviation is $n_{ij} - E_{ij}$.

Cell chi-square is $\dfrac{\left(n_{ij} - E_{ij}\right)^2}{E_{ij}}$.

Row Pct is row percent: $\dfrac{p_{ij}}{p_{\bullet j}}100\%$.

Col Pct is column percent: $\dfrac{p_{ij}}{p_{i\bullet}}100\%$.

❹ Chi-square test statistic

8.3.7.3 Analysis

The data is presented by a stacked bar chart below in Figure 8.23.

Figure 8.23 Example 8.5 Data in Stacked Bar Chart

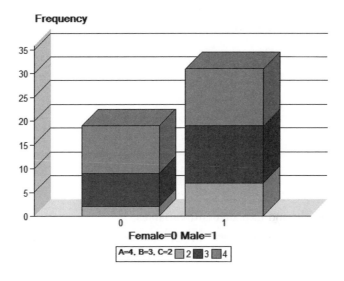

Example 8.5

H_0 : Gender and expected grade are independent.

H_1 : Gender and expected grade are dependent.

p-value = 0.4770. See ❹ in Output 8.5.

Since the p-value > 0.05, there is not sufficient evidence to reject the claim that gender and expected grade are independent.

The proportions of females and males in each of the expected grade categories do not differ significantly. The table below shows just the column percents.

Table of Gender by ExpectedGrd				
Gender(Female=0 Male=1)	**ExpectedGrd(A=4, B=3, C=2)**			
Col Pct	**2**	**3**	**4**	**Total**
0	22.22	36.84	45.45	
1	77.78	63.16	54.55	
Total	9	19	22	50

Also, the proportions of females that expect a C, a B, or an A do not differ significantly from the proportions of males that expect a C, a B, or an A. The table below shows just the row percents.

Table of Gender by ExpectedGrd				
Gender(Female=0 Male=1)	ExpectedGrd(A=4, B=3, C=2)			
Row Pct	2	3	4	Total
0	10.53	36.84	52.63	
1	22.58	38.71	38.71	
Total	9	19	22	50

8.4 Fisher's Exact Test

Fisher's Exact Test is an alternative to the Pearson chi-square test for 2×2 tables. It can be used for tests on two binomial proportions from independent populations and the test of independence.

For tests on two binomial proportions, the Fisher's Exact Test supports the three possible pairs of hypotheses:

$$H_0 : p_1 \geq p_2 \qquad H_0 : p_1 \leq p_2 \qquad H_0 : p_1 = p_2$$
$$H_1 : p_1 < p_2 \qquad H_1 : p_1 > p_2 \qquad H_1 : p_1 \neq p_2$$

It is automatically part of the output when the chi-square test is requested for a 2×2 table. This test should be considered when one or more expected cell frequencies are less than 5.

8.4.1 Test Statistic

In the theory for Fisher's Exact Test, the row and column totals are both treated as fixed. When the row and column totals are fixed, a single cell frequency determines all other cell frequencies in a 2×2 table. In Table 8.19, all cell frequencies depend on n_{11}, the observed *a-c* cell frequency.

The test statistic is n_{11}.

Table 8.19 2×2 Contingency Table

	c	d	Total
a	n_{11}	$n_{1\cdot} - n_{11}$	$n_{1\cdot}$
b	$n_{\cdot 1} - n_{11}$	$n_{2\cdot} - (n_{\cdot 1} - n_{11})$	$n_{2\cdot}$
Total	$n_{\cdot 1}$	$n_{\cdot 2}$	$n_{\cdot\cdot}$

8.4.2 *p*-Values

The *p*-values for Fisher's Exact Test are applications of the hypergeometric distribution. The population is all 2×2 tables that have the fixed row and column totals. The value of the random variable X is n_{11} for each table.

The following is the hypergeometric distribution in terms of Table 8.19. The probability is the same if the roles of the row and column totals are switched.

$$P(X = n_{11}) = \frac{\binom{n_{1.}}{n_{11}} \binom{n_{2.}}{n_{.1} - n_{11}}}{\binom{n_{..}}{n_{.1}}}, \text{ where } \max(0, n_{1.} + n_{.1} - n_{..}) \leq n_{11} \leq \min(n_{1.}, n_{.1})$$

- The mean of the hypergeometric distribution is $\dfrac{n_{1.} n_{.1}}{n_{..}}$.

- This is E_{11}, the expected *a-c* cell frequency.

The *p*-values for Fisher's Exact Test measure the degree to which the observed cell frequency n_{11} is less than, greater than, or different from the expected cell frequency E_{11}.

The technical definitions of the *p*-values are below. Cumulative hypergeometric probabilities can be computed with a SAS code expression: $P(X \leq x) = \textbf{\textit{probhypr}}(n_{..}, n_{1.}, n_{.1}, x)$. The *p*-value is computed using the expression in the "Detailed Solutions" section of "Example 8.6: Fisher's Exact Test."

❶ $H_0 : p_1 \geq p_2$ ❷ $H_0 : p_1 \leq p_2$ ❸ $H_0 : p_1 = p_2$
     $H_1 : p_1 < p_2$ $H_1 : p_1 > p_2$ $H_1 : p_1 \neq p_2$

❹ H_0 : The two sets of categories are independent.
     H_1 : The two sets of categories are not independent.

Fisher's Exact Test		
Cell (1,1) Frequency (F)	n_{11}	
Left-sided Pr <= F	$P(X \leq n_{11})$	❶
Right-sided Pr >= F	$P(X \geq n_{11})$	❷
Table Probability (P)	$P(X = n_{11})$	
Two-sided Pr <= P	Sum of all $P(X = x)$ where $P(X = x) \leq P(X = n_{11})$	❸❹

8.4.2.1 Instructions for Table Analysis

Fisher's Exact Test is automatically part of the output when the chi-square test is requested for a 2×2 table. In the relevant section, see Section 8.1.8.4, "Table Statistics > Association."

8.4.3 Example 8.6: Fisher's Exact Test

It is not obvious but one of the expected cell frequencies in the following table is less than 5. The user is warned of this in the output. The chi-square test is ignored and Fisher's Exact Test is used.

8.4.3.1 Patient Satisfaction

A hospital develops a home-based care program for disabled elderly patients. The program manages patient care after discharge from the hospital. The hospital hopes the program reduces the rate at which patients need to be readmitted.

A study examines the association between patient satisfaction with the program and being readmitted within 6 months of discharge. Fifty patients take part in the study.

The results are in the Home_care data set in Appendix 1.

- The satisfaction responses for patients in the program are in prog_sat column with s = 'satisfied' and u = 'unsatisfied'.

- The readmit information for patients in the program is in prog_readmit column with hosp = 'readmitted to the hospital within 6 months' and no = 'not readmitted to the hospital'.

The data is summarized in the contingency table below.

prog_readmit

prog_sat	hosp	no	Total
s	5	31	36
u	7	7	14
Total	12	38	50

This is an example of a one-population model. The row and column totals are randomly determined. The test of independence is appropriate here.

Example 8.6

Test the claim that patient satisfaction with the program and being readmitted within 6 months of discharge are independent. Let $\alpha = 0.05$.

Figure 8.24 Example 8.6 Data in Stacked Bar Chart

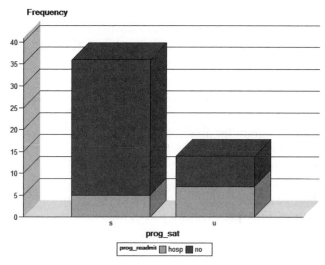

8.4.3.2 Detailed Solutions

Plan the task.

H_0 : Satisfaction and being readmitted are independent.

H_1 : Satisfaction and being readmitted are dependent.

$\alpha = 0.05$.

Compute the statistics.

The following probabilities are computed using the cumulative hypergeometric probability expression: $P(X \le x) = \text{probhypr}(50, 36, 12, x)$

x	$P(X \le x)$	$P(X = x)$	Probabilities $\le P(X = 5)$
0	0.0000000007	0.0000000007	0.0000000007
1	0.0000001087	0.0000001079	0.0000001079
2	0.0000053034	0.0000051947	0.0000051947
3	0.0001230490	0.0001177456	0.0001177456
4	0.0015801513	0.0014571023	0.0014571023
5	0.0122378141	0.0106576628	0.0106576628
6	0.0604193313	0.0481815172	
7	0.1980808090	0.1376614777	
8	0.4475922373	0.2495114283	
9	0.7298677925	0.2822755552	

x	$P(X \leq x)$	$P(X = x)$	Probabilities $\leq P(X = 5)$
10	0.9204037923	0.1905359998	
11	0.9896896104	0.0692858181	
12	1	0.0103103896	0.0103103896

p-value = sum of probabilities $\leq P(X = 5)$: ⠀⠀⠀⠀0.0225482037

Apply results.

Since the p-value < 0.05, there is sufficient evidence to reject the claim that satisfaction and being readmitted are independent.

8.4.4 Task Output, Interpretation, and Analysis

8.4.4.1 Task Output

Output 8.6 Table Analysis for Example 8.6

Table Analysis
Results

The FREQ Procedure

❶

Table of prog_sat by prog_readmit			
❷ prog_sat	prog_readmit		Total
❸ Frequency Expected Deviation Row Pct Col Pct	hosp	no	
s	5 8.64 -3.64 13.89 41.67	31 27.36 3.64 86.11 81.58	36
u	❹ 7 3.36 3.64 50.00 58.33	7 10.64 -3.64 50.00 18.42	14
Total	12	38	50

Statistics for Table of prog_sat by prog_readmit

Statistic	DF	Value	Prob
chi-square	1	7.2064	0.0073
Likelihood Ratio chi-square	1	6.6881	0.0097
Continuity Adj. chi-square	1	5.3626	0.0206
Mantel-Haenszel chi-square	1	7.0623	0.0079
Phi Coefficient		-0.3796	
Contingency Coefficient		0.3549	
Cramer's V		-0.3796	
WARNING: 25% of the cells have expected counts less than 5. chi-square may not be a valid test.			

❺

Fisher's Exact Test	
Cell (1,1) Frequency (F)	5
Left-sided Pr <= F	0.0122
Right-sided Pr >= F	0.9984
Table Probability (P)	0.0107
Two-sided Pr <= P	0.0225

❻

Sample Size = 50

8.4.4.2 Interpretation

❶ Table is defined by the prog_sat and prog_readmit variables.

❷ prog_sat is the row variable. prog_readmit is the column variable.

❸ Contents of table cells:

Frequency is the cell frequency or cell count n_{ij}.

Expected is the expected frequency E_{ij}.

Deviation is $n_{ij} - E_{ij}$.

Row Pct is row percent: $\dfrac{p_{ij}}{p_{\cdot j}}100\%$.

Col Pct is column percent: $\dfrac{p_{ij}}{p_{i\cdot}}100\%$.

❹ The expected count is less than 5: $E_{21} = 3.36$.

❺ Warning that the Expected Cell Frequency Rule has not been satisfied.

❻ Fisher's Exact Test *p*-value for the test of independence.

8.4.4.3 Analysis

H_0 : Satisfaction and being readmitted are independent.

H_1 : Satisfaction and being readmitted are dependent.

*p-v*alue = 0.0225. See ❻ in Output 8.6.

Since the p-value < 0.05, there is sufficient evidence to reject the claim that satisfaction and being readmitted are independent. The rates that satisfied patients and unsatisfied patients are readmitted are significantly different. The rates that satisfied patients occur among those readmitted and those not readmitted are significantly different.

Appendix 1

A1.1 SAS Code for Example 4.1 and Example 7.5

This section presents the Code Editor and the SAS code used to create results for Example 4.1 and Example 7.5. It does not discuss writing programs. An excellent introduction is *The Little SAS Book: A Primer*, *Third Edition*, by Lora D. Delwiche and Susan J. Slaughter.

A1.1.1 Opening the Code Editor

Each of the following opens the Code Editor. See Figure A.1.

1. From the Welcome to SAS Enterprise Guide window, click the New SAS Program icon ![icon].

2. From the menu bar, select **File ▶ New ▶ Code**.

3. From the Standard toolbar, select **Create New Item In Project ▶ Code**.

4. From the Project toolbar, click the **New Code**.

5. Right-click on a Process Flow window: **New ▶ Code**.

    The default program names are **Code**, **Code1**, **Code2**, …. A saved program takes on the name of its file.

    Program files can be opened from and saved to Windows folders, SAS libraries, and SAS Enterprise Guide binders.

Figure A.1 Code Editor with Code as the Default Program Name

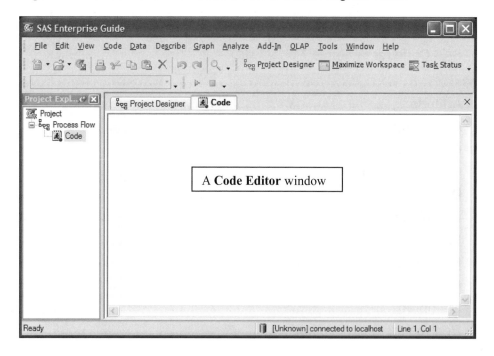

A1.1.2 Running a SAS Program

A program is executed by clicking **Run** on the Control toolbar. See Figure A.2 (top).

- The program in the Code Editor in Figure A.2 (top) produces the normally distributed weight values in Example 4.1.
    - ○ There is an asterisk by the program name — Code*. This indicates that changes have been made and not saved.
- The program has executed in Figure A.2 (middle).
    - ○ The result is the data set Weights.
    - ○ The log is listed in the Project Explorer.
- Figure A.2 (bottom) shows the resulting Project Designer icons.

Figure A.2 (Top) Program in Code Editor, (Middle) Program Results, (Bottom) Project Designer Icons

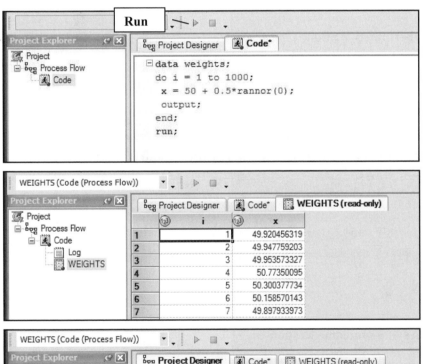

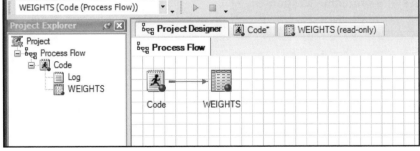

A1.1.3 SAS Code for Example 4.1

Normally Distributed Weights

```
data weights;
do i = 1 to 1000;
 x = 50 + 0.5*rannor(0);
output;
end;
run;
```

Means of Samples of Normally Distributed Weights

```
data xbar_weights;
array sample{30} x1-x30;
do i = 1 to 1000;
 do j = 1 to 30;
  sample{j}=50+.5*rannor(0);
 end;
 xbar = mean(of x1-x30);
 output;
end;
run;
```

Exponentially Distributed Waiting Times

```
data exponential_responses;
do i = 1 to 1000;
 x = 45*ranexp(0);
 output;
end;
run;
```

Means of Samples of Exponentially Distributed Waiting Times

```
data exp_xbar_responses;
array sample{30} x1-x30;
do i = 1 to 1000;
 do j = 1 to 30;
  sample{j}=45*ranexp(0);
 end;
 xbar = mean(of x1-x30);
 output;
end;
run;
```

Means of Samples of 5-Outcome Responses

```
data table_xbar_responses;
array sample{30} x1-x30;
do i = 1 to 1000;
 do j = 1 to 30;
  sample{j}= rantbl(0,.2,.2,.2,.2,.2);
 end;
 xbar = mean(of x1-x30);
 output;
end;
run;
```

Means of Samples of 2-Outcome Responses

```
data table_p_hat;
array sample{150} x1-x150;
do i = 1 to 1000;
 do j = 1 to 150;
  sample{j}=ranbin(0, 1,.6);
 end;
 p_hat = mean(of x1-x150);
 output;
end;
run;
```

A1.1.4 SAS Code for Example 7.5

The data set Ex07_05 is exported to the SASUSER library before running this program.

```
proc iml;
use sasuser.ex07_05;
read all var {homework} into x1;
read all var {commute} into x2;
read all var {final} into y;
n = nrow(y);
intercept = j(n,1,1);
x = intercept||x1||x2;
print x, y;
b = inv(x`*x)*x`*y;
invxpx = inv(x`*x);
diaghat = diag(x*inv(x`*x)*x`);
print b, invxpx, diaghat;
*Ex. 7.5.2;
yhat = x*b;
yhat_ybar = yhat - y[:];
residual = y - yhat;
yhat_ybar2 = yhat_ybar##2;
residual2 = residual##2;
print x1 x2 y yhat yhat_ybar residual yhat_ybar2 residual2;
ssmodel = yhat_ybar2[+];
sserror = residual2[+];
print ssmodel, sserror;
*Ex. 7.5.9;
mult_ex_7_5_09 = {1 65 10}*invxpx*{1, 65, 10};
print mult_ex_7_5_09;
*Ex. 7.5.10;
mult_ex_7_5_10 = 1 + {1 65 10}*invxpx*{1, 65, 10};
print mult_ex_7_5_10;
*Ex. 7.5.12;
xsub1 = (j(n-1,1,0)||i(n-1))*x;
ysub1 = (j(n-1,1,0)||i(n-1))*y;
bsub1 = inv(xsub1`*xsub1)*xsub1`*ysub1;
mserrorsub1 = (ysub1 - xsub1*bsub1)[##]/(n-4);
print mserrorsub1;
yhatsub1 = x*bsub1;
yhat_yhatsub1 = yhat - yhatsub1;
yhat_yhatsub12 = yhat_yhatsub1##2;
print x1 x2 y yhat yhatsub1 yhat_yhatsub1 yhat_yhatsub12;
sumyhat_yhatsub12 = yhat_yhatsub12[+];
print sumyhat_yhatsub12;
quit;
```

A1.2 Data Sets

A1.2.1 Attitude

Observation	Location	Gender	Work	Supervision	Quality	Years
1	Central	F	54	50	46	1
2	Central	F	53	52	51	4
3	Central	F	49	49	52	6
4	Central	F	51	52	53	5
5	Central	F	50	46	54	7
6	Central	M	45	35	54	5
7	Central	M	48	43	60	12
8	North	F	51	51	45	1
9	North	F	52	52	48	4
10	North	F	51	53	51	5
11	North	F	59	44	52	6
12	North	F	58	53	53	8
13	North	M	52	52	40	0
14	North	M	51	57	50	5
15	North	M	51	48	52	7
16	South	F	59	61	45	1
17	South	F	57	49	48	2
18	South	F	56	55	50	6
19	South	F	56	53	52	5
20	South	F	58	55	53	8
21	South	M	57	59	45	2
22	South	M	55	50	47	3
23	South	M	51	54	48	4
24	South	M	57	56	49	4

A1.2.2 Boys_Fitness

Observation	Time	BodyFat	VO2max	MaxO2AVdiff	MaxHR
1	8.52	18.9	50.3	13.3	201
2	12.25	23.6	42.3	12.4	206
3	7.15	10.4	58	8.9	198
4	11.05	14.7	49.5	14	190
5	10.62	16.3	49.2	13.6	211
6	10.25	22.4	43.9	14.8	212
7	7.79	14.5	51.8	11.5	181
8	10.17	22.6	43.7	12.1	214
9	10.26	20.2	45.7	8.4	180
10	10.77	15.7	43.5	12.2	189
11	12.36	19.8	39.4	14	200
12	11.02	15.4	49.7	15.7	195
13	10.88	16.7	51.1	13	193
14	12.72	21.6	36.1	13.5	205

Observation	Time	BodyFat	VO2max	MaxO2AVdiff	MaxHR
15	12.37	19.7	44	16.3	182
16	13.69	27.8	39.7	12.3	191
17	9.34	19.7	48.6	14.3	202
18	6.04	10	64.2	18.3	198
19	11.29	19.6	45.3	12.6	199
20	11.61	30	43.1	10.7	193
21	9.72	22.7	54.2	7.3	200
22	9.21	18.3	48.5	9.8	207
23	7.8	9.2	48.9	14.7	194
24	12.66	22.7	46	12.3	199
25	8.82	14.1	51.2	13.7	199
26	7.56	15.6	49	12.4	190
27	11.87	20	42	14.1	190
28	10.62	18.3	46.9	15.6	201
29	9.96	16.5	47.5	16.2	198
30	8.02	13.8	51.4	12.5	213

A1.2.3 Calc_predictors

Observation	Calc1final	SATmath	SATverb	HSgpa	Orientation
1	70	440	410	2.4	72
2	89	660	670	3.5	73
3	72	520	550	3.2	67
4	77	600	590	3	73
5	64	490	540	3.4	65
6	80	570	480	3.2	81
7	78	530	520	2.9	73
8	71	480	450	2.6	73
9	65	420	430	2.9	67
10	92	550	410	3.7	85
11	79	620	550	3.4	80
12	69	510	600	2.3	62
13	63	470	550	2.9	60
14	77	660	650	3.5	75
15	74	560	640	2.5	64
16	75	570	640	3.2	64
17	59	470	540	3.2	61
18	63	480	550	2.7	62
19	63	430	470	2.6	65
20	93	620	490	3.5	87

A1.2.4 Counseling_survey

Observation	score	importance	confidence	ability	time	reimbursement
1	3	1	1	1	1	1
2	5	5	5	6	5	3
3	7	4	6	6	6	3
4	1	1	2	2	7	7
5	5	5	5	5	7	7
6	1	1	1	1	5	4
7	6	7	7	7	1	2
8	2	3	5	3	7	6
9	5	2	3	4	2	3
10	4	6	6	6	6	3
11	7	6	7	3	3	4
12	5	6	6	4	6	6
13	5	4	6	4	1	1
14	5	5	5	2	1	2
15	3	5	6	4	5	4
16	3	3	2	3	3	6
17	5	5	4	2	2	2
18	3	3	3	1	3	4
19	3	3	3	2	5	2
20	2	1	1	1	6	7
21	5	2	6	6	6	2
22	2	2	1	3	4	6
23	7	7	7	7	2	2
24	6	6	6	6	5	6
25	3	1	4	3	7	6
26	6	7	7	6	3	6
27	4	3	4	2	5	2
28	5	7	7	6	2	7
29	4	1	1	3	1	2
30	5	6	5	3	3	5

A1.2.5 Defect_study

Observation	pct_def	dt_freq	dt_min	comp	chemA	chemB	chemC
1	16.8	4	12	40	10.7	0.6	1.9
2	7.9	3	4	40	13.1	0.1	0.2
3	10.6	5	3	50	15.9	0.4	2.9
4	8	1	7	44	16.9	0	1.2
5	12.6	2	4	40	11.2	0.5	0.8
6	15.5	2	8	44	10.7	0.9	2
7	7.3	2	2	50	15.5	0.4	2.2
8	11.4	3	1	43	11.8	0.4	1.2
9	16.4	4	7	41	14	1	0.9
10	7.1	3	15	42	17.3	0	1.7
11	17.1	8	22	49	15.8	0.8	2

Observation	pct_def	dt_freq	dt_min	comp	chemA	chemB	chemC
12	5.8	1	4	46	13.6	0.1	0.9
13	10.2	4	14	48	10.6	0.2	1.4
14	13.7	0	5	48	17.7	0.1	2.8
15	13.8	4	106	41	17.3	0.7	2.3
16	14.7	3	6	48	17.5	1	2
17	8.3	4	7	40	14.4	0.1	2
18	16.8	1	5	40	19.7	0.5	0.5
19	10.5	2	1	50	15.4	0.9	1.8
20	12.9	4	3	42	15.1	0.5	0.8
21	15.4	1	3	44	10.3	0.1	0.1
22	13.1	2	12	50	17.8	0.4	0.9
23	6.6	3	1	45	15.9	0.3	0.2
24	6.5	1	4	47	16.9	0.2	1.5
25	14.3	3	3	41	11.8	0.5	0.3
26	16.5	8	4	41	16.1	0.6	0.1
27	5.9	3	1	42	13.3	0	1.9
28	11.8	1	2	48	17.5	0.6	0.5
29	18	6	1	50	18.2	1	0.4
30	11.1	2	23	41	16.8	0.5	1.9
31	11.4	2	49	44	16.7	0.6	2
32	15.6	3	7	41	18.6	0.3	1.3
33	16	5	5	44	18	0.3	0.6
34	8.7	3	0	42	13.8	0.5	1.9
35	13.2	3	3	50	17	1	2.2
36	17.2	6	1	40	15.7	0.5	0.6

A1.2.6 DentalSurvey

Obs.	CommOne	CommTwo	Obs.	CommOne	CommTwo	Obs.	CommOne	CommTwo
1	N	N	41	N	N	81	N	N
2	N	N	42	N	N	82	N	N
3	N	N	43	N	N	83	N	N
4	N	N	44	N	N	84	N	N
5	N	N	45	N	N	85	N	N
6	N	N	46	N	N	86	N	N
7	C	N	47	N	N	87	N	N
8	N	C	48	N	N	88	N	N
9	N	C	49	N	N	89	C	C
10	N	N	50	N	N	90	N	N
11	N	C	51	N	N	91	N	C
12	N	N	52	N	N	92	N	N
13	N	N	53	N	N	93	N	N
14	N	N	54	N	N	94	N	C
15	N	N	55	N	N	95	N	N
16	N	N	56	N	N	96	N	C
17	N	N	57	N	C	97	N	N
18	N	N	58	N	N	98	C	N
19	N	N	59	C	C	99	N	N

Obs.	CommOne	CommTwo	Obs.	CommOne	CommTwo	Obs.	CommOne	CommTwo
20	N	N	60	N	N	100	N	N
21	N	N	61	N	N			
22	N	N	62	N	N			
23	N	N	63	N	N			
24	N	C	64	N	N			
25	N	N	65	C	C			
26	N	C	66	N	C			
27	N	N	67	N	N			
28	N	N	68	N	N			
29	N	N	69	N	N			
30	N	N	70	N	C			
31	N	N	71	N	N			
32	N	C	72	N	N			
33	C	N	73	N	C			
34	N	N	74	N	N			
35	N	N	75	N	N			
36	N	N	76	N	N			
37	N	N	77	N	N			
38	N	N	78	N	N			
39	N	N	79	N	N			
40	N	N	80	C	N			

A1.2.7   Early_education

Observation	cognitive	gender	ed_level	pretest	prog_quality
1	48	0	14	22	101
2	47	0	12	26	101
3	63	0	14	31	126
4	49	1	12	26	94
5	55	1	14	38	101
6	51	1	14	27	108
7	42	1	11	27	101
8	55	0	14	26	108
9	49	1	14	28	114
10	45	1	14	18	101
11	42	1	11	19	101
12	42	0	14	25	101
13	57	1	16	29	121
14	61	1	16	21	114
15	58	1	11	30	94
16	64	0	18	26	101
17	57	0	14	23	121
18	40	0	11	21	108
19	50	1	12	19	121
20	51	0	14	24	101
21	53	1	18	25	108
22	51	0	16	15	114
23	49	0	12	22	121

Observation	cognitive	gender	ed_level	pretest	prog_quality
24	52	0	14	28	101
25	59	1	14	23	121
26	54	1	14	30	121
27	59	1	14	28	114
28	58	1	16	18	114
29	53	0	14	25	114
30	59	0	16	29	114

A1.2.8 Headache

Observation	Treatment	Sex	Stress	QOL	Age	Baseline
1	N05	F	57	49	50	Severe
2	N05	F	55	42	33	Severe
3	N05	F	50	25	40	Severe
4	N05	F	56	70	47	Mild
5	N05	F	51	46	44	Moderate
6	N05	F	58	56	65	Moderate
7	N05	F	51	62	53	Mild
8	N05	F	52	42	43	Moderate
9	N05	M	57	50	42	Moderate
10	N05	M	43	46	46	Severe
11	N05	M	46	69	58	Mild
12	N05	M	49	72	65	Moderate
13	N05	M	43	70	55	Moderate
14	N05	M	58	47	40	Severe
15	N05	M	43	63	49	Mild
16	N05	M	50	58	58	Mild
17	N10	F	43	62	44	Moderate
18	N10	F	43	62	47	Moderate
19	N10	F	43	59	38	Severe
20	N10	F	43	75	50	Mild
21	N10	F	43	64	50	Moderate
22	N10	F	43	76	62	Mild
23	N10	F	43	73	48	Mild
24	N10	F	43	59	45	Severe
25	N10	M	43	61	44	Mild
26	N10	M	43	52	54	Severe
27	N10	M	43	65	43	Mild
28	N10	M	43	54	41	Severe
29	N10	M	43	58	47	Moderate
30	N10	M	43	55	42	Moderate
31	N10	M	43	61	49	Mild
32	N10	M	43	58	59	Moderate
33	PL	F	53	45	55	Mild
34	PL	F	54	30	35	Moderate
35	PL	F	56	28	38	Moderate
36	PL	F	59	18	38	Severe
37	PL	M	53	30	33	Severe

Observation	Treatment	Sex	Stress	QOL	Age	Baseline
38	PL	M	50	44	50	Moderate
39	PL	M	34	14	34	Moderate
40	PL	M	40	37	42	Mild
41	ST	F	52	46	39	Mild
42	ST	F	49	33	44	Severe
43	ST	F	45	45	42	Mild
44	ST	F	53	44	47	Moderate
45	ST	F	51	36	35	Moderate
46	ST	F	50	33	34	Severe
47	ST	M	36	56	39	Moderate
48	ST	M	49	45	50	Moderate
49	ST	M	45	44	55	Moderate
50	ST	M	47	47	46	Moderate
51	ST	M	51	40	33	Severe
52	ST	M	49	65	52	Mild

A1.2.9 Home_care

Observation	prog_sat	reg_sat	prog_readmit	reg_readmit
1	s	u	no	hosp
2	s	s	no	no
3	s	s	no	hosp
4	u	u	no	no
5	u	u	no	no
6	u	u	no	no
7	s	s	no	no
8	s	s	no	hosp
9	s	u	no	hosp
10	s	s	no	no
11	s	s	no	hosp
12	s	s	no	no
13	s	s	no	no
14	u	u	no	hosp
15	s	s	no	no
16	u	u	hosp	hosp
17	s	s	no	no
18	s	s	hosp	hosp
19	s	s	no	no
20	s	s	no	no
21	s	s	no	no

Observation	prog_sat	reg_sat	prog_readmit	reg_readmit
22	s	u	no	hosp
23	u	u	hosp	hosp
24	s	s	no	no
25	s	s	no	no
26	s	s	no	no
27	s	s	no	no
28	s	s	no	no
29	s	s	hosp	hosp
30	u	u	no	no
31	s	s	no	hosp
32	s	s	no	hosp
33	s	s	no	no
34	u	u	no	no
35	u	u	no	no
36	u	u	hosp	hosp
37	s	s	hosp	hosp
38	s	s	no	no
39	s	s	no	hosp
40	s	s	hosp	hosp
41	u	u	hosp	hosp
42	u	u	hosp	hosp
43	s	s	no	no
44	s	s	no	no
45	s	s	no	no
46	u	u	hosp	hosp
47	s	s	hosp	hosp
48	u	u	hosp	hosp
49	s	s	no	no
50	s	s	no	no

A1.2.10 Mathpred

Obs.	College-Math	HrsExtra	Absent	HSMath	SAT-Math	SAT-Verbal	Gender	Expected-Grd	Siblings	Handed-ness
1	87	8	4	100	793	702	1	4	1	0
2	81	1	4	81	616	647	0	4	2	0
3	72	1	7	78	586	607	0	4	2	1
4	89	2	4	74	574	655	1	3	3	0
5	65	0	5	67	502	551	0	3	1	0
6	66	8	3	66	481	596	1	2	1	0
7	88	6	7	81	628	668	1	3	1	0
8	77	1	4	67	506	584	1	3	1	1
9	75	5	9	80	598	555	0	4	2	0
10	72	1	6	68	485	562	1	2	1	0
11	76	8	3	78	599	660	1	3	4	0
12	67	2	10	77	560	535	0	3	0	0
13	84	1	2	86	644	538	1	3	1	0
14	97	4	3	78	595	630	0	4	2	0

Obs.	College-Math	HrsExtra	Absent	HSMath	SAT-Math	SAT-Verbal	Gender	Expected-Grd	Siblings	Handed-ness
15	79	1	4	73	543	577	0	4	0	0
16	66	5	7	65	480	572	0	2	1	0
17	82	3	3	79	577	578	0	4	1	0
18	72	7	7	68	492	523	1	2	0	0
19	85	3	6	87	664	633	1	4	2	0
20	65	0	7	68	512	689	1	2	2	0
21	85	4	4	70	489	526	1	3	2	0
22	92	5	5	78	595	628	1	3	1	0
23	71	0	4	79	585	565	1	4	2	0
24	66	1	8	72	519	583	1	4	2	0
25	82	8	2	87	675	683	1	4	2	0
26	66	8	9	76	581	694	1	4	0	0
27	73	8	8	87	639	620	0	3	2	0
28	76	7	6	83	622	566	1	3	1	0
29	68	8	2	68	489	466	0	2	1	0
30	68	7	3	66	488	596	0	3	1	0
31	75	4	7	65	461	619	1	4	2	0
32	71	3	5	67	468	463	0	4	1	0
33	92	4	3	85	661	589	0	3	4	1
34	76	6	3	64	440	432	1	2	1	0
35	81	6	8	74	565	659	1	4	1	0
36	77	6	5	76	591	637	0	3	1	0
37	84	5	3	69	495	530	1	4	1	1
38	93	5	2	82	565	437	1	3	3	0
39	79	6	5	76	535	496	1	4	1	0
40	44	7	7	75	516	390	0	4	2	0
41	77	4	4	64	475	575	1	4	0	0
42	89	5	2	76	541	505	1	3	1	0
43	75	8	3	90	681	540	1	2	2	0
44	62	0	5	67	494	598	0	4	3	0
45	67	5	5	68	485	423	0	3	1	0
46	90	2	6	74	568	722	1	4	1	0
47	77	2	1	73	525	555	0	4	2	0
48	79	3	5	79	568	499	1	3	2	0
49	95	5	3	92	676	521	1	2	2	0
50	73	2	5	68	471	448	1	3	6	0

A1.2.11 Real_estate

Observation	price	taxes	rooms	bedrooms	baths	lotsize	squarefeet	age
1	152	1666	8	4	2.5	0.38	2236	18
2	107	907	6	3	1	0.29	1660	44
3	189	1721	9	5	3.5	0.48	2902	19
4	175	1977	6	3	2.5	0.2	1635	1
5	358	2975	9	4	3.5	0.37	3400	7
6	210	2339	8	4	2.5	0.26	2079	1
7	650	5792	12	5	5	0.85	4800	4
8	439	3582	11	4	4.5	0.92	5508	24
9	375	3497	9	4	2.5	1.82	3150	4
10	315	3037	10	5	3	1.01	4000	24
11	298	2631	10	4	3.5	0.92	3372	30
12	250	2276	11	4	3	0.82	4000	24
13	238	2072	7	3	2.5	6.61	1944	4
14	230	2207	8	4	3	3.07	2835	23
15	209	2361	7	3	2	0.26	2047	1
16	198	1857	9	4	2.5	0.83	2814	36
17	190	2100	7	3	2.5	1	2050	1
18	187	2113	8	4	2.5	0.45	2035	0
19	180	2034	6	2	2	0.17	1600	1
20	182	2034	8	4	2.5	0.25	2072	1
21	175	2090	11	4	4	1.7	3390	24
22	160	1516	8	3	2	2.07	1724	28
23	153	1514	9	4	2.5	0.38	2270	18
24	130	1468	5	3	2	0.47	1150	1
25	130	1215	8	3	2.5	0.26	1885	25
26	120	1028	7	4	2	0.15	1714	81
27	96	1076	7	3	2	0.28	1450	40
28	79	502	5	3	1	0.22	1014	49
29	215	1984	3	2	1	0.74	2860	16

A1.2.12 Salaries

Observation	Salary	Gender	Age	Assoc	Full	YearsRk	AveCollSal
1	50.2	1	44	1	0	10	48
2	56.7	1	39	1	0	4	57
3	77	0	51	0	1	11	55
4	48.5	0	48	0	1	3	48
5	61.8	1	53	1	0	15	55
6	84.6	1	55	0	1	8	62
7	70.9	0	49	1	0	14	57
8	72.4	1	38	1	0	2	70
9	37.2	0	39	1	0	3	51
10	35.4	0	35	0	0	6	55
11	55.3	1	41	0	1	1	57
12	33.9	1	41	1	0	3	48

Observation	Salary	Gender	Age	Assoc	Full	YearsRk	AveCollSal
13	60.7	1	47	0	1	7	48
14	51.8	1	38	1	0	3	51
15	68	1	42	1	0	2	48
16	44.5	0	35	1	0	1	57
17	50.4	1	40	1	0	5	55
18	83.1	1	60	0	1	12	51
19	81.2	0	48	1	0	14	70
20	45.1	0	47	0	1	1	57
21	40.2	1	36	1	0	2	48
22	40.7	1	36	0	0	5	70
23	57.6	1	43	0	1	1	57
24	54.3	1	41	0	1	1	48
25	44.4	1	42	0	1	2	55
26	52.7	1	38	1	0	2	51
27	47	1	43	1	0	7	48
28	50.1	0	44	1	0	10	48
29	39	0	38	1	0	4	51
30	76.8	1	59	0	1	12	51
31	42	0	39	1	0	5	51
32	53.6	1	37	0	0	2	70
33	43.7	1	35	1	0	1	57
34	34	1	29	0	0	1	51
35	55	1	54	0	1	2	48
36	29.3	0	33	0	0	5	51
37	70	0	45	0	1	3	48
38	34.7	0	34	0	0	4	48

A1.2.13 Scrap3

Observation	line	part	speed	scrap
1	PL1	P11	1	15
2	PL1	P11	1	11
3	PL1	P11	1	9
4	PL1	P11	2	17
5	PL1	P11	2	14
6	PL1	P11	2	11
7	PL1	P11	3	14
8	PL1	P11	3	18
9	PL1	P11	3	17
10	PL1	P12	1	23
11	PL1	P12	1	11
12	PL1	P12	1	15
13	PL1	P12	2	13
14	PL1	P12	2	10
15	PL1	P12	2	13
16	PL1	P12	3	16
17	PL1	P12	3	18
18	PL1	P12	3	23

Observation	line	part	speed	scrap
19	PL2	P13	1	16
20	PL2	P13	1	19
21	PL2	P13	1	20
22	PL2	P13	2	21
23	PL2	P13	2	13
24	PL2	P13	2	23
25	PL2	P13	3	25
26	PL2	P13	3	22
27	PL2	P13	3	20
28	PL2	P14	1	21
29	PL2	P14	1	29
30	PL2	P14	1	12
31	PL2	P14	2	15
32	PL2	P14	2	15
33	PL2	P14	2	16
34	PL2	P14	3	24
35	PL2	P14	3	21
36	PL2	P14	3	19

A1.2.14 Trmt_delay

Observation	delay	age	ed	income	druguser	alcoholques	inperson
1	3	40	1	1	1	3	1
2	14	33	1	1	1	4	0
3	12	38	0	1	1	9	0
4	8	29	1	1	0	5	0
5	9	39	1	1	0	4	0
6	13	28	1	1	1	9	0
7	8	33	1	1	1	1	0
8	9	41	1	1	1	2	0
9	10	38	1	1	0	4	0
10	9	47	0	1	0	6	0
11	9	34	1	0	0	6	0
12	7	42	1	1	0	5	0
13	11	31	1	1	0	7	0
14	10	48	1	1	1	3	0
15	7	46	1	1	1	1	0
16	18	31	0	1	0	8	0
17	12	39	1	0	1	4	0
18	5	29	1	1	0	10	1
19	27	30	1	1	1	9	0
20	2	33	1	1	0	5	1
21	9	42	1	1	0	3	0
22	12	40	1	1	0	8	0
23	10	35	1	1	0	5	0
24	12	43	1	1	1	7	0
25	10	43	0	1	1	4	0

A1.2.15 Univ_alcohol_use

Observation	TestScore	Gender	Level	Grades	AveDrinkWk	Binge	Use30days
1	87	0	3	3.52	1	1	1
2	82	0	2	3.49	0	2	1
3	66	0	1	3.3	1	0	2
4	50	1	1	2.05	7	0	14
5	75	0	4	3.22	1	0	2
6	70	0	2	3.92	0	1	0
7	75	1	1	2.38	2	3	4
8	61	1	2	2.52	2	3	4
9	52	1	3	2.56	3	2	7
10	73	1	4	3.36	1	0	1
11	77	0	4	2.65	2	1	4
12	74	1	1	2.54	1	3	2
13	78	0	3	3.21	1	1	2
14	77	1	2	3.56	0	1	1
15	66	1	3	2.71	1	1	2
16	68	1	2	3.27	1	5	2
17	68	1	3	2.56	1	0	3
18	88	1	1	3.6	0	2	1
19	79	0	3	3.82	0	1	0
20	59	1	3	2.44	2	0	4
21	80	1	4	3.43	1	5	1
22	61	1	1	2.31	4	0	6
23	75	0	2	3.98	0	2	0
24	81	0	2	3.38	1	1	1
25	64	1	2	2.2	2	1	4
26	75	0	1	3.18	1	0	2
27	53	1	1	2.27	2	2	2
28	81	1	1	3.88	0	1	0
29	78	1	1	2.7	1	0	3
30	66	1	1	2.58	2	0	4
31	61	0	3	2.53	2	1	3
32	77	0	3	3.34	1	2	2
33	59	0	4	2.42	2	2	5
34	64	0	4	2.3	3	0	7
35	80	1	2	3.96	0	1	0

Index

A

active data sets 4, 6
Active Data toolbar 17
"Additional data" option (Linear Regression)
 565, 618
"Additional statistical value to show next to bar"
 option 123
Additional Statistics option (Linear Regression)
 566, 619
adjusted coefficient of determination 550–551,
 588, 654
 model selection method 647–648
Advanced Expression Editor 67, 81–87
 examples 87–94
Advanced option group (Bar Chart task) 123, 694
aggregate functions 84–86
alias for columns in queries 62
{All} qualifier 84
Allow multi-level formats (Classification
 variables) 141
alpha statistic 196
alternative hypotheses 480–485
 ANOVA, one-way parametric 359–360, 367
 ANOVA, three-way factorial 470–471
 ANOVA, two-way factorial 414–430, 428–
 429, 432–434
 based on ANOVA table 414–415
 binomial proportions 662–663
 Fisher's exact test 730
 homogeneity tests 694, 699–700
 independence tests 710, 713–714
 mean difference, estimation of 313–316
 means from independent populations,
 comparing 194–196, 199–200, 284–
 285, 288, 292–293
 median, estimation of 251, 257
 median difference, estimation of 348
 medians from independent populations,
 comparing 330–336
 multiple linear regression 576
 Pearson correlation coefficient 503–505
 population proportion, estimation of 224,
 234
 Spearman correlation coefficient 509–511
 two-way contingency tables 668
 variances from independent populations,
 comparing 278–279, 283

analysis of variance
 See ANOVA
analysis of variance tables
 See ANOVA tables
Analysis option group
 Nonparametric One-Way ANOVA task
 343–344
 One-Sample *t* Test task 213
 t Test task 324
 Two-Sample *t* Test task 301–302
analysis variables 135
Analysis variables (task role)
 Correlations task 517
 Distributions task 262
 One-Sample *t* Test task 212
 One-Way Frequencies task 238
 Standardize Data task 601
 Summary Statistics task 135
 Summary Tables task 166
 Two-Sample *t* Test task 300–301
AND connective 68–69
ANOVA (analysis of variance) 356–495
 See also hypothesis tests for ANOVA
 one-way nonparametric 479–495
 one-way parametric 357–406
 three-way factorial 469–479
 two-way factorial 406–469
ANOVA tables 360–364, 579–583
 hypothesis tests based on 414–430
 simple linear regression 540–542, 550–552
Appearance option group
 Bar Chart task 121–125
 Distributions task 263–264
Appearance options (Bar Chart task) 694
appending rows in data sets 42
arithmetic mean
 See mean
Ascending option (Classification variables)
 Summary Statistics task 141
 Summary Tables task 167
Association options, Table Analysis task 683,
 706, 720–721
asymmetric distributions
 See also exponentially distributed
 populations
 estimation of median and 272–273

H

I

Books Available from SAS Press

Advanced Log-Linear Models Using SAS®
by **Daniel Zelterman**

Analysis of Clinical Trials Using SAS®: A Practical Guide
by **Alex Dmitrienko, Geert Molenberghs, Walter Offen,** and
Christy Chuang-Stein

Annotate: Simply the Basics
by **Art Carpenter**

*Applied Multivariate Statistics with SAS® Software,
Second Edition*
by **Ravindra Khattree**
and **Dayanand N. Naik**

*Applied Statistics and the SAS® Programming Language,
Fifth Edition*
by **Ronald P. Cody**
and **Jeffrey K. Smith**

An Array of Challenges — Test Your SAS® Skills
by **Robert Virgile**

*Building Web Applications with SAS/IntrNet®: A Guide to the
Application Dispatcher*
by **Don Henderson**

*Carpenter's Complete Guide to the SAS® Macro Language,
Second Edition*
by **Art Carpenter**

Carpenter's Complete Guide to the SAS® REPORT Procedure
by **Art Carpenter**

The Cartoon Guide to Statistics
by **Larry Gonick**
and **Woollcott Smith**

*Categorical Data Analysis Using the SAS® System,
Second Edition*
by **Maura E. Stokes, Charles S. Davis,**
and **Gary G. Koch**

Cody's Data Cleaning Techniques Using SAS® Software
by **Ron Cody**

*Common Statistical Methods for Clinical Research with
SAS® Examples, Second Edition*
by **Glenn A. Walker**

The Complete Guide to SAS® Indexes
by **Michael A. Raithel**

*Data Management and Reporting Made Easy with
SAS® Learning Edition 2.0*
by **Sunil K. Gupta**

Data Preparation for Analytics Using SAS®
by **Gerhard Svolba**

*Debugging SAS® Programs: A Handbook of Tools and
Techniques*
by **Michele M. Burlew**

*Decision Trees for Business Intelligence and Data Mining: Using
SAS® Enterprise Miner™*
by **Barry de Ville**

*Efficiency: Improving the Performance of Your SAS®
Applications*
by **Robert Virgile**

Elementary Statistics Using JMP®
by **Sandra D. Schlotzhauer**

The Essential Guide to SAS® Dates and Times
by **Derek P. Morgan**

The Essential PROC SQL Handbook for SAS® Users
by **Katherine Prairie**

*Fixed Effects Regression Methods for Longitudinal Data
Using SAS®*
by **Paul D. Allison**

Genetic Analysis of Complex Traits Using SAS®
Edited by **Arnold M. Saxton**

A Handbook of Statistical Analyses Using SAS®, Second Edition
by **B.S. Everitt**
and **G. Der**

Health Care Data and SAS®
by **Marge Scerbo, Craig Dickstein,**
and **Alan Wilson**

The How-To Book for SAS/GRAPH® Software
by **Thomas Miron**

*In the Know ... SAS® Tips and Techniques From
Around the Globe, Second Edition*
by **Phil Mason**

Instant ODS: Style Templates for the Output Delivery System
by **Bernadette Johnson**

*Integrating Results through Meta-Analytic Review Using
SAS® Software*
by **Morgan C. Wang**
and **Brad J. Bushman**

Introduction to Data Mining Using SAS® Enterprise Miner™
by **Patricia B. Cerrito**

Learning SAS® by Example: A Programmer's Guide
by **Ron Cody**

Learning SAS® in the Computer Lab, Second Edition
by **Rebecca J. Elliott**

The Little SAS® Book: A Primer
by **Lora D. Delwiche**
and **Susan J. Slaughter**

The Little SAS® Book: A Primer, Second Edition
by **Lora D. Delwiche**
and **Susan J. Slaughter**
(updated to include SAS 7 features)

The Little SAS® Book: A Primer, Third Edition
by **Lora D. Delwiche**
and **Susan J. Slaughter**
(updated to include SAS 9.1 features)

The Little SAS® Book for Enterprise Guide® 3.0
by **Susan J. Slaughter**
and **Lora D. Delwiche**

The Little SAS® Book for Enterprise Guide® 4.1
by **Susan J. Slaughter**
and **Lora D. Delwiche**

Logistic Regression Using the SAS® System:
Theory and Application
by **Paul D. Allison**

Longitudinal Data and SAS®: A Programmer's Guide
by **Ron Cody**

Maps Made Easy Using SAS®
by **Mike Zdeb**

Models for Discrete Data
by **Daniel Zelterman**

Multiple Comparisons and Multiple Tests Using SAS®
Text and Workbook Set
(books in this set also sold separately)
by **Peter H. Westfall, Randall D. Tobias,**
Dror Rom, Russell D. Wolfinger,
and **Yosef Hochberg**

Multiple-Plot Displays: Simplified with Macros
by **Perry Watts**

Multivariate Data Reduction and Discrimination with
SAS® Software
by **Ravindra Khattree**
and **Dayanand N. Naik**

Output Delivery System: The Basics
by **Lauren E. Haworth**

Painless Windows: A Handbook for SAS® Users, Third Edition
by **Jodie Gilmore**
(updated to include SAS 8 and SAS 9.1 features)

Pharmaceutical Statistics Using SAS®: A Practical Guide
Edited by **Alex Dmitrienko, Christy Chuang-Stein,**
and **Ralph D'Agostino**

The Power of PROC FORMAT
by **Jonas V. Bilenas**

PROC SQL: Beyond the Basics Using SAS®
by **Kirk Paul Lafler**

PROC TABULATE by Example
by **Lauren E. Haworth**

Professional SAS® Programmer's Pocket Reference,
Fifth Edition
by **Rick Aster**

Professional SAS® Programming Shortcuts, Second Edition
by **Rick Aster**

Quick Results with SAS/GRAPH® Software
by **Arthur L. Carpenter**
and **Charles E. Shipp**

Quick Results with the Output Delivery System
by **Sunil K. Gupta**

Reading External Data Files Using SAS®: Examples Handbook
by **Michele M. Burlew**

Regression and ANOVA: An Integrated Approach Using
SAS® Software
by **Keith E. Muller**
and **Bethel A. Fetterman**

SAS® for Forecasting Time Series, Second Edition
by **John C. Brocklebank**
and **David A. Dickey**

SAS® for Linear Models, Fourth Edition
by **Ramon C. Littell, Walter W. Stroup,**
and **Rudolf J. Freund**

SAS® for Mixed Models, Second Edition
by **Ramon C. Littell, George A. Milliken, Walter W. Stroup,**
Russell D. Wolfinger, *and* **Oliver Schabenberger**

SAS® for Monte Carlo Studies: A Guide for Quantitative
Researchers
by **Xitao Fan, Ákos Felsővályi, Stephen A. Sivo,**
and **Sean C. Keenan**

SAS® Functions by Example
by **Ron Cody**

SAS® Guide to Report Writing, Second Edition
by **Michele M. Burlew**

SAS® Macro Programming Made Easy, Second Edition
by **Michele M. Burlew**

SAS® Programming by Example
by **Ron Cody**
and **Ray Pass**

SAS® Programming for Researchers and Social Scientists,
Second Edition
by **Paul E. Spector**

SAS® Programming in the Pharmaceutical Industry
by **Jack Shostak**

SAS® Survival Analysis Techniques for Medical Research,
Second Edition
by **Alan B. Cantor**

SAS® System for Elementary Statistical Analysis,
Second Edition
by **Sandra D. Schlotzhauer**
and **Ramon C. Littell**